DEVELOPMENTAL/ ADAPTED PHYSICAL EDUCATION

Making Ability Count

Third Edition

Carl B. Eichstaedt   *Illinois State University, Emeritus*

Leonard H. Kalakian   *Mankato State University*

Macmillan Publishing Company
New York

Maxwell Macmillan Canada
Toronto

Editor: Ann Castel
Developmental Editor: Molly Kyle
Production Supervisor: Publication Services, Inc.
Production Manager: Linda Greenberg
Cover Designer: Proof Positive / Farrowlyne Associates, Inc.
Cover Photograph: ©David Young Wolf / PhotoEdit

This book was set in 10/12 Janson by Publication Services, Inc.,
printed and bound by R. R. Donnelley & Sons. The cover was printed by
Lehigh Press.

Macmillan Publishing Company
866 Third Avenue, New York, New York 10022

Macmillan Publishing Company is
part of the Maxwell Communication
Group of Companies.

Maxwell Macmillan Canada, Inc.
1200 Eglinton Avenue East
Suite 200
Don Mills, Ontario M3C 3N1

Library of Congress Cataloging-in-Publication Data

Eichstaedt, Carl B.
    Developmental/adapted physical education : making ability count /
Carl B. Eichstaedt, Leonard H. Kalakian.—3rd ed.
        p.   cm.
    Includes bibliographical references and index.
    ISBN 0-02-331701-9
    1. Physical education for handicapped persons—United States.
2. Mainstreaming in education—United States.   I. Kalakian, Leonard
H. II. Title
GV445.E34   1993
371.9'04486—dc20   92-37930
                                                      CIP

Printing: 1 2 3 4 5 6 7   Year: 3 4 5 6 7 8 9

Preface

Developmental/Adapted Physical Education: Making Ability Count serves not only as the title of this book but also as its underlying statement of philosophy. This Third Edition was undertaken to provide a reliable and updated source of detailed information regarding the ever-expanding area of physical education for infants, toddlers, children, teenagers, and young adults with disabilities. Since 1986, extensive changes have occurred in methodology, teaching techniques, and legal requirements for individuals with disabilities. These educational changes have evolved from both empirical and experimental research. The federal laws P.L. 99-457, P.L. 101-476 (IDEA), and P.L. 101-336 (ADA) now provide even more exacting guidelines for the education of individuals with disabilities between the ages of birth and 21.

In the psychomotor domain, we are convinced that all students, disabled and nondisabled, should be taught using the developmental approach. We also believe that these methods are the foundation of all good physical education curricula. In revising the text, we assumed that, for the great majority of undergraduate and graduate physical education majors and minors, basic concepts of teaching developmental physical education have already been learned. It would be inappropriate, therefore, to repeat in this text the extensive developmental process of how to catch and throw a ball, or how to execute the overhand serve in volleyball. Even though we do review many basic skills, we acknowledge that other physical education and motor learning texts are written for this specific purpose.

We understand that all human beings climb a universal developmental ladder. The climb up this ladder is characterized by an orderly, sequential achievement of developmental milestones. The universality of human development is founded in the fact that relative ability or disability does *not* have a material impact on the sequence of developmental achievements. Relative ability or disability can, however, materially affect both the rate of developmental achievement and the potential for ultimate achievement.

The physical educator must have knowledge of human motor development as a basis for understanding developmental delays. When circumstances impede one's climb up the developmental ladder, the teacher must seek approaches to education that accommodate the learner's unique developmental needs. The curriculum thus must be adapted. The goal of adapting curriculum is to minimize or, if possible, eliminate the gap between developmental status and developmental potential.

Throughout the text, the guiding principle is that adaptations should be made only to the extent necessary to accommodate the learner's unique developmental needs. Too often, the task of teaching a learner with a disability who requires special attention is perceived in a negative context of what *cannot* be done. The negative context, the learner is perceived more as a "handicapped" person than as a person first who *happens* to have a disability. In contrast, the idea of "making ability count" places the person *before* the disability and shifts the emphasis to what the learner *can* do. This approach accentuates the positive.

As authors and teachers we receive questions continually from physical education, special education, and elementary classroom teachers on *how* certain activities should be taught and *which* activities should be taught to students with disabilities.

Other questions we often hear include the following:

What can I do to help, and what is contraindicated for these students?

What is acceptable and what is dangerous?

What are the limitations?

How can activities be modified when students with disabilities are
mainstreamed into traditional physical education classes?

Today's physical educator must be able to teach all children, including those with disabilities. In addition, the teacher must know how to perform valid and reliable assessment, how to write appropriate motor and fitness programs, how to suggest proper placement, and how to use various teaching methods and evaluation procedures. The Third Edition attempts to meet these meeds.

The multidisciplinary or transdisciplinary team approach is continually emphasized, as we include methods of incorporating special educators, physicians, administrators, therapists, parents, and students into a smoothly functioning unit. The physical educator must be able to use the vocabulary of the other professionals on the team. Without a thorough background in and understanding of disabling conditions, the physical educator risks being excluded (overtly or covertly) from the all-important multidisciplinary group. To address this issue, all chapters in the Third Edition have been expanded or revised. We have contacted national and state organizations that deal with different disabling conditions to ensure that we have included the latest terminology, the most recent research, new trends in rehabilitation, and exemplary teaching methods. Also, we have updated the comprehensive glossary to provide quick reference to key words and terms.

A new and comprehensive chapter on infants and toddlers from birth through 3 has been added to meet the needs of the physical educator and motor development specialist. Developmental milestones in one-year increments are provided, along with suggestions for motor assessment, program development, and physical activities for youngsters at-risk or with identified disabilities. Detailed reference is made to the *Individualized Family Service Plan (IFSP)* to provide individualized motor programs for infants and toddlers as required by P.L. 99-457 and P.L. 101-176 (IDEA).

We have completely revised the chapter on mental retardation and included expanded coverage of physical education for learners with severe and profound mental retardation. New (1991) physical fitness and motor performance norms are provided for students with mild mental retardation, moderate retardation, or Down syndrome between the ages of 6 and 21.

You will find updated coverage of key topics, including current information from the fields of therapy, early childhood education, rehabilitation, medicine, and learning disabilities. The concept of Regular Education Initiative (mainstreaming) is addressed, and ideas concerning integration of students with disabilities into traditional physical education classes are provided. Also, you will find specific information pertaining to congenital and acquired conditions such as AIDS, fetal alcohol syndrome, fragile "X" syndrome, and "crack babies." Additionally, information and programming is provided regarding students with multidisabling conditions and individuals who exhibit self-injurious behavior.

Finally, physical educators must never lose sight of the overall role they play in the total development of each child who comes under their guidance. The emotional, social, and cognitive benefits that accrue from positive experiences in an exciting physical education program should never be underestimated. No youngster should ever be excluded from participation in physical education. The Third Edition of *Developmental/Adapted Physical Education: Making Ability Count* was written with these basic tenets continually in mind.

My years as a public school physical educator, adapted physical education teacher, and athletic coach, plus my most recent tenure as a professor at Illinois State University, have given me 35 exciting years of teaching young people. I will continue to research and write in the field of adapted physical education. Again, I dedicated this Third Edition to my wife Donna (my inspiration and best friend) and also to our beautiful granddaughter, Carly, who has just turned 3 years old.

C.B.E.

ACKNOWLEDGMENTS

The authors express appreciation to the reviewers who assisted in the preparation of this new edition: Terry L. Rizzo, California State University, San Bernardino; Michael Orfitelli, St. Ambrose University; and Walter Davis, Kent State University.

Contents

Part I

DEVELOPMENT

Chapter 1

BUT FIRST I HAVE SOME QUESTIONS, PROFESSOR

The professor looked at his watch and closed his book of notes. The students picked up their backpacks and stored their course outlines, along with the new information they had collected from today's lecture. The first day was over. The professor felt that this would be a good group; several students provided personal comments, and others asked interesting questions. One young man told of his experience as a volunteer for his local Special Olympics team. Another student shared that she had an older brother who died from muscular dystrophy. Another girl was concerned over the impact of mainstreaming and wondered if she would really be able to teach physical education to kids with special needs. Other questions came fast and furious:

- Who are these students with disabilities?
- Why haven't we seen them in our schools?
- What causes disabilities?
- What different disabilities can we expect in our P.E. classes?
- Is physical education really required for *ALL* students with *ALL* types of disabilities?
- How do we assess students with disabilities?

As the professor returned to his office and sat at his desk, he thought that yes, there were many questions to answer regarding individuals with disabilities and their participation in physical education. When these P.E. majors graduate, they would be faced with a new challenge, one that would include their providing exciting and demanding physical education opportunities for children and teenagers with disabilities. The professor then turned his thoughts back to the completion of his next lecture in the area of Adapted Physical Education.

This chapter focuses on questions that physical education students often ask as they start their adapted physical education experience. When confronted by a new and challenging situation, we need to know where that situation may ultimately lead.

We are more inclined to ask questions when a new situation seems relatively removed from previous experiences. Often, a new situation brings us in contact with people whose life and educational needs differ from the norm. Particular concern arises when physical educators become responsible for developing and implementing programs for students with special needs.

Let us consider some important initial questions. As concerns arise, questions should be encouraged, for there is far less risk in asking a question than in allowing a possible harmful situation to develop as the result of an unasked question.

WHO ARE THOSE INDIVIDUALS WITH DISABILITIES?

They include, among others, individuals who are mentally retarded, orthopedically disabled, deaf or hard of hearing, blind or visually impaired, and speech impaired. *Disabled* is, however, a relative term. Some people with severe mental retardation are trained to assemble complex electronic components. Chris Burke, an actor with Down syndrome, has gained acclaim as a star of the hit television show "Life Goes On." Marlee Matlin, an actress who is deaf, won an Academy Award. Rick Allen, professional drummer for the rock band Def Leppard, has only one arm. A professional baseball pitcher for the California Angels, Jim Abbott, was born without a hand on his left arm. Country music entertainer Mel Tillis stutters. Each of these people is in some way disabled, yet in other important ways each is not.

You are very probably disabled in some fashion. Indeed, given the broad spectrum of human attributes and potentials, people are *not* created equal. There are few, if any, "plain vanilla" people (i.e., an average person, born of average parents, from an average neighborhood in an average community). Rather, each person is an individual with an array of capabilities and limitations. Each may, or may not, be capable of becoming a Bo Jackson or an Albert Einstein. Each faces life's challenges with a unique combination of aptitudes that may be assets or deficits.

When limitations occur in those areas of life that draw attention, they may become disabilities. Everyone has limitations, but a person with a disability may have limitations of sufficient magnitude to affect achievement negatively in terms of society's expectations.

Some disabilities may go virtually unnoticed, except under trying circumstances, whereas others may be so extreme that lifetime custodial care is required. Everyone is disabled to some degree. The question is: to what degree and in which area of human performance?

GENERAL CHARACTERISTICS OF A DISABLING CONDITION

How and when does an individual become disabled? Some persons become disabled during prenatal development or during birth. Deformation or partial formation of a limb usually occurs during prenatal development. Brain damage may result from a compressed umbilical cord during birth. All disabling conditions that develop during prenatal growth or during birth are **congenital.**

All disabilities that are not congenital are **acquired** and are incurred anytime after birth, usually as a result of illness or injury. Mental retardation resulting from meningitis is an example of a disability due to illness. Seizures that appear following a severe head injury are an accident-caused disability.

Do disabilities last forever? Not necessarily. Some disabling conditions are **acute** and may cause significant problems for a few weeks or months. A fractured collarbone is an example of an acute disability, a temporary condition from which complete recovery is possible.

Some disabling conditions are **chronic** (long-term, but not necessarily lifelong) and may persist for many years. Juvenile rheumatoid arthritis is a chronic disability that typically persists for years, yet when the disease is in complete remission, there is usually no residual joint damage and no disability remains.

Some disabling conditions are **permanent** and remain throughout life. Down syndrome, a frequent cause of mental retardation, is permanent.

Does the disability become worse? Not necessarily. Many permanently disabling conditions are **nonprogressive.** They do not increase in extent or severity. Cerebral palsy is a permanent but nonprogressive disabling condition.

Some disabilities do increase in extent or severity and are considered **progressive.** A condition may be progressively debilitating but may not necessarily be terminal. For example, certain arthritic conditions are chronically and progressively debilitating but are not fatal. Other disabilities are relentlessly progressive and may end in death. Among school-age children, muscular dystrophy (Duchenne type) is presently the most devastating example of a fatal progressive disability for which there is no known cure.

Do people with disabilities have special needs? The answer often expected is an unqualified "yes," but the more correct answer is "yes and no." For example, a child who is deaf may have special needs during a square dance unit but not during a gymnastics unit. Special needs vary for people with different disabling conditions, and needs vary among individuals with the same type of disability depending on the severity of the condition.

Generally, the person with a disability tends to be more like, rather than different from, the nondisabled. The person with a disability usually has some limitations and special needs, but not in every area and not even in most areas. Whenever the individual with a disability is capable of participation on an equal basis with the nondisabled, he or she is for the moment truly not disabled and has no special needs.

EDUCATION OF INDIVIDUALS WITH DISABILITIES: A BRIEF HISTORY

How have children with special needs been accommodated in education? Historically, the appropriateness of any school program for the child with a disabling condition has been determined by whether or not the child could reasonably be expected to experience safe and successful participation. The safe and successful participation philosophy is a decisive basis for judging program appropriateness. In reality, however, interpretation of these criteria has often been inadequate. Until recently, safe and successful participation in many school programs, including physical education, has been left to local interpretation, which sometimes meant no participation at all for the child with disabilities. In other instances, it has meant meaningful commitment sometimes backed by law. Most educators have struggled to make the most of often inadequate resources, both human and material, to meet the special needs of children and adolescents with disabilities.

Until recently, some children with disabilities were not merely isolated from a school program, but were excluded from school entirely. Parents of children with disabilities became accustomed to "sorry, but" excuses for a child's ineligibility for public education: "Sorry, but... your child has too serious a behavior problem... we are not able to provide special services for children who are moderately retarded... your child does not hear well enough... the facilities in our district were not designed for nonambulatory children." Until recently, parents had no alternative but to accept such explanations without recourse.

When children with disabilities were afforded public learning opportunities, they were often grouped categorically (segregated) according to their disabilities. Although generally well-intentioned, such efforts denied the individuality of children with special needs. Categorical grouping by disability created an atmosphere in which the individual child was overshadowed and obscured by the disability. Teachers, parents, and society often failed to perceive the total child. When the child's participation in such programs complied with the safe and successful participation criterion, little effort generally was made to determine *appropriateness* of the program in meeting the child's unique needs.

Categorical approaches tend to focus on the negative—on the disability—which emphasizes what the child cannot do. When concerns about individual needs arise, they then occur within the negative context of the general category, which fosters such categorical questions as: "What are the educational needs of children with cerebral palsy?" This general question ignores the individual child who happens to have cerebral palsy. The appropriate question is asked in a different context, which emphasizes the individual: "Here is a child who happens to have cerebral palsy. What are the unique educational needs of this child?"

Growing dissatisfaction with categorical approaches, owning to their insensitivity to individual needs, has provided the basis for opposition. As opposition gathered momentum, changes in the law occurred, which meant profound, positive changes in the education of people with special needs.

What is behind the current change in education of children and adolescents with disabilities? On November 29, 1975, Congress enacted Public Law 94-142, the Education for All Handicapped Children Act. In 1990, a new law was passed (P.L. 101-476) that changed the name of P.L. 94-142. Now this law is officially known as *Individuals with Disabilities Education Act* (I.D.E.A.). All parts of the original 1975 law are still intact (i.e., free appropriate public education, priority children, IEP, least restrictive environment, due process). Additionally, the mandates of P.L. 99-457 *Educational Amendments of 1986* ("at-risk" children—birth to 5 years of age) are integral components of I.D.E.A. (Cowden & Eason, 1991). The profound effects that this law is having and will have on the kind and quality of education for people with special needs is discussed here briefly so that we can compare the past with the emerging concept of adapted physical education. The full significance of I.D.E.A. in meeting the special needs of the child with a disability in physical education is analyzed in Chapter 2.

Through guarantees provided by I.D.E.A., children with special needs have been granted for the first time the right to receive a "free, appropriate public education in the least restrictive environment." **Free** means that a local education agency is now legally obligated to accept and educate a child with special needs without cost to the parent or guardian. **Appropriate** means that, by valid assessment and evaluation, education will be individualized to meet the child's unique needs. **Least restrictive environment** means that the child cannot be removed arbitrarily from the regular mainstream educational environment. The child is placed in a modified educational setting only when the results of individualized assessment and evaluation justify such placement. Above all, I.D.E.A. guarantees that the child's individual needs, rather than a categorical disability grouping, must determine appropriate education of the child.

The most significant addition to education of individuals with disabilities occurred on October 8, 1986, when Congress passed Public Law 99-457, *Education for All Handicapped Children Act Amendments of 1986.* This law, and especially the section known as Part H, is having a significant impact on the lives of our citizens—the families of infants and toddlers who are born with disabilities or are at high risk of being disabled (Hepp, 1991). Youngsters from birth to 3 are now being provided opportunities to increase their chances of leading productive and happy lives. Again, the financing of this education is coming from federal and state money. A thorough analysis of this law, regarding infants and toddlers, will be discussed in Chapter 4.

In what major ways is I.D.E.A. changing how teachers perceive the educational needs of children with disabilities? The repudiation of categorical approaches in favor of needs-based individualized education has created an awareness that *all* children follow similar developmental patterns characterized by order and sequence. Their accomplishments may be likened to achieving successive rungs on a developmental ladder. Emphasis on the word *all* implies that, regardless of abilities and disabilities, the ladder of human development is universal. Each individual has unique attributes and is faced with personalized, individual challenges. Those who are relatively nondisabled tend to climb life's developmental ladder with comparative ease. Those who are relatively disabled tend to experience greater difficulty.

A philosophy focused on the need to reach rungs of a universal developmental ladder encourages the educator to identify the child's developmental achievement level, and to determine how the child might best reach each successive stage (rung). Knowledge about the child's disability becomes one consideration, but not the major consideration, in determining how the child's education should proceed.

For the adapted physical educator, this means that all children with disabilities cannot be grouped arbitrarily in one physical education class, nor can children exhibiting the same categorical disability be grouped arbitrarily. Rather, physical education requirements must now be determined through valid assessment and evaluation. The child is then placed in a regular or adapted physical education setting based on results of the assessment process.

I.D.E.A. sounds comprehensive. Is it? The law is comprehensive and specific, but it poses particular concerns for physical educators. I.D.E.A. is first and foremost a **special education act,** and physical education is included as part of special education. Writers of the Individuals with Disabilities Education Act were not physical educators. They perceived physical education as purely an education of the physical phenomenon (i.e., physical and motor fitness; fundamental motor skills and patterns; and skills in aquatics, dance, and individual group games and sports, including intramural and lifetime sports). The law does not recognize the role of physical education in facilitating nonphysical outcomes of physical education experiences. Most physical educators include the elevation of self-esteem and social development as two important nonphysical outcomes. Difficulties associated with the objective measurement of such nonphysical outcomes are acknowledged as the reason for their exclusion from the law. Their significance, however, warrants their inclusion as parts of the physical education experience of all children.

Everyone has a self-concept. The esteem in which one holds that concept becomes one's level of self-esteem. Self-satisfaction is determined, at least in part, by how a person perceives that he or she is like others and is likable. Children who realize success and recognition through movement-centered experiences may enjoy a concomitant elevation of self-esteem. Particularly important is the child's perception of having achieved something significant in the eyes of others.

Helping a child to achieve a higher level of self-esteem through successful participation in physical education is not one of the school's I.D.E.A. physical education–related *legal* obligations. The law makes no mention of the role of physical education in striving for nonphysical outcomes. Despite the law, however, achieving greater self-esteem can be important to the child who, as a result of heightened self-esteem, spends more time actively pursuing communication with others.

Physical education experiences are thought to enhance social development, because the setting offers the child opportunities to gain experience and proficiency in functioning as a group member. With teacher guidance, the child forms concepts in the activity setting about cooperation, competition, giving and taking, leading and following, taking turns, abiding by rules, playing fair, and working together to achieve a common goal.

Physical education provides a basis for developing positive social traits, because competition and cooperation and give-and-take occur as teacher-guided experiences. Many school experiences outside the physical education setting are solitary, independent situations in which few opportunities exist for students to practice and learn social amenities under teacher guidance. The child with a disability often has relatively few opportunities for social development under any circumstances. Physical

Physical education group activities can stimulate cooperation and social development.

education, with its emphasis on individual-to-group relationships, seems to facilitate the socialization process of the child with special needs.

Although the law does not recognize social development as an outcome of the child's physical education, most physical educators do. To the extent that success in activities enhances self-esteem and activity experiences foster socialization, the child becomes educated through the physical. One noted adapted physical educator rejects the concept of education through the physical, indicating that such a concept tends to dichotomize the human being falsely into separate mind and body entities. We reject this notion, for movement is simply one of many educational media through which a child gains experience.

I.D.E.A. falls short in yet another way. It fails to recognize many children who have movement-centered special needs. For example, among such children are certain obese, underdeveloped, awkward, clumsy, and temporarily (acutely) disabled youngsters. Physical educators are obligated professionally, if not legally, to ensure that such children, who may be truly disabled, receive a physical education tailored to meet their unique needs.

Many physical educators would consider the Individual with Disabilities Education Act to be significantly more complete if it addressed the special physical education needs of all children and if certain non-movement–centered outcomes had been included. The law, however, does represent a giant step forward in the education of children with special needs, and this progress will undoubtedly be followed by

Positive physical education experiences can foster socialization.

subsequent steps on behalf of these children. As guarantees of a quality education for children with disabilities continue to evolve, the physical educator's voice should be assertive, articulate, and ever present when future curricula are proposed and legislation is drafted. If the educator does not assume this responsibility actively, who will?

How can I develop confidence and become comfortable working with infants, children, and adolescents with disabilities? A mystique seems to surround working with people who have disabilities. Teachers' basic insecurities often increase when they learn that they will be responsible for youngsters with disabilities. Veteran teachers are not immune. Most teachers who have little or no previous background in working with individuals with disabilities will experience apprehension when teaching children with special needs for the first time. Such apprehensions are consistent with human nature and are to be expected.

No magic formula exists for overcoming such apprehensions, but the in-depth theoretical and practical information in this text will help the reader to better understand people with special needs who, as individuals, sometimes have special needs in physical education. Even with this information, however, the preparation to teach adapted physical education is incomplete until one has had supervised, hands-on experience working with persons who have special needs. The major goals of this text are to complement the professor's expertise in preparing the teacher or future teacher for initial hands-on adapted physical education experiences and to serve as a future reference.

SUMMARY

Students who are new to developmental/adapted physical education commonly ask the questions answered in this chapter. The term *disabled* is defined broadly as any mental, emotional, or physical disadvantage that makes achievement unusually difficult. Being "disabled" is often an attitude imposed on individuals with disabilities by those who are without disabilities, including teachers. Physical education instructors must become familiar with the origin, duration, and severity of many disabling conditions, but even more importantly, they must learn to look beyond the disability and to develop appropriate and exciting physical education programs that help students maximize their performance potential. The most common reason for exclusion of youngsters with impairments from traditional physical education programs is the teacher's inability to understand that students with disabilities have the same physical and motor needs as their nondisabled peers.

I.D.E.A. emphasizes as its goal that every child with a disability be provided a free, appropriate education in the least restrictive environment. This law includes physical education in its definition of special education, and designates physical education as required for all children with disabilities.

I.D.E.A. guarantees that the student with a disability will receive needed special education services and will be educated in a setting as close to the mainstream as possible.

This law is explicit in its definition of disabling conditions that make the student eligible for special services, including physical education, but it is limited in its definition of physical education. Nonphysical outcomes (e.g., social and self-esteem development) are not considered a part of physical education. Many students perceived by physical educators as having special needs (e.g., perceptual disability, low fitness, obesity, poor motor skills) are not defined as disabled under the law. Such children are deemed disabled and thus eligible for I.D.E.A. services only if the disability is *organically based*. Despite these limitations, I.D.E.A. is acknowledged as a significant step forward in providing quality education for children with special needs.

REFERENCES

Cowden, J. E., & Eason, R. L. (1991). Legislative terminology affecting adapted physical education. *Journal of Physical Education, Recreation, and Dance, 62*(6), 34.

Hepp, E. S. (1991). Reflections of Part I: One state's experience. *Infants and Young Children, 4*(1), v–viii.

Chapter 2

EDUCATION FOR ALL CHILDREN WITH DISABILITIES: THE LAWS

 During the 19th century, federal laws concerning the individuals with disabilities were designed primarily to meet the needs of groups with specific disability problems such as deafness or blindness. Not until the 1920s were laws enacted to provide services for all people with disabilities. This was achieved through vocational rehabilitation legislation that was drafted to assist the many people disabled during World War I or injured while working in the rapidly growing industrial society. Legislation for individuals with disabilities over the next 35 years focused mainly, although not exclusively, on services and programs for persons who were blind. These early laws did little for the child with disabilities in the public schools.

EDUCATION OF INDIVIDUALS WITH DISABILITIES— 1954 TO 1973: A PRECEDENT IS SET

The increasing national concern for the needs of children with disabilities is of relatively recent origin. The initial impetus for establishing the right of the child with disabilities to an equal educational opportunity came in the historic 1954 Supreme Court school desegregation case, *Brown v. Board of Education.* The rationale behind this court decision was stated as follows: "In these days it is doubtful that any child may reasonably be expected to succeed in life if he is denied the opportunity for an education. Such an opportunity, where the state has undertaken to provide it, is a right which must be made available to all on equal terms."

Relying on the legal principles of the Brown decision, parents of children with disabilities demanded the child's constitutional rights to a free and appropriate education. The first major breakthrough in the form of direct congressional support came in 1965 with Title VI of the Elementary and Secondary Education Act (Public Law 89-750). This law, signed by President Lyndon Johnson, authorized grants to the states to initiate, expand, and improve educational programs for children with disabilities, and created a Bureau of Education for the Handicapped.

Although P.L. 89-750 was designed to provide educational opportunities for children with disabilities, many schools circumvented its directives. At this point, the courts exerted even more pressure. What was to become a national phenomenon began in 1971 when the Pennsylvania Association for Retarded Children filed suit (*P.A.R.C. v. Commonwealth of Pennsylvania*) on behalf of 13 children with mental retardation in that state. Citing guarantees in the U.S. Constitution of due process and equal protection under the laws, the suit argued that these children's access to public education should be equal to that afforded other children. In a consent agreement, the court ruled in favor of the children.

One year later (1972), the federal court in the District of Columbia made a similar ruling involving not only children with mental retardation but also the full range of disabling conditions. All children, said U.S. District Judge Joseph Waddy (*Mills v. Board of Education*), have a right to suitable publicly supported education, regardless of the degree of the child's mental, physical, or emotional disability or impairment. In response to arguments that this position would impose an intolerable financial burden on the community, Judge Waddy added the following: "If sufficient funds are not available to finance all of the services and programs needed and desirable in the system, then the available funds must be expended equitably in such a manner that no child is entirely excluded from a publicly supported education" (p. 1728).

During the next few years, an avalanche of suits followed as concerned groups in other jurisdictions asked the courts to enforce the constitutional rights of children with disabilities. The impact of these rulings has not only opened school doors but has also stimulated states to improve the quality and comprehensiveness of education offered to individuals with disabilities.

SECTION 504 OF THE REHABILITATION ACT OF 1973 (P.L. 93-112)

In September 1973, Congress passed a law that prohibits those agencies that receive federal funding from discrimination on the basis of disabling conditions. Section 504 states that "no otherwise qualified handicapped individual in the United States...shall, solely by reason of his handicap, be excluded from the participation in, be denied the benefits of, or be subjected to discrimination under any program or activity receiving Federal financial assistance" (p. 22676).

In April 1977, the U.S. Department of Health, Education, and Welfare issued the final Section 504 rules and regulations governing all recipients of federal funds, which included all elementary and secondary public schools. This law affects many facts of life in the United States and has a direct bearing on all individuals with disabilities. Joseph A. Califano, Jr., former secretary of HEW, is quoted in the *Federal Register* (April 23, 1977) as stating:

> Today I am issuing a regulation, pursuant to Section 504 of the Rehabilitation Act of 1973, that will open a new world of equal opportunity for more than 35 million handicapped Americans—the blind, the deaf, persons confined to wheelchairs, the mentally ill or retarded, and those with other handicaps.... The 504 Regulation attacks the discrimination, the demeaning practices and the injustices that have afflicted the nation's handicapped citizens. It reflects the recognition of Congress that most handicapped persons can lead proud and productive lives. It will usher in a new era of equality for handicapped individuals in which unfair barriers... will begin to fall before the force of law. (p. 32101)

This law provides that programs must be accessible to people with disabilities. It does not require that every building or part of a building be accessible, but that the whole program must be directly available. Structural changes must be undertaken only if alternatives, such as reassignment of classes or rooms, are not possible.

All buildings for which clearance was begun after June 3, 1977, must have been designed and constructed to be accessible to handicapped persons. Design standards of the American National Standards Institute determine minimal requirements for accessibility.

The implications of Section 504 for physical education become exceedingly clear, because emphasis is given to guarantee that no individual shall be excluded from, denied benefits of, or discriminated against in any program sponsored by recipients of federal funds. This is further emphasized in the rules and regulations and, although not specifically stated, includes all aspects of physical education instruction, intramurals, and interscholastic sports (Horvat, 1990).

Programmatic concerns emphasize that all people must have activities and learning experiences conducted in the least restrictive and most integrated setting feasible. Two restrictions are suggested to avoid in conducting programs: (1) Do not separate categorically individuals with disabling conditions from individuals without such conditions, and (2) do not indiscriminately place individuals with disabling conditions in special or segregated programs and activities or both.

Compliance with these suggestions is mandated by law, and when a student with a disability is denied the opportunity to participate, that individual has the legal right to sue the school for discrimination. If any public agency does not comply with Section 504, it jeopardizes its federal funds.

In a 1984 legal case in Pittsburgh, Pennsylvania, five students with physical disabilities, whose disabilities included hemophilia and spina bifida, were not receiving appropriate physical education opportunities. The case was brought to the U.S. Office of Civil Rights (OCR). The OCR determined that the students were receiving appropriate physical education, but were being denied other opportunities as defined in Section 504. After investigation, the OCR concluded that the students did qualify as persons with disabilities because each had a physical impairment that substantially limited one or more major life activities. The most critical

The international symbol of access.

point made was that the youngsters had undergone no preassessment, as required in P.L. 94-142, to determine their physical and motor needs. The students were not listed as "handicapped children" on the local school district's roster. The OCR and the school district reached an agreement establishing that these students be listed officially as "legally handicapped" students per P.L. 94-142. The students would thus fall under the requirements of *both* P.L. 94-142 and Section 504, and would be eligible for all benefits. In other words, P.L. 94-142 mandated physical education for all students with disabilities between the ages of 3 and 21. Section 504 does not list physical education as being specifically required, but the law does state that no program or activity can be denied to any person with a disability (National Consortium on Physical Education and Recreation for the Handicapped, 1985).

On February 22, 1984, P.L. 98-221 was passed to revise and extend the Rehabilitation Act of 1973. This new law was entitled the Rehabilitation Act Amendments of 1984. It calls specifically for continuation of the Architectural and Transportation Barriers Compliance Board. The board continues to review complaints concerning accessibility to buildings. All other major phases of the 1973 law, including access to programs, remain intact (Programs for the Handicapped, 1985).

EDUCATION AMENDMENTS OF 1974 (P.L. 93-380)

This landmark law authorized giving higher levels of educational monetary aid to the states. P.L. 93-380 identified particularly the principle of placing children in the least restrictive educational environment commensurate with their needs, and it required the state not only to establish a goal of providing full educational services to children with disabilities but also to develop a plan that indicated how and when the state expected to achieve that goal.

EDUCATION FOR ALL HANDICAPPED CHILDREN ACT OF 1975 (P.L. 94-142)

In 1975, P.L. 93-380 was broadened by enactment of an even more significant measure, the Education for All Handicapped Children Act, P.L. 94-142. (As has been previously stated, the new title, *Individuals with Disabilities Education Act*, should be used instead. It is commonly abbreviated as I.D.E.A.) Some positions established in the bill were significant. First, unlike other federal education laws, P.L. 94-142 had no expiration date and was regarded as a permanent instrument. Second, the act was not simply another expression of federal interest in special education programming; it also provided a specific commitment to all children with disabilities. Third, P.L. 94-142 set forth as national policy the proposition that education must be extended as a fundamental right to individuals with disabling conditions.

A full commitment by the local school district must be recognized as a right of a person with a disability. Moreover, that right cannot be abridged, even on such grounds as unavailability of necessary funds. Individuals with disabilities should be provided with an exciting, stimulating, and meaningful educational experience that is geared to their individual needs and aspirations.

Since its enactment on November 19, 1975, P.L. 94-142 has received tremendous attention, both positive and negative, from all branches of the educational community. Whatever one may think about the law, its provisions clearly have had far-reaching effects on every child with a disability.

Most provisions in the law were not new. The following key components were first identified in P.L. 93-380 and incorporated into P.L. 94-142: (1) **Child find** means that *all* children in the state, regardless of the severity of their disabilities, who need special education and related services must be located, identified, and evaluated. The importance of this provision extends to the moral and logical commitment that all children can learn if given appropriate educational opportunity, and that society can no longer use as an excuse that old cliche: "We didn't know they were there." Youngsters with disabilities, often ignored before, must be brought out of the closet and accounted for by local school districts. (2) A **least restrictive environment** refers to the place where each child with a disability is assigned educationally; it must be the most beneficial teaching and learning environment for the child. To the maximum extent possible, all children with disabilities should be given opportunities to be mainstreamed with those without disabilities. (Mainstreaming and its frequently confused interpretation are discussed and analyzed in Chapter 9.) Least restrictive environment emphasizes identifying the specific child's needs. Recognizing those needs before considering the most appropriate placement or placements is of utmost importance. These placements (note the plural) can be at different sites, but all must be identified and listed as necessary to meet adequately the child's individual needs.

Additional P.L. 94-142 regulations that govern major service areas required under the law ensure that the statutory requirement is met of making available to all children and adolescents with disabilities ages 3 to 21 a free and appropriate public education. Regulations also incorporate identical components from Section 504 guidelines:

> If placement in a public or private residential program is necessary to provide special education and related services to a handicapped child, the program, including non-medical care and room and board, must be at no cost to the parents of the child.... Nothing in these regulations...relieves an insurer or similar party (i.e., local school district) from an otherwise valid obligation to provide or pay for services provided to a handicapped child. (*Federal Register*, April 23, 1977, p. 42488)

With reference to residential programs, the courts and hearing examiners have concluded that residential programming is required when (1) more than 6 hours of instruction is necessary to meet the child's educational needs, (2) the severity of the

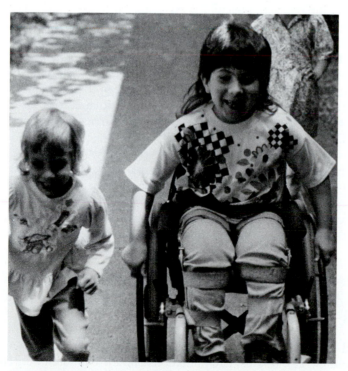

No individual shall be denied participation because of a disability. (Photograph courtesy of Gary Geiger)

child's language deficiency precludes meaningful benefit from pregroup learning and interaction with children without disabilities in the mainstream setting, and (3) social and emotional adjustment are poor in the mainstream setting (Silverstein, 1985).

Note that part B of P.L. 94-142 also required that *physical education be made available to every child with a disability who is receiving a free appropriate public education.* The child must participate either in the regular physical education program or, if necessary, in a specially designed physical education program.

The goal of offering *full educational opportunities* to children with disabilities is a key point of the law, and two top priority groups that must be served are identified. The first priority group is children who are not presently receiving any formal education, and the second is children with severe disabilities who are receiving a partial but inadequate or incomplete education. These children must "move to the head of the class" so they, too, will benefit from meaningful educational techniques. A major misunderstanding of a child's needs often stems from not looking specifically at each individual child's immediate needs—physical, emotional, social, and intellectual. Existing levels of ability and performance will almost always differ from child to child, and the individualized educational program should reflect these differences.

To meet the individual needs of a child with a disability, the law mandates and outlines a method for educators to follow. The **individualized educational program (IEP)** is a written document that must be developed by a team of professionals who are associated directly with the child. This written program must include five general components: (1) present level of educational performance, (2) annual goals and short-term objectivess, (3) specific educational services to be provided for the child and the extent to which the child can participate in regular educational activities, (4) starting date and duration of services, and (5) evaluative criteria and procedures for determining whether the program objectives have been achieved. (Chapter 5 discusses development of the physical education component of an IEP.)

P.L. 98-199, Education of the Handicapped Act Amendments of 1983, was signed on December 2, 1983, to revise and extend P.L. 94-142. The major purposes of the law were to (1) set a yearly spending ceiling for the state grants program, a permanently authorized program, (2) change the age range (at the state's discretion) of children eligible to receive special education and related services to include birth to age 3 years, and (3) establish grant authority for projects to help disabled youth make a successful transition from the public school system to adult life (Programs for the Handicapped, 1985). This new law retains *all* major components of P.L. 94-142.

EDUCATION FOR ALL HANDICAPPED CHILDREN ACT AMENDMENTS OF 1986 (P.L. 99-457)

Substantial gains have been made since 1975 in regard to education of youngsters with disabilities. The original age limitations included children between the ages of 3 and 21. P.L. 99-457 expands the age to infants and toddlers between birth and 3 years of age (Haring, 1990). Hutinger (1988) defines and describes the eligibility of infants and toddlers:

> Section 672 of PL 99-457 defines handicapped infants and toddlers as individuals from birth through 2 who are in need of early intervention services because they (a) are experiencing developmental delays as measured by appropriate diagnostic instruments and procedures in one or more of the following areas: cognitive development, physical development, language development, of self-help skills; or (b) have a diagnosed physical or mental condition that has a high probability of resulting in developmental delay. The term may also include...infants and toddlers who are 'at risk' for substantial developmental delays if early intervention services are not provided. (p. 37)

A new term was introduced with this law: the *individualized family service plan (IFSP)*. The IFSP recognizes the importance of parental involvement in the education of children. Parents must be given guidance in determining their child's needs and the services to be provided. Also, they will be actively involved in the assessment process and are strongly encouraged to assist in the development of the IFSP (Patton, Payne, & Beirne-Smith, 1990).

PHYSICAL EDUCATION AND RECREATION FOR THE CHILD WITH DISABILITIES

The report of the legislative committee of the National Consortium of Physical Education and Recreation for the Handicapped, "Analysis of Selected Federal and Domestic Programs: Implications for Physical Education and Recreation for the Handicapped" (1991) suggests the focus of physical education and recreation for individuals with disabilities.

> Government legislation should be designed to provide programs that will facilitate the ability of persons with handicaps to live independently in the community. Thus, it would be in the interest of legislatures to sponsor initiatives that improve the health of the handicapped and provide them with physical and recreational skills that would enable them to live independently in the community and reduce the need for further government support. (p. 1)

P.L. 94-142 requires that all children with disabilities be provided with a physical education program designed to meet individual and specific motor needs. The law clearly attempts to identify the importance of physical education in the total education of the child with a disability. As stated in the *Federal Register*, a government publication containing rules and regulations of the law, "Physical education services, specially designed if necessary, must be made available to every handicapped child receiving a free appropriate public education' (1977, p. 42489). This requirement is emphasized in section 121a14, which reads: "The term special education means specifically designed instruction, at no cost to the parent, to meet the unique needs of a handicapped child including...instruction in physical education" (1977, p. 42480).

In the same section, **physical education** is defined as follows:

> (i)...the development of: (A) physical and motor fitness; (B) fundamental motor skills and patterns; and (C) skills in aquatics, dance, individual and group games, and sports (including intramural and lifetime sports). (ii) The term includes special physical education, adapted physical education, movement education, and motor development. (1977, p. 42480)

The student's placement and involvement in classes with children with no disabilities is also emphasized in describing physical education. Support for this concept is reiterated in the law by the committee that formulated the bill:

> Special education as set forth in the Committee bill includes instruction in physical education, which is provided as a matter of course to all nonhandicapped children enrolled in public elementary and secondary schools. The Committee is concerned that although these services are available to and required of all children in our schools, they are often viewed as a luxury for handicapped children. The Committee expects the Commissioner of Education to take whatever action is necessary to assure that physical education services are available to all handicapped children and has specifically included physical education within the definition of special education to make clear that the Committee expects such service, especially designed where necessary, to be provided as an integral part of the educational program of every handicapped child. (1977, p. 42489)

Reinforcement of P.L. 94-142 is again found in the Vocational Rehabilitation Act of 1973, Section 504, and is explained in the *Federal Register* (May 4, 1977) as follows:

> A recipient[1] may offer to handicapped students physical education and athletic activities that are separate or different from those offered to non-handicapped students only if separation or differentiation is consistent with the requirements of section 84.34 and only if no qualified handicapped student is denied the opportunity to compete for teams or to participate in courses that are not separated or different. (p. 22682)

---

[1]As used here, the *recipient* is any agency, facility, or organization that receives federal funding.

Section 84.34 sanctions the participation of students with disabilities in separate academic, extracurricular, or nonacademic programs or activities, and the use of private or alternate facilities provided that (1) the education of the child in the regular environment with the use of supplementary aids and services cannot be achieved satisfactorily, (2) the student has the opportunity to participate with peers who are not disabled as much as is appropriate, (3) placement in an alternate or private facility is considered with regard to its proximity to the student's home, and (4) programs and services offered in the private or alternate facility are comparable to other facilities, services, and activities being offered by the recipient.

Although individual interpretations may vary to include certain vested interests, the law is clear when it states that any separate educational program in any curricular or extracurricular area may be provided to students with disabilities as long as they are also given the opportunity to participate in the regular programs, including organized and team sports, as appropriate. When participation in the regular programs is not appropriate, their participation in a comparable adapted program is allowable. Again, the key to appropriate placement begins with a thorough knowledge of the child's needs. Only then can the child be placed in an appropriate setting in which he or she learns efficiently and effectively.

With physical education instruction mandated as a part of special education under the P.L. 101-476 Individuals with Disabilities Education Act of 1990 and with further support from the civil rights legislation of the Americans with Disabilities Act of 1990, adapted physical education programs are now viewed by the law as an appropriate and nondiscriminatory means of meeting requirements to provide opportunities in a least restrictive environment. Failure to provide physical education to all students of the public school population is no longer justifiable.

Where does the money come from for these added services mandated by P.L. 101-476? Provisions between the state and local agencies have increased to a permanent 75 percent of appropriated money. This indicates a total and ongoing commitment by the federal government to support the law. The local school district must ensure and be able to prove that children with disabilities are being given an appropriate free public education. Furthermore, the local agency is expected to support educational services for children with disabilities to the same extent that it supports services for those with no disabilities. All children, disabled and nondisabled will receive identical monies for education. Beyond these monies, additional allotments will then be given to subsidize programs to meet the special needs of individuals with disabilities.

P.L. 101-476 funds cannot be used solely to initiate new programs or services for those children with disabilities. These experiences are assumed to be necessary components of an appropriate education, and as such should be initiated, regardless of cost, by local agencies. A lack of local school funds is not an acceptable reason for failure to meet the special educational needs of children.

Figure 2.1 summarizes the possible placement alternatives for children with disabilities, ranging from complete integration (mainstreaming) to complete individualization.

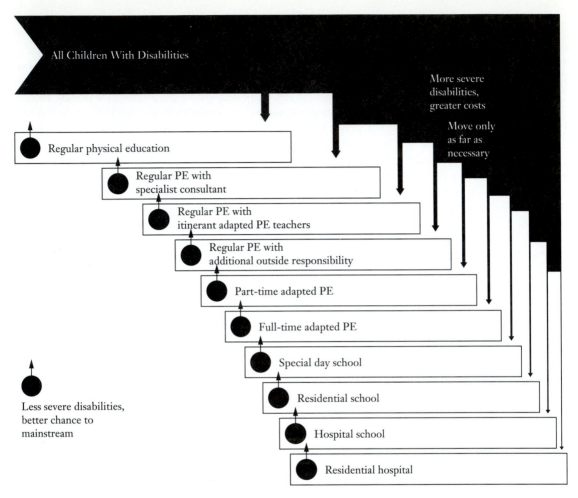

FIGURE 2.1   **Possible placement alternatives in physical education for children with disabilities. If, for whatever reason, a child must be transferred from a less restrictive to a more restrictive setting, the goal should be to return the student as soon as is feasible to the less restrictive environment.**

AMERICANS WITH DISABILITIES ACT OF 1990 (P.L. 101-336)

Americans with Disabilities Act of 1990 (ADA) replaces and includes all important aspects of Section 504 of the Vocational Rehabilitation Act of 1973. This federal law became operational on July 26, 1992. The law states, in essence, that individuals with disabilities *must be* provided equal opportunities in all aspects of life. Communities, schools, and employers are now required to comply with the mandates of ADA. For example, more stringent regulations are in effect regarding physical changes in buildings (restrooms, drinking fountains, ramps, elevators, and telephones), parking lots, parks, swimming pools, and schools.

Title I of this law pertains to employment policies for individuals with disabilities. Business owners must meet the following requirements:

- Existing facilities used by employees must be made readily accessible to and usable by persons with disabilities.

- Job restructuring, modifying work schedules, and reassignment to a vacant position must be utilized.

- Equipment, devices, examinations, training materials, and policies must be acquired or modified, and qualified readers or interpreters must be provided.

For students with disabilities who are moving into their transition phase from the public school into adult life, many new opportunities will become available. The role of public school physical education should become even more important in the physical development of these individuals.

With specific reference to physical education and athletic programs in the public schools, an individual cannot be denied access to classes or activities because of his or her disability. School administrators, teachers, or coaches cannot prevent people with disabilities from participating in an activity just because they are not able to perform *all* activities. If the people can do any part of the activity, then accomodations and adaptions must be made for them.

Violations of ADA could result in legal proceedings and could result in heavy monetary fines. Of more concern for public school entities is the possibility of losing all state and federal money.

PROBLEMS AND SOLUTIONS—THE LAW AND PHYSICAL EDUCATION FOR INDIVIDUALS WITH DISABILITIES

Laws, in their written form, can be confusing. Too often, teachers and school administrators have a distorted view of the law's true intent. Realistic and meaningful questions arise as to possible effects of the law on existing programs, curricula, faculty, finances, facilities, equipment, and most importantly, on the children.

Update, the monthly newsletter of the American Alliance for Health, Physical Education, Recreation and Dance (AAHPERD),[2] served as a clearing house for specific questions and answers concerning P.L. 94-142 and Section 504 of the Rehabilitation act. The AAHPERD unit on *Programs for the Handicapped* (1985) provided information about implementation of federal legislation affecting school physical education programs for children with disabilities. The following questions and responses were drawn from *Update* but are modified to clarify and highlight important points.

Question: Some state education agencies and state boards of education have asserted that physical education is not required for children with disabling conditions if it is not required for nondisabled students. Does this conflict with other interpretations of P.L. [101-476]?

Response: All children with disabilities must be assessed to determine whether the individual has special physical or motor needs or both. Specific physical education areas defined in the rules and regulations of P.L. [101-476] include development of physical and motor fitness, fundamental motor skills and patterns, and skills in aquatics, dance, individual and group games, and sports, including lifetime sports. The child with no special physical or motor needs is governed by the same requirements as those used for other students at the same grade level. If, after appropriate assessment procedures, an individual is identified as having special physical or motor needs, then that child must be given an individualized program, regardless of whether or not able-bodied students are required to take physical education. This is consistent with the provisions of the law, intent of Congress, and further interpretations regarding needed services. Whether those services are currently available or not, or whether such services are provided to able-bodied students does not affect the individualized program content (AAHPERD July/August 1979, p. 9).

Question: If a child with a disability is placed in a regular physical education class, must an IEP be developed for that child?

Response: No. A total IEP evolves from the initial assessment of the child. The recommendations of the multidisciplinary team (authors of the IEP) would indicate that the child does not need a specially designed adapted physical education program beyond the program provided for peers with no disabilities. The child therefore need only participate in the regular and comprehensive physical education program. That physical education program will meet all of the child's psychomotor needs, and will thus include positive reinforcement in the emotional, social, and intellectual domains (AAHPERD, June 1978, p. 6; January 1978, p. 6). If, for example, a child who is

---

[2]This organization was formerly termed the American Alliance for Health, Physical Education and Recreation (AAHPER). In 1980, the name was changed to reflect a growing involvement in dance. In this text, the abbreviation AAHPERD will be used for all references to the organization, regardless of the actual organization name at the time.

labeled as moderately mentally retarded tests at low average or above average levels in a general motor ability test battery and in a physical fitness test battery, then placement in a regular physical education class would seem appropriate.

Question: Must children be placed in regular physical education classes if their needs can be more effectively met in a separated setting such as an adapted physical education class?

Response: The fact that children are not mainstreamed in the regular program indicates that they have certain physical or motor needs or both that require a specially designed adapted physical education program. Placement decisions are based on previous physical fitness and on general motor ability assessment. Scheduling flexibility is of extreme importance in such situations. Learning opportunities are maximized when children are placed in different classes to meet weekly or daily needs. For example, the child with asthma who is allergic to swimming pool chemicals could be transferred temporarily to another activity that has similar basic strength and fitness components (arm, shoulder, and leg strength and cardiorespiratory endurance). The rules and regulations of P.L. [101-476] deal specifically with alternative placements in regular classes, special classes, home instruction, and even in hospitals and institutions (AAHPERD, November 1977, p. 13; June 1978, p. 6). Individuals with low motor skill ability often need short-term placement in a separate adapted physical education class where they can receive intensive and exacting instruction. The student's needs dictate placement. The adapted class is therefore *less* restrictive in this instance than the regular class would be. Both the setting and the time involved must be considered when applying the least restrictive environment mandate. Children identified as disabled who have been receiving special education services do not automatically need an adapted physical education program. As with any specially designed program, adapted physical education must be prescribed in the child's IEP. Before P.L. 94-142, a child with special needs was often labeled, placed, and *then* programmed. Now the process moves from assessment, to programming, and then to appropriate placement. No longer can placement be a function of organizational pattern or administrative inflexibility of the school system or the teacher. If a child cannot learn in one way, then the teacher must teach in another way that enables the child to learn (AAHPERD, January 1978, p. 5).

Question: Should a special education class consisting entirely of students who are grouped homogeneously according to specific disabling conditions (e.g., all moderately mentally retarded) be sent as a group to physical education class?

Response: Emphatically no! One of the main reasons for drafting P.L. 94-142 was to stop such indiscriminate placement and to force educators to look specifically at each child's unique needs. Each child must be placed according to individual, not group, needs. Grouping children categorically by disabling condition is not appropriate in terms of either the intent or letter of the law. Once a child has been assessed and found to possess physical and motor abilities consistent with those of children with no disabilities, then the school district should follow the same processes and procedures that govern all nondisabled children in its jurisdiction (AAHPERD, November 1978, p. 7). A child who is blind, for example, should not be placed automatically in an adapted physical education swimming class if his or her potential to learn swimming techniques is similar to that of children with no disabilities. Decisions regarding programs and placement must be based on present ability level (i.e., beginning swimmer, intermediate swimmer). Teachers and leaders must strive to identify children with special physical and motor needs that require attention, determine specific goals and objectives, and alter teaching methods to include appropriate activities, adaptations, and modifications. For example, a teaching technique modified for the child who is blind might involve moving the youngster's arms, rather than saying, "Watch me do this."

Question: What type of adapted physical education program can be provided without a special facility?

Response: When the needs of a child with a disability cannot be met in the regular class setting, then the adapted physical education placement become the least restrictive environment. Special program needs must be justified on the basis of IEP planning. Legal, legislative, philosophical, and programmatic trends are away from segregated facilities and special programs, except in cases in which a productive educational experience is not possible in the regular classroom (AAHPERD, January 1978, p. 5). For example, a 16-year-old youngster with spastic cerebral palsy might have great difficulty trying to participate in regular class units on volleyball and basketball. Extreme rule modification of either game would so restrict the participation of the nondisabled teenagers that the game would not fulfill their needs. That would be a violation of the goals of P.L. [101-476] and Section 504. Assuming that playing volleyball and basketball is essential for the motor development (i.e., agility, balance, explosive leg power, and eye-hand coordination) of all individuals, then these sports should be offered also to the child with a disability in a form commensurate with individual ability. The adapted physical educator will have to modify specific activities to allow for improvement and success for the individual with a disability. In this example, it is questionable if the regular program could span such extreme ability differences.

Placement in an adapted physical education class must ensure that the new program is as good or better than the regular class would be for the student. In the past, too many children with disabilities were given nonchallenging, irrelevant, and inappropriate activities. The adapted physical education program must *not* consist of handing out towels, keeping score, or maintaining equipment, nor will a watered-down activity program of checkers, chess, ping-pong, shuffleboard, or table games satisfy the mandates of P.L. [101-476].

Question: If a child is so disruptive that he makes it difficult for others to learn or function effectively, must he be kept in a given educational setting?

Response: No. The laws emphasize that when a child with a disability impairs the learning opportunity of another child, then placement is not considered appropriate (AAHPERD, January 1978, p. 5), and additional assessment is necessary. Assignment must be made to an alternative least restrictive setting (e.g., an adapted physical education class could afford a lower teacher-pupil ratio and thus provide a more individualized program).

Question: My 13-year-old daughter with autism is not getting physical education, which I requested during the IEP conference. I was told that gross motor activities are part of the classroom program. I asked for physical education in the gym or outdoors, not in the regular classroom. Doesn't my child have the right to participate in a program defined specifically as "physical education"?

Response: Physical education is the only curricular area in the definition of special education (P.L. 99-457). As such, physical and motor needs must be considered by every IEP planning committee. If, based on appropriate assessment, a child is found to have no special physical or motor needs, then nothing more need be done at the committee meeting. Ideally, the IEP form should indicate this and specify that the child is therefore subject to the same rules, regulations, and requirements as other students. A child with special physical or motor needs must be IEP-processed and programmed. It is important to distinguish between children with special needs who have specific goals and those who require adaptive devices, curricular adjustments, and method adaptations. In the latter case, a modification of rules may be all that is necessary to allow a child to remain in the regular class.

The purpose of physical activity must be considered. P.L. [101-476], its rules and regulations, and official interpretations all state clearly that physical education must be included. Physical and motor activities used for social or emotional purposes do not meet the intent or letter of the law, which insists on provision of a physical education. Indeed, physical activities should be encouraged for many reasons, including the academic and social, but these activities must be in addition to and not in place of activities designed to meet physical and motor needs.

A local education agency is therefore not fulfilling the mandates of either P.L. [101-476] or Section 504 if (1) no consideration is given to a child's physical and motor needs during the IEP committee meeting and in the IEP itself, or if (2) the child is being denied categorically the participation in physical education programs or activities comparable to those provided to nondisabled children (AAHPERD, May 1979, p. 3).

Question: If a regular or special education classroom teacher uses motor, physical, or recreational activities that reach certain students, has the physical education requirement been satisfied?

Response: No. To satisfy the requirements of P.L. [101-476], a certified physical education instructor must make a clear-cut effort to meet the child's motor needs. Although classroom teachers should be encouraged to provide additional physical and developmental activities, these opportunities are in addition to, and not in place of, instruction by a professional physical educator. Free play, recess, or recreational activities do not meet the intent of physical education for the IEP (AAHPERD, October 1978, p. 11; November 1977, p. 13).

Having trained physical educators is just as important as having trained driver education teachers. Although almost everyone can learn to drive a car without the aid of a trained educator, the student's safety and meaningful progression are left to chance.

Question: Do the same provisions that apply to children with disabilities also apply to students who are obese or malnourished, or who possess low levels of physical fitness or have poor motor development?

Response: Students not legally identified as disabled may also need an adapted physical education program to meet their needs effectively. Despite the need, however, there are no legal or binding statements requiring development of an IEP for these children. Additional P.L. [101-476] money is not available to support programs for such students. The rationale for hiring an adapted physical education specialist can be supported strongly when both disabled and nondisabled students require highly individualized instruction. Children who are obese may exhibit needs that cannot be met if they are always included in regular programs. The structured activities of specific units (i.e., gymnastics and tumbling) will not provide proper exertion to stimulate the cardiovascular system. A flexible physical education curriculum can result in a better program for all students. The assumption that a regular curriculum will meet the individual needs of all children is outdated. Physical education programs should include regular and adapted classes to provide a range of activities to meet the fluctuating and individual motor fitness needs of all children (AAHPERD, January 1978, p. 6).

Question: What can be done for students with disabilities who are excused completely from physical education because no adapted physical program exists?

Response: According to both P.L. 101-476 and Section 504, which mandate a free appropriate education for every child with a disability, no child should be excused from physical education. Both laws require that each child's special needs be met through individualized programs. P.L. 101-476 requires that this be done through a written IEP, which must include annual goals, short-term instructional objectives, a statement of specific special education and related services to be provided, dates for initiation of services and anticipated duration of services, and criteria and procedures by which achievement can be evaluated. Congressional intent is to provide every child with a disability with an appropriate physical education program. Interpretations of both laws indicate clearly that no justification exists for not meeting the identified needs of any child. The fact that a local education agency or school does not have a particular service is not an acceptable justification. Needed services are to be provided whether they are currently available or not; this is the responsibility of the local education agency. The interpretation includes adapted physical education if necessary (AAHPERD, January 1979, p. 5).

Question: How many persons (age 3 to 21) are considered to be legally disabled and eligible for P.L. [101-476] and Section 504 services?

Response: The numbers of children with disabilities served in the United States in 1989–1990 as compared with 1976–1977 are shown in Figure 2.2. The number of children birth through 21 who received special education and related services continued to grow during the 1988–1989 school year. The 4,587,370 children served represented a 2.1 percent increase over the number served in 1987–88. Nationwide, 6.7 percent of the general population between the ages of 3 and 21 received special education and related services. The percentage served varied across

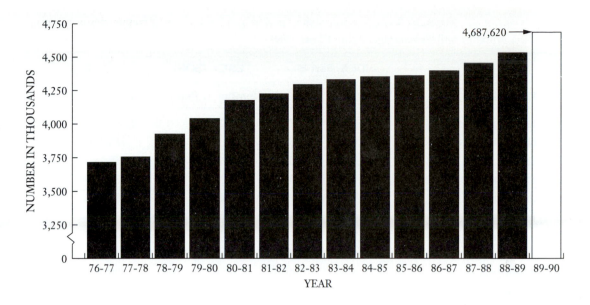

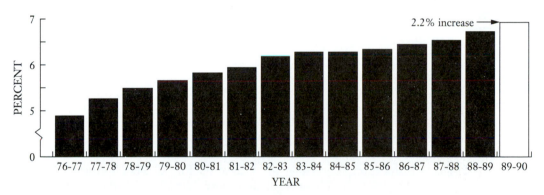

FIGURE 2.2   **Number and Percentage of Children Served under Chapter 1 (PL89-31) and IDEA-B, School Year 1976–1977 through 1989–1990.** *Note:* The figures represent children birth through 20 years old served under Chapter 1 of ESEA (SOP) and children 3 through 21 years old served under IDEA-B. For 1989–1990, the figures represent children (birth through 21 years) served under Chapter 1. *Source:* U.S. Department of Education, Office of Special Education, Data Analysis System (DANS).

individual states from a low of 4.0 percent to a high of 10.3 percent. Data for the 1988–1989 school year demonstrate a national increase in most disabling categories, except for mental retardation, which has decreased steadily over recent years (U.S. Department of Education, 1990). Comparisons of the numbers and percentages of disabling conditions are found in Table 2.1.

TABLE 2.1 **Students Age 6–21 Served under IDEA, Part B and Chapter 1 of ESEA (SOP), by Type of Disability: Number and Percentage, School Year 1989–90**

Type of Disability	IDEA, Part B		ESEA (SOP)		Total	
	Number	**Percent**	**Number**	**Percent**	**Number**	**Percent**
Specific learningdisabilities	2,038,720	98.7	26,172	1.3	2,064,892	100.0
Speech of languageimpairments	964,829	98.8	11,357	1.2	976,186	100.0
Mental retardation	507,331	89.6	58,819	10.4	566,150	100.0
Serious emotionaldisturbance	340,059	88.9	42,511	11.1	382,570	100.0
Multiple disabilities	67,500	76.7	20,456	23.3	87,956	100.0
Hearing impairments	41,003	70.5	17,161	29.5	58,164	100.0
Orthopedicimpairments	41,864	87.2	6,135	12.8	47,999	100.0
Other healthimpairments	49,233	92.6	3,932	7.4	53,165	100.0
Visual impairments	17,357	75.6	5,603	24.4	22,960	100.0
Deaf-blindness	813	49.8	821	50.2	1,634	100.0
All conditions	4,068,709	95.5	192,967	4.5	4,261,676	100.0

Source: U.S. Department of Education (1991). *13th Annual Report to Congress on the Implementation of Individuals with Disabilities Education Act.* Washington, D.C.

SUMMARY

On August 23, 1977, the *Federal Register* printed the final regulations of the U.S. Office of Education concerning the Education for All Handicapped Children Act of 1975 (P.L. 94-142). These regulations agree closely with the nondiscrimination requirements set forth in Section 504 of the Rehabilitation Act of 1973. Both laws require that (1) people with disabilities be provided a free and appropriate public education, (2) students with disabilities be educated with nondisabled students as appropriate, (3) education agencies identify and locate all unserved children with disabilities, (4) evaluation procedures be adopted to ensure appropriate classification and educational services, and (5) procedural safeguards be established. The penalties for noncompliance are severe and include severance of all federal financial assistance.

In 1990, P.L. 101-476 *Individuals with Disabilities Education Act* (I.D.E.A.) incorporated all the important points of P.L. 94-142 and P.L. 99-457. This legislation expands the age range to include birth through 21 and discards the use of the word "handicapped" and replaces it with "disabled." The law further guarantees public school services, not only to all students with disabilities, but also to those infants, toddlers, and young children diagnosed as being "at risk."

Specific legal implications surround the provision of special education, which is defined as specially designed instruction, to be offered at no cost to parents and tailored to meet the unique needs, including physical education, of the child with disabilities. Physical education is the only curricular area included in the defined elements of special education.

Physical education encompasses special physical education, adapted physical education, and motor development. A physical education program should provide for the development of physical and motor fitness, fundamental motor skills and patterns, body mechanics, individual and group games, and sport skills, which include intramural and lifetime sports, aquatics, dance, and movement education. Physical education must be made available to every child with a disability receiving a public education, and when necessary, must be provided for in the IEP. Technically, each child with a disability must have the opportunity to participate in the regular physical education program available to children without disabilities. Only after appropriate assessment can students be placed in a special class.

Achievement of the goals of P.L. 101-476 (94-142) appear to be progressing rather well. Not only have programs for children birth to 5 been expanded, but concern for what will happen to individuals with disabilities when they leave the public schools has also grown. Within the *Twelfth Annual Report to Congress on the Implementation of Public Law 94-142: The Education of All Handicapped Children* (U.S. Department of Education, 1990), the following statement is made:

> A key task of public schools is to successfully integrate each school-leaving generation into existing society, whether or not the students have handicaps. Toward that end, the Office of Special Education Programs' research on special education students in transition has been aimed at improving the current status and outcomes of such students in secondary school, further education, work, and independent living.... Through such efforts, OSEP's goal is to facilitate the movement of each student with a handicap from a school/home environment to the fullest possible participation in the society at large. (p. 108)

The federal and state governments have the financial backing and legal jurisdiction (P.L. 94-142/P.L. 101-476) to provide free and appropriate educational programs for all individuals with disabilities. The roles that physical education, recreation, and athletics can play in the overall development of individuals with disabilities must never be underestimated.

REFERENCES

AAHPERD. Questions and Answers: P.L. 94-142 and Section 504. *Update*, November 1977.
_____ *Update*, January 1978.
_____ *Update*, February 1978.
_____ *Update*, June 1978.
_____ *Update*, October 1978.

_____ *Update*, November 1978.

_____ *Update*, January 1979.

_____ *Update*, May 1979.

_____ *Update*, July/August 1979.

Brown v. Board of Education, 347 U.S. 483, 74 Ct. 686, 98 L. Ed. 873, 1954.

Cowden, J. E., & Eason, R. L. (1991). Legislative terminology affecting adapted physical education. *Journal of Physical Education, Recreation, and Dance, 62* (6), 34.

Federal Register (1977, April 23). Final regulations of education of handicapped children, implementation of Part B of the Education of the Handicapped Act. Department of Health, Education, and Welfare, Office of Education, 42(163), Part II, Section 121a302 Residential Placement, p. 42488.

_____ Section 121a301 (b) Free appropriate public education—methods and payments, p. 42488.

_____ Section 121a307 Physical education, p. 42489.

_____ Section 121a14 Special education, p. 42480.

_____ Rules and regulations—Section 504. Department of Health, Education, and Welfare, Office of Education, 42(65), Section 84.34 Participation of Students, p. 22682.

Federal Register. (1977, May 4).

Haring, N. G. (1990). Overview of special education. In N. G. Haring & L. McCormick (Eds.), *Exceptional children and youth*, 5th ed. (pp. 3–45). New York: Merrill/Macmillan.

Hepp, E. S. (1991). Reflections on Part I: One state's experience. *Infants and Young Children, 4*(1), v–viii.

Horvat, M. (1990). *Physical education and sport for exceptional students*. Dubuque, IA: Brown.

Hutinger, P. L. (1988). Linking screening, identification, and assessment with curriculum. In J. B. Jordan, J. J. Gallager, P. L. Hutinger, & M. B. Karnes (Eds.), *Early childhood special education* (pp. 29–66). Reston, VA: The Council for Exceptional Children/Division for Early Childhood.

Mills v. Board of Education of the District of Columbia. 348 F. Supp. 866 (D.D.C., 1972).

National Consortium on Physical Education and Recreation for the Handicapped. (1985 Spring). #504 applies to physically handicapped not in special education. *NCPERH Newsletter, 13(111)*, 1.

National Consortium of Physical Education and Recreation for the Handicapped. (1991, January 18). *Analysis of selected federal and domestic programs: Implications for physical education and recreation for the handicapped* (Report of the Legislative Committee). 1645 Old Town Road, Edgewater, MD: D. Auxter.

PARC v. Commonwealth of Pennsylvania, 334 F. Supp. 1257 (E.D. Pa. 1971) and F. Supp. 279 (E.D. Pa. 1972).

Patton, J. R., Payne, J. S., & Beirne-Smith, M. (1990). *Mental retardation* (3rd ed.). New York: Merrill/Macmillan.

Programs for the Handicapped. Clearinghouse on the Handicapped. Washington, D.C.: Department of Education/Office of Specialized Educational Services and Rehabilitation, Office of Information and Research for the Handicapped. January/February 1985, p. 12.

Public Law 93-112. *Rehabilitation Act of 1973*, Section 504, Title V, April 23, 1977.

Public Law 93-380. *Education Amendments of 1974*. 93rd Congress, August 21, 1974.

Public Law 94-142, *Education for All Handicapped Children Act of 1975*. 94th Congress, S.6 (20 USC 1401), November 29, 1975.

Public Law 98-199. *Education of the Handicapped Act Amendments of 1983.* 98th Congress, December 2, 1983.

Public Law 99-457, *Education of the handicapped act of 1986.* 99th Congress, October 6, 1986.

Public Law 101-476, *Individuals with disabilities education act.* 101st Congress, October 30, 1990.

Silverstein, R. (1985). The legal necessity for residential schools serving deaf, blind, and multiply impaired children. *Journal of Visual Impairment & Blindness,* 81(3):145–149.

U.S. Department of Education (1991). To assure the free and appropriate public education of all handicapped children. *Thirteenth Annual Report to Congress on the Implementation of the Education of the Handicapped Act.* Washington, DC: Office of Special Education Programs and Rehabilitative Services.

Chapter 3

PSYCHOSOCIAL ASPECTS
OF DISABILITY

I am America's child, a spastic slogging on demented limbs drooling I'll trade my PhD for a telephone voice.

(Bart Lanier Safford III, *An Obscured Radiance*)

This chapter investigates some psychosocial variables that influence the adjustment of individuals with disabilities. Sometimes greater degrees of disability are associated with greater adjustment problems, but this generalization is an oversimplification. Any study of psychosocial variables must be tempered by respect for the person's individuality and the disability's significance to that person. As Levine (1959) states:

> The extent of the [disability's] impact experienced by each individual is related to the significance which the disability possesses for him. This, in turn, will depend on the pattern of events in his life that have contributed to the values he holds, the way he perceives himself in relation to the rest of the world, and the form which his reactions to stress take. (p. 1)

SELF-CONCEPT

Self-concept is an important psychosocial variable that influences the disability's impact on the individual. Just as each person formulates attitudes about others, so each person also formulates attitudes about himself, which become his self-concept. Research in social psychology indicates consistently that arousal levels, motivation to achieve, and quality of interpersonal relationships are closely related to strength of self-concept. Researchers also assert that the strength of one's self-concept is governed by one's understanding of how the individual is perceived by others. This implies that if a feeling of self-worth is not shared by important others, it is of little value. Simply stated, "What I think about me depends largely on what I think you think about me."

Self-concept is a dynamic phenomenon. Among adults, self-concept is relatively stable; among young people, it is in a state of flux. A self-concept that is not improving may well be depreciating.

Self-concept is also a psychophysical phenomenon. No dichotomy exists between the mind and the body in a person's evaluation of self-worth. The individual

Meeting challenges and finding success in physical education can be good for self-concept.

with a disability who perceives his entire person as undesirable is unable to formulate a valid concept of self-worth. As Best, Carpignano, Sirvis, and Bigge (1991) state:

> A disabled person who grows up in a family with fixed attitudes toward disability, and living in a society which treats persons with disability as a disfavored minority, the person with the disabling condition is faced with preconceived, distorted perceptions of his state.... The fact that a disabled person may be different in appearance, behavior, or habits often suggests to others (and eventually to the person) that there is something deviant about him. (p. 111)

Distorted perceptions of self-worth and of deviance become, for some people with disabilities, the basis for a distorted, negative self-concept.

Best et al. state further that "if a disabled person can be perceived as 'a person with a disability' rather than as 'a disabled person,' there will be greater emphasis placed upon the person than upon the disability" (p. 111). When we focus primarily on the person and secondarily on the disability as only one of the person's numerous traits, we realize that many persons with a disability are not disabled at all times. Important others who perceive the individual's disability in a true context play a significant role in facilitating the individual's realistic, positive self-concept.

Dealing with the individual first and with the disability second does not avoid or ignore the disability. Treating the disability as if it were nonexistent does not allow the individual to accept limitations, to make an accurate appraisal of strengths and abilities, or to apply concerted effort toward achievable ends. (Best, Carpignano, Sirvis, and Bigge, 1991).

DEFENSE MECHANISMS

Realistic attitudes about one's disability avoid self-defeating behavior and inordinate reliance on defense mechanisms. Everyone relies on defense mechanisms to deal with stress. When a person relies consistently on defense mechanisms as an escape, however, the individual is perhaps unconsciously avoiding the source of stress. Reliance on the following defense mechanisms is common:

- **Regression**—The person, confronted by a threatening situation, returns to an earlier level of maturity or adjustment.
- **Repression**—The person purposefully, but unconsciously, forgets (obliterates from memory) events with which she is unable to cope.
- **Denial**—The person refuses to acknowledge the existence of real situations and circumstances. In repression, the person obliterates stressful situations and circumstances from his thoughts. In denial, the person may

acknowledge stressful situations and circumstances, but he denies that they have consequence or significance.

- **Rationalization**—The person creates "acceptable" reasons for events or circumstances because the true reasons are emotionally unacceptable.
- **Resignation**—The person gives up when confronted by seemingly insurmountable circumstances.
- **Becoming Dependent, Demanding**—The person requires unnecessary assistance to ensure that she gets attention, affection, and care from important others.

During stress, all persons rely to some extent on defense mechanisms. An over-reliance is, however, incompatible with healthy, adaptive attitudes toward the source of stress. Achieving healthy, adaptive attitudes facilitates one's ability to progress toward achievable ends. The adage that developing new habits is less difficult than breaking old ones merits consideration.

BODY IMAGE

The image of one's own body and the value of that image are significant in formulating self-concept. The body is the hub of one's identity. The individual's somatic limitations and strengths are variables that may alienate the individual from his environment. Among those individuals with physical disabilities, difficulty may arise in positively integrating a bodily disability into a healthy self-concept. Best, Bigge, and Sirvis (1990) confirm that social adjustment correlates negatively with self-concept when the disability is visible. The more visible the disability, the greater the difficulty in adjusting socially and developing a positive self-concept.

STRIVING FOR ACCEPTANCE OFTEN EXTRACTS ITS PRICE

Virtually everyone strives to be accepted by others and to count positively in another's life. People with or without disabilities can become trapped in their efforts to develop a false front that might be more acceptable to others. This behavior is self-defeating for the person with a disability, particularly if a false front is used to cover up certain traits. As Wright (1960) states:

> The price of trying above all to hide and forget is high. It is high because the effort is futile. A person cannot forget when reality requires him to take his disability into

account time and again. The vigilance required for covering up leads to strain, not only physically but also in interpersonal relations, for one must maintain a certain distance (social as well as physical) in order to fend off the frightening topic of the disability. . . . Trying to forget is the best way of remembering. (p. 24)

Wright (1960, pp. 36–37) points out that "acting like a normal person" is not the same as "feeling like a normal person" (i.e., a worthy human being). She concludes that "all too often, one pays a price for the apparent success when the motivation (to act like a normal person) is to prove that one is 'as good as anybody else.'" Any attempt to hide, forget, or cover up traits considered unacceptable will have a negative impact on a person's self-concept. Horney (1937) believes that a person wishing to obscure a disability often finds himself without associates. On the one hand, the person may resist association with other people with similar disabilities for fear of drawing attention to his disability. On the other hand, the person may avoid association with nondisabled persons for fear of differences being even more obvious. The person threatened by contact will avoid contact with either group. Given the need to feel "at home" with oneself, such a person is virtually homeless.

SEVERITY OF DISABILITY, ADJUSTMENT, AND SELF-CONCEPT

Empirical evidence suggests that severe disability does not necessarily go hand in hand with maladjustment. Conversely, mild disability offers no guarantee of positive adjustment. A person with mild disability, because he is relatively normal, may recognize greater potential for hiding his disability. The hiding process prompts denial and thwarts adjustment, because the person hiding a trait judged to be undesirable has already engaged in self-devaluation. Self-devaluation, in turn, negatively affects the self-concept. Persons with severe undeniable disabilities may have little recourse but to accept themselves as persons with a disability.

In either case, the person who does adjust may need to cling temporarily to the "normal ideal." It may be necessary to embrace that ideal before one can truly give it up and find satisfaction in being oneself.

The foregoing discussion is not intended to deny the significance of adjustment problems that confront the person with a severe disability. Persons with severe congenital disabilities often experience the least status in the social community. Persons with severe acquired disabilities experience a higher social status. It is hypothesized that a severe congenital disability, because it is present from birth, greatly limits experiences that ensure status in the community.

The degree and type of disability confronting the individual thus play a significant role in adjustment and self-concept development. Each person's unique individuality is, however, also significant in the adjustment and self-concept development process.

EMPATHY VERSUS SYMPATHY

Empathy and sympathy are similar in sound only. Recognizing the difference in the meaning of these words and the different concepts that they embody is critical for those who teach or otherwise function in a professional or personal relationship with people who have disabilities.

Empathy is the mature, genuine understanding of another's situation and circumstances. A saying in Native American lore speaks eloquently to the issue of empathy when the speaker admonishes, "Make no judgments about me until you have walked a mile in my moccasins." Empathy is the ability to understand another's thoughts or state of mind without actually having experienced the person's circumstances. Inability to empathize with another diminishes the teacher's potential to influence positively the learner's development. The ability to empathize goes beyond establishing rapport; it fosters insight, which creates an effective working relationship.

Sympathy is feeling sorry for another. It connotes, "Oh, you poor unfortunate fellow!" Sympathy is synonymous with pity; pity devalues worth, and devalued worth causes additional suffering. People want understanding, not pity.

Stories about outstanding achievements by persons with disabilities often unwittingly provoke sympathy and pity. The story of Pete Gray provides a case in point. Gray, who at age 6 lost an arm in a truck accident, became a major league baseball player. One newspaper account (cited in Rusk and Taylor, 1946) of Gray's achievement read as follows:

> Gray is an inspiration.... The mere fact that a one-armed ball player has crashed the big league opens up new and electrifying vistas for each of them [similarly handicapped persons]. If one can overcome his handicap in such fashion, there is hope for them all. (p. 140)

Reference to "them" effectively, though unwittingly, promotes the we-they dichotomy, which, based on disability alone, sets the disabled person apart from able-bodied persons. The last phrase, "there is hope for them all," drives home the stigma: Poor fellow. But don't worry. Even for people like you there is hope.

Inspirational messages should not be eliminated, but they should be tempered with empathy and an understanding that undertones can devalue the self-worth of the persons for whom the message is intended.

HANDLING OF DEATH IN OUR SOCIETY

Life's ultimate reality is death, yet death remains a reality with which many persons are unable to cope. Anxieties surrounding the imminent death of a terminally ill child are perplexing for everyone. People accept the death of older persons, but a child's death assaults reason. Human beings need to search philosophically for some purpose surrounding a child's death, yet an obsessive search disallows dealing with death's reality.

Some decades ago, most people in the United States were born and died at home. Three generations (children, parents, and grandparents) often lived together in a single dwelling, and the entire family was witness to birth, life, and death. Today, birth and death have been effectively obscured from human experience, because people are born and die in hospitals. Once, death was part of life's experiences; today, death has become taboo because of its physical remoteness. Although death in the home was not a welcome event, those who witnessed death were somewhat better prepared to accept its consequences as life's natural culmination.

TERMINAL ILLNESS IN CHILDREN

The dying child, if mature enough to grasp death's significance, and those affected by the child's death experience changes in attitude as death approaches. If adjustment time is sufficient, people can accept death as inevitable and imminent. The dying person often takes comfort in the closeness and presence of loved ones.

Attitudinal changes that lead to acceptance include anger, denial, bargaining (most often with God), and depression. Kübler-Ross (1969) believes that each stage, given sufficient time, is "worked through," with the person ultimately accepting death's arrival and reality. This working through is experienced by the dying person and by those affected.

Kübler-Ross says that the dying child often will single out one adult with whom to communicate feelings about death. That person is often not a parent but a teacher or therapist. Parents are not chosen because the child, sensitive to the parents' grief, does not wish to compound that grief. The selected person must be willing to accept the child's feelings, or the child will experience profound loneliness.

TEACHER'S ROLES

The teacher's roles are complex, for the teacher must communicate personally and sensitively with the child, the child's parents, and the child's friends. The teacher must recognize that his primary role is that of teacher to the dying child and teacher to the child's classmates. Responsibility is not only to the terminally ill child but also to the children who remain.

In coping with this situation, teachers must first work through their own thoughts and concepts about death. Best, Carpignano, Sirvis, and Bigge's work (1991) on the psychological aspects of physical disability, particularly implications of terminal illness, should be read. They suggest strategies and attitudes helpful to parents and professionals who work with terminally ill children:

- Treat all children the same. If children with cerebral palsy are disciplined, also discipline those with terminal illness.
- Be objective in goal setting, building toward attainable goals.
- Maintain mental health. Be available to those who are dying and to those who remain after the classmate's death.
- Develop an understanding of the Kübler-Ross stages of coping with death and how children, parents, and professionals may use them. Recognize that everyone does not progress at the same pace, and allow for individual differences in coping.
- Define your role as an educator, remembering that your role and responsibility are to teach. Included in that role is a responsibility as a human being to meet the personal needs of students. Your primary role, however, remains that of teacher.
- Respond to, and accept, your own feelings of anxiety, anger, guilt, and sorrow, and share these, when appropriate, with the children.
- Recognize the teacher as a catalyst for hope, but do not be foolishly optimistic.
- Prepare to answer the child's questions, such as "Am I going to die?" Such questions must be answered carefully and honestly in response to individual needs.
- Prepare yourself to deal with the behavior of youngsters who cannot act out physically, and thus may rebel verbally against the world.
- Establish rapport with professionals in medicine and mental health who can be valuable resources.
- Deal with yourself.

Teachers will find that the psychological problems manifested in children with terminal illnesses are more difficult to deal with. The affected youngsters and their peers, families, and teachers all need the insights that can be gained from death education programs. Wolery and Haring (1990) state the following:

> These programs [death education] can be incorporated into the curriculum so that younger children can learn from stories about the life cycle of plants and animals, and eventually, of people. Curricula must reflect age-related conceptualizations of death, because the child's knowledge of change, disappearance, and finality must be established before death is fully understood.... The teacher's task is to help the student with a terminal illness develop a concept of quality in a limited life-span....

Thus, curricula for students with muscular dystrophy, cystic fibrosis, and terminal cancer should stress development and achievement of attainable short-term goals. Overindulgence should be avoided at all costs. (pp. 310–311)

THE HELPING RELATIONSHIP

In a helping relationship, the person being helped is often assumed to be unable to help herself. The act of helping another can be easily interpreted as helplessness on the part of the person receiving assistance. The judgment of helplessness can be made by the helper, by the person being helped, or by persons observing the assistance. Because helping suggests a one-sided relationship, value judgments are made about the person receiving aid. The person who receives help consistently may be judged inferior to others who seem self-reliant and independent.

Virtually everyone needs help sometimes, and one's sensitivity to receiving help is highly individual. Most people respond positively to assistance if it is genuinely needed and is not offered primarily to satisfy the helper's ego.

A person with a disability usually desires minimum assistance and only when necessary. Before helping, always obtain the consent of the person involved. Do not assume that help is needed or wanted. Assistance, particularly unsolicited assistance, may be interpreted as denial of the person's independence. If a person desires help but uncertainty exists about what exactly is needed, the helper should simply ask. Assistance should be focused on the task, not on the relationship. Fuss and emotional display by the helper suggest ego feeding at the expense of the person receiving assistance.

Helping has psychological as well as physical impact on the recipient. The helper who understands clearly his own motivations will probably offer specific assistance only when needed, which is appreciated and which acknowledges the recipient's self-respect.

This chapter opened with five lines of poetry by Bart Lanier Safford III. We close this chapter with another of Safford's poems. Safford, who has cerebral palsy, has earned three degrees in higher education. In the opening excerpt, however, he placed his academic achievements in perspective in fewer than 20 words. For Safford and for those to whom he speaks, disability in psychosocial perspective is not pristine, abstract theory but an enduring fact of life. Safford, whose gift with words enables him to say more in a few words than others say in volumes, has written the following poem, which might well have been directed to physical education teachers or to those who coach persons with disabilities. His poem is entitled "The Baseball Manager and the Warm-up Jacket":

> In high school in Brooklyn
> I was the baseball manager,

proud as I could be
I chased baseballs,
gathered thrown bats,
handed out the towels
It was very important work
for a small spastic kid,
but I was a team member
When the team got
their warm-up jackets
I didn't get one
Only the regular team
got these jackets, and
surely not a manager
Eventually, I bought my own
but it was dark blue while
the official ones were green
Nobody ever said anything
to me about my blue jacket;
the guys were my friends
Yet it hurt me all year
to wear that blue jacket
among all those green ones
Even now, forty years after,
I still recall that jacket
and the memory goes on hurting.
      Bart Lanier Safford III
      from *An Obscured Radiance* (1978, p. 2)

SUMMARY

The psychosocial implications of disability can extend further than the direct impact of the disability itself. Disabilities of great proportion do not, however, always precipitate greater problems of psychosocial adjustment. The impact that any disability has on psychosocial well-being is largely an individual phenomenon.

When difficulties in adjustment are apparent, defense mechanisms may be used. These include regression, repression, denial, rationalization, resignation, and becoming dependent or demanding.

Teachers should strive to empathize with the person with disabilities. Sympathy denies the self-worth of the individual at whom it is directed and has a devaluing effect on the recipient's self-esteem. The person whose level of self-esteem wavers will find pity particularly devastating. Conversely, empathy reflects a mature effort to understand the circumstances and challenges confronting an individual. Sympathy is synonymous with pity, empathy with understanding.

The adapted physical educator may encounter students with terminal illness. In these circumstances, the teacher should be prepared to provide appropriate support to the dying child and to the child's peers. Both the dying child and the child's peers may rely heavily on the teacher. The educator must understand her own responses to death and must be prepared to deal with the children's responses.

In the adapted physical education setting, the teacher becomes involved in helping relationships. These relationships must preserve the recipient's self-esteem. Help should be offered only when needed and desired. Offering help too quickly in specific situations may deny the opportunity to achieve independence. In many instances, the teacher, uncertain of how much help is needed, should simply ask the student.

All people, irrespective of disability or nondisability, have psychosocial needs. Whether or not these needs are met determines the individual's adjustment to personal circumstances. Just as all able-bodied persons do not manifest positive psychosocial adjustment, so all persons with disability do not exhibit problematic adjustment. In facilitating all psychosocial adjustments, the individual's integrity must be preserved.

REFERENCES

Best, S., Bigge, J., & Sirvis, B. (1990). Physical and health impairments. In N. G. Haring & L. McCormick (Eds.), *Exceptional children and youth*, 5th ed. (pp. 283–324). New York: Merrill/Macmillan.

Best, S. J., Carpignano, J. L., Sirvis, B., & Bigge, J. L. (1991). Psychosocial aspects of disability. In J. L. Bigge, *Teaching individuals with physical and multiple disabilities*, 3rd ed. (pp. 110–137). New York: Merrill/Macmillan.

Horney, K. (1937). *The neurotic personality of our time*. New York: W. W. Norton.

Kübler-Ross, E. (1969). *On death and dying*. New York: Macmillan.

Levine, L. S. (1959, October). (as cited by Best, Carpignano, Sirvis, & Bigge) *The impact of disability*. Address to Oklahoma Rehabilitation Association Convention, Oklahoma City.

Rusk, H. A., & Taylor, E. J. (1946). *New hope for the handicapped*. New York: Harper & Row.

Safford, Bart Lanier III (1978). The baseball manager and the warm-up jacket. *Disabled USA* 2(2).

———. *An obscured radiance*. El Paso, TX.: Endeavors of Humanity Press, n.d.

Wolery, M., & Haring, T. G. (1990). Moderate, severe, and profound handicaps. In N. G. Haring & L. McCormick (Eds.), *Exceptional children and youth*, 5th ed. (pp. 239–280). New York: Merrill/Macmillan.

Wright, B. A. (1960). *Physical disability—A psychological approach*. New York: Harper & Row.

Chapter 4

INFANTS AND TODDLERS: BIRTH THROUGH AGE 3

 It was shortly after midnight on the day that Ann Jackson would be born, although no one knew it was to be her birthday. Her family—father, mother, and two older brothers— were asleep in the Jacksons' three-bedroom home in a Chicago suburb, although Mrs. Jackson shifted restlessly without fully waking.

At about 3 A.M., a sharp contraction forced the dark-haired, 41-year-old mother into consciousness. Not quite sure what she had felt, Martha Jackson lay awake in the dark, waiting, hoping that the pregnancy that had become so awkward and tiring was about to end. Six minutes. Seven minutes. Almost eight minutes later she felt again the crampy tightening in her abdomen, not painful, but strong and insistent.

After two more contractions she slid out of bed, started a pot of coffee for her husband, and sat down to write out a schedule for the day's routine that would have to proceed without her. About 4:30, convinced at last by the urgency and strength of the contractions that this was true labor, Martha tiptoed into the bedroom to awaken her husband Tom. While he dressed, she phoned Dr. Paxton and Sally Davidson, the next-door neighbor who had agreed to take care of the boys until Martha's mother arrived. Then the Jacksons left for the hospital.

As Dr. Paxton was to record later on that day, it was a normal labor, a routine delivery. Martha had only a single injection of a pain-relieving drug to make her relaxed and drowsy, plus the spinal anesthesia she had requested so she could watch her baby being born. At 11:48, drowsy, tired, and elated, Martha heard Dr. Paxton say, "Well, Mrs. Jackson, you have your little girl!"

Martha smiled. Then she asked, "Is she all right? Does she have the right number of fingers and toes and everything?" Martha hadn't heard the nurse say in a low voice to the obstetrician, "Apgar score at one minute—6." Or again, five minutes later, "Apgar still 6." Nor did she know that Dr. Paxton, after carefully checking over the infant, had left a note for the Jacksons' pediatrician: "Please get in touch with me as soon as you've examined the Jackson baby."

"I know what you're thinking," began Dr. Sullivan abruptly, early that evening when he telephoned Dr. Paxton. "The skin fold in the corner of the eyes. The short, curved little fingers. The single straight line on one palm. Her general limpness and flabbiness.

These are only signs, of course, and I hope I am wrong, but I think she has Down syndrome. Chromosome tests are definitely indicated."

"That's what I was afraid of," replied the obstetrician. "I haven't said anything to the parents. Will you talk to them? You know them better than I do and you'll be caring for the baby anyway—unless they decide to put the baby into an institution."

For the rest of her life, Martha would remember that moment and how her thoughts had stuck like a phonograph needle in a record groove, spinning out "Down syndrome... Down syndrome... Down syndrome" again and again. She did hear snatches of the words Dr. Sullivan was saying. "Too soon to be sure... Chromosome count will tell us definitely... Many things that can be done for her." From Tom, who was holding Martha's hand so tightly her fingers ached, came a torrent of agonized questions: "Just what is wrong with our baby?" "What makes you think so?" "How bad is it going to be?" "Won't she outgrow it if we start treatment right from the beginning?" "Aren't there special programs for babies like Ann?"

Dr. Sullivan assured the parents that children with Down syndrome were making wonderful gains in today's society. No longer are these youngsters relegated to institutional life. He explained that there are many excellent programs for baby Ann, and that he would contact the school district and inform them that the baby is eligible for PL 101-476 early intervention programs. The doctor emphasized that these programs are exceptional and specialize in infants who are considered "At-Risk." He suggested that these activities should start immediately. Also, he said he would give the Jacksons' name to the local support group for parents of children with Down syndrome, as he has had good success with this organization.

Tom and Martha Jackson were overwhelmed by the added complications and questions regarding their new baby. What can be done for the baby? What programs are available in this town? How much will it cost us? What are infant stimulation programs? Who will help us? But the Jacksons will find more people to help than they ever suspected—doctors, nurses, social workers, psychologists, genetic counselors, therapists, teachers, and other parents. Financial help is available for those who need it. Early childhood developmental programs will be written and include detailed planning with input from many professionals. Also, the Jacksons will become actively involved in writing and implementing the program for their baby. Motor and physical development will be important components of the ongoing activity plan, which will continue through Ann's toddler and preschool years.

Adapted with permission from Apgar and Beck (1974).

INTRODUCTION

All infants, toddlers, and young preschool-aged children experience a phenomenal amount of learning and physical development during the years from birth to age 3 years. Typically, youngsters grow and develop in orderly and predictable ways. They learn to move, to communicate, to play, to control their environment, and to be independent. But for some youngsters with disabilities, these early years can become a series of missed opportunities. Developmental milestones for children with no apparent delays in growth and development differ sharply with the progress experienced by most children with disabilities. In fact, Bouffard (1990) found that individuals labeled as "educable" (mildly) mentally retarded lag well behind nondisabled children in both fine and gross motor skills. Also, Semmler and Hunter (1990) believe that infants and young children with severe or profound degrees of mental retardation may be functioning at less than a quarter of their age in most skills.

Education and child development specialists agree that early intervention programs can provide meaningful opportunities for all children, which at one time were considered unnecessary. Heward and Orlansky (1992) have found that "not too many years ago professionals often told parents concerned about deficits in their child's development, 'Don't worry. Wait and see. She'll probably grow out of it.' As a result, the early years became a time when many handicapped children fell further and further behind their nonhandicapped peers" (p. 515). Today, a major thrust of special education programs is clearly defined as providing free and appropriate programs for young children with developmental disabilities from birth to age 5. Trohanis (1991) emphatically states that "this nation is on the threshold of providing more and better services to all eligible infants, toddlers, and preschoolers with special needs and their families" (p. v).

LAWS AND PROGRAMS FOR INFANTS, TODDLERS, AND PRESCHOOLERS

Federal funding of special education programs for children between the ages of 3 and 5 who possess disabilities is included in PL 101-476 *Individuals with Disabilities Education Act of 1990* (formerly known as the Education for All Handicapped Children Act). This law is being commonly referred to as "I.D.E.A." Additional federal funding for infants and toddlers (0 to 36 months) with disabilities has come into prominence with the passage of PL 99-457, Part H, *Education of Children with Disabilities Amendments of 1986* (Dunn, 1991). This law amended PL 94-142 and officially extends rights and provisions to infants, toddlers, and preschoolers. Title I of this law requires a statewide plan for comprehensive interdisciplinary services for youngsters from birth to age 3. States are required to develop a statewide plan that will ensure that all children with special needs, birth through 36 months, receive a comprehensive evaluation, an individualized family service plan (IFSP), and access to procedural safeguards (Eichstaedt & Lavay, 1992).

Title II of PL 99-457 expands its services to children between 3 and 5 years old. Youngsters must receive identical services and protections now being provided to school-aged children. These services include, in part, full and appropriate education, due process, court appeals, and attorney fees (McCubbin & Zittel, 1991).

One of the biggest concerns regarding PL 99-457 and the preschool program, since its original passage in 1986, has been that Congress has not funded the programs to their fullest authorization and the states must assume the financial responsibility for implementing the law. It is interesting to review what has happened in the past few years. In 1986 federal funding for PL 99-457 was $30 million. The 1990 fiscal budget of $330 million ($250 million for preschool and $80 million for early childhood) does represent a 1,100 percent increase (Early Intervention, 1990).

McCormick (1990) believes the most notable difference between PL 94-142 and PL 99-457, other than the target children, is the strong emphasis PL 99-457 places on providing support for *families* of the children involved. This law recognizes that a child is part of a family system and that early intervention is effective only when key family members are involved.

EARLY CHILDHOOD INTERVENTION PROGRAMS: A SHORT HISTORY

During the past 25 years, specific early childhood programs have come into prominence. Legal, social, and scientific factors have provided direction to support the need for early intervention programs. Early childhood programs such as the 1964 Project Head Start and the 1972 Brookline Early Education Project (BEEP) have demonstrated positive results. School districts were helped by the *Children's Early Assistance Act* of 1968. This law enabled several projects to develop, including the Handicapped Children's Early Education Programs (HCEEP). These projects represented a wide variety of curricular approaches and provided for many individuals with different disabling conditions. The results of HCEEP projects were reviewed by DeWeerd (1984) and it was concluded that 55 percent of the "at-risk" children were placed in "mainstreamed" settings and 67 percent achieved at average to above-average levels when they entered school after being involved in special early education training programs. Patton, Payne, and Beirne-Smith (1990) comment on the impact of early childhood programs: "Most special educators now agree that appropriate early intervention significantly impacts a child's intellectual capacity and potential to learn" (p. 264). A more detailed account of early childhood projects can be found in Antley and DuBose (1981) and Heward and Orlansky (1992).

Trohanis (1991) estimates that as of the 1988–1989 school year, over 321,000 children, representing 3.2 percent of the population ages 3 through 5 years, were served with free appropriate public education. "This...reflects a 21 percent increase since the passage of PL 99-457 [in 1986]" (p. v).

Some professionals believe the focus of early intervention programs should be on preparing children for transition to and maintenance in integrated programs. Emphasis on attempting to remediate developmental delays and deficits may not be justified (Garland & Linder, 1988). Skills must be developed that will help a child succeed in future settings. McCormick (1990, p. 90) suggests specific skills that should be major considerations when programming for youngsters with developmental disabilities.

Play activities can help little ones to develop needed skills.

- Independent work skills
- Group attending/participation skills
- Following class routines
- Following directions
- Functional communication skills
- Social/play skills

The thrust of early intervention programming has included all dimensions of developmental education. Natural growth and developmental motor patterns have been viewed as guidelines and norms for all children. Children with developmental disabilities are often compared to these norms. The information gathered from these comparisons allows for a more comprehensive writing of annual goals and short-term objectives.

COGNITIVE AND MOTOR LEARNING: A NATURAL MARRIAGE

Cognitive learning and motor learning are known to be interwoven and are at times difficult to differentiate. Payne and Isaacs (1991) state the following: "An awareness...is critical to a thorough understanding of motor development because cognitive and motor development constantly interact. Cognitive development strongly depends on the movement capabilities the individual has acquired; similarly, motor development depends on intellectual capabilities" (p. 21). For individuals with disabilities, not enough can be said for the inclusion of specific motor programs. Therefore, major components for intellectual stimulation, motor development, and motor learning should be found in all early childhood programs. Physicians, physical educators, special educators, child development specialists, and therapists would likely agree that much of the teaching and learning that occurs in infants, toddlers, and preschool children is related to indirect or specifically planned progressions through the use of established developmental motor milestones.

Today, the obligation of providing early childhood programs has become the direct responsibility of the public schools. Professionals who deal with infants and young children must be able to assess existing levels of motor development, write appropriate developmental programs, teach these programs, and, finally, evaluate the progress made by the children. For physical educators, most will need to be more specifically trained for this responsibility. It is strongly suggested that all university physical education major programs include detailed coursework pertaining to early childhood development, assessment, and programming. Ideally, a new and progressive challenge for all present and future physical educators would be to develop a working understanding of the motor domain of infants, toddlers, and preschool children. University programs that train *adapted* physical education specialists *must* include specific coursework pertaining to early childhood assessment and programming, thereby ensuring that highly trained *adapted* physical education specialists will possess the necessary expertise (Kelly, 1991).

EARLY INTERVENTION PROGRAMS: A RATIONALE

Kirk and Gallagher (1989) have found that early intervention programs can be extremely important. They list the following reasons:

- Early intervention programs help to identify additional disabilities.
- Early intervention seems to reduce the future costs of educating children with multiple or severe disabilities. There appears to be a correlation between the cost of educating children with disabilities and the age at which intervention begins. The earlier the intervention, the lower is the annual cost of providing educational services.

- Parents of children with disabilities need the services delivered by early intervention programs.

Gast and Wolery (1985) suggest other benefits of early intervention programs:

1. Early experiences influence all areas of functioning—motor, sensory, cognitive, and social.
2. Data support the notion that there are critical or optimal periods of central nervous system development during the first 3 years of life.
3. Early intervention can inhibit or prevent the atrophy of muscles, thus avoiding the development of contractures.
4. Failure to remedy one handicap can adversely affect other areas of development.
5. Most handicapping conditions become worse as the child grows without early intervention.
6. There is growing evidence that early intervention helps. (pp. 479–480)

INFANCY DEFINED

The first 22 days following birth is considered the neonatal period. This time is included in the period known as infancy and extends from birth through the first year of life and ends with onset of independent walking (Payne & Isaacs, 1991).

CHILDREN "AT-RISK"

Children who possess identifiable disabilities (e.g., Down syndrome) are obvious candidates for early intervention programs. A second major group of youngsters who could benefit from special programming includes those labeled as "at-risk."

At-risk pertains to youngsters who are not currently identified as disabled but are considered to have a greater than usual chance of developing a disability. The term is most often used with infants and preschoolers who, because of conditions surrounding their birth or their home environment, may experience developmental problems at a later time. Heward and Orlansky (1988) provide the following example:

> Physicians also use the terms *at risk* or *high risk* to identify pregnancies with a greater-than-normal probability of producing babies with handicaps. For example, a pregnancy may be considered high risk if the pregnant woman is above or below normal childbearing age, if she is a heavy user of alcohol, or if she is drug-dependent. (p. 4)

At-risk children can be divided into three general types:

- *Established risk*: children with known medical conditions that affect their lives

Some children will be easily identified as "at risk."

- *Suspect risk*: children with developmental histories suggestive of biological problems
- *Environmental risk*: children with no known medical or biological problems who experience life situations associated with potential problems (Patton & Polloway, 1990)

THE INDIVIDUALIZED FAMILY SERVICE PLAN (IFSP)

The development of an individualized family service plan is a major component of PL 99-457. The IFSP and the individualized educational plan (IEP) of PL 94-142 are developed by a multidisciplinary team after initial assessment information has been gathered. There are similarities between the two plans, but the IFSP places an emphasis on the inclusion of the family in both planning and in actively participating in the program (Edelman, 1990). Hutinger (1988, pp. 48–49) lists eight components of an IFSP (see Table 4.1). As would be expected, a statement regarding the child's present level of development must be included. Therefore, the motor performance

TABLE 4.1   **The Individualized Family Service Plan**

According to P.L. 99-457, the individual family service plan (IFSP) must contain the following:

1. A statement of the child's present levels of development (cognitive, speech and language, psychosocial, motor, and self-help).
2. A statement of the family's strengths and needs related to enhancing the child's development.
3. A statement of major outcomes expected to be achieved for the child and family.
4. The criteria, procedures, and timelines for determining progress.
5. The specific early intervention services necessary to meet the unique needs of the child and family, including the method, frequency, and intensity of service.
6. The projected dates for the initiation of services and expected duration.
7. The name of the case manager.
8. Procedures for the transition from early intervention into the preschool program.

Source: From "Screening, Identification, and Assessment" by P. L. Hutinger, 1988. In J. B. Jordan, J. J. Gallagher, P. L. Hutinger, & M. B. Karnes, *Early Childhood Special Education: Birth to Three* (pp. 48–49), Reston, VA: Council for Exceptional Children/ Division for Early Childhood. Reprinted by permission.

level of the child must be listed. Also necessary is the listing of *specific* early intervention activities to meet the unique needs of the child *and the family*, including method, frequency, and intensity of service. When planning these activities, the physical educator should follow appropriate developmental guidelines and look for specific motor milestones.

A major component of PL 99-457 involves direct participation by the parents. Teachers and therapists will likely be training parents to provide activities for the babies. Belsky, Goode, and Most (1980) found that maternal stimulation of their youngsters (ages 9 to 18 months) promoted exploratory skill as well as learning. The mothers in their study (N = 32) were taught to direct their children's attention to objects and events in the home and how to gain control over and focus attention. Belsky et al. concluded

> that infants learn from their mothers how to stimulate themselves. Since such skill is considered essential for initiating and maintaining self-directed exploration, infant play is the product of maternal stimulation.... that during the last quarter of the first year there would be an increase in mothers' physical and verbal attention-focusing behavior in response to their infants' budding curiosity and mobility. (p. 1169)

This study was conducted with nondisabled infants but the results have a definite relationship for youngsters who are at risk. Parental inclusion will still be imperative for maximum results to occur.

Healy (1990) summarizes the intent of cooperation among professionals working in early intervention programs when he states the following:

Just as the entire field of early intervention services has evolved through interdisciplinary understanding, encouragement, and participation, additional increases in participation in the fulfillment of Public Law 99-457 requires that all involved professionals understand the roles and responsibilities of physicians in the organization, delivery, and evaluation of early intervention services. Such understanding, coupled with ongoing, interdisciplinary, mutual support and encouragement, must become the standard for the development of the health and medical care components of all national, state, and community-based early intervention services. (p. vii)

ESTABLISHING A NEED FOR PROGRAMS OF MOTOR STIMULATION

For young children with developmental disabilities, common sense dictates that specific programs be planned and instituted as early in life as possible. This will help to ensure that motor development begins and continues toward reaching optimal

Early intervention allows children "at risk" to experience needed motor opportunities.

levels. One of the reasons for providing early childhood programs is that they have the potential to reduce many problems that often become entrenched if allowed to continue into later years. These individualized programs can provide opportunities for at-risk children who are likely to need adapted motor training. The writing and implementation of annual goals and short-term objectives should enable youngsters with developmental disabilities to attain higher motor skill levels than would be possible without early intervention programs. Hanson (1984) reinforces this concept when she states that, "without special, comprehensive intervention, children with known disability and those at high risk for developing problems may not develop early skills and relationships needed in order to lead productive lives" (p. 362).

HOW INFANTS DEVELOP

Over the past 20 years, developmental specialists have altered their thinking regarding how infants develop. They once believed that a baby's capacity to learn emerged slowly after birth. Infants were thought to be passive recipients of parental care. Some experts believed that child development took place primarily as a result of the "unfolding" of the child's inborn capacities; others felt that development was influenced primarily by the experiences the child encountered in the environment (Spitz, 1988). Now it is widely believed that infants develop through a continuing interaction between their inborn abilities and the stimulation they receive from their environment (Payne & Isaacs, 1991).

The National Information Center for Children and Youth with Handicaps (1988) list four critical points regarding how infants develop:

1. An infant's capacity to learn is present from birth.
2. Infants learn through social interaction.
3. Infants are active learners.
4. Infants affect their parents, just as parents affect infants.

Mussen, Conger, and Kagan (1980) propose an interesting set of questions regarding infant development and early intervention:

> What about those infants who do not have the opportunities for playful intervention? What aspects of caretaking are most important? Does an infant really need much besides a clean dry diaper, a bottle of milk, and a warm place to sleep? In poorly run, understaffed institutions, infants may receive no more than routine care. Seldom are they held, and rarely does anyone talk or play with them. As we would expect, children in such settings are retarded in language, less vocal, less socially acceptable, and less alert to changes around them. (p. 134)

Before 3 or 4 months, little measurable difference is seen between nondisabled babies and those raised in institutional settings. The greatest change occurs after infants reach 4 months of age. The babies in a poor institutional setting seem to be listless and apathetic, demonstrating little response to caretakers, toys, or other aspects of their external environment. Their curiosity for new experiences seems nonexistent. For example, behaviors that are most likely to be learned as a result of interactions with people (i.e., clinging, crying in distress, reaching for adults for holding and play, and vocalization) are clearly delayed or absent in institutionalized children (Hallahan & Kauffman, 1988).

Babies learn through a variety of stimulating experiences, but caution should be given regarding the intensity and type of stimulation. It is the controlled variety of the experiences that are critical and not the intensity of stimulation. An infant in a crowded one-room apartment encounters many sights and sounds simultaneously, whereas a baby in her own bedroom in a single-family home with a relatively quiet environment is presented with distinctive stimuli. Her mother's voice breaks the quiet of the bedroom when she talks directly to the baby. This seemingly simple approach will more likely catch her attention and teach her something than a voice over a television set in a sea of noise. It is this distinctive quality, not simply quantity of stimulation, that is effective in enriching an infant's intellectual development (Mussen, et al., 1980).

Belsky et al. (1980) have found that infants and toddlers can be greatly assisted by early stimulation programs that use the parents of the children. They suggest that when parents are preinstructed to use attention-focusing behavior, it will foster infant exploratory skill; moreover, physical actions will more concretely draw attention to an object/event and exert greater influence than do verbal strategies. They state: "This may be due to the fact that physical strategies are more successful in capturing and directing infant attention" (p. 1173).

Infants with immature or damaged nervous systems (i.e., delayed brain development or brain damage) may be unable to tolerate a great amount of stimulation. Gorski (1984) states: "Contrary to general myth, social interaction can produce as much stress in weak infants as can painful stimuli" (p. 70). Therefore, infant stimulation must be carefully monitored, and caregivers should follow prescribed guidelines of the pediatrician or therapist.

INFANTS WITH DEVELOPMENTAL DISABILITIES

Babies with developmental disabilities (DD) are likely to experience delays in both motor and cognitive development. DeGangi (1991) believes it is imperative to determine the extent of developmental delay of youngsters with DD. She recommends the following:

1. Evaluation of infant performance in sensorimotor and regulatory processes affecting functional learning and behaviors

2. Incorporation of parental observations regarding the influence of an infant's behaviors on his or her functioning within the family and home environment

3. Examination of parental characteristics (e.g., personality dimensions, interaction styles) and parental availability to be involved in the assessment and treatment process (p. 1)

MOTOR LEARNING

All children will experience many opportunities to learn motor skills if they are encouraged and allowed to move in their environment. Some youngsters, because of their disabilities, may need highly structured programs to ensure that *appropriate* movement experiences are provided. Individualized programs, formulated on basic principles of motor learning, are known to result in more successful outcomes. In Table 4.2, Lerner, Mardell-Czudnowski, and Goldenberg (1987) describe these principles as they apply to children with developmental disabilities.

PIAGET'S (1952) DEVELOPMENTAL LEARNING THEORY

A highly accepted theory of how children develop was developed by the Swiss psychologist, Jean Piaget (pe-ah-zhay). His main theme is that all intelligence has as its source the infant's motor actions on the environment. Through such infant-environment exchanges, inborn reflex mechanisms progressively fade and become integrated, eventually developing into internalized actions called mental operations. Mental operations are the ideas or strategies with which individuals learn to cope with the world.

TABLE 4.2 Principles of Motor Learning as They Affect Children with Disabilities

1. *Human learning begins with motor learning.* As human beings move, they learn. An understanding of the dynamics of learning necessarily involves an understanding of movement and motor development.

2. *There is a natural sequence of developmental motor stages.* Each stage must be successfully acquired by the child before the next stage is added.

3. *Academic and cognitive learning is based on successful motor learning experiences.* A child's academic and cognitive problems may be due to insufficient motor experiences and gaps in motor learning.

4. *Planned motor intervention can provide children with missing motor experiences.* Building motor skills prepares the child for academic and cognitive learning.

Source: From *Special Education* (3rd ed.) (p. 164) by J. Lerner, C. Mardell-Czudnowski, & D. Goldenberg, 1987, Englewood Cliffs, NJ: Prentice-Hall. Reprinted by permission.

A second central idea proposed by Piaget is that intellectual operations are acquired in a developmental sequence. His developmental sequences are divided into four major periods, with each divided into a number of stages, or subperiods. These stages are not constant as to chronological ages, and different societies will vary, but the stages are always taken in specific order. The four periods and their age equivalents are (1) sensorimotor (birth to 2 years), (2) preoperational (2 to 7 years), (3) concrete operations (7 to 11 years), and (4) formal operations (12 to 15 years through adulthood). These four periods are briefly discussed in Appendix 4A.

The *sensorimotor period* is the time the infant changes from a creature who responds through reflexes to one who can organize his activities in relation to his environment. It is important to mention that although Piaget suggested approximate age boundaries for each stage, they are only approximate, as he was not particularly concerned with establishing age norms. In the sensorimotor period the child deals with the environment mainly through physical acts. She understands objects in terms of the actions she associates with them. Thus, bottles and pacifiers are things to put into your mouth and suck, whereas rattles are things to shake. The sensorimotor period takes the infant from a reflexive, body-centered organism whose world is spaceless, timeless, and objectless to one with acquired behavior patterns and the ability to think, at least in a rudimentary, practical sense, about those objects and everyday events that are directly experienced. Langley (1989) states that "sensorimotor intelligence is the ability to solve problems through the integration of perception, postural adjustment, and movement prior to the acquisition of language" (p. 249).

GESELL'S (1964) MATURATIONAL CONCEPTS

Arnold Gesell used the term "maturation" to explain changes in the developing child over a period of time. Maturation referred to the developmental change controlled by genetic factors. He found that maturation sets limits on growth. Within these preestablished limits, learning could produce changes in behavior. Thus, development resulted from the combined influence of maturation and learning. Gesell strongly believed that if youngsters were forced to learn skills beyond their current maturational level, they would become frustrated and inevitably fail. Effective learning, according to Gesell, requires a match between the child's current developmental level and the types of activities provided to stimulate learning.

Gesell's strong, genetically dominated theories have been questioned because they do not give enough credit to the influence of environmental conditions. Most developmental specialists now recognize that maturation is strongly influenced by the environment. Additionally, it is generally accepted that the "environment affect" begins at conception.

Four major principles developed by Gesell are as follows:

1. Directionality
2. Functional Asymmetry

3. Self-Regulating Fluctuation

4. Motor Development

Teaching of motor skills can be enhanced through the understanding and use of Gesell's developmental concepts. For example, physical education instructors can add developmental behaviors between the entry and exit objectives of a task analysis (Bagnato, Neisworth, & Munson, 1989).

Berger and Yule (1987) believe the Gesell test battery can provide detailed information of current functioning and is able to detect severe mental disability within the first year of life. Eckert (1987) describes Gesell's motor milestones of infants:

- In the first quarter (4-16 weeks) of the first year the infant gains control of his twelve oculomotor muscles.

- In the second quarter (16-28 weeks) he comes in command of the muscles which support the head and move his arms. He reaches for things.

- In the third quarter (28-40 weeks) he gains command of his trunk and hands. He sits. He grasps, transfers, and manipulates objects.

- In the fourth quarter (40-52 weeks) he extends command to his legs and feet; to his forefinger and thumb. He pokes and plucks. He stands upright. (p. 127)

To summarize Gesell's maturational concepts, Eichstaedt and Lavay (1992) state the following:

Newborns are incapable of effectively resisting the pull of gravity. Their postures and movements are characterized by flexion, with varying degrees of abduction and adduction, depending on their position. The development of extension in the vertebrae and extremities allow the child to pull up against gravity and move into upright positions. Rotation appears slowly in lying, sitting, standing, and walking, and is critical for developing smooth, skilled transition from one position to another. (p. 325)

A general description of Gesell's maturational concepts can be found in Appendix 4B. The full *Gesell Developmental Schedules* are included in the writings of Knobloch and Pasamanick (1974).

MOTOR ASSESSMENT OF THE INFANT

Movement is the avenue through which infants interact with their environment. As discussed before, Piaget believed movement is closely tied to and interrelated with both perceptual and conceptual development. Additionally, movement is an integral component of tasks in other domains including mobility, play, and self-help. Thus, attainment of movement skill and development of adequate motor performance is an important aspect of developmental programming for infants and toddlers with disabilities. Assessing existing levels of motor performance of an infant becomes extremely important (Eason, 1991). Historically, physical or occupational therapists have been given the responsibility for conducting assessments of motor skills. However, there are many reasons why physical educators and special educators should be familiar with terminology, infant test batteries, and all phases of programmatic development. Smith (1989) suggests the following prerequisites for professionals who plan to work with infants and young children:

- Professionals who have a clear understanding of normal motor development and screening methods are better able to identify children who need a thorough motor assessment.

- Professionals who are knowledgeable in motor development and assessment are better able to identify children's current abilities and needs in motor functioning and can plan more adequate instructional programs.

- Professionals who understand neuromotor development and its application to motor skill development are better able to use equipment and apply intervention techniques across curricular domains.

- Professionals who are knowledgeable in motor assessment are better able to document child progress, monitor intervention strategies, evaluate program effectiveness, and identify subtle changes in children's motor skills, particularly those with motor disabilities.

- Professionals who understand and use terminology from relevant disciplines (i.e., adapted physical education, physical therapy, occupational therapy) are able to communicate more effectively with members of those disciplines. (p. 302)

Traditional neonatal assessment test batteries have been questioned because they suffer from two major limitations. First, most test batteries have been concerned with two outcomes, namely, whether newborn infants are normal or abnormal. The second limitation of traditional test batteries is that they have made conclusions based on single sources of information. Sheehan and Gallagher (1984) refer to the problem of early infant assessment when they state that "the limitations found in several neonatal assessment efforts are typified by using indices such as birthweight (2,000 or 1,500 grams), gestational age (37 weeks), or presence or absence of a particular problem (e.g., respiratory distress syndrome) to categorize infants as high risk or normal" (p. 87).

Although Sheehan and Gallagher (1984) believe that a large number of existing infant assessment batteries lack overall reliability and validity and represent a collection of items with little regard for sequencing, integration, and working of items, it is appropriate to become familiar with one of the most commonly used infant test batteries, the Apgar Neonatal Scoring System.

THE APGAR NEONATAL SCORING SYSTEM

The Apgar neonatal (newborn) scoring system was developed by Virginia Apgar (1953). Newborn children are assessed by using five test items during their first minute of life, and again after 5 minutes. Both scores are recorded on the child's records. The initial rating is done to determine if the infants need immediate emergency care. The second is of particular interest, as this score is somewhat predictive of possible brain damage and the likelihood for developmental delays (Apgar & Beck, 1972). Hanson (1984) warns that Apgar scores only serve to measure initial obstacles to normal postnatal adaptation. They do not directly assess an infant's neurological functioning, nor can these scores predict future developmental delays.

Usually delivery room nurses or anesthesiologists rate the baby on five measures, using a scale of 0 to 2 for each item (10 maximum points). The areas of interest include skin color, heart rate, reflex response, muscle tone, and respiratory effort. The letters in Apgar are commonly used to identify the five test measures: *A*ppearance, *P*ulse, *G*rimace, *A*ctivity, and *R*espiration. A general description of the Apgar test, including a breakdown of how points are given, is found in Appendix 4C.

DEVELOPMENTAL TEST BATTERIES

Motor assessment of infants requires extensive training and is usually completed by physical therapists, occupational therapists, or kinesiotherapists. Some adapted physical educators, with special training, are also capable of administering infant developmental scales. Traditional physical education instructors should become familiar with the general makeup of commonly used infant test batteries, but in most cases they will not be expected to test the youngsters.

There are many test batteries used for assessment of motor development of infants and toddlers. In the research completed by Jordan, Gallagher, Hutinger, and Karnes (1988) regarding assessment of infants between birth and 3, one test battery was indicated most often in the 72 instruments used by different agencies. The *Bayley Scales of Infant Development* (1969) was most frequently used.

Basically, all infant and young child developmental test batteries measure similar components, these being cognition, communication/language, social skills/adaptation, self-help, fine motor, and gross motor. A more extensive review of infant developmental test batteries can be found in Chapter 5.

PRIMARY INFANT REFLEXES

The word *reflex*, when used in reference to motor development, pertains to a specific movement or posture that occurs when a particular stimulus is given. Reflexes are present at birth in full-term infants but may not have developed in premature babies. The presence of primary reflexes indicates that the nervous system is working properly. Neonates are unable to control these reflexes. Often these reflexes are referred to as primary or primitive reflexes. Generally speaking, these actions protect and provide responses that help babies to feed or to grasp. A loud sound, a sensation of falling, a touching of the cheek, a stroking of the palm or sole of the foot will elicit a response that the youngsters cannot control. As weeks go by, and infant "learning" occurs, babies are able to override these reflexes and thus control their movements. For example, no longer will an infant begin uncontrolled sucking actions when his cheek is stroked. He will have overcome (integrated) this innate action and now can control when he wants to suck.

Infants who are born prematurely (less than 36 weeks or less than $5\frac{1}{2}$ pounds) or have experienced brain damage may not possess these primary reflexes. Their nervous systems are incomplete and the youngsters will need special care and attention, which is usually provided in modern neonatal care units. Both types of infants are considered high-risk babies and are prime candidates for early intervention programs such as those identified in P.L. 99-457 and P.L. 101-476.

Pyfer (1988) has determined there are at least 36 reflexes that are critical to normal motor development. She states that "fourteen of these reflexes appear during the first year of life and eventually enable a child to assume an upright position and begin to move about. If these reflexes do not appear, the child will not be able to lift his head, balance on all fours, sit, or turn the head toward the outstretched hand" (p. 38).

Winnick and Short (1985) describe the role that primary reflexes play in infants:

> If reflexes, when elicited, are uneven in strength, too weak or too strong, or inappropriate at a particular age, neurological dysfunction may be suspected. Various reflexive behaviors are quite predictable and are expected to appear at particular ages and to be inhibited, disappear, or be replaced by higher order reflexes at later ages. Failure of certain reflexes to disappear, be inhibited, or replaced may inhibit the development of voluntary movement. (p. 50)

If primary reflexes do appear but fail to be eliminated in a normal period of time, children will be slow to crawl, creep, stand, and walk. Additionally, each of these mobility patterns will be performed in a clumsy and awkward manner.

The following primary infant reflexes are taken from Eichstaedt and Lavay (1992).

- Palmer Grasp or Hand Grasp Reflex. (onset from birth to 3 months)
  Stimulus: A finger is stroked across the palm.
  Response: The fingers close tightly and remain closed.
  Significance: This supports the infant's ability to grasp objects but must fade before objects can be voluntarily released.
- Moro Reflex or Startle Reflex. (onset from birth to 4 months)
  Stimulus: The baby's head is allowed to fall back into teacher's hand, or baby hears a loud noise.

Response: The Arms (and sometimes the legs) move suddenly up and back, then are moved forward across the chest. As this reflex fades out, only slight arm movements are apparent.

Significance: The baby cannot use the arms for protection during a sudden loss of balance.

- Toe Grasp or Plantar Grasp. (onset from birth to 12 months)

  Stimulus: A slight pressure is given over the ball of the foot, or the baby is placed in a standing position.

  Response: The Toes curl in flexion and stay curled.

  Significance: This reflex must fade before the child will have good balance in the standing position.

- Asymmetric Tonic Neck Reflex (ATNR). (onset from 1 to 4 months)

  Stimulus: The head is turned to the side.

  Response: The arm and sometimes the leg on the face side (i.e., the side to which the head is turned) extend, and the arm and sometimes the leg on the opposite side flex.

  Significance: This reflex often assists the baby in reaching out for an object in a back-lying position; but must fade so as not to induce unwanted arm extension when head is turned to the side.

- Symmetric Tonic Neck Reflex (STNR). (onset from 6 to 8 months)

  Stimulus: Occurs with extension or flexion of the neck.

  Response: With neck extension, the arms tend to extend and the legs flex at the hips; with neck flexion, the arms tend to flex and the legs extend.

  Significance: This reflex provides assistance when learning to creep but must fade because all movements may be affected if they are initiated with head flexion or extension. For example, if children still possess a positive STNR at an age when they should be creeping on all fours, the abnormal reflex will cause unwanted elbow or hip bending. Thus, the children cannot move forward because of this unwanted limb flexion.

POSTURAL REFLEXES

Most infants will develop postural reflexes, although youngsters with brain damage may progress at significantly slower rates. Obviously, the more neurological damage the individuals possess, the longer it will take for the children to move through the necessary developmental milestones. Postural reflexes include body righting, equilibrium, and protective reactions. These reflexes begin to appear a few months after birth, and with nondisabled children continue through the first 5 years of life. For children with moderate, severe, and profound disabilities, postural reflexes are usually delayed for several more years. The role of physical education and therapy is to provide movement experiences that will help to fade unwanted reflexes, thus allowing the children to move forward and upward through the developmental milestones.

Postural reflex reactions are important because they (1) maintain the head in an upright position and (2) ensure alignment of body parts for normal movement. These reflexes persist throughout life, providing an automatic support system for individuals to perform voluntary actions. Postural reactions are classified according to their function, including (1) righting, (2) tilting, and (3) protective extension.

RIGHTING REACTIONS

Righting reactions allow for alignment of body parts to each other and the alignment of the body as a whole. Four major righting reactions are as follows:

1. Head Righting. (onset from 2 to 4 months)

    Stimulus: The child is held at the shoulders and tilted forward or sideward.

    Response: The child brings head to an upright position with the eyes parallel to the horizon.

    Significance: The ability to right the head in space is the first phase of development of postural control. A child with this ability requires less support when being carried and has greater freedom to visualize and survey the environment.

2. Neck Righting. (onset from 4 to 6 months)

    Stimulus: With the child in the supine position, the teacher/ therapist turns the child's head to one side.

    Response: First the child turns the shoulders, then the hips, in the same direction.

    Significance: This sequence of movements promotes the rolling pattern started when the head turns.

3. Landau Response. (onset from 4 to 6 months)

    Stimulus: While in the prone position, the child is suspended by the chest.

    Response: Initially the baby lifts only the head; later, the back and legs extend; the back also arches upward.

    Significance: In the prone position, this allows the child to push up on elbows and later to push up on hands.

4. Body Righting. (onset from 4 to 6 months).

    Stimulus: While the baby is in the supine position, the teacher/therapist bends one of the baby's legs and draws it up and across the other side.

    Response: The baby turns shoulders, then head, in the direction of the leg movement, thus completing a roll onto the stomach.

    Significance: This action encourages development of a rolling pattern.

PROTECTIVE EXTENSIVE REACTIONS

Protective extension reactions are often described as "parachute" actions, and when properly working, they involve automatic movements of the arms and/or legs to catch oneself after balance has been lost. These reactions begin at a time when babies are learning to sit, stand, and walk and are developing in a very sequential manner. There are four important protective extensive reactions.

1. Downward Extension Reaction (onset from 4 to 6 months)

    Stimulus: The baby, suspended vertically in the air, is suddenly lowered toward a supporting surface but without letting the feet actually contact the surface.

    Response: The legs extend quickly and move slightly apart. The toes are brought up in preparation of weight bearing.

2. Forward Arm Extension Reaction. (onset from 6 to 7 months)

    Stimulus: The baby is held horizontally in the air, with the face down, then moved suddenly toward a supporting surface.

    Response: The arms are quickly brought forward and weight is taken on open hands.

3. Sidewards Extension Reaction. (onset from 7 to 8 months)

    Stimulus: The baby is placed in a sitting position and is gently but firmly pushed to the side.

    Response: The arm, on the side the baby is falling, moves quickly to that side and the weight is taken on an open hand.

4. Backward Extension Reaction. (onset from 9 to 10 months)

    Stimulus: In a sitting position, the baby is pushed quickly backward at the shoulder.

    Response: On the side the shoulder is pushed, the arm extends behind the body and the weight is taken on an open hand.

Infant development of postural responses can be unpredictable, as described by Johnson-Martin, Jens, and Attermeier (1986):

Although there is considerable variety in rate and some variety in order of milestone attainment, infants gain skills in a similar manner....At any given point in development, babies will alternate between using established skills and experimenting with new ones. If left on their own, and not placed in positions that they cannot independently assume, they will generally stay within the limit of their motor ability. Their exploration of movement, then, is continually self-reinforcing....Bear in mind that motor development is not a strictly stepwise process. At any given time a child will have some skills at lower stages of development. The motor program should include a variety of activities in different positions. (pp. 32, 37)

What if children with developmental delays are not given appropriate early intervention programs? Are these delays permanent or are they reversible? Can specific motor programming help? Mussen et al. (1980) believe special programming should not be delayed:

It appears that retardation during the first year or two of life does not necessarily doom the child to permanent incompetence, for with the proper environment, children do have amazing powers of recovery. The secret is to find the proper environment to overcome the initial handicap in these children....Most of the information gathered by psychologists to date does not provide for the popular belief that the experiences of infancy create fixed behavior patterns that persist no matter what environmental circumstances follow. However, neither can we conclude that the experiences of infancy are of no consequence for later childhood. It is encouraging, however, to find that if the conditions that may have caused fearfulness and retardation during infancy are favorably changed during the years 2 to 6, dramatic changes can occur. (pp. 138–139)

LEARNING CHARACTERISTICS OF INFANTS

Regarding very young infants, Taylor and Valerie (1990) believe that the nature of learning develops in a way that turns experience into knowledge. The initial contact with adults, which they term *attachment,* usually begins between the ages of 3 and 6 months:

When an attachment has been formed with the prime caregiver the child is more likely to risk new experiences because he or she has a sense of basic trust....Without trust, the child can become a mistrusting and demanding person. It is essential that children find...a climate of trust if any learning is to take place. In such an environment the healthy tension needed to encourage children to move out, to investigate and explore leads to the acquisition of a sense of autonomy whereby they learn to deal with frustrations and to investigate them into the totality of learning without doubting their ability to overcome obstacles. (p. 16)

If there is no attachment between the baby and the parent by the time the child is 6 months old, difficulties are likely to develop in the form of learning delays.

MOTOR ACTIVITIES FOR INFANTS

It is extremely important to provide motor activities that are appropriate for the children's developmental levels and not their chronological ages. Norms developed for specific ages could lead to false assumptions. Johnson-Martin et al. (1986) have found that most youngsters with mental retardation (particularly if their IQs were less than 50) would have difficulty attaining a 6-month motor gain in a 6-month period.

Activity programs should emphasize the children's levels of performance and not be locked into specific age requirements. For example, as was once done in the Doman/Delacato patterning program, infants and toddlers were required, while in a prone position, to have their head, arms, and legs manually moved to simulate the crawling action, even though these same youngsters were already creeping, and in some cases even walking. Programs must emphasize existing levels of development and provide for individualized activities. Instructors should develop a daily plan for each child, with specific activities based on developmental progressions. Anderson, Hinjosa, and Strauch (1987) have found that children's movement is best observed when they are happy, playing, and producing natural patterns. When children are absorbed in pleasurable activities they are not focusing on the motor demands inherent in the activity. Teachers will be able to see (and record) more strengths and weaknesses than are usually produced in traditional motor assessment test batteries.

Activities should be simple, organized, and limited in scope to allow the teacher to handle the child most effectively. Anderson and coworkers (1987) suggest that:

> less complicated activities with fewer positioning requirements are effective and interfere less with handling. With the young infant (birth to 3 months), the therapist's face and voice can be effective play objects to stimulate visual fixation and tracking, thereby facilitating side-to-side rolling while the child lies supine. (p. 424)

Movement can be developed by using toys or objects to elicit touching, grasping, releasing, and placing. Similarly, posture patterns (rolling, sitting, all-fours) can be strengthened by stimulating the youngsters' interest in their favorite toys, brightly colored objects, and things that make noise.

The inclusion of play in the teaching of infants cannot be emphasized enough. Whaley (1990, p. 350) describes five progressive levels of play in regard to infant development.

- LEVEL I: *Complementary/Reciprocal Social Play*   The infant and adult engage in purely social play with the adult as the "object." The play is

Children are best observed when they are happy.

complementary and reciprocal in nature as smiles, sounds, and gazes are exchanged. Each partner in play relies on the other for the play to continue.

- LEVEL II: *Complementary/Reciprocal Play With Mutual Awareness* Exchanges are still dyadic [between the two] in nature, but attention now shifts to objects. The adult presents objects to the infant for interaction and the infant attends only to the object. Both participants have defined roles, but no social exchange occurs during the object play.

- LEVEL III: *Simple Social/Simple Object Play*   The infant can now manipulate and initiate his own object play. Exploration and manipulation of objects predominates. The parent is still vital in providing constant social input but not simultaneous with object manipulations.

- LEVEL IV: *Object Play with Mutual Regard*   The infant has the ability to attend to both objects and adults simultaneously and is now able to enter into "conversations" with adults about objects.

- LEVEL V: *Simple Parallel Play*   The infant engages in solitary object play with an adult nearby. No social interaction is needed to maintain the play. The child is able to engage in social play with peers at this point as well.

TASK ANALYSIS

Most motor skills can be broken down into smaller sequenced steps. This process is commonly referred to as task analysis. Many individualized motor programs for youngsters with disabilities are written using the part-to-whole technique of teaching, thus stressing the task analysis method. Davis and Burton (1991) are using the term *ecological task analysis* in an attempt to be more specific as they believe traditional models are too simplistic. Their model is shown in Figure 4.1.

Teachers will usually find that infants give signs when they are receptive and want to learn. The babies will give verbal "coos," gaze attentively with their eyes, and move their arms and legs in excited actions. These natural interactions appear to be signals and the baby is saying "I am happy, willing, and eager to learn." Hanson (1987) suggests the following:

> Don't just passively move your baby through exercises. Place the child in the designated situation or position, then give the child a chance to respond. For example, when you are rocking the child from side to side during trunk control exercises, tip the child slightly and wait for the child to right the head and body (bring head and body upright perpendicular to floor), rather than passively rocking the child back and forth. Both you and your baby will have more fun with each other if you take turns responding. (p. 90)

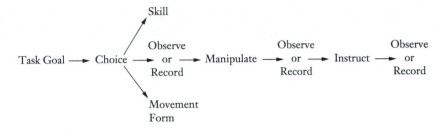

Steps:

1. Select and present the task goal—one of the functional movement categories. Structure the environment and provide verbal and other cues to the student that allow for an understanding of the task goal.

2. Provide choices—have the student practice the task, allowing him/her to choose the skill and the movement form. Observe and/or record the skill choice and movement form in qualitative measures and the performance outcome in quantitative or qualitative measures.

3. Identify the relevant task dimensions and performer variables. Manipulate one or two task dimensions to find the optimal performance level. Observe and/or record the skill choice, movement form, and performance outcomes in qualitative and/or quantitative measures, and compare results with previous measures.

4. Provide direct instruction in skill selection and movement form. Manipulate task variable to challenge the student. Observe and/or record the skill choice, movement form, and performance outcomes in qualitative and/or quantitative measures, and compare results with previous measures.

FIGURE 4.1   **Ecological task analysis model for assessment and instruction of movement tasks.** (*Source:* From "Ecological Task Analysis" by W. E. Davis and A. W. Burton, 1991, *Adapted Physical Activity Quarterly, 8* (2), p. 167. Copyright 1991 by Human Kinetics Publishers. Reprinted by permission.

MOTOR DEVELOPMENT AT 3 MONTHS

Infants will progress through motor milestones if given the opportunity. Table 4.3 lists motor actions and responses that are usually present at a developmental age of 3 months. Parents should be given a copy of the list and asked if their baby can do any of the items listed. Ask them to check the item if the baby consistently performs the task. Teachers should use the parent's completed list and continue with their own observations, being sure to record whenever the youngster consistently performs any new task. Generally speaking, a task is "learned" when the child responds correctly to a stimulus three out of four times on three consecutive days.

Daily activities should be planned that will stimulate the learning of new skills. Infants with disabilities may need more time to learn a task. Mental processing and short-term memory could be delayed and therefore more time will be required.

TABLE 4.3   **Developmental Motor Milestones at 3 Months**

**Age (in months)
or Date Mastered**

_____	1.	Bends and straightens arms and legs
_____	2.	Maintains head in midline position while on back
_____	3.	Head steady when held
_____	4.	Stops movement when noise is heard
_____	5.	Visually searches for sound
_____	6.	Turns head and searches or reaches for ear-level sound while lying down
_____	7.	Visually fixates for at least 3 seconds
_____	8.	Visually tracks object from side to side
_____	9.	Visually tracks object from forehead to chest
_____	10.	Visually tracks object moving in a circle
_____	11.	Shifts attention from one object to another
_____	12.	Looks for or reaches toward objects in sight that touch body
_____	13.	Moves hand to mouth
_____	14.	Responds differently to warm/cold; rough/smooth
_____	15.	Bats at object at chest level
_____	16.	Looks at hand or toy to one side
_____	17.	Looks at or manipulates toy placed in hands at midline
_____	18.	Raises both hands when toy is presented, hands partially open
_____	19.	Turns head from side to side in response to visual and/or auditory stimuli while in supine position

Lerner, Mardell-Czudnowski, and Goldenberg (1987) provide a sequence of prewalking behaviors and methods for infant stimulation (Table 4.4).

When moving, positioning, or handling babies, it is best to support them at the head, shoulders, or hips. Allow ample opportunity for the infants to perform as much of the movement as possible. The instructor should not "push" the youngsters too quickly, but allow them to think about what they are going to do. Johnson-Martin and coworkers (1986) suggest the following: "When bringing a child from back-lying to sitting, roll the child slowly to the side and give the child time to push up on his or her arm, even if he or she can only do this partially" (p. 38).

Babies possess a natural curiosity and will purposefully explore the surrounding area. To do this, most learn to control their head movements. Youngsters with disabilities may not be as inquisitive owing to brain damage or physical limitations. Nevertheless, all children will attempt some degree of trial and error exploration. This process is important as it requires the children to find new methods to touch, grasp, roll, and scoot forward and backward. Table 4.5 lists activities to increase head, arm, and leg control.

TABLE 4.4   **Sequence of Prewalking Gross Motor Behavior and Methods of Stimulation**

Motor Behavior	Method of Stimulating Motor Behavior
Head and Neck Control Turns head to side Raises head from prone position Supports head in an upright position	Stimulate the infant to raise head with the use of a moving light or noise
Sitting with Support Sits in a lap with minimal support Independently sits with prop (pillow) Independently sits in object with reduction of support	Gradually reduce the need for support and increase the length of time for nonsupport. Increasing reduction of support gives the infant a new situation to adjust to.
Rolling Over Rolls over from back to stomach	Place infant on back and guide roll to left or right
Raising Body Supports the upper body on forearm	Stimulate the infant by placing on stomach and using a noisy toy or colorful object to draw attention.
Sitting Without Support Sits in chair independently Sits on the floor independently	Gradually increase the length of time for nonsupported sitting and alternate a variety of places for sitting: floor, chair, highchair, swing, and jumperseat.
Precrawling Initiates forward movement—prone	Use a toy or food as an incentive and draw the infant's attention toward it.
Pull to a Sitting Position Pulls to a sitting position—prone Requires less adult support in task	The adult is an assist and support for the child. The adult will support the child in attempts to accomplish the task.
Creeping Locomotes forward on hands and knees	Offer objects to infant to increase distance accomplished.
Pull to Standing Position Pulls to standing position with support Pulls to stand with less physical support Uses objects as assist for pull to stand	Offer infant the use of adult support to pull to stand from a sitting position and reduce amount of support. Also make objects available for use as supports.
Sidestepping with Support Sidesteps around objects while standing	Encourage moving to left and right in moving around objects.
Standing with Support Stands with minimal adult assistance Stands using objects for adult support Stands without any support	Begin with physical support, and then the adults will gradually reduce support. First, hold with two hands and reduce to one hand and then to fingers.

(*continued*)

TABLE 4.4   (*continued*)

Motor Behavior	Method of Stimulating Motor Behavior
Walking Walks with back support Walks with front support Walks with object support Walks with support from side Walks without support Practices walking skills	Begin with front and back support of infant and gradually reduce physical support. Practice the skill with regularity.

Note: From *Special Education for the Early Childhood Years* (2nd ed.) (pp. 173–174) by J. Lerner, C. Mardell-Czudnowski, & D. Goldenberg, 1987, Englewood Cliffs, NJ: Prentice-Hall. Copyright Prentice-Hall. Reprinted by permission.

TABLE 4.5   **Activities to Increase Head, Arm, and Leg Control**

From the supine position:

- Hold legs at the knee and bend one leg and then the other. This encourages back and forth kicking.
- Stroke the arms and legs.
- Provide rattles and infant toys for the baby to hold and put into the mouth.
- Hang shiny, bright-colored objects high enough so they can be touched and batted with the arms and legs.
- Touch and stroke the hands and feet; also rub them together.
- Hold the baby's hands by putting your thumbs in the baby's hands. Gently pull the baby to a sitting position.
- Shake a rattle behind the baby's head so baby will look for the sound by turning the head and looking back.

From the prone position:

- Show the baby her favorite toy: in front; to the side.
- Pull one leg, then the other leg, to simulate scooting.
- Pull one arm, then the other arm, to simulate pulling.
- Turn the baby's head to the side.
- Holding the baby at the waist, move him up and down.
- Holding the baby at the waist, watch to see if she lifts her head upward.

From an upright position:

- Holding at the waist, swing gently through space.
- Holding at the waist, tilt the baby sideways, back, and forward.

INFANT CHARACTERISTICS AT 6 MONTHS

Shapiro, Palmer, and Capute (1987) have found that when an infant reaches the developmental level of 4 months, he should be able to visually follow a slow-moving object that is passed in front of him. Also, he should be making "cooing" noises and smile when he recognizes familiar faces. They suggest that if a baby does not demonstrate these actions at 4 months, then referral should be made for a more detailed observation and assessment. The implication is that there may be a developmental delay and early intervention programming is suggested.

MOTOR DEVELOPMENT AT 6 MONTHS

A checklist of developmental motor milestones that are normally found by the time a youngster reaches the developmental age of 6 months can be found in Table 4.6.

At a developmental age of 6 months, youngsters are able to use various means to move forward and backward. They are also beginning to use movements that lead to upright posture. Crawling (i.e., scooting on the stomach) and creeping (i.e., on all fours) actions are found to be quite different. Some babies only crawl, whereas others bypass crawling altogether. The weightbearing position of creeping, with its alternating arm and leg movements, is practiced and strengthened during crawling. Proficiency in these actions tend to develop a foundation for later phases of locomotion. Youngsters cannot be forced into these basic skills before their neuromuscular systems are ready. Some children with developmental disabilities have been known to possess significant delays in creeping. For example, Share and French (1982) have found that infants with Down syndrome may take as long as 15 months to develop the skill of creeping.

Activities to Improve Crawling and Creeping.   Children can be encouraged to crawl and creep by showing them their favorite toys or new objects that may be bright and shiny. For some reason, they also respond to stuffed animals and soft dolls. Their interest seems to compel them to move toward the object. As proficiency is gained, new challenges should be presented. For example, obstacles should be placed in front of the youngsters, such as increasing the height to crawl or creep over, or building low bridges to move under. Young children learn about their movement capacities by engaging in these simple locomotor skills. They also begin to understand about the size of their bodies by moving over, between, into, on, and under obstacles of different shapes.

Most babies are extremely interested in everything that moves; thus, they are likely to attempt to crawl and creep after a rolling ball. For added auditory stimulation, try using a ball that has bells or other noise-making parts. The following activities will tend to encourage movement:

- Both teacher and child crawl (or creep) after a ball that has been rolled away.

TABLE 4.6   **Developmental Motor Milestones at 6 Months**

**Age (in months)
or Date Mastered**

————	1. Reacts to tactile stimulation with movement
————	2. Turns head and searches toward source of sound while sitting; sound at ear level or shoulder level
————	3. Pulls cloth away from face
————	4. Pulls cloth from teacher's face
————	5. Plays with (e.g., shakes or bangs) toys placed in hand
————	6. Explores toys and responds to their differences
————	7. Does a previously learned task on verbal or gestural cue
————	8. Continues a movement if it is imitated by teacher
————	9. Grasps object in hand (not reflexive grasp)
————	10. Reaches out and grasps object near body
————	11. Displays extended reach and grasp
————	12. Rakes and scoops small objects (fingers against palm)
————	13. Plays with own feet and toes
————	14. Glances from one toy to another when toy is placed in each hand, or plays alternately with the toys
————	15. Brings hands together in midline
————	16. Places both hands on toy at midline
————	17. Transfers object from hand to hand
————	18. Extends arms, legs, head, and trunk in prone position
————	19. Bears weight on elbows in prone position
————	20. Rolls from stomach to back
————	21. Reaches while supported on one elbow
————	22. Supports self on hands with arms extended and head at 90°
————	23. Pivots in prone position
————	24. Rolls from back to stomach
————	25. Holds trunk steady when held upright

- The child crawls after the rolling ball that she has set into motion.
- The teacher rolls the ball in a different direction, sometimes close to the baby, and sometimes farther away.

Activities to Improve Manipulation.   Infants under the developmental age of 6 months should benefit from the following activities:

- Plastic bowls filled with discarded junk mail, plastic spoons, or blocks that can be easily handled will provide visual, auditory, tactual, and kinesthetic input. Obviously, the teacher and the parents must take care to ensure that these common household objects will not be potentially dangerous. For example, watch for pointed ends, parts that can be broken off, or small parts that can be swallowed.

- Plastic or rubber squeeze toys, soft cuddly animals, rattles, and teething toys can be used to develop object manipulation, which leads to the development of object concepts.

- Crib mobiles and other toys that are colorful, bright, and interesting, but not potentially harmful, and that can be hung tightly from the crib or playpen, will provide for early visual stimulation and exploration, which lead to tactual exploration of the toys.

- Radio, records, and music boxes can provide auditory input and encourage infants to move rhythmically in response to the music.

- Walkers with wheels, which support the baby, help to stimulate alternate leg action before the infant has developed sufficient balance and strength for standing and walking.

A need to use sitting, upright kneeling, and supported standing balance is surfacing at this time. The development of upright, postural skill can be enhanced and should be a part of the progressive program. A review of postural reflexes, righting reactions, and protective extensive reactions, found earlier in this chapter, should be reviewed. Included in this section are activities which can be used to develop the skill of balance.

INFANT CHARACTERISTICS AT 9 MONTHS

The developmental age of 9 months finds infants learning to master their bodies in prone, supine, and sitting positions, and the intermediate steps in between. Some are ready to use these skills to control their bodies in the upright positions of kneeling and standing.

The progression of infant locomotion skill is directly related to strength and balance. At 9 months, moving becomes extremely important to babies, and they play only for short periods on their stomachs, preferring to move by scooting and crawling. In a relatively short period of time, and in preparation of creeping, the youngsters will move into the "all fours" position and rock back and forth. This rocking motion requires both balance and reciprocal movements of the legs. From a sitting position, a backward protective extension action of the arms is now beginning. Good sitting balance is evident at this age and the children no longer rely on their hands for support. They can turn to look and grasp an object with good rotation of the trunk, or alternatively pivot in the sitting position.

Control in the upright position begins with kneeling. Youngsters are likely to move into this kneeling position from the creeping or sitting position. Hanson (1984) describes this development: "The infant shifts to one knee, freeing the opposite leg from weight. This leg is then free to be placed and have weight shifted onto it as the infant comes to a standing position with extended legs. This struggle is soon replaced with a fluid, effortless movement from kneeling to standing" (p. 333).

Motor Development at 9 Months.   Developmental motor milestones, which, again, can serve as a checklist for youngsters at the developmental age of 9 months, can be found in Table 4.7.

*TABLE 4.*7   **Developmental Motor Milestones at 9 Months**

Age (in months) or Date Mastered		
————	1.	Allows hands, feet, or body to be moved over rough textured surfaces
————	2.	Explores objects with fingers
————	3.	Plays in water
————	4.	Looks directly at noisemaker when sound is presented to the side at waist level
————	5.	Demonstrates appropriate activities with toys having obviously different properties
————	6.	Overcomes obstacles to get toys
————	7.	Raises arms to be picked up
————	8.	Consistently indicates desire to "get down"
————	9.	Reaches toward something to indicate "get down"
————	10.	Releases one object to take another
————	11.	Grasps, using thumb against index and middle finger
————	12.	Uses inferior pincer grasp (thumb against side of index finger)
————	13.	Uses index finger to poke
————	14.	Uses neat pincer grasp (thumb against tip of index finger)
————	15.	Claps hands
————	16.	Pulls forward on stomach (crawling)
————	17.	Pulls self to hands and knees
————	18.	Rocks forward and backwards in all-fours position
————	19.	Plays with toys in asymmetrical half-sitting, half-side lying position
————	20.	Moves to sitting position from stomach to all-four position

When attempting to determine if a child is developmentally delayed, Shapiro and coworkers (1987) suggest a more complete assessment be performed (by a physician or therapist) if the youngster does not attain the following skills or actions by the 9th month. They believe a child should be able to (1) turn to the sound of a bell or rattle, (2) babble, (3) transfer objects from one hand to another, (4) notice a small "bean-like" object, and (5) play with paper.

Activities to Improve Sitting to Standing to Walking.   Children can be helped to develop the skill of moving from either an all-fours or sitting position to standing upright. Place some toys on a couch or low chair. Hold a toy and show the youngster where you are placing it. Encourage the child to pull up to a standing position, thereby being able to see and grab the toy. If the baby is having trouble standing, encourage him to reach up from a kneeling position to grasp the toy while remaining on his knees. The teacher should move the toys farther each time so the child will have to extend himself and thus will need to explore ways of getting to the toys. Show him how to grasp an edge of the couch by putting his hand in the appropriate place. Teachers should always strive to reduce the amount of assistance given and encourage him to reach for the toy. This procedure should result in having the child stand upright.

To develop a child's skill of moving from hands and knees to hands and feet, and finally, to standing, place the youngster in an open space on a carpeted floor and encourage the child to stand by offering your hands or a favorite toy. If the child is hesitant and assistance is obviously needed, help the baby until she is able to do so alone. Give only as much assistance as necessary.

To develop the ability for a youngster to remove his hands from a support and stand independently, begin by having him hold onto the edge of a low chair or couch. Offer him a large toy, such as a stuffed animal, that must be held with both hands. Show him the toy at a close distance, but far enough away that he must use the edge of the chair for support while *leaning* to reach for the toy. As his balance and upright standing ability improve, move the animal farther away from the support, thus requiring him to let go of the support because he can no longer simply reach for the toy. Also, the teacher can play hand-clapping games while the youngster is standing to take the child's mind off of his practice standing and divert his attention to another task.

Activities to Improve Two-Hand Manipulation of Objects.   If a child is having difficulty reaching and grasping for objects at the midline of her body, she may need additional stimulation from the teacher. Hold a favorite toy at the midline within easy reach of the child. Encourage the youngster to look at the toy by moving it. If the child still does not become interested, try using a noisemaking toy such as a rattle. If the child does not reach for it, place her hands on it. The child may need to have her head and eyes turned to look directly at the toy. From behind, the teacher should gently grasp the youngster's head with both hands and turn the head in a direct line with the toy. This process requires the child to look at the object in question. Continue this action with different toys at different times.

Johnson-Martin and coworkers (1986) suggest the following teaching technique to increase a child's ability to bring the hands together at the midline of the body:

> If this behavior [grasping at the midline] is not observed in general free play, put something colorful and easy to remove on one of the child's hands or wrists (e.g., a stick-on bow, a yarn bracelet). Observe to see if the child brings the other hand to it to touch it. If the child does not, physically guide the two hands to the midline (by gently pushing the shoulders and upper arms). (p. 271)

The ability to reach and grasp objects is dependent on the babies' balance and ability to look at what they are doing. These youngsters are found to make exaggerated movements of their whole body and often overbalance in their attempts to reach out for an object. These exaggerated movements gradually diminish during the following months. Finnie (1975) describes a baby's action during this period:

> His ability to manipulate improves rapidly at this time, his grasp becoming more refined, he can now hold one object in each hand and transfer from one hand and bang two cubes together. He starts to take objects *out* of a container and tries unsuccessfully to pick up small objects. He starts to "drop" large objects onto the floor, a basic pattern for future release, but once they have been dropped he has no further interest in them. (p. 274)

Between the time infants begin to manipulate objects with their hands and the time they learn to walk, there are months during which the opportunity to use their hands is limited. This occurs because these youngsters need their hands for support. For these children, extra support may be used, such as bolsters, incline mats, or thick foam pads, thus allowing them to kneel against the support while playing with toys on the upper surface of the equipment.

Children are usually stimulated by toys that "do something." For example, pop beads provide both a challenge to pull apart or put together and generally make a "popping" sound. The teacher should show a child a string of pop beads. Demonstrate how to pull them apart and put them back together. Hand them to the youngster and, if necessary, physically give help to pull the beads apart. Because different types and sizes of pop beads require differing amounts of strength, the level of difficulty can provide new challenges, but all will work on the same principle of pulling apart or putting together.

INFANT CHARACTERISTICS AT 12 MONTHS

The 12-month motor developmental level is highlighted by the child being able to accomplish the following skills:

- The understanding of "no"
- Play patty-cake and peek-a-boo

- Grasp with the opposable thumb and forefinger
- Ring a bell

If the child has difficulty with these concepts, there may be a developmental delay and additional assessment is suggested. Shapiro and coworkers (1987) have found that "the 12-month-old who acts like a 9-month-old should not be seen as 3 months behind but as developing at a rate that is 75 percent of average. If the child maintains this rate of development, he will be 6 months behind at 2 years" (p. 217).

Youngsters at this age need repetition, but also change. Play situations should be varied and should present new problems that the youngsters can solve. One-year-old children develop an eagerness to solve unusual tasks. This is also the age when the infants begin their prewalking activities. Diem (1979) observes that

> children stand up when they are able to carry their own weight. We do not put the child in the standing position, but we help him little by little to stand by himself.... The first step is a difficult balance test, which requires many attempts. The child "runs" before he walks. He falls from one step into the other. The first steps are awkward and with straddled legs. A flowing walk must be practiced for a long time since it demands a sureness of body control and a refined coordination in the transition of completing a motion or movement.... The child sometimes disrupts his walking with crawling [creeping]—let him do this—this is a healthy change. (Section 1, #10)

Interaction between the teacher/parent/therapist and the infants involves face-to-face teaching. This process in the first half of the first year is likely to teach the youngsters the basics of attending, which are necessary to benefit from later stimulation. Belsky and coworkers (1980) state that

> such speculation raises the possibility of developmentally 'tracking' the attentional building blocks of exploratory competence from early infancy through the toddler period. The fact that all sorts of later achievements (e.g., reading) are dependent upon the capacity to maintain focused attention further suggests that exploratory skill may not only be a consequence of early parent-infant interaction but also an influence upon later development. (p. 1177)

Most youngsters who have been labeled as mildly mentally retarded and many of those with moderate mental retardation should be able to attain average developmental motor levels. Participation in early intervention programs should have a significant and positive influence on these children. A list of motor milestones often found in children who have reached their first birthday is found in Table 4.8.

Children with Down syndrome generally progress at slower rates than other youngsters of the same age. They usually will not have progressed through the crawling and creeping stages. Share and French (1982, p. 87) list seven developmental

TABLE 4.8 **Developmental Motor Milestones at 12 Months**

Age (in months) or Date Mastered	
————	1. Imitates building a two-block tower
————	2. Removes objects from container by reaching into container
————	3. Puts one or two objects in container
————	4. Plays with toys in mid-line; one hand holds toy and the other hand manipulates
————	5. Moves forward (creeps) on hands and knees
————	6. Raises one hand high while on hands and knees
————	7. Sits alone
————	8. Pulls self to standing position
————	9. Steps on sideways holding a support
————	10. Stoops to pick up a toy while holding on to a support
————	11. Removes hands from support and stands independently
————	12. Takes independent steps

milestones that children with Down syndrome generally are able to do by 12 months of age:

1. Sitting with head erect, but forward and unsteady (3 months)
2. Sits with head set forward (5 months)
3. On the verge of rolling over (5 months)
4. Rolls from back to stomach (7 months)
5. Rests weight on hands with chest off floor (7 months)
6. Maintains an erect sitting position (11 months)
7. Partially turns on stomach (12 months)

Esenther (1984) studied 40 infants with Down syndrome and found that when they were given "developmental coaching" (early infant intervention), 95 percent achieved certain hand skills criteria by 10 months of age, 92.5 percent achieved prewalking mobility by 10 months of age, and 40 percent achieved free walking by 18 months of age.

Infants with physical disabilities such as cerebral palsy, spina bifida, or blindness will likely be delayed in their developmental motor performance. Additionally, it was found that youngsters with severe or profound mental retardation will also show significant developmental delays. Inclusion in early stimulation and intervention programs are strongly recommended for these individuals.

THE TODDLER: THE SECOND YEAR OF MOTOR DEVELOPMENT (12 TO 24 MONTHS)

Once infants pass their first year, they usually move very quickly into the new and exciting world of the toddler. They are experiencing the emergence of new skills that are the combined effect of physical growth, biological maturation, perceptual learning, and intellectual learning. Physically, these toddlers are growing in both height and weight. Their bones and muscles are developing and their body proportions are changing.

The children will progress from being comparatively helpless infants, whose needs must be met by their parents, to toddlers who have begun to achieve some measure of independence and are able to take care of some of their own needs.

Motor skill learning is rapid during the early months of this period. By the time these youngsters reach their 2nd birthday, they should be fairly well coordinated and can walk effectively, including walking and running up and down stairs alone. They will be developing a growing sense of autonomy and competence because of their new skills and capabilities. During this 12-month period the average child will grow approximately 5 inches and gain about 5 or 6 pounds.

Teachers should encourage the toddlers' independence by allowing the youngsters reasonable freedom. Too often, parents and special education teachers tend to be overprotective of children with disabilities. This is particularly true when the little boys and girls are involved in motor development activities.

Realistically, for children with significant mental retardation, becoming more independent is directly related to the degree of brain damage and environmental learning opportunities. It is usually found that these youngsters will experience delays in memory; although muscular strength, balance, and body coordination may be adequate, they possess an inability to remember, and this will result in the children having less natural curiosity to explore. Eichstaedt and Lavay (1992) describe the infants with mental retardation:

> When observing random movement it is usually seen as purposeless and without direction. The growth of the muscle and nerve cells is very important, for these systems are the key to children's coordination and ability to make smooth and precise movements. During the second year, muscles develop and grow, providing a great increase in strength and also accounting for a larger portion of body weight. The brain is also growing and has increased in size and weight from about three-fourths of a pound to two and two-tenths pounds....Although the brain of the child with retardation is also growing, the highly sophisticated process of memory is delayed and learning is slow to follow. The integration and interpretation of information in the brain has slowed down and cognitive and motor learning tends to develop at a much slower pace. (p. 291)

For toddlers, the locomotor skill of walking is the most significant activity they will encounter during this 12-month period. Similar to earlier learned motor skills, walking depends primarily on physical development. Through practice and repetition in crawling, creeping, and standing, the youngsters develop muscular strength and balance, without which they will experience difficulty moving to the next level of locomotion. For children with mental retardation, they may not have the natural curiosity necessary to "want to" explore the environment. DePaepe and Croce (1987) state that,

> given normal motor control, most children acquire all of their basic subroutines (patterns) by the age of eight. Severely and multiply handicapped children with CNS [central nervous system] dysfunction, however, often lack these plans of action, and subsequently must be taught a plan of action through the systematic instruction of subroutines. (p. 158)

BALANCE AND EQUILIBRIUM

Balance and equilibrium are critical actions that directly affect infants in their progressions through creeping, kneeling, standing, and walking. The improvement of these skills is necessary for most locomotor patterns. Balance can be defined as the ability of an individual to position the body in response to the effects of gravity. The skill of balance is composed of three distinct parts: (1) static balance (e.g., standing on one foot), (2) dynamic balance (e.g., walking on a balance beam), and (3) balance with the surface moving (e.g., walking on a train in motion). Equilibrium is the combined process of assimilation and accommodation. *Assimilation* is the "taking in," or incorporation, of new experiences or concepts into prelearned, existing patterns. Toddlers will have an extensive stock of mechanisms they know how to use. When using them to respond to new stimuli, they are assimilating. *Accommodation* is the process by which youngster's structures change to manage new objects and situations. Children's changing actions reflect the structural change that has occurred. Assimilation and accommodation are constantly working together to produce changes in conceptualization of the external and internal worlds and the children's reactions to them. The state of balance between assimilation and accommodation is called *equilibrium*. Equilibrium reactions are reflexes that assist in the maintenance of an upright position when the center of gravity is suddenly moved beyond the base of support.

Perceptual-motor specialists generally agree that children with good balance skill are able to focus their attention on other tasks, such as catching a ball, while still being able to keep their balance. These theorists believe that "good" balance often indicates functional integrity of the nervous system (Eichstaedt & Kalakian, 1987). Seaman and DePauw (1989) describe characteristics of individuals with a dysfunction of balance and equilibrium:

> Signs of dysfunction are evidenced by difficulty in achieving and maintaining balance, a decreased ability in regaining balance, an inability to adjust quickly to changes in equilibrium, and an inability to avoid falling. Individuals will often assume awkward

postures to compensate for the lack of fully functional balance and equilibrium responses. (p. 53)

When developing specific motor activities for developing balance and equilibrium, it is possible to incorporate more than one attribute in the task. For example, reaching for a favorite toy can be used to divert the child's attention away from the balancing skill and still allow practice to occur. Only a small number of activities may be needed to favorably alter several attributes. Most eye-hand activities incorporate agility, locomotor movements, and object-problems. Youngsters with mental retardation, or those who are motor delayed, may need a variety of simple activities designed to improve a single attribute.

For children with disabilities, outcome variables can be identified at a number of programmatic levels. Haley and Baryza (1990) provide an excellent example of individualized programming:

> A specific child . . . who has significant problems in walking a distance of 50 ft as a result of balance deficits. . . . [For this youngster] changes in the quality of walking (improved control of stepping, more normal base of support) can be measured and related to the intervention program. Standing balance tests may also be used to determine improvements in stability and resistance to stumbling and falling. At a more functional level, recording the actual decrease in the frequency of falls or the amount of time needed to walk 50 ft provides an indication of adaptive change. Collectively, multiple outcome measures not only provide information on child improvement, but also suggest patterns of interdependence among different levels of outcome variables. Consistent efforts to capture progress at many levels through a comprehensive series of outcome measures provides for evaluation and refinement of the motor program. (p. 2)

Activities to Develop Balance and Equilibrium.   Evans (1980) suggests the following activities for developing balance skill.

- Have the child sit on the edge of a small box with feet off the floor.
- Position the child as above, with the arms extended to the side, then overhead.
- Have the child sit on a rocking board and maintain supported, sitting balance.
- Have the youngster stand on a rocking board, supported by the teacher who is holding the hands. Rock the board gently back and forth.

WALKING

While developing walking skills, Evans (1980) found that

> the broad-based gait characteristic of the very young child is often seen in retarded children . . . who are attempting to learn the skill of walking. Although the arms and

legs may be moving alternately, the walk appears stiff and inflexible and almost robot-like. (p. 24)

Johnson-Martin and coworkers (1986) suggest the following performance level, the approximate time which youngsters attain this balance skill, and criteria for mastery:

- Stands on one foot while hands are held (18 months).

  Criterion: With hands held, child raises one foot off floor and holds for 2-3 seconds; three consecutive days.

Developmental motor milestones for the approximate age of 18 months is shown in Table 4.9.

Johnson-Martin and coworkers (1986) also describe specific tasks usually accomplished at the developmental motor age of 24 months.

- Walks with one foot on a walking board and one foot on the floor (21 months). The walking board is 72 inches long, $2\frac{1}{2}$ inches wide, and four inches high.

  Criterion: Child walks full length of the board with one foot on the board and one foot on the floor; three times on 3 consecutive days.

- Stands on one foot without help (21 months).

TABLE 4.9   **Developmental Motor Milestones at 18 Months**

Age (in months) or Date Mastered		
_____	1.	Spreads soft material with fingers
_____	2.	Imitates building a six-block tower
_____	3.	Places two or more large round pegs in holes
_____	4.	Places small objects through a small hole in container
_____	5.	Holds dowel rod in one hand and puts ring over it
_____	6.	Places pencil through hole in piece of paper
_____	7.	Crawls downstairs, backwards
_____	8.	Moves from hands to knees, to hands and feet, to standing
_____	9.	Walks upstairs with railing
_____	10.	Unscrews small lids
_____	11.	Walks downstairs with railing
_____	12.	Stands on one foot while hands are held
_____	13.	Walks backwards

Criterion: Child lifts one foot off the floor and holds for 3–4 seconds; four times each session on 3 consecutive days.

- Walks on line independently, following the general direction (24 months). Ten-foot line painted or taped on floor, 45 inches wide; two side boards 72 inches long.

Criterion: Child walks entire length of the line independently; three trials on 3 consecutive days.

Additional checkpoints for the developmental age of 24 months are found in Table 4.10.

Many youngsters who are mildly mentally retarded experience no delay in acquiring the ability to walk, and the quality of their walking is identical to that of children who are nonretarded. This is not true for most toddlers who possess lower levels of mental retardation (i.e., Down syndrome, moderate, severe, profound). With these youngsters, significant walking delays are often present. Though behind their age peers, the youngsters labeled as moderate or with Down syndrome should

TABLE 4.10   **Developmental Motor Milestones at 24 Months**

Age (in months) or Date Mastered		
_____	1.	Pushes and plays with clay
_____	2.	Puts objects away in appropriate places
_____	3.	Uses "tools" to deal with spatial problems (extends height with a stool, extends reach with a stick)
_____	4.	Puts round, square, and triangular forms in form box when they are given simultaneously
_____	5.	Completes simple puzzles
_____	6.	Places square pegs in square holes
_____	7.	Puts loose pop beads together
_____	8.	Walks upstairs without railing, places both feet on one set at a time
_____	9.	Walks downstairs without railing, places both feet on one step at a time
_____	10.	Walks with one foot on walking board and one foot on floor
_____	11.	Stands on one foot without help
_____	12.	Walks on line independently, following the general direction
_____	13.	Jumps off step with both feet
_____	14.	Runs stiffly
_____	15.	Runs well

progress smoothly, and at 24 months they will fall less often than they did the month before. With ongoing developmental activities, they will learn the rudimentary skills of running, stopping suddenly, and even changing directions. It is also likely that within the upcoming year they will have mastered the ability to go up and down stairs, one step at a time, without holding on to the rail.

In contrast, for those children 3 to 5 years of age with severe mental retardation, locomotor patterns will resemble those of 18– to 30-month-old nonretarded youngsters. Those children with severe retardation should be able to walk fairly well, with few falls. They should be climbing into large chairs, onto the sofa, and onto the bed. They will probably be able to walk up stairs with assistance and to crawl backwards down stairs.

At 24 months, individuals classified as profoundly mentally retarded often display gross motor skills that initially involve learning to coordinate and overcome primary infant reflexes. Motor milestones do, however, tend to be seriously delayed. Three- to 5-year-old severely or profoundly retarded youngsters who are not able to walk independently are not uncommon. But improvement should be a constant goal. As they progress, they tend to gain control of their head, neck, and body. Next, they begin to bear weight in a standing position, usually by holding on to a parent, teacher, or piece of furniture. They will sit up when propped. Eventually, they will be able to sit without support, creep around the floor, pull to a standing position, take supported steps, and, hopefully, finally walk.

A distinct difference can be expected between youngsters labeled as *severe* and *profound*. The major difference is found in the greater progress made by those children classified as severe. Today, many of these youngsters are being placed into school settings, and for the most part are making remarkable progress. It is not uncommon to find individuals with severe retardation walking, running, and jumping.

Needless to say, appropriate early intervention is necessary for all toddlers, including those with disabilities. These youngsters should be involved in movement activities, as movement is still the very essence of their world.

THE YOUNG CHILD: THE THIRD YEAR OF MOTOR DEVELOPMENT (24 TO 36 MONTHS)

Between 24 and 36 months, young children learn about their relationship to space, make decisions to solve problems, follow directions, cooperate and play better with others, develop creative ability, and discover what they are all about. They are constantly making decisions, exploring, experimenting, and creating in their worlds of present and past experiences.

Young children in this developmental period seem eager to venture out on their own but still need constant supervision and protection by teachers and parents. With these youngsters, cooperation and sharing with others is beginning to surface, although these characteristics are still being learned. Taking turns must be stressed.

After their second birthday, children will begin active play.

Play with other children is basically parallel; that is, they choose to be in the company of other children but are still very possessive and tend not to share very well.

By the time they reach 36 months, most of the lingering traces of infancy have disappeared. The "grown-up" little boys and little girls have begun to move, look, talk, think, and act more like children than babies. Their growth rate has slowed down in comparison to when they were infants. The average weight gain during this 12-month period is approximately 4 or 5 pounds, and growth will be between 2 and 3 inches.

Block (1977) describes 3-year-old children:

Three is a delightful age. The child of this age is "not as knowing as four but he is transcending the infantilism of two." Most three-year-olds can build towers of nine blocks and can construct bridges of three blocks. They can catch a ball with arms the straight, copy circles, and draw straight lines.... [They] can balance briefly on one foot and are able to walk upstairs alternating the feet. Most have developed enough strength and coordination to be able to ride a tricycle. Jumping from a bottom stair may also be accomplished. Climbing is natural and easy since the three-year-old can grip well with his hands. Ladders, swings, and jungle gyms should be provided to develop skills. (p. 6)

MOTOR SKILL LEVELS OF THE 3-YEAR-OLD

Motor skills that develop during this period include the following:

- Walking on tiptoes
- Jumping from the bottom stair
- Standing on one foot
- Jumping on two feet
- Riding a tricycle using the pedals
- Changing feet walking upstairs
- Catching a ball using the chest

These motor skills are usually accomplished by 3-year-old children labeled as mildly mentally retarded, but for children with greater levels of mental retardation (including Down syndrome), the delay in development is as much as 12 to 30 months (Eichstaedt and Lavay, 1992). With specific reference to young children with Down syndrome, Woollacott and Shumway-Cook (1986) describe the cause of developmental delay. "The transition from primitive spinally controlled muscle response patterns to more integrated and coordinated movement patterns is delayed and/or absent in Down's syndrome children due to poor myelination of the descending cerebral and brainstem neurons and a reduction in the number of neurons in the higher nervous centers" (p. 45).

Share and French (1982) have compared motor skill differences between young children with Down syndrome (Ds) and nondisabled children (ND):

walking on tiptoes	Ds = 48 months	ND = 30 months
jumps up with both feet off floor		
	Ds = 54 months	ND = 30 months
jump from bottom stair	Ds = 54 months	ND = 36 months
riding tricycle	Ds = 60 months	ND = 36 months

THE YOUNG CHILD WITH DISABILITIES

Children labeled as mildly mentally retarded will be very close in height and weight to their nondisabled peers, but those with more neurological involvement will be significantly smaller in both height and weight. This maturation difference is also found in children with Down syndrome. Westling (1986) states the following:

It is likely that organic sources of brain impairment also affect growth impairment either directly or indirectly. Thus, while organically impaired individuals often have smaller than average bodies, cultural-familial [no biological brain damage] mildly mentally retarded individuals are usually about equal in size to their nonretarded chronological age peers. (p. 155)

It is interesting to note that physical delays in both height and weight appear closely aligned to the amount of extra movement these youngsters experience. Oelwein (1988) believes that grow gains increase when daily structured movement programs are provided for young children with Down syndrome. She has found that teachers, leaders, therapists, and parents involved in preplanned and ongoing movement activities agree that these children will significantly improve in all dimensions of cognitive, physical, social, and emotional growth.

Young children with mild and moderate disabilities should be concentrating on "readiness" skills (e.g., prerequisites for later learning). Hallahan and Kauffman (1988) believe the following:

Preschool classes for mildly retarded children start at a lower level, and the training may take as long as two or three years. Readiness skills include the abilities to:

1. Sit still and attend to the teacher
2. Discriminate auditory and visual stimuli
3. Follow directions
4. Develop language
5. Increase gross- and fine-motor coordination
6. Develop self-help skills
7. Interact with peers in group situations (pp. 70–71)

PLAY: THE AVENUE TO SUCCESS

Play becomes the fascination of young children who are quickly moving from the toddler stage. Most psychologists agree that the process of play is the dominant mode of activity for young children (Karrby, 1989). Through play, cultural standards and basic social norms are learned. Through play youngsters learn to transform their motives and needs into socially acceptable modes of dealing with their ever-expanding world. Block (1977) describes how play becomes invaluable for all types of development:

Through play a child learns socialization, direction-following, and the development of motor and language skills. His exposure broadens, and through this comes the opportunity to try new and exciting skills. The child's sense of autonomy is strengthened, and he develops self-confidence through having his efforts positively reinforced. Through movement play, the young child will develop interests and preferences as he matures. (p. 2)

For the toddler, play changes dramatically during the second year, developing from undifferentiated exploration and functional manipulation to more sophisticated

Through movement involving play, the young child will develop interests and preferences as he matures.

acts. Tamis-Lemonda and Bornstein (1990) contend that "over the short period of 12 to 18 months, sustained attention becomes longer, more controlled, and more focused. Specifically, children make rapid strides in coordinating attention and in disregarding extraneous environmental intrusions" (p. 86).

For the physical education teacher, there is no question as to the inclusion of play in programs. But as can be expected, much of a daily physical education program is quite structured, and "free" play is kept to a minimum. The children, particularly those with disabilities, are generally inserted into preplanned activities, so as to reach established goals according to their present needs.

Learning to move effectively is enhanced when the children are having fun. The medium of play can be a strong motivator. Therefore, movement activities for young children should include many opportunities involving games that are fun. For example, youngsters have always enjoyed games in which they pretend to be animals, including simple relays where they move and act like different animals (e.g.,

Learning to move effectively is enhanced when children are having fun.

bear walk, bunny hop, lame dog). Although these animal relays are designed to provide fun and interest, it is apparent that all dimensions of locomotion, agility, and muscular strength are being used. Thus, with imagination and thoughtful planning, physical education teachers have at their disposal an extensive source of play-oriented activities.

Cowden and Torrey (1990) suggest that teachers can increase socialization among preschool children by carefully selecting the toys to be used in the learning environment. They found in their study of 24 preschool children with disabilities (age range of 3 to 5 years) that providing toys a child prefers is an important consideration in developing socialization: "If they are social toys, increased socialization skills may be facilitated" (p. 179). Regarding their study, they concluded as follows:

> This study did address the child characteristics of gross and fine motor abilities and their effects on toy preference. Although many children exhibited vestibular, balance, and locomotor deficits, tricycles and other riding toys were the most highly preferred

toys. This finding was unexpected, due to the high level of gross motor ability required to play with these toys. Evidently the handicapped preschoolers preferred the sociability afforded by these riding toys even though they did not have the motor skills necessary to use these toys. Additionally, two social toys that required visual motor coordination and spatial awareness for appropriate play (dollhouse, dishes) were also chosen with moderate frequency. . . . It is possible that due to the children's motoric deficits, level of play most frequently remained nonsocial even though play was with toys that typically encourage social play. (p. 180)

ACTIVITIES FOR THE THREE-YEAR-OLD

The following activities are suggested to improve the overall locomotor, fundamental skill, strength, and endurance levels of young children between the developmental ages of 24 to 36 months.

Climbing:	monkey bars, ladders, climbers that can be raised or lowered, boxes, or stacked mats
Lifting:	wooden boxes, hollow blocks, suitcases, sand pails, boards, cardboard boxes, shopping bags, coffee cans . . . filled will sand or other objects
Pushing:	large blocks, large cardboard boxes, wagons, bolsters, medicine balls
Pulling:	on ropes, other children in wagons, ropes hanging from above
Strength:	carrying packages, hanging clothes on a line, mopping, sweeping, waxing, raking leaves, shoveling snow, picking up sticks and stones on the ground, moving furniture, carrying out small wastebaskets
Balancing:	balancing boards, boards set on different angles, bolsters, wide balance beams or wide boards
Riding:	tricycles, kiddie cars, wagons, swings, swinging nets
Swinging:	tire swings, spinning nets hung from above, swing nets, rope ladders
Rocking:	wooden or plastic horses, balancing boards, rocking chairs, see-saws
Sliding On:	slides, plastic mats, scooters
Running:	around objects, up and down small hills, large area to run straight, stopping, starting, dodging, and changing direction
Jumping:	Onto safety mats; from low stairs, from rebound boards, from wooden boxes, from large rubber inner tubes, over ropes
Locomotor Skill:	hopping, jumping, galloping, sliding over ropes laying on the floor, over mats, to a line; to the wall; to the hoop; to the teacher

SUMMARY

The worlds of the infant, toddler, and young child are exciting, and the ongoing developmental pace can only be described as challenging and fascinating. These youngsters will face new opportunities, with many difficult hurdles to overcome. A large proportion of these experiences will be in the motor domain and will demand a natural progression through developmental milestones. For youngsters with developmental disabilities, the path could be extra challenging.

For youngsters at risk between birth and 36 months, early childhood intervention programs have proven successful. These programs have provided individualized plans and activities to meet existing motor needs. P.L. 101-476 has now officially extended the educational responsibilities of infants, toddlers, and young children to the public schools. Therefore, programs (Individualized Family Service Plans) must be written and carried out for all youngsters with disabilities. Even those considered "at-risk" have become eligible for these special programs. Assessment, program writing, placement, teaching, and evaluation will not only involve teachers and therapists; now parents are integral components of the multidisciplinary team. A great variety of motor activities are likely to be included in all IFSPs, because controlled movement is extremely important for young children. All small boys and girls can be expected to progress through the traditional developmental milestones, whether they have developmental disabilities or not.

Infants (birth to 12 months) progress through infant reflexes into postural reflexes, and finally into the stages of crawling, creeping, kneeling, and standing. Manipulation skills will improve, and the youngsters will be able to better control objects and toys with their hands as they move closer to their first birthdays. *Toddlers* (12 to 24 months) will begin and end this period with rudimentary walking, which will lead into controlled walking, starting, stopping, changing directions, and running. Their balance and equilibrium will show marked improvement and, along with muscular strength, will provide the basis for continued progress. *Young children* (24 to 36 months) will move quickly away from "baby" characteristics and are truly on their way to becoming real preschoolers. They are learning to share and play within the realm of socially accepted standards.

With the close of the 36-month period, youngsters will be preparing to move into "preschool" activities; most of the children with developmental disabilities will have the opportunity to be integrated with nondisabled students. The ease with which this mainstreaming occurs is dependent on how far the youngsters have developed and how close they are to their nondisabled age peers. Early childhood intervention programs, including major portions devoted to motor skill and muscular strength development, can provide the needed stepping stone.

DISCUSSION QUESTIONS

1. In your school, what attempts are being made to develop comprehensive early childhood programs for infants, toddlers, and young children?

2. Who is responsible for the administration and financial implementation of the above programs?

3. When children with developmental disabilities reach the age of 36 months and have been provided with good motor skill activities, is it feasible to expect that most of these youngsters will be "ready" for integration into regular preschool programs?

4. What motor learning differences would you expect between infants who are developmentally disabled and their nondisabled peers?

5. What problems would you anticipate when professionals (special education teachers, therapists, physical educators, parents) meet for the first time regarding an "at risk" infant? What can be done to open the lines of communication and break down professional elitism?

6. What special training is needed for a physical educator who is planning to become professionally knowledgeable in the area of infants, toddlers, and young children?

7. Describe the progressive framework of developmental motor milestones.

REFERENCES

Anderson, J., Hinjosa, J., & Strauch, C. (1987). Integrating play in neurodevelopmental treatment. *The American Journal of Occupational Therapy, 41*, 421–426.

Antley, T. R., & DuBose, R. F. (1981). *A case for early intervention: Summary of program findings, longitudinal data, and cost effectiveness.* Seattle: Experimental Education Unit.

Apgar, V. (1953). Proposal for a new method of evaluating the newborn infant. *Anesthesia and Analgesia, 32*, 260–267.

Apgar, V., & Beck, J. (1972). *Is my baby all right?* New York: Pocket Books.

Bagnato, S. J., Neisworth, J. T., & Munson, S. M. (1989). *Linking: Developmental assessment and early intervention* (2nd ed.). Rockville, MD: Aspen.

Bailey, D. B., Jr., & Wolery, M. (1992). *Assessing infants and preschoolers with handicaps* (2nd ed.). New York: Merrill/Macmillan.

Bayley, N. (1969). *Bayley scales of infant development: Birth to two years.* New York: Psychological Corporation.

Belsky, J., Goode, M. K., & Most, R. K. (1980). Material stimulation and infant exploratory competence:Cross-sectional, correlational, and experimental analyses. *Child Development, 51*, 1163–1178.

Berger, M., & Yule, W. (1987). Psychometric approaches. In J. Hogg & N. V. Raynes (Eds.), *Assessment in mental handicap* (pp. 12–44). Cambridge, MA: Brookline.

Block, S. D. (1977). *Me and I'm great. Physical education for children three through eight.* Minneapolis: Burgess.

Bouffard, M. (1990). Movement problem solutions by educable mentally handicapped individuals. *Adapted Physical Activity Quarterly, 7*, 183–197.

Cowden, J. E., & Torrey, C. C. (1990). A comparison of isolate and social toys on play behaviors of handicapped preschoolers. *Adapted Physical Activity Quarterly, 7*, 170–182.

Davis, W. E., & Burton, A. W. (1991). Ecological task analysis: Translating movement behavior theory into practice. *Adapted Physical Activity Quarterly, 8*, 154–177.

DeGangi, G. A. (1991). Assessment of sensory, emotional, and attentional problems in regulatory-disordered infants: Part I. *Infants and Young Children, 3*, 1–8.

DePaepe, J., & Croce, R. V. (1987). Neurobehavioral intervention based on pediatric exercise and motor behavior. In L. Bowers, S. Klesius, & B. Price (Eds.), *Proceedings of the CIVITAN-I'M SPECIAL Network International Conference on Physical Education and Sport for Disabled Persons* (pp. 157–160). Tampa, FL.

DeWeerd, J. (1984). Introduction. In D. Assael (Ed.), *Handicapped children's early education program: 1982–83 overview and directory* (pp. vii–xvii). Technical Assistance Development System of Special Education Programs, U.S. Department of Education. Washington, D.C.: Government Printing Office.

Diem, L. (1979). *Children learn physical skills, Vol. 1: Birth to 3 years.* Reston, VA: American Alliance for Health, Physical Education, Recreation, and Dance.

Dunn, J. M. (1991). PL 99-457: Challenges and opportunities for physical education. *Journal of Physical Education, Recreation, & Dance, 62*(6), 33–34; 47.

Early Intervention. (1990, December). Progress and problems with part H implementation: A national perspective. *Quarterly Newsletter of the Illinois Early Childhood Intervention, 5*(1), 6.

Eason, R. L. (1991). Adapted physical education delivery model for infants and toddlers with disabilities. *Journal of Physical Education, Recreation, & Dance, 62*(6), 41–43; 47.

Eckert, H. M. (1987). *Motor development* (3rd ed.). Indianapolis: Benchmark.

Edelman, M. W. (1990). Broadening the view: Hopes and responsibilities. *Infants and Young Children, 3(1)*, vi–vii.

Eichstaedt, C. B. & Kalakian, L. H. (1987). *Developmental/Adapted physical education: Making ability count* (2nd ed.). New York: Macmillan.

Eichstaedt, C. B., & Lavay, B. (1992). *Physical activity for individuals with mental retardation: Infant to adult.* Champaign, IL: Human Kinetics.

Esenther, S. E. (1984). Developmental coaching of the Down syndrome infant. *The American Journal of Occupational Therapy, 38*, 440–445.

Evans, J. R. (1980). *They have to be carefully taught.* Reston, VA: The American Alliance for Health, Physical Education, Recreation, and Dance.

Finnie, N. R. (1975). *Handling the young cerebral palsied child at home* (2nd ed.). New York: Dutton.

Garland, C. W., & Linder, T. W. (1988). Administrative challenges in early intervention. In J. B. Jordan, J. J. Gallagher, P. L. Hutinger, & M. B. Karnes (Eds.), *Early childhood special education: Birth to three* (pp. 5–27). Reston, VA: Council for Exceptional Children/Division for Early Childhood.

Gast, D., & Wolery, M. (1985). Severe developmental disabilities. In W. Berdine & A. Blackhurst (Eds.), *An introduction to special education* (2nd ed.), pp. 469–520. Boston: Little, Brown.

Gesell, A. (1949). *Gesell developmental schedules.* New York: Psychological Corporation.

Gorski, P. A. (1984). Infants at risk. In M. J. Hanson (Ed.), *Atypical infant development* (pp. 57–80). Baltimore, MD: University Park Press.

Haley, S. M., & Baryza, M. J. (1990). A hierarchy of motor outcome assessment: Self-initiated movements through adaptive motor function. *Infants and Young Children, 3*(2), 1–14.

Hallahan, D. P., & Kaufmann, J. M. (1988). *Exceptional children* (4th ed.). Englewood Cliffs, NJ: Prentice-Hall.

Hanson, M. J. (Ed.). (1984). *Atypical infant development.* Baltimore: University Park Press.

Hanson, M. J. (1987). *Teaching the infant with Down syndrome* (2nd ed.). Austin, TX: Pro-Ed.

Healy, A. (1990). Physician participation in early intervention services. *Infants and Young Children, 3*(2), v–vii.

Heward, W. L., & Orlansky, M. D. (1992). *Exceptional children* (4th ed.). New York: Merrill/Macmillan.

Hutinger, P. L. (1988). Linking screening, identification, and assessment with curriculum. In J. B. Jordan, J. J. Gallagher, P. L. Hutinger, & M. B. Karnes (Eds.), *Early childhood special education: Birth to three* (pp. 29–66). Reston, VA: Council for Exceptional Children/Division for Early Childhood.

Johnson-Martin, N., Jens, K. G., & Attermeier, S. M. (1986). *The Carolina curriculum for handicapped infants and infants at risk.* Baltimore, MD: Brooks.

Jordan, J. B., Gallagher, J. J., Hutinger, P. L., & Karnes, M. B. (Eds.). (1988). *Early childhood special education: Birth to three.* Reston, VA: Council for Exceptional Children/Division for Early Childhood.

Karrby, G. (1989). Children's conception of their own play. *International Journal of Early Childhood, 21*(2), 49–54.

Kelly, L. (1991). Personal communication. March 25, 1991.

Kirk, S. A., & Gallagher, J. J. (1989). *Educating exceptional children* (6th ed.). Boston: Houghton Mifflin.

Knobloch, H., & Pasamanick, B. (1974). *Gesell and Amatruda's developmental diagnosis: The evaluation and management of normal and abnormal neuropsychologic development in infancy and early childhood* (3rd ed.). Hagerstown, MD: Harper & Row.

Langley, M. B. (1989). Assessing infant cognitive development. In D. B. Bailey Jr., & M. Wolery (Eds.), *Assessing infants and preschoolers with handicaps* (pp. 249–274). New York: Merrill/Macmillan.

Lerner, J., Mardell-Czudnowski, C., & Goldenberg, D. (1987). *Special education for the early childhood years* (2nd ed.). Englewood Cliffs, NJ: Prentice-Hall.

McCormick, L. (1990). Infants and young children with special needs. In N. G. Haring and L. McCormick (Eds.), *Exceptional children and youth,* 5th ed. (pp. 77–107). New York: Merrill/Macmillan.

McCubbin, J., & Zittel, L. (1991). PL 99-457: What the law is all about. *Journal of Physical Education, Recreation, and Dance, 62*(6), 35–37; 47.

Mussen, P. M., Conger, J. J., & Kagan, J. (1980). *Essentials of child development and personality.* New York: Harper & Row.

National Information Center for Children and Youth with Handicaps. (1988). Early intervention for children birth through 2 years. *News Digest, 10,* 1–10.

Oelwein, P. L. (1988). Preschool and kindergarten programs: Strategies for meeting objectives. In V. Dmitriev and P. L. Oelwein (Eds.), *Advances in Down syndrome* (pp. 131–157). Seattle: Special Child Publications.

Patton, J. R., Payne, J. S., & Beirne-Smith, M. (1990). *Mental retardation* (3rd ed.). New York: Merrill/Macmillan.

Patton, J. R., & Polloway, E. A. (1990). Mild mental retardation. In N. G. Haring and L. McCormick (Eds.), *Exceptional children and youth,* 5th ed. (pp. 195–237). New York: Merrill/Macmillan.

Payne, V. G., & Isaacs, L. D. (1991). -*Human motor development* (2nd ed.). Mountain View, CA: Mayfield.

Piaget, J. (1952). *The origins of intelligence in children.* New York: International Universities Press.

Pyfer, J. L. (1988). Teachers, don't let your students grow up to be clumsy adults. *Journal of Physical Education, Recreation, and Dance, 59,* 38–42.

Seaman, J. A., & DePauw, K. P. (1989). *The new adapted physical education* (2nd ed.). Mountain View, CA: Mayfield.

Semmler, C. J., & Hunter, J. G. (1990). *Early occupational therapy intervention: Neonates to three years.* Gaithersburg, MD: Aspen.

Shapiro, B. K., Palmer, F. B., & Capute, A. J. (1987). The early detection of mental retardation. *Clinical Pediatrics, 26,* 215–220.

Share, J., & French, R. (1982). *Motor development of Down syndrome children: Birth to six years.* Sherman Oaks, CA: Jack B. Share.

Sheehan, R., & Gallagher, R. J. (1984). Assessment of infants. In M. J. Hanson (Ed.), *Atypical infant development* (pp. 81–106). Baltimore, MD: University Park Press.

Smith, P. D. (1989). Assessing motor skills. In D. B. Bailey, Jr., & M. Wolery, *Assessing infants and preschoolers with handicaps* (pp. 301–338). New York: Merrill/Macmillan.

Spitz, H. H. (1988). Mental retardation as a thinking disorder: The rationalist alternative to empiricism. In N. W. Bray (Ed.), *International Review of Research in Mental Retardation* (pp. 1–32). New York: Academic Press.

Tamis-LeMonda, C. S., & Bornstein, M. H. (1990). Language, play, and attention at one year. *Infant Behavior and Development, 13,* 85–98.

Taylor, M., & Valerie, S. (1990). The learning needs of children. *International Journal of Early Childhood, 22(1),* 14–22.

Trohanis, P. (1991). Perspective. *Infants and Young Children, 3,* v–ix.

Westling, D. L. (1986). *Introduction to mental retardation.* Englewood Cliffs, NJ: Prentice-Hall.

Whaley, K. K. (1990). The emergence of social play in infancy: A proposed development sequence of infant-adult social play. *Early Childhood Research Quarterly, 5,* 347–358.

Winnick, J. P., & Short, F. X. (1985). *Physical fitness testing of the disabled—Project UNIQUE.* Champaign, IL: Human Kinetics.

Woollacott, M. H., & Shumway-Cook, A. (1986). The development of the postural and voluntary motor control systems in Down's syndrome children. In M. G. Wade (Ed.), *Motor skill acquisition of the mentally handicapped: Issues in research and training.* Amsterdam: North Holland.

APPENDIX 4A: FOUR MAJOR PERIODS OF PIAGET'S DEVELOPMENTAL THEORY

1. *Sensorimotor* (birth to 2 years).   The infant changes from a creature who responds through reflexes to one who can organize his activities in relation to his environment.

2. *Preoperational* (2 to 7 years).   The child begins to use symbols such as words, but is prelogical in her thinking because she is highly egocentric (self-centered).

3. *Concrete Operations* (7 to 11 years).   The youngster is beginning to understand and use concepts that help him deal with the immediate environment.

4. *Formal Operations* (12 to 15 years through adulthood).   The individual can now think in abstract terms and deal with hypothetical situations (Bailey and Wolery, 1992).

APPENDIX 4B: GESELL'S MATURATIONAL CONCEPTS

The four major principles developed by Gesell (1949) include the following:

1. Directionality

2. Functional Asymmetry

3. Self-regulating Fluctuation

4. Motor Development

The Principle of Directionality.   Development is governed by maturation. As in the case of fetal development, there are two distinct directions of growth: *cephalocaudal* (development proceeding from the head downward) and *proximodistal* (development from the trunk outward).

The Principle of Functional Asymmetry.   There is a strong tendency for infants to develop asymmetrically. This is seen as the development of "handedness"; most individuals will have a preferred side. People eat with the hand on the preferred side, throw a ball with that hand, and kick with the foot on that side.

The Principle of Self-Regulating Fluctuation.   Development of body systems does not proceed at an even pace. Although one system is growing and developing rapidly, another system may be dormant. Later, these two systems may reverse activity levels. There is a strong relationship between motor development and language development. Usually children don't begin talking extensively until after they have learned to walk; the two skills are rarely developed together. Later, after the language system is more firmly established, there are more advances in motor skills.

The Principle of Motor Development.   Motor development progresses from head to foot, moving outward from the midline. For example, the baby gains head control before he gains trunk control. Control of the body begins first in a horizontal plane, such as on the back and belly, and then progresses to the vertical position, such as sitting and standing.

Although Gesell's theories have been questioned, his Developmental Schedules are still considered to be viable tools for the assessment of youngsters between birth and 36 months. Bagnato, Neisworth, and Munson (1989) state that

> Gesell test behaviors . . . supported the usefulness of traditional developmental scales as reliable criterion-based measures of individual child progress and intervention effectiveness. They also demonstrated that a curriculum based on the same developmental landmarks as the assessment device could be used to track normative progress. (p. 30)

APPENDIX 4C: APGAR (1953) INFANT RATING SCALE

In appearance (A) the infant is given a score of 2 if the skin is completely pink; 1 if the body is pink but the arms are bluish; zero if the entire body is blue. It is important to note that babies of the Negroid race are, at birth, extremely pink in color. Therefore, skin color, in reference to a presence or lack of sufficient oxygen, is still an important variable.

If the heart rate (pulse-P) is higher than 100, 2 points are recorded; 1 point if less than 100 beats; and 0 if no beat is present.

For the baby who cries vigorously when given a light slap on the soles of the feet, 2 points are given; if the child grimaces (G) or gives only a slight cry, then 1 point is recorded. Finally, if no response is given, then 0 is listed.

A neonate who makes active motions will receive a score of 2 for muscle tone and activity (A); some movement of arms and legs rates a score of 1; a limp, motionless infant receives a 0. Infants with Down syndrome are often born with this limp and hanging appearance and are commonly referred to as "floppy babies."

Babies whose total score on the first test administration is between 4 and 6 usually need some immediate assistance to increase their initial attempts to breathe. A baby with a score of less than 4 is usually limp, unresponsive, pale, often not breathing, and possibly even without a heartbeat. The baby's throat will be quickly suctioned to open a clear pathway and the lungs will be artificially inflated as rapidly as possible. The infant may need assistance with breathing for several minutes until ready to sustain breathing alone.

Part II

ASSESSMENT AND INSTRUCTION

Chapter 5

INDIVIDUALIZED EDUCATIONAL PROGRAMMING: THE PROCESS AND THE PRODUCT

 "Pardon me, may I have your attention? Thank you for coming. I'd like to begin with the first staffing of the day." The teachers and therapists settled into their chairs, shuffled their papers, and looked up to Mr. March, the assistant director of special education who was serving as the leader of this multidisciplinary staffing. Mr. March continued: "A new student in the district, Jeanie McElmurry, is a 12-year-old female with spastic cerebral palsy and moderate mental retardation; she has had grand mal seizures, which are now under control. To begin with, Mrs. Barkwick, please present your findings regarding the results of the motor skill and physical fitness performance tests of the student." Mrs. Barkwick distributed copies of the test raw scores and percentiles and began her explanation.

An **individualized educational program (IEP)** is a detailed, written plan to meet the educational needs of a child with disabilities. It should contain all dimensions of a total education, including specific information regarding the intellectual, social, emotional, and physical programs for each child (Figure 5.1).

The underlying concept of the IEP is that students must have their most important and immediate needs identified if they are to receive the best education possible. This planning, therefore, is essential and must be completed before any programming, placement, or teaching can begin. Individualized teaching and learning have proved to be highly effective with both students with disabilities and those without.

OVERVIEW OF THE IEP, IFSP, AND LEGAL REQUIREMENTS

P.L. 94-142 required that an IEP be developed for students with disabilities between the ages of 3 and 21. Now, with the full inclusion of P.L. 99-457 (Title I, infants & toddlers, and Title II, ages 3 through 5) into P.L. 101-476, infants, toddlers,

MIDSTATE SPECIAL EDUCATION
INDIVIDUALIZED EDUCATIONAL PROGRAM

White—Building
Yellow—Parent
Goldenrod—Midstate
Pink—Regional Supervisor

19 _____ to _____ 19 _____

Student's name _____ Birthdate _____

Resident district _____ Building _____

Placement _____ Building _____

Type of Sp. Ed. Program _____

Date of initial placement _____

Date of IEP _____ Date of review _____

THE FOLLOWING PERSONS ATTENDED
IEP staffing/review:

Reg. Ed. Admin. _____

Standard Teacher _____

Special Teacher _____

Parent(s) _____

Student _____

Other (Title) _____

IEP Manager _____

Sp. Ed. Admin. _____

Psychologist _____

PE Teacher _____

SERVICES TO BE PROVIDED

Type	Start	Teacher or Itinerant	No. of Min. Per Week	No. of Weeks

Transportation:

Physical education:

Extent of time in standard program:

Vocational/Career Educ.

FIGURE 5.1   Example of the individualized education program planning form.

and preschool children with disabilities must be accounted for. Additionally, the new law provides for children who show signs of being "at risk." The newest change is the introduction of the *Individualized Family Service Plan* (IFSP), which provides for a child's individualized educational plan; it is identical in concept to the IEP of 94-142. Both the IFSP and the IEP are designed to show existing needs of the individuals involved and specific remediation programs. A major difference is that, within the IFSP, the parents *must* be integral members of the team and directly involved in all stages of planning and implementation (McCubbin & Zittel, 1991).

All local school districts receiving federal funds must write an annual IEP or IFSP for individuals with disabilities or infants and children who are "at risk." If a child is sent to a facility outside the school district, the IEP, its implementation, and total financial cost of education are still the responsibility of the local school board. For example, meeting the needs of a child labeled as severely multidisabled within the facilities of the local school district may not be possible. The school district and the parents should decide if the child will receive more effective educational opportunities in a state-operated developmental center. If the answer is *yes*, in most states, the total cost of educating this child must be paid by the local school district.

Some states have attempted to relieve the local school districts of financial responsibility for students with severe or profound disabilities who reside in state-operated developmental centers. These states have passed legislation to assume the entire cost of meeting the mandates of P.L. 101-476.

Illinois is experiencing positive results from special funding entitled The Orphanage Act (Illinois 14-7.03). At Lincoln Developmental Center, Lincoln, Illinois, 86 students with severe and profound disabilities are being educated effectively in classroom settings with a maximum of eight students in each class. One certified special eduation teacher and two teacher aides are assigned to each group. Daily physical education is provided by an approved adapted physical education teacher (Landis, 1991).

THE WRITTEN DOCUMENT

The IEP describes the educational plan and how education and related services will be provided. It must contain the following elements:

1. A statement of the child's present levels of educational performance
2. A statement of long-term educational performance goals to be achieved by the child at year end
3. A statement of short-term instructional objectives for each annual goal, which represent measurable intermediate steps between the child's present level of performance and the desired level
4. A statement of special education and related services to be provided, including the type of physical education program in which the child will

participate and any special media or materials required to implement the child's IEP

5. Initiation date and anticipated duration of special education and related services

6. Description of extent to which the child will participate in regular education programs

7. Justification for the child's educational placement

8. Objective criteria, evaluation procedures, and schedules for determining on an annual basis whether short-term instructional objectives have been achieved

Although the total IEP should stress improving intellectual abilities, it must also provide specific details regarding the student's physical and motor program. Physical educators, because of their psychomotor expertise, thus become the appropriate professionals to define the status of a child's present motor and fitness ability.

The components and depth or detail of an IEP may be more extensive than the general class planning that physical educators are currently using, and some terminology may be new, but the actual development of an IEP simply represents sound physical education planning. What the educator has always done for a large group of students must now be done for an individual child. Basically, the law asks educators, including physical educators, to provide the following: (1) a clear statement of the child's current levels of ability, (2) precise identification of the most important skills to be learned, (3) specific programming suggestions, (4) placement recommendation for the most effective program, and (5) how the child's progress will be evaluated.

DO ALL CHILDREN WITH DISABILITIES NEED AN IEP IN PHYSICAL EDUCATION?

Many children with disabilities can remain in the regular physical education class because they do not need a specially designed adapted program. For example, after assessing a 10-year-old girl with educable mental retardation, her levels of general motor ability and physical fitness were found to be comparable to those of her nondisabled peers. Presumably, therefore, she could learn physical skills as effectively as those youngsters in the mainstream, so she was placed into the regular program. In this child's case, the regular physical education curriculum was assumed to provide appropriate developmental sequences to meet the overall needs of all children her age. Consequently, because of her placement, an IEP was not needed for her physical education experience. In most cases, the IEP form will contain a specific section that identifies whether the student is to be placed in regular or adapted physical education (see Figure 5.1).

Individualized assessment determines individual need.

Conversely, when a child is found to possess unusually low levels of motor ability or fitness, it is necessary to write an IEP. In this case, performance dictates the need for special programming. The IEP will specify present levels of ability at which the most effective learning can occur and will list specific goals and objectives. For example, after testing, a boy with a learning disability was found to possess an extremely low level of perceptual motor ability, including catching and striking problems and deficiencies in static and dynamic balance. Because of these particular skill problems, one assumes that he cannot participate successfully and competitively with his normal age group. The most appropriate placement for this boy is an adapted physical education class with a more concentrated program that was written to improve performance in perceptual motor tasks.

These examples are at the extremes of full-time placement in either regular or adapted physical education. Most individuals with disabilities can perform or learn most activities in a regular physical education class with nondisabled peers. The boy with a hearing impairment could be placed for part of the time in the regular program, particularly when planned activities involve strength and cardiorespiratory

Static balance is often lacking in children with disabilities.

improvement. Weight training activities and endurance running would also provide opportunities for him to return to the mainstream. The IEP should identify those activities for which the boy can remain in the regular program (see Figure 5.1).

THE TRANSDISCIPLINARY TEAM

An IEP should be planned and written by those individuals most closely involved with the child's education. These professionals—teachers, school administrators, and support personnel—become the transdisciplinary team. Support personnel often includes physicians, therapists, psychologists, and social workers. The team works in cooperation and agreement with the child's parents, and when appropriate, with the child. For instance, it is appropriate for a 17-year-old boy who is blind to participate in planning his educational program, whereas a 4-year-old child with Down syndrome cannot provide meaningful input. This yearly face-to-face exchange of ideas and information serves as the basis for the child's complete educational program.

Lavay and French (1985) emphasize the extreme importance of communication among representatives of all disciplines. In fact, they stress the need for the adapted physical educator to become a driving force—the individual who takes responsibility for articulating the effort required in the motor and fitness areas. They make reference to the term, "transdisciplinary approach." In their view, an ongoing dialogue must be maintained among physical educators, medical personnel, regular and special educators, and psychologists. Eichstaedt and Lavay (1992) also believe that the transdisciplinary model is far more effective than the traditional multidisciplinary method. Bird (1990) compares the methods when he states, "When considering the differences among teaming approaches, these are best portrayed as points on a continuum rather than as discrete entities" (p. 288). Table 5.1 illustrates the unique differences found in teaming approaches for the development of IEPs.

Preplanning by the local school district is necessary so school personnel can discuss the following issues with the child's parents at the transdisciplinary staff conference: (1) child's eligibility, (2) present levels of educational performance, (3) annual goals, (4) supportive services, and (5) placement. Individuals responsible for implementing the child's IEP must also be identified and should attend the transdisciplinary staff conference.

The purpose of preplanning is to assure parents that the school has reviewed the child's case study evaluation, examined the child's needs, identified potential goals

TABLE 5.1   Continuum of Teaming Approaches for Development of Individualized Education Plans (IEP)

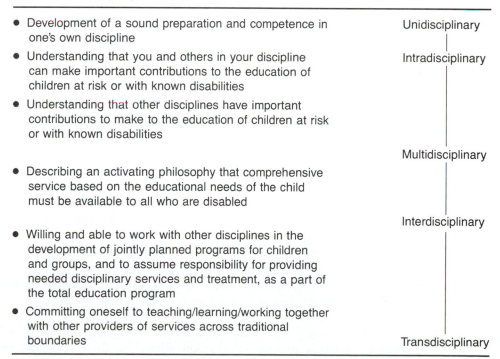

• Development of a sound preparation and competence in one's own discipline	Unidisciplinary
• Understanding that you and others in your discipline can make important contributions to the education of children at risk or with known disabilities	Intradisciplinary
• Understanding that other disciplines have important contributions to make to the education of children at risk or with known disabilities	
	Multidisciplinary
• Describing an activating philosophy that comprehensive service based on the educational needs of the child must be available to all who are disabled	
	Interdisciplinary
• Willing and able to work with other disciplines in the development of jointly planned programs for children and groups, and to assume responsibility for providing needed disciplinary services and treatment, as a part of the total education program	
• Committing oneself to teaching/learning/working together with other providers of services across traditional boundaries	
	Transdisciplinary

Adapted from *Staff Development Handbook: A Resource for the Transdisciplinary Process* by United Cerebral Palsy. Copyright 1976 by United Cerebral Palsy. Reprinted by permission of Unted Cerebral Palsy.

for the child, and considered placement and service options. By engaging in some preplanning, the transdisciplinary staff conference can be used to present program options to the child's parents and to discuss goals and needed services for the child.

The IEP planning process requires systematic organization so the educational program is individualized and student-oriented. The IEP provides a comprehensive plan for meeting the needs of the child.

Kirk and Gallagher (1989) outline an approach for developing and coordinating the IEP. They state that successful adaptation, both physical and social, is the primary goal of the process. Specifically, the process involves information gathering, data pooling, initial programming, periodic reassessment, and program modification. They emphasize total communication among child, family, and public school personnel. Adaptability and flexibility on the part of all involved personnel are necessary to facilitate efforts to meet each child's unique needs.

Heward and Orlansky (1988) identify three goals that should influence the exchange of knowledge and function among team members: (1) Consider the whole child. "Splintering" of the child along disciplinary lines must be avoided, that is, the old saying "the arms and legs to the physical educator, the joints to the physical therapist, and the brain to the teacher" is no longer appropriate. (2) Increased communication among team members should be a constant goal. (3) Maintain a positive attitude toward increased services to children regardless of fiscal constraint (i.e., when budgetary restrictions limit the number of full-time personnel, some disciplines may provide assistance on a consulting basis). These considerations do not imply that one individual or discipline must assume total responsibility for a child's program, but rather that team members share their information and, when appropriate, their skills to ensure consistency in the child's program.

Cooperation and better understanding among professionals is illustrated in the following examples:

Case 1: A physician mistakenly diagnosed a child severely involved with cerebral palsy as also being mentally retarded because he could not elicit any communication from the child. The classroom teacher, on the other hand, saw the child every day and was able to provide significant insights on reevaluation. The teacher knew that the child, who was quite intelligent, was terribly frightened by fear of failing. The child therefore gave the doctor a totally inaccurate picture during diagnostic examination.

Case 2: A physical educator augmented regular classroom instruction by incorporating simple group movement experiences. The classroom teacher supplied information to the physical educator regarding the social, emotional, and intellectual abilities of two new students. The physical educator also learned that the teacher wanted to develop geometric design concepts (squares, triangles, circles). For several weeks, the physical educator therefore included movement activities and games that involved geometric figures.

Parents and professionals can assist in the development of IEPs by collecting written data that provide information related to their discipline or to involvement with the child with disabilities. Some specific areas that warrant attention are (1) priorities for the IEP, (2) evaluation criteria, (3) suggested strategies for change,

(4) the child's strengths and limitations, (5) the child's special attitudes, (6) performance potential, (7) psycho-social development, (8) specific problems encountered by the student, (9) specific suggestions as to what others can do to facilitate skill development, and (10) recommendations for other support programs (Table 5.2).

All individuals involved in the conference should be able to state specific needs and objectives clearly to facilitate better understanding. The formal staff conference

TABLE 5.2   Specific Questions to Be Considered When Collecting Information for an Individualized Educational Program (IEP)

Specific Questions	Examples of Information Given for a Boy with Duchenne Muscular Dystrophy
1. Priorities of IEP	a. Maintain upper-body strength and endurance. b. Increase joint range of motion. c. Reduce joint contractures. d. Increase recreational skills.
2. Evaluation Criteria	a. Use hand dynamometer for strength evaluation. b. Use goniometer for joint range of motion. c. Use cupcake pan and tennis ball for eye-hand coordination. Time with stopwatch.
3. Suggested strategies for change	a. Include progressive exercises, allowing for ample rest periods. b. Involve in activities that use the hands. c. Modify games for play in wheelchair.
4. Child's strengths and limitations	a. Nonambulatory; must remain in wheelchair. b. Close supervision in swimming pool is a must. He cannot support himself in standing position.
5. Child's special attitudes	a. Positive mental attitude and enjoys physical education class.
6. Performance potential	a. Strength levels will decrease from the disease. b. Fatigue will set in after shorter periods of time.
7. Psychosocial evaluation	a. Very cooperative with peers and teachers. b. Eager to be involved in team activities.
8. Specific problems encountered by the student	a. Severe contractures of ankles and feet. b. Legs cannot be lifted by student.
9. Specific suggestions for what others can do to facilitate skill development	a. Allow student to wheel own wheelchair. b. Allow student to use arms and hands in all activities to maintain strength levels.
10. Recommendations for other support programs	a. Physical therapist should conduct additional exercises for reduction of contractures. b. The Business Education Department should begin training student to use typewriter and calculator.

should result in (1) identification of educational program priorities, (2) identification of persons who will provide necessary instruction, (3) understanding of the child's placement for most effective learning, and (4) choices of evaluation methods.

PARENTS' APPROVAL OF THE IEP

The IEP is deemed complete only after the parents sign the IEP approval sheet. This final step is usually a mere formality if the parents have been involved and informed during the initial phases of IEP development. If the parents are not pleased and do not agree with an aspect of the document, they are not required to sign the approval form. They have the right, ensured in P.L. 101-476, to challenge the school's decisions or the quality of services provided. This right is referred to as **due process provisions of the law**.

Specific examples of why some parents have disapproved of an IEP include the following:

- Evaluation was not appropriate.
- Parents' opinions concerning their child's education were not considered or addressed in planning conferences.
- IEP is deemed inappropriate based on evaluation.

The parent or parents also have the right to question whether the IEP is being followed carefully. According to a Special Olympics publication discussing implementation of P.L. 94-142 (1980), parental concerns often stem from one of the following:

- The school is not using special education services as specified in the IEP.
- The child is not showing any progress in the areas targeted for remediation.
- The school is delaying implementation of a service specified in the IEP.
- Racial, cultural, or disability biases have led to development of an inappropriate IEP.

All involved in writing an IEP must understand the legal steps that parents can take to challenge the school's IEP. Possible legal actions include (1) appeal to the local school district administration, (2) request for independent evaluation, (3) request for a hearing before an independent and neutral officer, (4) filing an administrative appeal, (5) filing a complaint to the Federal Office for Civil Rights, and (6) filing a lawsuit. Every attempt should be made to resolve disagreements and misunderstandings early so the child's program can be implemented quickly. It is always preferable to try to settle issues by working with local officials before proceeding to other action (Ekstrand & Edmister, 1984).

THE PHYSICAL EDUCATOR'S ROLE
ON THE TRANSDISCIPLINARY TEAM

The psychomotor area is an integral component of the child's IEP. All children with disabilities must therefore be assessed to determine (1) physical and motor fitness, (2) fundamental motor skills and patterns, and (3) skills in aquatics, dance, individual and group games, and lifetime sports. Because physical education instruction is a defined part of special education, the committee should review motor and physical fitness needs of each child to determine if a need exists for specially designed physical education programs. Too often, such assessment is completed by professionals other than the physical educator (e.g., the special educator or the physical therapist). Certified physical educators have been trained to assess, program, teach, and evaluate within all of these parameters; they must be involved at the beginning of the evaluation process, particularly if a motor problem exists. Figure 5.2 illustrates how a physical educator should participate in the initial phases of the IEP.

Physical educators must take the initiative to become actively involved in the development of each child's IEP. Stein (1977) lists ten suggestions for physical educators to follow when working with the transdisciplinary team:

1. Ensure that physical education is included in each child's IEP.
2. Volunteer information about the child's physical and motor development, and about social, emotional, and personal characteristics to the team for preparation of the IEP.
3. Be available to participate in planning conferences and show a personal interest in contributing actively to this process.
4. Make sure that children who need a specially designed physical education program receive such programs and are not inappropriately placed in regular programs.
5. Make sure that children are not programmed for specially designed physical education when their needs can be adequately and appropriately met in regular programs.
6. Remind the committee that every child with a disability does not need, want, or require specially designed physical education.
7. Remind the committee that certain specially designed physical education programs can be accomplished in regular classes, some with additional support and others without any supplementary assistance.
8. Primarily, remember and remind the committee of the specific nature of physical education as IEPs are planned and implemented.
9. See that placement flexibility is maintained so the child participates in regular physical education activities whenever possible and in specially designed programs as necessary.

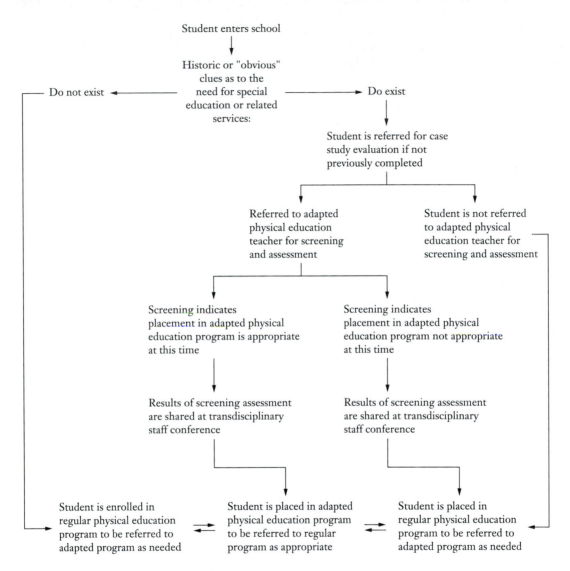

(At this level of the process, program success depends on ease with which students can transfer from the regular program into the adapted program and vice versa. Although most participants in the adapted program will be students with permanent disabilities, from time to time students with temporary disabilities, such as physical injuries or overweight and obesity, who might benefit from limited participation will be placed in the adapted program. To receive the greatest impact and benefit from the adapted physical education program, smooth transition between regular and adapted classes is essential.)

FIGURE 5.2   Model showing appropriate involvement of physical education in IEP development.

10. Remember that individualized education and one-to-one relationships are not synonymous.

THE THERAPIST'S ROLE IN DEVELOPING THE IEP

P.L. 101-476 clearly identifies physical and occupational therapies as **related services**. This means that therapists and their services cannot replace required physical education programming. Any prescribed therapy should be given *in addition* to the physical education class. If the specialized services of a therapist are identified as necessary in the child's IEP, then both physical education and therapy must be given.

Drawing clear lines between the roles of the adapted physical educator and the therapist is difficult, for similar responsibilities are often within the professional expertise of both. When the transdisciplinary team requests specific motor performance data, the physical educator is the committee member who should provide this information. The majority of children with disabilities can be tested effectively by the adapted or regular physical education teacher. When the severity or complexity of a disabling condition is beyond the physical educator's expertise, then the child's motor assessment should be done by a therapist. Table 5.3 provides a partial list of major disabling conditions and suggests areas of responsibility for the physical educator and therapist.

Some motor abilities can be evaluated by both teacher and therapist, but testing duplication of the same skill should be avoided. Through cooperation and sharing of information, the child will receive a more complete and effective evaluation. Skills to be assessed are shown in Table 5.4.

A well-coordinated schedule, including a cooperatively planned program, will provide for optimum growth and development. Each related service and teaching experience should contribute important and necessary motor experiences to the education of a child with disabilities.

TABLE 5.3 Partial list of Disabling Conditions and Areas of Assessment Responsibilities for Physical Educators and Therapists

Adapted Physical Educator	Therapist
Blind and visually impaired	Cerebral palsy (severely involved)[a]
Deaf and hearing impaired	Muscular dystrophy (Duchenne)[a]
Mentally Retarded (EMR, TMR, and Down syndrome)[a]	Severe congenital disabilities[a]
Behavior disorders	Mentally disabled (severe and profound, nonambulatory)[a]
Learning disabilities	Postoperative (extreme low levels of strength, endurance, and range of motion)[a]
Obese/overweight/underweight	

[a] Conditions that necessitate a physician's written prescription.

TABLE 5.4   **Comparative Areas of Expertise Between Therapist and Physical Educator**

Therapist	Physical Educator
Basic biological efficiency 　Strength 　Endurance 　Range of motion 　Flexibility 　Gross motor coordination	**Advanced locomotor skills, including degree of performance (How fast? How far? How many?)** 　Dynamic balance 　Jumping 　Hopping 　Galloping 　Running 　Skipping 　Leaping
Basic perceptual-motor skills 　Infant reflexes 　Sensory stimulation 　Conditioned reflexes 　Static balance 　Figure-ground relationships 　Spatial relationships 　Kinesthesis	**Advanced biological efficiency** 　Muscular strength 　Cardiovascular efficiency 　Gross motor coordination 　Agility 　Speed 　Reaction time
Basic locomotor skills 　Rolling 　Crawling 　Creeping 　Walking	**Eye-hand coordination skills** 　Throwing 　Catching 　Kicking 　Striking

SPECIFIC ASSESSMENT TECHNIQUES USED BY THERAPISTS

One distinctive technique used by therapists includes **muscle testing**, which is the subjective strength evaluation of specific muscles and muscle groups. The ratings usually are categorized as normal, good, fair, poor, trace, and zero. Muscle testing is designed to assess the extent and degree of weakness occurring from disorders that involve contractile muscles, myoneural junction, and lower motor neuron.

Analysis of a range of motion of a child with disabilities is also a specialty of the therapist. Children with restricted movement (i.e., children with cerebral palsy, muscular dystrophy, and postoperative conditions) can be measured with specific instruments. The goniometer measures joint angles and permits a fairly accurate comparison of joint angle before remediation with joint angle during rehabilitation. Many physical educators are trained to use the goniometer and to administer range-of-motion tests.

Evaluation of an individual's gait pattern (and teaching of gait) is also done by the therapist. Many children with permanent physical disabilities can learn or improve their walking patterns. These initial progressions are usually highly structured and demand a one-on-one teaching situation, often using orthotics (braces) or specialized parallel-bar walking equipment or both. The therapist has usually received special training to work in these areas.

A therapist's rehabilitation program can be conducted only with a physician's written approval. This written prescription consists of medical guidelines from which the therapist develops a plan of action. The physician may include statements such as, "Quad setting exercises for the rehabilitation of the right knee." This prescription allows the therapist (or adapted physical education teacher) to begin a progressive program with the student. Some prescriptions will be more detailed and specifically designate the rehabilitation program. If the doctor's prescription is too vague, the therapist should contact the physician before any program is initiated. Figure 5.3 provides a specific example of a written prescription. Figures 5.4 and 5.5 show how the IEP includes the services of the therapist.

Three types of therapist are commonly associated with physical development and rehabilitation: the registered kinesiotherapist (RKT), the registered physical therapist (RPT), and the registered occupational therapist (OTR).

The **kinesiotherapist** often possesses a degree in physical education to be eligible for certification and is quite often a certified physical education teacher as well. In many cases, this individual has an unusually strong background in both rehabilitation and physical education of students with disabilities. Specifically, the kinesiotherapist, in cooperation with a physician, applies principles, tools, techniques, and psychology of medically oriented physical education to assist individuals with

---

FROM THE DESK OF:

DONALD R. BROWN, M.D.
C. M. PETERSON,   M.D.
ROBERT F. SMITH,   M.D.

TELEPHONE 445-2120

Susan March

Spastic quadriplegia-cerebral palsy
Reduction of contractures and range of motion exercises for all extremeties
Place specific emphasis on extension activities

Robert F. Smith   9/10/92
PHYSICIAN   **DATE**

FIGURE 5.3   **Example of a written prescription from a physician for a student with cerebral palsy.**

INDIVIDUALIZED EDUCATIONAL PROGRAM
Sample Form

Student's Name: Fred Brown

IEP Manager's Name:

Initial Planning Conference Date:

Date for Review/Revision:

PRESENT LEVELS OF PERFORMANCE

Academics:
Not applicable

Speech/Language:
Says own name, Mommy, Daddy, go, baby; uses jargon otherwise

Motor:
Nonambulatory
Pincher grasps, palmar group

Social Behavior:
Parallel play
Follows directions to sit, lie down, etc.

Prevocational/Vocational:

Self-Help:
No dressing skills, cooperates, only finger feeds

Extent of Participation in Regular Education:
Possible lunch, Bus — may be in feeding program, may ride adapted bus

SERVICES TO BE PROVIDED FOR CURRENT YEAR

Type	Initiation Date	No. Minutes Per Week	No. Weeks
Physical therapy	9/3/87	150	40
Speech/Language Therapy	9/3/87	120	40

Placement:
Self-contained primary classroom for severely handicapped (below trainable)

Justification for Placement:
Needs low ratio, special attention, special equipment

FIGURE 5.4 The related services of the physical therapist are identified in a typical IEP.

IEP
Sample Form

Student's Name: Fred Brown

Implementer's Name:

Instructional Area: Mobility

Goal Statement: Transfer from wheelchair

SHORT-TERM INSTRUCTIONAL OBJECTIVES

Condition	Behavior	Criteria	Special Media and Materials	Evaluation/Schedule	Date Objective Mastered
1. With student sitting in wheelchair	1. Student transfers from wheelchair to floor	5 out of 5 trials for 5 consecutive days		Weekly	
2. With student sitting in wheelchair	2. Student transfers from wheelchair to chair	5 out of 5 trials for 5 consecutive days			
3. With student sitting in wheelchair	3. Student transfers to toilet	5 out of 5 trials for 5 consecutive days			
4. With student on the floor	4. Student climbs into wheelchair	5 out of 5 trials for 5 consecutive days			
5. With student sitting in a chair	5. Student transfers to wheelchair	5 out of 5 trials for 5 consecutive days			
6. With student sitting on toilet	6. Student transfers to wheelchair	5 out of 5 trials for 5 consecutive days			

FIGURE 5.5 The physical therapist has developed an individualized program of mobility for a child with a severe disability.

special physical and mental conditions. The therapist's ultimate goal is to accomplish prescribed treatment objectives in a rehabilitation or habilitation program. More recently, kinesiotherapists have also become involved in adapted physical education and perceptual-motor and related programs for children with special needs.

The **physical therapist** plans, implements, and evaluates treatment programs under physician supervision. Such programs typically include (1) exercises for increasing strength, endurance, coordination, and range of motion, (2) activities to facilitate motor capacity and learning, (3) instruction in use of assistive devices and activities relevant to daily living, and (4) application of physical agents such as heat or cold, ultrasound, or water to relieve pain or alter physiological status.

An **occupational therapist** evaluates clients, decides on treatment needs, develops treatment programs, and supervises the evaluation process—all under direct physician supervision. The programs usually attend to activities of daily living or those pertaining to occupational pursuits.

ASSESSMENT

Central to the IEP are the child's present levels of physical and motor performance: what the child can and cannot do. Because program planning, development, placement, teaching, and evaluation begin with assessment, testing must be valid, reliable, and easily administered, and the test results must be accurately interpreted. In planning the assessment, two basic questions must be asked:

1. *What information is needed to write an effective physical education program for a student with a disability?* The information needed to write the program will contain evaluation of such basic components as the child's strength, endurance, agility, flexibility, speed, eye-hand coordination, and balance.
2. *How will this information be collected?* Specific tests or test batteries must be selected to evaluate accurately the student's total motor performance. The results of these tests will contain specific data such as how many, how fast, how far.

A number of objective measures are desirable in the assessment process. Students, parents, teachers, and administrators understand objective test scores readily. The physical education teacher will be better able to describe and justify program recommendations in everyday language if objective scores are available.

BASIC PRINCIPLES OF ASSESSMENT

The student's placement in, and the direction and intensity of, the child's individualized physical education program is based on the student's present levels of ability. Placement in the least restrictive environment depends on the analysis of test scores and on observations. Important considerations involving the collection of data are as follows:

1. The test results should describe a specific component of the physical education program (e.g., balance, agility, strength).
2. Consider employing a variety of test batteries to assess more than one area (e.g., physical fitness tests, general motor ability tests, sport skill tests).
3. A competent professional should administer and interpret the tests.
4. Results must reflect the student's "true" achievement level. For example, a student with mental retardation may not understand the concept of "run as fast as you can" and therefore does not perform at maximum level. The test score would be misleading, and an inaccurate picture might develop.

Assessment of performance and achievement must be included as part of every physical education curriculum. Testing becomes crucial in diagnosing students' strengths and weaknesses. Each student's needs and the benefits of a specific physical education experience can be effectively evaluated only through a planned testing method.

Different assessment techniques are considered useful by physical educators. Kalakian and Horvat (in press) describe the following techniques and measures:

- **Informal techniques**—observation of student performance, self-testing activities, exploration activities; discussions with students, professionals, and volunteers who work with students; use of rating scales, checklists, inventories, questionnaires, and screening activities
- **Formal techniques**—tests for perceptual-motor functions, coordination, gross motor ability, physical fitness, cardiorespiratory function, anthropometric characteristics, and specific sport skills
- **Developmental measures**—tests for intelligence, learning ability, academic achievement, social-emotional behavior, speech, perception, adaptive behavior
- **Tests, examinations, and assessments by experts**—results of evaluations and assessments made by specialists, available to physical education teachers
- **Individual records**—data about each child organized for physical education program personnel; time allotted for specialists who have evaluated youngsters to meet with teachers to discuss appropriate activities and approaches that will meet each student's needs

To comply with P.L. 101-476 and to develop an effective and appropriate IEP, physical education instructors need to understand a variety of assessment methods. Although the administration of tests to children with disabilities is often considered difficult, most children with disabilities are able to be tested and can perform on the identical tests given to the nondisabled. To illustrate: children with mental retardation are often considered physically unable to function in regular physical education activities. This impression is not supported by fact, since most (60%) individuals with mental retardation are classified as mildly retarded. This means that of the population of mentally retarded, 6 out of 10 will be able to complete the same motor tests as the nondisabled (Eichstaedt and Lavay, 1992).

Eichstaedt, Wang, Polacek, and Dohrmann (1991) conducted a study of 4,448 males and females with mild or moderate mental retardation, or with Down syndrome. The ages of the subjects were between 6 and 21. Specific test items from the *AAHPERD Youth Fitness Test Battery* (1976) and the *AAHPERD Health Related Physical Fitness Test Battery* (1980) were administered to all subjects. The test items included were the standing long jump, flexed arm hang, 50-yard dash, shuttle run, sit-ups (with arms folded across the chest and knees bent), 6-minute run (ages 6–11), 9-minute run (ages 12–21), sit and reach, and skin folds (triceps, subscapular, calf). To provide additional information, several test items were added, including the stork stand, a 15-second basketball wall bounce (ages 6–11, 4 feet away from wall; ages 12–21, 6 feet away from wall), plus height and weight information. From the data gathered, Dohrmann and Wang (1990) concluded that the above test items are appropriate for administration to boys and girls between the ages of 6 and 21 with Down syndrome and also those subjects with mild and moderate mental retardation.

INADEQUATE TESTING CAN BE MISLEADING

Too often, a physical education department administers only one standardized test battery and expects the results to provide complete psychomotor information regarding the student. The inadequacy of such an assessment is further compounded if the tests are given only once a year. For example, at Average High School, U.S.A., the *AAHPERD Youth Fitness Test* (1976) is administered only in late spring. The scores provide information about student levels of performance involving abdominal and upper body strength and endurance, explosive leg power, speed, agility, and running endurance. Although this information is important, other areas covered in a comprehensive physical education program are missing (eye-hand coordination, balance, game and sport skills). These testing procedures are incomplete because all areas of general motor ability are not included. A well-planned curriculum must be based on complete assessment data. Program effectiveness (i.e., Does the curriculum meet the immediate needs of the students?) can be evaluated only if initial performance levels are determined and compared with final achievement. The school in this example should include additional tests such as balance and eye/hand coordination.

A testing program can be effective only when the people responsible for the overall curriculum understand the importance (and limitations) of test results. The authors of *Physical Fitness and Motor Skill Levels of Individuals with Mental Retardation: Mild, Moderate, and Down Syndrome Ages 6–21* (Eichstaedt, Wang, Polacek, & Dohrmann, 1991, p. 1) reemphasize an important point: "Too many educators in every sphere of every discipline fail to realize that a test battery in itself is not important—how it is used is all that really counts. It does no good and makes no sense to administer a physical fitness test, motor skill test, or developmental profile and then deposit the results in a drawer until the next year or until the test is administered again."

One often-asked question regarding the assessment of children with disabilities is, "Which test battery should I use for my youngsters?" The answer becomes mind-boggling because physical educators often look for a single approach, but in most instances, no one test battery effectively measures all dimensions of the psychomotor domain.

When identifying common components of general motor ability tests, strength, endurance, balance, speed, agility, and eye-hand coordination are most often listed. Although other components are also considered important, when accurately tested in those areas mentioned, children with poor motor skills and fitness can be identified.

Researchers agree (Rarick & Dobbins, 1975) that strength is the single most important element contributing to success in motor activity performance. Because of this, strength tests should be used. Most commonly identified areas of assessment are grip strength, upper body strength, abdominal strength, and explosive leg power.

Balance, both static and dynamic, is considered necessary in movement and skilled performance, such as running, throwing, jumping, and striking objects. Balance is also an integral component of test batteries and research as cited by Rarick, Dobbins, and Broadhead (1976), Bruininks (1978), Keogh and Sugden (1985), Werder and Kalakian (1985), Bailey and Wolery (1992), and Luftig (1989).

Speed and agility, together, are essential elements of psychomotor ability and are necessary for successful performance in play and sports. Specific reference is made to this in the research of Bruininks (1978), Cratty (1979), and Rarick, Dobbins, and Broadhead (1976).

Perceptual-motor ability (eye-hand and eye-foot coordination) is an extremely important component of general motor ability. Luftig (1989) states the following:

> Why, then, use perceptual-motor tests at all? One answer is that perceptual-motor tests do have some usefulness. . . . Children *do* experience perceptual-motor problems, and these problems often require remediation, not because they cause academic difficulties (and they may in some situations) but because the deficits cause problems for the individual. . . . For example, a child who experiences motor deficits may have difficulties in dressing and eating, skills that are needed for independent living. Likewise, a child who cannot catch a ball thrown at various speeds and heights may be ridiculed by peers during a game and begin to experience peer and emotional difficulties. Ask any eight-year-old who is struggling to learn the skills of baseball, and who is losing status with more accomplished peers, if there is a relationship between motor skills and social acceptance and listen to the response! (pp. 404–405)

Visual tracking of arm, hand, and foot movements is necessary for successful catching, throwing, striking, and kicking. Gallahue (1982), Sage (1984), and Payne and Isaacs (1991) stress the necessity to identify these abilities specifically when developing a complete motor picture of the individual.

A SHORT GENERAL MOTOR ABILITY TEST BATTERY

The test battery shown in Table 5.5 is a composite and modification of many test components designed to identify minimal levels of proficiency. A student who scores low becomes a potential candidate for individualized adapted physical education programming.

TABLE 5.5 **Minimal Levels of Performance when Determining Placement of Students for Adapted Physical Education**

Age	Upper Body Strength (Flexed Arm Hang) (seconds)		Explosive Leg Power (Standing Long Jump) (total inches)		Speed and Agility (Shuttle Run) (seconds)[a]		Balance (Stork Stand, Eyes Open) (seconds)		Eye-Hand Coordination (Basketball Wall Pass)[b]	
	Female	Male	Female	Male	Female	Male	Female	Male	Female	Male
6	1	1	12	15	17.4	16.4	4.0	4.5	5	5
7	1	2	16	17	16.8	15.8	5.5	5.5	5	6
8	2	4	19	19	16.3	15.3	5.5	5.0	6	8
9	3	4	21	24	12.5	14.8	6.5	5.5	9	11
10	3	5	22	26	12.5	13.9	6.0	5.5	11	13
11	3	6	24	28	12.1	12.8	6.5	5.5	12	15
12	3	6	29	32	12.0	12.5	5.0	5.5	12	15
13	3	5	30	35	12.0	12.0	6.0	5.5	12	16
14	3	7	32	36	11.8	12.0	6.0	5.0	13	16
15	4	6	32	38	12.0	12.0	6.0	6.0	13	16
16	3	9	32	38	12.0	12.2	6.5	6.0	12	16
17	3	9	32	38	12.0	11.4	6.5	6.5	12	16
18	4	9	32	38	12.1	11.5	7.0	6.5	12	16
19	4	9	32	38	12.2	11.5	8.0	7.0	12	16
20	4	9	32	38	12.3	11.4	9.0	8.0	12	16

[a] 30 ft by four trips.

[b] Total bounces completed in 15 sec from 4 ft away through age 11; total bounces completed in 15 sec from 6 ft away ages 12 and up.

STANDARDIZED OR NORM-REFERENCED TESTS

The standardized test, often called the norm-referenced test, is considered an exacting evaluation technique. These tests are the basis for comparative research and practice in the psychomotor area. Norm-referenced test batteries use standard scores (e.g., developmental age/mental age, developmental quotient/intelligence quotient, percentiles, T-scores) for the following purposes: (1) to describe an individual's functioning in terms of developmental expectancies for the individual's age, (2) to place the individual within some diagnostic category, and (3) to predict the individual's eventual outcome status (Bagnato, Neisworth, & Munson, 1989). This method of measuring performance enables physical educators to make comparisons between individuals with similar characteristics (i.e., age, sex, height, weight, disabling condition). An example of extensive research conducted to establish norm-referenced instruments is *Project UNIQUE*, reported by Winnick and Short (1985). They collected data from 23 states and the District of Columbia. The subjects tested were 3,914 children and youth ages 10 to 17. Nondisabled youngsters and youngsters with visual, auditory, and orthopedic impairments were included in the study. Percentile norms were established for physical fitness measures.

This type of test battery is valuable because it provides a better understanding of how to objectively evaluate a student's performance. The following items are commonly observed to identify specific levels of ability: (1) *time* (using a stopwatch) for agility run, endurance run, dash, skipping a given distance, holding a balance position; (2) *distance* (using a tape measure) for walking on a balance beam, ball is thrown, jumped, run in a given time; (3) *number* of times (watching and counting) a ball is bounced, sit-ups, pull-ups, or squat thrusts are performed; objects are picked up in a given time.

Standardized tests are extremely useful for preliminary classification of students into homogeneous groups, for diagnosis of weaknesses in specific areas of motor and physical performance, and for testing physical achievement (Johnson and Nelson 1986). The most common way to present standardized test results is by using percentiles. The results of many tests for children with disabilities are described in terms of percentile scores, which compare the student's performance with that of peers. For example, a percentile score of 35 means that 35 percent of the people taking the test had lower scores and 65 percent had higher scores.

When children score in the 25th percentile or lower, they may be strong candidates for individualized instruction or an adapted physical education program (Eichstaedt and Lavay, 1992). Sherrill (1986) suggests that most students scoring one standard deviation below the norm (at approximately the 16th percentile) could benefit from specialized instruction. Keogh and Sugden (1985) suggest that approximately 3 out of every 40 students in a regular physical education class will possess extreme levels of awkwardness. This number includes approximately 7.5 percent of every class. The use of objective test scores and percentiles thus provides valuable clues when one is trying to develop a total picture of a child's motor ability. This information is absolutely necessary when writing the IEP.

STANDARDIZED PHYSICAL FITNESS TEST BATTERIES

Instructors must be certain that standardized testing is not the only assessment used. The standardized test will provide initial (pretest) and final (posttest) levels of achievement, but is of little help when analyzing specific causes for success or failure.

For example, as 10-year-old boy with moderate mental retardation jumps 22 inches in the standing long jump test. This performance places him in the 25th percentile as determined by the norms established in *Physical Fitness and Motor Skill Levels of Individuals with Mental Retardation: Mild, Moderate, and Down Syndrome Ages 6–21* (Eichstaedt et al., 1991). Percentile ranking, by itself, does not provide enough information for future educational planning for IEP development. In this instance, it indicates only that the child definitely needs to improve this skill.

A youngster who has difficulty kicking a rolling ball (e.g., kick baseball) could have any one or all three of the following problems: (1) inability to balance for that fraction of a second that it takes to swing one's leg once the ball is rolling (i.e., inability to kick may stem from balance deficiency), (2) inability to judge speed and position of the ball and inability to coordinate perceptually the kicking action (i.e., swinging the leg too soon or too late), or (3) inability, when contact is made, to kick the ball very far because leg strength may be well below average.

In this situation, we see that more objective testing is necessary to determine specific levels of performance. The following tests might be administered: static and dynamic balance test (e.g., stork stand and balance beam walk), perceptual-motor tests (e.g., bounce a ball, catch a ball, kick a ball), and a leg strength test (e.g., standing long jump or Sargent jump test).

CRITERION-REFERENCED ASSESSMENT

Payne and Isaacs (1991) define criterion-referenced assessment as

> the "quality" of a person's performance. Because development proceeds along a predictable sequence of milestones, it is possible to determine where a person lies within this continuum. Thus, one major difference between norm-referenced and criterion-referenced assessments is that the latter compare people to themselves over time, whereas the former compare people to a standardized population at a given point in time. (p. 329)

Criterion-referenced assessment can help to determine an individual's performance level on many tasks that lead to a major or terminal skill. These assessments identify exactly what a student can and cannot do in a given skill. Consider students participating in "jungle relays." All students perform each of the following tasks for a distance of 20 ft: bear walk, bunny hop, frog leap, crab walk, snake wiggle, and lame dog walk. Children unable to support themselves with their arms for the entire distance (i.e., they stop or collapse) apparently possess low levels of hand, wrist, arm, and shoulder strength or low endurance level or both in comparison with other children who can perform the tasks. Ability to observe this weakness becomes the basis for criterion-referenced programming.

The instructor must become familiar with specific aspects or terms that are essential to an understanding of the criterion-referenced process. Writing a criterion-referenced program is similar in format to writing an IEP.

A **skill** can be compared to an annual goal. Ability to learn a skill will result in the child's being able to perform that skill in more advanced activities. Examples of skills are the mature skipping pattern, the mature run, and the mature overhand throw. After having learned the mature overhand throw, the student will be able to use this skill in games such as softball. All skills can be broken down into smaller components that are also observable and measurable.

The criterion-referenced approach requires the teacher to select appropriate short-term objectives (a list of specific activities) for the student. These objectives consist of three parts: (1) a **behavior** is the specific observable skill, such as skipping; (2) a **condition** states how and where the behavior should occur (e.g., with bare feet on a tumbling mat); and (3) a **criterion** establishes a certain standard of performance (e.g., 15 ft).

The advantage of this type of assessment is that it can be used to observe children actively at play. Each child can be closely watched and evaluated while performing different activities and games. For example, assessment could be occurring while 10- and 11-year-old students play a game that involves throwing. The instructor sees that one boy is not transferring his weight from the back to the front foot when throwing. This indicates that the child's level of overhand throwing is below average for his age. Skill activities that teach appropriate weight transfer must therefore be included in the youngster's program.

An *I CAN* evaluation sheet (Figure 5.6) shows how an entire class can be evaluated on the overhand throw. Note that specific levels of performance have been identified.

I CAN

CLASS PERFORMANCE SCORE SHEET
PERFORMANCE OBJECTIVE: OVERHAND THROW

SCORING

Assessment:
X = Achieved
O = Not achieved

Reassessment:
⊗ = Achieved
Ø = Not achieved

FOCAL POINTS
- a Overhand motion
- b Ball release
- a Eyes on target
- b Overhand motion
- a Arm exten./side orient.
- b Weight transfer
- c Hip and spine rotation
- d Follow through
- e Smooth integration

STD.
- 10 ft distance, 2/3 times
- 20 ft target at 15 ft, 2/3 times
- 2/3 times
- Angle of release 45°   age/sex norm., 2/3 times
- Accuracy   8 ft target at 50 ft, 2/3 times

PRIMARY RESPONSES
- N Nonattending
- NR No response
- UR Unrelated response
- O Other (specify in comments)

NAME	a	b	a	b	a	b	c	d	e	4	5	COMMENTS
1. John J.	⊗	X	⊗	⊗	Ø	⊗	⊗	Ø	Ø	Ø	Ø	Throws side arm
2. Katie	X	X	X	X	⊗	⊗	⊗	X	Ø	Ø	Ø	
3. Susan	X	X	X	X	X	X	X	X	X	X	Ø	Practice accuracy
4. Mark	X	X	X	X	Ø	X	Ø	⊗	Ø	Ø	Ø	Faces target
5. John S.	X	X	X	X	X	X	X	⊗	Ø	Ø	Ø	Follow through inconsistent
6. Scott	⊗	X	Ø	⊗	Ø	Ø	Ø	Ø	Ø	Ø	Ø	Throws underhand
7. Judy	X	X	Ø	X	Ø	Ø	Ø	Ø	Ø	Ø	Ø	Doesn't look at target
8. Cindy	X	X	X	X	⊗	X	⊗	X	Ø	Ø	Ø	Faces target
9. Kirk	X	X	X	X	X	X	X	X	Ø	Ø	Ø	Jerky
10. Joanie	X	X	X	X	X	⊗	⊗	X	Ø	Ø	Ø	
11. Larry	X	X	X	X	⊗	X	X	X	Ø	Ø	Ø	Arm Bent
12. Chuck	X	X	⊗	⊗	Ø	⊗	Ø	Ø	Ø	Ø	Ø	Throws underhand or side arm unless assisted
13. Linda	X	X	X	X	X	X	X	X	⊗	⊗	Ø	Nearly mature
14. Sherry	X	X	X	X	⊗	X	⊗	X	⊗	Ø	Ø	Inconsistent beginning position
15. Greg	X	X	X	X	X	X	X	X	⊗	⊗	⊗	Nearly mature

FIGURE 5.6 The mature overhand throw is broken down into its observable components and an entire class is evaluated. (Reprinted with permission from J. A. Wessell, *Planning Individualized Education Programs in Special Education*, Northbrook, IL: Hubbard Scientific Co., 1977, p. 44.)

After testing students on other specific objectives to determine what skills they possess, the instructor can develop an individualized program for each child. Tables 5.6, 5.7, and 5.8 list specific items and activities that one might incorporate in formal or informal assessment.

If a particular skill is too complex to assess, the objective should be further broken down. A child's problem with developing and mastering a skill may be quite elementary, particularly when the child does not possess enough upper body strength to throw a ball an acceptable distance. The child's program should then contain specific activities to develop this basic strength component (e.g., prone to standing drills, modified push-ups, bear walk, crab walk, tennis ball squeezes, weight training).

Criterion-referenced assessment follows the concept of mastery learning in which several specifically defined objectives are attempted by the students. Assessment

TABLE 5.6   **Developmental Profile Items**[a]

Adaptive Behavior	**Gross Motor**
Discrimination of stimuli	Balancing
Leisure-recreation	Ball Handling
Manipulate environment	Catching
Peers-playmates	Climbing
Basic Knowledge	Climbing stairs
Body awareness	Crawling
Spatial relationships	Creeping
Fine Motor	Hand clapping
Building towers	Hitting objects
Copying activities	Holding up head
Drawing	Hopping
Grasping	Jumping
Placing objects in container with one/both hands	Kicking objects
Stacking beads	Maintaining good posture
Tracing activities	Physical fitness activities
Turning pages of book	Reaching for object
Using small muscles of hands/fingers	Riding tricycle
	Rocking activities
	Rolling activities
	Running
	Sitting with and without support
	Swinging
	Throwing objects
	Tossing objects
	Walking

Source: Adapted from AAHPERD, *Testing for Impaired, Disabled, and Handicapped Individuals,* 1975, p. 25.

[a] Listed items and activities can be incorporated into formal or informal approaches for assessing each of these developmental characteristics to show growth and maturation of a child.

TABLE 5.7 Physical Fitness Test Items[a]

Agility
Leg thrusts
Shuttle run (30 and 15 ft)
Squat thrusts or burpee
Line jumps
Zigzag run

Balance
Balance board activities
Beam-rail-bench walks
Object balance activities
Hopping and skipping activities

Cardiorespiratory endurance
Bench step cycling
Hiking
Jogging
Rope jumping
300-yard run
600-yard run-walk
6- , 9- , 12-min runs
$\frac{1}{2}$- , 1- , $1\frac{1}{2}$-mi runs
Swimming activities

Explosive power arms and shoulders
Medicine ball throw
Softball throw
Volleyball throw

Flexibility
Back extension activities
Back lifts
Bend, twist, and touch
Floor touch
Head, chest raise (prone position)
Trunk flexion activiites
Windmill
Goniometer

General coordination
Ball bounce
Roll progression
Softball throw
Standing long jump
Running high jump

Leg power
Mountain climber
Squat jump
Standing long jump
Vertical jump
Wall jump

Muscular endurance abdominal
Curls
Isokinetic activities
Leg lifts
Sit-ups
V-sit

Physique
Classification index
Height
Somatotyping
Weight

Speed
Dashes (25 to 100 yd)
8-sec dash

Strength
Dynometer
Hand grip
Isometric activities
Isokinetic activities
Tensiometer

Source: Adapted from AAHPERD, *Testing for Impaired, Disabled, and Handicapped Individuals,* 1975, p. 75.

[a] Listed items and activities can be incorporated into formal or informal approaches for testing physical fitness components.

is conducted repeatedly to determine if objectives are being accomplished. Objectives should be revised continually to incorporate newly acquired motor skills.

The following example of how to establish and use criterion-referenced objectives involves an 11-year-old boy with mild ataxic cerebral palsy who is expected to play "kick baseball" in the regular 6th-grade physical education class, but he per-

TABLE 5.8   Motor Ability, Perceptual-Motor Development, and Psychomotor Test Items[a]

Balance dynamic
Balance board activities
Beam-rail-bench walks
Bounce board activities
Stepping stones
Locomotor activities
Stunts and self-testing activities
Trampoline activities
Hopping activities

Balance static
Balance Board activities
Beam-rail-bench walks
Stock stand series
Stunts and self-testing activities

Balance object
Carry object
Finger and wand activities
Stick activities

Fine motor coordination
Building
Grasping
Gripping
Lacing
Manipulating
Stacking
Tapping

Spatial-body perception
Bilateral activities
Body abstraction
Body awareness
Body localization
Directionality activities
Identification of body parts
Imitation of body movements
Laterality activities
Sensory-motor integration
Shape-size-form differentiation and discrimination

Gross motor eye-foot coordination
Climbing stairs
Kicking activities
Motor planning and sequencing
Rope jumping
Line jumping

Gross motor eye-hand coordination
Ball activities
Catching activities
Manipulative and manual activities
Motor planning and sequencing
Tapping activities
Target activities
Throwing activities

Gross motor coordination general
Calisthenic activities
Exercise
Simultaneous activities
Trampoline activities
Tumbling and apparatus activities

Gross motor fundamental movements

Balancing	Hopping	Shifting
Batting	Jumping	Sitting
Bouncing	Kicking	Sliding
Catching	Landing	Skipping
Climbing	Leaping	Standing
Crawling	Lifting	Striking
Creeping	Marching	Swinging
Dancing	Pulling	Throwing
Galloping	Pushing	Tossing
Hanging	Rolling	Walking
Hitting	Running	

Visual
Acuity
Constancy
Equilibrium
Figure-ground relationships
Ocular control and pursuit
Spatial relationships
Tracking

Source: Adapted from AAHPERD, Testing for Impaired, Disabled, and Handicapped Individuals, 1975, p. 44–45.

[a] Listed items and activities can be incorporated into formal or informal approaches for assessing each of these motor, perceptual-motor, and psychomotor functions.

forms very poorly. The physical education instructor observes that the student is not succeeding due to a lack of eye-foot coordination and balance. The instructor therefore establishes criterion-referenced objectives for the student. These objectives will serve as an assessment instrument and as a subsequent skill-building program. The written program will be developed as follows:

- **First objective:** Student will balance on one foot (behavior) for 5 sec, three out of four consecutive attempts (criterion).
- **Second objective:** Student will kick (behavior) a 10-in. ball that is stationary in front of him (condition) 30 ft in the air, four out of five consecutive attempts (criterion).
- **Third objective:** Student will kick (behavior) a 10-in. ball that is moving slowly toward him (condition) into an 8 × 24 ft soccer goal, four out of five consecutive attempts (criterion).

The instructor should note if additional skills of a more basic nature are needed to accomplish these objectives. Possibly the boy's leg strength is extremely poor, and appropriate hopping, jumping, and skipping activities should also be included in this program.

The *behavior*, *condition*, and *criterion* can always be modified. By using this type of assessment, the instructor can determine, on an individual basis, how students are doing, who needs more help in which areas, and who has acquired the necessary skills to advance to the next level of participation. When a child appears to need more time to learn with more opportunities for trial and error, the instructor may place the youngster in an adapted physical education class.

SUBJECTIVE ASSESSMENT

Criterion-referenced assessment requires that the teacher make subjective judgments about an individual's performance. The quality of these judgments is directly related to the knowledge and expertise of the instructor. Herein lies the main drawback of the criterion-referenced approach. The gymnastic or springboard diving judge can make a reliable subjective evaluation. These people are highly trained and are able to reproduce reliable and consistent scores in their specific areas of expertise. Although some experienced physical educators are able to determine student strengths and weaknesses with seeming accuracy, it is almost impossible to find a reliable consistency between the judgments of two or more instructors in all areas of physical education evaluation. It is therefore difficult to find agreement on the meaning of words such as "average" or "slow."

Seaman and DePauw (1989) provide an example of subjective evaluation: "An informal test of endurance may take the form of observing that, after three minutes of play in a soccer game, the student appears fatigued and cannot keep up with the other students. The observation that the student 'appears fatigued' is clearly judgmental" (p. 129).

Although subjective assessment is used extensively by physical educators, its contribution to the IEP is, by itself, inadequate. P.L. 101-476 states specifically that all assessment data must include criteria that are both appropriate and objective, thus subjective observations should be used only to supplement other objective or criterion-referenced assessment.

ASSESSMENT REVIEW

The assessment process must be completed before the transdisciplinary team can develop a student's IEP. Test results will reflect current performance and achievement levels of the individual. With completion of appropriate assessment, the first phase of the IEP is finished when the physical educator is able to supply the transdisciplinary team with the child's present level of physical fitness and motor ability. At this point the adapted physical educator, by virtue of his or her involvement in testing the child, should lead the discussion.

WRITING BASIC PHYSICAL FITNESS AND MOTOR PROFICIENCY OBJECTIVES INTO THE IEP

Fitness-oriented goals and objectives should appear on the student's IEP only if assessment ascertains that special fitness needs truly exist.

When assessment has identified low fitness levels among students who are guaranteed access to special services by P.L. 101-476, this becomes the basis for developing annual goals and short-term instructional objectives for each student. Annual goals should be stated in general terms that identify the area of physical education focus. Short-term instructional objectives should be stated in precise *behavioral* terms so both teacher and, when appropriate, student know unquestionably that the objective has been achieved. Short-term instructional objectives should be *developmentally sequenced* so achievement indicates step-by-step progress toward the annual goal.

ANNUAL GOALS

An **annual goal** relates to the student's current performance level and indicates what the student should be able to accomplish after 12 months in the program.

Teachers often ask the question, "How many goals should a child have?" There is no right answer; the number of goals a youngster should have depends on the child's specific needs. A child who is mildly mentally retarded may have only one or two goals, both of which address the child's need to improve strength and endurance. A youngster who is severely physically and mentally retarded has a greater number of needs and, therefore, a greater number of goals.

Specific examples of annual goals are to improve (1) upper body strength to the 35th percentile (2 pull-ups), (2) cardiorespiratory efficiency to the 15th percentile (1,250 yd in 9-min run), and (3) static balance to the 20th percentile (8 sec right/left total). Werder and Kalakian (1985, p. 108) list three annual goals for object control skills: (1) Student will demonstrate a mature overhand throw with distance (30 ft) and accuracy (10 ft diameter target). (2) Student will grasp a 4-in. nerf ball 9 out of 10 times. (3) Student will toe-kick a 10-in. playground ball for a distance of 20 ft, 4 of 5 times.

SHORT-TERM OBJECTIVES

Short-term objectives are intended to be intermediate or en route objectives between the student's current performance level and that suggested by the annual goals. They are not as detailed as the instructional objectives used in daily planning, but they are specific to particular performance areas. They are to be used in measuring progress. Some examples of short-term instructional objectives are as follows: (1) Given a mat, the student will perform 20 curl-ups with knees bent and hands behind head, in 30 sec, (2) given a 3-ft square, the student will demonstrate 9 of 10 vertical jumps with feet together, full arm swing, and maintain balance when landing, and (3) given a basketball, the student will dribble to a line 30 ft away and return in 15 sec.

Dauer and Pangrazi (1992) suggest the following guidelines when writing short-term objectives:

1. State the motor skill in behavioral terms, including positioning (e.g., 30- to 40-degree curl-ups with bent knees and hands clasped behind head).

2. Describe the "givens," the instructional cues, environmental boundaries, time limits, and equipment.

3. State criteria for attainment, the standard against which the student will be measured (e.g., 9 of 10 trials).

SUMMARY

An individualized educational program (IEP) is a written statement incorporating the following: (1) the child's present levels of educational performance, (2) annual goals and short-term instructional objectives established for that child, (3) specific special education services available, (4) extent to which the child can participate in the regular education program, (5) projected dates for initiation of services and anticipated duration of services, (6) objective criteria and evaluation procedures used, and (7) schedules for determining annually whether instructional objectives are being achieved.

Individualized physical education programming might be described as the prescription of exercises and activities based on diagnostic pretest results. The IEP becomes a direct plan of action to meet both immediate and long-range motor needs of the child with a disability (Figure 5.7).

NAME Warren   AGE 14   PE X   SWIM X
                      BIRTHDATE

LONG-TERM GOALS: • Mainstream for physical education and swimming.
                 • Participate in Adapted Physical Education classes for strength and range of motion
                   activities.

ANNUAL GOALS:

SCHOOL YR.	PROGRAM LEVEL	GOALS	COMMENTS
1986–87	Intermediate PE – 4	To improve upper body strength to the 35th percentile (2 push-ups) To increase elbow range of motion to the 85th percentile (160°)	May wish to use a wheelchair for some activities

OBJECTIVES: (INCLUDE PERFORMANCE CRITERIA)	STRATEGIES: (INCLUDE METHODS AND MATERIALS)	EVALUATION OF PERFORMANCE	COMPLETION DATE	
			ANT.	ACTUAL
Warren will . . . 1. perform on a 70% accuracy basis skills necessary for successful participation in flag football, basketball, modified volleyball, and softball.	1. Direct teaching and skill drills	1. Observations of performances. Skills tests.	6/87	
2. play each of the above sports in game situations on six different occasions.	2. Filmstrips, library books, officiating	2. Observations of performance. Written tests.	6/87	
Warren is an ATAXIC cerebral palsied male who walks with short crutches; he uses a wheelchair for some sports to free use of his hands. He has been mainstreamed once and after one unsuccessful semester returned to special school placement; intelligence is low normal. Motivation level is somewhat low. Sometimes Warren can be a real hard worker and other times he is really lazy—switch is not usually related to activity. He is an intermediate level swimmer.				

DATE ———— PERSON(S) RESPONSIBLE ————————

LEA REPRESENTATIVE ———————— POSITION ————

PARENT ———————— POSITION ————

FIGURE 5.7 **Example of an individualized educational program in physical education.** (Adapted from AAHPERD (1977), *Practical Pointers, 1* (7), 15.

Appropriate assessment is critical to success of the IEP; assessment must be thoroughly planned to achieve maximum results. The adapted physical educator is instrumental in the selection, administration, and interpretation of motor and fitness tests for students with disabilities. Test results should be forwarded to the transdisciplinary team for inclusion in the child's complete IEP.

REFERENCES

AAHPERD health related physical fitness test manual. Reston, Va.: AAHPERD, 1980.

Bagnato, S. J., Neisworth, J. Y., & Munson, S. M. (1989). *Linking. Developmental assessment and early intervention: Curriculum-based prescriptions* (2nd ed.). Rockville, MD: Aspen.

Bailey, D. B., Jr., & Wolery, M. (1992). *Assessing infants and preschoolers with handicaps* (2nd ed.). New York: Merrill/Macmillan.

Bird, A. K. (1990). Enhancing communication within a transdisciplinary model. In C. J. Semmler & J. G. Hunter (Eds.), *Early occupational therapy intervention: Neonates to three years* (pp. 288–304). Gaithersburg, MD: Aspen.

Broadhead, G. D., & Rarick, G. L. (1978). Family characteristics and gross motor traits in handicapped children. *Research Quarterly , 49* (4), 421–429.

Bruininks, R. H. (1978). *Bruininks-Oseretsky Test of Motor Proficiency: Examiner's manual.* Circle Pines, MN: American Guidance Service.

Cratty, B. J. (1979). *Perceptual and motor development in infants and children,* (2nd ed.). Englewood Cliffs, NJ: Prentice-Hall.

Dauer, V. P., & Pangrazi, R. P. (1992). *Dynamic physical education for elementary school children* (10th ed.). New York: Macmillan.

Dohrmann, P. F., & Wang, P. Y. (1990, July). *Physical fitness and motor skill levels of individuals with mental retardation: Mild, moderate, and Down syndrome ages 6–21.* Paper presented at the International Conference on Sport, Recreation, Fitness, and Health for Mentally Handicapped People, Vancouver, Canada.

Eichstaedt, C. B., & Lavay, B. (1992). *Physical activity for individuals with mental retardation: Infant through adult.* Champaign, IL: Human Kinetics.

Eichstaedt, C. B., Wang, P. Y., Polacek, J. J., & Dohrmann, P. F. (1991). *Physical fitness and motor skill levels of individuals with mental retardation: Mild, moderate, and Down syndrome ages 6–21.* Normal, IL: Illinois State University Printing Services.

Ekstrand, R. E., & Edmister, P. (1984, October). Mediation: A process that works. *Exceptional Children, 51* (2), 163–167.

Gallahue, D. L. (1982). *Understanding motor development in children.* New York: John Wiley & Sons.

Heward, W. L., & Orlansky, M. D. (1992). *Exceptional children* (4th ed.). New York: Merrill/Macmillan.

Johnson, B. L., & Nelson, J. K. (1986). *Practical measures for evaluation in physical education* (4th ed.). Minneapolis: Burgess Publishing.

Kalakian, L. H., & Horvat, M. (in press). *Assessment in adapted physical education* (2nd ed.). Dubuque, IA: Brown.

Keogh, J., & Sugden, D. (1985). *Movement skill development.* New York: Macmillan.

Kirk, S. A., & Gallagher, J. J. (1989). *Educating exceptional children* (6th ed.). Boston: Houghton Mifflin.

Landis, J. (1991, December 3). Personal communication. Lincoln Developmental Center, Lincoln, IL.

Lavay, B., & French, R. (1985, July/August). The special educator: Meeting goals through a transdisciplinary approach. *American Corrective Therapy Journal, 39* (4), 77–81.

Luftig, R. L. (1989). *Assessment of learners with special needs.* Boston: Allyn & Bacon.

McCubbin, J., & Zittel, L. (1991). PL 99-457: What the law is all about. *Journal of Physical Education, Recreation, & Dance, 62* (6), 35–37; 47.

Payne, V. G., & Isaacs, L. D. (1991). *Human motor development* (2nd ed.). Mountain View, CA: Mayfield.

Rarick, G. L., & Dobbins, D. A. (1975). Basic competencies in the motor performance of children 6–9 years of age. *Medicine and science in sport,* 7(2), 1–12.

Rarick, G. L., Dobbins, D. A., Broadhead, G. D. (1976). *The motor domain and its correlates in educationally handicapped children.* Englewood Cliffs, NJ: Prentice-Hall.

Sage, G. H. (1984). *Motor learning and control—A neurological approach.* Dubuque, IA: Wm. C. Brown.

Seaman, J. A., & DePauw, K. P. (1989). *The new adapted physical education: A developmental approach* (2nd ed.). Mountain View, CA: Mayfield.

Sherrill, C. (1986). *Adapted physical education and recreation: A multidisciplinary approach.* (3rd ed.). Dubuque, IA: Wm. C. Brown.

Special Olympics. (1980). *P.L. 94-142: It's the law—Physical education and recreation for the handicapped.* Washington, D.C.: Special Olympics.

Stein, J. U. (1977). Individualized educational programs. *Practical Pointers, 1* (6), 8–9.

United Cerebral Palsy. (1976). *Staff development handbook: A resource for the transdisciplinary process.* New York: United Cerebral Palsy Association, Inc.

Werder, J. K., & Kalakian, L. H. (1985). *Assessment in adapted physical education.* Minneapolis: Burgess Publishing.

Wessel, J. A. (1977). *Planning individual education programs in special education.* Northbrook, IL: Hubbard Scientific Co.

Winnick, J. P., & Short, F. X. (1985). *Physical fitness testing of the disabled—Project Unique.* Champaign, IL.: Human Kinetics Publishers.

Chapter 6

BASIC PHYSICAL AND MOTOR FITNESS: COMPONENT PARTS AND THEIR ASSESSMENT

All living organisms must survive in an environment surrounded by energy. Radiant, mechanical, and thermal energies are primary stimuli sources with which the organism must contend. Survival in such an energy surround is contingent on movement. If movement cannot be initiated independently, the organism is at the mercy of energy forces or is dependent on others for survival (Barsch, 1965).

Much of survival depends on movement. Independent living implies the ability to initiate movement independently to fulfill life's basic needs. Those who do not move efficiently or who must rely on others for their mobility are relatively dependent on others for survival.

Basic physical and motor proficiency form the basis of movement independence. Development of these proficiencies is *not* founded on the belief that all persons can achieve total movement independence, but rather on the belief that all persons must be afforded full opportunity to progress toward the *goal* of total movement independence.

To enable all persons to achieve movement independence commensurate with their unique potential, the physical educator must be able to (1) delineate the components of basic physical and motor proficiency, (2) measure proficiency by component, and (3) suggest activities to develop component proficiency.

DISSECTING FITNESS

The term **fitness** is global and can be divided into three subcategories: **physical fitness, motor fitness,** and **power,** or **explosive strength,** which is part motor and part physical fitness. Power is a combination of speed and strength (Figure 6.1).

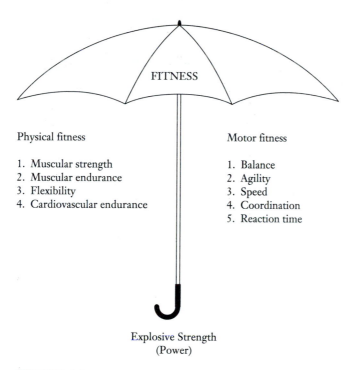

Physical fitness

1. Muscular strength
2. Muscular endurance
3. Flexibility
4. Cardiovascular endurance

Motor fitness

1. Balance
2. Agility
3. Speed
4. Coordination
5. Reaction time

Explosive Strength
(Power)

FIGURE 6.1

DIFFERENTIATING PHYSICAL AND MOTOR FITNESS

Physical fitness depends primarily on the functional integrity of the circulatory, respiratory, and muscular systems. Development of physical fitness is not directly associated with development of any specific motor skill. There are, however, indirect relationships. People who have good motor skills tend to have active life-styles, which stimulate physical fitness. Physical fitness cannot be learned as a motor skill. Rather, it is attained through physical exercise or training.

Motor fitness is identified closely with motor skill development. For example, balance is a motor performance component of fitness, and by developing appropriate motor skills, one might improve balance. Likewise, agility, which requires rapid direction change, is improved by developing skills that promote prompt, efficient direction change. Motor fitness components therefore differ from their organic counterparts in that the latter tend to be enhanced as the person's motor skill repertoire expands, whereas the former tend to improve primarily through physical exercise or training.

SPECIFICITY IN FITNESS

Because the term *fitness* has many specific components, it is misleading to speak in general terms about a person's degree of physical fitness. Greater accuracy is attained by considering a person's "fitness for a given task."

The components of fitness tend to represent different performance attributes that support fitness specificity and fitness for a given task. In practical terms, possessing good balance does not necessarily predict or guarantee strength, good agility does not necessarily predict or guarantee speed, explosive strength does not necessarily guarantee agility, and so forth. As a rule, a person is "fit for a given (specific) task" if that task is executed with a reasonable degree of skill, without undue fatigue, and with rapid recovery from exertion.

DEVELOPING FITNESS AND THE OVERLOAD PRINCIPLE

The overload principle implies that a body system or function can develop (i.e., increase capacity to function) only if work loads in excess of normal demands are experienced.

These practical observations indicate that overload is occurring:

1. Elevated breathing
2. Perspiration
3. Noticeably diminished performance
4. Strained facial expression
5. Flushed face
6. Elevated pulse rate

Overload is a highly individual phenomenon, so different levels of exercise stress will affect individuals differently. In establishing overload levels for people with disabilities, it is important that the task demand be almost beyond, yet still within, the person's grasp. The person with a disability who has not had successful experiences does not need to fail at yet another task demand, in this case one that is fitness oriented. Remember also that many students with disabilities do not possess average levels of strength or endurance. Overload for them should be at a relatively low level of intensity. A good rule to follow is this: A little more today than yesterday.

Winnick and Short (1985) believe that to increase strength, including strength of those with physically disabling conditions, overloading the muscles is necessary. Auxter and Pyfer (1985, p. 369) list five ways to achieve muscle overload: (1) increase number of repetitions or sets, (2) increase distance covered, (3) increase speed at which the exercise is performed, (4) increase number of minutes of continuous effort, and (5) decrease rest interval between activity sessions.

To determine the appropriate exercise or activity stress level for people with special needs (i.e., heart valve defect, cystic fibrosis, juvenile rheumatoid arthritis, Duchenne muscular dystrophy), the opinion of the person's physician should be sought. The physician can assist in ascertaining activity levels that bring the person to, but not past, the threshold of overload stress tolerance.

PHYSICAL FITNESS COMPONENTS

Strength refers to maximal or near-maximal muscular exertion of relatively brief duration. The duration is necessarily brief because intense, concentrated muscular effort is required. Pushing a stalled automobile is an example of an activity requiring strength. Another example is lifting oneself from the ground into a wheelchair. Virtually any activity that meets the criteria of brief duration and maximal or near maximal exertion will develop muscular strength. Repetitive (i.e., dynamic) exercise tends to develop strength when the resistance encountered permits only ten or fewer repetitions.

Strength development is important for all persons regardless of disability, because a certain amount of strength is required to do virtually everything. Indeed, minimal levels of strength must be achieved before minimal skill levels can be developed. For example, one cannot become proficient at working with crutches until minimal levels of grip and arm and shoulder girdle strength have been achieved. Without sufficient strength, even simple activities are difficult (Figure 6.2).

Flexibility refers to the ability of body segments to move through normal ranges of motion. Like strength, flexibility can be a major determinant of success in many physical and motor activities. Virtually all require a minimum degree of flexibility before the activity can be executed comfortably, correctly, and with minimum risk of muscle strain.

Unexpected muscle stretching beyond normal motion range may cause strain on a continuum from mild to strain so severe that surgical repair is needed. The range of motion through which a body can move comfortably is largely a function of the muscle stretching that an individual is accustomed to experiencing. Relative inactivity may precipitate loss of flexibility. Maintenance of flexibility in people with disabilities, is particularly important to the extent that such people may tend to have a sedentary lifestyle.

Flexibility maintenance is a lifelong need. Without flexibility, one's capacity to enjoy movement is reduced. Reduced enjoyment then fosters activity avoidance, reduced activity fosters further flexibility loss, and the cycle continues. Significant flexibility loss with advancing age is often due more to progressive inactivity than to advancing age.

Step on tube, flex arm

Like shooting a bow and arrow

Place tube around feet, lock knees, pull backward

Arms hold firm, extend neck backward (or sideways)

FIGURE 6.2   Strength development using inner tube strips. (Redrawn from Moran & Kalakian, 1977, p. 42.)

Flexibility development.

To foster flexibility through activity and exercise, it is important that muscles be stretched to, but not through, the discomfort threshold. Without discomfort, sufficient stretching does not occur to enhance flexibility (remember the overload principle). When one stretches beyond the initial discomfort sensation, however, muscles can be overextended to the point of injury.

Muscular endurance refers to submaximal muscular effort that continues for a relatively long period of time. Unlike strength activities, muscular endurance activities do not involve brief, all-out exertions. Rather, they require persistent, submaximal effort. Many activities in industry, workshops, domestic upkeep, and physical education require muscular endurance. Lifting medium-heavy weights or meeting medium-heavy resistance over an extended period involves muscular endurance.

Muscular endurance and muscular strength may be thought of as opposite extremes of a continuum. Most activities require relative strength or relative endurance and fall somewhere between the two extremes. Many activities that enhance strength can, with modest alteration, be used to develop muscular endurance. In strength-building activities, the resistance encountered must be sufficient to require immediate, near-maximal exertion. Because of the intensity of a strength activity, its duration is necessarily brief. A similar activity can be used to develop muscular endurance by simultaneously reducing the resistance and increasing the duration. Muscles then

Flexed arm hang requires strength and endurance. Here, a student with an upper extremity amputation, uses her prosthesis with assistance from her instructor.

fatigue gradually and the body's response is to increase muscular capacity for sub-maximal, protracted effort.

Cardiovascular endurance refers to the ability of the heart and circulatory system to adapt to the demands of prolonged, total body physical exertion. This fitness component is perhaps the most important of all, for it involves the functional integrity of vital organs. Because cardiovascular disease is the leading cause of death in the United States and is the very antithesis of a healthy and active life, the teacher of people with disabilities must stress development and maintenance of cardiovascular fitness.

Any activity that is sufficiently taxing to significantly elevate an individual's heart rate or more than 5 minutes is considered cardiovascular activity. To achieve noticeable results, the activity must be performed a minimum of 12 minutes per day, 3 days per week. Typical cardiovascular activities include prolonged walking, swimming, jogging, cycling, or crutch- or wheelchair-assisted ambulation.

Locomotor rhythm activities and dance are equally appropriate ways to stimulate cardiovascular development. Cardiovascular activities may be particularly taxing for some persons with paraplegia, because flaccid paralysis (in this case, in the lower extremities) prevents the "milking" action of muscles, which returns venous blood to the heart. This relative inability of lower extremity muscles to contract and relax may cause inordinate pooling of venous blood in the lower extremities. To put this condition in a broader context, consider the fact that an increasing number of highly conditioned athletes in wheelchairs consistently demonstrate the ability to "run" full marathons in times that are equal to or better than those of nondisabled runners in the same race.

Training studies and other research have demonstrated that youngsters with mental retardation, when offered appropriate programs, are able to achieve levels of physical fitness equal to those of their nonretarded peers (Hallahan & Kauffman, 1991).

MOTOR FITNESS COMPONENTS

Balance refers to the ability to maintain a proper relationship between one's points of support (i.e., hands and feet) and one's center of gravity. Balance may be either static or dynamic. **Static balance** involves balance in a stationary position. **Dynamic balance** involves balance with the body in motion. Either static or dynamic balance may occur on moving surfaces. All types of balancing are required in everyday life and can be replicated and practiced in physical education settings.

Some controversy exists as to whether balance is a general trait in the physical and motor performance area. Some believe that balance is highly specific to the task being executed (Ulrich & Ulrich, 1985). Salvia and Ysseldyke (1991) state that "balance training will improve *balance* functioning" (p. 322). Other researchers suggest that the balance trait is indeed general, and that general balance activities improve balance in the broad spectrum of motor performance (Payne & Isaacs, 1991). The issue of balance specificity has not been fully resolved. Pending resolution of the controversy, general balance activities should be considered helpful (Figure 6.3).

Agility refers to the ability to rapidly and effectively change direction. Agility is an important fitness component, especially in activities requiring sudden, unexpected direction changes. Agility is also an important means of sidestepping unexpected danger (e.g., jumping from the path of an oncoming car). In sports, agility is important when one must guard or "shadow" an opponent. Teachers can promote agility through a variety of games with low organization, tag games, and relays. Students can be told to mirror the random, rapid direction changes of another person. Any activity that requires rapid movement coupled with frequent direction change develops agility.

Three points of
support

One point of
support (swan)

Stand on right foot
(left foot forward),
stand on left foot
(right foot forward)

Balance on
one knee and foot

Balance on
knees

With hands on hips,
walk on tiptoes down
a line on the floor

Two points
of support

FIGURE 6.3   Examples of balance activities. (Redrawn from Moran & Kalakian,
1977, p. 47.)

Speed refers to the ability to traverse straight, short distances rapidly. Although speed is generally associated almost exclusively with running, it should be noted that speed is observed whenever the individual demonstrates any rapid, successive movement. Most fitness tests, however, rely on running as the primary means of assessing speed.

For purposes of assessing or enhancing speed, a distance of 50 yards is sufficient. This is considered a long enough distance to attain maximum speed while minimizing the influence of reaction time, and a short enough distance to avoid involvement of the variable of cardiovascular endurance.

In assessing speed among persons with motor involvement, including bipedal, crutch-assisted, and wheelchair-assisted ambulation, distances may be modified as individual needs dictate.

Coordination refers to the harmonious interaction of individual muscles and muscle groups to produce skilled movement patterns. It involves the ability of muscles to contract with proper intensity at the opportune moment and in proper sequence. Coordination is a twofold function of practice and properly directed effort resulting from effective instruction. Specific skills such as catching or hitting a ball are examples of the eye-hand type of coordination.

Reaction time refers to the elapsed time between activation of a stimulus and the organism's response. The stimulus may be auditory (buzzer), visual (hand signal), or tactile (touch). This component is the least modifiable and for that reason is often not emphasized.

Explosive strength (power) refers to a combination of speed and strength produced by the force and rapidity with which muscles are able to contract. This fitness component does not fall exclusively in either the organic or motor category but incorporates speed from motor performance fitness and strength from organic performance fitness. Power is used for throwing, kicking, running (start), striking, or self-propelling as in a jump, hop, or leap.

ASSESSING BASIC PHYSICAL AND MOTOR FITNESS

Assessment items, test batteries, and parts of batteries are available for the adapted physical educator. Identifying the specific component of physical and motor performance to be assessed and the characteristics of the person to be assessed are essential for selection of the proper item or battery.

Assessment tools are available for certain special populations and for the nondisabled population. In some instances, items or batteries designed for the nondisabled can be used appropriately to assess individuals with disabilities.

Some batteries are general and are used for screening. Others are more comprehensive and serve as diagnostic tools.

DIFFERENT WAYS OF REPORTING AND INTERPRETING TEST SCORES

Some test batteries are designed so the individual's score is compared with the scores of others. In such instances, the individual's score is compared with established norms. These tests are called **norm-referenced tests.** When using norm-referenced tests, the evaluator must be certain that the norms are derived from a group representative of the person to whom the norms are being applied. For example, extreme caution must be exercised when applying fitness norms for nondisabled persons to the performance of a person with moderate mental retardation. In contrast, if the instructor is attempting to determine if a student with disabilities can participate successfully in traditional, unrestricted physical education classes, then the teacher should use the test battery and norms designed for nondisabled students. For example, to determine if a boy with mild mental retardation can be integrated successfully in the regular physical education program, he might be given the *AAHPERD* Health Related Test battery, which is used for nondisabled youngsters. Raw scores and appropriate norm references would provide the information necessary for appropriate placement.

Some tests are **criterion referenced** (i.e., Physical Best; I Can). In these tests, a performance criterion is stated as a behavioral objective, and the person's performance is assessed with respect to conformance to the criterion. Both norm- and criterion-referenced instruments measuring fitness are discussed later in this chapter.

ASSESSMENT MUST NOT DISCRIMINATE UNFAIRLY

When administering tests and other evaluations to a child with impaired sensory, manual, or speaking skills, care must be taken to ensure that the test results accurately reflect the child's aptitude, achievement level, or whatever other factors the test purports to measure, rather than reflecting the child's impairment (unless specific skill impairment is the factor that the test measures).

When the physical or motor performance items are not appropriate to the specific capabilities or characteristics of the individual, then the instrument is worthless in that given situation. For example, sit-ups, used as a measure of muscular endurance, could discriminate unfairly against a person whose paralysis limits abdominal or hip flexor function. Instead, pull-ups, flexed arm hang, hang time, or parallel bar dips might be more appropriate endurance tests. For people who are blind or partially sighted, the shuttle run as a measure of agility should be replaced by the less discriminatory squat thrust (burpee). In assessing the physical and motor performance of people with mental retardation, test results should reflect actual physical or motor ability, not the individual's limited comprehension of task demands. In evaluating persons with special needs, the adapted physical educator must be sure that the results truly reflect what the test purports specifically to measure.

ASSESSMENT INSTRUMENTS

We do not offer an exhaustive delineation of physical and motor proficiency assessment tools in this text. Rather, we present selected tools as examples of available instruments. Each is intended for a specific population and may provide an initial reference in the search for additional and perhaps more appropriate instruments.

Some instruments function as *screening devices* but do not purport to be thoroughly diagnostic. Rather, they identify persons whose physical and motor performance fitness levels are less than adequate for safe, successful participation in a mainstream program. Although the definition of *adequacy* may vary, passing a screening test does not necessarily mean high or even moderate fitness. Passing may mean simply that the person has achieved the bare minimum.

Bruininks-Oseretsky Test of Motor Proficiency.   One screening test for basic motor proficiency is the short form of the *Bruininks-Oseretsky Test of Motor Proficiency* (Bruininks, 1978). The form includes 14 of the 46 items that appear on the Bruininks-Oseretsky long form. The long form is more comprehensive and is recommended as a motor proficiency diagnosis instrument. The short form may serve as an initial screening device when many children must be assessed in a short time. The instrument is designed for persons age $4\frac{1}{2}$ to $14\frac{1}{2}$ years. The short form yields both stanine and percentile rank scores and measures proficiency in the following components of motor behavior: running speed and agility, balance, bilateral coordination, upper limb coordination, strength,[1] lower limb coordination, response speed, visual-motor control, and upper limb speed and dexterity.

AAHPERD Youth Fitness Test.   A well known test that purports to measure physical and motor fitness is the *AAHPERD Youth Fitness Test* offered by the American Alliance for Health, Physical Education, Recreation and Dance (AAHPERD, 1976a). The test has existed since 1958 and has undergone revisions. In its present form, it includes national norms and assesses physical fitness of youngsters age 9 to 17+ years. Items include the following:

1. Flexed arm hang (girls; Figure 6.4) and pull-up (boys; Figure 6.5)—shoulder girdle muscular strength or muscular endurance, depending on student's fitness level at time of testing

2. Flexed knee sit-up–timed— number completed in 1 minute; abdominal and hip flexor strength or muscular endurance, depending on student's fitness level at time of testing

---

[1]Physical fitness literature from the physical education profession typically does not include strength and visual-motor control as measures of *motor* proficiency. Strength generally is considered organic fitness, whereas visual-motor control generally appears in batteries that assess perceptual-motor competence.

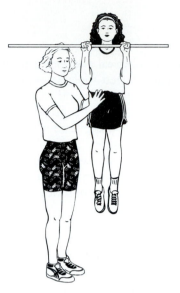

FIGURE 6.4 **Flexed arm hang.** (Redrawn from Moran & Kalakian, 1977, p. 51.)

FIGURE 6.5 **Palms away pull-up.** (Redrawn from Moran & Kalakian, 1977, p. 50.)

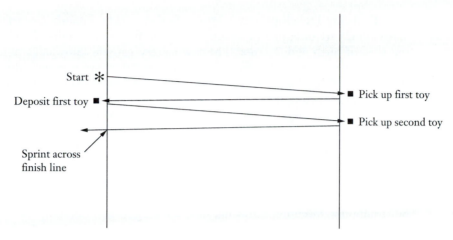

FIGURE 6.6   Ability run configuration. (Redrawn from Moran & Kalakian, 1977, p. 56.)

3. Shuttle run (Figure 6.6)—agility
4. Standing long jump—explosive strength
5. 50 yard dash—running speed
6. 1-mi or 9-min run for ages 10 to 12, $1\frac{1}{2}$-mi or 12-min run for ages 13 or older—cardiovascular endurance

AAHPERD (1980) published the *Health Related Physical Fitness Test.* This test is alleged to focus solely on items known to correlate with health. Items believed to be more directly related to the acquisition of motor skills are not on the test. Health-related physical fitness items include the following:

1. Triceps, subscapular, and abdominal skin fold (subcutaneous body fat)
2. Sit-ups (Figure 6.7) (abdominal and hip flexor strength and endurance)
3. Sit and reach (flexibility)
4. One-mile or 9-min for ages 10 to 12, $1\frac{1}{2}$-mile or 12-min run for ages 13 or older (cardiovascular endurance)

Arms folded
across chest

FIGURE 6.7   Flexed knee sit-up.

Peabody Developmental Motor Scales.   The *Peabody Developmental Motor Scales* (1983) are designed to identify gross and fine motor skills of children between the ages of birth and 7 years. The test battery gathers knowledge about the skills that the children have mastered, those skills that they are currently developing, and those not yet developed. Over 200 specific gross motor skills and 130 fine motor skills are listed through the 7-year developmental sequence. Suggested activities for improving and strengthening needed skills are also included.

Ohio State University Scale of Intra-Gross Motor Assessment (O.S.U. SIGMA).   This test battery was developed by Drs. Mike Loovis and Walt Ersing (1980). It is designed to assess the efficiency and maturity of children from preschool age through 14 years. Eleven gross motor skills were selected: walking, running, hopping, jumping, catching, throwing, stair climbing, ladder climbing, kicking, skipping, and striking.

Brigance Diagnostic Inventories.   This series includes three different test batteries, but the *Diagnostic Inventory of Early Development* (Brigance, 1978) contains a strong component of motor skill assessment. The test battery is designed for use with individuals who have developmental ages of less than 7 years. It is criterion referenced and also has norm referencing included. The following areas are identified: (1) 4 preambulatory motor sequences (i.e., supine, prone, sitting, and standing positions), (2) 13 gross motor sequences (e.g., walking, catching, rhythm), and (3) 9 fine motor sequences (e.g., eye-finger-hand manipulations, painting).

Physical Fitness and Motor Skill Levels of Individuals with Mental Retardation: Mild, Moderate, and Down Syndrome Ages 6–21.   This test battery was developed over a 10-year span by Eichstaedt, Wang, Polacek, and Dohrmann (1991) using subjects from the state of Illinois. The subjects (N = 4,464) were used to develop norms in both physical fitness and motor skill performance items. The items include height, weight, skin fold (tricep, subscapular, calf), sit and reach, modified sit-ups (knees flexed, arms folded across the chest), 6-minute run (ages 6–11), 9-minute run (ages 12–21), 50-yard dash, flexed arm hang, shuttle run, standing long jump, stork stand, and 15-second basketball wall bounce.

AAHPERD Physical Best.   AAHPERD developed the test battery *Physical Best* (1988) to meet needed revisions of its older test batteries. The test battery is similar to the 1980 *Health Related* test battery. With Physical Best, however, norms have been abandoned in favor of criterion referencing or the use of suggested health fitness standards. AAHPERD states that Physical Best is meant to replace all previously endorsed AAHPERD fitness tests. The test items include a 1-mile endurance run (or any aerobic endurance test that exceeds 6 minutes), body composition (sum of triceps and calf), flexibility (sit and reach), muscular strength and endurance (modified sit-ups in 60 seconds, with knees bent and arms crossed on the chest), and upper body strength and endurance (pull-ups).

Straight-back push-up (most difficult).

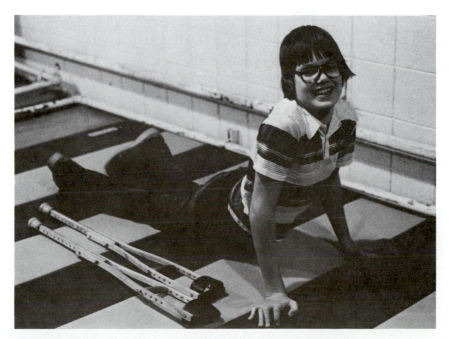

Straight-back push-up with knees touching ground (easiest).

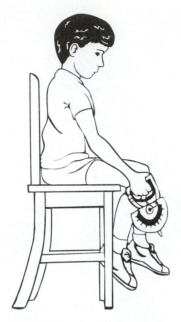

FIGURE 6.8 **Grip strength.**

OTHER COMMONLY ENCOUNTERED MEASURES OF FITNESS BY COMPONENT

STRENGTH

1. Push-ups (ranging from most difficult to easiest)
2. Parallel bar dips
3. Grip-strength dynamometer (Figure 6.8)

MUSCULAR ENDURANCE

Items that measure muscular strength will also measure endurance for students who are able to continue execution over an extended period. Generally, strength is measured when maximum repetitions fall below 10. Muscular endurance is measured as the student repeats executions beyond 10.

FLEXIBILITY

1. Back lifts. Measure height from floor while in maximum extension.
2. Shoulder rotation. Grasp the rope with both hands positioned shoulder width apart and with the rope passing in front of the body. Keeping arms

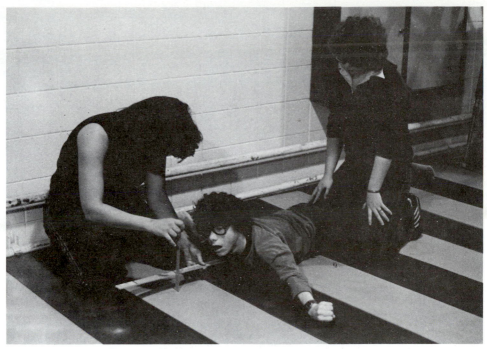

Back lifts measure flexibility.

straight, the student should rotate her arms up, over her head, and back until the rope rests against the buttocks. The rope should slide through her hands only to the extent necessary to execute the action correctly. A score is derived by subtracting shoulder width from the rope length required to execute shoulder rotation.

CARDIOVASCULAR ENDURANCE

Measures heavily relied on include 1- and $1\frac{1}{2}$-mile runs, and 9- and 12-minute runs (Figure 6.10). These are found in the *AAHPERD Health Related Test* Manual (AAHPERD, 1980) and in AAHPERD manuals modified for use with special populations (blind and visually impaired, mildly and moderately retarded) (Buell, 1973; AAHPERD, 1975, 1976b). One should remember that the norms provided by the early AAHPERD test batteries for individuals with mental retardation should not be used because they are over 15 years old and comparisons would be inappropriate.

BALANCE

1. Stork stand (Figure 6.11). Stand on flat foot, hands on hips, with opposite toe tucked behind the support knee. Score is number of seconds that the

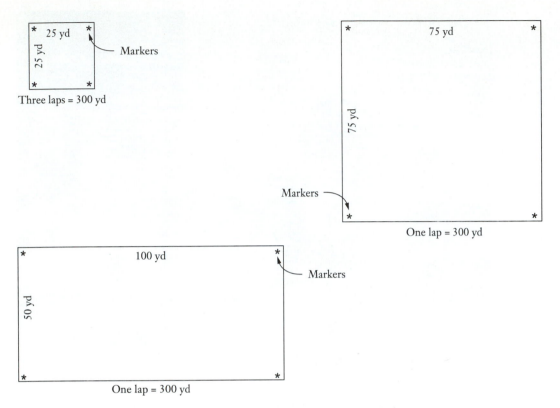

FIGURE 6.9   Suggested configurations for the 1- , 1½-mile and 9- , 12-minute run-walk. (Redrawn from Moran & Kalakian, 1977, p. 54.)

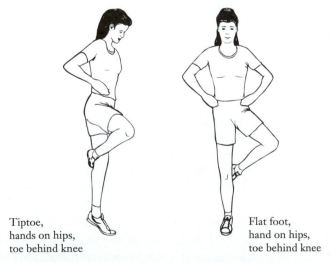

Tiptoe, hands on hips, toe behind knee

Flat foot, hand on hips, toe behind knee

FIGURE 6.10   Stork stand. (Redrawn from Moran & Kalakian, 1977, p. 55.)

student is able to maintain the correct stork-stand position. Ten seconds maximum. This test measures *static* balance.

2. Beam walking forward, backward, and sideward (observe both left foot lead and right foot lead in the sideward item). Take 6 steps in each of the 4 directions and receive a separate evaluation for each performance. During each of the 4 separate trials, each step on the beam scores 1 point, a step off the beam scores 0. Maximum score is 6 points per trial. Beam height and width must be standardized when comparisons between trials or between students are made. Among low-ability students, a stripe on the floor may replace the beam. This test measures *dynamic* balance.

COORDINATION

1. Throw ball for accuracy.

2. Throw ball in air and catch (ball should rise a distance approximately equal to the person's height). Ball must be thrown directly overhead, must be caught before it bounces, and must not require locomotion for catching. Ten trials are required, and one point is scored for each correct effort.

3. Alternate foot tap and hand clap. Person, while seated, alternately and rhythmically taps left and right foot. With rhythm established, person claps hands simultaneously with each tap. Each properly timed hand clap scores one point. Thirty seconds maximum.

4. Basketball wall bounce for time. The subject (age 6–11) stands behind a restraining line 4 feet away from a wall and "passes" the basketball against a solid wall and catches the ball on the rebound. This continues for 15 seconds, counting the number of hits against the wall. For subjects 12–21, the restraining line is 6 feet away.

SPEED

Speed is generally measured in dashes not to exceed 100 yards.

1. Tap pencil with preferred hand. (Note in 30 seconds number of dots the student makes on a piece of paper.)

2. Note in 30 sec number of hand claps the student executes.

3. Note in 30 sec number of foot taps made with the preferred foot.

4. Measure distance run during specific time period (e.g., 6-sec dash). Flying start may be incorporated to reduce influence of explosive strength or reaction time.

AGILITY

1. Time zigzag run, crutch-assisted ambulation, or chair wheeling through obstacle course.

2. During definite period of time, observe number of cones in zigzag run that the student maneuvers through successfully.

3. Use shuttle run in the *AAHPERD Physical Best Test*, but eliminate block handling to limit influence of eye-hand coordination on student's score (student touches the line with his foot).

4. Use the two-count burpee (stand, squat) when the relatively more complicated measures of agility might inadvertently measure intelligence.

EXPLOSIVE STRENGTH

1. Throw ball for distance from stationary position. (Stationary position reduces influence of throwing skill on performance.) Record score to nearest foot.

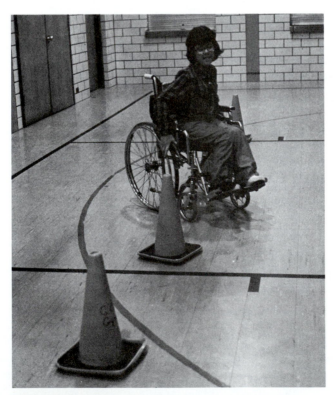

Wheelchair agility.

2. Throw medicine ball for distance (administer same as no. 1).

3. Throw for velocity at a wall target. Use a stopwatch to record elapsed time from release to impact for a designated distance. Consider only instances when ball strikes target. Impact within target area ensures that distance remains constant between trials and students. Record time to nearest tenth of second.

SELECTED ASSESSMENT BATTERIES FOR SPECIAL POPULATIONS

In discussing fitness assessment thus far, we have focused primarily on batteries and items not intended for any special population. The preceding items and batteries may, in many instances, be used appropriately for people with certain disabilities. For example, a person who is visually impaired, blind, hearing impaired, or deaf could be tested by using some of the regular *AAHPERD Physical Best Test* items. Items might include sit-ups, flexed arm hang, and one of the various endurance runs (For the endurance run, a child who is blind can run with a sighted partner who has a bell or similar noise-emitting device fixed to wrist or ankle). The person who is deaf should take the entire *AAHPERD Physical Best Test* designed for the nondisabled. The most significant modification required when using the regular *AAHPERD Physical Best Test* battery with a person who is deaf or hearing impaired involves visual cues in timed events.

When one must rely on batteries intended specifically for a special population, the following instruments should be considered:

BLIND AND PARTIALLY SIGHTED

Buell Test (CA[2] 8–18) (Buell, 1973).   Includes pull-ups (pull-ups for boys, flexed arm-hang for girls), sit-ups, 50-yard dash, 600-yard run-walk, and standing long jump. All items except 50-yard dash and 600-yard run-walk incorporate regular *AAHPERD* physical fitness test norms.

MENTALLY RETARDED

Special Fitness Test for the Mildly Mentally Retarded (CA 8-18) (AAHPERD, 1976b).   Includes flexed arm hang, sit-ups (straight leg is no longer recommended), shuttle run, 50-yard dash, 300-yard run-walk, standing long jump for distance, and softball throw for distance (See Chapter 12 on mental retardation for additional discussion of this battery).

---

[2]CA = chronological age.

Motor Fitness Test for the Moderately Mentally Retarded (CA 6-21) (AAHPERD 1975).   Includes flexed arm hang, sit-ups (bent knee in 30 sec.), 50-yard dash, 300-yard run-walk, standing long jump for distance, softball throw for distance, recording of height and weight, sitting bob and reach, hopping, skipping, and tumbling progression. This battery is discussed further in Chapter 12, Mental Retardation.

Physical Fitness and Motor Skill Levels of Individuals with Mental Retardation: Mild, Moderate, and Down Syndrome Ages 6–21.   This test battery was developed over a 10-year span by Eichstaedt, Wang, Polacek, and Dohrmann (1991) using subjects from the state of Illinois. The subjects (N = 4,464) were used to develop norms in both physical fitness and motor skill performance items. The items include height, weight, skin folds (tricep, subscapular, calf), sit and reach, modified sit-ups (knees flexed, arms folded across the chest), 6-minute run (ages 6–11), 9-minute run (ages 12–21), 50-yard dash, flexed arm hang, shuttle run, standing long jump, stork stand, and 15-second basketball wall bounce.

PHYSICALLY DISABLING CONDITIONS

Winnick and Short (Project UNIQUE, 1985) have developed national physical fitness and motor proficiency norms for people with sensory and orthopedic impairments (CA 10-17). The following disabilities are included: blind and visually impaired, deaf and hard of hearing, orthopedic amputee, congenital defects, spinal cord defects and injuries, and cerebral palsy.

Project UNIQUE normative data were collected nationwide as to type of disability, extent of disability, and whether the person was receiving education in a regular setting or an institution.

Many items in the UNIQUE battery are from the *AAHPERD Physical Best Test* for the nondisabled and from the 1980 *AAHPERD Health Related Physical Fitness Test*. The type and extent of the disability will provide the basis for determining whether the item is appropriate or requires modification to ensure suitability.

Another test that can be used to assess a child who is physically disabled was adapted from the work of Bobath and Bobath by the California Department of Public Health (1964). The battery measures basic motor control of people with cerebral palsy by assessing various positions and postures and culminating in the skill of walking.

FITNESS GAMES AND ACTIVITIES

Once teachers understand the basic components of physical and motor fitness, they can select activities that enhance specific proficiencies, particularly of students with low fitness. There is not room here to list or explain the many activity alternatives for people with different abilities, special needs, and varying potentials. We can, however, cite activities that are valuable for specific fitness development.

In selecting activities to enhance fitness teachers should use a "means to an end" philosophy. The activity is the means, and the fitness component is the end. By knowing which activities and experiences promote each component of physical fitness, teachers can develop a file of "means to an end" activities categorized according to fitness value. The following activities were selected for their specific fitness value.

Straddle Bowling
Component of fitness: Body coordination

Students participate in groups of three. One student stands in straddle position. Student in wheelchair may substitute by placing foot rests in the "up" position. One

Straddle bowling.

student bowls. One student retrieves. After each roll of the ball, students rotate. Bowler tries to roll ball between the other student's straddled legs. A ball between the legs scores 2 points; a ball that touches one leg but deflects outside the straddle scores 1 point. Distance rolled and scoring may be modified to suit each situation.

Squirrels in Trees
Components of fitness: Agility resulting from rapid change of direction in search of an unoccupied "tree"; explosive strength resulting from forcefully thrusting oneself into motion from a stationary start

Students are designated as either squirrels or trees. Trees face each other and clasp hands with arms extended. One squirrel is permitted inside each tree. Squirrels without trees are interspersed in the midst of the activity area. When the teacher calls out "squirrels change," trees raise arms on one side, and all squirrels ambulate to get into a tree (Those squirrels in trees must leave and seek a new tree). Only one squirrel is allowed per tree, leaving some squirrels always in the midst of the group. The object is not to get caught without a tree. The teacher should change designations often so all students have an opportunity to be active. (Figure 6.12).

FIGURE 6.11 Squirrels in trees. (Redrawn from Moran & Kalakian, 1977, p. 64.)

Circle Hook-On
Components of fitness: Cardiovascular endurance and agility

Three students form a circle. A fourth student remains outside the circle. One student, a member of the circle, is designated to be tagged by the student outside the circle. Circle players may maneuver in any way they wish so the pursuing child (tagger) cannot tag the designated circle member. Tagger cannot enter the circle. In avoiding the tagger, circle students cannot release clasped hands. If the designated child is tagged or if the circle players release their hand clasp, the tagger becomes part of the circle and one of the circle members then becomes the new tagger.

Jump the Shot
Components of fitness: Dynamic balance resulting from taking off and landing, explosive strength resulting from jumping, and cardiovascular endurance if activity is prolonged

Students form a circle. A student in the center swings a weighted rope while moving within the circle. A dampened towel wadded up and tied to a rope end functions as a safe yet sufficiently heavy weight. The student in the center gradually lengthens the rope until students forming the circle must jump over the shot. The shot should be swung midway between the ankle and knee. A child who entangles the rope by failing to jump takes the student's place in the center and swings the shot until another child misses.

For some children, the weighted rope swings much too rapidly, and repeated failure should be limited. For such students, a long fiberglass rod (which may be ordered from an equipment catalog or fashioned from a defunct spinning rod or long CB whip antenna) may replace the weighted rope. Using the rod, the student (or teacher) in the center can move the rod on the floor at a speed slow enough to be compatible with a child's jumping and balance capabilities. For some children, the rod might be stopped completely before the child jumps. As the child is momentarily airborne, the rod may be slid under his feet, thereby building success into the activity (Figure 6.13).

Inch Worm
Components of fitness: Hop extensor flexibility, muscular strength or endurance depending on individual's level of fitness and body coordination

The student assumes push-up position. Hands remain stationary, and feet step forward toward stationary hands. When the student is in as tight a pike as possible, the feet become stationary, and the hands walk forward until the starting push-up position is again assumed. Repeat (Figure 6.14).

FIGURE 6.12 **Jump the shot.** (Redrawn from Moran & Kalakian, 1977, p. 65.)

Hot Potato Relay and Tag
Component of fitness: Speed

Speed is generally considered a phenomenon of running. Actually, speed is involved whenever any body segment moves rapidly. In the hot potato relay, two circles are formed. A beanbag is the hot potato. At the signal, students pass the "hot potato" around the circle as rapidly as possible. In this game, all students can be seated so ambulators using crutch and wheelchair are not at a disadvantage. The group that first passes the hot potato around the entire circle for a specified number of times is the winner. Circles should be kept small so activity is intense. For purposes of skill development only, introducing competition may be of little value. In such situations, students can pass the hot potato as rapidly as possible with no need to win.

Tag activities requiring running or rapid ambulation appropriate to the child also develop speed. Tag games that involve running must have physical boundaries to confine the activity, thereby increasing the activity level. Boundaries should never be hazardous. Trees, building walls, and fences are unsafe boundaries. Line markings on a field, plastic bleach bottles, or the edge of a building shadow are appropriate, safe boundary markers.

Feet walk toward line, arms remain stationary

X

X = Reference point

Arms walk forward, feet remain stationary

X

X

FIGURE 6.13   **Inch worm.** (Redrawn from Moran & Kalakian, 1977, p. 65.)

SUMMARY

Basic physical and motor fitness provide the foundation for efficient movement, and should include 10 specific components. Nine of these tend to function as independent phenomena; proficiency in one component does not ensure proficiency in any other. The remaining component, power or explosive strength, is composed of muscular strength and speed, which function together.

Tests that measure fitness may be either norm or criterion referenced. Norms compare one person's performance with that of another (i.e., one may achieve some percentile for performance on a test item). Criterion referencing compares one person's performance with a preestablished, behaviorally stated performance criterion (i.e., if the performance criterion for overarm distance throwing is 20 ft, the student's actual throwing distance is compared with that criterion). Criterion-referenced instruments are particularly useful in testing special populations for which applicable norms have not been developed.

Tests of fitness can serve initially to screen persons who may need more thorough assessment. Assessment batteries that are more thorough are considered diagnostic. Diagnostic tests of physical and motor proficiency detect only the extent and focus of developmental delay. Such tests do not identify the specific reason or reasons underlying the deficient performance level.

Whenever fitness assessment is done for special populations, the tester must be sure that the administered test item does not discriminate on the basis of disability. For example, among persons with mental retardation, agility run times tend to correlate positively with IQ. The evaluator must therefore question whether the score is a valid measure of agility or is inaccurate because of the participant's limited understanding of the task. Student performance scores from test batteries must provide meaningful information if the adapted physical educator is to plan appropriate motor and fitness activities based on the instrument findings. Making subjective assumptions about performance levels is *not* desirable, particularly when many test batteries are now available to the physical educator.

When evaluating students, the instructor must include all dimensions of the psychomotor domain. For example, if a test battery assesses only physical fitness components, then the instructor must search out additional test items (from another test battery) that include motor skill performance (e.g., balance and eye-hand coordination).

Only after a total physical and motor fitness picture has been developed can appropriate activities be selected and included in the student's individualized physical education program. Posttesting also should be included in every individualized educational program to evaluate whether the selected activities had the desired effect on the child's development.

REFERENCES

AAHPERD. (1975). *Motor fitness testing manual for the moderately mentally retarded.* Reston, VA: AAHPERD.

——(1976a). *AAHPERD youth fitness test manual.* Reston, VA: AAHPERD.

——(1976b). *Special fitness test manual for mildly mentally retarded persons.* Reston, VA: AAHPERD.

——(1977). *Practical pointers 1* (6):10. Reston, VA: AAHPERD.

——(1980). *AAHPERD health related physical fitness test manual.* Reston, VA.: AAHPERD.

——(1988). *Physical best.* Reston, VA: AAHPERD.

Auxter, D., & Pyfer, J. (1985). *Principles and methods of adapted physical education and recreation,* (5th ed.). St. Louis: Times Mirror/Mosby College Publishing.

Barsch, R. (1965). *A movegenic curriculum.* Madison, WI: Bureau for Handicapped Children, 1965.

Brigance, A. (1978). *Diagnostic inventory of early development.* North Billerica, MA: Curriculum Associates.

Bruininks, R. H. (1978). *Bruininks-Oseretsky test of motor proficiency: Examiner's manual.* Circle Pines, MN: American Guidance Service.

Buell, C. (1973). *Physical education and recreation for the visually handicapped.* Reston, VA: AAHPERD.

California Department of Public Health, Bureau of Crippled Children Services. (1964). *Cerebral palsy assessment chart—Basic motor control.* Sacramento, CA: The Department.

Eichstaedt, C. B., & Lavay, B. (1992). *Physical activity for individuals with mental retardation: Infant to adult.* Champaign, IL: Human Kinetics.

Eichstaedt, C. B., Wang, P. Y., Polacek, J. J., & Dohrmann, P. F. (1991). *Physical fitness and motor skill levels of individuals with mental retardation: Mild, moderate, and Down syndrome, ages 6-21.* Normal, IL: Illinois State University Printing Services.

Hallahan, D. P., & Kauffman, J. M. (1991). *Exceptional children* (5th ed.). Englewood Cliffs, NJ: Prentice-Hall.

Loovis, M. E., & Ersing, W. F. (1980). *Assessing and programming gross motor development for children.* Loudonville, OH: Mohican Publishing.

Moran, J. M., & Kalakian, L. H. (1977). *Movement experiences for the mentally retarded or emotionally disturbed child* (2nd ed.). Minneapolis: Burgess Publishing.

Payne, V. G., & Isaacs, L. D. (1991). *Human motor development* (2nd ed.). Mountain View, CA: Mayfield.

Peabody Developmental Motor Scales (1983). Nashville, TN: George Peabody College.

Salvia, J., & Ysseldyke, J. E. (1991). *Assessment* (5th ed.). Boston: Houghton Mifflin.

Ulrich, B. D., & Ulrich, D. A. (1985). The role of balancing ability in performance of fundamental motor skills in 3- , 4- , and 5-year-old children. In J. E. Clark & J. H. Humphrey (Eds.), *Motor development—Current selected research* (Vol. I, p. 127). Princeton, NJ: Princeton Book Co.

Winnick, J. P., & Short, F. X. (1985). *Physical fitness testing of the disabled—Project UNIQUE.* Champaign, IL: Human Kinetics.

Chapter 7

FUNDAMENTAL MOTOR SKILLS

In about the third grade, I could neither catch nor throw a ball with the proficiency that would enhance my self-concept. By the time I finished third grade, I had come to detest that ball, because it was the source of all those feelings of inadequacy which, at the time, mattered most. One day, after an eternity of missed catches, inaccurate throws, strikeouts, and being chosen last (or being told by the team captain to play in the outfield because the ball seldom got that far), I managed to get that damned ball when nobody was looking. Intent upon punishing that ball for all it had done to me, I took it to the farthest corner of the playground and literally buried it. For a while, I felt good, because I knew my spheroid enemy, in its final resting place, couldn't hurt me any more. Unfortunately, our class soon got a new ball.

Len Kalakian

Movement behavior in humans is as indigenous to the pursuit of happiness as to survival itself. In fact, many motor behaviors are part of our biological heritage and enhance human survival potential. They emerge quite naturally without formal modeling or instruction.

All species have their respective repertoires of phylogenetic behaviors. Among birds, an obvious phylogenetic behavior is flying; among fish, swimming; among humans, walking. In each instance, the animal's survival would be threatened without the instinctive and timely appearance of its respective phylogenetic skills.

Because many phylogenetic skills are motor skills, movement is, indeed, indigenous to survival. This fact suggests, perhaps, why we admire skilled movement and those who move well.

Children recognize the significance of movement early in life and learn that movement competence often means recognition, acceptance, and friendship. This is unfortunately a two-edged sword. Just as those with good motor skills tend to gain positive attention, those who are unskilled go unrecognized or worse, are ridiculed. By making positive value judgments about people who possess desirable attributes, we consciously or unconsciously make negative value judgments about those who do not possess such attributes. As a result, possessors of positive attributes tend to perceive themselves as being valuable, whereas those without such attributes tend to perceive themselves as having lesser value. Self-worth becomes largely a reflection of how individuals perceive that they are valued by others.

Just as important as the psychosocial significance of skilled movement is the physiological significance. Normal amounts of activity on a regular basis are essential to normal growth and development. Furthermore, virtually all components of basic physical and motor proficiency essential for continued well-being require movement for maintenance. Although skill in movement is not essential for fitness, skill is often the necessary ingredient that motivates the individual to remain active and fit.

CAUSATIVE FACTORS OF LOW MOTOR SKILLS

Known causes underlying low motor skills can be categorized as follows: (1) attitudinal and environmental influences, (2) delayed development of the central nervous system (CNS), and (3) minimal neurological dysfunction. Rosenbaum (1991) believes that low motor skill performance can also occur if children have inadequate instruction or too few opportunities to practice. In many instances, low motor skills cannot be attributed to known causes.

Delineating three causes of this complex problem risks oversimplification. In many instances, low motor skills are the result of combined influences. For example, low motor skills originating from delayed CNS development may precipitate an attitude that causes conscious avoidance of activity and skill development. Long after the CNS has matured, a negative attitude may remain and influence activity involvement and skill development. A child whose low motor skills are founded in minimal neurological dysfunction (e.g., mild cerebral palsy) might become the focus of well-meaning but misdirected efforts to remediate a condition for which there is no cure. This child should have opportunities for skill development in accordance with potential. A realistic intervention program must be sensitive to limitations owing to a single cause. Unrealistic expectations result in the child's becoming a nonachiever for reasons that the child cannot control. Understanding the cause of low motor skill development focuses remedial efforts on the problem's source, rather than on the symptoms.

INTERVENTION FOR CHILDREN WITH LOW MOTOR SKILLS OWING TO ATTITUDINAL AND ENVIRONMENTAL INFLUENCES

Poor attitudes resulting in low motor skills can often be modified. Sometimes the child's attitudes toward physical education and motor skill development are a reflection of parental attitudes. In an old but apropos study, Zeller (1968) used the Wear Attitude Scale (Wear, 1955) to determine parental attitudes toward physical education. Children of parents responding to the Wear Scale were administered a six-category motor proficiency test including agility, balance, ball handling, and body image items. Results indicated that parents with positive attitudes tended to have children whose motor skills were high. Conversely, negative parental attitudes coincided with low motor skills among those children. Further analyses indicated that the parents' degree of activity participation also influenced their children's performance. Children with low motor skills tended to have parents who did not participate in activity.

These limited data do not prove conclusively that parental attitudes directly affect children's attitudes and participation patterns. They do, however, indicate that some attitude sharing between parents and children may occur. These results suggest that intervention programs for some children with low motor skills might also include efforts to modify parental attitudes toward physical education.

An "I can't" attitude among children with low motor skills tends to reinforce low achievement and is often the product of peer attitudes toward the nonachiever. The low achiever who is ridiculed and ostracized for awkwardness will avoid negative attention, which means avoiding physical education. This is the beginning of a physical education dropout. Every reasonable effort should be made to ensure that children with low motor skills do not become objects of verbal abuse. Such children are in need of significant psychosocial support to counteract the association between low motor skills and fragile or negative self-concept.

Pagenoff (1984) found that a 14-year-old student with spastic cerebral palsy was exceptionally self-conscious of others' observations that her physical appearance was different from her peers. Fearing failure, the youngster refused to perform many activities both in treatment and in extracurricular settings. Her development of self-esteem and of performance skills was therefore limited. The girl in Pagenoff's study was quoted as saying, "I'm deformed, no one wants me around. I can't do what my friends can." A 2-day-a-week program, which continued for 8 weeks, was planned for the girl. To ensure optimum performance, the immediate area surrounding the pool was off limits to anyone else during the treatment sessions. (The student had refused to perform swimming activities when her mother or outside observers were present.) After the girl completed the planned progressive program, Pagenoff found positive physiological and motor skill improvement, and found in addition that "The most significant changes were noted in self-image" (p. 472).

Even in an empathetic environment, children may not progress. In this case, they deserve a program tailored to meet their unique needs. Enlist peer teaching, a teacher aide, or an adapted physical education resource teacher. When special needs are more pronounced, consider placement, at least part-time, in a special class.

For these children, it is particularly important that special programming be challenging but not frustrating. Challenges should be reasonable, with progress often measured in inches rather than feet. The child should be prodded gently by sincere and regular encouragement. Progress, no matter how modest, should be recognized as an important accomplishment.

Fortunately, young people's attitudes toward skill development and physical education are often malleable. It is difficult, however, to determine whether attitudes

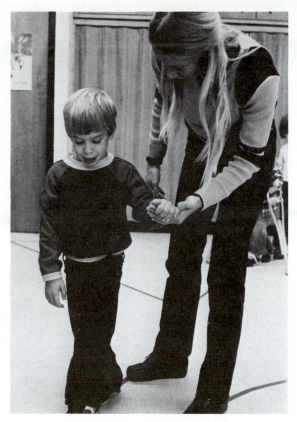

**The child should be prodded gently by sincere
and regular encouragement.**

improve because motor skills have improved or vice versa. In all likelihood, improved motor skills promote an improved attitude toward the activity, and the improved attitude in turn fosters a desire to improve motor skills further.

Attitudes, like habits, are often more easily formed than changed. This suggests that prevention is the best cure and that intervention, when necessary, should begin as early as possible.

INTERVENTION FOR CHILDREN WITH LOW MOTOR SKILLS OWING TO DELAYED CNS DEVELOPMENT

The child whose CNS develops more slowly than the norm will demonstrate motor proficiencies commensurate with the developmental status of the CNS. When attitudinal influences on the child are positive and one finds no reason to suspect neurological dysfunction, then delayed CNS development is the probable cause of low motor skills. In most instances, minor developmental delays reflect the normal range of CNS maturation at any age. At the normal CNS growth rate, maturation does not occur until age 8 or 9 (Rarick & Dobbins, 1975). Although an apparent developmental delay is not sufficient cause for alarm over CNS well-being, examination by a pediatrician or pediatric neurologist should be considered. Continuing delays or continued negative response to remediation indicate the need for medical evaluation.

Once the cause of low motor skills is attributed to delayed CNS development within normal parameters, intervention can follow one of two courses depending on individual circumstances. If delayed development has been accompanied by a history of low achievement in regular physical education, the child may need remediation to achieve present motor potential. This child needs to catch up! When the child's developmental delay is identified early, remediation to catch up will not be as necessary if a program is sensitive to the child's developmental pace and level. Such a child, by virtue of early diagnosis and prescription, may have little or no catching up to do. Even though the latter child may be behind his chronological age peers, he is not lagging in achievement according to potential. The developmental tasks confronting the former child may well be more formidable than those confronting the latter. Again, prevention is the best cure.

INTERVENTION FOR CHILDREN WITH LOW SKILLS OWING TO MINIMAL BRAIN DYSFUNCTION

The emergence and refinement of certain motor behaviors are indicators of CNS well-being. Delays in neurological development that are within normal parameters may delay certain motor behaviors; differentiating between these maturation delays and delays owing to minimal neurological dysfunction is important. In the former instance, time and sensitive instruction should diminish the problem gradually. In the latter case, neither time nor remediation offers complete resolution. Intervention efforts should focus on raising the child's skill level to present potential. Subsequent intervention efforts should focus on meeting the child's motor skill needs according to developmental status. It is important to recognize that an underlying neurological dysfunction is causing motor difficulties and will ultimately limit motor development potential.

When a child's low motor skills are founded in minimal neurological dysfunction, teachers, parents, and others must not make categorical judgments about what the child cannot do. Objectives for such a child must be realistic, and realistic objectives focus on ability rather than disability. Sparling et al. (1984) found a significant change occurring ($p < 0.01$) in the gross motor skill ability of neurologically impaired preschoolers when a planned program of "play" was provided for a 7-week period.

SCREENING, DIAGNOSIS, AND ACTIVITY PRESCRIPTION

The adapted physical educator is not expected to diagnose specific causative factors that underlie low motor skills, but the educator should be able to diagnose delays in specific motor proficiency areas and the extent of the delay.

Teacher or parent observation often identifies the rate of motor skill development as problematic. A screening device can be administered to confirm or allay suspicions. Possible screening tests for younger children include gross motor development scales that appear in the *Denver Developmental Screening Test* (Frankenburg et al., 1975). This screening device was developed to measure motor proficiencies of youngsters age 1 month to 6 years. Salvia and Ysseldyke (1991) suggest that *DDST* is an acceptable tool for screening, but they question the use of the norms derived from the full battery because they are quite old.

Regarding the use of gross and fine motor norm-referenced test batteries for infants and toddlers, Sugden and Keogh (1990) make an interesting observation:

> Despite their many limitations, data from gross and fine movement subscales of developmental examinations are the best source of information about general movement skill problems during the early years. A caution is that movement skill subscales are useful only to about 24 months, and because few movement achievements beyond 24 months are as distinct and observable as those in earlier months. Also, it is difficult to relate movement skill achievements on developmental examinations to achievements at later ages, because movement skills at later ages are not easily traced as an elaboration or extension of early movement skill achievements. It is difficult for all of these reasons to describe the nature and frequency of movement skill problems across the early years and to link early movement skill problems to later movement skill problems. (p. 146)

Werder and Kalakian (1985) believe the *DDST* should only be used with children between the ages of 4 and 6. Among older children (CA $4\frac{1}{2}$ to $14\frac{1}{2}$), the *Bruininks-Oseretsky Test of Motor Proficiency* (Bruininks, 1978) identifies specific areas of motor function and dysfunction (static balance, performance balance, speed and agility, response speed, and bilateral coordination). It is diagnostic in that it identifies general performance areas in which deficits exist. Once areas of performance deficit, including suspected causes, have been identified, specific activities can be prescribed to improve proficiency in those areas.

The Ohio State University SIGMA (*Scale of Intra-Gross Motor Assessment*) by Loovis and Ersing (1980) is a criterion-referenced assessment battery. It offers flexibility in assessing basic motor skill development of the nondisabled, children who are mentally retarded, and developmentally delayed children of preschool or elementary school age. The test battery includes 11 test items: walking, stair climbing, running, throwing, catching, jumping, hopping, skipping, striking, kicking, and ladder climbing.

LEARNING AND PERFORMANCE

Motor learning is the study of the processes involved in acquiring and perfecting motor skills. Motor skills are movements dependent on practice and experience for their performance (Payne & Isaacs, 1991).

Physical educators must be knowledgeable about the basics of motor learning to teach in ways compatible with the child's learning capabilities. Sound teaching practices are particularly vital when teaching children who demonstrate poor achievement in physical education.

By definition, a motor performance is skilled when a minimum amount of extraneous movement occurs. Schmidt (1991) uses Guthrie's definition of *skill* as the ability to bring about a predetermined outcome with maximum certainty and minimum outlay of time and energy.

When teaching motor skills, the teacher must recognize the difference between learning and performance. Although students may have learned what they must do to execute a skill properly, they may not have developed the motor responses

In evaluating the student with spastic cerebral palsy, the disparity between learning and performance must be a considered.

to transform their knowledge into action. When evaluating skill levels, particularly among low achievers, the teacher may find merit in reporting not only what can be performed, but also what has been learned.

MASSED VERSUS DISTRIBUTED PRACTICE

In **massed practice,** the learner practices a skill or skills over an extended period. In **distributed practice,** total practice time may be the same but practice periods are relatively brief and occur in greater number. For example, given the choice, the teacher should determine whether more learning will occur in four 30-min practice periods or in eight 15-min practice periods. Although total instruction time may remain the same, the amount of learning may not be the same. Students with relatively high skill levels often learn best in massed practice settings. When a high skill level is accompanied by high motivation, the student may persist in practice for an extended time. Children with relatively short attention spans and low skill levels often have low motivation and poor frustration tolerance as well. They learn best in distributed practice settings because the short practice periods accommodate their briefer concentration spans. The teacher can use inherently satisfying movement experiences to hold the child's attention while changing from distributed to massed practice situations. In so doing, the child may not only learn the desired skills but may also acquire an increased attention span.

There are no absolutes in selecting massed or distributed time blocks. Because children exhibit different learning characteristics, massed and distributed learning experiences should be prescribed on a child-by-child basis.

SPECIFICITY

Learning a motor skill tends to be a specific phenomenon. We learn only the skills that we practice, with little carry-over to other skills. The principle of specificity has many implications. It means that learning to throw a large ball first is *not* a prerequisite to learning to throw a small ball; the child probably should throw a small ball in the first place.

Breaking down a skill unnecessarily into what appear to be its component parts (i.e., beyond the developmental sequence for any given skill) may promote proficiency only in the component parts practiced. Specificity suggests that using gimmicks to teach motor skills may teach only proficiency in executing the gimmick. For example, telling students to position a tennis racket as if to scratch their back may teach back scratching with a tennis racket rather than serving. Specificity in practice suggests that the student should be directed to practice the whole skill. A guiding principle should be that, whenever possible, the ultimate skill to be learned should be practiced.

CEPHALOCAUDAL AND PROXIMODISTAL PROGRESSIONS

A child's ability to learn any motor skill depends largely on the nervous system's maturity. A skill presented prior to nervous system readiness for the task will not be learned.

The child's nervous system progresses in two directions. In the cephalocaudal progression, the nervous system matures first in the upper part of the body. Control is then achieved successively over the lower body parts. One example of cephalocaudal progression is demonstrated in the stages of learning to throw overarm. The first stage is characterized by arm action only. Successive stages extend to lower body segments, including body rotation, then weight shifts accompanied by leg and foot movements.

In the proximodistal progression, control is first achieved at the body midline, then gradually progresses distally to the arms, forearms, hands, and fingers. This progression is observed in learning to catch. Initial efforts are characterized primarily by the arms coming together in front of the body. Purposeful elbow, hand, or finger

Balance on lower extremities may be problematic in cases of delayed cephalocaudal progression.

action is not present. The second stage is characterized by a "scooping" response. Action occurs at the shoulders and elbows in an attempt to trap, or scoop, the ball into the chest. Finally, hand and finger actions are integrated with shoulder and arm actions.

Recognizing these progressions has practical significance for the physical educator, because complex skills requiring precise functions of lower extremities or distal members of upper extremities may be inappropriate for some children. Such children may be those whose low motor skills are founded in delayed CNS development.

GROSS AND FINE MOTOR CONTROL

Children tend to acquire and achieve control over gross motor skills before acquiring and achieving control over fine motor skills. This suggests that as children become older, they become progressively more capable of executing precise, fine motor movements. Children with low motor skills may not yet be neurologically able to develop precise, fine motor coordinations.

SUMMARIZING THE SKILL ACQUISITION PROCESS

Our effort to shed light on certain aspects of the skill acquisition process has been brief. In this text, only a few of the more significant factors influencing motor skill acquisition can be covered. Teachers in the adapted physical education area, who regularly encounter children with special needs, should undertake further study of motor learning theory. In this way they can apply their knowledge of motor learning theory selectively to individual students.

DEVELOPING FUNDAMENTAL MOTOR SKILLS

Children with low motor skills often experience difficulties in achieving even basic skill performance levels, yet acquisition of basic skills is essential. Such skills are the foundation of efficient movement.

Gallahue (1982) explains the goals of fundamental locomotor activities: "The child must be able to: (1) use any one of a number of types of movements to reach the goal; (2) shift from one type of movement to another when the situation demands it; and (3) alter each movement as the conditions of the environment change" (p. 180).

Keogh and Sugden (1985) have developed an interesting concept regarding motor development. They state the following:

> One problem in studying development is that we come to think of age as being development, that age becomes an agent of change, perhaps even the agent of change. It is easy to look at a graph of improved performance across age and think that age determines or influences change. We must remember that time itself is not causal and that age merely marks the passage of time or a period of time. Agents of change, such as biological processes or social interactions, function during the passage of time to determine or influence change. This means that we must consider what is happening during a given period of time rather than view age as an agent of change. To reiterate, age is merely time, and our problem is to identify and understand the changes in movement development across time. (p. 20)

Concern about motor development is well founded, for effortless locomotor patterns are the basis of an active life-style and of success in play, games, and sports. The basic motor skills are often identified as problematic in persons exhibiting poor motor patterns.

WALKING

Walking is the most used basic locomotor skill. It is incorporated in daily living to such an extent that one's walk is taken for granted. Physically and mechanically, walking is the least demanding of the upright locomotor skills; it is the first of the bipedal locomotor skills to appear in young children. If the walking skill is never mastered, the child may not be able to develop subsequent bipedal skills such as running, jumping, and skipping.

Mechanically correct walking begins with good posture, which requires an alignment of body segments resulting in minimum fatigue. Good posture is an individual matter. Body alignment that constitutes good posture for one person may not be the same for another. There are, however, key body alignment characteristics that imply effective posture in most individuals.

Good posture, whether standing or walking, is not necessarily characterized by ramrod straightness. Rather, spinal curves (thoracic, or upper spin, and lumbar, or lower spine) should be present but moderate. The thoracic curve should not create a forward protrusion of the head and neck. In posture exhibiting good thoracic curve, the ear is aligned directly above the shoulder. In posture exhibiting good lumbar curve, the individual should be able to stand with back, hips, and heels against the wall and *snugly* fit a hand (palm flat against the wall) between the lumbar region and the wall. If the hand fits loosely, the lumbar curve may be excessive.

An excessive lumbar curve often produces an excessive thoracic curve and vice versa. These excessive curves place undue stress on the posture muscles and ligaments that maintain the spinal column in an erect position. In addition, undue stress may also be placed on the last lumbar vertebra, which articulates with the pelvis. An excessive lumbar curve often causes lower back pain. An excessive thoracic curve is often accompanied by a sunken chest which, if sufficiently sunken, may create some breathing blockage.

In good posture, the feet should be pointed forward, which ensures an advantageous position to bear weight and facilitate locomotion.

Deviations from good posture should be assessed by a physical educator, physician, pediatrician, orthopedist, or physical therapist. Assessment will determine whether the child's posture problems are remediable. If they are, appropriate activities and exercises can be suggested.

Good posture characteristics are important to efficient walking. When walking, the child's arms should swing opposite from the legs. In mature walking, weight is transferred from the toe of the trailing foot to the heel of the lead foot. Arm, leg, and foot movement should be in the direction of the walk.

RUNNING

Running is the most rapid form of bipedal locomotion and is an integral part of many physical education and recreation activities. The child who learns to run well can enjoy success in many games and sports. In contrast, an inability to run well virtually ensures failure in many activities. Such failure can in turn result in avoidance of activities that could otherwise bring years of enjoyment and enhance health and fitness.

Skilled running implies the ability to run in a straight line. Any other direction than straight is counterproductive to speed. To visualize correct foot placement, a straight line should be drawn on the running surface. The line, approximately 2 in. wide and extending the full running distance, enables the child to observe proper foot placement as it occurs. To avoid failure for children whose feet seldom hit the line, lanes can be provided to direct proper foot contact. The lane should be 12 in. wide and should be narrowed gradually as the child's running skill improves.

In running, the feet should be pointed straight ahead. This placement maximizes foot leverage and thrust. Proper foot placement can be seen when the child runs a straight line in loose dirt. If the child is running on a hard surface, powdered chalk dusted on the shoe soles will indicate foot placement. The placement should be parallel to and preferably superimposed on the line. The most common error in foot placement is the toes-out position, which greatly reduces leverage, thrust, and therefore speed.

In running, the arms should swing opposite to the feet. Arm swing should be in a forward-backward plane, the direction of thrust. The head should remain stable and be pointed in the intended direction of travel. Left or right head rotation while running can be uncomfortable and makes staying on course difficult. Any rotation of the head back and forth is evident when children endeavor to run very fast.

Running requires forward lean to maintain forward momentum. Generally, the faster one runs, the greater the forward lean. When jogging comfortably, forward lean may be barely discernible. When sprinting forward, lean may be pronounced.

The student should endeavor to relax when running. Relaxation assists coordination and minimizes fatigue resulting from extraneous effort. Relaxation is indicated when jaw, hands, and fingers wobble loosely while running.

There are occasions in physical education or recreation activities when running backward may be required. This warrants some practice of backward running activities.

HOPPING

Hopping is rising and landing on the same foot. A student should be able to hop on either foot and in any direction. The nonhopping leg is off the floor, bent at the knee. Arms and the nonhopping leg aid in body balance. The arms, if not used for balance, aid in lifting the body for hopping. Using 3-, 4-, and 5-year-old children, Ulrich and Ulrich (1985) found that the level of hopping skill was directly related to the existing level of balance skill. In addition, significant positive correlations were found between balance and jumping.

Hopping is an important basic motor skill for safety. When a student is pushed or falls off balance in any direction other than directly forward or backward, hopping regains balance. The push or fall transfers weight onto one foot. Before balance is completely lost, the weighted foot and leg thrust the body momentarily into the air. While the body is airborne the same leg is aligned with the direction of travel, and on landing balance is regained.

Hopping is the most demanding of basic locomotor skills in terms of strength because it requires total body weight to be carried on one leg. For this reason, hopping is also the most demanding in terms of balance.

Children should be encouraged to hop in hopscotch-type games or in relays. Colorful marks or footprints can be drawn randomly on the playing surface, and the children told to hop from mark to mark. In the initial stages, marks on the playing surface should be placed close together. As hopping skill improves, marks should be placed farther apart in varying directions.

Children who fear losing their balance and falling may be timid about hopping from spot to spot. If the student cannot hop from mark to mark, have the child hop vertically on the same mark. Hold the child's hand to inspire confidence. Should difficulty persist, an assistant can hold the child's other hand. The child should, however, be supported only enough to ensure success. This enables the youngster to gain a feel for the skill much sooner.

When children hop, they hop naturally forward on the preferred foot. To ensure that hopping becomes a truly versatile skill, provide opportunities that encourage the child to hop on either foot in different directions.

SKIPPING

Skipping is the most complex of all basic locomotor skills. It involves alternation of the feet and a combination of one walking step followed by an immediate hop on the same foot.

The pattern for skipping is left foot—step, hop; right foot—step, hop. In fact, the verbal command "step-hop, step-hop, step-hop" provides a cue and the correct rhythm.

The arm swing for skipping is similar to the alternate arm swing used in walking and running. The arms maintain body balance and assist in obtaining height. To produce the desirable springy, joyful, carefree quality in skipping, movements should be performed on the balls of the feet.

Because skipping s a relatively complex motor skill, the teacher may need to employ more concrete modes of instruction. One mode involves the use of a full-length mirror. Teacher and student hold hands and stand side-by-side 15 ft from and facing the mirror. The child is instructed to step-hop simultaneously with the teacher. The teacher can cue the child verbally with "step-hop, step-hop." The mirror image and the verbal cues facilitate learning this skill. As the child progresses, the mirror can be eliminated. Teacher and student may continue to hold hands and skip to the verbal cue. Eventually, the verbal cue is sufficient for the child to skip alone. Finally, the child can skip along without the cue.

SLIDING

Sliding is the most effective locomotor skill for rapid lateral movement. It permits quick movement to one side, and facilitates a rapid stop and a return slide. Many games and activities require sliding as an appropriate motor skill. Such games involve situations in which one child is "it" and another child attempts to run past the tagger to reach a goal or safety zone. As the runner begins to switch direction in an effort to get past, "it" shadows the runner by sliding from side to side. If the tagger breaks prematurely into a run, thus committing herself to one direction, the runner can take off easily in the opposite direction and reach the goal.

Sliding is also important when catching a ball hit to one side of the fielder. If the ball is hit obviously to one side, the child may run to catch the ball. If the child is nearer to the ball, however, one or two slide steps are the quickest way to place the fielder in position to catch the ball.

The movement pattern for the slide is step-close-step. In sliding to the left, the left foot steps to the side followed by an immediate slide of the right foot next to the left. This sequence continues as long as a slide to the left is the objective. In sliding to the right, the right foot steps sideways, followed by a slide of the left foot next to the right.

Sliding can be taught easily if teacher and student face each other and hold hands. Instruct the child to imitate the teacher. The teacher should begin slowly to step-close-step sideways. As the child moves with the teacher, the tempo can be increased, and as the child's skill improves, teacher and student can work parallel but need not hold hands. Sliding can also be taught by using a full-length mirror; teacher and student then perform side-by-side.

GALLOPING

Galloping is a modification of sliding. It involves the same step-close-step foot pattern but is used in straight forward-backward or diagonal planes. Children can gallop in situations similar to those described for sliding. Whether one slides or gallops depends solely on movement direction. Step-close-step sideways or laterally is a slide. Step-close-step in any other direction becomes a gallop.

When galloping diagonally to the right, the right leg leads the step-close-step pattern. When galloping to the left, the left leg leads. When galloping forward or backward, either foot can lead.

Galloping is taught easily by using a full-length mirror. The child, beside the teacher, is instructed to imitate the teacher's movements. Another way to learn galloping is by walking with a limp. As the child begins limping, the tempo is increased gradually. A rapid limp using the step-close-step foot sequence is identical to the gallop.

To ensure versatility, provide galloping experiences in all directions. Ability to slide in either direction sideways and to gallop in all other directions enables the child to move quickly in all directions without having to commit to any one direction. When a specific direction is necessary, the child ceases to gallop or slide and breaks into a run.

LEAPING

Leaping is similar to running and is often used in conjunction with running. Running accentuates forward motion; leaping accentuates upward motion. In leaping, as in running, the child takes off on one foot and lands on the other foot. Although there is no set rule, a run becomes a leap when more effort is expended going upward than forward.

During takeoff and landing, weight should be concentrated on the ball of the foot. This provides maximum spring on takeoff and maximum cushion on landing. The knee bearing the weight on landing should be flexed slightly to avoid jarring on impact.

A leap can be used to surmount small obstacles such as a puddle or fallen log. Leaping can also be used to surmount greater obstacles or to catch a ball in flight.

In teaching children to leap, encourage the use of both left and right foot for takeoff. If the child can leap easily with either foot, the skill becomes more versatile.

Lengths of rope can be used to teach children to leap. Two ropes are stretched parallel. The distance between the ropes can be varied depending on the child's physical size and capability. The area between the ropes might be called "the river," and the child's objective is to leap across the river. Initially, the child should leap from a stationary position. As skill improves, the leap can be preceded by a walk or run. To make the obstacle more challenging as skill increases, the ropes an be placed farther apart or raised off the ground. If ropes are held above the ground, be sure that they can be released easily should a child trip.

Colorful marks on the floor can also be used to practice leaping. Random placement of the marks stimulates the children to leap for height and distance and in various directions.

JUMPING

Jumping is defined as taking off on either or both feet and landing on two feet. Jumping can occur from a stationary position or from a run. Although a jump can be in any direction, most jumping is vertical, straight ahead, or almost straight ahead.

The power necessary for a successful jump results from vigorous extension of the hips and knees and plantar flexion of the feet. The arms assist in lifting the body by swinging upward or forward in the desired direction. When landing, the body should be relaxed. The balls of the feet contact the ground first, and the knees and ankles bend to absorb the landing force. The arms may assist in balancing the body as the legs are extended and the jumper returns to standing position.

In teaching children to jump vertically, arrange a piece of rope to form a circle on the ground. The child should stand in the circle, jump vertically, and land inside the circle. To motivate children to jump straight up, suspend a brightly colored ball or familiar toy directly above the circle. Suspend it with elastic to prevent detachment when touched. The height of the ball or toy can be varied according to each child's vertical jumping capability.

In teaching children to jump forward, place two lengths of rope parallel, as when teaching youngsters to leap. In jumping across the two ropes, the child can take off using one foot or both feet. If the takeoff is on one foot, it can be preceded by a walking or running start.

Holding the child's hand as he jumps off a low step can also develop jumping skill. Variety and motivation can be added by painting colorful circles on the floor to use as landing targets and by increasing the number of step risers from which to jump. When jumping from steps above the first riser, the child should jump to the side rather than forward over lower risers.

Activities to improve general locomotor ability are illustrated in Figure 7.1.

KICKING

Kicking is a somewhat different motor skill. All skills discussed thus far are body projection skills. Each bipedal locomotor skill represents a means of projecting or moving one's body through space. Conversely, kicking is an object projection skill. The purpose of any object projection skill is to impart velocity to a projectile (e.g., a ball). Although one may project one's body through space in the execution of an

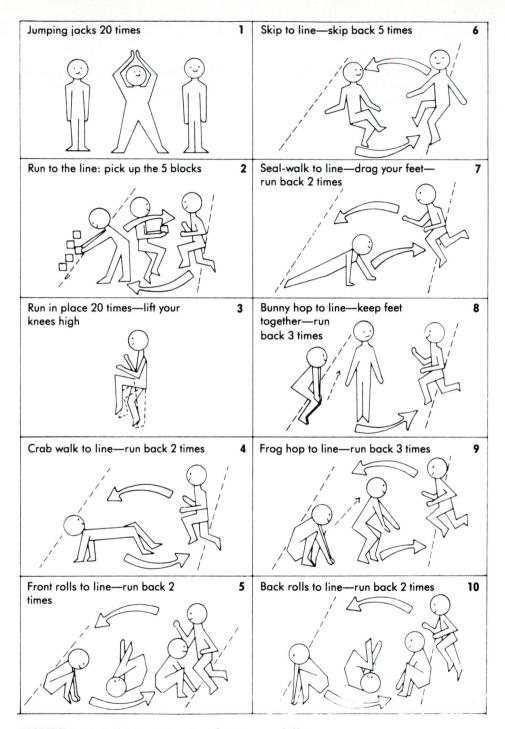

FIGURE 7.1 Activities to improve locomotor skills.

The following labels appear within the figure:

1. Jumping jacks 20 times
2. Run to the line: pick up the 5 blocks
3. Run in place 20 times—lift your knees high
4. Crab walk to line—run back 2 times
5. Front rolls to line—run back 2 times
6. Skip to line—skip back 5 times
7. Seal-walk to line—drag your feet—run back 2 times
8. Bunny hop to line—keep feet together—run back 3 times
9. Frog hop to line—run back 3 times
10. Back rolls to line—run back 2 times

object projection skill, the basic purpose is to control the projectile's velocity and accuracy.

Kicking requires eye-foot coordination. Until soccer became popular in the United States, most children seldom realized their full eye-foot coordination potential because kicking activities were emphasized less in our physical education classes.

A ball can be kicked from a walk, run, or stationary position. In any instance, it can be rolling or stationary. In all kicking, the eye must be kept on the ball to maintain contact, hence the use of eye-foot coordination.

The ankle of the kicking foot can be turned outward so that contact is made on the inside of the foot, or the ankle can be turned inward so that contact is made on the outside or top of the foot. The foot also can point straight ahead so that toe contact is made.

Controlling the ball is most difficult when toe contact is used. The small contact surface of the pointed toe makes the ball's direction unpredictable when the kicker is unskilled or only marginally skilled.

The height of the kicked ball is determined by placement of the nonkicking (supporting) foot. When the supporting foot is placed beside the ball, it will soar upward as well as forward. This occurs because the supporting foot is placed in such a way that the kicking foot can get well under (and scoop up) the ball. When the supporting foot is placed behind the ball, the ball will follow a low trajectory. This occurs because the position of the supporting foot does not permit the kicking foot to get too far under the ball.

In teaching children to kick, a wall can be used so the ball rebounds. In this way, little time is lost retrieving the ball. The direction of rebound tells the child immediately whether or not the ball was kicked in the intended direction. The children can also walk or run to kick an oncoming ball that has been rolled by the teacher, or they can form a circle and kick the ball back and forth. In either activity the ball can be kicked while it is moving, or stopped (trapped) and kicked from a stationary position.

DRIBBLING

A series of short kicks to move the ball from one play area to another is a form of dribbling. In dribbling with the feet, the primary concern is to keep the ball close to the feet and under control at all times. Dribbling is first performed while walking and then while running.

Dribbling can be taught by having children maneuver the ball to a point and back again. This activity can become a relay when children acquire more advanced dribbling skills.

Children should learn to kick with either foot; the child who kicks well with either foot is naturally more versatile. In teaching children with low motor skills to kick with a specific foot, tie a ribbon or similar colorful object to the kicking foot. This helps the child remember which foot to use. It also enables the teacher to determine at a glance whether or not the child is using the intended foot.

Modified kicking can be done by crutch walkers and wheelchair ambulators. For the former, a striking implement or surface is affixed to the crutch. For the latter, a plywood striking surface is affixed to the chair's footrests. Both modifications facilitate learning and enjoyment of games such as modified soccer in which many types of ambulators participating together can be accommodated.

STRIKING

Striking, like kicking, is an object projection skill. It involves the hand or some hand-held striking implement (e.g., bat, racket, club) to impart velocity to an object (e.g., ball, shuttlecock). Striking requires eye-hand coordination and, like kicking, requires keeping an eye on the object.

Initial striking experiences are most successful if the object is bright in color and stationary (e.g., ball against contrasting background placed on a batting tee). Such an arrangement minimizes the impact that visual tracking, spatial awareness, and figure-ground discrimination have on success. Although the child may eventually need to strike moving objects, striking stationary objects ensures success and continued interest in learning striking skills. When the child progresses to striking moving objects, the learner can begin by striking (volleying) a balloon or a slow-moving object that permits time for body movement and positioning.

Children who are blind or visually impaired can develop striking skills by using balls that jingle or beep electronically. A child with upper extremity orthopedic impairment, which affects grasp, can use rackets and paddles strapped securely to the preferred extremity.

To learn striking skills, children should be given implements of proper size and weight. A small child should not have an adult-sized implement. An implement that is too heavy for the user ensures failure. Striking surfaces can be enlarged to enhance success, but care must be taken to ensure that the implement remains easy to grasp and move.

THROWING

The underarm throw (toss) is the first throw observed in children. In the least mature underarm throwing attempts, only arm action is noted. Later, a follow-through with the right foot (right-handed thrower) accompanies arm action. Finally, the left foot steps forward in preparation as the throwing arm swings backward. As the throwing arm swings forward, the right foot moves forward in follow-through fashion. Common variations of throwing include bowling, serving a volleyball, and pitching horseshoes.

Of all throwing patterns, the overarm throw is the most effective in terms of velocity and distance. It is therefore the pattern most often used in throwing-related activities. An extensive study of overarm throwing skill development was made by Wild (1938), who found that four phases of overarm throwing are closely associated with chronological age. In children with low motor skills, these phases are also associated with chronological age, but the age at which each phase appears is later than that of normally progressing youngsters. Wild identified four throwing phases as follows:

> **Phase one** (CA 2–3 years). Throw involves the arm only. There appears to be no shift in body weight or rotation of the trunk. Both feet remain planted firmly on the ground.
>
> **Phase two** (CA $3\frac{1}{2}$–5 years). Throw differs from phase one in that body rotation has been added, which increases ball velocity. There is still no foot movement or weight shift.
>
> **Phase three** (CA 5–6 years). Throw involves body rotation but adds a step forward with the right foot (right-handed thrower).
>
> **Phase four** (CA $6\frac{1}{2}$ years and older). Left foot steps forward as the ball is being delivered. Weight is then transferred from the right to the left foot so that the right foot can step forward in follow-through motion as the ball is released.

Wild observed that many girls never progressed beyond phase three. Note, however, that Wild's observations occurred at a time when girls were not reinforced socially for effective throwing skills. A replication of Wild's studies today would be interesting to determine how far beyond the third phase most girls have progressed. His observation would probably no longer hold true.

Data indicate that throwing distance decreases as children are given larger balls to throw. Factors besides weight difference contribute to this phenomenon. When an excessively large ball is used, the child usually modifies her throwing pattern to accommodate the ball size. In fact, the theory of specificity suggests that learning to throw a large ball first may actually retard the skill acquisition process of throwing a small ball with mature overhand delivery. When the child switches from a large ball to a small ball, he must unlearn many large ball throwing skills before learning skills related to throwing a small ball. Two considerations are appropriate in teaching the child to throw: (1) the ball must accommodate the child's hand size, and (2) the ball should be the size that the child will throw most frequently. Teach the child to throw a large ball only if throwing a large ball is the objective.

BALL BOUNCING

Ball bouncing, or dribbling with the hands, plays a major role in many physical education and recreational activities. It requires concentration, visual tracking, and eye-hand coordination. While bouncing the ball, the child can stand still, walk, run, slide, or gallop.

In bouncing the ball, children should be instructed to tap, not slap it. A slapped ball bounces out of control. As the child becomes more highly skilled, she should be taught to bounce the ball with the thumb and fingertips, which affords greatest control.

Recordings with a heavily emphasized beat can be used to teach children to dribble. First, practice with the record to be sure that the tempo is neither too fast nor too slow. With the record on, demonstrate by bouncing the ball to the tempo in full view of the children. The teacher's participation along with the accentuated beat will give the children visual and auditory cues, which facilitate understanding the rhythmic pattern that underlies dribbling.

In the initial stages of dribbling, the child may use both hands simultaneously to thrust the ball toward the ground and then catch it with both hands. As the child progresses, he may soon be capable of dribbling with one hand. At this stage, the child should be taught to dribble with either hand to make the skill as versatile as possible (see Figure 7.2).

CATCHING

Developmentally, catching is more complex than throwing and is perfected only after throwing skills are learned. Catching challenges should conform to the child's developmental status. A rolled ball is easiest to catch. Following this, intercepting a ball bounced on the ground is relatively easy, particularly if the child has placed the ball in motion. Self-initiation of ball action eliminates many uncertainties associated with catching a ball that another has thrown. Finally, the child is ready to catch a ball thrown by another.

A common error in teaching children to catch is throwing the ball too slowly. When learning to catch, many children cue on the thrower, not on the ball. Throwing the ball initiates a catching response in the child. If the ball is thrown inordinately slowly, the catching response may occur before the ball has come within reach. When this occurs, the thrower should try to determine the time lapse between the throw and response initiation. The thrower should then adjust the velocity of the ball so it comes within reach at the precise time when the catching response is initiated. Should the ball arrive consistently before the catching response, the ball's velocity can be reduced. Should the ball's velocity need to be reduced, a balloon can be used.

Data indicate that ball size is significant when learning to catch. Du Randt (1985) found that a smaller ball size (e.g., the size of a tennis ball) stimulates the occurrence of a more mature catching response in 6- and 8-year-olds, but not in 4-year-olds. She states: "It is therefore recommended that 8- and 6-year-olds be encouraged to play with a small ball as often as possible, whereas 4-year-olds need not be confronted formally with a small ball until they are relatively proficient with a larger ball" (p. 42). Cratty (1989) reports reasonable success with 5-year-olds attempting to catch an 8-in. diameter ball. He cites little success with 5-year-olds catching a tennis ball. In each case, the ball was bounced to the child. The balls were, however, bounced from different distances, and the same children were not observed in each instance. Nevertheless, the data suggest that the larger ball is easier for 5-year-olds to catch because it provides a more substantial visual stimulus and offers greater surface area for catching.

Children learning to catch should be given balls with a rough surface. The roughness creates friction for hand contact.

For learners with limited manipulative ability, mittens and Velcro-covered balls can build success in catching activities. Velcro should also cover the mitten gras-

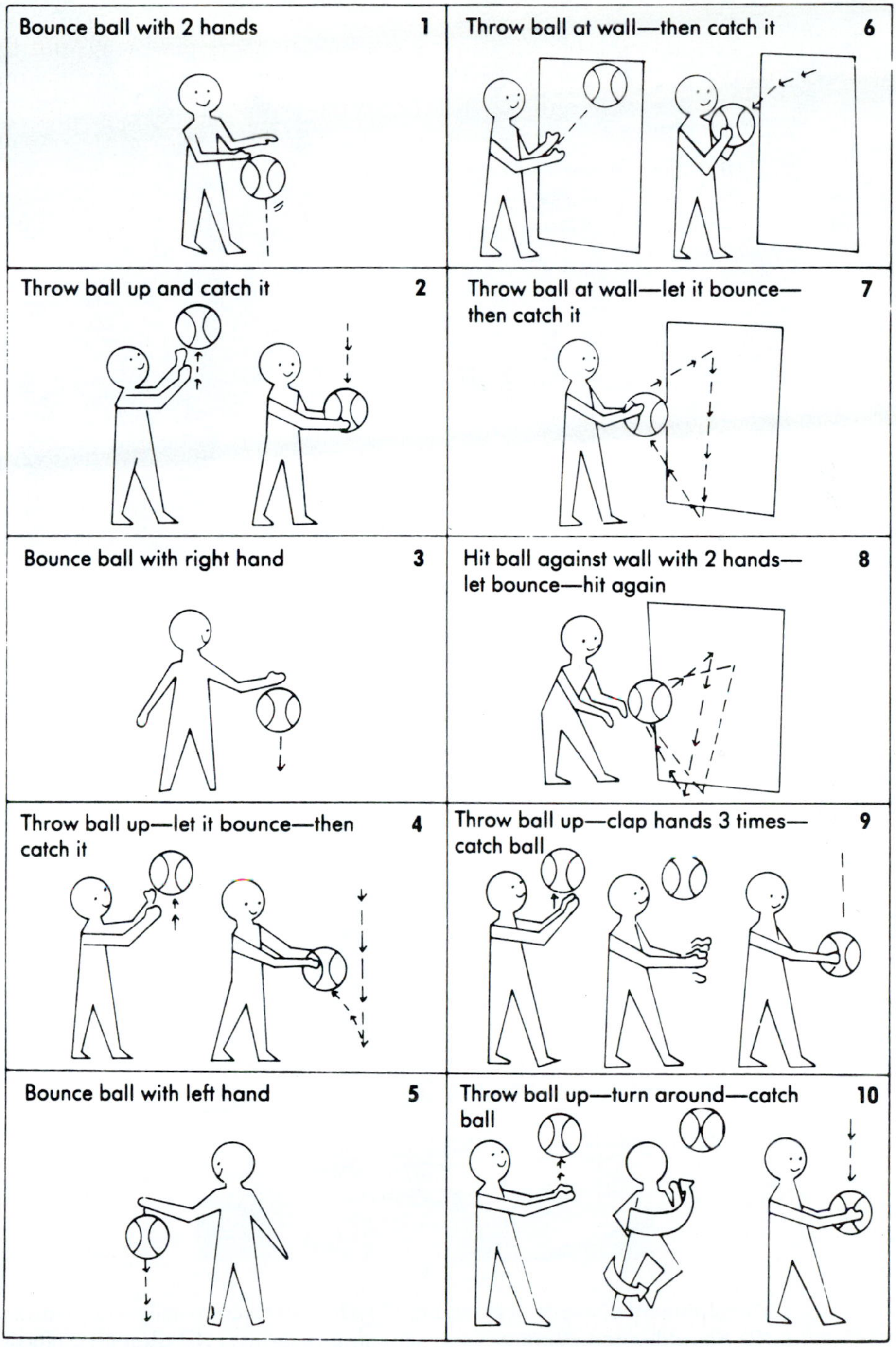

Bounce ball with 2 hands 1
Throw ball up and catch it 2
Bounce ball with right hand 3
Throw ball up—let it bounce—then catch it 4
Bounce ball with left hand 5
Throw ball at wall—then catch it 6
Throw ball at wall—let it bounce—then catch it 7
Hit ball against wall with 2 hands—let bounce—hit again 8
Throw ball up—clap hands 3 times—catch ball 9
Throw ball up—turn around—catch ball 10

FIGURE 7.2 **Activities to improve eye-hand coordination.**

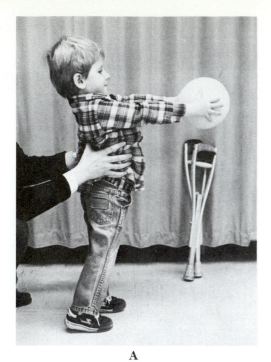

A

B

C

Developmental stages in catching. (A) Shoulder action only—immature response. (B) Shoulder and elbow action—scooping response. (C) Shoulder, elbow, wrist, and finger action—mature response.

A rolled ball is easiest to catch.

ping surfaces. When a Velcro-covered nerf, cloth, or whiffle ball contacts the mitten surfaces, it then sticks. The child thus experiences successful catching without demonstrating a prerequisite grasp.

Inflatable balls are easier to catch if partially deflated. A partially deflated ball is easier to grasp and does not hurt when missed. The child who is hurt by the ball while trying to learn to catch may soon concentrate more on avoiding than on catching the ball. Beanbags also serve to teach catching.

PUSHING, PULLING, LIFTING, AND CARRYING

When pushing, the body moves forward, near forward, or sideward against resistance. Body lean should be toward the object being pushed. One leg should be placed almost fully extended behind the object. This leg is a major force contributor during the push. The opposite leg is flexed to a somewhat greater degree and is placed ahead of the fully extended driving leg. It assists in the push but also facilitates balance.

During the push the body should form a nearly straight line from point of force application (foot to ground) to point of force application (hand to object). The straight body configuration pits bone against bone during the push, thus increasing efficiency of energy expenditure. In effective pushing, hip-knee extension is a major force contributor.

Objects with a high center of gravity and a small support base often topple over when pushed (or pulled). When pushing such objects, force should be applied near the base to avoid tipping.

The easiest airborne ball to catch is the one you bounce.

In pulling activities the body generally leans in the opposite direction, and grip strength is important. When pulling, one leg should be almost fully extended and relatively near the object. The opposite leg assumes a greater degree of flexion to assist in force application and in balance. As in pushing, hip-knee extension is a major force contributor. Additional pulling force results from simultaneous arm and shoulder action.

During pulling, the body should form a nearly straight line from point of force application (driving foot against the ground) to point of force application (one's grip on the object). Often, heavy or cumbersome objects can be pulled with greater efficiency if a rope is attached to the object. A top-heavy object should be pulled near the base to avoid toppling.

Lifting is a potentially dangerous activity, especially if the object to be lifted is heavy or cumbersome. Improper lifting techniques will result in lower back strain.

When an object is to be lifted, knowing the object's approximate weight is important. In preparing to lift, the child should be as near to the object as possible. Knees and hips should be flexed and help perpendicular or nearly perpendicular to the back. The major force should come from hip-knee extension and not from the back. With the back erect and with the lifting force coming from hip-knee extension, the possibility of back injury is minimized (i.e., head up–butt down). In lowering an object, the lifting procedure is simply reversed. The weight should be carried by the lower extremities (i.e., hip-knee flexion).

Once lifted, an object can be carried in many ways depending on its physical characteristics and weight. Objects with handles (e.g., suitcases) may require only one arm. Relatively small, lightweight objects can be carried under the arm. Larger, heavier objects may require both hands with the object resting against the front of the body. Heavy or cumbersome objects can be carried on one shoulder with the hands used to balance the object.

Whenever an object is too heavy or cumbersome for one person to manage, two or more persons should assist. Lifting and carrying principles remain the same for each individual, even though several individuals may be involved simultaneously. When more than one person participates in lifting or carrying, coordinating efforts is important. Signals should inform each helper when to lift, carry, and lower the object. Such a procedure minimizes wasted or misdirected effort and reduces the possibility of injury.

EVALUATING PROGRESS

Performance can be evaluated through anecdotal records, norm-referenced tests, and criterion-referenced tests.

Anecdotal records are valuable for recording improvements to which standardized tests are not sensitive. For example, anecdotal records can note increases in willingness to participate during class and to engage in active play with others during free time.

Norm-referenced tests (e.g., Bruininks-Oseretsky) are valuable in determining the extent to which a child's motor proficiencies continue to depart from the norm. Norm-referenced tests are of interest to parents who want to know "how my child is doing." Caution should be exercised, however, when using norm-referenced test results. Children with low motor skills may know that they are performing below the norm. Continued comparison with others, which is the basis of norm-referenced test interpretation, can serve only to embarrass the child.

Criterion-referenced tests measure progress according to developmentally sequenced performance criteria. Criterion-referenced instruments do not compare the child's performance with that of others, as do norm-referenced tests. Rather, the child's performance is evaluated in terms of improved performance measured against a behaviorally stated performance criteria. In effect, children become their own norm and thus do not experience unwanted or unnecessary comparisons. Four criterion-referenced test batteries that measure motor proficiency and are appropriate for children with low motor skills are *I CAN* (Wessel, 1976); *I CAN Primary Skills*

(Wessel, 1980); the *Test of Gross Motor Development* (Ulrich, 1985); and the *Achievement Based Curriculum Development in Physical Education* (Wessel & Kelly, 1986).

SUMMARY

Movement and acquisition of motor skills are fundamental elements of human behavior. Many fundamental motor skills that children and youth acquire under normal circumstances actually require little formal instruction. The major concern should be that opportunities exist for such skills to emerge and be perfected. For children with special motor development needs, these basic skills sometimes do not emerge naturally. The possible reasons for this include lack of opportunity for skill practice and developmental interruption owing to the nature and extent of a disability. Whenever such situations arise, special attention in physical education is indicated.

Motor skill acquisition has both physiological and psychosocial significance. Sufficient movement opportunities are essential for normal growth and development. Skilled movement is also significant as a means of communicating and establishing rapport with others.

Children with disabilities tend to manifest low motor skills disproportionately in comparison with the nondisabled population. Fundamental motor skills, often problematic among children with special needs, include body and object projection skills.

The physical educator must become familiar with the various skill categories, including a thorough understanding of each skill's significance and the developmental stages necessary for skill acquisition. Only then can the educator arrive at effective methods for facilitating skill acquisition and for modifying instruction to accommodate the learning characteristics of children with specific disabilities.

REFERENCES

Bruininks, R. H. (1978). *Bruininks-oseretsky test of motor proficiency: Examiner's manual.* Circle Pines, Minn.: American Guidance Service.

Cratty, B. J. (1989). *Adapted physical education in the mainstream* (2nd ed.). Denver: Love.

Du Randt, R. (1985). Ball-catching proficiency among 4- , 6- , and 8-year-old girls. In J. E. Clark & J. H. Humphrey (Eds.), *Motor development current selected research* (Vol. I). Princeton, N.J.: Princeton Book Company.

Frankenburg, W. K., Goldstein, A., & Camp, B. (1975) *Denver developmental screening test, reference manual* (revised 1975 ed.). Denver: LADOCA Project Publishing Foundation.

Gallahue, D. L. (1982). *Understanding motor development in children.* New York: John Wiley and Sons.

Keogh, J., & Sugden, D. (1985). *Movement skill development.* New York: Macmillan.

Loovis, M. E., & Ersing, W. F. (1980). *Assessing and programming gross motor development for children.* Loudonville, Ohio: Mohican Publishing.

Pagenoff, S. A. (1984, July). The use of aquatics with cerebral palsied adolescents. *The American Journal of Occupational Therapy, 38* (7), 469–473.

Payne, V. G., & Isaacs, L. D. (1991). *Human motor development: A lifespan approach* (2nd ed.). Mountain View, CA: Mayfield.

Rarick, G. L., and Dobbins, D. A. (1975). Basic components in the motor performance of children six to nine years of age. *Medicine and Science in Sports,* 7, 105–110.

Rosenbaum, D. A. (1991). *Human motor control.* San Diego: Academic Press.

Salvia, J., & Ysseldyke, J. E. (1991). *Assessment* (5th ed.). Boston: Houghton Mifflin.

Schmidt, R. A. (1991). *Motor learning and performance.* Champaign, IL: Human Kinetics.

Sparling, J. W., Walker, D. F., & Singdahlsen, J. (1984, September). Play techniques with neurologically impaired preschoolers. *The American Journal of Occupational Therapy, 38* (9), 603–612.

Sugden, D. A., & Keogh, J. F. (1990). *Problems in movement skill development.* Columbia, University of South Carolina Press.

Ulrich, D. A. (1985). *Test of gross motor development.* Austin, TX: PRO-ED.

Ulrich, B. D., & Ulrich, D. A. (1985). The role of balancing ability in performance of fundamental motor skills in 3- , 4- , and 5-year-old children. In J. E. Clark and J. H. Humphrey (Eds.) *Motor development — Current selected research,* (Vol. I). Princeton, NJ: Princeton Book Company.

Wear, C. L. (1975). Construction of equivalent forms of an attitude scale. *Research Quarterly, 26,* 113–119.

Werder, J. K., and Kalakian, L. H. (1985). *Assessment in adapted physical education.* Minneapolis: Burgess Publishing.

Wessel, J. A. (1976). *I CAN.* Northbrook, IL: Hubbard.

Wessel, J. A. (1980). *I CAN primary skills.* Northbrook, IL: Hubbard.

Wessel, J. A., & Kelly, L. (1986). *Achievement based curriculum development in physical education.* Philadelphia: Lea & Febiger.

Wild, M. (1938). The behavior patterns of throwing and some observations concerning its course of development. *Research Quarterly, 9,* 20–24.

Zeller, J. (1968). *The relationship between parental attitude toward physical education and physical performance of the child.* Unpublished master's thesis, University of California, Los Angeles (as cited by Cratty).

Chapter 8

PERCEPTUAL-MOTOR DEVELOPMENT

Danielle is a 7-year-old who seems lost in space. Even though her movements appear thoughtful and pensive, she often stumbles or bumps into objects. When she walks down the school halls, she bumps into other children. In the classroom, her achievements fall noticeably below those of her peers. Although she is in the second grade, she continues to reverse *p*s and *q*s, and *b*s and *d*s, and she has difficulty with reading comprehension. When asked to draw a person, she omits body parts, and draws other parts out of proportion. She is awkward in executing gross motor movements and, perhaps for this reason, avoids other children (and is avoided by other children) in active play. Her pediatrician and a pediatric neurologist concur that her developmental difficulties have no obvious medical explanation.

Tommy is a 9-year-old with a marginal (35 decibel) conductive hearing loss. A hearing aid has been helpful in overcoming Tommy's amplification problem. Although his vestibular apparatus has not been affected by his hearing impairment, Tommy has poor balance when executing many motor skills. Both gross and fine motor coordinations are noticeably immature when compared with others. He seldom initiates active play, and those activities that he does select are solitary and sedentary. His achievements in school are below average, and his teacher states that he is not achieving in accordance with his potential.

Children like Danielle and Tommy are far from unique. Danielle's developmental delays seem particularly perplexing because nothing is apparently "wrong." Tommy's developmental delays are less baffling, but are disproportionate to his hearing loss, much of which has been restored.

What plausible explanations might shed light on the whys of such developmental delays? One possible, though controversial, explanation is suggested, at least in part, by perceptual-motor theory. Although perceptual-motor theorists vary, a common theme is that perceptual competence evolves initially through movement and in large measure determines readiness to undertake subsequent, more complex learning challenges.

Perceptual-motor theory is just that—theory. Its advocates and critics are equally vociferous. One perceptual-motor theorist, the late Newell C. Kephart, proposed that all learning has its basis in movement. One critic, Bryant J. Cratty (1986), criticizes proponents like Kephart as "movement messiahs."

We have developed this chapter with an awareness that a controversy does indeed exist concerning the merits of perceptual-motor theory and practice. Some programs are based on this theory, however, and are likely to continue. This requires that perceptual-motor development theory be scrutinized.

DEFINITIONS AND RATIONALE

Perception is the interpretation of information (sensory stimuli) monitored by the nervous system. Gallahue (1982) defines the term **perceptual-motor** in the following way: "In its broadest sense a perceptual-motor act is any voluntary movement that relies on sensory data to process information used in the performance of that act. In other words, all voluntary movement may be viewed as perceptual-motor in nature" (p. 14). Rosenbaum (1991) describes the perceptual-motor process:

> We move to be able to perceive, just as we perceive to be able to move....One reason perception benefits from movement is that movement allows for the transport of sensory receptors. We turn our eyes and our heads so we can take in visual information from a wide range of locations. We walk to new locations to see and hear what is going on there. We use our hands to feel objects or bring the objects to locations where we can inspect them further. (p. 22)

Perceptual-motor efficiency is the ability to interpret sensory stimuli resulting from movement. Perceptual-motor efficiency may involve perceiving through movement (e.g., the interpretation of a tactile sensation as roughness) or making appropriate motor responses to sensory input (e.g., placing the hands in proper position to catch a ball).

The key word in the definition of perceptual-motor efficiency is **interpretation.** Interpretation is important because sensory experiences alone have no meaning. They are merely electrical impulses traveling from sensory input mechanisms (e.g., the eyes) along nerve pathways to the brain. The ability to discriminate among countless sensory experiences is interpretation, hence perception.

Perception and translating perception into concept is how an individual organizes and systematizes his environment. When perceptions and concepts are adequate, the individual can communicate with the environment. When precepts and concepts are inadequate, one's ability to communicate with the environment is inadequate. This inadequacy in communicating with the environment is thought to result from an inability to derive meaning from sensory information. In other words, the brain must learn (memorize) past movement experiences, and this only occurs from numerous trials. Without the benefit of repetition, the brain will never possess the backlog necessary for individuals to become proficient in motor skills (Payne & Isaacs, 1991).

Dummer (1985) believes that to succeed at a motor task, the individual must (1) recognize the current task to be either like or unlike previously learned skills, (2) retrieve from memory examples of past similar movements and sensory consequences, (3) decide on a motor plan for the current task by interpolating new response specifications from past response specifications and movement outcomes, (4) execute the motor plan, (5) correct the movement in progress by updating the motor plan (if the movement is more than one reaction time in duration), (6) evaluate the completed movement in terms of both actual outcome and sensory consequences, and (7) update and revise the motor schema.

In perceptual-motor theory, perception is thought to arise from action connoting movement. Movement is thought to be the primary means by which the child encounters sensory experiences in early learning. The child who does not move ably experiences some sensory deprivation. Because perception evolves out of sensory experiences, movement that produces sensory experiences is considered an important component of early learning.

An experienced observer will note that an infant's interactions with her surroundings are almost exclusively motor. The child gathers perceptual information about the world primarily through motor experiences. As the child moves, sensory experiences are encountered, and perception through motion gives meaning and order to a world characterized by sensory chaos.

Development of perceptual competence through movement may be likened to the scaffold required to build a house. Movement is the scaffold and perceptual competence is the house. The scaffold is necessary to build the house. Once the house is built, however, the scaffold is no longer needed. Although movement is important to achieve many other objectives, it has fulfilled it purpose as a scaffold to build perceptual competence. Without the scaffold (movement) the house (perceptual competence) might never become functional.

In reference to perceptual-motor learning, a quotation from Kerr (1985) provides an interesting comparison:

> The term "motor capacity" is an intuitively relevant concept which eludes definition. To use a computer analogy, one can enhance the performance of a computer by changing either the hardware or the software. One can increase the computer's memory storage—the capacity of the system—or one can write more programs which can function within the existing capacity of the system. Thus, improvement in the motor performance of a child could reflect changes in motor capacity—for example, the ability to store or process larger amounts of motor information—or it could reflect the adoption of new strategies which would allow the child to process information at a faster rate or would require the processing of less information due to an improved selection or sampling process. (pp. 45–46)

Thomas (1984) agrees with Kerr and states that "if memory is compared to a computer, then the size of the computer does not change; however, the programming becomes better, and more knowledge and programs are available" (p. 92).

Perceptual-motor inadequacies can be observed in a child whose sensory mechanisms are intact (e.g., an able-bodied child with normal eyesight whose immature visual perceptual-motor development prevents successful catching) or in a child whose sensory mechanisms are partially or totally nonfunctioning (e.g., a visually impaired or blind child whose disability prevents successful catching).

In the former child's case, perceptual-motor inadequacies may be the result of inadequate sensory experiences. Kephart (1960) suggests that as society becomes more civilized, it restricts its children's freedom of movement. He states that restrictions result in perceptual inadequacies owing to deprivation of movement-centered sensory experiences. In the case of a child with a disability, impairment may prevent initial motor-based environmental exploration, which in turn delays acquisition of perceptual-motor and cognitive skills. The child, however, may still learn depending on the site, extent, and severity of the disability, although an optimal level of skill may not be attainable.

Considerable evidence exists that memory plays an important part in the motor learning process. In particular, encoding, rehearsal, and organization are all memory functions that younger children use less effectively than older children, and older children use these processes less efficiently than adults. Thomas (1984) states the following:

> Experience is in large part the knowledge base in LTS (long term storage). In general, children have less knowledge than do adults, but research shows that when children have a larger knowledge base than do adults, children's performance is better. Thus, enriching the knowledge base through varied movement experiences should be a major objective of teachers and coaches. Remember that the base of knowledge about movement not only includes movement patterns themselves but also how, why, and when to use these movements. Thus, cognition is a vital and important part of the effective acquisition and performance of motor skills: The correlation between memory, understanding, cognition, and motor learning may be a major reason why mentally handicapped children have difficulty when attempting to learn motor skills. (p. 101)

WHAT DOES THE LITERATURE SAY?

The literature suggests associations between motor experiences and perceptual, motor, and intellectual capabilities. In recent years, acceptance of the perceptual-motor rationale and allegiance to perceptual-motor theorists and practitioners have increased. For some educators and parents of children with special needs, the perceptual-motor rationale has become a panacea. Rather than indict or deny validity of perceptual-motor theory, we need to explore and evaluate the issues with scholarly scrutiny.

ITARD

Jean-Marc Itard (1801), a French physician, was perhaps the first person to try effecting positive changes in human behavior by training of the senses. His work was undertaken early in the 19th century when he was responsible for a 12-year-old boy captured in the forests of Aveyron. The boy, named Victor, had been diagnosed by a physician as being severely retarded. Itard endeavored to work with the boy by using intensive, systematic sensory and motor training. Although this training resulted in marked changes in the boy's behavior, Victor never learned to speak or live independently in Parisian society. Itard viewed his efforts as a failure, but his work with Victor marks the first scientific attempt to teach a child with special needs through particular sensory and movement-centered experiences.

SEGUIN

Edovard Seguin (a student of Itard's) and his contemporaries who followed Itard's teachings were called **sensationalists** or **environmentalists.** They believed that an environment, enriched with sensory experiences, would effect positive behavioral changes in people with special needs (i.e., persons with mental retardation). Seguin emphasized sensory experiences and the maturing of sensory perception through movement-centered experiences. He also espoused education through perception development rather than through abstract reasoning, because he believed that perceptions evolved through sensory experiences that result from muscular activity. Seguin (1907) stated his theory in this way: "The physiological education of the senses must precede the psychological education of the mind.... The physiological education of the senses is the royal road to education of the intellect."

MONTESSORI

Deteressa Maria Montessori was an early proponent of movement experiences as a means of acquainting the child with his environment. She believed that the child must become proficient in walking, balancing, and coordinating movements through motor activities. The Montessori approach to education (1912) emphasizes sensory training and contends that a child's intellectual development is founded in observing, comparing, and judging environmental phenomena. Sensory experience, which occurs through movement, is purported to acquaint the child with the environment and to develop intelligence. It is of interest to note that Montessori's initial work and research was done with children who were mentally retarded. She was a great advocate of "muscular education" and believed that without this development many youngsters with mental retardation could not go about their daily routines. She held the concept that, through movement, children seek the exercise that helps to organize and coordinate behaviors in order that purposeful learning can take place. Her theories and programs are still used today, but the student population tends to lean toward young "gifted" children whose parents believe that the Montessori Method will provide different challenges not offered in traditional educational programs.

PIAGET

Jean Piaget is perhaps the most renowned scholar to have studied the nature of learning. Piaget, in observing his own children, became convinced that their intellects developed initially not through coping with abstractions, but from thought spawned by movement-centered experiences. According to Piaget (1936), such movement-centered experiences constitute the first of four developmental periods through which the child passes to achieve intellectual potential. The first period, the *sensorimotor* period, is concerned principally with the sequence of interrelated sensorimotor experiences believed to be the foundation of perceptual and symbolic fluency development. Initially, movement is random. Soon, thoughts spring from movements (i.e., mind follows hand). Eventually, movements spring from thoughts (i.e., mind leads hand). Piaget believes that adequate development during the sensorimotor period is prerequisite to more complex forms of cognitive development.

BARSCH

Ray H. Barsch, a special educator, theorizes that perceptual development is the basis of intellect. He believes that perceptual fluency owes its functional integrity to efficient movement patterns.

Earlier work by Barsch culminated in his *movigenic theory*. This theory correlates learning ability with movement efficiency. The movigenic theory involves the study of movement patterns, their origins and development, and how they relate and contribute to learning.

Movigenic theory speculates that movement efficiency is the primary principle underlying the human organism, which learns first to move so it can move to learn. As the organism moves, it matures, and symbolic fluency (i.e., ability to deal with abstractions) replaces motor-based modes of experience and comprehension. Major tenets of Barsch's movigenic theory (1965) are stated in part as follows:

> All living organisms must survive in an energy surround. Radiant mechanical and thermal energies represent the primary sources with which the organism must contend. . . . Survival in such an energy surround is contingent upon movement. The organism must move to survive. If movement cannot occur from independent initiation, the organism is at the mercy of the energy forces or dependently reliant upon others for survival. . . . The pull of gravity represents the major force to be resolved by the human organism in developing patterns of movements to promote survival. . . . Building an adequate repertoire of movement patterns for survival in a variable uncertain energy surround requires walking, crawling, hopping, running, squatting, rolling, etc. . . . The terrain of movement is space. Each individual must organize a visual space volume, an auditory space and a kinesthetic space volume. Failure to organize each spatial volume results in some constricting penalty to the survival efficiency of the organism. . . . Efficient patterns of movement then become crucial to communicative proficiency. (p. 15)

To develop movement efficiency and thereby perceptual awareness, Barsch prescribes activities in 12 categories: (1) muscular strength, (2) dynamic balance, (3) spatial awareness, (4) body awareness, (5) visual dynamics, (6) auditory dynamics, (7) kinesthesia, (8) tactile dynamics, (9) bilaterality, (10) rhythm, (11) flexibility, and (12) motor planning.

VERNON

M. D. Vernon (1962) alleges that perception primarily influences development of knowledge about, and phenomena identification in, the environment. He believes that initial perception results from motor experiences. Motor contact provides the child's initial experiences of similarities and differences in environment.

TAYLOR

J. G. Taylor (1962) suggests that spatial orientation (awareness of one's body in space in relation to other objects) depends largely on organism mobility. He contends that movement enables one to experience concretely the relationships between distances and sizes of objects. He believes that, until the child experiences the environment from many vantage points, her perceptual perspectives remain immature.

KEPHART

Newell C. Kephart, a special educator, believes that well-integrated patterns of motor behavior are prerequisite to environmental exploration and learning. In his view, motor proficiency is therefore essential to development of perceptual integrity, including laterality, directionality, postural flexibility, body image, and ocular control. Kephart contends that inadequate development of motor proficiencies inhibits the child's later development of the ability to perform more sophisticated tasks. His belief is based on the assumption that acquisition of learning tools is a hierarchical process and that advanced learning depends on fundamental, motor-based experiences.

In Kephart's opinion, separation of perceptual experiences from motor experiences is probably not possible. He stresses combining perceptual and motor experiences so the child can match perceptual and motor information. Perceptual inefficiency is alleged to correlate with academic failure.

He believes that a child engages in more complex motor activity to develop increasingly more complex perceptual competencies. Kephart alleges that activity and resultant perceptual competence become increasingly complex in the following hierarchical order:

- **Posture and Balance.** Kephart, like Barsch, believes that achieving control over the force of gravity represents the most basic conflict that confronts the human organism. Kephart surmises that without posture and balance, the child is not ready for efficient movement. Children with poor posture and balance are incapable of the most rudimentary forms of movement, and therefore are not ready to learn through movement. Kephart believes that the child with poor balance, who should be learning through movement-centered experiences, is instead distracted by poor balance. Efficient posture and balance set the stage for locomotion.

- **Locomotion.** Through locomotion skills, children can explore their environment. They are no longer limited to those sensory experiences within reach. The child with efficient locomotion moves freely in quest of sensory experiences; organizing and systematizing those experiences gives meaning to the child's world. Inefficient locomotion limits movement and requires concentration on the mastery of locomotor skills. The child's attention is drawn away from the productive encounter with sensory experiences.

- **Contact.** Although contact experiences often occur before locomotion, they are limited in quantity and quality by immobility. Once the child has achieved proficiency in locomotion, contact (manipulative) experiences increase and enable the child to understand objects.

- **Receipt and Propulsion.** Following contact (manipulative) experiences, the child propels objects by throwing, kicking, and striking, and receives objects by catching. Through these activities, Kephart believes that the child acquires an understanding of size, velocity, direction, and distance.

The goal of perceptual-motor experience, according to Kephart, is for the child to make *motor generalizations*, which involve the ability to apply learned perceptual competence to other life situations. To Kephart the skills are not as important as the ability to generalize precepts and concepts derived from those skills.

Hallahan and Kauffman (1991) have found that many developmental psychologists have disagreed with Kephart and maintain that visual development occurs chronologically before motor skills. Additionally, critics question Kephart's methods and other process training programs on the grounds that they have not documented their effectiveness. It is largely on the basis of these criticisms that process training is not as popular as it once was.

AYRES

A. J. Ayres (1960, 1972, 1977) believes that the integrity of higher brain centers (i.e., the cortex) is dependent on the supporting integrity of lower brain centers. Ayres points out that kinesthetic, vestibular, and tactile stimulation activities affect the brain stem and produce improved cortical functions. She contends that both motor and academic tasks are cortical functions that can be improved through her activity-centered programs. Her procedures are appropriate only for children with learning difficulties and sensorimotor deficits. According to Ayres, the child with learning difficulties who exhibits sound sensorimotor behavior should respond positively to other treatment (she does not specify).

Ayres is associated with "sensory integration," a phrase implying that a person's motor responses are appropriate to the sensory input. Through improved sensorimotor integration, the individual's central nervous system (CNS) supposedly achieves a higher degree of functional sophistication, which results in improved motor and academic performance.

In questioning the validity of Ayres' premises, Cratty (1989) notes that Ayres' research indicates that academic learning, including auditory perception and reading proficiency, appears to function *independently* of sensory integration proficiencies. In effect, Ayres found that kinesthetic, tactile, and vestibular proficiencies are *not* predictive of auditory perception or language and reading proficiencies. For this reason, Cratty questions Ayres' allegations that improvements in kinesthetic, tactile, and vestibular functions will result in improved academic performance.

Ayres' approach to treating learning disorders through movement-centered experiences is similar to that of Kephart and Barsch. Although specifics differ, each believes that perceptual and academic functions will respond positively to sensori-motor experiences.

Cratty (1989) negatively summarizes Ayres' sensory integration theory:

> The writings of Dr. Ayres possibly, even probably, have useful clinical methods, including tactile stimulation, to be applied to the severely handicapped. Overall, though, the promises held for sensory integration therapy are not reflected in the clinical-descriptive research presently available. It may be a useful clinical tool, but only in the hands of one who is prepared to obtain additional data and can carefully interpret the results. When asked about the validity of these methods, physical educators might direct the questioner to data-based literature and current reviews of sensory integration. (p. 82)

GETMAN

G. N. Getman suggests that children who do not develop minimal levels of coordination or neuromuscular control will experience difficulty or failure when confronted with formal academic tasks. Getman, an optometrist, is concerned with the role that movement plays in a child's visual readiness skills. Getman and Kane (1964) believe that cognitive development is preceded by "physiological readiness" to learn:

> Remedial instruction assumes (or ignores) physiological readiness to profit from instruction. Apparently the remedy seems to be not to keep working on the second story of the house of learning, but to repair the foundations so that they can support greater learning weights above. Physiological readiness cannot be skipped over any more than a second story of a house can rest on a shaky, inadequate foundation. (p. 1)

DOMAN AND DELACATO

Doman and Delacato (Delacato, 1959) have developed a motor therapy program called *neurological organization*. Although the authors of this theory are not proponents of perceptual-motor development, they believe that their program of "patterning" improves the learning abilities of children with brain injuries. The Doman-Delacato theory states that failure to learn may be the result of inadequate neurological organization of the central nervous system, diagnosed by the absence of specific motor patterns. Delacato purports to determine inadequate neurological organization through motor testing, and to remedy that inadequacy with a strictly supervised program of motor activity.

According to these authors, brain hemisphere dominance results from concentration on activities that stimulate the dominant side. A primary concern in achieving neurological organization is hemispheric dominance. Conversely, they recommend avoidance of activities that stimulate the nondominant hemisphere, because such activities might interfere with establishment of cerebral dominance.

The program espoused by Delacato is the most controversial of motor therapies. Research and thought in the professional community do not support his neurological organization theory and practice. Support is substantial, however, in the lay community, particularly among parents who believe the Delacato's methods have positively influenced their children with special needs.

QUESTIONING THE VALIDITY OF PERCEPTUAL-MOTOR THEORY AND PRACTICE

Perceptual-motor practice as a tool for learning is supported more by seemingly logical theoretical musings than by scientific evidence. Indeed, when carefully controlled studies are reviewed, one finds cause to question the claims made by prominent perceptual-motor advocates.

Cratty (1989) has been relentless in his efforts to determine the efficacy of perceptual-motor theories and practices. He concludes that perceptual-motor advocates have oversimplified or misunderstood the child's developmental process. He recognizes, however, that behavioral attributes are often affected positively by perceptual-motor experiences. He suggests that the child may improve performance simply as a result of such factors as receiving attention (social stimulation), developing a longer attention span, or developing coordination that improves handwriting.

Salvia and Ysseldyke (1991) make a strong statement regarding perceptual motor training: "There is a tremendous lack of empirical evidence to support the claim that specific perceptual-motor training facilitates the acquisition of academic skills or improves the chances of academic success. Perceptual-motor training will improve *perceptual-motor* functioning" (p. 322).

For children who experience a perceptual disorder, the problem results from an inability to use one or more of the senses to recognize, discriminate, and interpret stimuli (Haring & McCormick, 1990). Regarding children labeled as "clumsy or severely awkward," Sudgen and Keogh (1990) estimate that through unselected samples covering the early school years, 5% to 9% would fit into this low-performance category.

Heightened perceptual awareness, as espoused by perceptual-motor advocates, may not necessarily contribute to the desired results. The desired outcomes may result instead from social development, improved self-concept, and increased attention span.

The literature indicates that motor experiences may be a catalyst that stimulates functional development. The fact that many children who encounter learning difficulties also exhibit perceptual-motor deficits is sufficient reason to consider perceptual-motor programming for some children with special needs.

COMPONENTS OF PERCEPTUAL-MOTOR EFFICIENCY

Perceptual-motor efficiency, like physical fitness, is a general term that covers a broad spectrum of perceptual attributes. Unlike the components of physical and motor fitness, however, the components of perceptual-motor efficiency seem closely inter-related. For example, locomotor awareness is dependent on visual perception, posture is related to balance, tactile perception to body awareness, and so on. Components of perceptual-motor efficiency are discussed separately to ensure that the total picture does not obscure individual components. When, therefore, a balance activity is suggested, that activity should produce tactile perception, body awareness, visual perception, and kinesthetic experiences simultaneously. This will hold true for almost any activity that fosters perceptual-motor efficiency.

Components of perceptual-motor efficiency include balance, postural and locomotor awareness, visual perception (including localization, tracking, and spatial awareness), auditory perception, kinesthetic perception, tactile perception, body awareness, laterality, and directionality.

BALANCE

Balance is important because the ability to control one's center of gravity is critical to development of skilled movement patterns. A person has good balance when an effective working relationship can be maintained between points of support and center of gravity. Three types of balance (Figure 8.1) are static balance (e.g., standing on one foot), dynamic balance (e.g., walking the balance beam), and balance with the medium moving (e.g., walking on a bus in motion). Perceptual-motor advocates generally allege that persons with good balance can focus attention on more important tasks and keep their balance. These theorists believe that good balance often indicates functional integrity of the nervous system.

Most tests of physical and motor ability include balance in the test battery, but controversy exists as to whether general balance is a motor performance factor. Critics suggest that balance is highly specific, and that any specific balance assessment item measure only the *specific* motor skill being observed. Balance activities are pre-

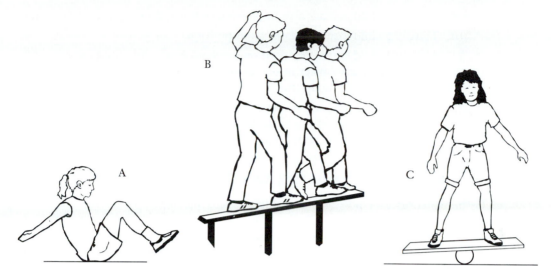

FIGURE 8.1   Three types of balance. (A) Static balance. (B) Dynamic balance. (C) Balance with the medium moving. (Redrawn from Moran & Kalakian, 1977, pp. 47, 48.)

sented here despite this controversy, because the possibility of achieving a number of desirable results transcends the controversy.

The following activities are recommended:

1. Have the child assume and maintain various body configurations on a static surface.
2. Have the child attempt to maintain various body configurations while on a moving surface (tilt board or lazy Susan).
3. Have the child maintain balance by contacting the surface with any three body parts (e.g., both knees and one hand).
4. Have the child tuck-sit with feet and buttocks touching the floor, with buttocks only touching the floor, and V-sit and pass a ball under the legs.
5. Have the child straddle a large padded barrel and maintain balance as the barrel is rolled to the left and right.
6. Have the child sit on a T-stool. Engage in progressively more distracting activities (i.e., manipulative activities) as balance improves.
7. Have the child assume the stork stand position (left foot, then right foot). Variations include eyes closed, on tiptoe, hands on hips, hands over head, hand free to aid in balancing.
8. Have the child assume a pike from the back lying position (V-sit).

9. Have the child assume a swan position (left leg, then right leg).

10. Have the child assume a knee swan position.

11. Have the child sit (or stand on one or both feet) while holding a moderately heavy object in one or both hands. Have the child move the object around the body (this constantly shifts one's center of gravity).

12. Have the child sit back-to-back with a partner, partner's arms interlocked, feet drawn in toward the buttocks. At a given signal, both partners rise simultaneously and carefully to a back-to-back position.

POSTURAL AND LOCOMOTOR AWARENESS

The human organism possesses the ability, need, and desire to move. Almost all human functions exhibit some movement component. In turn, movement is the primary medium through which humans find purpose and achieve objectives. Barsch (1965) suggests that locomotion is entwined inseparably with human survival potential. When an individual experiences movement deficits, Barsch suggest that that individual then become dependent on others for survival.

Because perception occurs through movement, the ability to select and control movement (i.e., postural and locomotor awareness) becomes significant when teaching children. Postural and locomotor awareness activities assist the individual in realizing movement potential. The more effectively one can move, the more one is able to make direct contact with and take control of (rather than being controlled by) the environment. Postural and locomotor awareness, a facilitator of effective movement, precipitates comfortable feelings as one moves through the environment. Secure, threat-free movement minimizes stress. Easy movement also minimizes distractions, thus maximizing perceptual fluency.

Postural and locomotor awareness in children is developed by ensuring that movement opportunities exist. For a variety of reasons, ranging from overprotection to misdirected effort to ignorance of the child's needs, movement experiences are sometimes not available to children with special needs.

As previously pointed out, postural awareness involves the ability to cope effectively with the force of gravity. Control of gravitational force manifests itself in the child's ability to assume and maintain appropriate postural attitudes. Postural awareness among children with special needs and particularly among children with orthopedic disabilities is highly individual. Postural skills are the foundation for locomotion and may have to be developed using a brace, crutch, prosthesis, or wheelchair-assisted ambulation. The goal is not a predesignated postural model but is rather an individualized goal that considers the person's anatomical and physiological strengths.

Development of locomotor awareness is also highly individual among children with special needs. The gait, locomotor skills, and needs of a child with cerebral palsy differ from those of a child with spina bifida who walks using braces and crutches. People using wheelchairs require different skills from those who walk with an above-knee prosthesis. All ambulation is not walking, and all walking is not bipedal.

Effective ambulation for any child must be determined within the context of the child's anatomical, physiological, and, sometime, psychological needs. Some people capable of brace- and crutch-assisted walking opt for wheelchair ambulation because it is physically less taxing or because they believe that sitting ambulation appears more normal to others than dragging paralyzed limbs behind crutches.

In perceptual-motor development, ambulation is important because it allows exploration of the environment. Exploration leads in turn to stimulation of the senses and thus to perceptual development.

The following activities are suggested for development of postural and loco-motor awareness.

1. Children may participate in rolling (e.g., log roll), crawling, creeping, walking, hopping (using both left and right feet), galloping (in all directions and leading with both left and right foot), sliding, jumping, leaping, running, and skipping activities. These skills can be taught directly or experienced in almost all activities. Movement versatility and experimentation should be encouraged.

2. Wheelchair ambulators may move to predesignated stations. Circular, straight, zigzag, and random direction patterns should be used. Such activities are equally applicable for nonwheelchair ambulators.

3. Include change in direction and pace (e.g., fast-slow, stop-start, left-right, backward-forward) in all activities.

4. Ask all ambulators to respond to the teacher's movements. Alternate between characteristic ambulation, use of crutches, and a wheelchair.

5. Have children walk, hop, leap, or jump between designated spots.

6. Roll a ball toward but out of reach of the child. Ask the child to intercept the ball before the ball stops (i.e., stop the ball with chair wheel, crutch, foot, or hands). Encourage the child to get to the ball as soon as possible.

7. Have the child demonstrate several different ways to move from point *A* to point *B*.

8. Have children crawl through tunnels and mazes.

9. Have children bounce on a bounce board, trampoline, or other device. Those unable to bounce may experience bouncing by sitting or lying (whichever is appropriate) on the trampoline bed, and by being bounced gently by the teacher.

10. Have children walk on sinking tires (i.e., automobile tires without rims).

11. Pair children with like individuals (or dissimilar) with disabilities. Designate one as the leader who makes some purposeful motion. The other imitates the purposeful motion (if disabilities are similar) or makes an alternate motion to accomplish the same objective (if disabilities are dissimilar).

Footprints on floor designate where to step.

12. Have children ambulate on level and uneven terrain. Help each child discover the skills of ambulation appropriate to her unique needs.

VISUAL PERCEPTION

Visual perception is more than seeing; it involves making value judgments and interpreting what one sees. Because persons rely heavily on the sensory modality (sight), the ability to derive meaning from visual perception is of utmost importance.

The development of visual perception is considered to be dependent on a broad base of motor experiences. Visual perceptual-motor experiences occur when one simultaneously sees and manipulates an object. Manipulation, the motor component, is important because there is concreteness in the physical manipulation of objects. The relative concreteness of physically manipulating an object coupled with the simultaneous visual experience develops a visual impression about that object. These simultaneous impressions and judgments provide the basis for visual perceptual-motor efficiency.

As visual perception becomes more acute and visual impressions are firmly established, physical manipulation becomes less crucial. Repeated visual perceptual-motor experiences eventually render the motor component unnecessary or less necessary. For example, a child who manipulates a stuffed toy also concentrates visually on the toy. The visual information about the toy is reinforced and augmented by the tactual sensations. Eventually, visual information alone provides sufficient sensory input to make an accurate visual judgment (perception).

When objects start to move in the environment, youngsters encounter more visual problems to solve. The child must *detect* motion and *track* moving objects, as well as *predict* their future locations. Keogh and Sugden (1985) state the following: "When an object is moving they [the children] also must use all of the visual skills needed when the environment is stationary and do so more continuously. The object is no longer a static picture of a moment in time; it is constantly changing and thus requires continuous perceptual *reorganization*, for example, we must be able to know that other persons are walking, must be able to keep them in sight, and must be able to know where they will be in another few steps" (p. 289).

Movement experiences are vital when developing **visual tracking and fixating** capabilities. Visual tracking involves willful direction and focusing of one's eyes from one visual stimulus to another (e.g., reading from left to right across a page). The visual tracking experience actually is *not* uninterrupted eye movement, but is in fact composed of minute, sequential fixations as the eyes pursue a visual stimulus. In the tracking process, the most meaningful visual information comes during the points of fixation. Another form of visual tracking involves directing and focusing one's eyes on a single moving stimulus such as a moving automobile or a thrown ball. Either experience may be further complicated by the individual's moving simultaneously. Yet another form of visual tracking occurs when one's eyes are directed and focused on a stationary object while the viewer is moving. Physical education and recreation movement experiences provide many opportunities for enhancing visual-motor coordination, visual tracking, and visual fixating capabilities.

Visual spatial awareness facilitates making judgments about distances between objects and between oneself and the objects. Spatial awareness evolves as a result of experiencing distances while moving. Having experienced distances as a concomitant outcome of movement, the individual eventually understands distances without actually having to travel them.

Visual spatial awareness allows correct interpretation of perceptual distortions. Perception of any phenomenon changes as one's vantage point changes. For example, a ball at the far end of the gymnasium appears extremely small, yet may be identical in size to a larger ball appearing in the foreground. Visual spatial awareness not only facilitates a judgment of the distant ball's characteristics, but also of one's distance from the ball. Physical education and recreation skills that encourage movement through and exploration of the environment are conducive to the development of visual spatial awareness.

Figure-ground discrimination is the ability to focus and concentrate visually on a specific stimulus when many stimuli are being received simultaneously. A figure-ground discrimination problem involves focusing on one ball against a cluttered background. A baseball catcher might experience difficulty seeing a ball thrown from the outfield against a background of variously colored signs or against the outfield fence. The ball (the figure) and the multicolored signs (the ground) are the components in the figure-ground problem.

Children rely heavily on visual perception to learn, and their learning environment, both formal and informal, is replete with figure-ground challenges. Movement-centered experiences in which the teacher controls figure-ground relationships can significantly improve the child's figure-ground discrimination. Through gradually increased background complexity (or decrease in the object's stimulus value), the child can achieve greater figure-ground awareness.

The following activities are suggested to develop visual perception and its components:

1. Provide opportunities for children to play with numerous objects. Whenever possible, children should be permitted to sort through, see, and simultaneously manipulate objects in the environment.

2. Have the child ambulate across a room and visually spot a brightly colored picture on the wall. The picture can be of the child's own making, which is a visual perceptual-motor experience.

3. Ask the child to finger-trace drawings prepared by the teacher. Forms to be traced might include straight lines followed by geometric forms. Place a picture of an automobile on one side of a page with a garage on the other side. Draw parallel lines approximately 1 in. apart to connect the automobile with the garage. Ask the child to trace the path of the car into the garage. Create similar additional examples.

4. Place large numbers, letters, or geometric forms on the play surface. Ask the child to walk heel to toe on the lines that form the figures.

5. Have the child stand at varying distances from a wall and roll, throw, or bounce a brightly colored ball at the wall. Have the child retrieve the ball. Emphasize visual concentration on the ball. Vary the background to control the figure-ground relationship between ball and wall.

6. Place a ladder horizontally on the ground or a few inches above the ground. Ask the child to walk the length of the ladder stepping between, but not touching, the rungs, or have the child stop *on* the rungs.

7. Hold a broomstick at different heights, depending on the capability and characteristics of the child, and have the child duck under, step over, or slip around but not touch the stick.

8. Tie the ends of a 10-ft rope together so the rope forms a circle. Place the rope circle on the ground. Pretend that the circle is a mud puddle, and have the children leap or jump across (but not into) the puddle.

9. Have assistants hold two tightly stretched, parallel ropes at approximately elbow height and slightly more than shoulder width apart. Have the child ambulate forward (backward, sideways) between the ropes but not touch either rope.

Student stepping over wand.

10. Have children push a small ball as they creep around the playing surface.

11. Have the child throw two different-colored objects simultaneously. One or both hands may be used. Have the child determine, without traversing the distance, which object went the farthest. Use reference cues in the form of lines perpendicular to the object's trajectory to assist the child in making distance judgments. To judge distance initially, the child may actually have to traverse the distances traveled by the objects.

12. Have each child place one shoe (or mitten) in a pile. Stir the pile. Have the children compare and visually identify their own clothing article. Have each child retrieve his article and put it on.

AUDITORY PERCEPTION

Auditory perception is more than hearing. It is the ability to translate what one hears into meaningful information. The ability to understand sound develops, in some measure, from the ability to move. Movement produces sound and sets the stage for auditory perception development. From movement experiences, a child observes that different movements cause different sounds and she comes to understand the cause-effect relationship between movement and the sounds created.

The child also realizes similarities and differences in sounds that emanate from different objects. The mass and consistency of objects create different sounds when the objects are manipulated, but the objects remain mute until accidentally or purposefully contacted and manipulated.

Initially, the individual encounters through movement many auditory sensations that stimulate auditory perception. This sound perception, linked inseparably with motor experiences, becomes auditory perceptual-motor awareness.

Repeated auditory perceptual-motor experiences enable the individual to comprehend sounds caused by someone or something else. Having learned through motor experience that circumstances result in sound emissions, the individual does not need to create sound or to be in its immediate vicinity to make a value judgment about the sound. The motor component in auditory perception becomes less crucial, and the individual's repertoire of sound and auditory perception experiences provides understanding of sound concepts merely by hearing them.

Auditory spatial awareness is related closely to and depends on movement experiences. Precepts and concepts of up-down, near-far, behind-in front, and left-right develop as movement capabilities allow exploration of a sound-filled environment. The individual, through movement, soon understands that sound emanate from different directions and that sounds change over distances as one moves nearer-farther from a sound source (i.e., the sound seems to become progressively louder-quieter). Soon, the child, having perceived sound from many vantage points, becomes adept at judging the distance, direction, direction of travel, and characteristics of the sound.

The following activities are suggested to develop auditory perceptual-motor efficiency and its components:

1. Rhythm band activities that promote auditory perceptual-motor awareness, because rhythm instruments demonstrate cause-effect relationships between movement and sound.

2. Rhythm and dance activities that require movement toward, away from, and around sound sources and provide auditory spatial orientation.

3. Exercises in which the child keeps time with an audible cadence.

4. Creative motor responses to recorded sounds of various animals.

5. Activities in which the child makes an appropriate quantity of motor responses on hearing a number of sounds (e.g., the child may be asked to execute as many hops as there are drumbeats).

6. Activities in which the child is asked to make appropriate responses to sounds (e.g., Walk when you hear the bell; stop when you hear the whistle).

7. Activity that involves analyzing the origin of a sound. Show the child two small, clean paint cans. Place two marbles in one can and seal the lid. Place one marble in the other can and seal the lid. Now mix up the cans so the child does not know which can is which. Have her shake and manipulate each can and then guess how many marbles are in each.

8. Activities in which children play with balls that have sound producers inside. As the ball is manipulated, cause-effect relationships are fostered between movement and sound. Sound emissions from the ball as it is rolled and thrown allow children to track the sound. Tracking the movement of sound develops auditory spatial awareness.

9. Auditory experiences in which sounds range in intensity from quiet to loud. Have children become as small as possible when sounds are quiet; have them become progressively larger as sound becomes more intense. Use recorded music and control the volume, or sounds of a drum, tom-tom, or tambourine can be altered by varying striking strength.

10. Auditory experiences in which the pitch ranges from low to high. Have children become as small as possible when pitch is low and as large as possible when pitch is high. Notes or chords from a piano are appropriate.

11. Activities in which blindfolded children are asked to turn toward (ambulate toward) a sound.

12. Activities in which children play with balls of various weights and materials. The child should realize that construction materials, weight, and size contribute to the sounds that things make. Such play might involve different playing surfaces (e.g., turf, wood, rubber, asphalt, concrete) to help the child realize that dissimilar surfaces also affect sound. These activities help the child learn to discriminate among sounds and to judge an object by the sounds it makes.

KINESTHETIC PERCEPTION

Kinesthetic Perception is an awareness of one's body position in space. It enables one to conceptualize configurations that the body assumes and the body's relationship to its immediate environment. Kinesthetic perception is involved in judgments such as whether or not one is moving, and if moving, how rapidly. It provides awareness of the body's form whether moving or standing still. If moving, kinesthetic perception helps determine whether one is moving forward, backward, sideways, at an angle, in an arc, or in any combination. If the individual is airborne, it enables determination of speed, trajectory, and distance from the surface. In these situations, kinesthetic perception is an important safety skill.

Kinesthetic perception is an extension of the previously discussed perceptual-motor attribute of postural and locomotor awareness. Postural maintenance and locomotion require competence in kinesthetic perception. Postural and locomotor awareness are, however, extremely basic and cannot be the sole stimulant for development of kinesthetic perception.

Almost any activity that requires an awareness and control of body position in space stimulates kinesthetic perception. Sage (1984) warns that participation in general activities may not always provoke kinesthetic development: "Practice in a wide variety of motor activities will presumably result in some improved body

A

B

(A) Ask children to become tall when the music is loud.
(B) Have them become small when the music is quiet.

sitional control, balance, and movement control, but large general improvements in kinesthesis probably do not occur" (p. 184). The instructor should remember that if a student has a static balance weakness, then the prescribed activities should relate specifically to static balance.

Activities that enhance kinesthetic perception should be challenging yet not frustrating to the children. The following are examples of motor activities and equipment typically used to enhance kinesthetic perception:

1. Almost all motor activities that provide sensations of movement.

2. Activities requiring changes in body or body segment direction, starting and stopping, or fast-slow movement.

3. Playground equipment, including slides, swings, spring-mounted rocking horses, and jungle gyms.

4. Activities in which the child tries to stand on one foot with eyes closed and not lose balance. Children exhibiting low levels of kinesthetic perception may have to do this skill with eyes open. Another variation for more highly skilled children involves standing on the tiptoe of the supporting leg. Eyes may be open or closed, depending on the child's performance level.

5. Activities that provide opportunity to crawl and creep through improvised tunnels. Children should not touch the top or sides of the tunnel. More highly skilled children may be able to crawl and creep backward through the tunnel.

6. Activities in which the child holds a 24-in. rope in her hands. The rope should hang in front of the body like a jump rope, with the lower part of the rope at approximately knee height. Have the child jump forward over the rope so that, on completion of the jump, the child's body is in front of the rope.

7. Activities in which the child walks a circle marked on the playing surface. After several trials, have the child walk the circle without looking at the line. As necessary, suggest that the child look at the line for reorientation.

8. Activities in which the child lies on a safety mat with a line drawn down its center. Have the child lie flat on the mat with arms at sides and body extended. Have the child logroll down the length of the mat, straight to the end rather than off to the side. Have the child roll to the left and right.

9. Activities with scooter boards that enable the child to propel across the playing surface, preferably a smooth floor. The child may sit or lie on the scooter board and propel in any direction (Figure 8.2).

10. Activities with balancing devices including beams, balance (vestibular) boards, bounce boards, and lazy Susans.

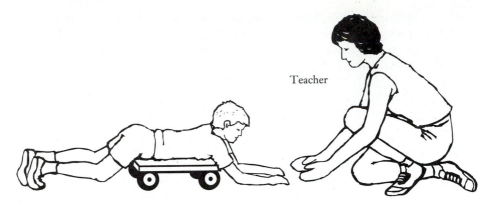

Teacher

FIGURE 8.2   **Scooter activity with teacher assistance.** (Reprinted from Moran & Kalakian, 1977, p. 73.)

11. Activities in which the child ambulates through a zigzag obstacle course, trying not to touch any object marking the course.

12. Activities in which the child leans in different directions, one direction at a time, trying not to lose balance. The children can stand, kneel, or assume an all-fours position. Coincidentally, the children form concepts about the body position that is most stable.

Scooter activity without assistance.

TACTILE PERCEPTION

Tactile perception is the ability to interpret sensations of touch. Touching, feeling, and manipulating objects are dependent on movement to experience tactual sensations. Certainly tactile sensations are experienced by passive as well as active persons, but tactile experiences are more numerous when actively pursued.

Tactile awareness is important for learners who, regardless of chronological age, are in the early stages of coping with abstractions. Tactile experiences tend to be concrete. To experience tactually, one touches, feels, holds, or manipulates. Such actual physical contact provides concrete knowledge of the world.

Tactual perception is important in developing manual dexterity and fine motor skill. Tactile perception is the primary informant when determining how an object has been grasped. It is also the primary informant when one formulates judgments about objects that cannot be seen but can be touched.

Tactile perception serves as an adjunct to visual perception. Simultaneously seeing and feeling are often more informative than a single perception from either sensory modality.

Because tactile perception is prompted by action, it is facilitated by movement experiences that emphasize the sensation of touch. The following activities exemplify tactile perception through motor experience:

1. Place several familiar objects in a paper bag. Have the child identify objects by feel before pulling them from the bag.

2. Fill two pans with water, one warm and one cool. Have the child immerse her hands in one pan and then in the other. Have her determine which pan of water is warmer. Repeat this activity using foot and elbow contacts.

3. Have the child touch objects with his feet, and without visual or other sensory input, identify the things touched.

4. Permit the child to walk barefoot over different surfaces—smooth, rough, warm, cool, damp, or dry.

5. Have children roll, crawl, and creep over different textured surfaces (e.g., tile floor, lawn, safety mats, gymnasium floor, carpet). If possible, have them roll, crawl, and creep over many varied surfaces during a relatively short time. This experience enables a child to perceive tactile sensations with the entire body, rather than just hands or feet.

6. Place a length of tape in a straight line on the floor. Permit the child to walk barefoot, and without looking for the tape, feel the tape with his feet.

7. Place a piece of tape approximately 2 in. square on the flat surface of a $1 \times 12 \times 12$-in. board. Place the board in the child's lap, tape side down. Have the child feel the tape side of the board with her fingers

and tell her to stop feeling as soon as she locates the tape. Have her hold that spot and turn the board over to see if she did in fact locate the tape.

8. Have the child play with several differently shaped and textured toys. Encourage the child to simultaneously manipulate and look. Tactual sensations supplement and enhance visual perception and vice versa.

9. Have the child string beads. For some children whose manual dexterity and tactile perceptions are somewhat lacking, use bolts or blocks of wood with large holes. As manual dexterity and tactual awareness improve, substitute smaller objects and lighter rope or string.

10. Place three square blocks or balls of different sizes (same texture) inside a bag. Have the child (without looking) feel each object, and pull the largest object from the bag. The child should then empty the bag to see if the choice was correct.

11. Encourage children to engage in sand play for tactile stimulation.

12. Touch the child's back or other body parts with one or more fingers. Without visual access to the experience, have the child identify how many fingers are pressing against her body. Other sensations involving tactile discrimination without aid of visual cues might include warm-cool, wet-dry, rough-smooth, or soft-firm.

Sand play provides tactile stimulation.

BODY AWARENESS

Body awareness, sometimes called **body image**, refers to an awareness of body parts and segments. It encompasses the ability to name body parts and an awareness of one's body parts as one moves.

Body awareness is an important initial step in becoming aware of one's environment. Essentially, one must know oneself before organizing and systematizing the external world. This suggests that body awareness must be established before establishing the components to be discussed next—laterality and directionality.

Body awareness activities focus attention on body segments and parts. Such activities help the individual to understand that the body has two sides that work together, in opposition, or individually. Body awareness activities also focus attention on capabilities and limitations of body parts and segments. The following are examples of motor activities used to develop body awareness:

1. Swimming activities promote body awareness through the sensation of movement through water.

2. Have the child identify ears, eyes, hips, nose, arms, knees, elbows, toes, ankles, and shoulders.

3. Place a bright-colored ribbon or loose elastic band on a body part or segment to draw attention to it as the child moves about.

4. Attach a jingle bell to various body parts and segments. The bell's jingle calls attention to that body part or segment. This activity is most successful when working with one child or with a small group of children. With larger groups, the noise is a distraction.

5. Have the child execute several elementary motor skills while watching his image in a mirror.

6. Have the child pose or move before a mirror, then have her attempt to draw a picture of her movement.

7. Have children stand facing the teacher. Provide adequate space between children so movements can be made freely. Tell them to "Do as I do." Move your arms and legs in various combinations. Movements may be unilateral, bilateral, and cross-lateral (e.g., left arm only, right arm and left arm simultaneously, left arm and right leg simultaneously).

8. Have the child lie on his back and move one or more body parts by sliding them along the floor. Point to (do not touch) the body parts to be moved, so the child does not get tactual cues. Have the child make unilateral, bilateral, and cross-lateral movements. Movement patterns in this activity resemble patterns experienced when playing angels in the snow.

9. Secure a weighted belt to a body segment while the child participates in several motor experiences. The weight should be heavy enough to

Observing one's shadow develops body awareness.

create an awareness of that segment but not so heavy that it inhibits movements. The belt may be moved from segment to segment.

10. Have the children stand facing a wall or screen with their backs to an overhead projector. Turn on the projector so they see their body image shadowed against the wall or screen. Have them move in a variety of ways for an immediate cause-effect feedback, which develops body awareness.

11. Introduce and play games or activities like hokey pokey, which requires the child to activate one body part at a time.

12. Have the children engage in activities before a large window fan (or outdoors on a breezy day). Air movement, like water resistance, enables children to feel various body segments as they move.

LATERALITY AND DIRECTIONALITY

Laterality is an internal awareness that the body has a left and right side. **Directionality** is the extension of laterality into the external world. Directionality is thought to develop largely as a result of movement experience. In the hierarchy of perceptual-motor development, body image or body awareness emerges first, followed by laterality. Laterality development is thought to be the foundation of the subsequent emergence of directionality.

Establishing lateral preference is believed to be important to development of laterality. Well-established lateral preference enables the individual to distinguish between left and right. Certain learning difficulties are thought to result in part from a lack of lateral preference or from a mixed preference. A common problem associated with laterality inadequacies is reversals. Common reversals include substitution of a *p* for a *q* and vice versa, or substitution or a *b* for a *d* and vice versa. A child who does not have well-established left-right orientation may perceive little or no difference between these letters.

Another theory regarding reversals supports the view that development of body awareness is sequential—first laterality, the directionality. Until he is cognizant of body parts and segments (body image), the child cannot become fully aware that the body has sides (laterality). Until laterality enables the child to deal with the concept of sidedness in internal space (the body), he is unready to deal with the complex concepts of sidedness and direction in external space (the environment). The child who has not full conceptualized sidedness and direction in external space may, for example, view *b*s and *d*s or *p*s and *q*s as simply undifferentiated circles with lines attached. He may unwittingly write "bog" instead of "dog." The child who unknowingly holds a picture book upside down does not understand sidedness, including "up" and "down."

Directionality is also thought to give dimension to space. A child with good directionality development may be capable of conceptualizing right-left, above-below, in front-behind, and various combinations.

Directionality and spatial orientation or awareness are closely related perceptual attributes. Each gives dimension to space and enables the child to determine where he is in relation to other phenomena in the environment. Motor experiences that enhance development of laterality and directionality include the following:

1. Provide a variety of throwing and kicking experiences that encourage selection and use of the dominant or preferred side of the body.

2. Have the child participate in rhythm and dance activities that require movement in many directions.

3. Encourage movement activities in all conceivable directions, using each of the basic locomotor skills.

4. Have the child wad up a 10-ft segment of rope and throw it high in the air. When the rope lands on the playing surface, have the child walk heel to toe from one end of the rope to the other.

5. Draw or tape geometric figures, letters, numbers, and words on the playing surface. Have the child walk heel to toe along the full length of the lines that comprise each figure.

6. Have the child walk forward and backward on a balance beam. The child may perform before a full-length mirror to help conceptualize direction changes.

7. Have the child walk in both directions sideways on the balance beam. Be sure that she walks with the left foot as the lead foot and then with the right foot as the lead foot.

8. Place safety mats on the playing surface, and have children roll from one end of the mat to the other, rolling both to left and right.

9. Draw a straight line or lane on the playing surface. Provide an old tire or hula hoop and have the child roll the tire or hoop straight down the line or between the lines that form the lane. The child may walk sideways, forward, or backward in performing this activity.

10. Place brightly colored circles randomly on the floor. Have the child leap, hop, or jump in any order he chooses from one circle to another. Encourage movement in all directions if the child does not do so spontaneously.

11. Have the child respond similarly to the teacher or a peer who is making rapid, sequential direction changes (i.e., forward-backward, right-left, forward diagonal left-right, backward diagonal left-right).

12. Have the child respond to large flash cards that have arrows pointing in different directions.

EVALUATING PERCEPTUAL-MOTOR EFFICIENCY

All motor activities possess some perceptual-motor component, some activities more than others. Success with any activity in the motor performance domain depends on the person's level of perceptual-motor competence.

Perceptual-motor assessment typically serves one of several purposes. In some cases, the perceptual-motor skills of an entire class of students are assessed in an effort to identify those having perceptual-motor difficulties. Appropriate physical education training programs can then be developed to prevent further learning difficulties. Students who perform poorly on these tests are said to demonstrate perceptual-motor problems, which are thought to contribute negatively to academic learning capabilities. In other cases, youngsters having academic problems are assessed in an effort to identify the extent to which perceptual-motor difficulties may be causing lack of academic success. Finally, identification of perceptual-motor disabilities is imperative so the adapted physical educator can begin immediate remediation activities for the "clumsy, awkward" child. A lack of smooth and efficient body movement has left many youngsters with tremendous feelings of inferiority. For these children, who so often experience failure in physical education class, the future looks grim unless appropriate programming is initiated immediately! The negative carry over must not be underestimated. Some professionals believe that a major part of an individual's personality is affected adversely if the youngster is forced continually to take part in frustrating motor activities at which she always fails.

Although assessment identifies physical and motor deficiencies, it does not generate labels or identify causes of deficiency. For example, deficiencies may be symptoms of deeper underlying causes. Werder and Kalakian (1985, p. 17) list the following possible reasons for poor performance: "(1) attitudinal or environmental influences, (2) emotional or behavioral disturbances, (3) minimal neurological dysfunction (i.e., mild ataxia), (4) delayed development of the central nervous system, (5) muscular weakness, and (6) structural abnormalities." The instructor must consider using the team approach, that is, calling on allied professionals including therapists, the special educator, the school nurse, and the child's pediatrician.

Tests and survey of perceptual-motor efficiency vary in sophistication. Authorities tend to agree that more definitive perceptual-motor assessment tools are needed, but Salvia and Ysseldyke (1991) issue this warning:

> What the majority of the research *has* shown is that perceptual-motor tests are unreliable. We do not know what they measure, because they do not measure anything consistently. Unlike the majority of intelligence and achievement tests, the tests used to assess perceptual-motor skills in children are technically inadequate. ...The real danger is that the reliance on such tests in planning interventions for children may actually lead to assigning children to activities that do them absolutely no good. (p. 305)

Those tests currently in existence are primarily screening devices and evaluation guides for perceptual-motor assessment and programming.

The *Purdue Perceptual-Motor Survey* (Roach & Kephart, 1966) was developed to qualitatively assess the perceptual-motor abilities of children in the early grades. These authors state that "the survey was not designed for diagnosis, per se, but to allow the clinician to observe perceptual-motor behavior in a series of behavioral performances" (p. 11). Owing to vagueness in scoring criteria and because more than one perceptual component is present in many of the survey's 22 items, interpretations of results should be made with caution. All survey items are rated on a 4-point scale. Subtests of the survey focus on posture and balance, body image and differentiation, perceptual-motor integration, ocular control, and form perception. Salvia and Ysseldyke (1991) conclude the following:

> Because standardization was limited, and the norms are out of date, the survey cannot be used for the purpose of making normative comparisons. Although good test-retest reliability has been demonstrated, validity of the scale is questionable. Individual teachers must judge whether they are willing to accept the author's contention that

the development of adequate perceptual-motor skills is a necessary prerequisite to the acquisition of academic skills. Such a claim is, to date, without support. (p. 321)

The following items are laden with perceptual-motor components and are suggested as screening tools in the initial identification of children with deficits (Taylor, 1989). As noted before, perceptual- motor activities often do not isolate a single perceptual-motor component. Although some items can be measured objectively (i.e., number of seconds the child remains balanced), others call for subjective judgments that are only as good as the teacher's judgmental consistency and powers of observation. The following items are suggested for consideration in perceptual-motor assessment:

Balance

Item	Performance Criteria
Stork stand (10 sec maximum).	Number of seconds child remains balanced. Removal of hands from hips, nonsupporting foot from side of supporting leg, or hopping is considered loss of balance.
Sitting tuck balance (10 sec maximum).	Number of seconds child can hold this position without touching feet to floor or rolling onto back.

Sitting tuck balance.

FIGURE 8.3   Teeter board balance.
(Reprinted from Moran and Kalakian,
1977, p. 429.)

Vertical stick balance on index finger of preferred hand from sitting position (10 sec maximum).	Number of seconds child can maintain stick in upright position.
Teeter board (10 sec maximum).	Record number of times edges of teeter board touch the floor. Fewer touches are interpreted as better performance (Figure 8.3).
Child stands motionless with eyes closed (10 sec maximum).	Note excessive swaying in an effort to remain balanced. Note flexion in knees, hips, and ankles (need to maintain balance by lowering center of gravity), removal of hands from sides, facial expressions signaling difficulty, need to take a step, and opened eyes.

Postural and Locomotor Awareness

Item	**Performance Criteria**
Child walks heel-to-toe (forward and backward) along 1-in. wide line 10 ft in length (minimum of ten heel-to-toe contacts required).	Note any movements that appear excessive or extraneous. Note number of missed heel-to-toe contacts. Note number of steps totally missing the line.

Heel-toe walking on a 1-in. wide line.

Child crawls (total body in contact with floor). Child creeps (hands and knees position).

In either case, note preference for homolateral pattern (arm and leg on same side move simultaneously) or for cross-lateral pattern (arm and opposite leg move simultaneously). Note any deviations in simultaneous arm-leg movement (e.g., arm movement, delay, then leg movement). Evaluate ability to move in a straight line. Note any extraneous or abortive movements (Figure 8.4).

Crawl

Creep

FIGURE 8.4 **Crawling and creeping.** (Reprinted from Moran & Kalakian, 1977, p. 74.)

Bipedal locomotion.	Walking, hopping (preferred and nonpreferred foot), jumping, leaping, galloping (right and left foot lead, forward and backward), sliding (left and right), running, skipping.
Rolling, right and left (maximum of five complete rolls in each direction).	Place two parallel lines on the floor approximately 1 ft wider apart than the child is tall. Ask the child to roll in logroll fashion parallel to and between the lines. Note ability to roll without touching either line. Note extraneous or abortive movements.
Crossover walking (forward and backward) along 1-in wide line 10 ft in length (maximum of five contacts with each foot in each direction).	Child stands on left side of line. Child steps diagonally with right foot, placing it on left side of line. Child now steps diagonally with left foot, placing it on right side of line. Note number of foot contacts by both left and right foot, in both forward and backward directions, that cross completely over the line.

Visual

Item	**Performance Criteria**
Pendulum ball suspended on 2-ft string (three trials maximum).	Place ball in lateral motion (approximately 180-degree arc). Child must intercept ball with index finger before ball completes three cycles.
Horizontal ladder fashioned from tagboard, contrasting background (10 rungs).	Note child's ability to step between, but not on, rungs.
Horizontal ladder fashioned from tagboard, blending background (10 rungs).	Note child's ability to step between, but not on, rungs.
Child catches rolled ball (five trials).	Child seated in straddle position must successfully grasp the ball, which has been rolled from a distance of 10 ft, with both hands. Note number of successful catches.

Child catches thrown ball (five trials).	Child in standing position must successfully grasp ball with both hands. Catching by trapping ball between arms and chest should be noted as a relatively less sophisticated response. Ball should be thrown from approximately 6 to 8 ft and should arrive at chest height. Record number of successful catches.

Auditory

Item	Performance Criteria
Child shakes cans.	In each of two cans of the same size, place one and three marbles, respectively. Replace lids on cans. Ask child to shake each can and to designate which has the greater number of noisemaking objects inside.
Child walks to drum or metronome cadence (20 beats maximum, 10 beats per foot).	Child must walk in a straight line in time to the beat. Establish beat and let child move to get in time with the beat before counting begins. Note number of foot contacts that strike the surface simultaneously with the drum or metronome cadence.
Child faces sound source (five trials).	Tape a circle 15 ft in diameter on the floor. Add 12 radials from the axis (e.g., one o'clock, two o'clock). Child, blindfolded, stands on circle axis. Teacher at edge of circle shakes a rattle. Child must turn toward sound source. Sound should emanate from a different spot on the circle's periphery for each of the five trials. For each trial, record, to the nearest radial, the discrepancy between direction that the child faces and direction from which the sound has come. Discrepancies for five trials are totaled. Lower score is interpreted as better performance.

"Which ball is larger?"

Tactile

Item	Performance Criteria
Grab bag (six trials).	Place three similarly textured but differently shaped objects familiar to the child in a bag. Identify specifically shaped object to be retrieved from the bag. Child reaches into the bag without looking, and tries to retrieve the specific object requested. Object is replaced in bag. Ask for another object. Ask randomly for each object twice. Note number of correct responses.
Rough-smooth (three trials).	Two object, one rough, one smooth (e.g., sandpaper, typing paper) are placed out

of child's view. Child is asked to manipulate each object and to identify which is smoother. Two out of three correct trials scores a pass.

Pennies in a cup (20 sec).	Using preferred hand, child picks up pennies one at a time and places as many pennies as possible into a cup in the allotted time.
Large-small (three trials).	Two objects similar in every way but size are placed out of the child's view. Child is asked to manipulate and identify the larger of the two objects. Two out of three correct trials scores a pass.
Soft-hard (three trials).	Same as large-small item, except objects are dissimilar only in consistency (e.g., hard and soft or spongy ball). Two out of three trials scores a pass.

Kinesthetic

Item	**Performance Criteria**
Heel click (three trials).	Child jumps vertically into the air and clicks heels as many times as possible before landing. Record trials.
Jump and knee touch (three trials).	Child jumps vertically and touches knees once before landing. Two out of three successful trials scores a pass.
Jog in place, heel touch (maximum 10 foot contacts for each foot).	Child jogs in place and attempts to touch right hand to right heel (left hand to left heel) each time the heel rises from the jogging surface. Seven out of ten (for each foot) scores a pass.
Bounce board (maximum 10 bounces).	Circumscribe 12-in circle on center of bounce board surface. Note child's ability to bounce rhythmically in place. Record number of contacts in which rhythm is not broken and at least part of both feet simultaneously contact some portion of the circle.

Straddle jump and arm raise (10 sec maximum).

Child begins rhythmic straddle jumping (feet out to side, feet together). As feet assume straddle position, straight arms parallel to each other are raised forward to shoulder height. When feet come together, arms lower to starting position. Allow child to get rhythm going before commencing 10-sec count. Count number of correct cycles demonstrated during 10-sec period.

Body Awareness

Item	Performance Criteria
Identification of body parts (simple).	Have child touch nose, hips, stomach, knees, feet, elbows, ankles, ears, shoulder, eyes, and mouth. Note any incorrect or uncertain responses.
Identification of body parts (complex).	At the same time, touch your nose and knee (e.g., left hand to nose, right hand to right knee), hip and knee, eye and ear, stomach and foot. Note any incorrect or uncertain responses.
Angels in the snow.	Ask child, lying on back with feet together and arms at sides, to move body segments as requested;

    Right arm only (lateral)
    Left arm only (lateral)
    Both arms simultaneously (bilateral)
    Right leg only (lateral)
    Left leg only (lateral)
    Both legs simultaneously (bilateral)
    Right arm, left leg simultaneously
      (cross-lateral)
    Left arm, right leg simultaneously
      (cross-lateral)

Note incorrect responses, extraneous movement of other segments, unsure or abortive movements.

"Touch your shoulder and your ear."

"Touch your ear and your eye."

Fist I.

Have a child make fist with preferred hand. Point randomly to (but do not touch) each of the five fingers one at a time and ask child to point that finger only. Note any pointing of incorrect finger, opening of hand, or pointing of more than one finger. Record number of correct responses.

Fist II.

Have child make fist. Ask child to open fist sequentially, one finger at a time until hand is entirely open, starting with the thumb. Note number of fingers opened in proper sequence only.

Laterality and Directionality

Item	Performance Criteria

Establishment of lateral preference.

Note informally the child's preference or lack of preference for a given hand or foot. Try to differentiate between children who might show mixed preference but have already established a strong lateral preference and those whose mixed preference more truly reflects relatively less mature lateral preference development. Suggested activities to observe include writing, drawing, eating, throwing, catching, kicking, striking, pushing, pulling, hopping, galloping, and sliding.

Follow me (stationary).

Stand before the child and assume different stationary body poses (e.g., hands over head, hands to sides, hands to front, one arm up–other arm down, hands on hips and bend to left-right-front-back). Feet straddled–feet together, half straddle left foot only–right foot only, forward straddle one foot forward–one foot back. Note whether child parallels exactly or mirrors teacher's pose. Parallel responses show relatively more sophisticated response. Mirrored response is thought to be of little concern provided mirroring is constant over entire observation period. Note particularly any unsure responses or any combination of responses that sometimes are parallel and other times are mirrored.

Follow me (locomotor).

Circumscribe two squares approximately 8 ft on a side in a side-by-side position on the floor. Stand in one square and have child stand in other. Move to various parts of the square with the child endeavoring to imitate your movements precisely. Stand in each of the square's corners randomly and on each of the lines midway between each of the corners. Note child's ability to replicate your movements. Score a point for each correct response.

When using any perceptual-motor test battery, accuracy is important. Objective-based assessments (i.e., how far, how many, how fast) are valuable tools for the adapted physical educator. Reuschlein and Vogel (1985) state the following: "The qualitative standards...are generalizable to children...since they are elements of performance that define skilled or unskilled performance. As such, they form the basis for systematic and quantitative performance at a level that is consistent with the innate ability levels of individual children." (p. 151).

SUMMARY

Perceptual-motor theory and practice reflect the premise that perceptual competence is initially achieved largely through the medium of movement. Although the specific interpretations of various perceptual-motor theorists and practitioners cited here may differ, the basic tenet remains constant.

A considerable degree of controversy arises over whether development of perceptual competence through movement automatically translates into heightened readiness for academic challenges.

Unlike the components of physical and motor fitness, the various components that constitute perceptual-motor efficiency are closely interrelated. Nevertheless, the physical educator can create activities that focus on development of proficiency in each component.

Methods of assessing perceptual-motor efficiency vary in sophistication, and more definitive tools are needed. At the present time, the *Purdue Perceptual-Motor Survey* is the most frequently used instrument.

As an adjunct to existing instruments, teachers are encouraged to design their own assessments using selections from the assessment items and performance criteria in this chapter as a starting point. Three to five ways of measuring proficiency for each perceptual component are recommended.

REFERENCES

Ayres, A. J. (1960). Occupational therapy for motor disorders of the central nervous system. *Rehabilitation Literature* 21, 302–310.

_____. (1972). Types of sensory integrative dysfunction among disabled learners. *American Journal of Occupational Therapy, 26,* 13–18.

_____. (1977). Cluster Analyses of Measures of Sensory Integration. *American Journal of Occupational Therapy, 31,* 362–366.

Barsch, R. H. (1965). *A movegenic curriculum.* Madison, WI.: Bureau for Handicapped Children.

Cratty, B. J. (1986). *Perceptual and motor development in infants and children* (3rd ed.). Englewood Cliffs, NJ: Prentice-Hall.

Cratty, B. J. (1989). *Adapted physical education in the mainstream* (2nd ed.). Denver: Love.

Delacato, C. (1959). *The treatment and prevention of reading problems.* Springfield, IL. Charles C. Thomas.

Dummer, G. M. (1985). Developmental differences in motor schema formation. In J.E. Clark & J.H. Humphrey, (Eds.), *Motor-development—Current selected research,* (Vol. I), (pp. xx–77). Princeton, NJ: Princeton Book Company.

Gallahue, D. L. (1982). *Understanding motor development in children.* New York: John Wiley & Sons.

Getman, G. N., & Kane, E. R. (1964). *The physiology of readiness.* Minneapolis: Program to Accelerate School Readiness.

Hallahan, D. P., & Kauffman, J. M. (1991). *Exceptional children: Introduction to special education* (5th ed.). Englewood Cliffs, NJ Prentice-Hall.

Haring, N. G., & McCormick, L. (Eds.). (1990). *Exceptional children and youth* (5th ed). New York: Merrill Macmillan.

Itard, J. M. (1801). *The wild boy of Aveyron.* New York: Appleton-Century-Crofts.

Keogh, J., & Sugden, D. (1985). *Movement skill development.* New York: Macmillan.

Kephart, N. C. (1960). *The slow learner in the classroom.* Columbus, OH: Charles E. Merrill.

Kerr, R. (1985) Fitts' Law and motor control in children. In *Motor Development—Current Selected Research,* (Vol. I), (pp. 185–207). J.E. Clark & J.H. Humphrey (Eds.), Princeton, N.J.: Princeton Book Company.

Montessori, D. M. (1912). *The Montessori Method.* New York: Frederick A. Stokes.

Moran, J. M., & Kalakian, L. H. (1977). *Movement experiences for the mentally retarded or emotionally disturbed child,* (2nd ed). Minneapolis: Burgess Publishing.

Payne, V. G., & Isaacs, L. D. (1991). *Human motor development* (2nd ed.). Mountain View, CA: Mayfield.

Piaget, J. (1936). *The origin of intelligence in children.* New York: New York University Press.

Reuschlein, P. L., & Vogel, P. G. (1985). Motor performance and physical fitness status of regular and special education student. In J. E. Clark & J. H. Humphrey (Eds.), *Motor development: Current selected research, Vol I.* Princeton, NJ: Princeton Book Co.

Roach, E., & Kephart, N.(Eds). (1966). *The Purdue-Perceptual Motor Survey.* Columbus, OH: Charles E. Merrill.

Rosembaum, D. A. (1991). *Human motor control.* San Diego, CA: Academic Press.

Sage, G. H. (1984). *Motor learning and control—A neuropsychological approach.* Dubuque, IA: Wm. C. Brown.

Salvia, J., & Ysseldyke, J. E. (1991). *Assessment* (5th ed.). Boston: Houghton Mifflin.

Seguin, E. (1907). *Idiocy, its treatment by the physiological method.* New York: Columbia University Press.

Sugden, D. A., & Keogh, J. F. (1990). *Problems in movement skill development.* Columbia, University of South Carolina Press.

Taylor, J. G. (1962). *The behavioral basis for perception.* New Haven, CT: Yale University Press.

Taylor, J.G. (1989). *Assessment of exceptional students: Educational and psychological procedures* (2nd ed.). Englewood Cliffs, NJ: Prentice-Hall.

Thomas, J. R. (1984). *Motor development during childhood and adolescence.* Minneapolis: Burgess Publishing.

Vernon, M. D. (1962). The psychology of perception. Baltimore: Penguin Books.

Werder, J. K., & Kalakian, L. H. (1985). *Assessment in adapted physical education.* Minneapolis: Burgess Publishing.

Chapter 9

MAINSTREAMING AND THE LEAST RESTRICTIVE ENVIRONMENT

Jim Rose, his wife, Donna, and their two children, John (12) and Courtney (10), were considering moving to Deerfield, Illinois. One major concern regarding their future move was the quality of the school system. Mr. Rose said to the principal, "We want our children to be in a good school, with good teachers. Our daughter has special needs but we feel she has the ability to be successful in school if given the right classes and teachers. Does your school have specially trained teachers to work with Courtney's needs, including both academic and physical? Is the school accessible? That is, can Courtney's wheelchair get to all classrooms, the lunchroom, the gym, and the locker rooms? How can we be assured she will get appropriate programs? Please explain your school's ideas regarding mainstreaming. How do you determine which classes are best for her? Will she have the opportunity to be in small classes that emphasize Courtney's individual needs? We know she has major motor problems; do you have a special physical education program? We don't want her dumped into a large P.E. class and told that it will be socially better for her."

The principal paused, then said: "Welcome to Deerfield, Mr. and Mrs. Rose. We have the school you are looking for. Let me explain, as we take a tour of the school."

Current federal and state legislation uses the term **least restrictive environment** to suggest that the regular class offers less restriction of opportunities for learning (Hallahan & Kauffman, 1991). **Mainstreaming,** often used synonymously with the phrase *least restrictive environment*, is the practice of providing educational services for children with disabilities in integrated settings with their nondisabled peers (Eichstaedt & Lavay, 1992). This means that individuals, regardless of type or severity of disabling condition, should participate in activities with nondisabled students whenever possible. Mainstreaming is the movement of children with disabilities out of segregated special education classes and into classes with nondisabled peers (Figure 9.1).

An assessment of the least restrictive environment (LRE) provisions of Public Law 101-476 requires an examination of the settings in which children with disabili-

**Adapted physical education teachers soon
learn that students with disabilities are just
like nondisabled kids.**

ties are served, the options available to children with various disabling conditions, and the decision-making processes used to place children in appropriate settings. During the 1988–1989 school year, large numbers of students with disabilities were served in relatively less restrictive settings. Almost 69 percent of all children with disabilities received most of their education in regular schools. Another 25 percent received services in separate classes within a regular education building (Figure 9.1). Together, these settings accounted for 4,687,620 children (ages 0–21) who received special education services. Slightly more than 7 percent of all children with disabilities were educated in separate schools or in other environments (i.e., home, hospitals, institutions). Furthermore, most children with disabilities were educated in public rather than in private settings (U.S. Department of Education, 1991).

RESEARCH AND MAINSTREAMING

In recent years, the growing interest in mainstreaming has produced controversy. Many special educators and investigators still believe that traditional, self-contained,

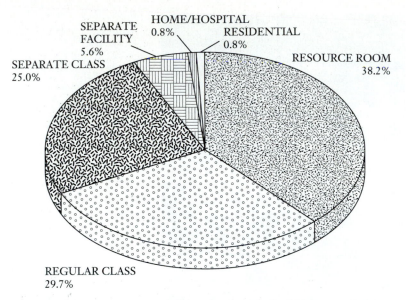

FIGURE 9.1   Percentage of all students with disabilities age 3–21 served in six educational placements.
Note: Includes data from 50 states and Puerto Rico. *Source:* U.S. Department of Education, Office of Special Education Programs, Data Analysis System (DANS) (1991).

segregated classrooms remain the most appropriate placement for children with special needs. On the other hand, criticism of traditional methods often centers on the possible negative effects of segregation on the child's self-image and social relationships.

A new thrust has emerged in relation to children with more severe disabilities and their integration in regular public school settings. Brinker and Thorpe (1984) used 13 school districts ($N = 245$) and found that over and above functional level, the degree of integration (measured by interaction with nondisabled students) was a significant predictor ($p > .025$) of educational progress as measured by the proportion of individualized educational program (IEP) objectives met. They consider integration an important aspect of the curriculum for students with severe disabilities (age 3–22 years).

In the 1970s, children with severe disabilities were usually the responsibility of private schools or institutions. The idea of mainstreaming had, however, gained wide acceptance by the late 1970s, but cautions were then being voiced. MacMillan and Becker (1977) state the following:

> It is assumed that the regular classroom teacher can deal with a wide range of individual differences, and that either the curriculum accommodates a diversity of needs and interests or can be adapted readily to do so. It is interesting to note

that in the past these children failed in the regular classroom, and now they are being required to return to the same setting. We question whether regular education has changed sufficiently to warrant the apparent optimism regarding the educational plight of the handicapped learner. One cannot lose sight of the fact that traditionally these have been 'hard to teach' children, and to delabel and mainstream does nothing to alter the fact. (p. 209)

Abramson (1980) found little support for mainstreaming as a means of improving the social acceptability or academic performance of children with disabilities. Although few would argue against the need for mainstreaming in principle, implementation of the mainstreaming concept is no easy matter. Hallahan and Kauffman (1991) suggest that the mere establishment of special classes does not bring about miracle cures for children with special needs, nor does the abolition of these classes.

Research focused on mainstreaming in physical education has been widely accepted over the past few years. Initially, concern was expressed regarding the effectiveness of physical educators with traditional teaching styles and their ability or desire to teach students with disabling conditions (Morreau and Eichstaedt, 1983). Full integration is unquestionably desirable, but many physical educators have difficulty when they attempt to mainstream the majority of students with disabilities. Mizen and Linton (in DePaepe and Lavay, 1985, p. 44) state the following: "By the very nature of their program physical education teachers are constantly reminded that teaching children with handicaps in a mainstreaming program can be frustrating and disappointing." Although this statement seems foreboding, they conclude their comments by saying: "The time has come to meet the challenge" (1983, p. 63). Marston and Leslie (1983) determined that a strong correlation exists between positive teacher attitudes toward individuals with disabilities and direct teacher involvement with students with disabilities. Those not directly teaching students with disabilities retained their negative attitudes. Jansma and Schultz (1982) suggest the use of a mainstreaming attitude inventory to evaluate the attitudes of those physical educators who may teach students with disabilities.

There is strong evidence that attitudes of both nondisabled and youngsters with disabilities improve when they are placed together in a physical education setting (Karper and Martinek, 1982; Morreau and Eichstaedt, 1983).

THE LAW AND MAINSTREAMING

Mainstreaming represents one level in the continuum of services required by the least restrictive environment mandate in P.L. 101-476, the Individuals with Disabilities Education Act, and P.L. 101-336, Americans with Disabilities Act of 1990 (ADA). The rules and regulations of P.L. 101-476 require that each public agency ensure a continuum of alternative placements to meet the needs of children with disabilities for special education and related services. Instruction in regular classes, in special classes, and in special schools, home instruction, and instruction in hospitals and institutions are all on this continuum. These requirements are consistent with P.L. 101-336 provisions that mandate program accessibility and appropriate accommodations so individuals with disabilities can participate to the maximum degree possible with nondisabled peers.

Most states have included mainstreaming in their school codes. The following statements are typical: (1) The child shall be placed in an appropriate educational program that is least restrictive for interaction with nondisabled children. (2) Students receiving special education services must attend school in the same buildings as nondisabled students. Special classes and separate schooling are permitted only when the nature or severity of the child's disability prohibits education in regular classes. (3) When a child is removed from a special education program and placed in a regular classroom, the local school district must help to make the transition successful.

Mainstreaming has three basic thrusts: (1) removal of labels, (2) desegregation, and (3) more effective programming. Although all three concerns are being addressed by public school physical educators, the main thrust of mainstreaming thus far has been class placement. Educators are examining specifically how much time the child with disabilities is spending in the regular class environment.

SOCIAL OR PHYSICAL DEVELOPMENT?

Often, the primary goal in placing children with disabilities in a regular physical education class is not the attainment of physical fitness or enhancement of motor development, but rather to promote acceptable social behavior by exposure to appropriate peer models or to provide competitive situations that the child must ultimately experience. Although these are meaningful goals for a child with disabilities, they should be recognized for what they are: social and not physical education goals. An evaluation of mainstreamed education must therefore begin with a clear statement as to whether placing the child with a disability in a regular class will go beyond social opportunities to actually promote the student's physical improvement.

IS MAINSTREAMING APPROPRIATE FOR ALL INDIVIDUALS WITH DISABILITIES?

Controversy exists within educational circles regarding implementation of mainstreaming. The key questions are: (1) who is to be mainstreamed, and (2) is mainstreaming the most appropriate placement for all children? Teachers are concerned that children with disabilities may be "dumped" in regular classes. Although this practice is completely contrary to the intent of the laws, some administrators are misinterpreting the laws and are requiring all children with disabilities to remain in regular physical education classes.

Many professionals view mainstreaming as the primary method by which educators can assist children with disabilities to achieve normalization. Studies beginning in the 1950s and continuing into the 1980s emphasized research on the effectiveness of special education classes and mainly used individuals with mild disabilities as subjects. These efficacy studies typically produced conflicting results, showing social but not academic benefits. For example, the efficacy studies typically found that individuals with mild disabilities learned as much or more academically in integrated traditional classes compared to segregated special education classes but that traditional class placement tended to result in *lower* acceptance of these students by their nondisabled peers. Hallahan and Kauffman (1991, p. 57) make reference to these early studies:

> In spite of the serious flaws in many efficacy studies and the inconclusive findings of the research, many now view these studies as an indictment of special classes. Special classes—even those that students may attend for only part of the school day—segregate exceptional children from their peers. Because segregation is unethical unless its benefits have been demonstrated and because, some argue, no benefits of special classes have been demonstrated, the case is closed: Special classes are indefensible (Wang, Reynolds, & Walberg, 1989). Others are more cautious, pointing out that we have not resolved all the problems in making special classes effective. (Vergason & Anderegg, 1989)

Physical education instructors are faced with the dilemma in which *all* youngsters with *all* degrees and types of disabilities are being placed into their programs. In fact, the concept of *Regular Education Initiative* (REI), for students with mild disabilities, is strongly endorsed and financially supported by the U.S. Department of Education. Madeleine C. Will, former Assistant Secretary for Special Education and Rehabilitation Services, argued that many, and perhaps all, children with mild disabilities could be educated within the framework of the regular education program if that program were properly structured and staffed (Kirk & Gallagher, 1989). *Project Choices* and *Parents for Inclusive Communities* (PIC) are receiving considerable attention from certain teaching professionals and parents, all with the same goal to mainstream all children with severe and profound disabilities into regular programs. Regarding programs such as these, Dohrmann (1991) expresses concerns regarding improper mainstreaming in physical education: "I continually hear elementary P.E. teachers complain that children have been placed back into the very environment in which they failed." Major questions regarding mass and nonselective mainstreaming are identified by Patton, Payne, and Beirne-Smith (1990):

- In light of the presumed benefits of having students who are disabled educated as much as possible with their nondisabled peers, we still lack a solid research base that supports this idea.

- There may be more interest in mainstreaming students than in what happens to them afterward.

- If the population of the mildly disabled has changed over the last few years, then there are two notes of caution: (1) Earlier research on mainstreaming students who are mildly disabled is probably not applicable to the present population; and (2) this new, lower functioning group of individuals with severe disabilities is probably not as capable of being mainstreamed as the earlier one. (p. 82)

Complications also arise when attempting to use the directives of PL 101-476. For instance, to begin an IEP, specific information regarding the present level of performance of each student must be gathered. This clearly indicates that each student with a disability is to be given a series of motor skill and physical fitness tests, and these results must be included in the IEP document. In the past, these scores were used to determine if special placement was necessary, perhaps into an adapted physical education class. The IEP, with its annual goals and short-term objectives, is probably incompatible with the *traditional* physical education curricula. The regular program makes certain assumptions, the greatest being that distinct age groups (e.g., 14-year-old sophomore girls and boys) will bring with them comparative homogeneous levels of performance; seldom will the range of abilities go beyond two developmental years in either direction. Activities are planned with this assumption in mind. Age-appropriate activities are of great concern and large deviations from the norm lead to boredom (on the high side) and failure and frustration (on the low side). Special programs, within the context of an overall physical education program, have been developed to meet the special needs of the students at the extremes. Competitive athletics, for example, allows for highly motor-skilled individuals to be challenged with appropriate intensities, thus allowing for the maximum benefits. Likewise, an adapted physical education program is provided for those individuals who are performing at the extreme lower end of the motor continuum. Again, the students will have individualized motor and physical fitness plans written to meet their immediate needs. Anything less would relegate the students to significantly lower gains in the motor and fitness areas. Individualized adapted physical education classes can offer the following:

- Smaller class size; better student-to-teacher ratio
- Specialized equipment; which cannot be easily moved to all areas
- Activities designed to meet individualized needs; so students will not have to be shackled to 3-week units of, say, basketball
- Specially trained teachers; will understand unique motor and fitness needs, how to assess them, and how to provide different age-appropriate and stimulating opportunities

One distinct problem that arises from mainstreaming is the strong possibility that regular classroom teachers and, in some states, special education classroom teachers are expected to teach motor skill and physical fitness activities to youngsters with disabilities. The obvious flaw is the serious lack of special training of these traditional teachers.

On the positive side regarding mainstreaming, the general indication is that most students with *mild* disabilities are functioning relatively well in regular physical education classes with their age peers (Eichstaedt, 1991; Reynolds, 1989). It is another story for the individuals with the more serious disabilities. Rizzo and Vispoel (1991) determined that physical education teachers' attitudes toward students with disabilities were directly related to perceived competence in teaching students with disabilities. Also, they found that, of their physical education teacher subjects (N = 94), students with learning disabilities were viewed more favorably than students with educable (mild) mental retardation or behavior disorders.

Additional problems begin to surface when medical contraindications of students with severe disabilities become evident. The legal responsibilities are often overwhelming and the potential for student injury is ever present. School administrators should seriously question if their physical education instructors are capable of meeting the unique needs of individuals with severe and profound disabilities. Anything less could result in youngsters being placed into programs of potential danger, not to mention legal constraints arising from this questionable placement. Again, the crux of the problem is the lack of training of thousands of regular physical education teachers. Extensive and intensive in-service training appears to be the most viable alternative, but in the meantime, total mainstreaming must be viewed very cautiously for those individuals with the most severe disabling conditions.

It is unrealistic to expect *all* children with disabilities to benefit from placement in a regular physical education class for *all* activities. Most comprehensive physical education curricula contain activities to meet the total psychomotor needs of a particular age group, but the individualized needs of individuals with disabilities are not always considered in initial program planning. Many activities are compatible with the needs of the child with disabilities, whereas others require modification. For example, a student labeled as trainable (moderate) mentally retarded may experience difficulty playing a version of basketball in which team strategy is important.

Children with disabilities should be placed in activities in which they can participate actively. Exclusion from or severe modification of an activity may indicate that the child's ability has not been considered properly and that the placement is inappropriate.

Gardner (1978) emphasizes that continued and consistent failure does not develop positive attitudes. He states the following: "An emotionally disturbed, mentally retarded, or learning disabled child cannot learn achievement orientation, to be relaxed, satisfied, friendly, or to be free of anxiety, and related defensive behavior patterns in an environment that promotes excessive failure. A child with severe visual or auditory problems cannot learn to like himself, to relate warmly to others, or to accept his own sensory limitations realistically if he experiences a preponderance of failure" (p. 128).

Mainstreaming students with disabilities into public school physical education programs is feasible and in certain instances desirable if personnel have a positive attitude and if appropriate, flexible program planning and activity modifications are made when necessary (Block, 1991).

Random, inappropriate, and hasty placement can be physically, socially, and emotionally detrimental to the child with a disability. When, however, children with disabilities can participate safely, successfully, and with personal satisfaction, then, and only then, should they be placed in the regular program.

THE LEAST RESTRICTIVE ENVIRONMENT

A *least restrictive environment* provides the best match between a child and a specific learning program. An ideal combination should promote maximum development and functioning in the physical education curriculum. Movement experiences may occur through large group instruction (mass techniques with everyone doing similar tasks), through individualized experiences within the regular class (in-class grouping), or

The effective adapted physical education teacher must identify the motor needs of a child with a disability. This child shows a marked weakness of the upper body for which specific upper body exercises have been prescribed.

through a highly individualized small class setting designed especially for a particular child. In the small class, such as an adapted physical education section, the individual child and his immediate psychomotor and fitness needs take precedence. In other words, the least restrictive environment must be interpreted as that place where the child learns best.

A *most restrictive environment* is that place where the child with a disability is assigned unnecessarily, a place that is distinctly different and physically separate from the setting in which nondisabled students are being taught. Although an institution may be the most appropriate (and least restrictive) environment for a relatively small number of people with severe or profound disabilities, an institution is the most restrictive environment for most individuals with disabilities.

PLACEMENT ALTERNATIVES

Any decision regarding the most appropriate placement should not be considered a simple choice between regular and adapted physical education programs. Neither should placement be considered final once a decision is made. Rather, practitioners should continually examine those placement alternatives, which, when implemented, will produce a least restrictive environment that enables the child to learn effectively and completely. For example, a girl with mental retardation with normal levels of physical fitness may be successful in regular activities that involve strength, speed, and endurance but may perform poorly in activities that require striking with a racket (e.g., badminton, tennis). Her motor performance could be almost two standard deviations below that of an average child. Instead of instruction in racket sports, she should be taught more basic activities involving eye-hand coordination. Her performance indicates that she is not yet ready to use an implement but should learn first to hit an object with her hands. An adapted physical education class can provide meaningful activities at her ability level. When a child's needs call for a more effective learning environment, the regular program may provide some activities and an adapted class the others.

Stein (1976) explains that although mainstreaming can produce positive results, it is not the only alternative. He states: "Some activities lend themselves more readily to mainstreaming than others. For example, exploratory activities, tumbling, gymnastics ... are excellent for this process, since success or failure does not depend on the performance or ability of others" (p. 43).

PLACEMENT IN THE REGULAR PROGRAM

For a child with a disability to receive maximum benefits from a regular class, two conditions must be satisfied. First, the child's physical needs must be compatible with the instruction level that is offered to the nondisabled children. Incompatibility, for example, is evident when a child is assigned to play shuffleboard while classmates are engaged in volleyball. The basic skills developed by playing volleyball (i.e., eye-hand coordination, explosive leg power, agility) are not acquired by playing shuffleboard. Alternative activities should help the student to develop similar skills (Table 9.1).

Second, the teacher must be able to modify regular class instructional practices to accommodate the child with abilities that are quite different from those of other students. Such modifications may not be appropriate when extreme differences of ability exist between the child with a disability and the others. For example, placing a child in a wheelchair in a regular volleyball class is usually inappropriate. In-class grouping by ability levels may provide a viable alternative, but students with extreme disabilities should be placed in an adapted physical education class where a better opportunity for success exists, and where the obvious frustration of a watered-down activity is not experienced (Eichstaedt & Lavay, 1992).

The Illinois Office of Education, Department of Special Education (1991) has developed a model that supports flexible placement with a continuum of alternatives. Based on assessment data, placement alternatives should be considered and the individual assigned to the regular or adapted physical education class as each student's needs dictate. Suggested transitional placement should occur as follows: (1) The child should remain in a regular physical education class with supplementary adapted programming available when modifications in activities, equipment, facilities, or in the performer's role are impractical or not possible. For example, a student with perceptual motor disability may need adapted programming when regular pro-

TABLE 9.1   **Alternative Activities for Volleyball**

Basic Fundamental Skill	Alternative Activities
Eye-hand coordination	Wall volley Sidewalk tennis 4-Square Balloon volley Tether ball
Explosive leg power	Line jump Vertical wall jump Hopscotch Hopping relays Hop tag
Agility	Belly-back-stand Line jump Shuttle run Obstacle run Boomerang

gram activities require well-developed visual-motor skills, as in badminton or tennis. In yet another example, a student with a perceptual motor impairment may need adapted programming when the regular program activities require an acute sense of balance, as in tumbling and gymnastics. (2) The child should be placed in an adapted physical education class with supplementary regular programming when modifications in the regular program activities, equipment, or facilities or in the performer's role are possible. For example, a student with visual impairment can use a handrail or guide rope to participate in bowling with normal-vision students, or a student with cerebral palsy can use flotation devices to participate in the regular swimming program.

These proposed transitional placements allow the child with special needs to participate in a least restrictive physical education environment.

ORGANIZATION AND ADMINISTRATION OF A FLEXIBLE CURRICULUM

Many children with disabilities have unfortunately been placed in learning environments because of their disabling label (e.g., only children with EMR in the class). This practice does not consider each child's individual motor differences or each child's diverse physical needs. For example, although mental ability is below normal range, the child's motor ability may be quite adequate and he might participate successfully in a traditional physical education program.

The identification and placement of children with disabilities are two major obstacles for school administrators. Performance levels, and not diagnostic group labels, should determine organization and administration of appropriate physical education experiences. Hobbs (1975) summarizes this position:

> In schools that are most responsive to individual differences in abilities, interests, and learning styles of children, the mainstream is actually many streams, sometimes as many streams as there are individual children, sometimes several streams as groups are formed for special purposes, sometimes one stream only as concerns of all converge. We see no advantage in dumping exceptional children into an undifferentiated mainstream; but we see great advantage to all children, exceptional children included, in an educational program modulated to the needs of individual children, singly, in small groups, or all together. Such a flexible arrangement may well result in functional separations of exceptional children from time to time, but the governing principle would apply to all children: school programs should be responsive to the learning requirements of individual children, and groupings should serve this end. (p. 197)

Mainstreaming is not intended to change the special child so that she fits into the regular classroom, but rather to change the nature of the regular classroom so it becomes more accommodating to all children.

THE TEACHER'S RESPONSIBILITY

Once a child with disabilities is retained in the regular class for a specific purpose (e.g., tumbling to develop agility, balance, and kinesthetic awareness), the logical question is whether the ongoing lessons will meet the stated goals of the IEP. What steps can the teacher take to accomplish goals that were established for the child?

The question has no simple answer, because the material offered to a child with disabilities or to any child, depends largely on the teaching strategies of the instructor. The teacher may develop a learning environment that enables students to progress at their own rate or that provides all students with identical opportunities. (The teaching approach of "what's good for one is good for all" is usually not conducive to meeting individual needs.)

The National Information Center for Handicapped Children and Youth (1983, p. 1) cautions that "placing students with handicaps into the 'mainstream,' or regular class, does not guarantee that they will be liked, or chosen as friends by their non-handicapped peers. Without careful attention by sensitive teachers, such a placement could even be a harmful experience."

Mercer (1990) identifies two major problem areas regarding mainstreaming children with disabilities: (1) the teacher's attitude toward the child, and (2) the teacher's ability to teach the child. Awareness sessions, including actual contact with individuals with disabilities, are necessary if teachers are to overcome their natural fears and misconceptions about children with disabilities. All undergraduate physical education majors should participate in awareness sessions. This also must be a priority for in-service and retraining experiences for already certified physical educators.

Research shows that the majority of teachers believe that they are not equipped to deal with youngsters with disabilities. Melograno and Loovis (1991) have found through their longitudinal study of Ohio physical education teachers (N = 242) that teachers lacked the ability to provide appropriate physical education for students with disabilities. Additionally, these same teachers indicated a general need for assistance in learning how to administer and interpret motor behavior assessments for students with disabilities. It is therefore extremely important that the physical education teacher become knowledgeable about children with disabilities. A close working relationship should be established with the special educator who has been trained and will be able to answer questions about most disabling conditions (e.g., What causes Down syndrome? Is it a disease? Will the child become progressively worse? Will the child have difficulty understanding instructions?). The special educator should act as a consultant when specific information about a child is required (e.g., Is Susie cooperative? Is she shy? Does she have many friends? What makes her happy? What makes her unhappy?).

TEACHING TECHNIQUES FOR SUCCESSFUL MAINSTREAMING

One central impediment to mainstreaming—competition—is deeply ingrained in our educational system. Many classroom procedures, management programs, and curricular materials emphasize the selection and sorting functions of the schools; that is, schools, both officially and tacitly, sort out the able from the less able and rank students according to specific criteria. Physical educators should truly question the validity of grading students by their performance levels. This process inevitably leads to failure for a significant number of individuals when they are compared with the norm. Although these same individuals may try their best, their skills do not permit them to reach acceptable levels. If the basic goal of physical educators is to develop positive attitudes toward physical activity, then everything possible must be done to motivate the less skilled and the child with disabilities. The concept of zero-fail should be an integral component of all physical education programs.

Successful mainstreaming begins with a total picture of an individual's present level of physical fitness and general motor ability. These ability levels, determined by using appropriate testing instruments, indicate the child's proper placement. Werder and Kalakian (1985) believe that assessment in adapted physical education should focus on identifying the needs of students with motor difficulties and on measuring the progress of students who cannot safely or successfully participate in the traditional mainstream physical education program. Certain individuals will be difficult to assess because of their emotional and social skill levels. The questions asked in Figure 9.2 can assist in placement.

A large class size, often typical of the regular program, may necessitate the use of alternate teaching methods to integrate the child with disabilities. Alternate methods might include (1) circuit or station organizational patterns, (2) a buddy system that pairs a child with a disability with an able-bodied partner for specific activities, (3) peer tutoring, (4) contract techniques using problem-solving, exploratory, and movement education activities, (5) use of paraprofessionals, aides, volunteers, parents, and older students, and (6) elective programs in which students select activities or units according to their interests and abilities.

SUMMARY

Mainstreaming, now a top priority in public schools, provides an exciting opportunity for youngsters with disabilities if cautiously administered. It does not mean simply including all children with disabilities in the regular physical education program. Mainstreaming should be a carefully executed process by which the physical needs of the child with disabilities are identified and met. Moderate and severe degrees of motor disability may require a flexible combination of several alternatives with each

TO: PHYSICAL EDUCATION INSTRUCTORS
FROM: ADAPTED PHYSICAL EDUCATION INSTRUCTOR
RE: POSSIBLE CANDIDATES FOR ADAPTED PHYSICAL EDUCATION PROGRAMMING

STUDENT _____   GRADE LEVEL _____

COUNSELOR _____   PE INSTRUCTOR _____

PLEASE ANSWER THE FOLLOWING QUESTIONS PERTAINING TO THE STUDENT

YES   NO   SOMETIMES   1. Is this student rejected by classmates because of ability?

YES   NO   SOMETIMES   2. Does this student avoid competive games and activities?

YES   NO   SOMETIMES   3. Does this student continually finish toward the bottom of the class on
                                        skill tests and/or physical fitness tests?

YES   NO   SOMETIMES   4. Does this student have difficulty when playing ball games?

YES   NO   SOMETIMES   5. Does this student seem sincerely happy to be in physical education class?
                                        (Does the student outwardly enjoy most activities? Is it difficult to deter-
                                        mine the individual's true feelings?)

YES   NO   SOMETIMES   6. Does this student make negative comments about physical education?

SPECIFIC REASONS FOR REFERRAL

_____ Excessive overweight

_____ Excessive underweight

_____ Lacks coordination

_____ Lacks strength

_____ Poor posture

_____ Poor physical fitness

_____ Class adjustment (In your opinion, would he/she benefit from a more individualized
                              program?)

FIGURE 9.2   **Answers to these questions will aid in identification of the students'
adapted physical education needs.**

one contributing to the child's education. The indiscriminate placement of individuals with disabilities in regular classes for which they are not ready is as inappropriate as the exclusion from regular classes of those students with disabilities who are ready for the challenge of physical activity with nondisabled peers.

Jones, Gottlieb, Guskin, and Yoshida (1978) stress that the effectiveness of any mainstream program for children with disabilities can be measured only by *what* is being taught, which is far more important than *where* the students are being taught.

Students should not be shuffled between rigid, narrowly conceived experiences, which ensure that a certain percentage of children will fail. The concept of "zero-reject," or "zero-fail," must be practiced by all physical educators. Ideally, mainstreaming will become the impetus for examining and redesigning special education and many other aspects of our school system.

REFERENCES

Abramson, M. (1980). Implications of mainstreaming: A challenge for special education. In L. Mann & D. A. Sabatino (Eds.), *The fourth review of special education* (pp. 39–47). New York: Grune and Stratton.

Block, M. (1991, November). *Integration of individuals with disabilities into the traditional physical education program.* Paper presented at the annual meeting of the Illinois Association for Health, Physical Education, Recreation, and Dance, Arlington Heights, IL.

Brinker, R. P., & Thorpe, M. E. (1984). Integration of severely handicapped students and the proportion of IEP objectives achieved. *Exceptional Children, 51*(2), 168–175.

DePaepe, J. L., & Lavay, B. W. (1985). A bibliography of mainstreaming in physical education. *The Physical Educator, 42*(1), 41–45.

Dohrmann, P. F. (1991, November). *Elementary physical education and children with disabilities.* Paper presented at the annual meeting of the Illinois Association for Health, Physical Education, Recreation, and Dance, Arlington Heights, IL.

Eichstaedt, C. B. (1991, November). *Adapted physical education: A state of the art.* Paper presented at the annual meeting of the Illinois Association for Health, Physical Education, Recreation, and Dance, Arlington Heights, IL.

Eichstaedt, C. B., & Lavay, B. (1992). *Physical activities for individuals with mental retardation: Infant through adult.* Champaign, IL: Human Kinetics.

Gardner, W. I. (1978). *Learning and behavior characteristics of exceptional children and youth* (2nd ed.). Boston: Allyn and Bacon.

Hallahan, D. P., & Kauffman, J. M. (1991). *Exceptional children* (5th ed.). Englewood Cliffs, NJ: Prentice-Hall.

Hobbs, L. (1975). *The future of children.* San Francisco: Jossey-Bass.

Illinois Office of Education. (1991). *Illinois state rules and regulations to govern the administration and operation of special education.* Springfield: Illinois State Board of Education.

Jansma, P., & Schultz, B. (1982). Validation and use of a mainstreaming attitude inventory with physical educators. *American Corrective Therapy Journal, 36,* 150–158.

Jones, R. L., Gottlieb, J., Guskin, S., & Yoshida, R. K. (1978). Evaluating mainstreaming programs: Models, caveats, considerations, and guidelines. *Exceptional Children, 44*(8), 588–601.

Karper, W. B., & Martinek, T. J. (1982). Differential influences of various instructional factors on self-concepts of handicapped and non-handicapped children in mainstreamed physical education classes. *Perceptual and Motor Skills, 54,* 831–835.

MacMillan, D. L., & Becker L. D. (1977). Mainstreaming the mildly handicapped learner. In R. D. Kneedler & S. G. Tarver (Eds.), *Changing perspectives in special education* (pp. 212–231). Columbus, Oh: Charles E. Merrill.

Marston, R., & Leslie, D. (1983). Teacher perceptions from mainstreamed versus non-mainstreamed handicapped and non-handicapped teaching environments. *The Physical Educator, 40,* 8–15.

Melograno, V. J., & Loovis, E. M. (1991). Status of physical education for handicapped students: A comparative analysis of teachers in 1980 and 1988. *Adapted Physical Activity Quarterly, 8*(1), 28–42.

Mercer, C. D. (1990). Learning disabilities. In N. G. Haring & L. McCormick (Eds.), *Exceptional children and youth* (5th ed.; pp. 109–151). New York: Merrill/Macmillan.

Mizen, D. W., & Linton, N. (1983). Guess who's coming to PE: Six steps to more effective mainstreaming. *JOPERD, 54,* 63–65.

Morreau, L. E., & Eichstaedt, C. B. (1983). Least restrictive programming and placement in physical education. *American Corrective Therapy Journal, 37*(1), 7–17.

National Information Center for Handicapped Children and Youth. (1983). *Attitudes:* Washington, DC: The Center.

Patton, J. R., Payne, J. S., & Beirne-Smith, M. (1990). *Mental retardation* (3rd ed.). New York: Merrill/Macmillan.

Public Law 94-142. *Education for All Handicapped Children Act of 1975.* 94th Congress, S.6 (20 USC 1401), November 29, 1975.

Reynolds, M. C. (1989). A historical perspective: The delivery of special education to mildly disabled and at risk students. *Remedial and Special Education, 10*(6), 7–11.

Rizzo, T. L., & Vispoel, W. P. (1991). Physical educators' attributes and attitudes toward teaching students with handicaps. *Adapted Physical Activity Quarterly, 8*(1), 4–11.

Shotel, J. R., Iano, R. P., & McGettigan, J. F. (1972). Teacher attitudes associated with integration of handicapped children. *Exceptional Children, 38,* 677–683.

Stein, J. U. (1976). Sense and nonsense about mainstreaming. *JOPER, 47*(1), 43.

U.S. Department of Education (1991). To assure the free appropriate public education of all handicapped children. *Thirteenth Annual Report to Congress on the Implementation of the Education of the Handicapped Children Act.* Washington, DC.

Vergason, G. A., & Anderegg, M. L. (1989). Save the baby! A response to "Integrating the children of the second system." Cited in D. P. Hallahan & J. M. Kauffman, *Exceptional children* (5th ed.; p. 57). Englewood Cliffs, NJ: Prentice-Hall.

Wang, M. C., Reynolds, M. C., & Walberg, H. J. (1989). Who benefits from segregation and murky water? Cited in D. P. Hallahan & J. M. Kauffman, *Exceptional children* (5th ed., p. 57). Englewood Cliffs, NJ: Prentice-Hall.

Werder, J. K., & Kalakian, L. H. (1985). *Assessment in adapted physical education.* Minneapolis: Burgess Publishing.

Part III

CONDITIONS

Chapter 10

LEARNING DISABILITIES

...and report cards I was always afraid to show
Mama'd come to school
and as I'd sit there softly cryin'
Teacher'd say he's just not tryin'
Got a good head if he'd apply it
but you know yourself
it's always somewhere else
I'd build me a castle
with dragons and kings
and I'd ride off with them
As I stood by my window
and I looked out on those
Brooklyn roads
> *Neil Diamond, "Brooklyn Roads"*
> *©1970 Stonebridge Music.*
> *All rights reserved.*
> *Used by permission.*

In 1985 the Association for Children and Adults with Learning Disabilities adopted a definition of **specific learning disabilities** that stresses the potential of these disabilities to affect people throughout their lives:

> Specific Learning Disabilities is a chronic condition of presumed neurological origin which selectively interferes with the development, integration, and/or demonstration of verbal and/or non-verbal abilities. Specific Learning Disabilities exists as a distinct handicapping condition in the presence of average to superior intelligence, adequate sensory and motor systems, and adequate learning opportunities. The condition varies in its manifestations and in degree of severity. Throughout life the condition can affect self-esteem, education, vocation, socialization, and/or daily living activities.

> (*National Information Center for Handicapped Children and Youth 1985, p.2*)

259

POSSIBLE CAUSES AND DIAGNOSIS

The number of students with learning disabilities receiving special services pursuant to federal mandates has risen dramatically in recent years. The number has increased from just over 750,000 to just under 2,000,000 in 1990 (U.S. Department of Education, 1991).

The child with a learning disability possesses at least average intellectual abilities. In fact, some children with learning disabilities exhibit potential that exceeds the norm. Children are designated as having a possible learning disability when normal potential and opportunity exist but achievement is not in accordance with potential. Among children with learning disabilities, difficulties stem *not* from deprivation of information (i.e., negative environmental influences or sensory modality incapacity), but from *inability to utilize information adequately*. These children are identified as having emotional, motoric, sensorial, and intellectual integrity, but are unable to learn in the usual manner.

Learning disabilities have been attributed to various causes. As yet, the genesis of learning disabilities is not understood, and children with learning disabilities are homogeneous only to the extent that all underachieve despite seemingly typical potential and opportunity to learn. Cause-related theories range from genetic heredity to environmental deprivation to chemical imbalance. In some, the disability is believed to reside in the peripheral nervous system's inability to convert sensations accurately into electrical impulses. In such cases, the brain may be receiving portrayals of reality that are, in fact, distorted. Torgesen and Licht (1983) have postulated that children with learning disabilities do not process information within the brain with the same facility as do children without learning disabilities. Research by Kerr and Hughes (1987), however, suggests that the origin of learning difficulties among persons with learning disabilities lies elsewhere. They suggest that learning and performance deficits experienced by children with learning disabilities are the result of dysfunctions at either the input or output level rather than at the information processing level in between. In a few persons, learning disabilities may be associated with difficulties experienced during pregnancy or delivery. Inadequate prenatal care, prenatal maternal malnutrition, difficult delivery, prematurity, temporary anoxia at time of delivery, and Rh incompatibility are among complications seen in a disproportionate number of persons with learning disabilities. Although cause-and-effect relationships between these factors and the occurrence of learning disabilities cannot be drawn readily in many instances, such relationships are still suspected.

Learning disorders are generally categorized as **verbal** and **nonverbal.** Verbal underachievement is characterized by disabilities in spoken language, reading, written language, and arithmetic. Characteristic nonverbal disabilities involve motor dysfunctions, problems of perception, problems of attention (distractibility and disinhibition), hyperactivity, perseveration, and social imperceptions. Disorders in more than one performance area occur frequently. This phenomenon suggests a possible interrelationship among the various dysfunctions.

For designation purposes, children with learning disabilities exhibit intelligence quotient (IQ) of 90 or above. In diagnosing learning disabilities, an IQ test and achievement tests are administered. Once IQ has been determined to be average or above, achievement tests are administered. Discrepancies between achievement potential, indicated by comparison of IQ scores with actual achievement as measured by achievement test scores, become the primary basis for the learning disabilities diagnosis.

Diagnosis of learning disability is a relatively new phenomenon. Until recently, children with learning disabilities were often misclassified as mentally retarded, emotionally disturbed, slow, or lazy. Incorrect diagnoses then led to improper educational placement and continued underachievement.

Although our understanding of learning disabilities is still incomplete, we are now aware that learning disabilities do exist independent of other conditions that affect learning and have similar symptoms. Disability, as used in the term *learning disability* does *not* mean incapacity. Children with learning disabilities *can learn* in accordance with their potential provided that their unique learning needs are understood and accommodated.

A variety of characteristics have been associated with youngsters who have learning disabilities. A national task force tallied numerous labels and terms related to this area and found 99 characteristics reported in the literature. The 10 most frequently reported symptoms were (1) hyperactivity, (2) perceptual-motor impairments, (3) emotional lability (frequent shifts in emotional mood), (4) general coordination deficits, (5) disorders of attention (short attention span, distractibility, perseveration), (6) impulsivity, (7) disorders of memory and thinking, (8) specific academic problems in reading, arithmetic, writing, spelling, (9) disorders of speech and hearing, and (10) equivocal neurological signs and electroencephalographic (EEG) irregularities (Hallahan and Kauffman 1991).

Children with learning disabilities, as a group, experience emotional difficulties to a greater degree than do peers who do not have learning disabilities. Walser and Richmond (1973) report that as many as 76 percent of children who have learning disabilities also have emotional disturbances. Whether learning difficulties among children with learning disabilities cause observed emotional disturbances or visa versa remains to be fully answered. Regardless, physical education may benefit such children to the extent that emotional disturbance is a function of frustration and low self-esteem, and positive activity experiences hold potential for helping students feel better about themselves.

Learning disabilities have implications for physical education. Many difficulties experienced by children with learning disabilities are revealed in movement-centered expression. Children with learning disabilities often exhibit difficulties with balance and coordination. These children have problems organizing time and space, which precipitates awkward and dysrhythmic movements. Writing and drawing problems involve an inability to execute fine motor coordinations.

Development of cognitive and verbal behaviors in children with learning disabilities affects their performance in physical education. Texts by Keogh and Sugden

(1985), Thomas (1984), Sage (1984), and Gallahue (1982), although not intended specifically for the teachers of persons with learning disabilities, focus on learning through movement. Traditionally, development of such behaviors has been the responsibility of the classroom teacher. Efforts by the physical educator to reinforce cognitive and verbal learning are most successful when coordinated with efforts of the classroom teacher.

Children with learning disabilities often manifest behavioral disturbances that have implications for physical education. Some children exhibit emotional disturbances, short attention spans, distractibility, and hyperactivity. Recognizing and understanding causes of these behavioral traits enables the teacher to plan success-oriented physical education experiences.

This chapter focuses on (1) delineating specific learning and behavioral disorders among children with learning disabilities, (2) identifying teaching methods to accommodate these special learning needs, and (3) citing specific teaching strategies and remedial activities for physical education.

NONVERBAL DISORDERS

DISORDERS OF MOTOR FUNCTION

Deficits in motor ability are particularly distressing to children with learning disabilities. Many experience feelings of ineptness in the presence of friends, peers, and significant others, because awkwardness sets them apart. Much frustration among children with learning disabilities who manifest motor dysfunction stems from inability to translate knowledge into required movement. Examples include inability to coordinate body motions on a swing, climb a jungle gym, tie shoes, or ride a bicycle or tricycle. Children with learning disabilities often experience difficulty in weaving individual body parts into coordinated body motion.

Such dysfunctions may stem from more than one cause. Although dysfunctions may be due to motor mechanisms, the child may also be trying to learn from visual cues, and may not be able to function when relying on visual cues. In another example, the child who does not function well when relying on auditory cues will not experience success in an environment where sound provides the primary sensory input.

Achievement tests administered to diagnose learning disabilities should yield information that determines functioning and dysfunctioning sensory modalities. This information should influence communication approaches chosen for use with each child. For example, visual cues may be emphasized when teaching a student who, through assessment, has been found to have difficulty processing auditory cues. Later, two or more sensory modalities (e.g., visual and auditory) may be stimulated simultaneously. At this point, the teacher may simultaneously demonstrate and explain.

Here, information received by the student's preferred sensory modality may actually facilitate the student's becoming better able to understand information received by a nonpreferred modality (Schmitz, 1989).

Motor dysfunction may be associated with deficits in coordination, balance, agility, body image, tactile and kinesthetic awareness, spatial awareness, laterality, directionality, motor planning, and dysrhythmia. With the exception of motor planning and dysrhythmia, many activities to rehabilitate basic motor and perceptual-motor deficits are found in Chapters 6 and 8. To habilitate motor planning when the child presently cannot execute a series of movements required for task completion, begin with discrete activities followed by serial activities. A **discrete movement** is a single motor act executed once (e.g., bounce the ball and catch it). Following discrete skills, the child should execute movements in **simple series** in which the same skill is repeated. Dribbling a ball or continuous hopping are examples. Next, the child should execute tasks in **complex series**. This requires execution of many different discrete acts in sequential order.

Motor planning would appear to bear some similarity to the classroom-related competence termed "sequential thinking." The final, desired result of motor planning and sequential thinking is the ability to **execute behaviors in proper sequential order**. For instance, some children with learning disabilities are unable to follow necessary steps to complete tasks required for long division. Given that there might be some association between sequential thinking and motor planning, movement experiences requiring motor planning should be included in the special programming, including special education programming, of certain children with learning disabilities.

The child with a learning disability who has **dysrhythmia** has difficulty organizing time. Tasks that require rhythm capabilities begin with noncomplex discrete acts (finger tapping, foot tapping, hand clapping). Initially, only a single cycle of a skill may be possible. Gradually, more cycles of a skill can be executed in correct rhythm.

The child with dysrhythmia often needs concrete cues to achieve and maintain rhythmic performance. However, among children with learning disabilities who manifest dysrhythmia, certain sensory modalities may not be functioning properly and, therefore, may not be providing meaningful information. When this occurs, the teacher should determine which sensory modalities are functioning adequately. She can then begin cuing the child's better functioning sensory modalities for purposes of establishing and improving rhythmic behavior in the student. Cues may be auditory, visual, kinesthetic, or tactile. Once rhythmic behavior is established using cues from the better functioning sensory modality, these can be paired simultaneously with cues from the functioning sensory modality to reinforce information being processed by the dysfunctioning modality. As proficiency improves, gradually "fade" cues from the stronger modality, and gently shift emphasis to and dependence on the modality being habilitated.

Once rhythmic capabilities show improvement through reliance on heavily accented cues, gradually reduce the intensity of the cues. The objective should be a

Execution of discrete acts in sequential order. (A) "Go to the barrel." (B) "Place the beanbag in the barrel." (C) "Return to your chair." (D) "Sit down".

gradual fading that will not precipitate reversal to dysrhythmic behavior. For auditory cue fading, gradually reduce the volume of sounds that are heavily rhythmic. For visual cue fading, gradually alter an arm gesture to a hand or finger gesture. The goal of rhythm learning, which is accomplished to varying degrees by children with dysrhythmia, is achieving intrinsic or self-control of rhythm maintenance.

Early studies by Kephart, Getman, and Delacato produced theories that stated, in general, that motor activities, properly applied, could help young children overcome delays or disabilities in academic endeavors. However, researchers have not been able to prove a correlation between improvement of motor abilities and increased intellectual capacity. Cratty (1979) supports the case that good motor programs can have positive effects on academic performance. He states, "Although motor activity itself may not enhance learning in a direct way through movement, there are components of the motor task (i.e., doing *something* for increased periods of time) that may indeed positively transfer to academic learning. An increased number of studies suggest that (1) attention span influences learning, and (2) attention span may be improved by various techniques available to the classroom teacher" (p. 42). Gallahue

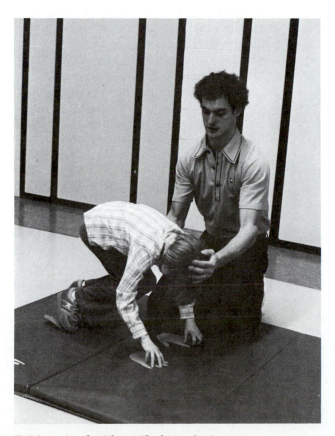

Pairing visual with tactile-kinesthetic cues.

(1982) agrees with Cratty and states, "... the value of perceptual-motor experiences to a general state of readiness should not be dismissed. Enhancement of body, spatial, directional, and temporal awareness as a means of guiding the child toward improved movement control and efficiency in fundamental movement is worthwhile in itself. Practice in perceptual-motor activities will enhance perceptual-motor abilities. Whether these abilities have a *direct* effect on academic performance is questionable. One can be assured, however, that they do play an important role in developing and refining the child's movement abilities" (p. 317).

Further assistance in teaching children with learning disabilities with motor dysfunction can be found in Chapter 7, Fundamental Motor Skills.

PROBLEMS OF ATTENTION

Distractibility.   Many children with learning disabilities are unable to concentrate on appropriate tasks. For children termed **distractible**, the typical learning environment is often overstimulating. Lights, bright colors, extraneous noises, and nonessential equipment and supplies all draw the distractible child's attention away from tasks. When teaching these children, remove nonessential stimuli from the learning environment. Equipment not in use should be put away; equipment to be used should be available only when needed. Whenever possible, activity should take place in a room or gym with softly colored walls without pictures. When outdoors, distractions are more difficult to control.

When using record equipment, ensure that records do not have distracting scratches. If the spoken word is important, there should be no background music. If rhythm is important, the recording should not include talking or singing.

For distractible children, limit the space in which activity occurs. When working one-on-one with the distractible child, have the child stand close to, and facing, a screen or wall to create a nondistracting visual field. To avoid having the teacher's visual presence be an unnecessary distraction, the teacher may stand behind the child.

Concurrent with reducing distractions in the learning environment, the stimulus value of objects used for teaching should be enhanced. For example, a ball used for teaching should be a color that contrasts with the room.

Exuberant praise for tasks well done may be contraindicated because it, too, may be distracting. A low-keyed "well done" or "that's good" is not only sufficient, but more appropriate.

For distractible children, situations that include unpredictable movements by players or balls simultaneously in motion are contraindicated. By controlling the quantity and variety of environmental stimuli, the child may learn gradually to deal with more than one stimulus at a time.

Disinhibition.   The child with **disinhibition**, like the child who is distractible, also exhibits attention problems (i.e., is distractible). However, inattention in the child who is *only* distractible is often more covert than it is in the child who is also disinhibited. At times, the child with disinhibition will verbalize a thought that has just come to mind. Because such utterances are usually out of context with the activity, others often dismiss the child as being odd or strange.

Carlton and Rainey (1984) suggest that disinhibition behaviors may be reduced by establishing routines for the child at school and at home. Routines reduce anxieties over uncertainties in the environment. Attention shifts and drifts into daydreaming sometimes reflect the child's need to escape anxiety, which can be decreased through routine, thereby perhaps reducing disinhibition. The routine in physical education may require starting and ending each class in the same way. Special clothing, worn only for physical education, can help establish a frame of reference during physical education periods. Yahraes (1982) agrees with Carlton and Rainey when he states:

> Remember that many learning disabled children need calm, "structured" surroundings. Schedule an activity—eating, playing, doing school work, reading with an adult—at the same time every day. In school, such a child is likely to do better in very small groups. Try to seat him or her in a spot that will minimize distraction from activities of other students. For children with little or no sense of space or direction, some teachers have found it useful to mark off the desk space on the floor with adhesive tape. The markings help the child to understand where he or she belongs and to gradually comprehend the meaning of left, right, back, and front (p. 22).

Because it is appropriate that the teacher often stand near the disinhibited child, the teacher can note shifts in attention as they occur. At that time, the child's attention should be gently, but firmly, reverted to appropriate tasks.

Another means to reduce disinhibition is behavior modification. Ways to reinforce desired behavior, in this case attentive behavior, are presented in Chapter 11, Modifying Behavior in Physical Education Settings.

Hyperactivity.   Recent years have witnessed an increase in numbers of children identified as being hyperactive (Churton, 1987). **Hyperactivity** may be a sexlinked inherited trait given that the ratio of boys to girls manifesting this condition is 4:1. Barkley (1984) estimates that 3 to 25 percent of children manifest hyperactive (sometimes called hyperkinetic) behavior. The wide percentage range cited above likely is the result of at least three reasons: (1) some agencies may be more aggressive in identifying people who have disabilities, (2) hyperactivity is not recognized as a categorical disability in many agencies, and (3) different agencies may rely on different criteria for identifying people who manifest hyperactivity. Symptoms of hyperactivity (also referred to as **attention deficit disorder** by Prazar and Friedman [1985]) may surface when the child begins regular school classes. Parents may not have noticed attention problems in the preschool years because the child was not required to concentrate in a room with other children.

The child who is hyperactive seems always to be in motion. These children find sitting or standing still for any length of time difficult or impossible. Children who are hyperactive will tap their feet, tap their pencils, and manipulate or exploit any object within reach. Such children routinely interfere with other children.

Hyperactivity in any child varies from day to day. Mood changes may reflect environmental influences, failure to take prescribed medications, or efforts to change medication or dosage to achieve more effective behavior control.

In most cases, hyperactivity disappears when the child reaches adolescence. Although hyperactivity will eventually pass, its effects on learning during critical early years may persist. For this reason, managing hyperactivity has both short- and long-term significance.

Efforts to manage hyperactivity are similar to those used to manage distractibility. The space in which activity occurs should be no larger than necessary to accommodate essential movement. Distractions, indeed, any source of unwanted activity, should be eliminated. Particularly with hyperactive children, equipment should be provided only when it is to be used. Verbal instructions should be brief to limit inordinate demands for sitting or standing still. For the hyperactive child, an error is committed if activity is used to help "blow off steam." These children often are not in control of their behavior. High-key activity intended to blow off steam will often backfire, and the child may become even more hyperactive and distractible. In effect, misdirected efforts to blow off steam may, in fact, fan the flames.

The physical education environment for children who are hyperactive must be structured to control the child's opportunity to make choices. For example, rather than ask children to get balls, the balls should be handed out. As the child becomes able to self-manage behavior in the physical education environment, the structure can be relaxed gradually.

On days when hyperactivity is a particular problem, activities should remain low key. At these times, activities that excite the child or call for creativity are contraindicated. Sometimes, pairing the child who is hyperactive with a youngster who is not hyperactive controls unwanted activity.

Occasionally, the child's ability to self-manage hyperactive behavior should be determined. This could be done by offering the child a cookie (or some other intense reinforcer) and the child, to receive the cookie, must abandon the unwanted behavior. If the child preempts the undesired behavior to accept the cookie, the youngster has demonstrated self-control. As the child learns to control behavior to achieve positive consequences (e.g., a cookie), the teacher can rely more on behavior modification to achieve desired changes.

Perseveration.   **Perseveration** is *uncontrolled* persistence in an activity. The child who perseverates is unable to stop an activity once it has begun.

Perseveration is different in character from long attention span, which implies the ability to persist in *purposeful* behavior. With perseveration, the child is out of control and continues an activity that never had, or has long since lost its purpose. Children who perseverate may incessantly rock, tap fingers, tap hands, tap feet, blink, cry, or laugh. The possible perseverations are limitless. The unifying characteristic is that, in all cases, the child is out of control and the behavior continues without purpose.

In a physical education setting, the child who perseverates may run but cannot stop. For example, the child may run, but may not be able to combine the run with a leap or jump. The youngster may begin dribbling a ball, but may not be able to stop. If asked to execute one forward roll, the child will persist in executing five or six.

In physical education, the child who perseverates should be given activities in which motor responses are varied and change often. Changes may occur in required motor response and in the pace. The child should be eased gradually into activity in which *limited* persistence is required.

The child who perseverates will often need a cue to interrupt the unwanted behavior. Verbal cues ("Stop!"), visual cues (hand gestures), or tactile-kinesthetic cues (a tap on the shoulder) are examples.

When perseveration occurs predictably during a given activity, the child should be diverted from those circumstances. If ball bouncing evokes perseveration, the child, for the time being at least, should avoid ball bouncing. To avoid perseveration-evoking activity, the teacher should control task requirements and be prepared to intervene on a moments notice.

SOCIAL IMPERCEPTION

Children with learning disabilities who manifest **social imperception** are unable to comprehend the meaning of their actions or those of others. They are unable to interpret social expressions, gestures, and body language. These children often exhibit quantities and types of affection that are inappropriate. Social imperception may surface, for example, when the child "crashes" an orderly line and is then angered by the angry response. The child's "in line" behavior may be controlled in the teacher's presence, but when the teacher is absent, the child is likely to misbehave. These children have difficulty making and keeping friends. They do not understand the implications of their actions, and classmates tire of the child's continued inconsideration.

Structure and close supervision are necessary for children with social imperception. The child should be taught in small groups so that social dynamics can be monitored. The social implications of the child's activity and behavior must be explained. Repeated efforts must be made to show the child how social amenities, practiced in physical education, have relevance in other relationships as well.

The responses to social imperception should be empathetic but not permissive. The teacher must be understanding but firm in dealing with the child's socialization.

VERBAL DISORDERS

DISORDERS OF AUDITORY LANGUAGE

Auditory language deficits manifest themselves in problems of receptive and expressive language and in auditory memory problems. The child with a **receptive**

language disorder (i.e., *receptive aphasia*) has difficulty understanding the spoken word. For these children, words should be used sparingly at first. Instruction should be conveyed in phrases or simple sentences. As one means of expanding the child's receptive language capabilities, the teacher may gradually shift toward reliance on verbal cues. In many instances, the child will benefit from visual instructions that accompany verbal instructions. Visual supplements to verbal instructions could be pictures, demonstrations, or gestures. Tactile and kinesthetic cues are also indicated.

Use caution in substituting words that have similar meanings. For instance, the receptive aphasic child may respond when the teacher says "*throw* the ball," but may not respond to "*pitch* the ball." Likewise, the child may understand "big" but not "large," or "small" but not "little." The physical educator can expand the child's receptive language by consciously pairing a word that the child comprehends with another of similar meaning: "This is a big ball. It is also a *large* ball. Big and large are the same."

Articulate words clearly for children with receptive language disorders. Slurred words, idioms, and slang are a problem for them. Idioms and metaphors are particularly difficult, often impossible, for the child to decipher. To interpret verbal communication, the receptive aphasic child should be near the speaker so that sounds can be plainly heard. In this position, the youngster can capitalize on visual cues including lip movements, facial expressions, gestures, and body language. Acoustics in the teaching environment should be good, and the environment should be free of extraneous sounds.

Children with **expressive aphasia** (expressive language problems) understand language but are unable to verbalize that understanding. These children tend to be nonverbal. When they do verbalize, they exhibit limited vocabulary, incomplete phraseology, and poor syntax.

Because movement experiences often seem to give satisfaction and a sense of well-being to children with expressive aphasia, such exercises can become a major source of conversation and vocabulary development. Many children with learning disabilities exhibit greater tendency to talk when engaged in activity or when the conversation turns to activity.

Children with **auditory memory problems** may be unable to follow more than one direction at a time. They also may be unable to carry out an instruction when time lapses between the instruction and the desired action.

For children with auditory memory difficulties, verbal instructions should immediately precede the desired response. When the child experiences difficulty in carrying out more than one direction at a time, the teacher must exercise caution in giving sequential verbal directions. Once the child performs a single verbal instruction on a consistent basis, two directions at one time may be given (e.g., go to Heather, and join hands). Gradually, the number of instructions may be increased.

The child with auditory memory difficulties typically is better able to perform multistaged auditory directions when mentally and physically fresh (i.e., early in the day, early in the period). As the school day or period wears on, the child may demonstrate less mature patterns of auditory memory behavior.

DISORDERS OF WRITTEN LANGUAGE

Difficulties in written expression may reflect lack of comprehension and also problems of fine motor coordination. Writing deficiencies are also known to result, in part, from a dissociation condition.

The child exhibiting **dissociation** is unable to visualize how parts merge to form a whole. Dissociation in movement is characterized by disintegrated responses or responses that overlook certain body segments. Dissociation in writing is manifested by letters or words written in disjointed fashion. The word *dog*, for example, might be written as shown in Figure 10.1.

Remediating writing problems founded in lack of fine motor coordination and dissociation should concern the physical educator. To help remedy these problems, manipulative activities that use fine hand and finger muscles and activities that develop tactile and kinesthetic awareness of the hands and fingers are indicated. Ball handling and sand play are two examples of such activities. To select activities to promote fine motor coordination in a particular child, an occupational therapist should be consulted. To help remedy dissociation problems, activities that require total body action should be considered. When children experience total body action (e.g., as in running, swimming, jumping jacks), they may begin to understand the association of body parts by sensing their body parts working simultaneously. Other relevant activities include having students walk on lines that form geometric shapes, letters, or words. To make shapes, use tape that contrasts in color with the gym floor. Finally, children can be encouraged to develop writing skills by writing their own safety rules and by writing about their physical education experiences.

DISORDERS OF ARITHMETIC

To assist the child with a learning disability who has an **arithmetic disorder**, give the child measured scorekeeping responsibilities. This activity is motivating and will increase the child's interest in dealing with numbers and number concepts. The child may also learn number concepts when instructed to hop five times or throw a ball at a target five times. A number card that requires an appropriate number of responses (e.g., clap your hands as many times as the number indicates) teaches number concepts.

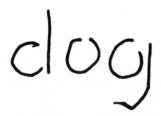

**FIGURE 10.1   Dissocia-
tion in writing**

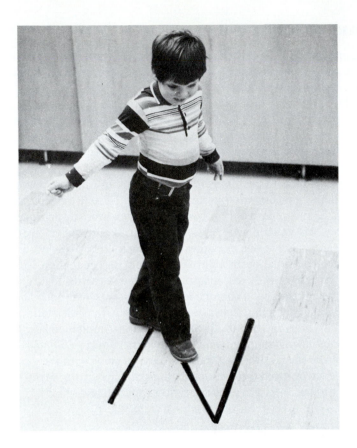

Heel-to-toe walking on letters—a concrete experience.

Ask the child to use a tape measure and to outline the dimensions of a court. On the floor, place adjoining squares with numbers inside and ask the child to hop into two, three, or four squares, then total the points.

Number concepts are also learned through playing games (e.g., first, second, and third base; half court; quarters of play; nine innings; three strikes). The physical educator should be able to include many activities in which arithmetic and number concepts are learned through movement.

DISORDERS OF READING

Many children with learning disabilities experience difficulty in understanding the printed word. The child may understand the spoken word but be unable to recognize printed words. Inability to comprehend the written word is termed **dyslexia** (a Greek word meaning "word blindness").

The physical educator can reinforce reading skills for children with dyslexia by integrating written words and sentences with verbal directions. Signs that say "stop," "go," "fast," and "slow," when used simultaneously with the spoken word, provide help. Drawings accompanied by an appropriate printed word or phrase (e.g., four push-ups, run in place, touch toes) are appropriate for some activities. Students can read aloud their own simple written safety rules.

Children should be encouraged to read about sports, particularly the involvement of young people in sports, to stimulate interest in reading. A child who does not like to read, for whatever reason, may tend to want to read about the subject she likes. Stories about game and sports often motivate reading interest.

SUMMARY

Children with learning disabilities possess average or above average intelligence. For these children, difficulties in learning arise from an inability to assimilate available information. Although the learning and behavioral manifestations of learning disabilities are identifiable, the root causes are not understood.

The term *learning disabilities* covers a variety of *verbal* and *nonverbal* disorders. Verbal behaviors include disorders of written and spoken language, reading, and arithmetic. Nonverbal disorders include problems of perception, inattention, hyperactivity, perseveration, and social imperception. Each disorder has implications for learning in physical education.

Remember that motor disabilities have a strong influence on how children feel about themselves and how other children accept or reject them. Should a youngster possess low levels of motor ability, and should individualized physical education programming be called for, placement in the adapted physical education class is indicated. Meyen (1982) warns, "To place a learning disabled child in a regular class where the disability will be further debilitating is foolish. For example, the child with difficulty in spatial orientation, directionality, and gross and fine motor coordination easily can become the subject of ridicule and failure if integrated into regular physical education class. The child's needs for physical education are vastly different from those of peers who may be ready for highly coordinated physical activities and competitive sports"(p. 340).

When learning disabilities are manifested in verbal disorders, activities can be prescribed in which verbal learning and verbal concepts are inculcated. This capitalizes on the motivating nature of movement experiences to help overcome learning frustrations in problematic verbal areas. In dealing with children who have nonverbal disorders, Chapters 7 and 20 are particularly helpful. Effective methods of managing the difficult behaviors of some children with learning disabilities are discussed in Chapter 11.

REFERENCES

Barkley, R. (1984). Effects of age and ritalin dosage on the mother-child interaction of hyperactive children. *Journal of Consulting and Clinical Psychology, 52,* 750–758.

Cratty, B. J. (1979). *Perceptual and motor development in infants and children,* (2nd ed.). Englewood Cliffs, N.J.: Prentice-Hall.

Carlton, G., and Rainey, D. (1984). Teaching learning disabled children to help themselves. *The Directive Teacher, 6*(1), 8–9.

Churton, M. W. (1989). Hyperkinesis: A review of literature. *Adapted Physical Activity Quarterly, 6,* 313–327.

Gallahue, D. L. (1982). *Understanding motor development in children.* New York: John Wiley & Sons.

Hallahan, D. P., & Kauffman, J. M. (1991). *Exceptional children* (5th ed.). Englewood Cliffs, N.J.: Prentice-Hall.

Keogh, J., & Sugden, D. (1985). *Movement skill development.* New York: Macmillan.

Kerr, R. & Hughes, K. (1987). Movement difficulty and learning disabled children. *Adapted Physical Activity Quarterly, 4,* 72–79

Meyen, E. L. (1982). *Exceptional children and youth, an introduction,* (2nd ed.). Denver: Love Publishing.

National Information Center for Handicapped Children and Youth. *News Digest,* June 1985, p. 2.

Prazar, G., & Friedman, S. B. (1985). Behavioral problems in children and adolescents. In R. B. Conn (Ed.), *Current Diagnosis,* 7 (pp. 1066–1070). Philadelphia: W. G. Saunders.

Sage, G. H. (1984). *Motor learning and control.* Dubuque, Iowa: Wm. C. Brown Publishers.

Schmitz, N. B. (1989, November/ December) Children with learning disabilities and the dance/movement class. *Journal for Physical Education, Recreation, and Dance, 2,* 59–61.

Thomas, J. R. (1984). *Motor development during childhood and adolescence.* Minneapolis: Burgess Publishing.

Torgeson, J., & Licht, B. (1983). The learning disabled child as inactive learner: Retrospect and prospect. In McKinney, J. & Feagans, L. (Eds.), *Current Topics in Learning Disabilities.* Norwood, NJ: Albex.

Walser, S., & Richmond, J. (1973). The epidemiology of learning disorders. *Pediatric Clinicians of North America, 20,* 549–566.

Yahraes, H. (1982). *Learning disabilities: problems and progress.* (Pamphlet no. 578). New York: Public Affairs Committee.

U.S. Department of Education (1991). *Thirteenth Annual Report to Congress on the Implementation of the Education of the Handicapped Act.* Washington, DC: Office of Special Education Programs.

Chapter 11

EMOTIONAL DISTURBANCE AND BEHAVIOR DISORDERS

I can still feel the panic when I hear the phone ring...I automatically think someone is calling to tell me my son has just hurt a kid, or broken a window ...even though things are better now. The teacher he has now has made a tremendous difference...I can get through a day without constant fear.

(Common Sense From Closer Look, 1979, p. 1)

One Day in the Lives of American Children: 1,293 teenagers will give birth; 6 teens will commit suicide; 1,849 children will be abused; 3,288 children will choose to run away from home; 1,629 children will be incarcerated in adult jails; 2,989 children will see parents divorce.

(Children's Defense Fund, 1989)

To imply that a child has an emotional disturbance is like saying that the child has a fever. Behavioral problems sufficient to be considered emotional disturbance have, like fevers, many causes and degrees of severity. Depending on the criteria used to define **emotional disturbance,** 2 to 22 percent of school-age youth manifest one or more of the conditions. Specific figures gathered from Public Law 101-476 data for 1989–1990 show that 9 percent of children with disabilities between the ages of 6 and 21 are labeled as being seriously emotionally disturbed (U.S. Department of Education, 1991).

P.L. 94-142 defines serious emotional disturbance as follows:

(i) A condition exhibiting one or more of the following characteristics over a long period of time and to a marked degree, which adversely affects educational performance: (1) an inability to learn which cannot be explained by intellectual, sensory, or health factors, (2) an inability to build or maintain satisfactory interpersonal relationships with peers and teachers, (3) inappropriate types of behavior or feelings under normal circumstances, (4) a general pervasive mood of unhappiness or depression, and (5) a tendency to develop physical symptoms or fears associated with personal or school problems.

(ii)   The term includes children who are schizophrenic. The term does not include children who are socially maladjusted unless it is determined that they are seriously emotionally disturbed. *(Federal Register 42*, August 23, 1977, pp. 42478–42479)

The original definition included individuals who were classified as being autistic. Today these youngsters are classified under the federal grouping of "other health impaired."

An inability to learn is perhaps the single most commonly observed characteristic of all who are labeled as emotionally disturbed. When all other factors that could impede learning have been eliminated, emotional disturbance becomes suspect. An inability to build or maintain interpersonal relationships includes more than an inability to get along with others. Such persons appear shy and do not convey warmth or sympathy toward others. They do not work well or play well either alone or with others. Children exhibiting unsatisfactory relationships usually are quite visible to their peers. When inappropriate types of behavior or feelings appear in these youngsters, they are often deemed "odd" by others. Such children may be overly aggressive and hyperactive, or overly passive and hypoactive. Mood variations may range from detachment to tantrums. General moods of unhappiness or depression are extremely common and are operative most of the time. These children experience virtually no joy in life with the possible exception of causing unhappiness in others. Finally, the tendency to develop illnesses, pains, or fears associated with personal or school problems is common. The anxieties stemming from perceived stress, whether real or not real, are sufficient to evoke psychosomatic illness ranging from nausea to headaches to ulcers.

Terms used to describe severe behavior problems include *socially maladjusted, emotionally disturbed, emotionally handicapped, psychological disorders*, and *behavior disorders*. Although there is inconsistency in both terminology and main points of emphasis, most definitions seem to agree that being emotionally disturbed involves the following: (1) behavior that goes to an extreme—behavior that is not just slightly different from the usual, (2) a problem that is ongoing—one that does not disappear, and (3) behavior that is unacceptable because of social or cultural expectations (Hallahan and Kauffman, 1991).

The Council for Exceptional Children (CEC) has determined to use the term "behavior disordered," as is evident in their subgroup entitled Council for Children with Behavioral Disorders. Whatever term is used, the fact is that these youngsters and teenagers have extreme social-interpersonal and/or intrapersonal problems.

A distinction must be made between *having* an emotional disturbance and *being* emotionally disturbed. Having an emotional disturbance in response to frustration, disappointment, or sadness is expected and normal. Striking out in a softball game is frustrating. Receiving a B instead of an A is disappointing. Experiencing the death of a friend evokes sadness. Responses to these situations are more or less disturbing, but these disturbances are transient and are consistent with normal expectations.

In contrast, being emotionally disturbed is characterized by behavior that is disordered to a *marked* degree and occurs over an extended period of time. Emotional disturbance generally does not go away of its own accord, and often becomes more pronounced in the absence of intervention.

Although it is important to differentiate between being emotionally disturbed and having an emotional disturbance, this task is often difficult, particularly during the early stages, because early symptoms are usually present in everyone's behavior. According to Bower (1969, p. 178) "what one is attempting to define is the beginning of a process and not the ending—the sniffles and sneezes—as it were, rather than the full fever." Although true emotional disturbance is often difficult to diagnose in its initial stages, particularly in less than severe cases, timeliness of diagnosis is essential for effective intervention.

DEGREES OF EMOTIONAL DISTURBANCE

Degrees of emotional disturbance include behavior disorders, neuroses, and psychoses. Less severe forms of emotional disturbance may not require remediation or are remediable through educational procedures, but more serious forms require direct medical or psychiatric intervention. In the latter instances, educational procedures may supplement medical or psychiatric methods, with education often having to occur in relatively specialized settings.

BEHAVIOR DISORDERS

Children with behavior disorders exhibit a variety of symptomatic behaviors. Although these behaviors are varied, they remain fixed over time and tend toward extremes. Terms that identify behavior disorders often overlap in definition, and in many instances, behavior disorders are interrelated. Common symptoms include delinquency, hypoactivity, withdrawal, pervasive anxiety, social maladjustment, aggression, tantrums, truancy, running away, extreme mood shifts, hypersensitivity, and hyperactivity.

Four distinct categories of behavior disorders have been identified by Hardman, Drew, Egan, and Wolf (1990):

1. *Conduct disorders:* overt aggression, both verbal and physical; disruptiveness; negativism; irresponsibility; and defiance of authority. All are deviations from expected behavior of the school and other social institutions.

2. *Anxiety-withdrawal:* overanxiety, social withdrawal, seclusiveness, shyness, sensitivity, and other behaviors implying a retreat from the environment rather than a negative response to it.

3. ***Immaturity:*** self preoccupation, short attention span, passivity, daydreaming, sluggishness, and other behavior not in accord with developmental expectations.

4. ***Socialized aggression:*** gang activities, cooperative stealing, truancy, and other manifestations of participation in a delinquent subculture (p. 135).

Behavior disorders have been difficult to identify objectively. The American Psychiatric Association (APA) (1987) provide an excellent format to help when attempting to list specific situations relating to students with behavior problems (see Table 11.1).

For students who cannot get along in school, generalizing about why this behavior occurs is extremely difficult. The oversimplification is for the school to blame the parents and for the parents to blame the school. Children with behavior disorders come from all economic levels of society, the very rich to the very poor. Every school has a small percentage of students who do not conform to the norms. These students seem to be searching for something that the school, the parents, other students, or the community are not able to provide.

TABLE 11.1   Diagnostic Criteria for Identification of Behavior Disorders

A disturbance of conduct lasting at least 6 months, during which at least three of the following have been present:

- has stolen without confrontation of a victim on more than one occasion (including forgery)
- has run away from home overnight at least twice while living in parental-surrogate home (or once without returning)
- often lies (other than to avoid physical or sexual abuse)
- deliberately engaged in fire-setting
- is often truant from school (for older person, absent from work)
- has broken into someone else's house, building, or car
- has deliberately destroyed other's property (other than fire-setting)
- has been physically cruel to animals
- has forced someone into sexual activity with him or her
- has used a weapon in more than one fight
- often initiates physical fights
- has stolen with confrontation of a victim (e.g., mugging, purse-snatching, extortion, armed robbery)
- has been physically cruel to people

Source: From *American Psychiatric Association: Diagnostic and Statistical Manual of Mental Disorders* (3rd ed., revised, 1987, p. 55). Washington, DC: The Association. Adapted by permission.

Successful experiences are difficult for these children to accomplish. Too often, adolescents with emotional disturbances seem to search for activities that are considered antisocial or against the law. They tend to enjoy shocking everyone with whom they come in contact. They curse, fight, drink, use drugs, talk of their sexual exploits, and are usually negative toward anything considered by society as positive.

The adapted physical educator is faced with a difficult task. Remember, however, that all students will respond to positive and successful experiences. If the student is unable to meet the social obligations of the traditional physical education class, that is, cooperating with instructors and students, being on time, complying with established regulations, following game rules, and contributing to a "team effort," then the student must be placed in an individualized adapted physical education class. Figure 11.1 shows the range of physical education class placement alternatives for students with behavior disorders.

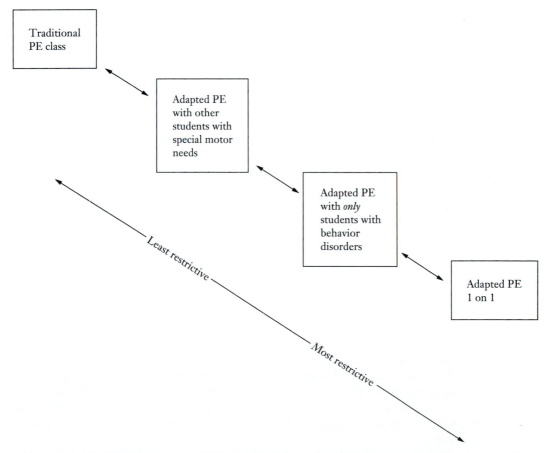

FIGURE 11.1 **Appropriate PE placement of students with behavioral disorders.**

IMPLICATIONS FOR PHYSICAL EDUCATION

To remediate behavior disorders, the root cause must be understood. Hyperactivity, for example, may require drug therapy to improve behavior. L. B. Silver (1984, p. 75) believes that proper medication can calm many children who are hyperactive or easily distracted. "Literally hundreds of studies have been done ... and the findings are consistent. There is improved attention span and decreased muscle-activity level. I feel safe in saying that psychostimulants (medications) are appropriate treatment when used correctly and followed up regularly." He also stresses that medication improves concentration and some motor skills.

Hypoactivity, withdrawal, or hypersensitivity may be a manifestation of a negative and fragile self-concept. Truancy may result from a fear of school failure, and delinquent behavior may result from a need for peer recognition. The child may perceive running away as less threatening than the home or school environment. All of these conditions, alone or in combination, are sufficient to precipitate social maladjustment.

The physical educator can mediate hyperactivity or aggressive behavior by structuring the child's learning environment. Often, this behavior is the result of having to make choices. Requiring children to sit while the teacher is speaking reduces disruptive or inattentive behavior. Requiring children to sit apart so they cannot reach each other further reduces disruption. For example, Earl is continually bothering his classmates to the detriment of both himself and his peers. The teacher should plan to reinforce Earl's behavior when he remains quiet or participates positively in assigned tasks. Such planned reinforcement by the teacher for being quiet and for other appropriate task-related behaviors could render unnecessary other less desirable procedures involving punishment. Imposing a penalty on Earl for bothering others at designated times only demonstrates to the youngster what he should *not* do, not what he *should* do.

The teacher must consciously plan activities that counteract the behavior disorder. For example, children who are hyperactive could engage in "catsup races" in which the person moving slowest is considered successful. Avoid placing overly aggressive children in activities that are highly competitive and overexciting. For the child with behavior problems, activities should demonstrate cooperation (e.g., building a pyramid) rather than competition (e.g., dodgeball). Conscious relaxation techniques can also be used effectively. The child's attention should be focused on a situation, and the youngster should be encouraged to calm down. Specific methods of relaxation (hatha-yoga) are described in Chapter 14.

Manifestations of inadequacy, such as hypoactivity, hypersensitivity, and withdrawal, can be mediated through the acquisition of motor skills that are important for positive recognition. The child may become more active once her skill levels are perceived as social assets. As motor skills improve, hypersensitivity and withdrawal may diminish in response to a gradually improving self-concept and increased positive recognition.

Pervasive anxiety related to physical education may result from the child's oversensitivity to being hurt, either physically or emotionally, by negative activity experiences. The youngster probably needs to engage in activities that develop fundamental motor skills. Skill development allows less fearful participation to take place gradually. As confidence grows, the child's participation will contribute to the diminishment of anxieties.

Social maladjustment is often the result of a child's lacking the skills that facilitate the socialization process. During the school years, significant socialization occurs through play, which is a movement-centered phenomenon. The child with average motor skills is capable of participating successfully as a group member or on a team active in games or contests. Social adjustment is a by-product of efficient movement, which draws young people together in problem-solving situations. The child with social maladjustment often is poorly skilled and remains on the fringes of activities that could contribute positively to alleviation of his problems.

High-school-age students with behavior disorders often seem to revert, in at least one socioemotional characteristic, to a level found in very young children. In other words, they tend to be egocentric. The adapted physical education instructor should understand this deep-seated problem and attempt to meet it in a direct approach. Individuals are unlikely to want to share with others, or to contribute to a team effort, or to follow rules established for the good of everyone. Repeated conversations with teenagers with behavior disorders reveal a striking conclusion on the part of these youngsters: "If it doesn't help me, why should I do it?" These persons want and need to be self-satisfied. They want to be better looking, stronger, and smarter than everyone else, and their craving will not be diminished until the teacher recognizes this driving compulsion. For this reason, individualized activities in which students can work alone (i.e., weight training) tend to be more beneficial because the youngster does not have to share or cooperate for the good of others. The intrinsic value of weight training as a way to "feel good" is documented repeatedly by individuals engrossed in this sport. This activity should provide a deep feeling of self-attainment, thus helping to fulfill the driving need to feel good about oneself. In addition, both the long-range goals and the short-term objectives of a weight training program are ideal when attempting to meet the individualized needs of these students. These activities facilitate self-confidence, and thus help the student move closer to that day when he is able to take part in more socially oriented physical education activities. The instructor should be aware that this socialization process may take weeks, months, or even years, depending on the severity of the emotional disturbance.

The adapted physical education instructor should develop an individualized program with each student assisting in program planning and development. As socially maladjusted children acquire better motor skills, focus still should remain on the individual's skill development. Once motor skill improves, this development permits truly successful activity participation, then the introduction of activities requiring cooperation among children is important. Activities of a "New Games" nature are excellent because they require cooperation to achieve a common goal. These activities also do not designate winners or losers. The individual with social maladjustments does not need to be designated a loser.

Behavior disorder symptoms and their causes suggest poor self-concept as a recurring factor. Teachers and clinicians often say, "Show me a child with a behavior disorder and I'll show you a child harboring a poor self-concept." Recognition that this association exists is the reason for including self-concept enhancement activities in remedial programs for children with behavior disorders. Physical education can make a unique contribution to the child's therapy. By acquiring efficient motor skills, the child becomes proficient in one aspect of human behavior that is almost universally admired. Good motor skills contribute to positive recognition from peers, parents, teachers, and important others. The child's growing awareness that his "likability quotient" is rising generates a cause-effect elevation in self-concept and interpersonal relationships.

Any behavior disorder, regardless of cause or symptom, is relatively more remediable during its early stages. In effect, "the time to bend the twig is when it is young." For children with behavior disorders, physical education presents "twig-bending" opportunities. Acquired motor skills offer concrete indicators to the child that she does have self-worth. Because humans are movement-centered, each time a child moves with skill and is recognized positively, that child's worth is apparent.

Teachers must communicate their expectations to students clearly and firmly. Nothing is gained by beating around the bush or keeping the student guessing as to what the teacher has in mind regarding behavior, goals, and expectations. The student should know what is expected at all times.

BEHAVIOR MODIFICATION

Carr, Robinson, Taylor, and Carlson (1990) describe the process of attempting to modify behavior. "The positive approach to treating severe behavior problems involves the use of interventions that are designed to make socially desirable responses more probable. As these responses become more probable, challenging behaviors including aggression, self-injury, tantrums, and property destruction become less probable" (p. 2).

Behavior management programs are based on the procedures to strengthen, maintain, or weaken a behavior (Eichstaedt & Lavay, 1992). Adaptive behaviors are defined as the degree of effectiveness with which persons meet the established standards of personal independence and social responsibility expected for age and cultural group (McGrew, Ittenbach, Bruininks, & Hill, 1991). Maladaptive behaviors, those that usually get individuals into trouble, are described by Morreau (1985): "Maladaptive behaviors are behaviors which interfere with a person's execution of such tasks [social responsibility]—for example, behaviors which are socially unpleasant, interfere with one's ability to cope, or are repetitive or unusual" (p. 106). Almost everything we do in life is controlled by consequences. Because behavior is also influenced by consequences, a given behavior can be modified by changing the consequences that are associated with it.

For example, a child involved in modified floor hockey might consciously remain on the fringes of the activity in which relatively little participation is ensured. This child is behaving according to expected consequences surrounding that action. Perhaps the child is avoiding energetic activity from fear of ridicule or of being hurt. Aversion to either outcome is sufficient to keep the child from the center of involvement. On the fringes, risk of ridicule or injury (however real or imagined) is greatly diminished. By avoiding the activity, the child experiences temporary relief from anxieties and fear of embarrassment or injury. Specific components of this situation in which the possible consequences of a behavior control that behavior are diagrammed in Figure 11.2.

In another situation, a child might be involved in the midst of activity. If the child perceives involvement as having positive consequences, the participatory behavior will continue.

For example, when a child catches a ball and receives a smiling "good catch" response, positive consequences have resulted from the behavior. The child will probably continue to play catch. Specific components of this situation in which the consequences of the given behavior controlled that behavior are diagrammed in Figure 11.3.

In another situation, a child is removed from activity because her behavior has been inappropriate. For example, the child may have deliberately struck or pushed another child. Antisocial behavior has resulted in a consequence of removal from activity. If removal is aversive, the child may modify her behavior to avoid removal from activity for similar reasons in the future. Specific components of this situation in which the consequences of the given behavior may control that behavior in future are outlined in Figure 11.4.

These situations provide three examples of how consequences of behavior may influence further exhibition of that behavior. In the first instance, fear of ridicule and injury resulted in what behavioral psychologists call **aversive stimuli.** By avoiding the midst of the activity, a behavior termed an **avoidance response,** the child escapes the aversive stimulus. When the child's response to an ongoing stimulus is escape or avoidance, the behavior has been **negatively reinforced.**

SETTING: Modified Floor Hockey

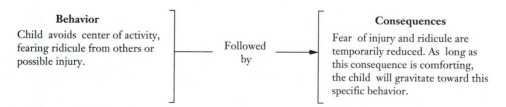

Behavior

Child avoids center of activity, fearing ridicule from others or possible injury.

Followed
by

Consequences

Fear of injury and ridicule are temporarily reduced. As long as this consequence is comforting, the child will gravitate toward this specific behavior.

FIGURE 11.2

SETTING: Child and a Friend Playing Catch

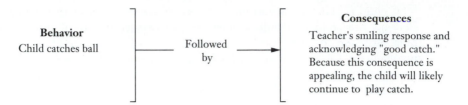

Behavior
Child catches ball

Followed
by

Consequences
Teacher's smiling response and
acknowledging "good catch."
Because this consequence is
appealing, the child will likely
continue to play catch.

FIGURE 11.3

In the second situation, the child's behavior was characterized by **approach** rather than avoidance. In this example, the child engaged in activity because a continued positive response was generated. Whenever the child engages in behavior because the behavior generates positive consequences, the behavior is said to be **positively reinforced.**

In the third situation, the child's inappropriate pushing resulted in removal from the activity. The consequence of this behavior, removal from activity, was calculated to be aversive to the child. In future instances, the child is expected to avoid behavior or behaviors that result in removal. When a consequence that is aversive to the child *follows* an undesirable behavior, that consequence is called **punishment.**

Both positive and negative reinforcement can *increase* and *maintain* the frequency of a given behavior. In positive reinforcement, a behavior increases in frequency as the direct result of a desirable consequence (e.g., food, recognition, money, praise, tokens, ribbons, patches or emblems, or privileges). In negative reinforcement, a behavior *increases* in frequency to avoid an undesirable situation (e.g., putting on a coat when cold, wearing sunglasses on a bright day, remaining on the fringe of an activity to avoid ridicule and embarrassment, feigning illness on the day of a swim-

SETTING: Group Activity (Modified Soccer)

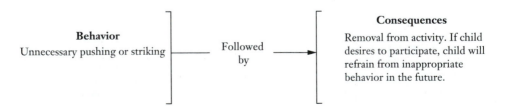

Behavior
Unnecessary pushing or striking

Followed
by

Consequences
Removal from activity. If child
desires to participate, child will
refrain from inappropriate
behavior in the future.

FIGURE 11.4

ming lesson owing to fear of water). In punishment, a behavior *decreases* in frequency to avoid aversive consequences (e.g., staying after school for disruptive behavior). Lavay (1985) believes that the physical education environment is an ideal setting in which to foster positive experiences and a genuine appreciation of physical education activities.

It is important to recognize that negative reinforcement and punishment, though often confused and used synonymously, are not the same. The examples demonstrate the basic differences. Negative reinforcement, like positive reinforcement, functions to *increase* a behavior, while punishment functions to *decrease* the frequency of a given behavior.

ALL REINFORCERS ARE NOT CREATED EQUAL

We know that the consequences of behavior are capable of modifying behavior, but some consequences, whether positive or negative, are more *intense* than others. For instance, what is intensely satisfying, dissatisfying, or punishing for one person may not necessarily be the same for another.

If the consequence of a behavior has little relationship to the individual's likes or dislikes, wants or needs, it will have little impact on that individual's behavior. This is an important point to keep in mind when trying to modify behavior in an educational setting. For example, consider a situation in which the teacher tries to improve some component of a child's motor skill. Were the child marginally motivated or incapable of dealing with relatively abstract reinforcement (e.g., knowing how well she is progressing, or verbal praise), abstract reinforcement would not be particularly effective. To get this child's attention, a considerably more intense reinforcer or consequence should be used. Possible reinforcers might be edibles (food or drink) or tangibles (awards such as stars, ribbons, emblems, or wall charts).

Eichstaedt and Lavay (1992) list several methods for the application of reinforcers.

1. *Tangible reinforcers* are concrete rewards and usually given immediately following performance of the desired behavior. Administration of tangible reinforcers can present teaching problems and is most effective for young children or low-functioning individuals with mental retardation.

2. *Token economy system* is when the student is given a chip or point, which may later be exchanged for items that are of value to the student.

3. *Tally sheets* are a method for keeping track of points earned. If students are capable, they should keep track of their own points.

4. *Reinforcement menus* are a list of high-preference activities made available to students to choose from when they meet a specific criteria of performance or perform the desired behavior.

5. *No cost reinforcers* describes the physical education setting with its variety of equipment. The student can select from an assortment of readily available high-preference reinforcers. The instructor can give structured free time, allowing students to engage in various activities of their own choosing. (p. 120)

Long-term reliance on intense reinforcers, however, should be avoided. As student skill, interest, and attention improve, intense reinforcers should be replaced with less intense but equally effective reinforcers such as verbal encouragement and praise. In effect, move from reliance on *extrinsic* motivation to reliance on relatively *intrinsic* motivation. This is important, because long-term changes in behavior are more likely to occur when motivation to continue the behavior is self-imposed.

Punishment often is used to reduce the frequency of a child's disruptive behavior because it is effective. Punishment is, however, temporary; the undesired behavior remains subdued only as long as the threat of punishment exists. In other words, "while the cat's away, the mice will play."

Because punishment resolves problems only temporarily, more permanent means of reducing the frequency of an undesired behavior must be found. For instance, a child might be punished (e.g., made to sit on the sidelines) for exhibiting overly aggressive behavior; or as an alternative, he might be positively reinforced (rewarded) for engaging in activity *incompatible* with the undesired response. One behavior is incompatible with another whenever both behaviors cannot be done at the same time. When a disruptive child is positively reinforced for attentiveness, attentive behavior will increase. Attentiveness is incompatible with disruption, and thus disruption should be reduced. This positive approach is desirable because (1) behavior improves as a result of positive rather than negative consequences, and (2) positive consequences or positive reinforcement generally provide the most effective means to influence long-term changes in behavior.

People generally prefer to exhibit behavior that generates positive consequences. Some children, however, may not find positive consequences or reinforcement forthcoming. When a child does not gain attention or recognition in acceptable ways, he may seek attention in a less acceptable manner. When this occurs, the teacher may quite naturally respond with aversive consequences (punishment). Punishment in any form, even though aversive, represents attention, and attention, even though aversive in this instance, is more desirable to some children than no attention at all. In this situation, the teacher, in an effort to reduce unwanted behavior through punishment, has drawn attention to that behavior and created a situation that is positively reinforcing. Under these circumstances, even the smallest increments of good behavior should be positively reinforced. Positive reinforcement, coupled with ignoring (not reinforcing) undesirable acts, may improve the child's behavior.

Time Out.   **Time out** refers to the procedure of temporarily removing the child from an enjoyable situation following an inappropriate behavior. In the physical education setting, the child who persists in disruptive behavior is told to sit outside the playing area, and is told why he must sit out on the side. For example, "No, Johnny, sit on the side for 3 minutes because you hit Bobby." When the time limit is up, it is critical that the instructor ask the youngster if he is ready to return to the game, and if he knows *why* he was told to sit out. The student must respond to the teacher's questions before returning to the activity.

The length of time used for a time out is contingent on the degree of misbehavior and on the mental and chronological age of the student. Fox (1982) describes the use of time out as follows: "The duration of the time-out is prespecified and relatively brief. The general rule of thumb is the younger the student, the shorter the duration of time." In most cases, the typical time is less than 5 minutes.

Briskin and Gardner (1968) used the time out (TO) procedure with a 9-year-old child as described in the following account:

> This child was described as hyperactive, disruptive, and difficult to control in the school setting. Specific inappropriate behaviors included screaming and throwing things in fits of anger, crying or whining when not getting her way, not waiting her turn to engage in art projects and physical activities, hitting, biting, grabbing, rough pushing, not responding to verbal instructions, and leaving the room, group, or activity without reason or permission. After an observational period revealed the average frequency of these behaviors in structured and unstructured activity periods throughout the school day, a TO procedure was initiated. Whenever any of these behaviors occurred during the three structured periods, Lisa was immediately removed from the classroom and seated outside for a two-minute period. The only verbal interaction during the TO consisted of a short statement informing Lisa why she was taken from the classroom: "You pushed Jill, you must sit in the chair." "You are whining; sit in the chair." Following the two-minute period, she was returned to the classroom.
>
> As a means of strengthening desired behaviors to replace inappropriate ones, an additional procedure was used of providing prompt teacher praise and other forms of social interactions following occurrences of appropriate behaviors. Although initially Lisa voiced her objections when placed in TO, she soon accepted the action as an unpleasant consequence which she produced by her own disruptive behaviors. Within a few days inappropriate behavior was reduced from an average of 31 percent to 2 percent of the time spent at school. There was a concurrent increase in appropriate behavior which was maintained over a follow-up period. It is interesting to note that improvement in Lisa's behavior had pronounced positive effect on the teacher, aides, other children, and on Lisa's mother. All interacted more readily with Lisa and provided her with the social attention which apparently was quite valuable to her. (pp. 84–85)

Another example of the successful use of time-out procedures is noted by Watson (1972). This example involved the modification of temper tantrums in a child who was profoundly retarded and psychotic. From the beginning of a temper tantrum, the youngster was ignored completely by everyone in the environment for 5 minutes.

As a result, the weekly tantrum frequency dropped, within about 3 weeks, from approximately 50 tantrums per week to a level of infrequent occurrence.

Fox (1982) cautions, however, about improper use of time outs. He states, "Some students will actually misbehave in order to receive time out, since they prefer the time out over the required educational activity.... However, if the density of reinforcement during the activity is high, the student will be less motivated to misbehave in order to escape or avoid it" (p. 74). In other words, the adapted physical educator must keep the activity interesting, stimulating, and rewarding for students; they should miss the activity when they spend time outside the setting.

DEVIANT BEHAVIOR

Some behaviors are serious enough to warrant immediate action on the part of the instructor or leader. Behavior becomes problematic if it causes physical harm to the person or to others, or if it seriously disrupts the teacher's overall instruction and classroom management. In some cases, severe behavior problems include aggressive and violent actions directed against other people and against property or tantrums such as yelling, crying, and whining that occur over a period of time and with great intensity (Carr, Robinson, Taylor, & Carlson, 1990). However, not all behavior that is viewed as problematic meets the criterion of being dangerous or seriously disruptive to the learning or work environment (Browder, 1991). Evans and Meyer (1985) devised a three-level model that classifies deviant behavior:

Level I: Urgent behaviors that require immediate social attention. These rare, excessive behaviors are clearly evident to the student's teachers and are likely to result in permanent physical damage or death.

Level II: Serious behaviors that require formal consideration. These problematic behaviors exist despite implementation of a well-designed educational program. The behaviors may interfere with the rights of others or the person's instruction, can become more serious without intervention, and may be of great concern to teachers.

Level III: Excess behaviors that may reflect "normal deviation." Often, these behaviors will not be targeted for instruction because modifying them creates more of a disturbance in the learning environment than does tolerating them. However, these excesses may be targeted if they create negative social consequences for the student.

With reference to these levels of behavior, an adapted checklist has been developed by Evans and Meyer (1985) (see Table 11.2).

SELF-INJURIOUS OR STEREOTYPIC BEHAVIOR

Self-injurious behavior (SIB) is most often found in individuals with severe or profound behavior problems. SIB is described by Hallahan and Kauffman (1991): "Some

TABLE 11.2 Checklist to Identify and Classify Deviant Problem Behavior

Level I. Urgent behaviors requiring immediate social attention

_____ 1. Is the student's behavior life threatening or does it cause irreversible physical harm to the student?

If yes, implement instruction to train incompatible skills, prevent the occurrence of the behavior, and if necessary, decelerate behavior. Define, measure, and analyze the behavior and begin social skills assessment.
If no, consider Level II.

Level II. Serious behaviors requiring formal consideration

_____ 1. Does the behavior interfere with learning?

_____ 2. Is the behavior likely to become serious if not modified?

_____ 3. Is the behavior dangerous to others?

_____ 4. Is the behavior of concern to caregivers?

If yes, define, measure, and analyze the behavior and begin social skills assessment.
If no, consider Level III.

Level III. Behaviors that reflect "normal deviation"

_____ 1. Is the behavior not improving or getting worse?

_____ 2. Has the behavior been a problem for some time?

_____ 3. Does the behavior damage materials?

_____ 4. Does the behavior interfere with community acceptance?

_____ 5. Would other behavior improve if this behavior improved?

If yes, define, measure, and analyze the behavior, and begin social skills assessment. Consider the cost versus benefits of decelerating this behavior.
If no, consider this to be "normal deviation." Informally monitor its existence as other skills are developed.

Source: *An Educative Approach to Behavior Problems* by L.D. Evans and L.H. Meyer, 1985, Baltimore: Brooks. Reprinted by permission.

children with severe emotional/behavior disorders injure themselves purposely and repeatedly to such an extent that they must be kept in restraints so they will not mutilate and/or slowly kill themselves" (p. 195). Snell (1993) provides several examples of SIB: hitting one's head or banging it on objects, biting various parts of the body, pulling hair, scratching, and poking eyes. Of these, the most common are head banging, hand biting, and eye poking.

Favell, McGimsey, and Snell (1982) identify several less common examples of unacceptable social behavior that, if not controlled, would exclude individuals from being mainstreamed: repeated vomiting, rumination (vomiting and swallowing vomitus), pica (eating inedible objects), and coprophagia (eating feces). It is estimated that approximately 5 to 15 percent of the population with severe or profound mental retardation exhibit self-injurious behavior.

Gorman-Smith and Matson (1985) add the less injurious stereotypic behaviors such as mouthing (putting fingers and hands in mouth), body rocking, head movements (moving the head back and forth), wall patting, and object manipulations. When reviewing studies to determine the treatments used to reduce self-injurious and stereotyped behaviors, the following methods were identified:

Air splints. Placement of air bags, typically used as a temporary cast on an arm or a leg, as a means of physical restraint.

Differential reinforcement of other behaviors (DRO). Reinforcing a person for not exhibiting a stereotyped behavior during a prearranged interval of time.

Facial screening. Placing a cloth over the eyes for a brief period of time (i.e., 30 seconds), contingent on the beginning of the unwanted stereotyped behavior.

Icing. Placing an ice bag on the face or arm for a few seconds when the stereotyped behavior begins.

Lemon juice. Squirting lemon juice in the mouth, contingent on the occurrence of a stereotyped behavior such as ruminating or biting.

Overcorrection. A type of work and effort procedure that consists of two phases— *restitution* and *positive practice.* Restitution involves improving an environment to a condition vastly superior to its previous condition (i.e., cleaning up a mess and then other parts of a room). Positive practice consists of practicing new, alternative appropriate behaviors many times (i.e., an individual who had a toileting accident would be required to practice walking to and sitting on the potty 10 times).

Physical restraint. Preventing self-hitting or kicking by either holding or other mechanical means.

Self-monitoring. The individual counts her own stereotyped responses.

Shock. Shocking a person when he is performing self-injurious behavior. Typically, electrodes are placed approximately an inch or so apart on the arm or leg (this is very controversial and is used only as a last resort).

Time out. Removal of the individual from an activity.

Vibratory stimulation. Sensory reinforcement given if the person does not elicit unwanted behavior.

Water mist. Procedure similar to lemon juice treatment.

Self-restraint. Person restricts or prevents her own movement by wrapping her own body parts in clothing, objects, or other body parts.

Of the listed procedures, Gorman-Smith and Matson (1985) found that unwanted behaviors were reduced most often when (1) differential reinforcement of other behaviors, (2) lemon juice therapy, (3) time out, (4) air splints, and (5) differential reinforcement plus overcorrection were used.

McClure, Moss, McPeters, and Kirkpatrick (1986) developed a training procedure for reinforcing positive behaviors and reducing negative behaviors of a 9-year-old male who was labeled as being profoundly mentally retarded and constantly finger sucking ("hand mouthing"). This behavior is not uncommon in infants but is considered undesirable because the prolonged contact of the hand and mouth often produces health problems such as salivary dermatitis, sores, and bad breath. Also, negative effects occur because this particular behavior is incompatible with many forms of developmental training and social interaction.

This boy learned to turn on either a cassette recorder that played children's music or a vibrator touching the back of his head. Significant results were observed by reinforcing desired behaviors and eliminating his finger sucking habit. McClure et al. (1986) note the following: "Of particular interest is that this form of treatment... provided the subject with a rare opportunity to control his environment" (p. 219).

Self-restraint by individuals is comparatively common and is most often found in conjunction with self-injurious behavior. Isley, Kartsonis, McCurley, Weisz, and Roberts (1991) describe three major categories of self-restraint:

1. Restricting the movement of body parts by wrapping, holding, placing, or entangling these body parts in inanimate objects such as bed linens or one's own or another's clothing

2. Behaviors in which one part or movement restrains another, such as clasping/folding hands or arms behind the head or over the chest

3. Behaviors that do not themselves restrict movement, but effectively produce forms of restraint. For example, (1) gesturing for, verbally requesting, or self-positioning in mechanical restraints, (2) cooperating during the replacement of restraints, (3) wearing particular apparel, or (4) holding objects.

Isley et al. (1991) conclude their review of research pertaining to self-restraint and SIB by stating the following:

> All investigations to date have assumed a relationship between self-restraint and SIB. Some studies have hypothesized that self-restraint is maintained by the contingencies of negative reinforcement, suggesting that self-restraint functions to terminate or to avoid SIB. Although equivocal, data from these studies seem to support this hypothesis.... Encouraging existing forms of self-restraint or teaching self-restraining behaviors to clients to manage SIB are interesting possibilities for clinicians, especially considering the strong reinforcing properties they may possess. (p. 94)

POSITIVE REINFORCEMENT AND LONG-TERM POSITIVE CHANGE

Positive reinforcement is the most efficient means of producing permanent behavioral change. Behavior that is punished remains subdued only as long as the threat of punishment is a consequence of behavior. Remove the threat of punishment, and the punished behavior will return. In many respects, punishment is treating a symptom of the problem rather than the problem cause. Likewise, negative reinforcement is not an efficient means of modifying behavior, because it requires a constant, on-going negative consequence to produce a desired behavior. Take away the negative consequence, and the desired behavior also will disappear.

With positive reinforcement, the child will strive to achieve a desirable consequence of behavior. Often, the child needs no prodding to seek positive reinforcement or reward. She will initiate good behavior, because positive consequences mean satisfaction. Only in positive reinforcement does the child have a positive reason to continue the desired behavior.

The instructor is the key to positive reinforcement, particularly for children who are having trouble identifying with appropriate behaviors. The students must have their reinforcers personalized. If they receive a star for a certain accomplishment, that star is even more valuable if the recognition is strongly reinforced by verbal praise from the instructor. M&Ms, Froot Loops, and star charts may be replaced easily by a strong hug and a squeeze, and an enthusiastic comment such as, "I liked the way you dressed for PE today."

CONDITIONING RESPONSES IN CHILDREN

Conditioning responses were first explored systematically by the Russian scientist Pavlov. Because Pavlov's conclusions resulted from working with animals, some aversion exists to applying Pavlovian principles to educational settings. Actually, Pavlov's principles do apply to human behavior, and understanding these principles can assist the adapted physical educator in establishing a learning environment conducive to producing desirable behavior changes.

Pavlov demonstrated that responses could be **conditioned** by pairing events. In effect, experiencing one event signals the impending occurrence of another. Let us examine this phenomenon in an educational setting. The child who wears a particular piece of clothing only during physical education associates (pairs) that clothing with activity and physical education. This serves two purposes: (1) It signals when behavior and activity levels appropriate to physical education are expected, and (2) its absence signals that physical education activity is not appropriate (e.g., once the child has returned to the classroom). This approach of pairing events is particularly appropriate with youngsters who are mentally retarded or children with behavior disorders who experience difficulty in dealing with different arousal levels in various settings.

Physical education classes should begin and end in a consistent manner. The child then recognizes when the physical education period has come and gone by the activities that consistently begin and end each class. This helps the child achieve a level of arousal appropriate to the physical education or classroom setting. The final activity in any physical education class should be one in which everybody can find success. This leaves the child with a positive attitude about physical education and a desire to return again soon.

The adapted physical education instructor will often be assigned to teach the student who is unsuccessful in the traditional program. The student may be labeled uncooperative, disruptive, aggressive, withdrawn, and so forth. The regular physical education teacher was probably faced with the traditional problems. As he might explain, "I don't have time to discipline this student," or "This student won't listen to me." The following statement is often heard: "The student doesn't like PE, why should I have to force him to like it? If he doesn't conform—then I'll flunk him."

Students are frequently blamed for their inability to conform or follow the traditional program. Too many students are expected to enjoy and to never question the procedures of the teacher. The "hard-nosed drill sergeant" instructor will inevitably punish with some negative act those who are unable or not willing to conform. Extra push-ups, running laps around the gym or field, or detentions after school are common practices in many programs. In reference to negative student attitudes, one hypothesis is that the program or the teacher's approach may be the true cause of most youngsters' negative responses.

To identify why students are disruptive, one must be precise when labeling inappropriate behavior. Terms such as aggressive, uncooperative, hyperactive, or withdrawn need to be more specific. As Taylor and Marholin (1980) state, "Behaviors presented in terms of traits, personality characteristics, and labels are too general and open to idiosyncratic interpretation to be of much value" (p. 273). Taylor (1984) suggests that *aggression* might be better described as "strikes out at others with fists or other objects" or "verbally abuses others by using curse words or a loud tone of voice." Similarly, *hyperactivity* might be more specifically stated as "gets out of line at inappropriate times" or "does not sit still when rules are being given" (p. 25).

Operant conditioning is a method used to increase the probability that a behavior will be strengthened, maintained, or weakened. First, the adapted physical educator must identify specifically the behavior in question. After identification, the desired behavior must then be properly reinforced. Eichstaedt and Lavay (1992) list five concerns:

1. Precise identification of the desired behavior must be measurable and observable.
2. Students must understand the reinforcement as well as why they are being reinforced.
3. Timing of the reinforcement is extremely important. At first, the student may need to be reinforced immediately so as not to become confused.
4. Individualize the reinforcement. What may be reinforcing to one student may not reinforce another.
5. Application of reinforcement must be consistent and direct. The particular behavior to be changed must be reinforced consistently. (p. 136)

The most important reinforcer is the positive and enthusiastic teacher. All children respond to a smiling face, a positive comment, and when appropriate, a hug, a squeeze, or a "high five." Instructors should, however, be extremely careful when making comments to students that they do not make the common mistake of continually telling every student "good job." Rewards should come when the student accomplishes the task *as desired.* If the youngster does not meet the task appropriately, the teacher is responsible for explaining or showing how to improve the skill. Instructors often will say "good job," when in reality the child has given a good effort but has not performed correctly. It is instead the teacher's responsibility to tell *how* to improve the task. For example, if the student is attempting a flank vault on the vaulting side horse and does not get her legs perfectly straight, the teacher must tell the student how to improve the vault. If the student does not understand by verbal comments, then show by demonstration. If there is still a communication problem, the instructor must provide physical guidance, that is, hands-on instruction. At this point, if and when the student accomplishes the skill in the correct manner, the instructor should, with genuine enthusiasm, reward the student with verbal and physical rewards. "Great vaulting! Did you feel it? Try it again." The hug or the "give me five" is also a major part of a job well done. Direct eye contact is extremely important and must be maintained throughout discussion with the youngster.

As Lavay (1983) states, "In physical education, alternative teaching strategies are needed with students who are undisciplined and seem disinterested. . . . controlling student discipline and promoting interest in physical education, exists to those physical educators able to systematically incorporate behavior management programs in their teaching. In short, behavior management is simply good teaching!" (p. 31).

Seaman and DePauw (1989) provide an excellent description of behavior modification and its process (Figure 11.5). In this chapter, we offer only a brief, practical introduction to some major tenets of behavior modification. The fact that all behavior is controlled by consequences and that consequences can be controlled suggests that all teachers should understand behavior modification. By so doing, the teacher can avoid becoming the unwitting facilitator of undesirable behavior, and can become a more effective architect of the educational setting. Specifically, we encourage enrollment in at least one class that focuses on the modification of behavior in practical settings.

NEUROSES

Neuroses come in many forms and tend to be relatively common, particularly among adults. Among the most common neuroses are **phobias,** which are defined as fears that have no basis in reality.

Many superstitions provide examples of phobia-related behavior. Examples of such phobias are fear of black cats, walking under ladders, broken mirrors, and Friday the 13th. Such phobias, however, represent only minor aberrations in behavior and generally do not become the focus of therapy or remediation.

Other phobias such as fear of confinement in small enclosures (e.g., elevators) or fear of heights can become serious and pervasive enough to limit the pursuit of a

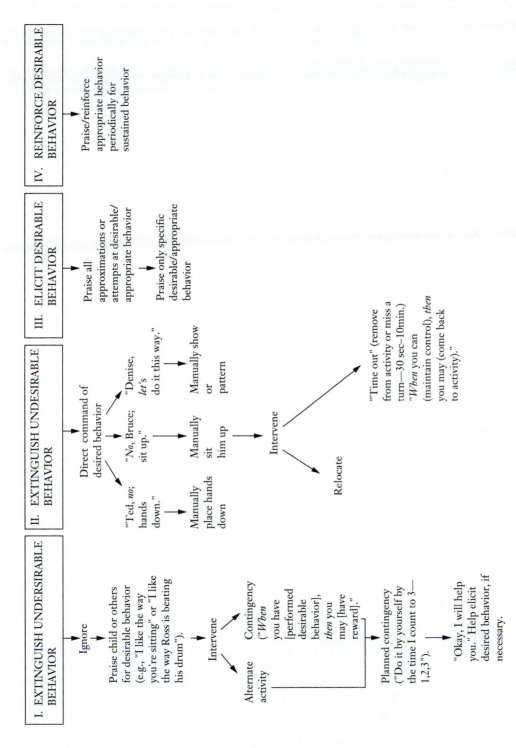

FIGURE 11.5 **Behavior management flow chart diagrams key objectives: to extinguish undesirable behavior, to elicit desirable behavior, and to reinforce desirable behavior.** (Used with permission from J. A. Seaman and K. P. DePauw, *The New Adapted Physical Education* (2nd ed.). Palo Alto, Calif.: Mayfield Publishing, 1989, p. 276).

normal life-style. Among the more serious phobias occurring in certain school-age children is fear of school, or **school phobia.**

School phobia is a phenomenon that evokes feelings in the child ranging from fear to terror. Phobia related to school attendance is probably symptomatic of deep-seated problems in the child's family relationships. The child's fear of school is believed to be primarily the product of anxiety over separation from parents (i.e., separation anxiety). The fact that school is the object of the phobia appears incidental to the fact that school is the site where the child spends the majority of time away from parents.

The separation anxiety involved in school phobia stems from the fear, which is very real to the child, that the parent may go away or be seriously harmed while the child is at school. Separation anxiety tends to be less of a problem in families that have strong and secure interpersonal relationships. Systematic planning will aid in the remediation of school phobias and is important to a positive prognosis. When intervention occurs at the onset of symptoms, the opportunity for complete remission appears most favorable. Treatment delayed by even a semester has been demonstrated to require prolonged therapeutic attention. The most serious problems are noted among children whose symptoms have been ignored during the early years. The prognosis is then poor, particularly among adolescents whose long-term symptoms have been ignored.

The specific term *school phobia* does not include aversions to school attendance founded more directly in school-related problems (e.g., nonachievement, shyness, truancy, awkwardness).

Neurosis also may manifest itself in **obsessions.** Obsessions are characterized by preoccupations in thought; they typically involve traits that would be perceived as desirable if they were not carried to extremes. Often-observed obsessions are eating, not eating, neatness, cleanliness, and achievement. Obsessions lead to behaviors that are termed **compulsive.** Compulsive behavior is the overt manifestation of obsession. Persons who exhibit such behavior are therefore termed **obsessive-compulsive.**

Obsessive-compulsive behavior often manifests itself in quirks of movement behavior. Twitches of the head and neck, blinking, and facial grimacing are examples of such behavior. One problem in treating obsessive-compulsive behavior is that the observed behavior may be merely the outward sign of some deep-seated psychological trauma. In such cases, effective remediation requires identification and amelioration of the underlying problem.

Another form of compulsion occurring primarily among adolescent females is **anorexia nervosa.** The main symptom is total appetite loss, which stems from an extreme fear of ingesting food. Left untreated, the youngster with anorexia may starve to death. The causes of anorexia nervosa are not thoroughly understood. Some believe that the condition results from a compulsive desire to avoid obesity. Among some adolescent females, extreme anxiety exists over physiological, including sexual, maturation. This anxiety manifests itself in loss of appetite, which, in turn, preempts physiological maturation. Therapy generally is medically oriented, long, and complex.

IMPLICATIONS FOR PHYSICAL EDUCATION

The implication of neurotic behavior for physical education differs in accordance with the specific neurosis. Neuroses such as fear of heights, fear of enclosures, and obsessive-compulsive behaviors have direct implications for physical education. Neuroses such as school phobia and anorexia nervosa have indirect implications.

In the latter situations, the physical educator should focus on empathetic psychological support for the child who will undergo psychological or psychiatric treatment or both. Although physical education may not directly affect the remediation of such neuroses, it can, through proper emphasis, ensure that students are not subjected to activities that evoke unnecessary added stress. Demands made on these youngsters must reflect concern for the individual's bouts with the perplexities of the neurosis. Physical education challenges should reflect cooperative efforts among understanding peers. Whenever possible, it is desirable to pair or group the child with neurosis with peers who show maturity in accommodating individual differences.

When evaluating such a child with neurosis, criterion-referenced rather than norm-referenced assessments should be used. The criterion-referenced instrument does not compare the child's performance with others. Instead, the child's performance becomes the norm, thereby avoiding anxiety over comparisons with others.

For persons with fear of heights, fear of enclosures, or obsessive-compulsive behaviors, the physical educator may have more direct impact on remediation. The child who fears heights may be coaxed gradually by empathetic support and positive reinforcement to experience activities above the gym or playground surface. For example, practice for walking a balance beam may begin by walking on a line. Next, the child may walk on a 2 × 4 in. board that remains directly in contact with the surface. Gradually, the board may be elevated above the surface. Throughout the progression, provide direct manual support, but only as needed. Gradually decrease manual support while continuing encouragement of the child's self-reliance.

Fear of enclosures can be mediated by activities that occur in open areas with few children. As progress permits, activities should be moved to relatively enclosed indoor settings. In each setting, increased numbers of children may be introduced into the learning environment, thereby gradually acclimatizing the child to enclosure and enclosures shared by others. For the child who fears enclosures, be sure to avoid darkness, blindfolding, or physical confinement during the early stages of intervention.

Obsessive-compulsive behaviors may be mediated somewhat by engaging the child in activities that preempt the child's acting out of the obsession. Involvement in activity sufficiently demanding to preoccupy the child should reduce unwanted compulsive behaviors. Activities that are incompatible with the undesired behavior are also appropriate. For example, if the child's obsessive-compulsive behavior manifests itself in blinking or head and neck twitching, employ archery or a similar activity that requires head and eye steadiness. This may be particularly effective if positive reinforcement is forthcoming for behavior that results in performance accuracy.

PSYCHOSES

Psychosis constitutes the most serious form of emotional disturbance. Its effect on personality is so pervasive that intense psychiatric attention is usually indicated. Although people with neurosis may exhibit personality problems, they are generally able to function independently. People with psychosis, however, are so severely or profoundly hindered by personality disturbance that, without intervention, leading a normal life may never be possible. Early recognition and treatment are of paramount importance. Even with the most competent psychological and psychiatric intervention, however, the person with psychosis may never fully recover and may require long-term supervision.

Four forms of schizophrenia constitute the most common kinds of psychosis (Randels and Marco, 1985). They represent the types of psychosis for which the *adaptive* behavior will function appropriately in an adapted physical education setting.

The individual with **catatonic schizophrenia** assumes a posture and does not move for extended periods. The person in a catatonic state will not relate to, or otherwise acknowledge, the presence of others. She draws inward, excluding all else. Except for wide-open eyes, this person appears to be in deep sleep. Sherrill (1986) reports that persons who recover from catatonia recall that the catatonic state is characterized by some awareness of external activity. Their recollection, however, indicates that they were incapable of responding in a meaningful manner.

The individual with **paranoid schizophrenia** harbors deep-seated fright, including fear of others. In some cases, the paranoid schizophrenic's extreme fears are exhibited in hostility toward others. This behavior is a manifestation of the individual's belief that others present a real and constant threat. At some stage in the progression of paranoid schizophrenia, the person reveals inflated feelings of self-importance. In a hospital, the patient might believe, for example, that he is the doctor or hospital administrator. It is not uncommon to assume the personage of a famous person. Virtually all of this person's overt responses are tempered by the distorted belief that no one can be trusted.

Hebephrenic schizophrenia is characterized by the person's exhibiting behaviors that are not age appropriate. The hebephrenic schizophrenic regresses in behavior to a stage when life is perceived as having been less threatening. Inability to cope with adult stress and responsibility is believed to be the cause of hebephrenic schizophrenia. Childlike behaviors and mannerisms include gibberish, baby talk, inappropriate giggling, thumb sucking, escape into fantasies, and use of nonsensical word phrases.

People with **undifferentiated schizophrenia** do not manifest behaviors that permit clear-cut designation as to type. These persons exhibit behaviors characteristic of two or all three schizophrenias.

For further information concerning schizophrenia, consult the American Schizophrenia Foundation, Box 160, Ann Arbor, MI 48107.

IMPLICATIONS FOR PHYSICAL EDUCATION

When working with the child who is schizophrenic, do not become overwhelmed or angered by incongruous and disintegrated behaviors. On the contrary, the teacher's temperament must be marked by steadiness and empathy. Because teachers see children on a regular basis, they are in an advantageous position to influence the child's recovery process. A display of steady temperament from the teacher in a world otherwise characterized by chaos and disarray may be one of the few constants on which the recovering child can depend.

Empathy must not be misconstrued as synonymous with sympathy or permissiveness. The ability to empathize enables the teacher to perceive the child's dilemma through the eyes and mind of the child. Empathy facilitates understanding of the child's circumstances.

Harsh discipline may drive the schizophrenic child into withdrawal and is contraindicated, but this caution should not be misconstrued as advocating permissiveness. The schizophrenic child needs limits and must experience firm intervention when limits are exceeded. Permissiveness fails to fulfill this need and in fact may precipitate reversions to maladaptive behavior. Firmness means not tolerating inappropriate behavior while avoiding punitive measures that might precipitate withdrawal.

When the child's behavior is inappropriate, the child's attention should be drawn to an activity different from that which precipitated the maladaptive behavior. Timely and abrupt "changes of scenery" assist the child in regaining behavior control.

When possible, the teacher should avoid activities suspected of evoking schizophrenic responses. For example, if swimming evokes symptoms of catatonia or paranoia, avoid aquatic activities for that child. Instead, draw the child gradually toward aquatic experiences through successive approximations. Have the child squeeze wet sponges, then experience face washing with a wet towel. Subsequently, the child can engage in limited water play (e.g., with toy boats in a sink) or sit with feet immersed in water. Have the child sit at the side of the pool, then dangle legs in the water, and finally, enter the water with a teacher or aide in whom the child has confidence. At each stage in the approximation process, be firm (but not punitive), gently prodding, and provide intense reinforcement for behaviors that show progress toward the norm.

Avoid permissive responses to the child's fantasies, hallucinations, and other maladaptive behavior. Permitting unchecked reversions to such behavior disserves psychiatric efforts and the child's recovery. Be ready to call the child back to reality. The verbal command "Listen to me," or "Look at me," may be sufficient. The child's head may need to be gently held to force eye contact. Should the child's eyes continue to wander, gently realign the child's head so that eye contact is reestablished, then, in close proximity to the child's eyes and speaking directly to the child, say "Listen to me."

Engaging the child alone in a reasonably challenging motor activity often will facilitate an attention shift to reality. For example, the child may be placed on the second or third rung of a climbing apparatus, then commanded, "Climb down." Because such a task requires concentration to negotiate the descent, the child may experience an attention shift back to reality.

The child with schizophrenia, during initial contact with physical education, requires a carefully structured environment that offers security so the youngster can

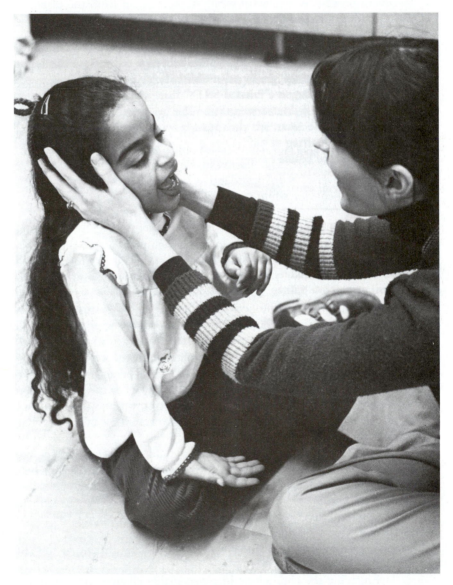

Establish eye contact to gain and maintain attention.

know what to expect from the surroundings. Knowing what to expect enables her to experience some reality, which ceases to be threatening. Positive experiences based in reality, although minimal at first, enable the schizophrenic child to realize that she can cope with reality.

SUMMARY

Estimates of the number of school-age youth with emotional disturbances in the United States differ because the definition of *emotional disturbance* varies among estimators. The 1989–1990 figures indicate that 382,570 students between the ages of 6 and 21 were labeled as being seriously emotionally disturbed, which represents 9 percent of all students with disabilities (U.S. Department of Education, 1991).

Emotional disturbance is a general term covering a broad spectrum of abnormal personality characteristics, which differ greatly in cause and degree. Having an emotional disturbance must be differentiated from being emotionally disturbed. In the former circumstance, behavior is neither aberrant nor chronic. In the latter, however, behavior is manifested to a marked degree and over an extended period of time.

Children labeled as emotionally disturbed with behavior disorders exhibit behaviors that become fixed and tend toward extremes. Twelve types of behavior disorder have been delineated. Certain of these behaviors may be remediable as a result of medical supervision (e.g., attention deficit disorder) whereas for others remediation may be primarily in the educational model. In the former instance, the teacher's role in remediation may be simply supportive, whereas in the latter, it may be primary.

In some behavior disorders, there is indication that the individual possesses an egocentric personality and a poor self-concept. These are often the underlying causes of deviant behavior. Adolescents with this type of behavior disorder should be directed toward individualized physical education activities (e.g., weight training) that improve self-concept.

Good behavior management for children labeled as emotionally disturbed has much in common with good behavior management for all children. The best preventive action any physical education teacher can take is to make sure that the gym or playing field is a happy place where students take pride in their work and learn to treat others with respect. An exciting teacher, who uses a stimulating program, seldom has problems with students.

Neuroses discussed were phobias, obsessions, and anorexia nervosa. In cases of neuroses, the implications for physical education vary in accordance with both type and severity of condition. In all instances, however, the teacher should endeavor to be empathetic. Allowing the child's neurotic behavior disorder to trigger feelings of anger in the teacher, although understandable, is counterproductive.

Children with neuroses should be engaged in cooperative rather than competitive activities and can be paired productively with nondisabled peers who have demonstrated a propensity for maturity. In many instances, behavior modification techniques can help alter the neurotic behavior.

Psychoses are the most severe forms of emotional disturbance. The four types of schizophrenia (i.e., catatonic, paranoid, hebephrenic, and undifferentiated) are the most common psychoses. Without considerable special help, both medical and educational, the person with a psychotic personality may never achieve functional independence. Even with intervention, recovery is not guaranteed. These people must not be expected to function in a mainstream physical education setting. Individualized attention in a special setting generally provides the most effective basis for safe, successful participation and gradual progress toward reality.

The consequences of any given behavior control that behavior. To the degree that the consequences of a child's behavior can be modified, the teacher can channel or mold that behavior.

Three major consequences of behavior include *positive reinforcement, negative reinforcement,* and *punishment*. Whenever possible, the teacher should rely on positive reinforcement, because it is most likely to influence long-term behavioral change.

The consequences of behavior, whether positive, negative, or punishment, vary in intensity. In any case, the reinforcement must be of sufficient intensity (e.g., consequence) to gain the child's attention. In certain instances, intense reinforcement may be necessary to gain the child's attention initially.

The principles underlying behavior modification are universally applicable. The teacher should rely heavily on behavior modification techniques. Reliance on these techniques is particularly important when behavior problems are significant (e.g., low motivation, bizarre behavior, emotional disturbance), but the principles of behavior modification are *always* in effect, whether or not they are consciously manipulated by the teacher.

Finally, the abridged approach to behavior modification presented in this chapter must not foster the assumption that behavior modification is simple. This text does not permit more extensive coverage. All teachers, particularly those who teach in settings in which student behavior is seriously problematic, should pursue further, in-depth study of the principles and practices of behavior modification.

REFERENCES

American Psychiatric Association. (1987). *Diagnostic and statistical manual of mental disorders* (3rd ed., revised). Washington, DC: The Association.

Briskin, A. S., & Gardner, W. I. (1968). Social reinforcement in reducing inappropriate behavior. *Young Children, 24,* 84–85.

Browder, D. M. (1991). *Assessment of individuals with severe disabilities.* Baltimore, MD: Brookes.

Carr, E. G., Robinson, S., Taylor, J. C., & Carlson, J. I. (1990). *Positive approaches to the treatment of severe behavior problems in persons with developmental disabilities: A review and analysis of reinforcement and stimulus-based procedures* (Monograph of The Association for Persons with Severe Handicaps No. 4). Seattle, WA: The Association for Persons with Severe Handicaps (TASH).

Children's Defense Fund. (1989). *A vision for America's future: An agenda for the 1990s.* Washington, DC: The Fund.

Common Sense From Closer Look. (1979, Fall). Forgotten Children... A Costly Crisis. Washington, DC: The Parents' Campaign for Handicapped Children and Youth.

Eichstaedt, C. B., & Lavay, B. (1992). *Physical activity for individuals with mental retardation: Infancy through adulthood.* Champaign, IL: Human Kinetics.

Evans, I. M., & Meyer, L. H. (1985). *An educative approach to behavior problems: A practical decision model for interventions with severely handicapped learners.* Baltimore, MD: Brookes.

Favell, J. E., McGimsey, J. F., & Snell, R. M. (1982). Treatment of self-injury by providing alternate sensory activities. *Analysis and Intervention in Developmental Disabilities, 2* (3), 83–104.

Federal Register. (1977, August). Final regulations of education of handicapped children, implementation of Part B of the Education of the Handicapped Act. Department of Health, Education, and Welfare. Office of Education, 42(163), Part II, Section 121a.5, Definitions, pp. 42478–42479.

Fox, R. M. (1982). *Decreasing behaviors of severely retarded and autistic persons.* Champaign, IL: Research Press.

Gorman-Smith, D., & Matson J. L. (1985). A review of treatment research for self-injurious and stereotyped responding. *Journal of Mental Deficiency Research, 29,* 295–308.

Hallahan, D. P., & Kauffman, J. M. (1991). *Exceptional children: Introduction to special education* (5th ed.). Englewood Cliffs, NJ: Prentice-Hall.

Hardman, M. L., Drew, C. J., Egan, M. W., & Wolf, B. (1990). *Human exceptionality: Society, school, & family* (3rd ed.). Boston: Allyn & Bacon.

Isley, E. M., Kartsonis, C., McCurley, C. M., Weisz, K. E., & Roberts, M. S. (1991). Self-restraint: A review of etiology and applications in mentally retarded adults with self-injury. *Research in Developmental Disabilities, 12,* 87–95.

Lavay, B. (1985). Help! Class out of control. *Kansas Association for Health, Physical Education, Recreation, and Dance Journal 53*(2):29–31.

McClure, J. T., Moss, R. A., McPeters, J. W., & Kirkpatrick, M. A. (1986). Reduction of hand mouthing by a boy with profound mental retardation. *Mental Retardation, 24,* 219–222.

McGrew, K. S., Ittenbach, R. F., Bruininks, R. H., & Hill, B. K. (1991). Factor structure of maladaptive behavior across the lifespan of persons with mental retardation. *Research in Developmental Disabilities, 12,* 181–199.

Morreau, L. E. (1985). Assessing and managing problem behaviors. In K. C. Lakin & R. H. Bruininks (Eds.), *Strategies for achieving community integration of developmentally disabled citizens* (pp. 105–127). Baltimore, MD: Brookes.

Randels, P. M., & Marco, L. A. (1985). Schizophrenia. In R. B. Conn (Ed.), *Current Diagnosis 7, p. 926,* Philadelphia: W. B. Saunders.

Seaman, J. A., & DePauw, K. P. (1989). *The new adapted physical education* (2nd ed). Mountain View, CA: Mayfield.

Sherrill, C. (1986). *Adapted physical education and recreation: A multidisciplinary approach,* (3rd ed.). Dubuque, IA: Wm. C. Brown.

Silver, L. B. (1984). *The misunderstood child: A guide for parents of learning disabled children.* Bethesda, MD.: National Institute of Mental Health.

Snell, M. E. (1993). *Systematic instruction of persons with severe handicaps* (4th ed.). New York: Merrill/Macmillan.

Taylor, R. L. (1984). *Assessment of exceptional students: Educational and psychological procedures.* Englewood Cliffs, NJ: Prentice-Hall.

Taylor, R. L., & Marholin, D. (1980). A functional approach to the assessment of learning disabilities. *Education and Treatment of Children, 3,* 271–278.

U.S. Department of Education. (1991). *Thirteenth annual report to congress on the implementation of the education of the handicapped act.* Washington, DC: Office of Special Education Programs, U.S. Office of Special Education and Rehabilitative Services.

Watson, L. S. (1972). *How to use behavior modification with mentally retarded and autistic children.* Columbus, OH: Behavior Modification Technology.

Chapter 12

MENTAL RETARDATION

"What are we going to do?" asked Mrs. Johnson. "They say we will be integrating all kids with disabilities into our regular P.E. classes, and that includes those with the most severe mental handicaps. You know, those kids with Down syndrome and some others in wheelchairs who can't even walk. How can they take part in our regular classes, like volleyball, tennis, and touch football? I know nothing about their abilities—what they can do and what they can't do. Will I hurt them and will I be liable if they do get hurt?"

"Now wait a minute," said Jill Anderson, the physical education director at Deerfield High School, "are you so sure that these kids with mental retardation are going to be so different? You know how we've made a commitment to meet the physical and motor needs of every student in school, so why should this be such a catastrophe? These youngsters have the very same physical and motor needs as our nondisabled students, and to be more accurate, have greater needs that only our P.E. department can provide. We are planning several in-service workshops before school gets started next fall. The adapted P.E. teacher from Edwards School will fill us in on the little things we need to know to get started. When I talked to him regarding the workshops I stressed the importance of providing "grassroots" approaches for these kids. He said he would start at the beginning and begin with generalizations that would fit most of the students with disabilities, including those with mild or moderate mental retardation, and also those students with Down syndrome. He assured me that these kids were more alike than different and that even those with the label of severe or profound mental retardation would benefit greatly from our individualized P.E. activities. Assessment will need to be done so that we can determine beginning levels of motor performance. He will help us to get started in this area and will be available when we begin this testing. Finally, he stated that we will learn to work with the pediatricians and how to seek their input regarding activities we should and should not do. He also emphasized that our professional physical education background will serve as the basis for assessment, program writing, and teaching."

Jill said she has greatest confidence in her staff and believes that they will weather this storm with few problems because they possess the professional dedication and ability to provide meaningful P.E. opportunities for all students regardless of the mental and physical challenges they bring with them. Jill Anderson believes that good physical education teachers are stimulated by difficult challenges and that her staff will open new horizons in motor activities for teenagers labeled as mentally retarded.

The adapted physical educator who teaches individuals with mental retardation must know about the nature and causes of mental retardation. Equally important, however, is the educator's awareness that persons with mental retardation must not be stigmatized by descriptive data. Individual aptitudes, attitudes, and temperament are as typical of individuals with mental retardation as of individuals with average intellect.

Hallahan and Kauffman (1991) observe the following:

> The once popular stereotype of the retarded person as a clumsy, drooling, helpless creature . . . is simply not true. First, most children classified as mentally retarded are *mildly* retarded and look like the hypothetical average child living next door. Second, it can be misleading to characterize even the more severely retarded as helpless. With advanced methods of providing education and vocational training, we are finding that retarded people are capable of leading more independent lives than was previously thought possible. Given appropriate preparation, many are able to live and work with relatively small amounts of help from others. (p. 78)

In learning about physical and motor performance characteristics of children and adolescents with mental retardation, some generalization can be made. It is important, however, to emphasize the person's individuality. Some persons with retardation cannot achieve physical and motor proficiencies commensurate with their chronological age; others achieve proficiencies that equal or surpass their nonretarded, chronological age peers.

Julian Stein relates an apropos story about the bumblebee, which, according to data gathered scientifically in wind tunnel experiments, cannot fly. The bumblebee's body is too heavy, its wings too short and without adequate surface area or correct configuration. The bumblebee is not, however, privy to this scientific information and does fly. The lesson is that many persons with mental retardation, like bumblebees, often achieve significantly beyond what is expected.

Teachers and parents must ensure that accomplishments of children with mental retardation are not a product of limited expectation. Limited expectations or opportunity deprivation results in limited learning and performance, and becomes a self-fulfilling prophecy. Certainly expectations must be tempered with realism; however, low achievement expectations that result in unnecessarily low achievement are readily evident.

TERMINOLOGY

Authors, researchers, and professionals who deal with individuals who are mentally retarded appear to be in agreement regarding the use of the term *retarded* in place of other words such as disabled, impaired, or handicapped. Although many professionals and parents believe the term is extremely stigmatizing, the majority of books, articles, and professional organizations pertaining to individuals with mental retardation have committed to the use of retarded or retardation as the accepted word. For example, the American Association on Mental Retardation recently changed its name, which for years included in the final word of its title "Deficiency." Also, three major special education text books (Drew, Hardman, & Logan, 1988; Luftig, 1987; Patton, Payne, & Beirne-Smith, 1990) use the phrase mental retardation in the titles of their books. Finally, the Council for Exceptional Children has renamed one of its major branches to that of the Division of Mental Retardation. Thus, this chapter will use the more accepted phrase when referring to individuals with mental retardation, thus replacing other common descriptors.

A DEFINITION

The definition of *mental retardation* put forth by the American Association on Mental Retardation bears the distinction of being the legal definition of mental retardation: "Mental retardation refers to significantly subaverage general intellectual functioning which exists concurrently with deficits in adaptive behavior and manifested during the developmental period" (Grossman, 1983, p. 11). This definition is also the most frequently used definition of mental retardation in the professional literature (Patton, Payne, & Beirne-Smith, 1990).

When, during the developmental period, an individual's intellectual and behavioral adaptations to society fall significantly below the norm, that person is designated as mentally retarded.

The major components of the definition of mental retardation can be further described as follows:

- *General intellectual functioning* refers to the results found by appropriate testing of individuals by qualified diagnosticians and the use of one or more standardized general intellectual test batteries developed to measure intellectual quotient (IQ). General intelligence is "reflected in the pervasive manner in which we respond to everyday challenges, the speed with which we can learn and the complexity and scope of material we can understand, the curiosity and interest we show in a range of subjects or in one engrossing problem, the intricacy of the problems we can solve." (Spitz, 1988, p. 2)
- *Significantly subaverage* refers to an I.Q. of 70 or below, although an upper limit is often extended to 75 or more, depending on the reliability of the particular test battery used. (Grossman, 1983)
- *Deficits in adaptive behavior* are viewed as outstanding limitations in a person's effectiveness in responding to the standards of maturation,

learning, personal dependence, and/or social responsibility that are generally found for children of similar age and cultural group. Again, these deficits are determined by clinical assessment and, in most cases, standardized scales. Examples and comparisons of adaptive and maladaptive behavior are given in Table 12.1.

- *Developmental period* is that time between conception and 18 years of age.

Although the definition of mental retardation has been universally accepted, Zigler and Hodapp (1986) believe that a working definition is practically impossible. They state the following:

Social adaptation is not a well-defined construct; it varies across subcultural groups, changing societal expectations for various groups, and important life changes for each individual (e.g., losing a job). Since this sort of imprecision may spare some

TABLE 12.1   Adaptive and Maladaptive Behavior as Determined by American Association on Mental Retardation[a]

Part I	Measures
Physical development	Physical development
Cognitive development	Language
	Number and time concepts
Functional skills	Independent living
	Economic skills
	Vocational skills
Volitional domains	Self-direction
	Responsibility
Socializaton	Socialization
Part II	**Measures**
Social maladaptation	Violent and destructive behaviors
	Antisocial behaviors
	Rebellious behavior
	Untrustworthy behavior
Personal maladaptation	Odd mannerisms
	Eccentric habits
	Odd speech patterns
	Self-abusive behavior
	Hyperactive behavior

[a] Adapted from *Teaching the Mentally Retarded Student* (p. 12) by R.L. Luftig, Boston: Allyn and Bacon. Reprinted by permission of Allyn and Bacon, Publisher.

individuals from and subject others to the mental retardation label, it creates a poorly defined clinical entity. It also makes the job of describing the mentally retarded population virtually impossible. (p. 91)

The American Association on Mental Retardation is in the process of revising its definition of mental retardation. The proposed definition refers to substantial limitations in certain personal capabilities. Mental retardation is manifested as significantly subaverage intellectual functioning, existing concurrently with related disabilities in two or more of the following adaptive skill areas: communication, self-care, home living, social skills, community use, self-direction, health and safety, functional academics, and work. Mental retardation begins before age 18 but may not always be of lifelong duration (Eichstaedt and Lavay, 1992).

DEFICITS IN INTELLECTUAL ADAPTATIONS

Intellectual adaptations significantly below the norm are defined as those that fall two standard deviations[1] below the mean, or average intelligence quotient (average IQ 100) (Eichstaedt and Lavay, 1992).

Three commonly accepted measures of intelligence are the **Stanford-Binet** and **Cattell scales** (each with a standard deviation of 16) and the **Wechsler scale** (standard deviation of 15). Intellectual deficits suggesting mental retardation, as measured by two standard deviations below the mean criterion for each of the above intelligence scales, would be as follows:

Stanford-Binet or Cattel   100   (Average IQ)
(1 SD = 16)   −32   (2 SDs below average IQ)
                            ―――
                             68

An IQ of 68 as measured by the Stanford-Binet or Cattell thus denotes two standard deviations below the average intelligence of 100. Intellectual function below this point as measured by the Stanford-Binet or Cattell is considered suggestive of mental retardation.

An IQ of 70 as measured by the Wechsler scale denotes two standard deviations below the average intelligence of 100.

Wechsler   100   (Average IQ)
(1 SD = 15)   −30   (2 SDs below average IQ)
                ―――
                 70

---

[1]Standard deviation (SD) is the measure that denotes the tendency for individual test scores to deviate from the mean, or average, score. The higher the standard deviation, the more spread or varied are the scores from the average. The lower the standard deviation, the more concentrated or clustered are the scores around the average.

Intellectual function below this point as measured by the Wechsler would be considered suggestive of mental retardation.

In examining a normal distribution of intelligence across the general population, we find that two standard deviations below the mean fall at the 2.28th percentile. This means that about 98 percent of the general population (97.72 percent, to be exact) have IQs above the two standard deviations below the mean cutoff. Conversely, roughly 2 percent (2.28 percent, to be exact) have IQs *below* the two standard deviations below the mean cutoff. This is how the American Association on Mental Retardation (AAMR) (1983) arrives at 2.3 (2.28 rounded off to 2.3) as the percentage of persons who, by reason of subnormal intellect, may be considered mentally retarded (Figure 12.1). This percentage of the U.S. population presently represents in excess of 6 million people. Of this total, 566,150 were between the ages of 6 and 21 for the 1989–1990 school year (U.S. Department of Education, 1991). This number represents 13.3 percent of all students with disabilities between the ages of 6 and 21. These figures are lower than in previous years because of differences in classification methods between states. Many youngsters who in the past were labeled mentally retarded have been reclassified into other disabling groups because of controversy regarding the inappropriate use of standardized IQ test batteries with certain minority groups. Also, this total number of students with mental retardation does not include those youngsters below the age of 6, which will increase the total. The impact of P.L. 101-476 (IDEA), which now mandates special education for all children with disabilities between *birth* and 21, is sure to be felt in the coming years.

Degrees of mental retardation recognized by the AAMR are mild (designated Level I), moderate (designated Level II), severe (designated Level III), and profound (designated Level IV) (Table 12.2).

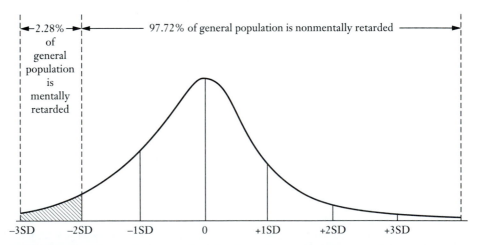

FIGURE 12.1   A normal curve showing percent in general population of individuals who are mentally retarded and nonmentally retarded.

TABLE 12.2   **AAMR Designated Levels of Mental Retardation and Respective Intelligence Quotient Ranges**

| Level | Degree of Retardation | IQ Ranges | |
		Stanford-Binet or Cattell	Wechsler
I	Mild	67–52	69–55
II	Moderate	51–36	54–40
III	Severe	35–20	39–25
IV	Profound	19–below	24–below

MENTAL AGE AS AN INDICATOR OF INTELLECTUAL FUNCTION

One practical appraisal of a person's functional intellectual status is to determine the individual's *mental age*. IQ scores are sometimes perceived as abstract statistics, but a measure of mental age can be a concrete indicator of intellectual maturity. A person with a mental age of 7, regardless of chronological age, can be expected to function as an average 7-year-old. Although mental age provides primarily an estimate of academic status, it also supplies valuable information for the adapted physical educator who must determine the child's ability to deal with movement-centered or movement-related problems. Table 12.3 indicates the mental age expectancy level for each degree of mental retardation.

If not readily available, mental age can be estimated from the child's IQ and chronological age in months. A good rule of thumb to be used in estimating children's mental age is to multiply the age in months by the last IQ record and divide by 100. Thus, a child tested at 10 years (120 months) who had an IQ of 70 would have a mental age of 7 years (84 months).

TABLE 12.3   **Mental Age Expectancy by Level of Retardation**

Level	Degree of Retardation	Mental Age Expectancy (years)	School Grade Equivalence
I	Mild (EMR)	8–12	3rd to 6th grade
II	Moderate (TMR)	4–7	Preschool to 2nd grade
III	Severe	2–3	
IV	Profound	0–2	

CHARACTERISTICS OF CHILDREN BY LEVEL OF RETARDATION

The intellectual deficit aspect of mental retardation is a disability of degrees. The disability may be so slight as to go unnoticed except when ability to deal with complex problems is required, or it may be so severe as to require complete custodial care. Most people (approximately 60 percent) with intellectual deficits are termed mildly or educable mentally retarded.

The person with **educable** retardation (mild, EMR) is usually not apparent during preschool years. Once in school, however, the child's delayed development becomes apparent. As a teenager, the child's mental age is comparable to that of an intellectually average child in grade school. As adults, these persons blend readily into society and within limitations can achieve economic and social independence.

People with **moderate** or **trainable** (TMR) levels of mental retardation manifest developmental delays that become apparent during early childhood. For these children, instructional emphasis is on systematic, repeated, rote experiences, which the child learns more by habit formation than by reasoning. Whereas the goal of education promotes concept formation and abstract reasoning, training tends to foster appropriate conditioned responses. The child or adult labeled as moderately retarded can achieve social and economic semi-independence, with support from others becoming necessary when stress levels are elevated.

Individuals with *severe mental retardation* require constant supervision and support. They may achieve modest communication skills and may learn some self-care skills. Work can be undertaken by some, but usually under close supervision. Persons with severe retardation function effectively only when supervision is constant and the environment is highly structured.

Persons with *profound retardation* are totally dependent on others for self-care. Communication abilities are grossly inadequate and there is little socialization or interaction. Lifelong, complete supervision is required.

The U.S. Department of Education (USDE) (P.L. 101-476, 1990) describes children and youth with severe disability conditions as youngsters who, because of the intensity of their physical, mental, or emotional problems, need highly specialized educational, social, psychological, and medical services in order to maximize their full potential for useful and meaningful participation in society and for self-fulfillment. The term includes individuals labeled as severely and profoundly mentally retarded. Thus, children labeled as "severely disabled" are likely to experience severe speech, language, and/or perceptual-cognitive delays, and exhibit abnormal behavior such as failure to respond to pronounced social stimuli. These children may also have extremely fragile physiological conditions.

Wolery and Haring (1990) refer to the U.S.D.E. definition of severely disabled as follows:

> This definition was not intended to imply that all severely handicapped children possess such challenging behaviors—the vast majority do not. It was developed

to clarify that even children with the most severe behavioral, learning, and medical problems were entitled to educational services in the least restrictive environment possible. (p. 246)

PREVALENCE DURING SCHOOL YEARS

The fact that mild and moderate retardation become apparent when the person is confronted by complex, abstract problems explains why these conditions are usually identified during the school years. Before and after the school years, identification drops markedly, suggesting that nonschool demands on learning and social adaptation are less acute. The preschool and postschool years permit children and adults with disabilities to seek and find functional levels within their potential and incentive.

DEFICITS IN ADAPTIVE BEHAVIOR

The AAMR definition of mental retardation includes maladaptive behavior among the identification criteria. Some researchers believe that the major components of adaptive behavior and maladaptive behavior can be dichotomized and delineated. They cite **adaptive behavior** as exemplified by independent functioning, physical development, economic development, language development, number and time concepts, domestic activity, vocational activity, self-direction, responsibility, and socialization.

They cite **maladaptive behavior** as exemplified by violent and destructive behavior, antisocial behavior, rebellious behavior, untrustworthy behavior, withdrawal, stereotyped behavior and odd mannerisms, inappropriate interpersonal manners, unacceptable or eccentric habits, unacceptable vocal mannerisms, self-abusive behavior, hyperactive tendencies, sexually aberrant behavior, psychological disturbances, and use of medication.[2]

Assessment of social maturity and immaturity, or adaptive and maladaptive behavior, may be undertaken using social maturity and adaptive behavior developmental scales. Although adapted physical educators would not be involved directly in administering these scales, educators should understand the meaning and the implications of maladaptive behaviors as they relate to mental retardation and how assessment can be undertaken. The more thoroughly the adapted physical educator understands the *total child*, the more effectively the educator will find the root causes of the child's behavior and thus avoid ineffective remediation attempts.

---

[2]Reference is to illicit use (chemical dependency).

CAUSES OF RETARDATION

Although many causes of retardation exist, most persons with mental retardation (80–90 percent) present no demonstrable pathology. Among such persons, the exact cause or causes of mental retardation remain elusive. Among those who manifest a pathology, the following causative factors have been identified.

Good prenatal care has been identified as essential for reducing the possibility of babies being born with disabilities. Services should include encouragement and provision for prenatal care and access to prenatal diagnosis. Baroff (1991) expresses concern when he states the following:

> Unfortunately, what is standard and routine care in our society is related to socioeconomic status, and the quality of care, prenatal as well as postnatal, available to or utilized by economically disadvantaged families often leaves much to be desired. This is starkly reflected in social class and racial differences in the use of prenatal care and in the frequency of low-birth-weight babies and the high mortality rates among the poor. (p. 34)

In 1987 a survey was conducted by the U.S. General Accounting Office that found that 63 percent of poor women had inadequate prenatal care as opposed to only 19 percent of more affluent women. The study defined "inadequate care" as a failure to begin prenatal care during the first three months of pregnancy or having less than nine medical examinations over the course during the pregnancy. The major differences between the two groups was a nearly doubled frequency of low-birth-weight infants, infants weighing less than $5\frac{1}{2}$ pounds at birth (12.4 versus 6.8 percent).

CULTURAL/FAMILIAL RETARDATION

Example: No Brain Damage but IQs Below 70.   The "nature/nurture" controversy has been in existence for many years. Proponents of the familial (nature) theory believe that offspring *inherit* their low intellectual potential. That is, parents who have lower IQs will tend to have children with similar low IQs. Spitz (1988) states, "intellectual potential is inherent in the brain, waiting to be tapped, not *given* by the environment. If it were produced by sensory training, 180 years of effort with retarded persons who have all their senses intact would have shown by now more favorable results" (p. 5). Spitz continues, "at present there is no way in which the efficiency of the central nervous system can be upgraded to any meaningful degree beyond the somewhat flexible but still limited restraints set by the individual's genotype [inherited traits]" (p. 24).

In contrast, the cultural (nurture) theorists believe that intelligence is quite flexible and can be developed or improved to greater levels of performance. Spitz (1988) describes Feuerstein, Rand, and Hoffman's (1979) concept of cultural influences on learning:

It is Feuerstein's contention that the crucial determinant of cognitive development is the "mediated learning experience"; that is to say, although children can develop intellectually from direct exposure to stimuli, only when a component, caring person explains the experience (mediates between the experience and the child) will the child really benefit to the greatest extent possible. Feuerstein considers native intellectual endowment only in the sense that more poorly endowed individuals require a larger investment of time and greater ingenuity on the part of the mediator than do less well endowed individuals. (p. 17)

The controversy continues, but teachers should not be intensely concerned with either extreme. Rather, they should be aware that some children will possess lower levels of intelligence regardless of the cause. According to Eichstaedt and Lavay (1992), "the outlook for individuals with mental retardation would be devastatingly bleak if nothing could be done to enhance their potential. Outstanding education and training become essential if society expects each child with a disability to reach the highest levels possible" (p. 15).

INFECTIONS (PRENATAL OR POSTNATAL)

Example (Prenatal): Acquired Immune Deficiency Syndrome (AIDS).   AIDS is caused by the human immune deficiency virus (HIV), and most children contract the disease from the mother who is infected with HIV. The condition causes severely impaired organs that will function as the child's immune system. Additionally, the infection produces damage to the fetal brain, resulting in mental retardation with developmental delays and deterioration of motor skills. More information regarding motor programming for children with AIDS is found in chapter 18, Acquired Conditions.

Example (Prenatal): Cytomegalovirus.   Cytomegalovirus (CMV) is a common intrauterine herpes infection which occurs in approximately 1 percent of all live births. It is highest in lower socioeconomic groups, with approximately 36,000 infants born with CMV each year. (Alford, 1988). Ten percent of these instances result in severe mental retardation as the uncontrolled virus produces an extremely high fever, often involving encephalitis, and could result in microcephalus or hydrocephalus.

For teachers, therapists, and pregnant women working with infants and toddlers, Blackman (1990b) warns that CMV is a chronic infection and may be transmitted in body secretions and urine for several years after birth. He states, "It is now known that children, especially toddlers, in group care settings are commonly infected with CMV, though they show no symptoms. Good hygienic practices, especially handwashing and proper disposal of diapers, can stop transmission to adults" (p. 94).

Example (Prenatal): Rubella.   Mothers who contract German measles (rubella) during the first three months (trimester) of pregnancy often give birth to children with a variety of congenital defects. Among these are deafness, cataracts, cardiac malfunctions, and mental retardation. Mental retardation is estimated to develop in 12 percent of prenatal children exposed to maternal rubella.

Example (Postnatal): Meningitis.   Meningitis, an inflammation of membranous brain tissue, is believed to cause mental retardation among some affected children. In looking at samples of children who have survived meningitis, data suggest a distribution of intelligence that approaches near or low normal.

Example (Postnatal): Encephalitis.   Encephalitis is almost exclusively caused by a virus and in its worst scenario causes destruction of brain cells. The symptom will always include an extremely high body temperature which, if uncontrolled, can exceed 106° C. If the fever continues for 12 hours or more, the brain cells of a small child begin to destruct. The final results are often mental retardation and seizures. This brain damage could also produce blindness, deafness, hydrocephalus, or cerebral palsy (Wolraich, 1990).

Example (Postnatal): Hepatitis B Virus (HBV).   Individuals at highest risk of catching HBV are caregivers dealing with individuals living in group homes, hospitals, or institutions. Residents of these facilities often possess severe or profound mental retardation in addition to multidisabling conditions.

The disease is transmitted by infected blood, serum, or saliva coming into contact with cuts or breaks in the skin. For example, if an infected or carrier student should bite the teacher and break the skin, there is a good chance that the virus will be passed on to the instructor. Thus, it is an excellent practice that teachers working with these special populations be inoculated. The highest standards of cleanliness must be maintained, including hand, arm, face, and neck washing by caregivers. Current thinking indicates that HBV is *not* spread through the following: drinking fountains, swimming pools, toilet seats, common school contact, social contact in workshops, coughing, or sneezing.

People with Down syndrome have been shown to be at increased risk of catching and being carriers of the hepatitis B virus. Studies indicate that the defense system of the individuals with Down syndrome more often responds negatively to the presence of this virus (Weber, 1985). Pueschel, Bodenheimer, Giesswein, and Dean (1991) question whether individuals with Down syndrome who are raised at home are more likely to possess HBV than others. They state, "We did not observe an increased prevalence of hepatitis B surface antigen or antibody in the study group [$N = 180$ noninstitutionalized persons with Down syndrome] and there was no significant difference between the Down syndrome and comparison groups" (p. 243).

Advanced complications from the disease lead to chronic liver problems and sometimes death. Statewide immunization programs for both residents and caregivers have and are being conducted to reduce the chance of contracting or spreading HBV.

TERATOGENS (TEŔ-AH-TÓ-JENS)

Teratogens are agents or factors that cause congenital malformations in the developing fetus, caused by diseases and/or substance abuse of the mother. Teratogens are generally most detrimental between 3 and 8 weeks of gestation.

Example: Fetal Alcohol Syndrome.   Fetal alcohol syndrome (FAS) is strongly linked to mental retardation. Scott (1988) lists FAS as one of the three most common causes of biological mental retardation. It is now clear that the excessive use of alcohol by pregnant women can result in a wide spectrum of fetal abnormalities. The current evidence suggests that the average consumption of as little as two drinks per day in the early parts of pregnancy or periodic binge drinking in early pregnancy may be associated with recognizable (although milder) abnormalities in a significant percentage of exposed newborns (Hanson and Bartley, 1985). Blackman (1990c) states the following:

> Since such organs as the brain and the heart are formed during the first trimester, it is clear that the consumption of alcohol during early pregnancy is cause for major concern. Alcohol can injure the fetus throughout the entire pregnancy, however.... It has been estimated that between 50 and 75 percent of infants born to chronically alcoholic women may be affected with FAS. (p. 141)

Children with fetal alcohol syndrome are physically delayed in growth and are thus shorter in height, lower in weight, and smaller in head circumference. Because of poor brain growth, children with FAS attain an average IQ of only 65 and frequently experience poor gross and fine motor coordination (Payne and Isaacs, 1991).

Example: Cocaine or "Crack Babies."   The use of cocaine has increased dramatically in American society and it is estimated that as many as 1 in 10 newborns in some urban areas will be affected. The narcotic is taken into the body by "snorting" through the nose, intravenous injection, or smoking in the form of "crack." The most damaging result is destruction of fetal brain cells caused by a lack of oxygen (anoxia) from ongoing constriction of blood vessels. Additionally, the fetus is likely to experience poor nutrition as a result of, again, constriction of the blood vessels. This often results in a low birth weight, shorter birth length, and smaller head circumference. Because of destruction of the brain and central nervous system, cocaine babies often score low on the neonatal APGAR test of infant reflexes. Mental retardation as well as poor gross and fine motor coordination are commonly experienced in these youngsters.

PRENATAL TRAUMA OR PHYSICAL DEFECTS

Example: Irradiation.   Exposure to high levels of radioactive substances during pregnancy creates greater risk of abnormal fetal development. Mental retardation is among the defects associated with maternal exposure to excessive doses of radiation.

INJURY OR ANOXIA AT BIRTH

Example: Difficult or Complicated Labor.   During difficult or prolonged passage through the birth canal, the fetus faces increased risk of cerebral damage. During delivery and prior to the child's breathing independently, umbilical cord compression or placental hemorrhage may occur. Either complication can deprive the fetus's brain of needed oxygen.

POSTNATAL INJURY

Example: Blow to the Skull.   It is estimated that over one million children are victims of child abuse or neglect. Child abuse is defined as physical or mental injury, sexual exploitation, negligent treatment, or maltreatment of a child under the age of 18 by a person who is responsible for the child's welfare. Blackman (1990a) states, "As many as 1,500 children die each year from child abuse.... Approximately one-third of abused children have signs of central nervous system damage, one-half to two-thirds have intellectual impairment" (pp. 67–68).

METABOLIC ERRORS

Example: Phenylketonuria (PKU).   This disorder involves an inability of the child's body to metabolize protein. This metabolic defect allows substances that destroy brain tissue to accumulate in the body. Fortunately, PKU can be detected immediately after birth through a simple urine test. Retardation is then avoidable with control of the child's diet.

CHROMOSOMAL DISORDERS

Example: Fragile X (Martin-Bell) Syndrome.   Fragile X syndrome is within the group of X-linked recessive disorders and is identified by one or more genes found on the X chromosome. This condition occurs more in males than in females. Spitz (1988) believes that fragile X syndrome rivals Down syndrome as a major genetic cause of mental retardation. Rogers and Simensen (1987) state, "[fragile] (X) syndrome may account for up to 10 percent of all mental retardation" (p. 455). The syndrome derives its name from a delicate site on the X chromosome of affected individuals, as the tips of the long arm of the chromosome appear "pinched." Measurements of intelligence range from mild to moderate retardation, and children have no neurological abnormalities (Grossman and Tarjan, 1987).

  Example: Down Syndrome.   Down syndrome is the most common clinically defined cause of mental retardation. Down syndrome may result from the child's having 47 instead of the usual 46 chromosomes. Chromosomes normally align in pairs. When the additional chromosome becomes attached to pair 21, Down syndrome, termed **Trisomy 21,** usually occurs (up to 95 percent of all cases).
  Some children with Down syndrome do have only 46 chromosomes. Among such children, a portion of chromosome 21 aligns with another chromosome, usually number 15 or 22. This chromosomal anomaly is termed **translocation.**

A third cause of Down syndrome, termed **mosaicism,** occurs when the individual has cells with different chromosome numbers. This difference occurs when, during cell division, one cell erroneously retains chromosome 21 intended for its sister cell. The sister cell dies, and the cell with the additional chromosome survives to generate additional abnormal cells.

Approximately 13 percent of all pregnancies occur in women over 35 years of age. About half of all babies with Down syndrome are born to women in this age group, one in every 300. Between the ages of 40 and 45, a woman's chance of bearing a child with Down syndrome is 1 in 100, and women 45 years and older have a 1 in 40 chance. It is interesting to note that reports from Texas, British Columbia, Japan, and Denmark show that only about 20 percent of infants with Down syndrome were born to older women. In general, women younger than 35 are responsible for more than 90 percent of all births, and they are having 65 to 80 percent of babies with Down syndrome. Although the mother's age is an important factor, note that approximately 25 percent of all babies with Down syndrome can be attributed to a faulty sperm of the father. If the male's sperm or the female's eggs are exposed to physical or chemical forces, such as radiation or viruses, then it is theorized that as the individuals age, their physiological ability to produce normal healthy sperm or eggs decreases. The exact etiology of Down syndrome is, however, still uncertain.

The physical features of Down syndrome are clearly recognizable. In addition to the characteristic almond-shaped eye features, the most common diagnostic physical features are a fold in the skin in the corner of the eyes (epicanthal fold); a tongue too large for the small oral cavity; close-set, deep eyes that are often strabismic (crosseyed); flaccidity (hypotonicity) of muscles (i.e., muscles appear to have little tone); thick, stubby hands; very small fingers; and short stature (bone growth stops at approximately 16 years of age). In a 1991 study, Eichstaedt, Wang, Polacek, and Dohrmann sampled Illinois individuals with Down syndrome (males $n = 313$; females $n = 232$) between the ages of 6 and 19 to determine, in part, height and weight figures. At age 19 the median male height was 5 ft 1 in., and females were 4 ft 10 in. tall. These figures indicate that both males and females appear to be at least 1 inch taller than older statistics. Overweight and obesity tend to be major problems for teenagers with Down syndrome. For example, females with Down syndrome (age 16) averaged 126 pounds as compared to girls who are nonretarded, who weigh 121 pounds. Five pounds seems insignificant until a height comparison reveals that the girls with Down syndrome are over seven inches shorter. This can only mean that females with Down syndrome are carrying too much weight on their short frames. Similar unhealthy comparisons are found with the males. Table 12.4 provides height and weight comparisons of girls and boys nonretarded or with Down syndrome between the ages of 6 and 19.

When children reach their plateau in height, it is critical to maintain close supervision of diet through the child's parents and pediatrician, because individuals with Down syndrome will have a tendency to gain excessive amounts of weight.

Approximately 40 percent of infants with Down syndrome have congenital heart defects. The majority of cardiac problems can be surgically corrected. Another

TABLE 12.4 **Comparison of Height (Inches) and Weight (Pounds) of Males and Females Nonretarded or with Down Syndrome, Ages 6–19**

Males					Females			
Nonretarded[a]		Down Synd.[b]			Nonretarded[a]		Down Synd.[b]	
Ht	Wt	Ht	Wt	Age	Ht	Wt	Ht	Wt
44.00	44.00	45.00	47.12	6	44.00	42.00	—	—
47.00	50.00	44.50	52.40	7	46.50	48.50	—	—
49.00	55.00	45.30	56.30	8	49.00	55.00	46.20	65.00
52.00	62.50	48.46	61.27	9	51.00	61.00	46.95	60.88
53.50	68.50	50.40	65.15	10	53.50	69.00	53.40	60.00
56.00	77.00	54.10	94.40	11	55.50	76.00	52.47	79.50
57.50	83.00	56.25	89.22	12	57.50	84.00	53.00	78.00
59.50	91.00	57.10	93.00	13	60.50	99.00	56.00	96.45
63.00	108.00	60.05	101.25	14	63.50	114.50	58.21	89.25
65.50	122.50	61.17	126.46	15	64.00	119.00	57.51	101.48
66.60	131.00	59.56	128.21	16	64.50	121.50	57.10	126.20
67.50	138.50	60.00	137.53	17	65.00	125.00	58.00	133.04
68.00	143.00	60.20	145.49	18	65.50	128.00	58.89	140.44
—	—	61.00	137.00	19	—	—	58.00	142.00

[a] Norms for the nonretarded from *Nutrition for Fitness and Sports* (pp. A56–57) by M.H. Williams, 1983, Dubuque, IA: W.C. Brown. Copyright W.C. Brown. Adapted by permission.

[b] Norms for individuals with Down syndrome from *Physical Fitness and Motor Skill Levels of Individuals with Mental Retardation: Mild, Moderate, and Down Syndrome Ages 6–21* by C.B. Eichstaedt, P.Y. Wang, J.J. Polacek, & P.F. Dohrmann, 1991, Normal, IL: Illinois State University Printing Services.

congenital defect, **atlantoaxial instability (AAI)** has been identified as potentially dangerous for approximately 10 to 20 percent of all individuals with Down syndrome. This condition is defined as a malalignment or natural displacement of the C1 vertebra in relation to the C2 vertebra. An enlarged space between the vertebrae allows excessive movement. If the individual should hyperextend or radically flex the neck, the spinal cord is exposed to possible damage. The international office of the Special Olympics Incorporated, now requires all persons with Down syndrome to be x-rayed before participating in competitive activities. Any individual who has AAI is not permitted to take part in gymnastics, diving, butterfly stroke in swimming, diving start in swimming, high jump, pentathlon, soccer, or any warm-up exercise placing potential pressure on the head or neck.

Share and French (1982) attribute the deficits in motor skill of children with Down syndrome to hypotonia (i.e., lack of muscle tone). They theorize that this deficit is related to a smaller cerebellum or cerebellar impairment. Remember that the function of the cerebellum is directly related to synthesizing movement coordination in the body. In addition, thyroid and pituitary deficiencies are often found in these youngsters. Coleman (1988) has found that in the middle childhood years, some children with Down syndrome tend to become overweight, sluggish, and dry skinned. She believes that in most cases these problems are caused by hypothyroidism and suggests that by the time these individuals reach adulthood, between 15 and 40 percent will have evidence of subnormal thyroxine and raised thyrotropin levels. Coleman (1988) states, "It is currently recommended that every Down syndrome child have a thyroid study every year. In case of a rapid development of obesity or dullness, a thyroid profile should be taken immediately" (pp. 14–15). Peuschel, Jackson, Giesswein, Dean, and Pezzullo (1991) suggest that because thyroid dysfunctions in individuals with Down syndrome are more common than in general population, periodic thyroid hormone function tests should be performed, particularly as the persons advance in age.

The congenital and physical constraints of persons with Down syndrome have important implications for physical fitness and motor skill development. Owing to these constraints, the attainment of above average physical fitness and motor skills is difficult for individuals with Down syndrome.

Eichstaedt, Wang, Polacek, and Dohrmann (1991) found that children and teenagers with Down syndrome (ages 6–21 years) fall below the 10th percentile on all items in the *AAHPERD Health Related Physical Fitness Test* battery (1980). These items measure cardiorespiratory endurance, abdominal and hip flexion strength and endurance, excessive adipose tissue, and higher back and hamstring flexibility. The researchers confirmed that individuals with Down syndrome are far more flexible than other nonretarded and other people with mental retardation. This facility is negative from the standpoint of coordinated movement and speed, both of which are related directly to degree of tonus of body ligaments and tendons. The hyperflexibility of youngsters with Down syndrome is therefore not a desirable trait. Evidence does exist, however, that this condition can be improved through progressive strength programs.

Adapted physical educators must keep in mind the physical constraints of students with Down syndrome when they make activity selections. For example, small hands and fingers can make catching and throwing difficult. When teaching throwing, the instructor should show the youngsters how to hold the ball with three fingers across the seams, instead of teaching the regular two-finger grip. When foot problems are encountered, long periods of running may be difficult, and the adapted physical educator should choose alternative activities such as stationary bicycle riding or swimming. Koranda (1991) believes that muscular development needs to be stimulated by exercises, by marching to music, and by the use of trampolines, on which many youngsters with Down syndrome become quite good. Scholl (1991) has found that use of the trampoline is extremely valuable. He believes that this activity contributes greatly to improved balance and motor planning. Swimming is also an enjoyable and helpful activity that can be taught to these children, even at an early age.

When children reach their plateau in height, it is critical to maintain close supervision of diet, because individuals with Down syndrome have a tendency to gain weight. Glaze (1985) indicates that both males and females between ages 13 and 18 continue to gain weight despite the fact that they reached maximum height in their early teens.

Share and French (1982) list developmental progressions of specific gross motor skills for children with Down syndrome between the ages of birth and 6 years (Table 12.5).

TABLE 12.5   **Developmental Progression of Specific Gross Motor Skills of Children with Down Syndrome**

| | Age of Onset (in months) | | | |
	Normal	Down Syndrome	Difference in Months	Norm Rate (%)
Motor Skill				
1. Sitting				
Sits with head erect, but thrust forward and unsteady	3	3	0	100
Sits with head set forward	4	5	1	80
Maintains an erect sitting position	7	11	4	64
2. Standing				
While supported, bears small fraction of weight momentarily	3	3	0	100
Stands and maintains balance briefly, with hands held	8	13	5	61
Uses rail of crib to pull self to a standing position	10	18	8	56
3. Rolling				
On the verge of rolling over	4	5	2	1
Rolls from back to stomach	6	7	1	86
4. Rests weight on hands with chest off crib or surface	5	7	2	71
5. Partially turns on stomach	8	12	4	67
6. Creeps				
Creeps on hands and knees	10	15	5	67
Creeps up at least one or two steps	15	24	9	63
7. Walks				
Moves around freely while holding onto a rail or with both hands held	12	21	9	57
Walks with only one hand held	13	27	14	48
Walks a few steps without assistance, starting and stopping	15	30	15	60
Walks and seldom falls	18	30	12	60
Walks upstairs with one hand held	18	55	37	33
Walks downstairs with one hand held	21	36	15	58
Walks on tiptoes after demonstration	30	48	18	63
Alternated feet when going upstairs in adult fashion	36	54	18	67
Walks on a walking board	42	72+	30	58+
8. Seats self in small chair	18	30	12	60
9. Throwing				
Throws a ball	18	30	12	60
Throws overhand	48	72	24	67

Source: Reprinted with permission from Share and French, 1982.

TABLE 12.5 (continued)   **Developmental Progression of Specific Gross Motor Skills of Children with Down Syndrome**

| | Age of Onset (in months) | | | |
Motor Skill	Normal	Down Syndrome	Difference in Months	Norm Rate (%)
10. Squats while playing	21	36	15	58
11. Kicks a large ball after demonstration	21	36	15	58
12. Runs well without falling (still not fast)	24	36	15	58
13. Jumping and hopping				
Jumps up with both feet off the floor after demonstration	30	48	18	63
Jumps from bottom stair, landing erect	36	54	18	67
Jumps while running	48	72+	24	67+
Hops on one foot	54	72+	18	75+
14. Rides a tricycle using pedals	36	60	24	60
15. Skipping				
Skips with one foot forward	48	72+	24	67+
Skips, alternating lead foot	60	72+	12	83+

Winnick (1979) has identified major physical and motor characteristics of children with Down syndrome and the resulting implications for movement experiences (Table 12.6).

MOTOR CHARACTERISTICS

Although children with mental retardation generally achieve at lower levels of physical and motor performance, they tend to be more similar to their chronological age peers in physical and motor performance than in any other single respect. These youngsters appear to have greatest achievement potential in this domain. Although physical and motor performance deficits do exist, such deficits are often more a matter of impoverished opportunity than impoverished potential. Many persons with retardation, particularly those with mild classifications, often demonstrate levels of physical and motor proficiency that approximate those of their chronological age peers. Because physical education is, indeed, part of special education (a primary service under Public Law 101-476), improved physical and motor performances among individuals with mental retardation should become a reality.

TABLE 12.6 Characteristics of the Child with Down Syndrome

Characteristics	Implications for Movement Experiences
Lag in physical growth. (Growth ceases at an earlier than normal age and generally results in shorter height and smaller overall stature.) Lag is evident in motor development.	The child may need to participate in activities geared for younger age groups.
The circulatory system is less well developed. Arteries are often narrow and thinner than normal, and less vascular proliferation is evidenced. Many children (especially boys) exhibit congenital heart disorders, heart murmurs and septum defects being the most common.	Although there is a need for the development of endurance, youngsters will have difficulty in endurance activities. It is necessary for all children to have a medical exam and for the instructor to develop a program with medical consultation.
Poor respiration and susceptibility to respiratory infections (Underdeveloped jaw causes mouth to be too small for normal-sized tongue, inducing mouth breathing.)	Poor respiration may impede participation in endurance activities.
Perceptual disabilities.	Children may be clumsy and awkward. Activities to develop perceptual abilities should be emphasized.
Poor balance.	Because balance is important in most physical and motor activities, lack of balance will affect performance ability. Children need balance training.
Enjoyment of music and rhythmic activities.	The instructor should include rhythmic activities in the program to provide successful and enjoyable experiences and should use music as an aid in teaching.
Obesity.	General overall participation in activities that enhance weight reduction is recommended.
Flabbiness. (Hypotonicity, particularly associated with newborn infants.)	The instructor should provide opportunity for movement experiences at early ages and activities to increase strength at later ages.
Protruding abdomen, lack of muscle and ligament support around the joints, and pronated ankles.	Activities to enhance body alignment and to increase muscle and ligament support around the joints and abdominal exercises are recommended.
Ability to mimic.	Instructor should demonstrate activities and ask children to imitate them.

Source: Reprinted with permission from Winnick, J. P. *Early Movement Experiences and Development: Habilitation and Remediation.* Philadelphia: W. B. Saunders, 1979, p. 229.

Although data are available regarding intellectual and behavioral characteristics of people with mental retardation, less data are available about their physical and motor performance characteristics. Until recently, the education of these youngsters and teenagers, under the guise of special education, was a classroom-centered phenomenon. Focus was largely on classroom-developed competencies for reading, writing, language, numbers, self-help, and socialization. The primary emphasis was on the child's mental retardation as a problem of intellect. The result of these attitudes has been the relative deemphasis of the child's movement-centered needs and potentials. Block (1991) states, "It is not unreasonable to suggest that the average child with Down syndrome today who is reared at home and who receives early intervention is completely different from the child with Down syndrome reared prior to 1970" (p. 180).

Before 1977 physical education of individuals with mental retardation seemed only a modest priority. This deemphasis occurred in part because many physical educators, although they taught children with special needs, perceived themselves primarily as teachers of children with physical and orthopedic disabilities. Most of these teachers did not consider themselves prepared to deal with the physical and motor performance needs of children with mental retardation. As a result, the physical education needs of these children often were not met.

Until recently, most information gathered in the physical education domain focused on the child's physical growth: collections of anthropometric data including length, height, weight, width, girth, and body fat. Little information was available regarding motor performance.

In reference to his review of research dealing with physical fitness and individuals with mental retardation, Newell (1985) states, "The mentally retarded are generally less active than nonretarded individuals, and this alone contributes to many of the performance differences typically reported in studies with physical fitness orientation" (p. 185).

Thomas (1984) refers to the motor learning problems that affect children with mental retardation (MR). She states the following:

> Training studies and other research have manipulated behavior to produce "normal" performance in MR individuals. That is, MR children can perform qualitatively like their chronological age counterparts when taught or forced to do so. Generalization and transfer are the greatest challenge for remediation. MR individuals can be both cued to attend and forced to rehearse, and exhibit normal retention. With more time (or trials), MR students can reach and maintain mastery. These individuals probably have less experience stored in LTS [long-term storage] than do normal individuals, and have increased difficulty in placing information there. They also have little knowledge about memory and ways to facilitate memory. All of these factors are alterable. (p. 182)

In other words, with appropriate teacher cues, adequate trials, and enough practice time, students with mental retardation can and will develop long-term memory storage in relation to learning motor skills.

Newell (1985) identifies the problem of past research related to motor skills learning and subjects with mental retardation as follows: "Of more specific concern to the consideration of skill acquisition in the mentally retarded, is the realization that a very small range of motor skills have been utilized for analysis (often a key press or a simple unidimensional movement) and that problems of learning have been eliminated by the motor performance orientation" (p. 186).

Sugden and Keogh (1990) found that children with mental retardation do not spontaneously exhibit an ability to remember movement cues. When students are prompted through instruction in the use of a strategy to recall movement, accuracy of recall was superior to the recall of other students with mental retardation who did not receive instruction. Horgan (1985) believes that the issue of spontaneity (i.e., acting without thinking) in adopting memory strategies for the recall of movement cues is fundamental to understanding memory structure of individuals with mental retardation. He substantiates his contention by his 1983 study in which he found no differences between his instruction subjects with mental retardation and two nonretarded instruction groups. His findings support the notion that people with mental retardation can make improvements in their movement accuracy equal to the improvements of their nonretarded counterparts. He qualifies his findings by stating that "the retarded *must* be made aware of effective means to assist them in coding, processing, and retaining movement information" (Horgan 1985, p. 201).

When analyzing developmental delays, researchers tend to place much emphasis on the role of reaction time. Henderson and Illingworth (1991) confirmed in their study of 18 children with Down syndrome (M age = 144.3 months) that their subjects did indeed have a significantly slower reaction time than control groups of both disabled and nondisabled children.

A question often arises as to whether individuals with Down syndrome can improve in motor performance. There appears to be little question regarding the untapped potential of these people. Although developmental delays are often extensive, early intervention has been attributed to excellent results.

Perceptual problems appear to be greater in children with Down syndrome. Block (1991) states, "While perceptual problems most likely do exist, the success or failure of children with DS in tasks requiring the analysis and interpretation of sensory information may reflect more the task conditions and strategies used rather than specific perceptual deficits" (p. 184).

Thombs and Sugden (1991) analyzed 40 children and adolescents with Down syndrome (ages between 6 and 16) and concluded that manual tasks do improve as age increases. They state the following:

> The results here demonstrate that skilled performance, as measured by a number of variables—speed, strategies, types of grip—does change between the ages of 6 and 16 years. It is doubtful that the tasks were influenced by such factors as body size or strength, and thus it is to the processes involved in the control of skill that we should be looking to explain these differences.... The results from this study form an optimistic note because naturally occurring changes were taking place within the

age groups studied, suggesting that even more enhancement is possible with specific forms of remediation. (pp. 252–253).

Francis and Rarick (1963) were among the first physical educators who sought systematically to determine physical and motor performance characteristics of children with mental retardation. Their data were drawn from (1) children classified as mentally retarded and assigned to special classes (IQ range 50–90), and (2) institutionalized children (IQ range 15–50). The researchers undertook to do the following: (1) determine age and sex trends in gross motor abilities, (2) compare motor achievement levels, (3) determine if interrelationships among gross motor functions of children with retardation were different from those among functions of children who are nonretarded, (4) determine possible relationships between motor performance and mental retardation, and (5) devise tests of gross motor performance to be used for institutionalized children of very low intelligence. Although Francis and Rarick's comments are almost 30 years old, they still are appropriate today.

IS THERE A RELATIONSHIP BETWEEN MOTOR AND COGNITIVE DEVELOPMENT?

In recent years, investigators have endeavored to determine the precise nature of the motor development-cognitive development relationship. Thomas (1984) identifies one problem of the child with mental retardation in regard to motor learning. She states that "the same system controls all learning and memory, whether cognitive, motor, or affective. A problem in the memory system may affect motor skill acquisition in infinite ways, including less understanding of task variables or verbal instructions, poor motor planning, slower processing, and inadequate socialization" (p. 175).

Cratty (1974) cautions against making overzealous claims for the role that physical education plays in the intellectual development of children with mental retardation. He suggests several possible positive outcomes of physical education for these children:

1. Movement capabilities often lead to vocational opportunities for children who are retarded.
2. Remediation of motor problems, coupled with learning of play skills, can lead to helpful social interactions among children who are retarded and between children who are retarded and nonretarded.
3. Physical activities help the child who is retarded to achieve success in skills that have performance levels easily discernible both by the youth and by his observing teacher.

4. Academic tasks, when used to motivate physical activities, can be a powerful tool for improving academic abilities in children who are retarded.

5. Sustained and intensive programs of sensory-motor activity, coupled with other kinds of sensory stimulation, have been shown to improve basic adaptive behaviors of some youngsters who are profoundly and severely retarded.

6. When applied properly, various kinds of relaxation training involving reduction of excess muscular tensions may help reduce hyperactivity in some youngsters who are retarded.

7. Rhythmic motor activities may help some youngsters who are retarded to grasp concepts of self-control and pacing, and may enhance rhythmic components of language, writing and reading.

8. Physical education programs, coupled with proper levels of exercise, can improve fitness of youngsters who are retarded and improve significantly performance of basic physical skills such as running, jumping, and swimming. Acquisition of these skills may in turn enhance significantly the child's self-concept.

COMMUNICATING AND RELATING IN A PHYSICAL EDUCATION SETTING

Children who are mentally retarded, like most nonretarded peers, are usually willing to obey the teacher if they understand what is being asked. The problem of understanding is, however, encountered often when the child with retardation is confronted with communication abstractions. Language is a collection of abstract verbal symbols that have no "built-in" meaning. The word "ball" is an abstraction without meaning until the symbol is connected with the concrete object. Children with mental retardation are not effective learners when abstracts are used. This explains the observed tendency in individuals with mental retardation toward nonverbal expression.[3]

Eichstaedt and Lavay (1992) warn that some youngsters with mental retardation may not understand the concepts of competition and trying their hardest. They simply do not comprehend statements such as "Run as *fast* as you can," or "Jump as *high* as you can," or "Do as many sit-ups as fast as you can." This is particularly true of

---

[3]Note the difference between *verbal* and *vocal*. *Verbal* implies the ability to use language purposefully. Many children with mental retardation are good "word callers"— they use words, phrases, or sentences without understanding. "Word calling" or uttering sounds without meaning is *vocalizing*. The child's propensity for vocalizing gives a false impression of the child's ability to understand. To determine whether the child is verbalizing or vocalizing, observe whether appropriate, purposeful activity accompanies an utterance or ask the child to repeat or relate *in the child's own words* something just said.

students who function at or below the lower range of students with moderate retardation. These individuals usually do not comprehend the significance of maximum performance. For such persons, strong, extrinsic motivators and reinforcers may be necessary to evoke the best response.

USE OF SHORT SENTENCES AND SINGLE-SYLLABLE WORDS

When using language to communicate with children who are retarded, use single-syllable or few-syllable words and short sentences. Avoid slurring words (i.e., the subconscious running together of words, which make them difficult to understand), and avoid slang. Use consistency and repetition when communicating. Language should be consistent in that words should not be subconsciously interchanged. "Get the big ball" might be understood, but "get the large ball" might not be. Synonyms should be used in the physical education setting only when a conscious, controlled effort is being made to develop vocabulary. Language repetition is important as a way to give children who are retarded more than one opportunity to understand what has been said.

USING PHYSICAL EDUCATION TO HELP OVERCOME NONVERBAL BEHAVIOR

Children who are mentally retarded who are nonverbal or who use language sparsely often will become more verbal as a result of a successful physical education experience. Because these children are similar to their nonretarded peers both physically and motorically, they often achieve movement-centered performance gains with relative ease. Success usually elevates self-concept, which may motivate the child to become a part of activity. Many activities in turn stimulate language use, and the child intensifies verbal communication. It is not uncommon for a nonverbal child to become more verbal during activity or when the conversation turns to activity. The child's willingness to verbalize about enjoyable physical education experiences should be used as a valuable adjunct to language development.

PROBLEM OF NEWNESS

Children who are mentally retarded tend to be comfortable with consistency and repetition. Newness represents a departure from these factors and can be a stressful obstacle in the child's learning environment. To children who are mentally retarded, newness often means failure and uncertainty, so the child may consciously avoid any departure from what is comfortable and known. To guide the child into activities within, but presently beyond, his grasp, avoid unnecessary references to newness. This should eliminate or at least reduce psychological barriers associated with uncertainty that complicate the learning process. Newness must be introduced in small increments, with progress measured (and praised) in inches rather than feet.

New or challenging experiences should be introduced early in a class period and early in the day, when children are mentally alert and physically fresh. This is especially important among children who are retarded whose attention spans and physical stamina may be limited.

Whenever possible, new activities in physical education should be introduced when subsequent physical education periods follow relatively soon. Because children with retardation often have short retention spans, new activities require immediate follow-up or they may be forgotten. Both quantity of intervening experiences and elapsed time between physical education classes can have a negative impact on the retention of new knowledge and skills.

ATTENTION SPAN

The child's attention span should be considered when presenting activities. Generally, the attention span of children with retardation is shorter than that of intellectually average children, but children who are retarded may remain interested in activities of their own choosing for a disproportionately long time. This raises the question of whether the children's attention span is truly short or whether teachers do not know how to or what maintains their interest. One plausible explanation for the child's short attention span, particularly when engaged in teacher-directed activities, might be the child's lack of communication skills. Children cannot be expected to remain interested in an activity that they simply do not understand. Children who do not understand a verbal instruction may need a *visual model*. If a visual model is too abstract for comprehension, use *tactile cues* such as gently nudging the appropriate body part in the proper direction. Children who remain unable to execute a skill may need *actual physical assistance* (kinesthetic patterning) through the entire skill.

Before the children lose interest, change to a different activity or curtail the day's physical education instruction. A timely change or curtailment of activity serves a twofold purpose: (1) it renders the activity worthwhile because it did not become boring, and (2) it eliminates discipline problems stemming from loss of interest.

THE NEED FOR STRUCTURE

For a child who is mentally retarded there is a need for structure in the learning environment to control variety and quantity of choices that the child must make.

Children should be encouraged to make choices in accordance with their abilities and particularly when choice making is a desired result of the activity period. Choices that the children make should be a function of the learning environment structure and should be controlled by the teacher.

Examples of appropriate structuring include (1) having children hold hands to form a circle, (2) supplying a geometric figure on which the child can stand so she knows where to stand, (3) placing a colored ribbon around the hand (foot) when consistent use is desired, (4) having the whistle mean stop, turn around, sit down, and listen to the teacher, (5) not giving the child a piece of equipment (e.g., a ball) until the child is to use it, (6) selecting activities in which all children participate all of the time, while avoiding activities that eliminate children (those eliminated first often need physical education most), and (7) not asking a question unless you truly expect an answer. Avoid saying "do you want to play _____ ?" unless you are prepared to deal with a possible "no" answer. Say, "We are going to play_____." Even more confusing is the question "What shall we play?"

Need for structure will vary for different activities and for different children. Even a seemingly unstructured physical education environment should be consciously created (i.e., structured) by the teacher.

PRAISE AND RECOGNITION

Children who are mentally retarded, like all children, thrive on praise and recognition. Take advantage of every reasonable opportunity to praise a child's accomplishments, and especially praise efforts that precede accomplishments. Even a small effort or minor accomplishment may, in fact, be enormous for a particular child. For children who too often experience failure, praise is a most effective antidote to withdrawal, low motivation, and low self-esteem. Praise should be given publicly so that the child derives satisfaction from knowing that others are aware of her achievement.

Although praise is effective when given in public, reprimands are more effective if given privately. A reprimand among peers, which the child interprets as embarrassing, may cause needless lowering of self-esteem and unnecessary withdrawal. For some children, public reprimand may contribute to disruptive behavior because the child is seeking attention. In either case, address the child's behavior problem in private on a one-to-one basis. When speaking to the child, particularly in one-to-one communications, meet the child at his own level; kneel and talk eye-to-eye if necessary.

CULMINATING ACTIVITIES

The final activity in the children's physical education day should be familiar and one in which all can participate successfully. A child who leaves the physical education environment feeling good about the experience will wish to return another day.

Often a quiet activity is appropriate. High-key activities near the end of a physical education period often evoke inappropriate levels of arousal, which the children carry back to the classroom. The classroom teacher is then obliged to deal with the child's emotions before commencing instruction.

USE OF MENTAL AGE IN SELECTING ACTIVITIES

Children who are mentally retarded often find activities more interesting and comprehensible when the activities are compatible with their mental age. When selecting activities for older retarded children or young adults, avoid activities that the older child perceives as "kid's stuff." The learner's negative perception of such activities does not motivate, improve self-esteem, or establish rapport with the teacher.

Often, the teacher need change only the name of a game or the character names to shed the game's "kid stuff" image. This is particularly true when the developmental level requires loosely-organized games suited to nonretarded elementary-age children.

ASSESSING PHYSICAL AND MOTOR PERFORMANCE

Pursuant to P.L. 101-476, adapted physical education must focus on development of (1) physical, and motor proficiencies, (2) fundamental motor skills, and (3) skills in aquatics, dance, and individual and group games and sports (including intramural and lifetime sports).

Basic components of physical and motor proficiency were discussed in detail in Chapter 6. (See sections entitled "Organic Performance Components of Fitness" and "Motor Performance Components of Fitness.")

Tables 12.7 and 12.8 show a few examples of physical and motor performance activities arranged by fitness component. Successful performance in one component

TABLE 12.7   Physical (Organic) Proficiency Activities Arranged by Component

Muscular Strength	Muscular Endurance	Cardiovascular Endurance	Flexibility
Isometrics	Backlifts[b]	Jogging	Split
Use of weights	Leglifts[b]	Walking	Straddle split
Pull-ups[a]	Pull-ups[b]	Swimming	Toe touch
Push-ups[a]	Push-ups[b]	Cycling	Windmill
	Sit-ups[b]	Jumping rope	Trunk twister
		Stair climbing	
		Extended wheelchair ambulation	

[a]These activities use muscular strength when fitness is low (i.e., child unable to repeat approximately 10).
[b]These activities use muscular endurance when fitness is high (i.e., child able to execute repetitions beyond 10).

TABLE 12.8   **Motor Proficiency Activities Arranged by Component**

Balance	Coordination	Agility	Speed	Explosive Strength
Stork stand	Ball throw	Zigzag run	Any activities	Long jump
Balance beam	Dribbling	Shuttle run	requiring	Vertical jump
Hop and land	Manipulative	Squat thrust	relatively short	High jump
without losing	activities	Mirroring	bursts of speed	Throwing for
balance	Catching	actions of	(e.g., running,	velocity
V-sit (bent	Jumping jack	teacher	wheelchair	
knees if		changing	dashes)	
necessary)		directions		

does *not* ensure or even suggest successful performance in another. If a performance deficit occurs in any component, the physical educator must understand which specific activities will improve performance of that component. For example, strength activities will develop strength but not coordination, or muscular endurance. Agility activities, which teach direction change capabilities, will not enhance flexibility.

Lavay (1988) suggests several considerations when testing individuals with mental retardation (p. 12):

1. Because they have limited mental ability and a short attention span, this population has difficulty understanding and following complicated test directions.

2. Many of these persons, because of their limited mental ability, are not intrinsically motivated and therefore lack motivation to try their best.

3. Inexperience with being tested may make these persons feel extremely uncomfortable around test equipment. Professionals must conduct orientation sessions and have a sufficient number of practice trials to allow these persons to feel comfortable during testing.

4. Tests appropriate to the general population are often used indiscriminately with this population, regardless of whether they can comprehend test directions.

FUNDAMENTAL MOTOR SKILLS

Comprehensive assessment of the child who is mentally retarded requires evaluation of fundamental motor skills. Development of these basic motor skills (Table 12.9) increases the child's movement versatility in many activities. Conversely, children who lack fundamental motor skills cannot experience success in many physical education activities. Children who are retarded often experience more than their share of failure. When they show deficits in the most basic motor skills, skill development is required.

TABLE 12.9   **Basic Motor Development Skills**

Locomotor Skills	Receipt and Propulsion Skills	Axial Skills
Crawling	Throwing	Bending
Creeping	Catching	Twisting
Walking	Manipulating	Stretching
Running	Kicking	Pirouetting
Hopping	Striking	Swinging
Leaping	Dribbling (hand and feet)	Lifting
Jumping	Pushing	
Galloping	Pulling	
Sliding		
Skipping		

SKILL IN AQUATICS, DANCE, AND INDIVIDUAL AND GROUP GAMES AND SPORTS, INCLUDING INTRAMURAL AND LIFETIME SPORTS

The adapted physical educator will be asked to assess the needs of children with mental retardation in aquatics, dance, and individual and group games and sports. Standard tools for assessing these skills are readily available.

HOW DOES ONE SELECT OR CONSTRUCT AN ASSESSMENT INSTRUMENT?

In selecting an assessment instrument for use with individuals with disabilities, the adapted physical educator must know which aspects of physical or motor performance are to be evaluated. Some standard tests are available. In other instances tests must be constructed. When tests require construction because those available are unsuitable, determine first which components of physical or motor proficiency or which motor skills are to be evaluated. After making that determination, select performance items that evaluate performance in the specific area. For example, if coordination is to be assessed, observe the child skipping, dribbling, or following a pursuit rotor. [4] Here, *criterion references* might be used to evaluate the child's performance. A performance criterion would be stated in behavioral terms. The child would then be assessed and periodically reassessed regarding achievement of the stated criterion. Examples of criterion referencing are as follows:

---

[4]The pursuit rotor resembles a phonograph with a small metallic disk positioned on and toward the outside of the turntable. The child, holding a metal-tipped stylus, attempts to maintain stylus contact with the disk as it revolves. Successful pursuit is calculated by continued contact between the moving disk and stylus as a measure of coordination.

Performance Component— Coordination	Actual Level of Performance
Example One—The child will dribble an 8-in. playground ball, using the preferred hand, 10 consecutive times without a break in rhythm.	_____
Example Two—The child will skip for 15 sec without a break in stride.	_____

The extent to which the child achieves the performance criterion determines the child's proficiency with respect to the skill in question. Criterion-referenced observation can be created for all aspects of performance in the physical or motor and motor skill performance domains.

In many instances, standardized or norm-referenced tests are also appropriate. Norms with which the child's performance can be compared generally accompany such tests. The following are a few available tests often used to assess physical or motor and motor skill proficiencies.

Health Related Physical Fitness Test Battery (AAHPERD).   The test battery (AAHPERD, 1980) established norms for nondisabled children between the ages of 5 and 17. Test items include modified sit-ups, distance run (1 mi or 9 min run, $1\frac{1}{2}$ mi or 12 min run), sit and reach, and the sum of adipose skin folds. Norms for the four test items are provided.

Test of Gross Motor Development   This test battery (Ulrich, 1985) measures 12 fundamental motor skills in areas of locomotion and object control in children of the ages of 3 through 10 years. The test items include run, gallop, hop, leap, skip, slide, two-hand strike, stationary bounce, catch, kick, and throw. Both criterion-referenced and norm standards are given. Although the test is standardized for children without disabilities, it can be used to compare the fundamental motor skill development of youngsters with mild and moderate mental retardation with their nonretarded age peers (Eichstaedt & Lavay, 1992).

Special Fitness Test for Mildly Mentally Retarded Persons (AAHPERD. This test battery (AAHPERD, 1976b) was developed to assess individuals with mild mental retardation between the ages of 8 and 18 years, and included seven test items and norms for both boys and girls. The test battery was developed by G. Lawrence Rarick and was administered throughout the country to over 4,200 subjects. The raw data were gathered over 18 years ago and the norms are out of date and are not appropriate for today's students.

Motor Fitness Test for the Moderately Mentally Retarded (AAHPERD). This test battery (AAHPERD, 1976a) was conducted by Leon Johnson and Ben

Londeree in 1972–1973 and used 1,097 subjects ranging from 6 to 21 years throughout the state of Missouri. In addition to the general test items used in the 1976 AAHPERD Young Fitness Test battery, these researchers included other data such as height and weight and selected fundamental motor skill items. The sit and reach, hopping, skipping, tumbling, and a target throw were used. From the raw scores, norms were developed. A problem surfaces because scores from both children with Down syndrome and others with moderate mental retardation were combined and give a composite picture of these two groups. Additionally, the number of students sampled is far too few to produce any valid conclusions, let alone norm-referenced tables. Finally, these norms are approximately 20 years old, which would give sufficient reason to exclude their use.

Physical Fitness and Motor Skill Test Battery for Individuals with Mental Retardation.   Eichstaedt, Wang, Polacek, and Dohrmann (1991) combined the Health Related Physical Fitness Test Battery (1980), the Youth Fitness Test Battery (1976), and the Physical Best Test Battery (1988) to develop a 12-item test battery for individuals with mental retardation (mild, moderate, or Down syndrome) between the ages of 6 and 21 (see Table 12.10). These researchers gathered data from 4,464 subjects in Illinois using certified physical education teachers and Special Olympics coaches to administer the test (see Table 12.11). It was determined that the three subject groups averaged fewer sit-ups, ran less yardage, and possessed more adipose tissue than peer individuals who were not retarded. Additionally, individuals with mental retardation jumped shorter, ran slower, maintained less static balance, and had poorer eye-hand coordination than youngsters with no retardation. Youngsters with Down syndrome were by far more flexible than all others, including the nonretarded individuals. Generally speaking, when comparing persons with moderate retardation and Down syndrome, it was concluded that the two groups are distinct and different

TABLE 12.10   **Test Items and Components Measured in Test Battery Conducted by Eichstaedt, Wang, Polacek, and Dohrmann (1991)**

Item	Component Measured
Triceps skinfold	Adipose tissue
Subscapular skinfold	Adipose tissue
Calf skinfold	Adipose tissue
Sit & reach	Trunk & hip flexibility
6-minute run (ages 6–11)	Cardiorespiratory efficiency
9-minute run (ages 12–21)	Cardiorespiratory efficiency
50-yard dash	Running speed
Flexed arm hang	Upper body strength
Shuttle run	Speed and agility
Standing long jump	Explosive leg power
Stork stand	Static balance
Basketball wall bounce	Eye-hand coordination

TABLE 12.11   Subjects from Eichstaedt, Wang, Polacek, and Dohrmann (1991)

Number of subjects: $N = 4,464$

Age range: 6 years through 21 years

Mildly mentally retarded:

females	=	494
males	=	557
total	=	1,051

Moderately mentally retarded:

females	=	917
males	=	1,379
total	=	2,296

Down syndrome:

females	=	537
males	=	580
total	=	1,117

Sample drawn from 127 Illinois schools, agencies, and Special Olympic groups.

populations and care should be taken when grouping them together for physical education purposes. Youngsters with Down syndrome usually fell below the 10th percentile when compared with nonretarded peers. It was concluded that most people with mild mental retardation could be active members of regular physical education classes but that their physical fitness and fundamental motor skill levels are likely to be below average. For persons with moderate mental retardation or Down syndrome, participation in regular physical education classes will be extremely difficult, and successful competition with nonretarded age peers will be challenging.

This research project includes graph comparisons between the three groups for all test items, ages 6 to 21, for both girls and boys. Height and weight tables are included. Ninety-eight norm-referenced tables are given along with complete test item descriptions and instructions. Copies of the 170-page project can be purchased ($10.00) by contacting Jerry Polacek, Department of HPERD, Illinois State University, Normal, IL 61761.

Eichstaedt (1991) concludes, using comparisons from earlier studies (Wang & Eichstaedt, 1980; Polacek, Wang, & Eichstaedt, 1985), that little or no positive change has occurred in a 10-year period involving Illinois children and teenagers with mental retardation (mild, moderate, or Down syndrome). In some cases the scores have gotten worse. If P.L. 101-476 is having any positive effect on improving physical fitness or motor skill, it isn't happening in Illinois. To make matters worse, it should be acknowledged that Illinois is the only state in the union that still maintains a "daily physical education" mandate for all public school children. National longitudinal studies should be conducted to provide an accurate picture of the present physical fitness and fundamental motor skill levels of individuals with mental retardation.

Special Olympics pagentry.

Bruininks' Revision of the Oseretsky Scale of Motor Development.   Oseretsky developed the original motor development scale. In 1948 Sloan (1955) revised the original test to improve its validity for practical settings. The most recent revision by Bruininks (1978) represents the most precise adaptation of the original scale. Bruininks alleges that specific motor behaviors fall into broad, general categories that comprise subtests of the composite test. Both subtest and composite test scores can be reported and used in the assessment process.

Bruininks has also developed a short form of the test that can be used as a quick, though less precise, measure of motor ability. Only items considered to be representative of each subtest are included in the short form. The short form may be used for initial screening or when administering the entire battery is not feasible.

The test measures motor ability in the $4\frac{1}{2}$ to $14\frac{1}{2}$ age range. Test results are interpreted in terms of motor age, stanines, and percentiles. A 9-year-old child performing at a $7\frac{1}{2}$-year-old level would thus be exhibiting a $1\frac{1}{2}$-year deficit in motor development as measured by the test.

Denver Developmental Screening Test.

Denver Developmental Screening Test.   For many children with mental retardation, the physical and motor development tests and the motor skill performance tests previously mentioned are inappropriate. For these children, mental age, chronological age, or present level of physical and motor ability may be well below the ability levels measured by the instruments described. For these children, however, an assessment of physical and motor capabilities is essential, and such assessment can be done by using one of the available developmental scales.

Among the most used development scales is the *Denver Developmental Screening Test* (Frankenburg et al., 1975). This test measures developmental status among children from birth to 6 years. Gross motor, fine motor, language, and personal and social developmental status can be assessed. The results of any subtest enable the teacher to judge the extent to which observed behaviors are comparable to those of nonretarded children at any chronological age level from birth to 6 years. The test's reliability and validity are accurate for a screening device, although the norms are questionable (Salvia & Ysseldyke, 1991).

BRIGANCE Diagnostic Inventory of Early Development.   This test battery (Brigance, 1978) was designed to assess children whose developmental levels range from birth to 7 years. It is used to evaluate a wide range of curriculum areas including preambulatory motor skills and behaviors, gross motor skills and behaviors, and fine motor skills and behaviors. The inventory is developmentally sequenced, and comprehensive. All test items are written in behavioral format, allowing the teacher to easily design annual goals and short-term objectives. The BRIGANCE is commonly used with individuals labeled as severely and profoundly mentally retarded (Koranda, 1991).

I CAN.   The *I CAN* program (Wessel, 1976, 1979, 1980) provides assessment items, activity prescriptions, and teaching strategies. *I CAN* materials have been field-tested among children labeled as trainable and severely retarded (CA 5–14). Either physical education specialists or classroom teachers can use the materials. *I CAN* facilitates development of a child's individualized educational program (IEP) pursuant to P.L. 101-476. Specific *I CAN* programs focus on fundamental skills, body management, health and fitness, aquatics, and leisure and recreation, including team sports, dance and individual sports, backyard and neighborhood activities, and outdoor activities. The 1980 series includes preprimary motor and play skills.

Special Olympic International Sport Skill Instructional Program Manuals.
An individual sport skill guide is available (Special Olympics Inc., 1989) for each of the 22 sports that Special Olympics offers to individuals with mental retardation. Each manual includes a subjective assessment section (checklist) designed to determine present levels of performance. There is also a motor activity training program for persons with severe disabilities.

TRANSLATING ASSESSMENT INTO INDIVIDUALIZED EDUCATION

Assessment based both on observations and on formal data-gathering procedures provides insight into a child's physical education status and potential. This information also provides insights on development of the child's physical education in the most appropriate (i.e., least restrictive) environment. Evaluation of assessment data should determine (1) whether special services are indicated for physical education, (2) whether related services such as physical therapy, occupational therapy, or special transportation arrangements might benefit the child, (3) annual goals, and (4) short-term instructional objectives. A complete description of the IEP process is found in Chapter 5.

INCENTIVES TO ENCOURAGE EFFORT AND ACHIEVEMENT

Motivational charts should be created and placed where they are visible. Use stars to signify levels of achievement and effort.

Designate a "Student of the Week" and display the student's activity efforts, accomplishments, interest, or a combination of these on a bulletin board with the student's photograph. Certificates or ribbons can also serve as tangible recognition of the student's efforts.

BEYOND THE PHYSICAL EDUCATION CLASS, WHAT NEXT?

Although some children with mental retardation will not develop physical or motor proficiencies measurable beyond the early childhood level on the developmental scales, others will be able to participate in special and regular intramural and interschool athletic activities. P.L. 101-476 includes sports and intramurals as part of physical education, and Section 504 of the Vocational Rehabilitation Act of 1973 guarantees the child access to any school program provided that the child is capable of safe and successful participation. Mental retardation alone is no longer an acceptable criterion for excluding a child from intramural or athletic program participation.

Persons who are mentally retarded are becoming more visible in regular school sport programs. They are often capable of physical and motor performance commensurate with their nonretarded, chronological age peers. If a person who is retarded is capable of participating safely and successfully as a member of the school's regular athletic team, no justifiable reason exists for denying that person such an opportunity.

The Special Olympics International (SOI) program, sponsored by the Joseph P. Kennedy, Jr. Foundation, has enhanced opportunities for persons who are mentally retarded to develop athletic skills and enjoy athletic experiences. The Special Olympics oath, "Let me win, but if I cannot win, let me be brave in the attempt," embodies the Special Olympics' emphasis on participation. SOI reports that any one year over 1 million persons with mental retardation (minimum age of 8 years) participate in Special Olympics activities. Ten official sports are offered in the summer and six in the winter. There are also six demonstration sports provided (see Table 12.12). SOI has made a strong commitment toward training and certification of coaches. From 1980 to 1991 over 140,000 coaches were certified through SOI sport training schools. Excellent sport skill training guides are available from SOI for all 22 official and demonstration sports.

Special Olympics has also developed year-round fitness and sport skill development programs. These programs enhance both fitness for living and competence in Special Olympics sport events.

Children with mental retardation mainstreamed into regular school interscholastic athletic programs generally are not eligible for participation in Special Olympics. An objective of Special Olympics is to encourage and enable the participant's "graduation" into a regular school sport program.

Further information about Special Olympics programs is available from local Special Olympic chapters, the state director, or from the national office.

SUMMARY

Mental retardation is a disability of degrees. In its milder forms, it may escape notice during early years. In more severe forms, constant, lifelong custodial care may be indicated.

TABLE 12.12 Official Summer, Winter, and Demonstration Sports Sponsored by the Special Olympics International

Official Summer Sports	Official Winter Sports	Demonstration Sports
Aquatics	Alpine skiing	Canoeing
Athletic	Cross-country skiing	Cycling
Basketball	Figure skating	Team handball
Bowling	Speed skating	Table tennis
Equestrian	Floor hockey	Tennis
Gymnastics	Poly hockey	Power lifting
Roller skating		
Football (soccer)		
Softball		
Volleyball		

Causes of mental retardation are many; the most common *identifiable* cause is Down syndrome. The cause in the majority of cases, however, cannot be pinpointed, because there is no apparent brain damage.

Although persons with mental retardation generally achieve lower levels of physical and motor proficiency than do their chronological age peers who are nonretarded, they are more like their nondisabled peers in physical and motor proficiency than in any other respect. It is often difficult to ascertain the extent to which performance deficits are a function of impoverished intellect or lack of opportunity. Data indicate that physical and motor proficiencies can often approach lower performance levels of the nonretarded when quality physical education is provided.

Persons who are retarded are capable of achieving both significant nonphysical and motor proficiency results. In the nonphysical realm, self-esteem may improve markedly as proficiencies are developed that are important to the child and others. Physical education facilitates the socialization process by providing opportunities for give-and-take in group-centered settings. The inherently motivating nature of motor activities should stimulate achievement in conversation in the three Rs.

A number of special teaching methodologies are appropriate for instruction of people with mental retardation. Teachers are urged to use short sentences and to consider attention span when presenting activities. The child who is mentally retarded has a special need for structure in the learning environment. Teachers must also keep in mind that any newness often stress the child who may have come to associate anything new with failure.

Meeting the mandates of P.L. 101-476 makes assessment a necessity. In selecting an assessment instrument, the educator must first identify which aspects of physical or motor performance are to be evaluated. When appropriate standardized tests are unavailable, criterion references can be used to evaluate performance. Standardized tests are often used to evaluate the performance of those with mental retardation.

Achievement in physical education can be reinforced by incentives, which may include inexpensive tangibles such as badges, ribbons, certificates, or wall charts. The incentive program provided by the Special Olympics International is also recommended. Finally, the opportunity for sports participation is recommended through involvement in the Special Olympics program.

REFERENCES

AAHPERD. (1976a). *Motor fitness testing manual for moderately mentally retarded.* Reston, VA: The Alliance.

AAHPERD. (1976b). *Special fitness test manual for mildly mentally retarded persons.* Reston, VA: The Alliance.

AAHPERD. (1988). *Physical best.* Reston, VA: The Alliance.

—. *AAHPERD Health related physical fitness test manual.* (1980). Reston, VA: AAHPERD.

Alford, C. A. (1988). Chronic perinatal infections and mental retardation. In J. F. Kavanagh, (Ed.), *Understanding mental retardation: Research accomplishments and new frontiers* (pp. 137–148). Baltimore: Brooks.

American Association on Mental Retardation. (1983). *Classification in mental retardation.* Washington, D.C.: The Association.

Baroff, G. S. (1991). *Developmental disabilities.* Austin, TX: Pro-Ed.

Blackman, J. A. (1990a). Child abuse and neglect. In J. A. Blackman (Ed.), *Medical aspects of developmental disabilities in children birth to three* (2nd ed., pp. 67–70). Rockville, MD: Aspen.

Blackman, J. A. (1990b). Congenital infections. In J. A. Blackman (Ed.), *Medical aspects of developmental disabilities in children birth to three* (2nd ed., 89–95). Rockville, MD: Aspen.

Blackman, J. A. (1990c). Fetal alcohol syndrome. In J. A. Blackman (Ed.), *Medical aspects of developmental disabilities in children birth to three* (2nd ed., pp. 141–142). Rockville, MD: Aspen.

Block, M. E. (1991). Motor development in children with Down syndrome: A review of the literature. *Adapted Physical Activity Quarterly, 8,* 179–209.

Brigance, A. (1978). *The BRIGANCE diagnostic inventory of early development.* North Billerica, MA: Curriculum Associates.

Bruininks, R. H. (1978). *Bruininks-Oseretsky test of motor proficiency: Examiner's manual.* Circle Pines, Minn: American Guidance Service.

Coleman, M. (1988). Medical care of children and adults with Down syndrome. In V. Dmitriev and P. L. Oelwein (Eds.), *Advances in Down Syndrome* (pp. 7–18). Seattle: Special Child.

Cratty, B. J. (1974). *Motor activity in the education of retardates* (2nd ed.). Philadelphia: Lea & Febiger.

Drew, C. J., Hardman, M. L., & Logan, D. R. (1992). *Mental retardation* (5th ed.). New York,: Merrill/Macmillan.

Eichstaedt, C. B. (1991, October). *Adapted physical education in Illinois: A State of the art.* Paper presented at annual convention of the Illinois Association for Health, Physical Education, Recreation and Dance. Arlington Heights, IL.

Eichstaedt, C. B., & Lavay, B. (1992). *Physical activity for individuals with mental retardation: Infancy through adulthood.* Champaign, IL: Human Kinetics.

Eichstaedt, C. B., Wang, P. Y., Polacek, J. J. , & Dohrmann, P. F. (1991). *Physical fitness and motor skill levels of individuals with mental retardation: Mild, moderate, and Down syndrome ages 6–21.* Normal, IL: Illinois State University Printing Services.

Feuerstein, R., Rand, Y., & Hoffman. M. (1979). *The dynamic assessment of retarded performers: The learning potential assessment device, theory, instruments, and techniques.* Baltimore: University Park Press.

Francis, R., and Rarick, G. L. (1963). *Motor characteristics of the mentally retarded.* Washington, D.C.: U.S. Office of Education, Cooperative Research Branch.

Frankenburg, W. K., Goldstein, A., & Camp B. (1975). *Denver developmental screening test: Reference manual,* (rev.) Denver: LADOCA Project and Publishing Foundation.

Glaze, R. E. (1985). *Height and weight of Down syndrome children as compared to normal children aged ten to eighteen.* Unpublished masters study, Illinois State University, Normal, IL.

Grossman, H. J. (Ed.). (1983). *Classification in mental retardation.* Washington, D.C.: American Association on Mental Deficiency.

Grossman, H. J., & Tarjan, G. (Eds.). (1987). *AMA handbook on mental retardation.* Chicago: American Medical Association.

Hallahan, D. P., & Kauffman, J. M. (1991). *Exceptional children* (5th ed.). Englewood Cliffs, NJ: Prentice Hall.

Hanson, J. W., & Bartley, J. A. (1985). Teratogenic agents. In R. B. Conn (Ed.), *Current diagnosis* 7 (pp. 1289–1295). Philadelphia: Saunders.

Henderson, S. E., & Illingworth, J. A. (1991). Prolongation of simple manual and vocal reaction times in Down syndrome. *Adapted Physical Activity Quarterly, 8,* 234–241.

Horgan, J. S. (1983) Mnemonic strategy instruction in coding, processing and recall of movement related cues by the mentally retarded. *Perceptual and Motor Skills, 57,* 547–557.

———. (1985). Issues in memory for movement with mentally retarded children. In J. E. Clark and J. H. Humphrey (Eds.), *Motor Development: Current Selected Research*, (Vol. I) Princeton, NJ: Princeton Book Co.

Koranda, P. (1991, October). *Physical education programs for students with severe and profound mental retardation.* Paper presented at the annual convention of the Illinois Association for Health, Physical Education, Recreation, and Dance. Arlington Heights, IL.

Lavay, B. (1988). Cardiovascular fitness testing for adults with mental retardation (research application). *Palaestra, 5,* 12.

Luftig, R. L. (1987). *Teaching the mentally retarded student. Curriculum methods and strategies.* Boston: Allyn & Bacon.

Newell, K. M. (1985). Motor skill acquisition and mental retardation: Overview of traditional and current orientations. In J. E. Clark & J. H. Humphrey (Eds.), *Motor development: Current selected research* (Vol. I, pp. 183–192). Princeton, NJ: Princeton Books.

Patton, J. R., Payne, J. S., & Beirne-Smith, M. (1990). *Mental retardation* (3rd ed.). New York: Merrill/Macmillan.

Payne, V. G., & Isaacs, L. D. (1991). *Human motor development* (2nd ed.). Mountain View, CA: Mayfield.

Polacek, J. J., Wang, P. Y., & Eichstaedt, C. B. (1985). *A study of physical and health related fitness levels of mild, moderate, and Down syndrome students in Illinois.* Normal, IL: Illinois State University Printing Services.

Pueschel, S. M., Bodenheimer, H. C., Jr., Giesswein, P., & Dean, M. K. (1991). The prevalence of hepatitis B surface antigen and antibody in home-reared individuals with Down syndrome. *Research in Developmental Disabilities, 12,* 243–249.

Pueschel, S. M., Jackson, M. D., Giesswein, P., Dean, M. K., & Pezzullo, J. C. (1991). Thyroid function in Down syndrome. *Research in Developmental Disabilities, 12,* 287–296.

Rogers, R. C., & Simensen, R. J. (1987). Fragile X syndrome: A common etiology of mental retardation. *American Journal of Mental Retardation, 91,* 445–449.

Salvia, J., & Ysseldyke, J. E. (1991). *Assessment* (5th ed.). Boston: Houghton Mifflin.

Scholl, R. A. (1991, October). *Physical education and sport for students with Down syndrome.* Paper presented at the annual convention of the Illinois Association for Health, Physical Education, Recreation, and Dance. Arlington Heights, IL.

Scott, K. G. (1988). Theoretical epidemiology: Environment and lifestyle. In J. F. Kavanagh (Ed.), *Understanding mental retardation* (pp. 23–33). Baltimore, MD: Brooks.

Share, J. & French, R. (1982). *Motor development of Down syndrome children: Birth to six years.* Sherman Oaks, CA.: J. B. Share.

Sloan, W. (1955). The Lincoln-Oseretsky motor development scale. *Genetic Psychology Monographs, 51,* 183–252.

Special Olympics International. (1985). *Sport skill instructional manuals.* Washington, D.C.: Special Olympics.

Spitz, H. H. (1988). Mental retardation as a thinking disorder: The rationalist alternative to empiricism. In N. W. Bray. (Ed.), *International Review of Research in Mental Retardation* (pp. 1–32). New York: Academic Press.

Sugden, D. A., & Keogh, J. F. (1990). *Problems in movement skill development.* Columbia, SC: University of South Carolina Press.

Thomas, K. T. (1984). Applying Knowledge of Motor Development to Mentally Retarded Children. In J. R. Thomas (Ed.), *Motor development during childhood and adolescence.* Minneapolis: Burgess Publishing.

Thombs, B., & Sugden, D. (1991). Manual skills in Down syndrome children ages 6 to 16 years. *Adapted Physical Activity Quarterly, 8,* 242–254.

Ulrich, D. (1985). *Test of gross motor development.* Austin, TX: Pro-Ed.

U.S. Department of Education. (1991) *To assure the free appropriate public education of all children with disabilities. Thirteenth annual report to Congress on the implementation of the Individuals with Disabilities Education Act.* Washington, D.C.: The Department.

Wang, P. Y., & Eichstaedt, C. B. (1980). *A study of physical fitness levels of mentally handicapped children and adolescents in Illinois.* Normal, IL: Illinois State University Printing Services.

Weber, L. (February, 1985). Facts about hepatitis B. *ARC facts.* (Available from Association for Retarded Citizens, Arlington, TX)

Wessel, J. (1976). *I CAN.* Northbrook, IL.: Hubbard Scientific Co.

——. (1979). *I CAN: Primary skills.* Northbrook, IL.: Hubbard Scientific Co.

——. (1980). *I CAN: Preprimary motor and play skills.* East Lansing, MI.: Instructional Media Center, Michigan State University.

Williams, M. H. (1983). *Nutrition for fitness and sports.* Dubuque, IA: W. L. Brown.

Winnick, J., & Jansma, P. (1978). *Physical education inservice resources manual for all handicapped children act* (P.L. 94–142), Brockport, NY: by authors.

Wolery, M., & Haring, T. G. (1990). Moderate, severe, and profound handicaps. In N. G. Haring and L. McCormick (Eds.), *Exceptional children and youth* (5th ed., pp. 239–280). New York : Merrill/Macmillan.

Wolraich, M. L. (1990). Encephalitis and meningitis. In J. A. Blackman (Ed.), *Medical aspects of developmental disabilities in children birth to three* (2nd ed., pp. 117–120). Rockville, MD: Aspen.

Zigler, W. B., & Hodapp, R. M. (1986). *Understanding mental retardation.* New York: Cambridge University Press.

Chapter 13

HEARING IMPAIRMENTS

 An interview with Jimmy, age 12. Diagnosis: mild hearing loss (43 dB).

Question: Have you ever had problems when playing sports?
Response: I went into a game once and the kid told me where to play. I did not hear him and the coach yelled at me.
Question: If you cannot hear the directions, do you tell the teacher you cannot hear?
Response: No. I do not want to be embarrassed.
Question: Has it happened a lot?
Response: Yes. The other day we were playing some games and all the kids had numbers. We had to go out and get the ball and see who could make the first shot. I did not understand. I did not hear the directions so I just had to watch and see how to play. I wasn't very happy.

Individuals with hearing impairment must learn to cope—to develop their social, emotional, and physical personalities—without normal hearing. Success usually requires the ability to communicate effectively. Hearing loss makes the educational hurdle difficult. The physical educator has a challenging opportunity to help those with hearing impairment to develop a more normal way of life.

Many recreational activities readily available to the nondisabled are often missed by individuals with hearing impairment. For example, the students with hearing impairment cannot totally enjoy television, radio, records, movies, or concerts.

Through physical education, the potential arises for enjoyment through movement: from grace and beauty (dance) to intense physical exertion (athletic competition), from recreational individualism (jogging) to recreational adult competition (bowling or golf). Moving and doing replace sitting and listening. Physical education must provide individuals with hearing impairment with opportunities to learn and enjoy movement skills to establish a solid foundation for future leisure time activities, sports, and individual pursuits.

Because the majority of children with hearing impairment possess at least average motor ability, they are able to participate successfully in regular physical education classes. Individuals who are deaf have excelled in statewide and national gymnastics, dance, and wrestling competitions in which they competed with people who are nondisabled.

Motor deficiencies of the child with a hearing impairment generally stem from not having played with other children and not having participated in early childhood activities. Overprotective parents, while eager to seek educational (intellectual) endeavors for their children, sometimes overlook the importance of organized movement activities. Not being able to run, jump, or play as well as the children in the peer group who are nondisabled is further compounded if the child is not offered (or is denied because of disability) a comprehensive developmental physical education program. Motor deficiencies become strikingly evident as the child grows. The child with hearing impairment must have stimulating movement experiences as soon as the hearing deficiency is diagnosed. Delayed intervention too often ensures that the child's motor abilities will be below the national norms for children who are nondisabled.

HOW MANY?

The number of children who are either deaf or possess hearing impairment, and who were provided special education services in the United States (ages of 6 to 21) during the school year 1989–1990, was 58,164 (U.S. Department of Education, 1991). This number represents 1.4 percent of all disabling conditions.

The National Information Center on Deafness (1991) estimates that one out of every eight students with hearing impairment will be classified as *deaf* (90 dB or greater hearing loss).

HEARING IMPAIRED DEFINED

The term **hearing impairment** identifies individuals with measurable hearing loss resulting from defects in the hearing apparatus or process. Four descriptive variables are used to identify specific subgroups: (1) degree of hearing impairment, (2) age of onset of hearing impairment, (3) type of hearing impairment, and (4) etiology of hearing impairment.

Hallahan and Kauffman (1991) list terms often used by school officials regarding individuals with hearing impairments.

- *Hearing impairment* is a generic term indicating a hearing disability that may range in severity from mild to profound: It includes the subsets of *deaf* and *hard of hearing*.

- A person labeled as *deaf* is one whose disability precludes successful processing of linguistic information through audition, with or without a hearing aid.

- A person who is *hard of hearing* is one who, generally with the use of a hearing aid, has residual hearing sufficient to enable successful processing of linguistic information through audition.

Distinction between levels of hearing loss is measured with an audiometer, an instrument that gauges the loudness of sound in units called decibels (dB).

Individuals who have a **moderate hearing loss** (less than 70 dB) are often considered "hard of hearing," whereas those who have a **profound loss** (greater than 90 dB) are considered deaf. The category **severe loss** (71 to 89 dB) is a transition category between hard of hearing and deaf. Table 13.1 lists classifications and educational implications of hearing loss.

Quigley and Kretschmer (1982) advise caution when determining the differences between deaf and hard of hearing. They state the following:

> We stress again the need for clearly stated definitions or at least descriptions of deaf individuals.... It is inappropriate to generalize findings obtained with what we would term hard-of-hearing individuals (less than 90 dB) to deaf individuals (greater than 90 dB). It should be recognized that 90 dB is a somewhat arbitrary line. Other authors use varying points on the decibel scale to define "deaf."... The important point is that the sensorineural impairment is of sufficient severity that the individual, even with amplification, must rely on vision as the primary channel for receptive communication. We contend that any impairment of less than 90 dB is not sufficient severity to produce such an effect and, therefore, should not be classified as deaf. (p. 104)

Figure 13.1 shows the distribution of hearing impaired students in the United States by degree of hearing loss (Gallaudet Research Institute, 1991).

Special educators also distinguish between deafness and less severe levels of hearing loss by how the child learns language. Deaf children who have little or no hearing ability during the first 3 years of life will not have learned language in the normal way; these children are classified as educationally deaf (prelingually deaf). Children who become hearing impaired *after* 3 years of life will, in most cases, have learned language in the usual way. These youngsters are considered to be advanced in their ability to understand and articulate new language experiences (Lowenbraun and Thompson, 1990). The Gallaudet Research Institute (1991) estimates that 94% of all hearing losses occur before age 3.

The physical educator should obtain school medical records (often available through the school nurse) to develop a complete picture of the child with hearing

TABLE 13.1   **Classifications and Educational Implications of Hearing Loss**

Classification	Decibels (ISO)[a]	Educational Implications
Normal	−10 to 26	
Slight	27 to 40	Student needs favorable seating and lighting; may have difficulty hearing faint or distant speech; will not usually experience difficulty in school situations.
Mild	41 to 55	Needs hearing aid in some cases; favorable seating and possible special class placement, specially for primary children; understands conversational speech at distance of 3–5 ft; may miss as much as 50% of class discussions.
Moderate	56 to 70	Needs hearing aid by evaluation and auditory training; lip reading instruction; conversation must be loud to be understood; will have increasing difficulty with school situations requiring participation in group discussions.
Severe	71 to 89	Needs full-time special program for children who are deaf with emphasis on all language skills, concept development, lip reading, and speech; individual hearing aid by evaluation; may hear loud voices about 1 ft from ear.
Profound	90+	Needs full-time special education program for children who are deaf, with emphasis on all language skills, concept development, lip reading, and speech; continuous appraisal of needs in regard to oral and manual communication; relies on vision rather than hearing as primary avenue for communication; speech and language are likely to deteriorate.

Source: Modified from Bernero, R. J., and Bothwell, H. *Relationship of Hearing Impairment to Educational Needs.* Illinois Department of Public Health and the Office of the Superintendent of Public Instruction, 1966.

[a]ISO = International Standards Organization.

impairment (e.g., cause of deafness, age at which deafness occurred, use of hearing aid, degree of hearing loss, balance difficulties, eye-hand coordination problems). When the degree of hearing loss is recorded in a student's medical file and only one score is noted, that score is for the better ear.

In a 1981 research project, Sarff, Ray, and Bagwell found that 32 percent of their fourth-, fifth-, and sixth-grade subjects had minimal hearing loss (10 to 40 dB loss). Seventy-five percent of the sixth-grade students who had minimal hearing loss were *also* deficient in one or more of the basic academic skill areas of reading, language arts, or mathematics. This 3-year longitudinal study showed that students improved their achievement significantly after amplification of the teacher's voice. This research highlights the importance that hearing plays in learning. Even minimal

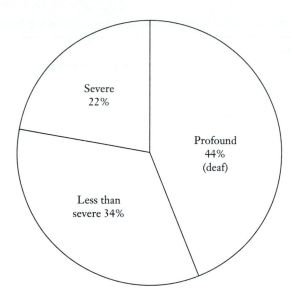

FIGURE 13.1   **U.S. distribution of students with hearing impairment by degree of hearing loss.**

hearing loss must be identified early if teachers are to meet the educational needs of the child.

ANATOMY AND PHYSIOLOGY OF THE EAR

Figure 13.2 shows a diagram of the ear. Hearing involves two basic components: (1) the reception and conduction of sound waves, and (2) the nerve function by which impulses are set up and transmitted to the brain.

Individuals hear in three ways. First, the auricle (fleshy, outside ear) directs sound waves through the ear canal. Sound waves vibrate the eardrum, which vibrates across three small bones of the middle ear. The stapes, the innermost of the three small bones, moves in and out against the oval window, stimulating the fluid in the cochlea. This, in turn, stimulates nerves that lead to the brain. A second method of hearing involves the sound waves passing through the eardrum (or a hole in the eardrum) to a secondary eardrum covering the oval window. This covering vibrates fluid in the cochlea, which in turn stimulates nerves leading to the brain. A third way to hear occurs when the bones of the skull that surround the ear carry sound waves directly to the inner ear, striking the cochlea. This method is often associated with use of a hearing aid, which is placed behind the outer ear and is grounded directly on the mastoid bone. The cochlea, where all sound waves must ultimately go, contains over 25,000 hairlike sensory receptors. These generate nerve impulses to the brain.

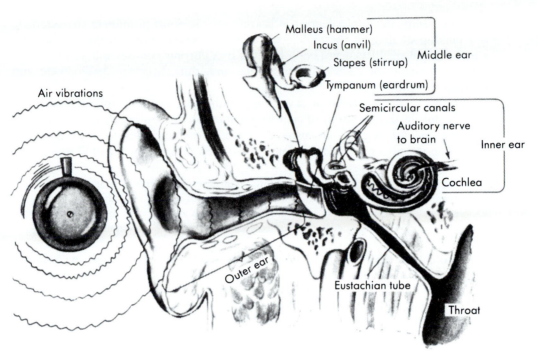

FIGURE 13.2   **The human ear.**

ETIOLOGY OF HEARING IMPAIRMENT

Among the causes of hearing impairment are heredity, accident, and illness. An unborn child can inherit hearing loss from the parents. In about 50 percent of all cases of deafness, genetic factors are a probable cause. Accidents, illness, and ototoxic drugs are responsible for hearing loss in the remaining cases. Rubella or other viral infections contracted by the pregnant mother may cause destruction of parts of the hearing apparatus of the fetus. Complications during the birth process, such as anoxia, may also affect hearing. Illness or infection may cause permanent deafness in young children. For example, mumps, although mostly controlled in the United States, is one of the leading causes of unilateral sensorineural deafness in children and young adults (Kacica and Harrison, 1990). Loss of vestibular reactions may accompany the hearing loss (Marcy, 1980). Central hearing loss can occur from congenital brain abnormalities, tumors, or lesions of the central nervous system.

OTITIS MEDIA

By far the most common cause of conductive hearing impairment in children under the age of 6 is otitis media (middle ear disease) (Kahn, 1990). This inflammatory infection results in various degrees of hearing loss; its most prominent characteristic is a buildup of fluid in the middle ear space. Recurrent otitis media can become a major problem. Blackman (1990) believes that chronic, severe, and perhaps even moderate middle ear disease affects hearing and, thus, language development and learning in general.

Otitis media is treated by several approaches: (a) low doses of antibiotics, especially during those seasons of cold winter months, (b) antihistamines and decongestants, and (c) surgical placement of tubes in the eardrums to allow drainage. Regarding the placement of tubes into the ears, Blackman states the following:

> Surgical drainage of the middle ear (myringotomy) and insertion of tubes into the eardrum are also controversial. Although there is yet no uncontestable research to support their effectiveness, these procedures—when appropriate—appear to improve the function of the middle ear and decrease the number of infections. (p. 195)

Coleman (1988) has found that approximately 60% of children with Down syndrome will have otitis media in early childhood. She explains the potential dangers:

> It has been reported that any child with chronic or severe otitis media (even if he or she is an otherwise normal individual) may manifest some delay in speech and language development, have auditory processing deficits, disturbance in auditory integration, and is likely to have reading disorders and even poor reading skills. The middle ear infusions which are so common in Down syndrome children may be one important factor in the language delay in these children which in the past has been attributed solely to their retardation. (p. 12)

New medical and surgical techniques to correct conductive hearing loss have greatly improved the prognosis within the last few years. Current research involving the cochlear implant may provide a way to medically correct profound sensorineural hearing loss. The cochlear implant is a unit that is surgically placed in the ear. Unlike a hearing aid, the implant does not change electrical impulses back to sounds, but allows electrical impulses to be carried directly through the auditory system to the brain. Lowenbraun and Thompson (1990) have found the following: "Implant users have stated that sounds heard through an implant are different from sounds heard through a hearing aid" (p. 398).

HEARING DEFECTS

If any part of the ear structure fails to function normally, partial or total deafness results. Deafness may be caused by either conduction or nerve failure. **Conductive deafness** is caused temporarily by a simple swelling due to infection in the external auditory canal. Nearly all forms of conductive deafness can be corrected by use of an electronic hearing aid. Deafness due to nerve deterioration is more serious. Sound is conducted to the inner ear, but an abnormality there, in the auditory nerve, or in the brain prevents the proper electrical signal from being generated, transmitted, or received.

Sensorineural deafness results from damage to the microscopic sensory hair cells of the inner ear or to the nerves. This type of hearing loss often affects certain frequencies more than others. Even with amplification to increase sound level, the person still perceives distorted sound. This distortion, which accompanies some forms of sensorineural deafness, can be so severe that successful use of a hearing aid is impossible.

Central deafness is attributed to damage or impairment to the nerves of the central nervous system.

Mixed hearing losses are those in which impairment occurs both in the outer or middle and inner ear. Table 13.2 lists definitions, causes, and treatment of various types of hearing impairment.

ACOUSTICAL TRAUMA

In modern society, we are assaulted by extremely high levels of noise pollution. Intense exposure to high-decibel noise over an extended period of time can cause serious hearing impairment. Loud rock music, home power tools, and industrial noise are all potential causes of acoustic trauma (Figure 13.3). Whereas industrial noise used to cause most of acquired hearing loss (not attributed to aging), ear specialists say that recreational noise—from rock concerts to auto racing—has become the major threat to hearing today.

Acquired hearing loss is usually gradual, subtle, and cumulative. Extremely high levels of sound, as experienced when listening to amplified rock music (110 to 130 dB), is known to damage the delicate hearing mechanism of the ear. Depending on length and intensity of exposure, damage can be temporary or permanent. When damage is permanent, the sensory hair cells in the inner ear lose their ability to relay sound. Dr. Hawley Jackson (1985), a Long Beach, California, otologist states, "Kids often say that they have ringing in their ears for days after going to a rock concert. Ringing is an indication of trauma or injury to your inner ear. Ringing is your body telling you that you have damaged your hearing"(p. 1). Ear specialists warn that one risks hearing loss if exposed to 95 to 100 dB for 2 hours or more (Petryshyn, 1991).

The Federal Occupational Safety and Health Administration has set standards to determine when damage could occur. Sustained sound over 85 dB, the equivalent of heavy street traffic, is enough to impair hearing gradually. An average person can probably withstand a noise level of 85 dB for 7 to 8 hours per day without damage. A few more decibels, however, can make a significant difference. If the noise level increases to 90 dB, a 3-hour-per-day exposure can be damaging.

TABLE 13.2   **Definitions, Causes and Treatment of Hearing Impairments**

	Type		
	Conductive	**Sensorineural**	**Central**
Definition	Those conditions arising from some mechanical blockage of sound transmission in the outer or middle ear (outside central nervous system).	Conditions arising from damage to neural pathways between inner ear and brain: 1. Congenital—nerve injured or destroyed before or during birth. 2. Acquired or adventitious—hearing loss occurring after birth.	Any interference with sound transmission from brain stem to and including auditory cortex.
Cause	Physical obstruction (e.g., impacted wax or middle ear infection) to conduction of sound waves to inner ear. Major cause of conductive hearing loss related to middle ear pathology is *otitis media,* inflammation or infection of the middle ear.	1. Genetic factors, Rh blood factor, premature birth, and diseases such as German measles, mumps, or influenza (when contracted by mother during early pregnancy). 2. Complications of childhood diseases such as spinal meningitis, encephalitis, scarlet fever, or influenza, or accident that damages nervous system so hearing ability is affected.	Diseases of the brain that affect auditory pathway (e.g., cerebral tumor or abscess, arteriosclerosis, cerebral hemorrhage, and multiple sclerosis).
Treatment and Prognosis	Hearing may be seriously impaired, but deafness is never total. Hearing aids improve hearing loss that results from conduction difficulties.	Usually more serious than conductive loss and less likely to be improved by medical treatment. Proper treatment usually involves educational as well as medical intervention.	Patient can "hear" but does not understand what he hears. Generally treated as a form of receptive language disorder (i.e., aphasia).

Source: Adapted from AAHPERD 1976, p. 3.

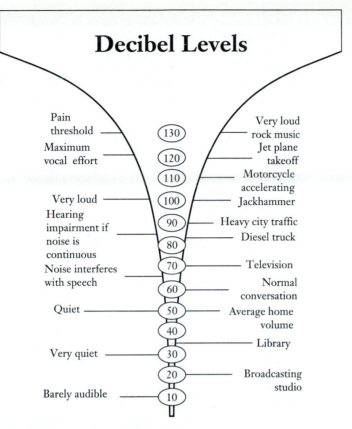

Decibel Levels

Pain threshold	130	Very loud rock music
Maximum vocal effort	120	Jet plane takeoff
	110	Motorcycle accelerating
Very loud	100	Jackhammer
Hearing impairment if noise is continuous	90	Heavy city traffic
	80	Diesel truck
Noise interferes with speech	70	Television
	60	Normal conversation
Quiet	50	Average home volume
	40	Library
Very quiet	30	
	20	Broadcasting studio
Barely audible	10	

FIGURE 13.3 **Comparative decibel levels.**

PHYSICAL EDUCATION: ADAPTED OR REGULAR?

Most children with hearing impairment can perform successfully in the regular, unrestricted physical education class. Physiologically, they usually possess adequate physical development. They should not be placed in an adapted physical education setting without reliable and valid assessment. Accurate testing of general motor ability should be completed before the individual is programmed for and placed.

Vance (1968) found that although girls with normal hearing scored higher than girls who are deaf on seven of nine selected motor tests, only two of the tests were significant at the 0.05 level. He questions whether inferior motor ability is inherent in those who are congenitally deaf. Inferior ability may result instead from limited variety of experiences, from differences in child-rearing practices, or from inadequate training of deaf children at an early age. In the past, children with hearing impairment were not offered a comprehensive physical education or movement-oriented program supervised by a qualified physical educator. Marked differences may have developed in people who have hearing impairments simply from lack of participation and *not* because of poor innate motor ability.

Gallaudet College in Washington, D.C., is an institution of higher learning for people who are deaf. The college gave all incoming freshmen a national physical fitness test. After 1 year of physical education, the students were retested and surpassed the national averages for hearing students. Arnheim and Sinclair (1979) believe that the child with hearing impairment can overcome significant movement difficulties: "The most important sense organs to the acquisition of skilled movement are organs of vision, touch, and kinesthesis.... Hearing, or audition, is important but not as important as the aforementioned three sense organs" (p. 5). A concentrated perceptual-motor program that stresses vision and kinesthesis will enable children with hearing impairment to participate successfully in physical activities with their nondisabled peers.

Activities that stress development of vision and kinesthesis must be provided. (Photograph courtesy of C.B. Eichstaedt)

FUNDAMENTAL MOTOR SKILLS

Brundt and Broadhead (1982) conducted an extensive study of 154 boys and girls with hearing impairments of greater than 60 dB, ranging in age from 7 through 14. They used the Short Form of the Bruininks-Oseretsky Test of Motor Proficiency (Bruininks, 1978) and administered 14 fundamental motor skill test items. Comparisons were made to nondisabled students. Table 13.3 shows comparisons between boys, girls, hearing impaired, and non-hearing impaired.

Shephard (1990) comments on the 1982 study by Brundt and Broadhead: "[These researchers] found that deaf students [loss > 60dB] had significant deficits on such simple psychomotor tasks as standing on the preferred leg, walking forward heel-to-toe on a balance beam, jumping up and clapping the hands.... The lack of balance inevitably had a negative impact upon most tests of skilled motor performance" (pp. 114–115).

BALANCE AND THE HEARING IMPAIRED

Too often we assume that all children with hearing impairment possess significant balance deficiencies. Indeed, destruction or impairment of the inner ear can leave

TABLE 13.3 **Comparison of Fundamental Motor Skills of Hearing Impaired and Non-hearing Impaired Children**

Fundamental Motor Skill	Age (yrs)	Males		Females	
		H.I.	NonH.I.	H.I.	NonH.I.
Standing on one leg on balance beam (seconds)	7	3.50	8.14	3.14	8.38
	8	4.67	8.27	6.00	8.56
	10	5.75	9.17	6.75	9.25
	12	4.47	9.07	7.81	9.98
	14	6.44	9.61	8.00	9.25
Walking forward heel to toe on balance beam (steps)	7	1.00	4.35	.86	4.53
	8	1.17	4.80	1.40	4.54
	10	1.00	5.14	2.75	5.38
	12	2.80	5.68	3.00	5.44
	14	3.11	5.09	3.00	5.83
Jumping up and clapping hands (claps)	7	1.75	1.84	1.71	1.81
	8	1.67	2.27	1.60	2.20
	10	1.88	2.76	2.25	2.66
	12	2.20	3.18	2.00	2.88
	14	2.72	3.39	2.50	3.33

Source: Abridged from D. Brundt and G. D. Broadhead (1982), Motor proficiency traits of deaf children. *Research Quarterly for Exercise and Sport, 53,* 236–238.

the child with a distinct balance problem, but not all hearing impairments stem from inner ear difficulties. Unless the semicircular canals, which contain the corti and the endolymph organs, are damaged, balance is not necessarily affected.

Balance is affected by vision, muscle proprioceptors, and the vestibular mechanism of the inner ear. The importance of vision in maintaining balance is emphasized by Guyton (1971): "After complete destruction of the vestibular apparatuses, and even loss of most proprioceptive information from the body, a person can still use his visual mechanisms effectively for maintaining equilibrium" (p. 470).

Lindsey and O'Neal (1976) compared the static balance of 8-year-old children who were deaf and normal hearing and found that vision played an important role in balance. Elimination of visual input on static balance tasks increased task difficulty for people who were deaf and people with normal hearing, but the people who were deaf were more seriously impaired. Grimsley (1972) also identifies vision as a major contributor to balance performance. Using a dynabalometer, he compared the balance of children with normal hearing, congenital deafness, and acquired deafness, and concluded that exclusion of visual input impairs balance performance. Grimsley's study also determined that children who are deaf can learn a balance skill as well as their peers who have normal hearing.

Balance, or the ability to maintain equilibrium in the presence of disrupting conditions (Cratty, 1989), is a basic yet complex skill composed of several performance units. Deficiency in balance ability has a negative influence on more complex skills such as running, hopping, and jumping, as well as the highly coordinated activities of throwing and catching.

Two distinct measures of balance characterize general motor ability: One is **static balance** (e.g., standing in place on one foot) and the other is **dynamic balance** (e.g., walking on a balance beam). When one compares trends observed in tests of static and dynamic balance, and when one consults correlative or factorial studies comparing these two measures, one finds that the two types of balance are indeed independent and distinctly different (Cratty, 1989).

In a discussion of how damage to the vestibular mechanism affects dynamic balance in activities that involve running agility, Guyton (1979) makes the following statement:

> ... a person can still maintain his equilibrium provided he moves slowly. This is accomplished mainly by means of proprioceptor information from the limbs and surfaces of the body and visual information from the eyes.... If he begins to fall forward, the pressure on the anterior parts of his feet increases, stimulating the pressure receptors. This information transmitted to his brain helps to correct the imbalance. At the same time, his eyes also detect the lack of equilibrium, and this information too helps to correct the situation. Unfortunately, the visual and proprioceptor systems for maintaining equilibrium are not organized for rapid action, which explains why a person without his vestibular apparatuses must move slowly (p. 311).

This problem becomes significant when a youngster attempts to change directions, as when playing a game of tag or touch football. Among children who have

**Kinesthesis, including balance, is necessary to perform
successfully the act of throwing. (Photograph courtesy of
Gary Geiger and the Illinois Special Olympics)**

been diagnosed as having temporary or permanent vestibular damage, the physical
education teacher should be aware that activities involving rapid change of direction
may be difficult for that student. This problem should not be interpreted as one
about which the teacher can do nothing. The instructor must now provide extensive
skills work and drills to "overload" the child's proprioceptor and visual systems, thus
attempting to compensate for vestibular weaknesses. Figure 13.4 shows the vestibular
mechanism of the semicircular canals in the inner ear.

The vestibular mechanism, the cerebellum, the proprioceptors in the muscles,
tendons, and joints serve to regulate posture, equilibrium, muscle tone, and the
orientation of the head and body in space. Although mixed results exist regarding
the effectiveness of vestibular stimulation for infants, it is of interest to note the
findings of Ottenbacher (1985). His review of research listed 18 studies containing
44 hypotheses that evaluated the efficacy of vestibular stimulation on infants at-risk
and young children with overt developmental delays. He concluded the following:

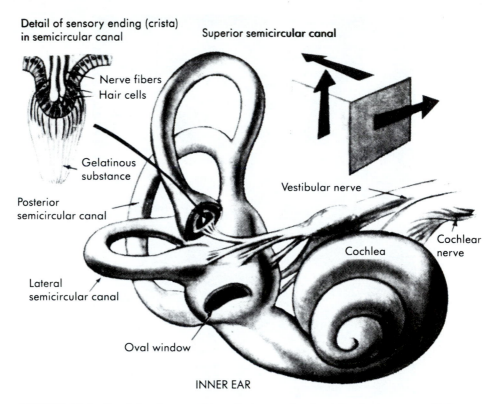

Detail of sensory ending (crista) in semicircular canal

Superior semicircular canal

Nerve fibers
Hair cells

Gelatinous substance

Posterior semicircular canal

Vestibular nerve

Cochlea

Cochlear nerve

Lateral semicircular canal

Oval window

INNER EAR

FIGURE 13.4   **Semicircular canal (vestibular mechanism) in the inner ear. Cube indicates that regardless of position of head or direction of head movement, information will be transmitted to the brain.**

"An analysis of the results of these tests, using methods of meta-analysis, revealed that subjects receiving vestibular stimulation performed significantly better than members of control or comparison groups who did not receive such stimulation" (p. 119).

All children with hearing impairment who have obvious balance problems must be tested to determine their static and dynamic levels of balance ability.

TESTS OF BALANCE

STATIC BALANCE

Several tests for static balance are valid and reliable. Arnheim and Sinclair (1979) evaluated 1563 boys and girls between the ages of 4 and 12 by using a modified version of the "stork stand" and a homemade balance board. Test descriptions and norms are shown in Figure 13.5 and Table 13.4, respectively.

Flat foot,
hand on hips

FIGURE 13.5
Stork stand test.
(Adapted from
Arnheim & Sin-
clair, 1979, p. 123.
Drawing from
Moran & Kalakian,
1977, p. 55.)

TABLE 13.4   **Static Balance**[a]

Male Percentiles					Age	Female Percentiles				
10	30	50	70	90		10	30	50	70	90
9	14	17	19	20	4	8	12	16	19	21
9	17	19	22	23	5	10	15	17	20	24
12	19	21	24	27	6	10	17	21	23	25
11	20	22	26	29	7	12	18	21	24	26
11	20	23	27	30	8	12	20	24	27	28
11	18	21	26	31	9	13	18	22	26	33
10	19	24	25	31	10	10	18	23	26	31
12	20	22	27	29	11	12	18	21	25	29
11	17	21	26	29	12	12	16	21	24	28

Source: Adapted from Arnheim and Sinclair, 1979.

[a]It should be noted that any child scoring in the 30th percentile or lower (as indicated in the boxed area above) is considered to possess a major balance disability. Adapted programming involving static balance activities is therefore necessary.

DYNAMIC BALANCE

Past research is vague about which dynamic balance testing scales are best. The purpose of initial general motor screening is, however, to identify individuals with distinct motor disabilities. A general forward walking balance beam test will identify those individuals with dynamic balance problems. (See Table 13.5.)

Stewart, Dummer, and Haubenstricker (1990) warn teachers to be very careful when giving oral instructions in the administration of standardized test batteries to individuals who are deaf. They list several concerns:

1. Spoken instructions alone are inadequate for motor skill test administration for most students who are labeled as severely or profoundly deaf.

2. Where modifications have been incorporated into instructions, measures must be taken to ensure that all subjects understand what is expected of them. To accomplish this, teachers might enlist the aid of a teacher who is familiar with the subjects, communication and motor skill abilities.

3. Modifications of instructions must not put students who are deaf at a disadvantage when their performance is compared to hearing students. For example, verbal reinforcement is often used to encourage hearing students to run faster, jump higher, or run further. (p. 237)

ACTIVITIES FOR IMPROVEMENT OF STATIC AND DYNAMIC BALANCE

To remedy major balance deficits, additional practice sessions should be scheduled. Individual sessions of 5 to 20 min should be held before or after school, at

TABLE 13.5 **Dynamic Balance (Walking Forward Heel to Toe on Four-Inch Balance Beam)**[a]

Male	Age	Female
1[b]	4	1
1	5	1
2	6	2
2	7	3
2	8	3
2	9	3
3	10	3
4	11	4
4	12	4

[a]Any child scoring less than the minimal levels listed above is considered to possess a major dynamic balance disability. Adapted programming involving dynamic balance activities is therefore necessary.

[b]Number of correct steps taken.

recess, during the lunch hour, or during study hall. These sessions would consist of exercises planned by both teacher and student. Encourage the parents' cooperation to improve skills by practicing at home. Table 13.6 lists activities for home and classroom.

Static and dynamic balance can be practiced by using positions and movements such as kneeling, sitting, standing, walking, galloping, hopping, skipping, leaping, running, and jumping. Balance is an important aspect of kinesthesis, the sense of the body's position in space. Balance is therefore a critical skill to improve.

STATIC OR STATIONARY BALANCE SKILLS

Students should learn to control their bodies in stationary positions. Many balance activities that are comparatively easy to perform with the eyes open become difficult to do with the eyes closed. The balance skill should be practiced with the eyes closed, because this requires exclusive use of body proprioceptors and vestibular mechanisms. Static balance (Figure 13.6) can be taught individually or with full class participation.

DYNAMIC OR MOVING BALANCE SKILLS

The simple skills of hopping, leaping, jumping, and running require balance proficiency, particularly when chasing, stopping, starting, and dodging. The child with low proficiency in dynamic balance will have difficulty competing successfully unless activities to improve balance deficiencies are planned. The program should stress take-off from one or both feet and landing in a gentle, controlled manner. Learners should practice jumping for distance and height. Their bodies must be under control when airborne and when landing. Explosive power for the jump comes from the upper and lower leg muscles, with a strong thrust from the foot and ankle. Some students will be deficient in muscular leg power, so leg strengthening exercises should be included for these students.

During a controlled landing, executed with good balance, the weight is absorbed gradually by the ankle, knee, and hip joints, which bend as toes and feet touch the ground. The arms and shoulders also absorb weight and provide for smooth integration of the total skill. Figures 13.7 and 13.8 show a progression of dynamic balance skills.

TEACHING SUGGESTIONS

1. Be sure students are aware that a child who is hearing impaired may need assistance.
2. Teacher and students should learn the child's name sign.
3. Be sure that directions and explanations are clearly understood by the student. Manual signs and demonstrations reinforce directions.

TABLE 13.6 **Adapted Activities for Home and Classroom**

Balance

1. Children assume hand and knee position on floor.
    a. Each child raises one hand in air; alternate hands.
    b. Each child raises one leg in air; alternate.
    c. Each child raises right arm and right leg; alternate sides.
2. Children balance on tiptoes for count of ten.
3. Children stand on one foot for count of five; alternate feet.
4. Rocking horse—children stand with hands on hips and feet astride; lean forward keeping knees stiff—and lifting heels from floor; rock backward lifting toes from floor.
5. Children walk forward and backward on knees.
6. Children jump on right foot with eyes closed; alternate feet.
7. Children stand on both feet with eyes closed, jump and turn while in air (use $\frac{1}{4}$ and $\frac{1}{2}$ turns only).
8. Use suggested balance activities described on pp. 365–368.

Basic Body Movements

1. Children practice walking; check that arms and legs alternate and swing freely; music may be added.
    a. Walk fast.
    b. Walk slow.
2. Children walk on tiptoes with arms over head.
3. Children walk backward bringing knees up high.
4. Children walk sideways using shuffle step (slide).
5. Children walk sideways using crossover step.
6. Children walk backward on tiptoes with arms over head.
7. Children walk in squatting position.
8. Children alternate between walking "small" and walking "tall."
9. Children place big toes together and walk.
10. Children place heels together and walk.
11. Children walk on heels, slow and fast.
12. Children, with feet together, jump forward one step, backward one step, forward three steps, sideways to left and right.

Eye-Foot Coordination

1. Place strips of masking tape on floor.
    a. Children walk forward heel to toe.
    b. Children walk forward on tiptoes.
    c. Children walk forward with giant steps.
    d. Children walk sideways each direction on tiptoes.
    e. Children walk backward.
    f. Children straddle tape while walking.
    g. Children use crossover step.
2. Lay pieces of rope in looping pattern and direct children to step in loops without touching rope.
3. Children sit on chairs facing partners, roll ball back and forth between each other by catching and pushing the ball with feet only.
4. Play hopscotch.

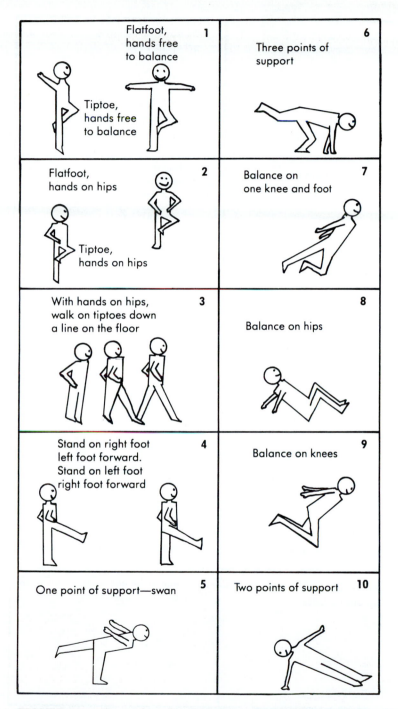

FIGURE 13.6 Examples of static balance. (Copyrighted by C. B. Eichstaedt, 1979.)

FIGURE 13.7 Locomotor activities to improve dynamic balance. (Copyrighted by C. B. Eichstaedt, 1979.)

FIGURE 13.8 (Copyrighted by C. B. Eichstaedt, 1979.)

FIGURE 13.8   *(continued)*

4. Show the student how to perform the action. The teacher should guide the child's body through the desired movement if necessary.

5. For safety, be sure that students know exactly what they are to do. Do not assume that they understand the first time an activity is explained. Students with hearing impairment may be embarrassed to admit that they do not understand and may nod their heads "yes" along with everybody else. Dangerous activities, such as those that require spotting, must be explained clearly and demonstrated visually before the activity begins.

6. Avoid lengthy explanations and constant changes in rules and regulations.

7. Hand signals are absolutely necessary. All students should use official athletic hand signals, even when playing without a referee.

8. Always know the location of the students who are hearing impaired in the teaching area.

9. Stewart, Robinson, and McCarthy (1991) suggest that technical modifications be made to replace auditory cues used to control games

and races. For example, at national, international, and even some regional competitions, swimming and running events are started with lights.

SPECIAL MOTOR ACTIVITIES FOR STUDENTS WITH HEARING IMPAIRMENT

Many activities are needed to motivate and foster positive attitudes when the child is placed in the individualized adapted physical education class. Long-range goals will ultimately be attained through short-term objectives. Interesting and continuing activities are important.

DANCE AND CREATIVE MOVEMENT

Individuals with hearing impairments, including those who are totally deaf, can learn new rhythms and complicated dances. A drum or other striking implement is extremely valuable for teaching rhythm to children with different degrees of hearing loss. They learn to feel the vibrations from the air compression, and the vibrations serve as a cue to movement. It is very difficult for persons who are deaf to dance by feeling vibrations in the floor. Although the person with hearing impairment may be skillful at receiving tactile cues, floor vibrations are not very useful because most dance forms involve airborne movement. The individual with hearing impairment learns to dance by counting specific beats (e.g., three-fourths time). Music is then added for the hearing audience who may be watching the performance.

SWIMMING

Some children may have ventilation tubes or prescribed medicine in their ears. For these children, avoid underwater swimming skills and submersion activities. Other swimming activities are encouraged. For those with tubes or medication, cotton in the ears and a tight bathing cap will generally keep water out of the ears. Quick immersion usually does not get the cotton wet (see section on hearing aids).

The swimming student will not easily be able to lip-read because of distance from the poolside speaker. A buddy system should be used, and lifeguards should know which students have hearing impairment.

BASKETBALL

When playing basketball, hearing team members should hold up arms or give visual signals to indicate to students with hearing impairment that play has stopped.

TOUCH OR REGULAR FOOTBALL

Students with hearing impairment must learn to respond to movement of teammates or opponents. They should learn silent signal counting by working with the quarterback. Because students who are deaf cannot hear an official's whistle, they should be taught the same rules of not "piling on" that hearing players learn.

GYMNASTICS AND TUMBLING

The child with hearing impairment needs to learn by observing skills and activities—one good demonstration may be worth ten thousand words. Manual assistance is extremely helpful also.

TRAMPOLINE

Trampoline jumping is an excellent activity for those with balance deficits. For example, the simple stunts of the jumping, seat drop, hand/knee drop, and the front drop are designed to allow youngsters to practice basic jumping development while stimulating the balance components of the vestibular mechanism, the proprioceptors, and vision. Body turning and twisting actions are encouraged, such as the combination of jump, half/turn, jump. Body coordination is enhanced when the student learns to perform basic skills in combination (i.e., hand/knee drop to front drop; seat drop to front drop; seat turntable). Do not give verbal instructions while the child is moving or bouncing on the trampoline because speech reading is then impossible.

Many school administrators have discouraged the use of trampolines because of the potential for injury. However, the positive influence of safe and controlled use of the trampoline must be emphasized; there is no better piece of equipment for jumping, stopping, and controlling one's body in space. For students with balance and body coordination delays, basic elementary trampoline skills should constitute the program; advanced skills such as somersaults *must not* be attempted. The "knee drop," once thought of as a beginning skill, is now considered potentially dangerous and should not be taught.

COMPETITIVE ATHLETICS

Competitive sport is intensely demanding and individuals who plan to compete at this level must dedicate themselves to the rigors of athletic training. Athletic coaches will expect maximum effort from their athletes. Whether the participants are deaf or of normal hearing, nothing of lesser intensity should be expected. The involvement of individuals with hearing impairments in competitive athletics with their nondisabled peers is highly encouraged. Coaches of normal hearing teams are continually expressing positive comments regarding the athletic performance of individuals on their teams who are deaf.

Although the positive impact of mainstreaming is being felt, some professionals believe that competition in sport should be between teams with similar disabilities (e.g., deaf teams playing against deaf teams). In reference to the highly competitive World Games for the Deaf (WGD), Stewart (1991) states the following:

> The Games [WGD] carry with them a message about diversity for all people, deaf or hearing; deaf sport has carved a niche for itself within the world or sport—one that underscores cultural distinctiveness of deaf individuals. Deaf athletes competing in the WGD and other deaf games come in contact with a sizable number of other athletes who share the experience of deafness, most of whom use sign language as their preferred means of communication. This commonality, peculiar to the deaf community, is the primary reason deaf games were established and will continue to exist. (p. 19)

The World Games for the Deaf include 13 summer and 4 winter events. Stewart, Dummer, and Haubenstricker (1990) summarize as follows: "Sign language is the communication of choice in deaf communities all over the world...World Games for the Deaf in their isolation from non-deaf sport organizations should be treasured for what they are" (p. 23).

Another strong negative feeling regarding integration of individuals with hearing impairment into regular physical education classes is presented by Butterfield (1991). He believes that students who are deaf might be better served in schools whose major population and teachers are highly skilled in using American Sign Language (ASL):

> It is time to rethink the meaning of least restrictive environment when making placement decisions affecting deaf children. A narrow interpretation of P.L. 94-142 is a disservice to deaf children, and in a broader sense to the deaf community. Moreover, physical education and sport within the context of the residential school is a linchpin of deaf culture and provides a means for deaf children to grow, learn, and engage in self-actualizing behavior. (p. 101)

HEARING AIDS

Hearing aids for sound amplification are effective correction for certain hearing disorders, such as a conductive loss in the external or middle ear. A **hearing aid** is a small, personalized unit that increases sound. Israel (1975) describes several styles:

> The traditional body-type aid consists of a small pocketworn unit (containing the microphone, amplifier, volume control, and battery). The unit is connected to the ear by a cord, at the end of which is the loudspeaker (usually referred to as the "button" or "receiver"). The ear-level type hooks around the top and back of the ear and contains all the basic components...in a single shell. The eyeglass type is similar to

the ear-level type, but is built into the temple portion of a pair of eyeglasses. The all-in-the-ear type is a subminiature aid which fits directly into the...hollow portion of the outer ear. All these aids require some form of ear mold and none...are invisible to the observer. (p. 22)

Hearing aids can be worn in one ear (monaural) or in both ears (binaural) and are designed to meet each person's need. The y-chord, which includes wires attached to an instrument worn on the body, is popular with many students.

In reference to advances in hearing aids, Osnowitz (1985) states the following: "The industry has undergone radical change.... Hearing aid makers have refined the technology required to put the entire hearing aid inside a person's ear, and in some cases entirely inside the ear canal.... It puts the components closer to the eardrum" (p. 4a).

Kahn (1990) believes the extent of hearing loss also determines the specific type of hearing aid that suits the child best. The relative proportions of binaural and y-cord use increase steadily with severity of hearing loss. Monaural aid decreases correspondingly, although monaural aids still account for the majority of use even among students with profound hearing loss.

Children who wear hearing aids obtain different levels of effectiveness, and some may even give a false impression that they are benefiting from its use when they in fact are not. If the aid is functioning properly, the child's auditory input will be improved.

The hearing aid should be used during physical education activities unless possible damage to the unit could occur or the unit inhibits activity. The child's hearing aid can be held securely by an elastic "tube top." This allows the child to run and jump without bouncing or jarring the hearing aid against his chest.

Activities such as basketball or touch football are rough enough to cause a sharp blow to the player's chest. The hearing aid therefore should be removed for safety during such activities. If wires are used for the hearing aid, the teacher may have difficulty spotting the child who is tumbling or vaulting. The hearing aid should be removed in these instances.

TOTAL COMMUNICATION AND THE PHYSICAL EDUCATION TEACHER

Sign language is now accepted as part of the education of children with hearing impairment. Significant educational advances result when children who are deaf are exposed to a combination of communication methods (oral, speechreading, lipreading), amplification of sound (hearing aids), fingerspelling, and signing, rather than an exclusive focus on any one of the highly controversial extremes of rigid oral or rigid manual communication (Moores, 1987).

AMERICAN SIGN LANGUAGE (ASL)

ASL or Ameslan has been identified as a major factor that identifies and characterizes individuals who are deaf as a unique subculture. Butterfield (1991) describes ASL as follows:

> ASL has been the subject of much study since the early 1960s and is recognized by many scholars as a genuine language that relies on visual rather than auditory encoding and decoding. Competence in ASL is requisite for membership in the deaf community. (p. 95)

Like the English language, ASL is considered a true language and has passed all rigors pertaining to its respectability and acceptance. ASL possesses its own grammar and structure and is able to communicate subtle nuances of abstractions in addition to describing concrete objects (Craft, 1990).

ASL is not a manual version of the English language, nor is it a worldwide sign language. Its differences are noted by Miller and Allaire (1987):

(a) It does not use English word order (the statement "There is food in the store" would be expressed in ASL as "It store have food");

(b) it has no form of the verb *to be*;

(c) it has no passive voice;

(d) it uses no articles;

(e) it marks verb tense for whole conversation or segment, not for individual verbs;

(f) it does not have signs for pronouns, but establishes the intended referent(s) in space; and

(g) it can use movement in space to convey in one sign a subject + verb + object statement that would require three words in English. (p. 274)

Because communication is vital, sign language and fingerspelling are necessary instruction tools for physical education instruction. Eichstaedt and Lavay (1992) suggest that regular classroom teachers who deal with children with hearing impairment should be given training programs to learn signing and fingerspelling. Because signing is desirable, a workable composite of approximately 50 signs used commonly in physical education and athletics will assist the instructor of students who are hearing impaired (Figure 13.9).

Physical educators frequently use a single word or phrase to explain, encourage, correct, or control learning situations. Some familiar expressions are: "Jump over, run to your left, come to me." "Good girl! Try again." "Crawl under. No, watch me." "Stop! Begin again." "Sit down, stand up, run to boys." Such commonly used activity words are converted easily to signs, can be learned readily, and should become workable tools for every physical educator.

In many typical physical education situations, the student with hearing impairment should be directly in front of the instructor so directions and commands will be

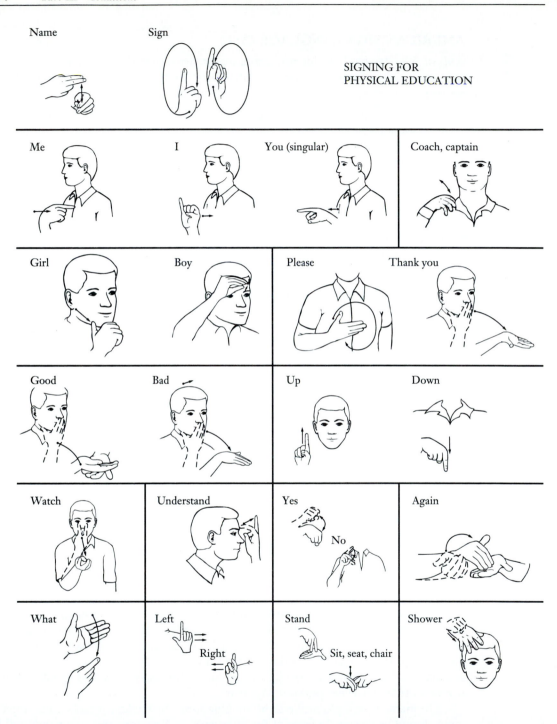

FIGURE 13.9   A working composite of approximately 50 signs which will greatly assist the instructor of students with hearing impairment. (Adapted from Eichstaedt & Seiler, 1978, pp. 20–21; modified by Howorka, 1986.)

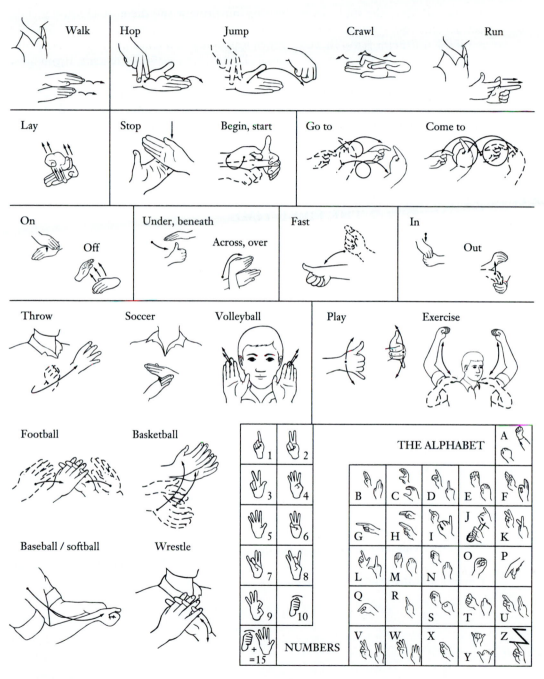

FIGURE 13.9   *(continued)*

understood. Both the student with hearing impairment and the normal hearing child can benefit from signing. Many children with hearing impairment can read lips, but not if the instructor is too far away. When explaining new concepts, rules, stratagems, or skills, use simple terms. Avoid unusual cliches or idiomatic statements. If you must use idioms, explain what they mean.

Students with hearing impairment will be unable to lip-read from the outfield, from across the swimming pool, or from the other end of the basketball floor. Use consistent signs and gestures as you would for students who are nondisabled.

MEETING THE INDIVIDUAL WHO IS HEARING IMPAIRED FOR THE FIRST TIME

Ask the person, "Can you read my lips?" If the individual says *yes*, continue conversation in a normal voice; do not shout. Speak distinctly but do not overenunciate your words. Face the person and do not turn your head while speaking. Do not cover your mouth or speak with something in your mouth. People with a mustache are more difficult to understand. If the individual does not understand, use a paper and pencil.

If you do not understand what a person who is hearing impaired is trying to say, ask her to repeat the statements. Pretending to understand when you do not only leads to confusion and frustration. If you cannot understand, ask the individual to write.

FINGERSPELLING

The basic English alphabet can be learned in a short time. It is easier to fingerspell than to read fingerspelling. The dominant hand, held at shoulder level with palm out, spells the letters. Spelling slowly increases accuracy and eliminates confusion. When receiving, if a letter is lost, continue interpretation; the remaining letters may suggest the total word. Figure 13.9 shows the alphabet finger positions both as the receiver and the sender view them.

SIGNING

Most signs are for concept only—the idea and not the word is stressed. The concept of *good* is signed in the following way: The left hand is open, palm up before the chest. The right hand, also open, touches the lips. The right hand is brought down so the back rests on the left palm (see Figure 13.9).

Signing often requires shortening extraneous words or deletion of word endings. "Go out to left field" is simply "go" and then point to left field. Use common everyday gestures because most students with hearing impairment are familiar with them. Pointing, motioning, demonstrating, and signaling are perfectly acceptable (Moores, 1987).

Formal signing and fingerspelling as explained in *A Basic Course in Manual Communication* (O'Rourke, 1973) can serve as the foundation for communication with individuals who are hearing impaired. *The Joy of Signing* (Riekenhof, 1985) is an excellent illustrated source for learning sign language and the alphabet. *The American Sign Language Dictionary* (1987) by Sternberg provides 3,300 signs and over 4,000 illustrations.

DEAF/BLIND

When double disabilities occur, the consequences are multiplied. In the case of the double disability of individuals being both deaf and blind, the two primary sensory inputs are missing. Often, these youngsters are labeled as severely disabled. Craft (1990) defines these individuals as multisensory deprived. This condition leads to severe communication problems and resultant educational delays. A child who is deaf learns much through observation and imitation. For a child who is only blind, learning occurs through tactual and verbal communication from others. For the child who is both deaf and blind, the world is experienced in vibrations, air currents, temperature changes, smells, and a great many tactile sensations and sensations within the digestive system, muscles, joints, and vestibular mechanism.

For the child who is congenitally blind, it is extremely difficult to understand the physical and social environment. For the person who is congenitally deaf, communication becomes the major hurdle. The combination of being both deaf and blind leaves the child physically and socially isolated from the environment.

P.L. 101-476 includes a specific definition of the deaf/blind classification:

> both auditory and visual handicaps, the combination of which causes such severe communication and other developmental and educational problems that they cannot properly be accommodated in special education programs solely for the child with hearing impairment or for the child with visual impairment.

As the definition describes, individuals who are deaf/blind have a combination of hearing and seeing impairments but are not necessarily totally deaf or completely blind. Several factors must be considered when attempting to understand the educational needs of children who are deaf and blind. First, these youngsters are not usually entirely deaf or entirely blind; the common understanding of deaf/blindness is that a person has such auditory and visual impairment as to be unable to communicate or be educated in traditional ways. Second, the child who is born blind and becomes deaf later in life has different problems from one who is born deaf and becomes blind later.

A common etiology of deaf/blindness has been traced to rubella (German measles), which causes infection of the mother during the first 3 months (the first trimester) of her pregnancy. The rubella virus crosses the placenta and produces developmental abnormalities of the eyes, ears, heart, brain, and bone in up to 40% of cases without interrupting the pregnancy. It should be stressed that these destructive conditions of rubella will only cause problems to an unborn fetus and will have no negative effect on young children. Another cause of blindness is retinitis pigmentosa (RP); it is the most common of all inherited disorders of the retina of the eye. RP sometimes occurs in children who are congenitally deaf. When this combination of congenital deafness and gradual retinitis pigmentosa occurs, it is known as *Usher's syndrome* and is a major cause among adolescents and adults of deaf/blindness (Heward & Orlansky, 1992).

Educational programs require instruction in basic skills and are similar to those for other children with severe and profound disabilities. The major emphasis should be on communication and should involve some form of tactual intervention, including the child writing on the palm of the teacher, speechreading, sign language, and gestures. For some students, teaching them to speak should also be attempted. Total communication is accepted as the most viable method of communication. This would include sign language when the child has enough vision to see signs; the Tadoma method, in which the individual places the fingers on the speaker's lips with the thumb on the speaker's throat in order to "lip-read"; fingerspelling, where the teacher spells each word and the child feels with both hands; tracing out a printed letter by the teacher on the palm of the student's hand or some other part of the body; use of Braille; and finally, if there is enough vision, large printing.

Heward and Orlansky (1988) point out:

> An educational program for deaf children is often inappropriate for a child who also has limited vision, because many methods of instruction and communication rely heavily on the use of sight. Programs for visually impaired students, on the other hand, usually require good hearing because much instruction is auditory. Most students who are classified as deaf/blind do have some residual vision and/or hearing. However, they frequently have other physical, intellectual, and behavioral disabilities along with their impaired sight and vision. (pp. 378–388)

After communication, the next greatest problem is mobility. It is very important to help children to effectively use any residual vision or hearing. These children will likely experience balance difficulties and have trouble walking a straight line. Static and dynamic balance activities should be offered daily, including basic sitting, kneeling, creeping, and standing positions. Balance boards, swinging cradles and nets, rotary movements, and rocking on a large cage ball can provide meaningful vestibular and proprioceptor stimulation. The children should be given the opportunity to explore, manipulate, and play with different pieces of equipment. Toys that provide tactual stimulation are important. For example, use differently textured surfaces that are smooth or rough; objects that are big or small, heavy or light; implements that vibrate, such as a hand-held vibrator; and boxes or cans that shake and rattle. Different foods can serve as learning experiences and can also be used for reinforcement purposes. Whipped cream, honey, jam, and jello are fun (in most cases) and taste good. Allow the youngsters to select those toys that give them the most satisfaction. Teachers can observe what the child truly enjoys and can use that toy or food for reward when on command the youngster completes a specific task. Immediate feedback is important. Physical reinforcement may be necessary when the child's level of stimulus/reward is very basic. These prompts should be "faded out" and replaced with either physical or verbal reinforcements (i.e., hugs, touches, high five). These too, should eventually fade out of the behavior modification plan, and the reward should be successful participation in the designated task.

Craft (1990) suggests that students who are deaf/blind can participate in most sports on a recreational basis and lists weight lifting, dancing, roller skating, swimming, skiing, bowling, hiking, and canoeing as possibilities: "In order to enjoy these and other sports, students need the prerequisite skills and immediate feedback on the success of their efforts" (p. 224).

Regarding the teaching of motor skills, Dunn and Fait (1989) describe teaching a student who is deaf/blind to reach for a ball: "With the student in a seated position... tap the student's elbows as a signal to reach for the ball. If the student fails to reach, as requested, the instructor would then take student's hands and physically assist the child to retrieve the ball. Additional feedback would be provided by moving the student's head up and down to indicate yes or side to side to indicate no" (p. 235).

The senses of seeing and hearing are undoubtedly the two primary avenues by which information is absorbed by infants and children. When these senses are not available, whether they never existed or are lost or severely limited, the child is restricted to a very small environment. Smithdas (1981), a person who is deaf/blind, stated the following: "The world literally shrinks; it is only as large as he can reach with his fingertips or by using his remaining secondary senses to touch, taste, smell, and kinesthetic awareness that he can broaden his field of information and gain additional knowledge" (p. 38).

The adapted physical educator must work closely with the special education classroom teacher, therapists, and parents to coordinate motor activity programs. Valuable time can be saved if common information is shared, such as methods of communication, likes and dislikes of the student, rewards used, and existing behavior modification plans.

SUMMARY

Hearing impairment in various degrees constitutes one of the most common disabilities affecting school-age children. Eight out of every 1000 students under age 20 have significant hearing loss. Hearing disabilities range from slight to total loss of sound perception. Statistics indicate that only 1 out of every 8 children with hearing impairment is deaf.

No motor activities should be excluded from physical education programs. Students may possess low levels of static or dynamic balance or low levels of both, but the great majority possess normal motor and physical capabilities. All youngsters with hearing impairment should be properly assessed and given the same test battery as children with normal hearing.

Students with hearing impairment have a communication disability and may have difficulty being able to understand verbal instruction. All physical educators should be able to use minimal fingerspelling and signing to facilitate communication with students who are hearing impaired.

REFERENCES

AAHPERD. (1976, June). *Physical education, recreation, and sports for the individual with hearing impairments.* Reston, VA: AAHPERD.

Arnheim, D., & Sinclair, W. A. (1979). *The clumsy child* (2nd ed.). St. Louis: C. V. Mosby.

Blackman, J. A. (1990). *Medical aspects of developmental disabilities in children birth to three* (2nd ed.). Rockville, MD: Aspen.

Bruininks, R. H. (1978). *Bruininks-Oseretsky test of motor proficiency: Examiner's manual.* Circle Pines, MN: American Guidance Service.

Brundt, D., & Broadhead, G. D. (1982). Motor proficiency traits of deaf children. *Research Quarterly for Exercise and Sport, 53,* 236–238.

Butterfield, S. A. (1991). Physical education and sport for the deaf: Rethinking the least restrictive environment. *Adapted Physical Activity Quarterly, 8,* 95–102.

Coleman, M. (1988). Medical care of children and adults with Down syndrome. In V. Dmitriev & P. L. Oelwein (Eds.), *Advances in Down syndrome* (pp. 7–18). Seattle: Special Child.

Craft, D. H. (1990). Sensory impairments. In J. P. Winnick (Ed.), *Adapted physical education and sport* (pp. 209–228). Champaign, IL: Human Kinetics.

Cratty, B. J. (1979). *Perceptual and motor development in infants and children* (2nd ed.). Englewood Cliffs, NJ: Prentice-Hall.

Cratty, B. J. (1989). *Adapted physical education in the mainstream* (2nd ed.). Denver: Love.

Dunn, J., & Fait, H. (1989). *Special physical education* (6th ed.). Dubuque, IA: Brown.

Eichstaedt, C. B. & Lavay, B. W. (1992). *Physical activity for individuals with mental retardation: Infancy through adulthood.* Champaign, IL: Human Kinetics.

Eichstaedt, C. B., & Seiler, P. (1978). Communicating with hearing impaired individuals in a physical education setting. *JOPER, 49*(5), 19–21.

Gallaudet Research Institute. (1991). Today's hearing impaired children and youth: A demographic and academic profile. Washington, DC: The Institute.

Grimsley, R. (1972). *The effects of visual cueness and visual deprivation upon the acquisition and rate of learning of a balance skill among deaf individuals.* Doctoral dissertation, University of Georgia, Athens, GA.

Guyton, A. C. (1971). *Basic human physiology: Normal function and mechanisms of disease.* Philadelphia: W. B. Saunders.

Guyton, A. C. (1979). *Physiology of the human body,* (5th ed.). Philadelphia: W. B. Saunders.

Hallahan, D. P., & Kauffman, J. M. (1991). *Exceptional children* (5th ed.). Englewood Cliffs, NJ: Prentice Hall.

Heward, W. L., & Orlansky, M. D. (1992). *Exceptional children* (4th ed.). New York: Merrill/Macmillan.

Israel, R. H. (1975). The hearing aid. *Volta Review,* 77 (1), 22.

Jackson, H. (1985, March). In W. Murray, *Chicago Tribune,* Section 6, pp. 1, 4–5, 24.

Kacica, M., & Harrison, C. J. (1990). Mumps. In R. E. Rakel (Ed.), *Conn's current therapy 1990* (pp. 96–98). Philadelphia: Saunders.

Kahn, G. (1990). Hearing impairment. In J. A. Blackman (Ed.), *Medical aspects of developmental disabilities in children birth to three* (pp. 191–195). Rockville, MD: Aspen.

Karchmer, M. A., & Kirwin, L. A. (1977). *The use of hearing aids by hearing impaired students in the United States.* Washington, DC: Office of Demographic Studies, Gallaudet College.

Lindsey, D., & O'Neal, J. (1976). Static and dynamic balance skills of eight year old deaf and hearing children. *American Annals of the Deaf, 121*(1), 49–55.

Lowenbraun, S., & Thompson, M. D. (1990). Hearing impairments. In N. G. Haring & L. McCormick (Eds.), *Exceptional children and youth* (5th ed.; pp. 362–401). New York: Merrill/Macmillan.

Marcy, M. (1980). Mumps. In H. F. Conn and R. B. Conn, Jr. (Eds.), *Current Diagnosis 6,* (pp. 996–1002). Philadelphia: W. B. Saunders.

Miller, J., & Allaire, J. (1987). Augmentative communication. In M. E. Snell (Ed.), *Systematic instruction of persons with severe handicaps* (3rd ed.; pp. 273–297). New York: Merrill/Macmillan.

Moores, D. F. (1987). *Educating the deaf* (3rd ed.). Boston: Houghton Mifflin.

Moran, J. M., & Kalakian, L. H. (1977). *Movement experiences for the mentally retarded or emotionally disturbed child,* (2nd ed.). Minneapolis: Burgess Publishing.

National Information Center on Deafness. (1991). *Deafness: A fact sheet.* Washington, DC: Gallaudet College.

O'Rourke, T. J. (1973). *A basic course in manual communication.* Silver Spring, MD: National Association of the Deaf.

Osnowitz, P. (1985, December 10). Hearing aids open deaf world. In J. Williams, *The Daily Pantagraph* (p. 4a, 10).

Ottenbacher, K. (1985). Developmental implications of clinically applied vestibular stimulation. *Physical Therapy, 63,* 338–342.

Petryshyn, W. A. (1991, September 30). Getting an earful. In *The Pantagraph* (p. C1).

Quigley, S. P., & Kretschmer, R. E. (1982). *The education of deaf children.* Baltimore: University Park Press.

Riekenhof, L. L. (1985). *The joy of signing.* Springfield, MO: Gospel Printing House.

Sarff, L. S., Ray, H. F., & Bagwell, C. L. (1981, October). Why not amplification in every classroom? *Hearing Aid Journal,* pp. 43–52.

Shephard, R. J. (1990). *Fitness in special populations.* Champaign, IL: Human Kinetics.

Smithdas, R. (1981). Psychological aspects of deaf-blindness. In S. R. Walsh & R. Holzberg (Eds.), *Understanding and educating the deaf-blind/severely and profoundly handicapped: An international perspective.* Springfield, IL: Thomas.

Sternberg, M. L. A. (1987). *American sign language dictionary.* New York: Harper & Row.

Stewart, D. A. (1991). Reflections on the 1991 world winter games for the deaf. *Palaestra, 8(1),* 18–23.

Stewart, D. A., Dummer, G. M., & Haubenstricker, J. L. (1990). Review of administration procedures used to assess the motor skills of deaf children and youth. *Adapted Physical Activity Quarterly*, 7, 231–239.

Stewart, D. A., Robinson, J., & McCarthy, D. (1991). Participation in deaf sport: Characteristics of elite deaf athletes. *Adapted Physical Activity Quarterly*, *8*, 136–145.

U.S. Department of Education. (1991). *Thirteenth annual report to Congress on the implementation of the individuals with disabilities education act*. Washington, DC: Office of Special Education Programs, U.S. Office of Special Education and Rehabilitative Services.

Vance, P. C. (1968). Motor characteristics of deaf children. Unpublished doctoral dissertation, Colorado State University. *Dissertation Abstracts International*, p. 1145–A.

Chapter 14

VISUAL DISABILITIES

 John Novotny has been blind since the age of 2 as a result of a rare eye disease that forced the removal of both eyes. The disability, however, has not limited his athletic endeavors in the least as he enjoys skiing, wrestling, distance running, weight lifting, bicycling, and beep baseball. John, who runs to stay in condition, considers himself a "jock" and credits his parents for never restricting him. "My family always treated me exactly as they'd treat anyone else. If I wanted to try something, they would say 'go ahead.' That environment and encouragement had a lot to do with my decisions to participate in athletics." John was one of seven skiers representing the United States in the 1980 Olympics for Individuals with Physical Disabilities.

Approximately 6.4 million persons in the United States have some visual disability, that is, they have less than normal vision even with corrective lenses. Of these, 1.7 million are severely visually impaired—they are either legally blind or function as if they were legally blind. Approximately 400,000 of those with severe visual impairment have no usable vision at all.

In the 1989–1990 school year, the actual number of students (ages 6–21) who had visual impairments served by Public Laws 101–476 and 89–313 was 22,960 (U.S. Department of Education, 1991). This represents one of the smallest groups of children with disabilities. The only smaller group is of individuals with the deaf-blind classification. The majority of children with visual disabilities in the United States attend public school, and a need exists for all students with visual disabilities to be integrated into sighted society.

DEFINITIONS

The term **visual disability** covers three general categories: **blind, legally blind,** and **partially sighted.** The American Foundation for the Blind prefers that the word **blind** be used to describe a complete loss of sight, and that all other degrees of visual loss be described as **visual impairment.**

383

Legally blind describes visual acuity (clarity or clearness) that does not exceed 20/200 in the *better eye* with corrective lenses or a visual field of less than a 20-degree peripheral angle. Simply put, a person is legally blind if he can see at a distance of 20 ft what a person with normal vision can see at 200 ft. Table 14.1 lists specific degrees and definitions of visual acuity, ranging from normal vision to total blindness.

Persons identified as **partially sighted** (often referred to as **functionally blind**) must possess a visual acuity of better than 20/200 but not greater than 20/70 in the better eye after correction. Although these individuals may have a great deal of useful vision, they may be unable to read newspapers or to see a television image.

Students are disabled to the degree that the visual impairment prevents them from living as they wish. A person with visual impairment who wants to participate in games such as tennis or racquetball will find poor vision more of a problem than the person who enjoys jogging or swimming. In other words, people are severely disabled when they consider themselves to be severely disabled.

TABLE 14.1   **Degree of Visual Acuity**

Visual Acuity	Description
Normal vision: 20/12 to 20/25	Healthy young adults average better than 20/20 acuity.
Near-normal vision: 20/30 to 20/70	Causes no serious problems, usually explored for potential improvement or possible early disease.
Moderate low vision: 20/80 to 20/160	Strong reading glasses or magnifiers usually provide adequate reading speed.
Severe low vision ("legal blindness"): 20/200 to CF10′[a]	Gross orientation and mobility generally adequate, but difficulty with traffic signs, bus numbers, etc. High-power magnifiers for reading.
Profound low vision: CF8′ to CF4′	Increasing problems with visual orientation and mobility. White cane useful. Highly motivated individuals can read visually with extreme magnification. Others rely on braille, talking books, or radio.
Near blindness: less than CF4′	Vision unreliable except under ideal circumstances. Must rely on nonvisual aids.
Total blindness (no light perception):	Must rely on other senses entirely.

Source: Modified from *California Department of Education and Rehabilitation Manual,* 2nd ed., Sacramento, California: Department of Developmental Services, 1978, p. 29.

[a]CF = central field

PHYSIOLOGY OF THE EYE

The eyeball is the receiving unit of the visual system. The eye is protected by the lids and rests in a bony pyramid (orbit or socket) filled with fat. The fat absorbs shock and facilitates eye movement, which is accomplished by four rectus muscles. The muscles provide motion upward, downward, toward the nose, and away from the nose. Two oblique muscles provide angular as well as upward and downward movement.

The eyeball has three layers (see Figure 14.1 for a cross section of the eye). The strong outermost protective coat is composed of the cornea (clear window and major refractive surface) and opaque sclera (white in color). The middle coat (uvea) carries the blood supply in its three structures: (1) the iris, which gives color to eyes, (2) the ciliary body, which produces the fluid of the aqueous humor and allows adjustment for distant vision (i.e., accommodation), and (3) the choroid, the blood supply for the retina. The front segment of the inner coat contains pigment that prevents light scattering, and in its posterior portion, the retina, which is the receptor organ. From the retina, nerve fibers form the optic nerve and carry impulses to the brain, which

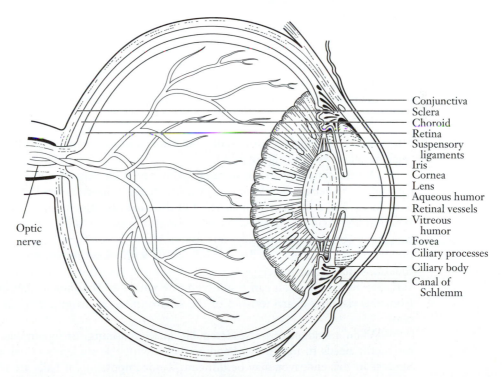

FIGURE 14.1 **Cross section of the human eye.**

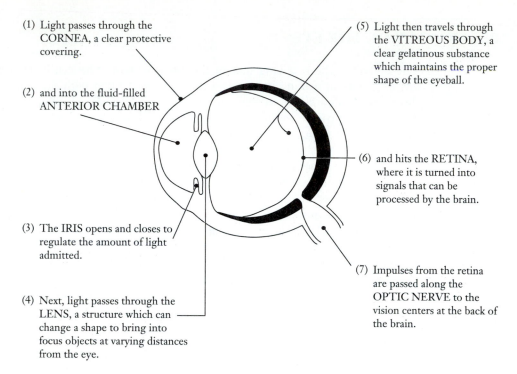

(1) Light passes through the CORNEA, a clear protective covering.

(2) and into the fluid-filled ANTERIOR CHAMBER

(3) The IRIS opens and closes to regulate the amount of light admitted.

(4) Next, light passes through the LENS, a structure which can change a shape to bring into focus objects at varying distances from the eye.

(5) Light then travels through the VITREOUS BODY, a clear gelatinous substance which maintains the proper shape of the eyeball.

(6) and hits the RETINA, where it is turned into signals that can be processed by the brain.

(7) Impulses from the retina are passed along the OPTIC NERVE to the vision centers at the back of the brain.

FIGURE 14.2   **How light is transmitted to the brain. (Reprinted with permission of Aspen Systems Corporation, copyright 1990, from D. P. Schor. Visual Impairment. In** J. A. Blackman, *Medical Aspects of Developmental Disabilities in Children Birth to Three*, p. 269.**)**

integrates these impulses with input from other sense systems and projects composite images, called **vision** (Figure 14.2).

Optical functions are associated primarily with physiological control of the external and internal muscles of the eye, which aid in fixation, tracking, accommodation, focus, and movement. Impairment or disease in the tissues or structures restricts function and produces irregular development of muscular skills. Often, several functions may occur simultaneously; one function may be uniform whereas others occur intermittently from day to day. In individuals with visual impairments, some visual functions may occur under certain conditions only and not in other situations. This variation in eye function can result from the nature of the impairment or disease or from the visibility characteristics of the environment or from a combination of the two.

When a student possesses irregular, malfunctioning, or incomplete vision, the instructor needs to match eye-hand activities with the student's visual ability level. Success in this endeavor may be difficult, if not impossible, if balls are too small, or move too fast, or if the environment is dark. Student frustration can be avoided if the instructor modifies equipment, rules, or playing area accordingly.

CAUSES OF VISUAL DEFECTS

Table 14.2 describes common visual disabilities. Diseases of the retina cause the greatest loss of vision and contribute to approximately 40 percent of all blindness. The retina and the optic nerve are outgrowths of the brain and do not regenerate when injured.

TABLE 14.2   **Common Visual Abnormalities**

Term	Description
Albinism	Herediatry condition characterized by a lack of pigment throughout the body, including the eyes. It is usually accompanied by a nystagmus condition (see below). Children with albinism are very sensitive to light and must sometimes wear tinted glasses.
Amblyopia	Commonly called "lazy eye," an eye deviation in which the wandering eye does not focus on the same object as the good eye.
Astigmatism	Blurred vision caused by defective curvature of refractive surfaces of the eye, as a result of which light rays are not sharply focused on retina.
Cataract	Condition in which the normally transparent lens of the eye becomes cloudy or opaque.
Glaucoma	Condition in which fluid pressure inside the eye is too high. Depending on the type of glaucoma, visual loss may be gradual, sudden, or present at birth. When visual loss is gradual, it begins with decreasing peripheral vision.
Hyperopia	Condition in which the eyeball is too short from front to back, causing farsightedness.
Myopia	Condition in which the eyeball is too long from front to back, causing nearsightedness.
Nystagmus	Involuntary, rapid movement of the eyeballs from side to side, up and down, in a rotary motion, or in a combination of these.
Retinitis pigmentosa	Hereditary degeneration of the retina beginning with night blindness and producing a gradual loss of peripheral vision. Although some persons with this disease lose all vision, many do retain some central vision.
Retrolental fibroplasia (Retinopathy of prematurity)	Visual impairment caused by oxygen given to incubated premature babies.
Strabismus	Eyes not simultaneously directed to the same object as a result of muscle imbalance of the eyeball. Crossed or deviated eyes are examples.

Source: Adapted from Corn and Martinez 1977, pp. 23–24.

Detachment of the retina occurs when the retina detaches from the choroid and floats in vitreous space. Prolonged detachment results in permanent visual loss following reattachment. This condition can be caused by a tumor, fluid underneath the retina, or strands of vitreous humor attached to the retina, which contract and detach the retina, as in diabetes. The condition often results from unknown causes as well. In idiopathic detachment, holes occur in the retina edges because of vitreous pressure. Vitreous fluid flows through these holes, stripping the retina away from the choroid. If the detachment continues, all central vision will be lost.

Surgical repair of a detached retina requires closing holes by diathermy and sewing plastic over the holes, thereby allowing the choroid to once again contact the retina. Fluid is released by puncture, and in most cases the retina returns to normal. Approximately 60 percent of people with a detached retina in one eye will develop the condition in the other eye. Untreated retinal detachments usually result in blindness, glaucoma, or phthisis bulbi (shrinking and wasting of the eyeball), with resultant enucleation (surgical removal).

Premature infants who are placed in incubators are also susceptible to detached retina. In this case, the blood vessels in the infant's retina become accustomed to the high levels of pure oxygen administered in incubators. When the baby is returned to natural room air, too little oxygen is available for transfer by existing blood vessels to the infant's system. New blood vessels then grow, not on the retina but toward the center of the eye, and scar tissue develops. Immediate surgery is necessary, but the condition often is not diagnosed soon enough for surgery to be effective. New surgical procedures are being used, but the prognosis is questionable. Machemer (1985) states, "One cannot expect full vision even if the retina is completely reattached, since many alterations have occurred in the retina during the disease's progress" (p. 188).

A child with retinal detachment must not jar or bump the head or eyes. Running and jumping are therefore contraindicated, but other noncompetitive activities are encouraged. All activities should be checked with the physician prior to participation.

During the past several years, a major preventive campaign has been undertaken to vaccinate school-age children throughout the United States against *rubella*, or German measles. This precaution is not only to safeguard the children but to protect their mothers as well. As a childhood disease, rubella is usually quite mild, but when the virus attacks women in the first 3 months of pregnancy, its effects on the unborn child can be devastating. In the rubella epidemic of 1964 and 1965, almost 40,000 unborn children were affected by rubella. One of the common prenatal results of the virus is the formation of congenital cataracts. Many of today's young adults with multiple disabilities were conceived during this epidemic. In addition to loss of vision, they often exhibit symptoms of deafness, heart conditions, mental retardation, and neurological impairment. When planning a physical education program for individuals who are blind, the physical educator must make sure that the child's physician provides specific information regarding any additional disabling condition that the child may possess.

Eye injuries are exceptionally common, particularly in physical education classes and competitive athletics. Every year more than 35,000 Americans lose some degree of sight from sports injuries. More than one-third of sports eye injuries occur in young adults ages 15 to 24. Baseball is the leading cause of sports eye injuries in children 5 to 14.

To emphasize how potentially dangerous some physical education activities can be, it is estimated that a tennis ball can travel over 110 miles per hour, racquet balls over 125 mph, and badminton shuttlecocks at 145 mph. Many believe that 90 percent of all eye injuries could be prevented by simply wearing eye protection. Safety glasses, made with industrial strength, impact-resistant lenses and sturdy frames, are recommended for noncontact activities. For racket sports, one-piece, specially designed plastic frames with polycarbonate lenses are highly recommended (American Optometric Association, 1992).

VISUAL AIDS: GLASSES AND CONTACT LENSES

Many visual aids are available for youngsters with severe visual impairments. These include headborne aids (which look like ordinary glasses), contact lenses, magnifiers (hand-held and on stands), telescopic lenses, and optical enlargers. Contact lenses do not supply sufficient magnification for the most severe impairments. Eyeglasses, therefore, should be worn during most physical education activities. For safety, all eyeglasses should have unbreakable plastic or case-hardened lenses. Pop-out lenses or protective coverings over the glasses can also be used.

PROFESSIONALS WHO WORK WITH INDIVIDUALS WITH VISUAL DISABILITIES

Ophthalmologist—A physician who specializes in diagnosis and treatment of defects and diseases of the eye. Physical education activity restrictions should come from this physician.

Optometrist—A licensed, nonmedical practitioner who measures refractive errors (irregularities in the size or shape of the eyeball, or surface of the cornea) and eye muscle disturbances. The optometrist's treatment is limited to prescribing and fitting glasses.

Optician—A maker of glasses who grinds lenses according to prescription, fits them into frames, and adjusts frames to the wearer.

Orientation and mobility specialist—One who teaches visually impaired students how to familiarize themselves with new surroundings and to travel independently; also works with young children to develop concepts to body image and spatial awareness. The services of this individual are especially helpful to the very young or a person who is newly blinded.

COMMON CONCERNS ABOUT VISION

1. Glasses do not always correct limited vision. Some children with limited vision may be aided by corrective lenses, but correction is not possible for many, and many who benefit from correction will still have limited vision.
2. Holding a book close to the eyes does not harm vision. This is often done by children with visual disabilities to compensate for print size.
3. If a television if functioning properly, sitting close will not harm the eyes.
4. Sight cannot be conserved. Unless informed otherwise, encourage a child to use her eyes.
5. Dim light will not harm the eyes. Because of some eye conditions (e.g., cataracts or albinism), a child may require dim lighting to feel more comfortable.
6. Loss of vision in one eye does not reduce vision by 50 percent. Although there is loss of vision on the affected side and a general loss of depth perception, a loss of half of the visual system has *not* occurred.

PHYSICAL ACTIVITY—HOW MUCH AND FOR WHOM?

Students who are blind and partially sighted can participate in many of the same physical activities that sighted individuals enjoy provided that the children with the visual impairment have learned basic motor skills, possess minimal levels of physical fitness, and have had some opportunities for interesting movement experiences.

Concern has been expressed that students who are blind are not given appropriate physical education opportunities. Seelye (1983) found that only 46 percent of the students (who are blind) in her study tested above minimal levels of physical fitness, whereas 95 percent of sighted children and 84 percent of subjects with partial sight passed the test. She states, "Apparently, existing school and home activities weren't meeting their [blind students] needs. The . . . students were not allowed to participate in physical education activities designed for sighted students—either because the teacher believed they were unable to participate or because they were actually unable to do so" (p. 117).

Teachers tend to set students with visual disabilities apart as being different from sighted students. They believe (often based on misunderstanding or lack of knowledge) that students who are blind and partially sighted must be coddled, that their motor abilities are limited, and that their activities must be restricted. In reality, if students with visual problems are given the opportunities, they can live life as fully as others. The quality of their physical well-being depends largely on the availability of good physical education programming.

Some students with visual disabilities may be reluctant to attempt new activities for fear of failure or bodily injury. The student needs support and encouragement from teachers, peers, and family to realize the joy of becoming involved with nondisabled people through physical education and recreational experiences. The physical educator should discuss with the student the possible fears and apprehensions surrounding new physical encounters. The student may be cautious and exhibit a reluctance to try new activities. The teacher's role is to instill confidence with verbal and tactual explanations. Given an understanding approach, the student often becomes enthusiastic.

REGULAR OR ADAPTED PHYSICAL EDUCATION... OR BOTH?

Initially, the student with visual impairment must be assessed for general motor ability and physical fitness. Outstanding deficits, observed by objective, criterion-referenced, and subjective testing, should be noted and recorded. These results serve as the basis for appropriate placement in physical education classes. As with other disabling conditions, placement is likely to be in a combination of regular and adapted physical education classes.

Most students with severe visual impairments will use tactual and auditory perception to explore, recognize, and learn. The physical education teacher should use these same sensory skills to provide an individualized program that enables the student to regain self-confidence and develop new motor proficiencies. The adapted physical education specialist should evaluate motor, tactual, and perceptual capabilities, and should provide instruction in perceptual skills and physical functioning.

The individual with visual disabilities can succeed in the regular class with nondisabled children when jogging, distance running, sprinting, weight training, swimming, gymnastics, wrestling, and tumbling are offered. For participation in team-oriented visual-motor activities, such as softball or volleyball, extreme modification is required if the student is to participate. It is questionable also if such modification is beneficial to the nondisabled students. The severity of an individual's disability will dictate the student's ability to participate in eye-hand coordination activities in the regular class. When the student with disabilities is relegated to menial and watered-down activities, however, the child has been inappropriately placed.

Adapted physical education placement should allow for the special adaptation of certain games and sports to make them more suitable for the student. Beep balls, wiffle balls with bells inside, or beach balls with noisemakers are useful equipment when adapting activities for students with visual disabilities.

When the student is placed in a regular physical education class, determine if the child can engage in effective physical competition and meaningful social interaction. Although the child may need to cope with visual and emotional stresses not usually encountered by nondisabled students, the chances are that he will soon become a fully participating class member if emphasis is put on individual improvement and not on specific levels of performance. For example, if the student improves cross-country performance by reducing his time by 5 percent (i.e., $1\frac{1}{2}$ mi run pretest 12:10, posttest 11:34), a significant gain was made, and participation in the regular class therefore proved successful. The only modification involves the "buddy system," in which the student who is blind holds the arm of a sighted person during events such as the $1\frac{1}{2}$ mi run.

UNIQUE CHARACTERISTICS OF INDIVIDUALS WHO ARE BLIND

Mannerisms or "blindisms" are often exhibited by individuals who are blind. These are repetitive or stereotyped movements not directed toward attainment of any identifiable goal. Cratty (1989) observed 200 children who were blind and reported a number of rocking movements. Interchild comparisons showed a range of postures, stances, and accompanying body movements.

Common mannerisms identified in the literature are (1) bending the head forward, (2) waving fingers in front of the face, (3) putting fist or fingers in the eyes, (4) rocking backward and forward, (5) whirling rapidly around and around, and (6) hitting or slapping oneself.

It appears that certain activities reduce the occurrence of mannerisms, and in some cases the mannerisms cease completely. Children who are blind show few, if any, mannerisms while eating, playing on swings, deeply absorbed in activity, or listening to records. The frequency of mannerisms increases when children become angry, frustrated, bored, anxious, or excited. Mannerisms also increase slightly when children are left alone.

Past research generally supports the assumption that mannerisms result from a lack of appropriate stimulation. By providing interesting and challenging activities, the adapted physical educator can help the child to replace unacceptable mannerisms. As with other disabling conditions, the educator should stress activities that develop the following psychomotor components: balance and coordination, posture and gait, ability to walk a straight line, dexterity or agility, stamina or endurance, and reaction time.

INTERNAL (KINESTHESIS) AND EXTERNAL ORIENTATION

Children with severe visual disabilities may need orientation training to help them recognize the environment and its temporal and spatial relationships. These students often possess certain habits, including poor posture (head drop, head thrust, rounded shoulders, forward tilt of pelvis) and a shuffling gait resulting from tight hamstrings and pronated feet. These characteristics develop when children have no visual model after which to pattern themselves. After a few years of repeated poor posture, bad habits become permanent. The adapted physical educator must provide constant positive correction and remind the individual to stand erect and walk with the feet in proper placement.

Exercises are best performed in reference to a vertical surface such as a wall. Sensation of limb position in space is aided by exercising in front of a large fan. The correct "feel" of the upright position can be learned only through repeated stimulation of body proprioceptors. Tumbling, trampoline, or other activities that increase kinesthetic awareness can lay the groundwork for posture improvement. Sensory stimulation activities, such as using a full-sized mannequin to demonstrate body parts and position, help the student acquire an appropriate body image. A sequential program of balancing that progresses from crawling and creeping to standing balance may be needed to reinforce specific psychomotor patterns.

MOBILITY TRAINING

Mobility training is based on an understanding of six basic concepts: right, left, up, down, forward, and backward. Table 14.3 identifies the developmental progressions between the ages of 2 and 6 for children who are blind.

The adapted physical education instructor should stress two important hearing skills, sound discrimination and sound location, as well as improving degrees of concentration, memorization, retention, and environmental awareness. Students who are severely visually impaired should be given practice in walking unaided in a straight line while maintaining good posture (Klee and Klee, 1985).

THE SIXTH SENSE

Persons who are blind sometimes seem to have a "sixth sense," or develop more acute hearing or more sensitive smell and touch than nondisabled people. At one time, the belief was common that people who could not see could tell colors by using their fingertips or could develop a special sensitivity wherein the skin produced its own little "eyes." None of this is true, but many persons who are blind do develop, through necessity and training, other senses to a greater degree than sighted individuals. The adapted physical education program should provide activities that bombard the individual's available senses. Many trial and error experiences will usually be necessary for permanent motor learning to occur. For example, children with normal motor ability learn the beginning trampoline

TABLE 14.3   Determinants for Mobility Training—Developmental
Progressions of Children Who are Blind Between the Ages of 2 and 6

Skill	Age (months)
Walks sideways	14
Points to four body parts	18
Walks straight line	18–30
Walks backward	20–30
Walks on tiptoe	20–30
Moves from one room to another without difficulty	24
Moves about yard without difficulty	24
Hops on two feet	25–30
Distance jumps 14 to 24 in.	28–30
Hops on one foot	30
Balances on either foot for 5 sec	31–36
Runs	36–48
Comprehends "on top of," "under," "inside"	42
Comprehends texture	48
Identifies most body parts	48–60
Learns left from right	60–72
Identifies variety of objects by tactual exploration	60–72

Source: Adapted from Ferrell 1979, p. 148.

skills of bouncing, stopping, and starting in a few minutes, but children who are blind need more trials to stimulate kinesthetic awareness.

Sighted people rely on sight to perform many activities that could be learned through other senses. For example, the coins in one's pocket can be identified through touch, but a sighted person will look to ascertain their value. Without dependence on sight, the person must organize and process the sense information through another framework, which provides a reasonably reliable and realistic impression of the environment and becomes the basis for analysis and intellectual judgment. Here, the major difference between persons who are *congenitally* blind and *adventitiously* blind becomes apparent. Children who are born blind or who become blind before age 4 will not have enough visual memory to coordinate their sensory perceptions. Children who are adventitiously blind (blinded later in life through disease or accident) rely on the same sensory input as the former group but within the framework of visual memory. The child who once had sight remembers the appearance of a ball, a basketball backboard, a swimming pool, and a climbing rope if these were experienced before blindness.

Hearing provides identification, direction, distance, size, and structure. Students who are visually disabled learn to identify sounds and to discriminate and select those that are important and useful. They learn to localize sounds and to use sound reflection, sound shadows, and echo location. This phenomenon is called **object perception.** The ability to perceive extremely close objects by feeling a sensation change or pressure on the face can be developed by anyone who can hear, whether sighted or blind.

Touch, or tactual stimulation, involves anything touched by any part of the body or anything that touches the body. The student learns about the object's size, weight, volume, density, texture, and surface through tactual exploration. Important to touch are the sensations of hot and cold, changes in air current, and changes in temperature.

Kinesthetic awareness is useful for detecting lateral tilts in surfaces, gradients, distances, changes in position, movement, and posture. Equilibrium is vital to balance and turning. Because children who are blind have difficulty with vertical perception, they must rely on information provided by muscle proprioceptors and the inner ear vestibular mechanism. For those youngsters who are ambulatory but possess poorly developed body concepts and movements, practice must be provided that involves early sensorimotor activities, such as crawling, half-kneeling, squatting, and climbing. Senitz, McBride, Adrian, and Semmler (1990) have found that children who are blind often have little interest in fine motor skills. Thus, instructors must continuously encourage development by placing objects into the children's hands and having them stack blocks, nest cups, and do puzzles.

Complex sensory information is learned through interaction of the senses. The tactile discrimination of shape and form occurs through kinesthetic awareness when one feels the position of a batting tee. Kinesthesis makes many habitual activities automatic. A person who is blind relies on kinesthesis to put on a gym shoe and to get from the locker room to the gymnasium without counting steps.

STUDENTS WHO ARE CONGENITALLY BLIND

The child who is congenitally blind may possess distinct motor ability deficiencies. According to research, these children usually need to improve large muscle control and balance.

Learning reflects experience, that is, interaction with the environment. The absence of motor development in individuals who are congenitally blind is difficult to explain but probably reflects a general lack of learning experience. Gagné (1970) stresses "learning by doing," that is, learning concepts in actual situations. The most widely accepted motor development theories about children who are blind emphasize two main points. First, they are unaware of the movement potential of many parts of their bodies because they lack opportunities to experience movement. Parents as well as school personnel often limit the congenitally blind child's physical experiences. P.L. 101–476 should ensure that all students who are blind receive appropriate and necessary physical education experiences. Second, motor development specialists claim that overprotection may hamper the child's motor development by instilling fear of bodily harm or by preventing practice. Hallahan and Kauffman (1991) have found that early visual experience of spatial relationships establishes a method of processing information, which affects all subsequent cognitive and motor learning experiences. Because children who are blind cannot see objects or movement, it is extremely difficult for them to copy or imitate. For example, if the adapted physical education instructor wants the students to imitate "lame dogs," few students who are congenitally blind will understand what the teacher means. Only through touching, feeling, and modeling can the child understand this concept.

The child who is blind who does not explore the environment by reaching out or moving toward objects or by other nonvisual stimuli usually becomes accustomed to stationary activities or to being guided in movement through space. Children who are blind cannot see to imitate the motor performance of others, so they cannot benefit from demonstrations of skilled movement. These students generally have a poor body image. For children who are blind to move skillfully and efficiently, they need to understand their bodies and body parts in relation to the surrounding space.

THE ADVENTITIOUS, OR NEWLY BLINDED

Persons who become newly blinded must come to terms with their new circumstances and develop new skills. The person must strive for alertness beyond that of most sighted persons. The individual will no longer be able to walk, run, and jump as she used to. Simple acts become complex undertakings, to be thought through and planned in advance, and therefore many movement opportunities must be provided by the physical education teacher.

INDIVIDUALS WHO ARE VISUALLY IMPAIRED OR PARTIALLY SIGHTED ARE NOT BLIND

Remember that persons who are visually impaired can see. They may not see distant objects, and their vision may be blurred or they may have restricted visual fields, but most can localize contrasting light and dark. Physical education instructors must be as conscientious about teaching these students to use their residual vision as they are about teaching the other senses to students who are blind.

The student who can localize light can move about indoors and locate lights, windows, and doors. Some students with visual impairment, although unable to read words or numbers on a Universal Weight Lifting Machine, can set the amount of weight by memorizing the number of 10-lb plates and inserting the holding pin appropriately.

TEACHING TECHNIQUES

The child learns tasks involving manipulation of materials, equipment, or his own body more quickly if his hands are placed and guided through the movement required to complete the task and if the teacher provides tactual as well as verbal feedback.

The teacher needs to speak clearly and loudly enough to be easily understood. A blatant violation of this is nodding the head in response to a question from a child who is blind. The teacher must not use ambiguous statements such as "Throw the ball over there," and must not point or use nonverbal gestures. A quiet-spoken teacher may be giving inappropriate feedback to a student's performance. This teacher must learn to praise through voice or tactile contact, or the student may not receive the message.

B. F. Skinner once claimed that the most valid proof of effective teaching is knowing that students have learned a skill so well that they can perform it without thinking. Walking is so automatic that most people never think about it until a critical situation arises. We become very conscious of walking, however, when we maneuver on an icy sidewalk—our steps become short and our pace slows because we are acutely aware of not wanting to slip and fall. Too often physical education teachers do not provide enough practice sessions for total learning to occur. Extensive practice is essential for all slow motor learners.

SPECIFIC SUGGESTIONS FOR TEACHING INDIVIDUALS WITH VISUAL DISABILITIES

Introduce the student to classmates. Other students will have questions that the student with visual disabilities may wish to answer. Shaking hands does not have to be awkward. Anticipate the situation and encourage contact between the student and others.

If the student prefers not to bring attention to her disability, she may use special aids and assistance only when absolutely necessary. In general, the teacher should respect the child's wishes, but if the child obviously requires aids or assistance, discuss these needs with the child's special education teacher.

When the student with visual disabilities brings adaptive aids into the physical education area, encourage the use of the aids and answer questions that others have about them.

When approaching an unfamiliar student who is blind, always state your name. Voices are not easy to identify, particularly in noisy areas. When a person who is blind is alone in the area, announce your entry, especially if you are wearing gym shoes or walking on a grassy field.

Do not shout at a student who is blind. These persons are not hard of hearing. When uncertain about whether assistance is needed by the student, ask. Offering help is always appropriate.

When speaking to the person who has visual disabilities it is acceptable to use words such as *see*, *look*, or even *blind*. These words are part of everyone's vocabulary. The child who is blind will use them to express feelings regarding *seeing*, and in phrases such as "*See* you tomorrow."

The adapted physical education teacher must provide extra locker space to accommodate any special aids, such as the student's cane. A lock with a key is preferable to a combination lock. The key can be worn around the student's neck or carried by the instructor. The locker should be easily identifiable by position, as at the end of the row. Assist the student to the locker room, the showers, toilets, and activity areas. Most students will learn the routine and floor patterns quickly. Be constantly aware of unusual hazards such as stairways, objects protruding from walls, and slippery floors. Use verbal cues to guide the student around the activity area (Eichstaedt & Lavay, 1992).

Encourage the student to assume leadership roles (i.e., team captain or activity leader) just you would any nondisabled student. Because children are sensitive to peer criticism, be aware of this problem and encourage positive interactions between the students. The child who is blind may not be aware of events, such as facial expressions or arm movements. Verbal cues become extremely necessary when working with students who have visual disabilities.

Disciplinary rules apply equally to students who are visually impaired and students who are nondisabled.

MANUAL ASSISTANCE, OR THE SIGHTED GUIDE

Assistance for the student who is blind is appropriate. The individual may choose (or need) to have a sighted guide. For safety, the person who is blind should grasp the guide's upper arm, above the elbow, with the thumb on the outside and the fingers on the inside of the guide's arm. A younger child can hold an adult's wrist. Both student and guide should hold upper arms close to the body, which automatically positions the student one-half step behind the guide. This is also an acceptable position for jogging or running.

When approaching doorways or objects, the guide should press his elbow close to his body or behind his body so that the student understands to walk directly behind the guide. Verbal cues are important. Inform the student when approaching stairways or curbs and whether ascending or descending.

BODY IMAGE AND SPATIAL AWARENESS

Failure to develop body image and a sense of position in space are common problems of the child who is visually impaired. Limited vision does not enable one to see mirror reflections, which help in understanding body contours. Movement limitations and irregularities limit one's exploration of one's body potential and the conception of how one's body relates to the world.

Beginning instruction starts with stroking the child's different body parts. A terry cloth, silk scarf, velvet glove, or feather can be used. Each part should be stroked gently and named. For example, stroke the leg and say, "Suzie's leg." Repeat the action with the opposite leg. As this is done repeatedly, body awareness increases. The stroking routine also reduces the tactile defensiveness commonly found in children who are blind. Introduce the child's hands to various textures; use sand, whipped cream, flour, and corn meal.

The child's proprioceptors must be developed to maintain static and dynamic balance. The body must experience different and unusual balance situations. The instructor should increase the child's proprioceptive awareness by attaching small weights, such as beanbags or sandbags, to the body. The added weight requires more effort to move, thus intensifying awareness of those parts.

The child's relationship to space must be clarified. This sense develops early when auditory stimuli help determine direction and distance of objects. Talk to the child from different positions around the room. Use a beep ball to let the student experience differences in direction of movement. Let the student throw objects to assist in learning the concept of up and down. Have the child throw or drop an object; pick it up, hand it back to the child, and have the youngster do it again. In this way the child experiences space, a concept that should be reinforced by the instructor through sound, touch, and movement.

The child who is blind cannot see or copy images and therefore must be taught to feel. Imagery plays an important role in stimulating and understanding movement. For the youngster, tactual stimuli suggest certain qualities of movement. Skills involved in locomotion (walking, hopping, galloping, sliding, and jumping) help children to sense movement. The qualities of lightness, heaviness, softness, and hardness assist in feeling movement. Tactual materials such as clay, wire, rubber bands, and balloons allow children to understand these concepts.

Clay can assume many shapes and is self-contained. It has the quality of heaviness. It can be made into numerous shapes such as flat, long, round, and thin.

Wire is hard, but pliable and flexible; thin, but strong; long, but form producing. It can be shaped, but its major feature is hardness. When shaping wire, the student becomes aware of the interaction between muscle resistance and skeletal articulation. The student knows that force will change the wire's shape. The child can imagine this force as muscle strength and the wire's firmness as resistance of the skeletal frame. The concepts of bend/straighten, toward/away from, right/left, and parallel/perpendicular can be taught using wire.

Rubber bands establish an image of elasticity. They provide an opportunity to experience flexibility, "stretchiness," and contracting ability of the child's muscles. A rubber band has no specific dimensions; it can be stretched up, down, forward, backward, and sideward. As the student moves, this action is compared with elasticity and lightness.

Balloons produce images of both lightness and airiness. Body shape can imitate a balloon that is flat and shriveled before inflation. Movement is experienced as traveling lightly off the floor at different levels. A balloon can explode, suggesting jumps and leaps from a crouched position, followed by collapse.

These stimuli alone provide an infinite number of movement possibilities and should enable students who are blind to experience movement shapes and qualities. They also enable the teacher to introduce a movement vocabulary.

The following suggestions may serve as a guide when using clay, wire, rubber bands, or balloons. Structure each lesson to encourage time for relaxation and breathing exercises; explore a new movement (e.g., time and energy factors, body involvement, relationship of body parts); create imitations (e.g., "Move as if you were carrying something heavy," "Crawl on the floor, like a worm"); and verbally analyze where the movement occurs in the body.

Encourage the students to move in response to suggested emotions (happy, sad, angry, funny); to act out words (descriptive words such as lazy, sleepy, sticky; or action words such as wiggle, crawl, bounce, shiver, squirm); and to experience movement sequences (dropping and falling, holding and stopping, tearing and breaking). For locomotion the students should be encouraged to move from place to place, including different levels or heights (high, medium, or low to the ground, tall or short), to interpret different sizes or shapes during movement and to move to a beat or a piece of music.

GROSS BODY MOVEMENT

Gross body movements usually precede fine motor coordination activities and should be encouraged at an early age. Place the child on a bare floor or mat and allow free movement, assisting when necessary. Rolling, scooting, crawling, and other gross movements involve the entire muscular system. Place the child on her back and guide her into rolling and gradually toward creeping independence.

Various activities and toys can also develop body control. Simple, guided gymnastics and postural exercises are effective. Swimming fosters movement exploration and body self-awareness while developing coordination. Heavy toys develop muscle strength and endurance. Large beach balls, rocking boats, swings, teeter-totters, hobby horses, animals filled with sand, medicine balls, and boxes filled with heavy material all stimulate mobility, balance, and strength.

If the student's walking techniques are poor, improvement is necessary to run effectively. Teach the child to maintain balance without spreading the feet. Encourage

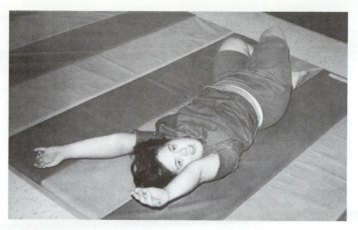

Gross body movements, such as rolling, should be encouraged.

free arm movement by swinging the child's arms during a walk. Reinforce the heel-toe technique by having the child begin steps with the heel, roll to the balls of the feet, and end on the toes. Discourage the child from shuffling the feet. If necessary, move the child's feet up and down to demonstrate walking without shuffling. Walking on a mattress helps the student learn to lift the feet.

DEVELOPING CONCEPTS

When attempting to develop concepts of size, such as big and little, use items familiar to the student. Do not talk about a "little" ball and then provide only a small ball. Children learn more quickly by experiencing concept comparisons. Provide the student with several examples of a concept and one example that does not fit the concept. The nonexamples allow the child to eliminate certain attributes and reinforce common characteristics.

Concepts should be taught that stimulate greater environmental awareness. For instance, the child should learn comparisons—big child-little ball, little child-big tree. Action concepts can be taught by having the student respond physically to action verbs. When a story mentions the act of spinning around and around, the student can sit on the floor and experience spinning.

Students with visual disabilities and additional physical impairments may need assistance to explore their world. Their environment may be small because of insufficient mobility. If they have severe vision loss, their concepts of the world are even more limited.

METHODS TO INCREASE VISUAL TRACKING

There are four basic ways to improve the child's ability to catch, kick, and strike objects. These include (1) increased ball size, (2) structured programming and repetition, (3) increased lighting, and (4) appropriate figure-ground contrasts (Gardner, 1985).

Increasing the size of the object being tracked assists visually impaired youngsters. An example would be using an inflated beach ball instead of a volleyball. Not only is the ball larger, but it also moves more slowly. This combination should enhance the student's chances of success.

Sugden and Keogh (1990) explain the process of improving visual tracking through repetition. The concept includes systematic instruction and opportunities to "learn" how the ball looks as it travels through space. They believe that visual functioning is enhanced, including the improvement of speed and accuracy, through extensive trial and error. In other words, the child's performance improves through practice while motor learning is occurring.

The instructor should consider improving the lighting in the gymnasium. Increasing bulb wattage and replacing any dead bulbs in the ceiling lights are possible solutions to lighting problems. These adjustments may be all that is necessary for successful participation. Inadequate light may also be experienced when the children are outside on a dark and gloomy day, or toward evening when the sun has gone down. Adjusting the class time or, on a gloomy day, changing the setting to indoors can help solve such problems.

The ball color and background against which it is thrown contribute to the success of a visually impaired child. For example, brown or tan colored balls are much more difficult to see than white or yellow balls. Kligerman (1981) conducted an experiment using figure-ground reversals with populations of children with cerebral palsy, learning disabled, and visually impaired. The use of a light foreground on a dark background improved the visual and perceptual motor functioning of these students.

Gardner (1985) finds that the background color (i.e., yellow chalk on a green chalkboard) enhances the ability of a child with visual impairment to read the writing on a chalkboard. Another important finding of his study is that the amount of luminance contrast available is critical. How dark the foreground is in comparison with the background, or vice versa, is the major contrast factor controlling visibility for individuals with visual impairment. Consideration must therefore be given to the actual color and hue of the gymnasium and playroom walls. They must be of sufficient contrast to provide an appropriate background when students with visual disabilities are attempting to track a moving object such as a ball or badminton birdie.

A SPECIAL EXERCISE PROGRAM

Many adults with visual disabilities do not get enough physical activity and are therefore not physically fit. Because physical activity patterns are formed in early childhood, the child who is visually impaired must be exposed to many athletic and developmental activities. Strength, muscle tone, and flexibility can be improved by performing specific exercises that are commonly identified with hatha-yoga (Krebs, 1979). The student needs to develop good hand and finger coordination, head and neck control, and skill in using body parts.

Many body image and spatial movement concepts that seeing children learn automatically (e.g., bending, stretching, and reaching exercises) reinforce academic skills such as reading readiness (e.g., left to right and top to bottom progression), printing and cursive handwriting (e.g., muscle strength from stretching wrists and fingers), mathematics (counting), and geometry (parallel, triangle, line, and straight).

The following exercises do not involve special equipment. They can be practiced in the gymnasium, outdoors, in the classroom, or at home. All movements should be gentle and never forced; the child should perform the exercises slowly. The breath is never held and breathing is done through the nostrils rather than through the mouth. The amount of time that each exercise is held can be decreased or increased according to the student's progress.

GENERAL EXERCISES

Krebs (1979) suggests the following exercises:

Breathing (Figure 14.3A).   (1) Sit with head, neck, and back in a straight line and pull the shoulders back. Cross the legs. Place then hands palms down on the knees. (2) Breathe in (through the nose) as the abdomen ("tummy") pushes out like a balloon. (3) Breathe out and pull in the abdomen. (4) Place hands flat on abdomen sideways, with fingers together and fingertips touching, to feel the movements.

Slow, controlled, rhythmic breathing should accompany all exercises. Check for proper posture before beginning the breathing exercise. Begin inhalation and exhalation, each to the count of three. Start with five complete rounds (inhalation and exhalation). Visually check the student's abdominal region and hand for proper movements (the fingers should come apart as the abdomen is expanded on inhalation). This exercise may also be practiced while lying on the back with the face upward. Breathing exercises are very relaxing and increase efficiency of the lungs.

Neck Rolls (Figure 14.3B).   (1) Sit with head, neck, and back in a straight line and pull the shoulders back. Cross the legs. Place the hands palms down on the knees. (2) Let the head drop forward with the chin pointing down, toward the chest. Keep the back straight. (3) Slowly roll the head to the right shoulder so the ear is pointing down toward the shoulder. (4) Roll the head backward so the nose is pointing toward the ceiling. (5) Roll the head to the left shoulder so the ear is pointing down toward the shoulder. (6) Roll the head forward with the chin pointing down toward the chest and repeat steps 3 through 5.

Neck rolls should be done slowly with continuous movement. Begin with two complete rolls to the right, then reverse the instructions for the left side. Neck rolls stretch the muscles of the neck, improve posture, and relieve tension.

FIGURE 14.3   **General exercises: (A) breathing, (B) neck rolls, (C) tiptoe stretch, (D) tree, (E) triangle, (F) hero, (G) standing forward bend, (H) frog, (I) cobra, (J) bow, (K) seated forward bend, and (L) relaxation.**

Tiptoe Stretch (Figure 14.3C). (1) Stand up straight with arms straight down touching the body sides. Place feet together; pull abdomen in and shoulders back. Make sure that head, neck, and back are in a straight line. (2) Rise up on the toes. Keep both legs straight. (3) Stretch arms and hands up slowly over the head until fingers are pointing up, toward the ceiling. Place palms together and keep elbows straight. (4) Hold to the count of five. (5) Slowly lower arms straight down by sides and rest heels back on floor.

If students have difficulty at first, have them practice against a wall. Balancing a book on the head will help students correct postural alignment problems. This exercise strengthens the toes and ankles, tones the leg muscles, and improves balance ability. Posture (standing and walking) can be improved by practicing the Tiptoe Stretch exercise.

Tree (Figure 14.3D). (1) Stand up straight with arms straight down touching body sides. Place feet together and pull abdomen in and shoulders back. Make sure that head, neck, and back are in a straight line. (2) Place sole (bottom) of right foot high up on inside of left thigh. Keep left leg straight. (3) Stretch arms and hands up over head with fingers pointing up, toward ceiling. Place palms together and keep elbows straight. (4) Hold to count of five. (5) Lower right foot to the floor. Arms are lowered gradually until they are straight down, touching sides. (6) Place sole of left foot high on inside of right thigh, keeping right leg straight. Repeat steps 3 through 5.

Triangle (Figure 14.3E). (1) Stand up straight with arms straight down touching sides. Place feet together and pull abdomen in and shoulders back. Make sure that head, neck, and back are in a straight line. (2) Jump, spreading legs apart to right and left sides. (3) Raise arms straight up 90 degrees, sideways, in line with shoulders and parallel to floor. Keep palms facing down toward floor and fingers stretched straight out to sides. (4) Turn right foot so it is pointing toward the right and bend down sideways, toward floor. Place right hand on ankle. Keep both legs straight. (5) Stretch left arm up with fingertips pointing toward ceiling and palm forward. Left arm should be in line with right shoulder. (6) Point nose toward hand in air. (7) Hold to count of five. (8) Slowly straighten by raising body up sideways, then jump so feet are together. (9) Repeat reversing instructions for left side.

Students should try to keep both legs (knees) straight and bend sideways while doing this exercise. The arms and fingers should be stretched straight up. The Triangle develops chest, leg, and hip muscles, stretches side and back muscles, and strengthens ankles.

Hero (Figure 14.3F). (1) Stand up straight with arms straight down touching sides. Place feet together and pull abdomen in and shoulders back. Make sure that head, neck, and back are in a straight line. (2) Jump, spreading legs apart to right and left sides. (3) Raise arms straight up sideways in line with shoulders (parallel to floor). Keep palms facing down toward floor and fingers stretched straight out to sides. (4) Turn right foot so it points toward right, and turn head so nose is pointing toward right hand. (5) Bend right knee slowly so that thigh is parallel to floor. Keep left leg straight. (6) Hold to count of five. (7) Slowly straighten knee and jump so feet are again together with legs straight and arms straight down at sides. (8) Repeat, reversing instructions for left side.

In this exercise, the fingers and arms should be stretched out sideways, while the pelvic area faces forward. The Hero exercise strengthens leg and back muscles and tones abdominal muscles.

Standing Forward Bend (Figure 14.3G).   (1) Stand up straight with arms straight down touching sides. Place feet together and pull abdomen in and shoulders back. Make sure that head, neck, and back are in a straight line. (2) Bend slowly forward from waist. Bring head down toward knees, and let arms and hands reach down toward floor. Keep legs straight. (3) Hold to count of five. (4) Raise the body slowly, keeping head down until body is erect. (5) Place hands pointing straight down by sides.

The Standing Forward Bend should be done very slowly. Students should only bend as far forward as they comfortably can while keeping the knees straight. This exercise improves posture and relaxes tight neck and back muscles.

Frog (Figure 14.3H).   (1) Sit on floor with legs together and straight out in front, and hands, palms down, resting on floor beside hips. (2) Bring soles of feet together. (3) Place hands around the feet and pull feet toward the body. (4) Hold to count of five or ten. (5) Straighten legs and rest hands on floor beside hips.

Check for correct posture before starting the Frog. Students should try to bring knees as close to floor as possible without pushing the knees down. This exercise increases the leg flexibility for activities such as running and jumping.

Cobra (Figure 14.3I).   (1) Lie face down, flat on floor. Keep body in a straight line with arms straight down by sides. Put feet together with toes pointing back, away from body. (2) Place hands with palms down on floor, under shoulders. Elbows are bent by sides, and forehead ins on the floor. (3) Slowly lift forehead, nose, and chin off floor. (4) Bring head up and back so nose is pointing toward ceiling. (5) Keep elbows bent and hold to count of five. (6) Lower head slowly to floor. (7) Place arms straight down by sides.

The pubic bones remain in contact with the floor during this exercise. The Cobra expands the chest, strengthens the wrists, and tones the spinal region.

Bow (Figure 14.3J).   (1) Lie face down, flat on floor. Keep body in a straight line and arms straight down by sides. (2) Hold ankles with hands. (3) Raise chest, knees, and thighs off floor. Keep nose pointing forward. (4) Hold to count of three. (5) Gently remove hands from ankles and return to starting position.

The arms should be straight in this exercise. The Bow eases tension in back and shoulders, and stretches chest and abdominal muscles.

Seated Forward Bend (Figure 14.3K).   (1) Sit on floor with legs together and straight out in front and hands, palms down, resting on floor beside hips. Pull shoulders back and keep head, neck, and back in straight line. (2) Raise hands up, straight over head, with fingers pointing toward ceiling. (3) Bend forward slowly from waist. Keep legs straight and together. (4) Hold legs (or ankles) with hands. (5) Hold to count of five. (6) Slowly raise body and hands to position 2. (7) Lower hands, palms down, so they rest on floor beside hips.

At first the back may be rounded when students do this exercise. Practice, relaxing, and normal breathing will gradually enable the children to flatten the back. The knees should not bend. The Seated Forward Bend strengthens abdominal muscles, stretches hamstrings, increases spinal flexibility, and massages abdominal organs.

Relaxation (Figure 14.3L).   (1) Lie flat on back with feet slightly apart, toes pointing away from each other and arms straight down by sides with palms up. (2) Close the eyes and open mouth slightly. Continue to breathe through nose. (3) Wiggle feet. Relax feet. (4) Raise legs, keeping them straight, a little above floor. Lower legs slowly to floor. Relax legs. (5) Raise arms straight up, a little above floor. Lower arms slowly to floor. Relax arms. (6) Stretch fingers. Relax fingers. (7) Roll head gently from side to side (ear on floor). (8) Make a silly face and stick out your tongue. Relax face. (9) Relax entire body. Lie quietly for a few minutes. (10) Roll onto left side. Pull knees up to chest. Sit up slowly.

Students who have difficulty relaxing should concentrate on the breathing (inhalation and exhalation). Relaxation eases body tension and is restful yet energizing.

PHYSICAL FITNESS FOR INDIVIDUALS WHO ARE BLIND

For the student who is totally blind, quick vigorous movement in an unfamiliar or physically complex area increases the risk of collision or falling and suffering injury. The amount of healthful, invigorating physical activity (i.e., brisk walking, jogging, running, climbing, or hiking) performed by these students often declines sharply or becomes nonexistent if the children are not stimulated by daily activities. Lack of appropriate physical education opportunities causes loss of stamina, strength, and agility. Without these, students may settle for a daily routine that consists of sitting, standing, lying down, and walking slowly over short distances. This low level of participation is totally insufficient to stimulate vital organs. In the absence of an effective cardiorespiratory program, the incidence of future heart disease and muscle atrophy rises significantly. The low physical fitness level of many persons who are blind means fewer calories burned, yet food may become a primary source of personal gratification to the sedentary individual. Obesity, which has complex side effects, often results (Weitzman 1985). Regardless of weight, once one's body composition starts to shift away from lean muscle toward fat, one's strength-to-weight ratio falls sharply, and relatively easy physical activity may seem strenuous and fatiguing.

Weitzman (1985) suggests the following brisk walking program for individuals who are blind:

> Because walking is low intensity exercise (which is what makes is safe), much more of it must be done to stimulate the body to develop greater efficiency and stamina. The ratio of walking three miles at an 18 minute per mile pace gives virtually the same aerobic benefit as running a mile in eight minutes and consumes twice as many calories. Compared to sitting, standing, or shuffling along, walking at a brisk pace forces the cardiovascular-pulmonary system to process two to three times as much oxygen and aerate the body. Over a period of four months, walking three to five miles daily will stimulate the adaptive changes at the tissue level.... The ability to work longer and harder without fatigue increases. (pp. 97–98)

The Braille Institute of America in Los Angeles developed a walking program for its students. Instructors found that all students, after program participation, were able to walk farther and faster without serious fatigue. The students also demonstrated gains in agility through their improved performance on the Braille Institute Youth Center obstacle course. Students were occasionally overheard boasting about their new physical accomplishments. A few students enjoyed, perhaps for the first time in their lives, the feeling of physical and ethical superiority over the majority of indolent, sighted persons (Weitzman, 1985).

SPECIAL EQUIPMENT

Many pieces of physical education and athletic equipment can be altered to allow students with visual impairment to participate in regular or adapted activities.

Balls should be yellow or bright orange so they can be located easily. Large softballs, preferably 16 in. in diameter, should be used. These balls travel shorter distances at reduced speeds and can be seen more easily. Medicine balls and cage balls can also be included in the class equipment.

Audible balls emit a beeping sound for easy location. They should be rugged enough for kicking, throwing, dropping, or hitting. The sound, which is activated by removing a small plug, is generated by a battery-powered solid-state circuit with the components properly located within to maintain balance. Different sized audible balls are available, including basketballs, soccer balls, softballs, and playground balls. The **National Beep Baseball Association** was developed to encourage individuals who are blind to compete in softball. Special equipment includes a beep softball (16-in.), cone-shaped rubber bases with internal buzzers, batting tee, and blindfolds for partially sighted and nondisabled players.

A beep baseball contest lasts for six innings unless more are needed to break a tie. A team has three outs per inning. The first and third bases are 4-ft-high rubber or pliable plastic cones, and are placed 90 ft down their respective lines and 5 ft off the foul line. This is to prevent a runner from colliding with a defensive fielder (Figure 14.4). There is no second base as in regulation baseball or softball. The bases contain sounding units that give off a buzzing sound when activated. The batter does not know which base will be turned on. When the ball is hit, the umpire activates one of the bases. The runner must identify the correct sound cone and run to it before the ball is fielded by a defensive player. If the runner is safe, a run is scored. In other words, there is no running from one base to another. Players do one of three things when batting. (1) They hit the ball and earn a safe call scoring a run. (2) They hit the ball and make an out if they are retired by the defense. (3) They strike out. The batter is allowed five, rather than the traditional three, strikes, and the fifth strike must be a clean miss.

To better understand how the game is played, keep in mind that each team has its own sighted pitcher and catcher. The catcher sets the target where the batter normally swings. The pitcher attempts to place the ball on the hitter's bat; the ball is pitched from a distance of 20 ft. According to the rules, a pitcher is obligated to verbalize two words clearly. He must say "ready" just before the ball is about to be

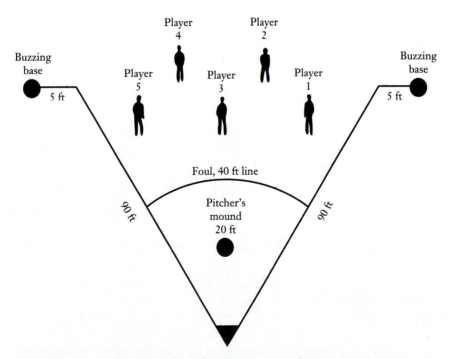

FIGURE 14.4 Beep baseball field dimensions and player placement.

released. This alerts all players that the ball may soon be hit. As the ball is being released, the pitcher says, "pitch." The batter allows a split second of time to pass before swinging. If contact is made, one of the two bases is activated, and the game then becomes a race between the runner and the defense. Note that a hit ball must travel at least 40 ft to be considered fair. A hit ball that does not reach the 40-ft line is counted as a foul. A hit ball that rebounds off the pitcher is ruled no pitch (1983 World Series of Beep Baseball).

Most Beep Baseball equipment is available through Telephone Pioneers of America. Local telephone offices can usually provide information regarding specific contacts.

Other special sport equipment enables persons who are visually impaired to participate in a variety of sports. A description of some of this equipment follows:

An *audible goal-locator* is a motor driven noisemaker that emits clicking sounds. It plugs into a regular electrical outlet and can be attached to a basketball backboard or soccer goal, or can be used to provide orientation in a swimming pool or gymnasium.

Guide wires enable running at top speed without fear of tripping over objects or curbs. The person grasps a short rope tied to a metal ring, which slides along a wire stretched 100 yd without intervening supports. The athlete can run back and forth to develop endurance.

Bowling rails are usually aluminum poles 9 ft long, 36 in. high, with $\frac{7}{8}$-in. diameter rail. The rail includes formed metal bases into which four bowling balls are placed for ballast. This equipment is portable; the parts slide together easily.

ATHLETIC COMPETITION

The U.S. Association for Blind Athletes holds national championships. The sports include goalball, gymnastics, judo, powerlifting, tandem cycling, track and field, wrestling, alpine skiing, Nordic skiing, speed skating, and marathon running (Adams and McCubbin, 1991). The goal of this association is to develop independence in persons who are blind and visually impaired through athletic programs that do not have unnecessary restrictions. The organization sponsors athletes in national and international competition and organizes informational programs to raise public awareness. To be eligible to compete nationally, a person must have $\frac{1}{20}$th or less normal vision.

SUMMARY

The adapted physical educator must be able to evaluate motor, tactual, and perceptual capabilities of students with visual disabilities. If students are to have a positive attitude toward physical activity, then perceptual-motor skills, coordination, balance, activities for orientation training, mobility skills, and physical fitness must be taught. Lifetime sports and recreational games should be an integral part of the curriculum.

Equipment and program adaptations are often necessary if students with visual impairments are to be placed in regular programs to the greatest extent possible. Physical educators have in fact found that accidents and injuries occur less among students who are blind than among the rest of the student body.

Because tactile, kinesthetic, and auditory perception are the major ways in which individuals with visual disabilities explore, recognize, and learn, the adapted physical educator's main focus should be on improving physical performance through the training of these senses. When this occurs, students regain self-confidence and feelings of independence and discover that they can enjoy the psychomotor world.

REFERENCES

Adams, R. C., & McCubbin, J. A. (1991). *Games, sports, and exercises for the physically disabled* (4th ed.). Philadelphia: Lea & Febiger.

American Optometric Association (1992). *Safety in sport*. (Pamphlet no. 421). New York: American Optometric Association.

Corn, A. L., & Martinez, I. (1977). *When you have a visually handicapped child in your classroom: Suggestions for teachers*. New York: American Foundation for the Blind.

Cratty, B. J. (1989). *Adapted physical education in the mainstream* (2nd ed.). Denver: Love.

Eichstaedt, C. B., & Lavay, B. W. (1992). *Physical activity for individuals with mental retardation: Infancy through adulthood*. Champaign, IL: Human Kinetics.

Ferrell, K. A. (1979). Orientation and mobility for preschool children: What we have and what we need. *Journal of Visual Impairment and Blindness, 73*(4), 148.

Gagné, R. M. (1970). *The conditions of learning*. New York: Holt, Rinehart & Winston.

Gardner, L. R. (1985, February). Low vision enhancement: The use of figure-ground reversals with visually impaired children. *Journal of Visual Impairment and Blindness, 79*(2), 64–69.

Hallahan, D. P., & Kauffman, J. M. (1991). *Exceptional children* (5th ed.). Englewood Cliffs, NJ: Prentice Hall.

Klee, K., and Klee, R. (1985, March). Group training in basic orientation, mobility and hearing skills. *Journal of Visual Impairment and Blindness, 79*(3), 100–103.

Kligerman, J. (1981). *The effects of color reversal on stimulus and response materials on the performance of learning disabled and normal learning children on the Bender Gestalt Test*. Unpublished Doctoral Dissertation, Columbia University, New York, N.Y.

Krebs, C. S. (1979). Hatha yoga for visually impaired students. *Journal of Visual Impairment and Blindness, 73*(6), 209–216.

Machemer, R. (1985, April). RPB Seminar highlights latest research findings. *Journal of Visual Impairment and Blindness, 79*(4), 188.

1983 World Series of Beep Baseball. (1983, August 25–27). *Beep Baseball in a nutshell: Batting and fielding*. St. Louis Park, Minn.: The World Series Program, 25–27 August 1983.

Schor, D. P. (1990). Visual impairment. In J. A. Blackman (Ed.), *Medical aspects of developmental disabilities in children birth to three*, (pp. 269–273). Rockville, MD: Aspen.

Seelye, W. (1983, March). Physical fitness of blind and visually impaired Detroit Public School children. *Journal of Visual Impairment and Blindness, 77*(3), 117–118.

Senitz, C., McBride, B., Adrian, J., & Semmler, C. J. (1990). Visually impaired children. In C. J. Semmler & J. G. Hunter (Eds.), *Early occupational therapy intervention. Neonates to three years* (pp. 262–274). Gaithersburg, MD: Aspen.

Sugden, D. A., & Keogh, J. F. (1990). *Problems in movement skill development.* Columbia: University of South Carolina.

U.S. Department of Education (1991). *Thirteenth annual report to Congress on the implementation of the Education of the Handicapped Act.* Washington, DC: Office of Special Education Programs.

Weitzman, D. M. (1985, March). An aerobic walking program to promote physical fitness in older blind adults. *Journal of Visual Impairment and Blindness,* 79(3), 97–99.

Chapter 15

SEIZURES AND CONVULSIVE DISORDERS

Greg Coker swims without fear of another convulsive seizure, determined that he won't be denied a normal life. Greg, a freshman in high school, dreamed of being an Olympic swimmer. That all changed in February when Coker, then living in Illinois, had a disabling skiing accident on a Colorado slope. He suffered a fractured skull, resulting in brain damage and the resultant convulsive seizures.

"Sure, I've had dreams of swimming the breast stroke in the Olympics, but I know it's not going to happen," Coker said. "But I can try and go to state on my high school team. I've got four years and I swear I'm going to get there. I've cried sometimes because I'm so frustrated that I'm different, but really, I'm no different from anybody else. When I swim, I won't use epilepsy as an excuse. I can go as hard as anybody on the team, and I know as long as I take my medicine I'm in complete control of my body and I won't have seizures."

Questions often asked are, Is it appropriate for a child who has seizures to participate in physical education activities? Will developmental exercises and physical fitness activities precipitate a seizure? What happens if the child's head is bumped during a game? What should I do when a convulsion occurs? Will competitive games cause undue stress? Is it better to assign the individual to a study hall or a class involving sedentary activities such as checkers, chess, or shuffleboard?

These questions plague physical educators, parents, physicians, and individuals who have seizures. Today, researchers and the medical profession have an extensive understanding of the intricacies of seizure disorders. As a result, a more positive approach is taken to activity for youngsters who are seizure-prone.

DEFINITION

A seizure is defined as a sudden and disorderly discharge of nerve cells in the brain, which is associated with an abrupt alternation in motor function, behavior, sensation, and/or consciousness (Coulter, 1991).

The word *epilepsy* is a general term for more than 20 different types of seizure disorders produced by brief, temporary changes in the normal functioning of the brain's electrical system. The Epilepsy Foundation of America (1990b) states, "These brief malfunctions mean that more than usual amount of electrical energy passes between cells. The sudden overload may stay in just one small area of the brain, or it may swamp the whole system" (p. 1). The Epilepsy Foundation offers information and assistance by phoning the following number: 1-800-EFA-1000.

Many professionals believe that the word *epilepsy* is very stigmatizing and are preferring to substitute terms such as *seizures* and *convulsive disorders* when describing these conditions.

Adams and McCubbin (1991) believe that people labeled as having seizure disorders are victims of society. They state the following:

> As a result of public prejudice, ignorance, and superstition, many persons with seizure disorders are denied the opportunity to receive an education and to work, and many do not receive proper medical care. This group of people is often perceived as having gross brain damage, uncontrolled convulsions, psychologic peculiarities, and mental retardation. While only a small percentage are so severely disabled, this erroneous public image perpetuates fear and misunderstanding of the disorder. (p. 93)

Seizures are estimated to occur in 1 to 2% of the U.S. population (Epilepsy Foundation of America, 1990a). Medical authorities state that approximately 1 in 50 school-age children has seizures. Seizures occur in children of all races and age groups and afflict both sexes. **Seizure disorder** (commonly called **epilepsy**) is not a disease and is not contagious. Of all new cases, 80% occur before the age of 18 years (Mennonite Hospital Tel-Med Program, 1992).

In the nervous system, all movement and activity is initiated by electrical discharges in the brain. In most people the excitability of the nerve cell is controlled by an intricate system of checks and balances so the discharge level seldom gets out of control. There is, however, a level at which these controls cease to operate, and an uncontrolled discharge then produces a seizure. In some individuals, this level is lower than in others, and may vary depending on such factors as time of day, onset of illness, fatigue, or emotional stress.

None of us is able to control our environment. We all respond differently to emotional situations. For example, the opossum may seem to "play possum" to confuse its attacker. In reality, the opossum is overcome with fear and simply faints, thereby giving the impression of being dead. When humans experience emotional situations that they cannot endure, they, like the turtle, pull into their shells and hide. Their emotional threshold has been overcome, the brain "turns off" the world, and the child faints. One hypothesis is that the seizure-prone individual possesses a lower emotional threshold and thus experiences seizures when under stress.

ABNORMAL BRAIN WAVE PATTERNS

Abnormalities of brain function during seizures cause abnormal brain wave patterns. Three anomalous patterns caused by different types of seizures are shown in the electroencephalographic (EEG) recordings in Figure 15.1. The second recording shows a spike and dome picture that occurs during **absence** or **petit mal** (or *pet-tee mahl*) seizures. A person in this condition becomes suddenly unconscious for 3 to 10 seconds. These episodes may occur every few minutes or every few hours, or the person may function for months without a seizure. Absence seizures result from abnormality of the reticular activating system of the brain. Transmission of normal alpha waves to the cerebral cortex is stopped temporarily. Instead, the spike and dome pattern is transmitted, and the person "falls asleep" for a few seconds until the alpha wave pattern is reintroduced.

The third recording in Figure 15.1 shows the brain wave pattern in tonic-clonic grand mal (*grahn mahl*) seizures. In this condition, the cerebral cortex becomes extremely excited when it must send many strong signals throughout the brain at the same time. When these signals reach the motor cortex, they cause rhythmic move-

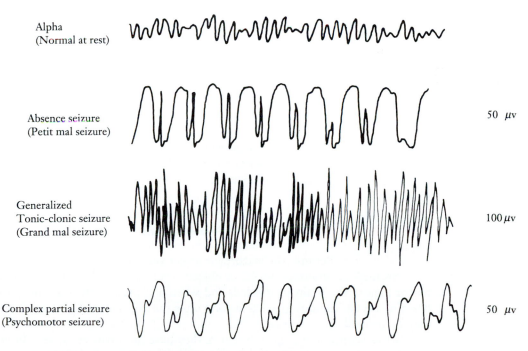

Alpha
(Normal at rest)

Absence seizure
(Petit mal seizure)   50 μv

Generalized
Tonic-clonic seizure
(Grand mal seizure)   100 μv

Complex partial seizure
(Psychomotor seizure)   50 μv

FIGURE 15.1 **Normal (alpha) and abnormal brain wave patterns as seen on an electroencephalogram. (Modified from Guyton 1979, p. 343.)**

ments, called **clonic convulsions,** throughout the body. Tonic-clonic or **grand mal** seizure results from abnormal reverberating cycles that develop in the reticular activating system. One portion of the brain stimulates another portion, which stimulates a third portion, which restimulates the first portion. The cycle continues for 2 to 3 minutes until the neurons of the system fatigue and the reverberation ceases. At the beginning of a grand mal attack, individuals may experience violent, abnormal, hallucinatory thoughts. Once most of the brain is involved, the person no longer has any conscious thoughts because signals are being transmitted in all directions rather than through discrete thought circuits. Even though the brain is violently active, the person becomes unconscious of his surroundings. Following a severe and prolonged attack, the brain and the muscles are so fatigued that individuals often sleep for at least a few minutes and sometimes as long as 24 hours (Guyton, 1971).

The most common characteristic of this disorder is the **seizure**. The seizure is, however, merely a symptom of the condition. In the past, some of the words used to describe a seizure were "epileptic convulsion," "spell," "fit," and "attack." "Seizure" is defined medically as an episode of impaired consciousness, which may or may not be associated with convulsive movements. Some loss of consciousness almost always occurs during a seizure. The individual's brain turns off the outside world because of an inability to control the overabundance of electrical (nerve) activity. These individuals possess a low convulsive threshold. It is important to understand that such conditions are common and can be treated. For the majority of children who have seizure disorder, limiting activities is not necessary.

ETIOLOGY

Children and adolescents who experience seizures are in one of two general categories: (1) those who have experienced brain damage (lesion), or (2) those who have inherited a low threshold for seizures. Some of the possible causes of seizures are identified in Table 15.1.

Lesions can occur as a result of any damage to the brain. A direct blow to the head during an accident, disease, an extremely high fever, or lack of oxygen (anoxia) are all possible causes of brain damage. The resultant seizures are termed *symptomatic, acquired,* or *focal,* because the seizure cause is easily identified.

Seizures are common when an object penetrates the skull, especially when the motor area of the brain is affected, and when a depressed fracture and intracranial bleeding occur. Seizures may occur soon after the injury (usually within 2 weeks) but may be delayed up to 1 year.

Most seizures are *idiopathic*; that is, they have no apparent cause. These seizures may be inherited, as some older studies show that parents of children with seizure disorder often have unusual EEG readings. Porter (1990) states the following:

TABLE 15.1   Causes of Seizures Occurring at Different Ages

Neonatal (first month)

Birth injury—anoxia or hemorrhage
Congenital abnormalities
Metabolic disorders—hypoglycemia, hypocalcemia
Meningitis and other infection

Infancy (1 to 6 months)

As above
Infantile spasms

Early Childhood (6 months to 3 years)

Febrile (high fever) seizures
Birth injuries
Infection
Trauma
Poisons and metabolic defects
Cerebral degenerations

Childhood and Adolescence

Idiopathic
Birth injury
Trauma
Infection
Cerebral degenerations

Source: Modified from Laidlaw and Richens 1976, p. 33.

Future scientific advances are likely to identify inherited susceptibility as a principle cause of epilepsy. Although there is considerable evidence that absence seizures, for example, are an extension of an autosomal dominant gene, the role of genetic factors in epilepsy has been wholly unexplored. (p. 791)

Seizures are commonly classified within specific age groups. Table 15.2 identifies these classifications by age group.

DIAGNOSIS

Neurologists determine whether or not an individual has the potential for seizures. Careful neurological examination may reveal specific brain lesion or tumor. These tests involve safe and painless x rays, EEG, computer tomography (CT), and the newer magnetic resonance imaging (MRI) (Eichstaedt & Lavay, 1992). Physicians, using CT scanning and MRI, are now able to identify tumors, cerebral atrophy,

TABLE 15.2   Etiology and Age: Convulsive Disorders

	Newborn	Infancy	Childhood	Adolescence
Severe perinatal injury	————————	————————		
Metabolic defects	————————	————————		
Congenital malformation		————————	————————	
Infection		————————	————————	
Genetic			————————	————————
Perinatal injury	————————	————————		
Genetic disease	————————	————————	————————	
Myoclonic syndromes	————————	————————	————————	
Postnatal trauma			————————	————————
Brain tumor				
Vascular disease				

hydrocephalus, infarctions (dead cells), subdural hematomas (bruises), cystic lesions, and arteriovenous malformations, all of which may be the cause of seizures. CT and MRI scanning are most helpful in diagnosing children who have partial (focal) seizures.

Once the condition is diagnosed, the physician makes a thorough evaluation to determine what is causing the seizures. Even if the main cause can be identified and treated, however, most individuals who suffer from seizure disorder require ongoing treatment with antiepileptic drugs (Horvat, 1990).

If a diagnosis is confirmed, the EEG may reveal that the excessive discharges always begin in the same brain area. For example, irregular EEG waves may occur only in a small area of the temporal lobe. If this area can be identified specifically, that small portion of the brain may be removed.

Vinning (1990) believes that surgery is appropriate for children whose seizures cannot be controlled through medication. She states, "In those individuals whose seizures are intractable [resistant to control] and/or who are experiencing life-altering side effects, the search for abnormal brain tissue and the potential for surgical reme-diation should be considered" (p. 807).

TYPES OF SEIZURES

The system known as the International Classification of Seizures identifies two major categories of convulsive disorder: (1) partial seizures (e.g., psychomotor), and (2) generalized seizures (e.g., petit mal and grand mal) (Vinning, 1990).

Partial seizures are limited to one part of the brain; generalized seizures imply that all brain cells are involved. Among children and adolescents, generalized seizures are more common. One type of generalized tonic-clonic seizure (grand mal) consists of a convulsion combined with a complete loss of consciousness. Another type, absence (petit mal) resembles a brief period of fixed staring.

Seizures are classified by observable characteristics. Four varieties are commonly found in school-age individuals (see Table 15.3).

ABSENCE (PETIT MAL) SEIZURES

Absence **petit mal** seizures are identified by a temporary loss of consciousness without convulsions. These seizures last for a few seconds only. Minor rhythmic movements of the eyes or eyelids are the only observable symptoms. Consciousness is regained, but total amnesia exists for the brief period of attack. The person may look around for a moment and then resume previous activity. If engaged in listening before the attack, the person experiencing the seizure will have missed only a sentence or two. The absence petit mal seizure usually occurs only in childhood, and is the most common type of seizure in school-age children.

The following account is taken from a case study of a female teenager who experienced absence petit mal seizures (Alvarez, 1972):

> Sure, I have always had brief spells of being "out" for a half a minute. There are seconds when I am gone, and then I return. I have brief vacant intervals.... Often I must have been unconscious for a few seconds...I have vacant spells in my thoughts that scare the life out of me. I am slow in my work because of the momentary spells when I know nothing. Often after such a spell I wonder what happened to me.

TABLE 15.3   **Most Common Child and Adolescent Seizure Classifications**

International Classification of Epileptic Seizures (Abridged)	"Old Terms"
I. Partial Seizures	
A. Complex partial seizures (with impairment of consciousness)	Psychomotor seizures
II. Generalized seizures (Convulsive or Nonconvulsive)	
A. Absence seizures	Petit mal seizures
B. Myoclonic seizures	Minor motor seizures
C. Clonic seizures	Grand mal seizures
D. Tonic seizures	Grand mal seizures
E. Tonic-clonic seizures	Grand mal seizures
F. Atonic seizures	Akinetic, drop seizures

Source: Modified from Vinning, E. P. G. (1990). Epilepsy in infants and children. In R. E. Rakel (Ed.), *Conn's current therapy 1990* (pp. 792–796). Philadelphia: Saunders.

Sometimes my vision shuts off for a few seconds. And, brief spells of unconsciousness interfere with my reading, because I miss a number of words. Once, when I was reading, I woke to find my book on the floor of the room... and I knew I must have had some sort of spell in which I was "out." Too often also, I must keep going unconscious because I drop things and break them. (p. 138)

Such seizures fortunately disappear in adult life. The use of medication is extremely successful for youngsters who experience absence petit mal seizures; control of seizures is effective in up to 80% of all cases (Coulter, 1991).

GENERALIZED TONIC-CLONIC GRAND MAL SEIZURES

Generalized tonic-clonic **grand mal** seizures are probably responsible for most of the misunderstanding and fear that surround convulsive disorders. The seizure that accompanies all tonic-clonic grand mal seizures is alarming to observe. Remember, however, that the individual feels no pain because of unconsciousness. Approximately 10% of all seizures are tonic-clonic.

Some people who have tonic-clonic grand mal seizures experience a vague, poorly described warning that a seizure is about to occur. This warning is called an **aura**. Not all grand mal seizures are preceded by an aura; for some individuals, seizure occurs without warning. The adapted physical education teacher should ask each child if seizure onset is predictable. The child should be instructed to inform the teacher immediately when he experiences an aura. Such warnings give the instructor time to prepare for the seizure by removing the child to a less hazardous place and having the child lie down.

Injuries from seizures can occur from a fall to the floor or from striking the head or other body parts on a hard surface (e.g., floors, walls, gymnastic equipment, tables). Any advance seizure warning could prevent a falling injury. Emergency procedures to follow during a tonic-clonic grand mal seizure are discussed on pages 427–428.

Three types of brain wave patterns appear during a grand mal seizure. Initially the brain experiences fast activity and starts "buzzing." This begins the **tonic phase,** during which the child may cry out or make a gasping, gurgling sound. These sounds arise because the respiratory muscles are contracting. If standing, the individual will fall with boardlike rigidity in the direction in which he is leaning. After falling the child will lie rigid, and because tonic contraction somewhat inhibits breathing, he may become blue. The child may also bite the inside of the mouth or tongue, or may urinate or defecate if the bladder or bowel is full.

The tonic phase progresses quickly into a rapid jerking of the muscles. These generalized spasms are the convulsive or **clonic phase**. During the spasms, the person may gasp for air between convulsive movements. Swallowing does not occur, so the child may froth at the mouth because of saliva buildup.

These movements gradually slow and disappear, and the individual seems to relax. The brain waves are at highest intensity and are most erratic during the tonic-clonic phases of the seizure. When these phases pass, the person then experiences the **postseizure stupor phase**. If a brain wave recording were made during this phase, it would show very, very slow movement, for the brain is exhausted, as are all of the body muscles. The seizure stops because the body is physically and mentally unable to continue and is literally "fatigued out"—all available energy has been used.

A tonic-clonic grand mal seizure can last for a few seconds or many minutes. The longer the individual continues in the convulsive state, the more fatigued she will be during the postseizure phase. Following the convulsion, the person may complain of a headache or a tired feeling. If the seizure has been extremely violent or prolonged, the child may ask to sleep. This is common, and the individual should be allowed to sleep. The sleeping phase allows the child's body to recover from an exhausting experience.

For most individuals, on any given day a seizure is a single happening, but some persons do experience one tonic-clonic grand mal seizure after another. This critical situation is called **status epilepticus**. Immediate emergency medical care should be obtained. Although deaths do occur when individuals experience status epilepticus, the condition is usually encountered only in severely involved seizure-prone individuals whose seizure disorder is poorly controlled by medication. Status epilepticus is comparatively rare.

COMPLEX PARTIAL PSYCHOMOTOR SEIZURES

Few young children have complex partial psychomotor seizures (Wright, 1975) (see Figure 15.1 for EEG brain wave patterns). Persons experiencing a **complex partial seizure** usually behave in a confused and irrational manner: they may wander around, make aimless gestures, or repeat whatever action was being performed when the seizure began. The following case history (Livingston, 1963) identifies a typical complex partial psychomotor experience of a 16-year-old female. Her father gave the following description of her "spells."

> My daughter and I were sitting in the restaurant eating lunch. . . . Suddenly she stopped talking and complained of feeling funny in the stomach . . . she had a blank and dazed expression in her eyes which lasted for a moment . . . she began repeating the questions: "Where am I?" "What day is this?" "What time is it?" She continued to repeat these questions . . . for about fifteen minutes. Then she . . . took a fork and began hitting it against the table . . . for about ten minutes. Following this she sat down again and then she seemed to relax. . . . For a moment she appeared somewhat confused, but then recovered completely. I spoke to her frequently during the course of the spell, but she did not seem to hear me and she did not answer the questions. When she recovered completely, I asked her what happened and she had no recollection of the disturbance. (p. 36)

During a complex partial psychomotor seizure, the individual may become involved in abnormal behavior, mutter meaningless phrases, or appear wide-eyed and terrified. During this state, the person may respond to a question, but usually does not understand the question and the reply is often inappropriate. Individuals may repeat prelearned material, count, or state their name over and over again.

Behavior abnormalities are three times as common in individuals with psychomotor seizure disorder as in persons with other forms of seizure disorder. In an estimated one-fourth of all psychomotor episodes, the person actually moves around. The potential for danger is evident if the person walks or runs into a dangerous environment (e.g., toward a flight of stairs, glass windows, or doors). The teacher should restrain the child so that injury does not occur. The idea that the person, while experiencing this type of seizure, might injure others intentionally is totally *incorrect*. In reality, the person is unaware of what is happening. Another child, positioned in the path of the person with a seizure disorder, could conceivably be bumped or possibly knocked down by accident. Restraint is therefore necessary for the safety of both the child and others.

ATONIC AKINETIC SEIZURES

Atonic drop or **akinetic seizure** describes a condition common in children in which the youngster falls unconscious to the floor. A second type of drop attack occurs when a sudden weakness of the legs forces the child to fall to the knees, but consciousness is not lost. Atonic seizures are usually recurring, but they are brief and not of a convulsive nature. During the seizure, the student generally falls forward and injury to forehead or chin can result. To prevent injury, these children should, when ambulating, wear protective head devices with padded straps for the chin.

Although there are other, less common forms of convulsive disorder, tonic-clonic grand mal, absence petit mal, partial psychomotor, and atonic drop seizures are the most common types found among school-age children.

INFANTILE SPASMS

Infantile spasms are clusters of quick, sudden movements that usually begin between 3 months and 2 years. High body temperature and fever can cause these seizures. Typically, if the child is sitting up, the head will fall forward, and the arms will also flex forward. If lying down, the knees will be drawn up, and the arms and head will flex forward as if reaching for support (Epilepsy Foundation of America, 1990a).

MEDICATION

Most children with seizure disorder must take medication to control the occurrence of seizures. These medications are **anticonvulsants**, which limit the spread of abnormal electrical discharges in the brain. Anticonvulsants are neither sedatives nor tranquilizers. Table 15.4 lists the common anticonvulsants, their uses, and side effects.

TABLE 15.4 Common Anticonvulsants, Their Use, and Side Effects

Type of Drug		Type of Seizure	Common Side Effects
Brand Name	**Generic Name**		
Dilantin (dī-LAN-tin)	Phenytoin (fee-nit-o-in)	Grand mal Psychomotor	Unsteady gait, blurred vision, double vision, gum hypertrophy, increased hair growth in females
Luminal	Phenobarbital (fee-no-bar-ba-tol)	Grand mal Psychomotor	Hyperactivity or irritability in young children, sluggishness in school-age children
Primidone (pry-mo-dōne)	Mysoline (my-so-leen)	Grand mal Psychomotor	Stomach upsets, dizziness, drowsiness, irritability (temper outbursts)
Tegretol[a]	Carbamazepine (car-ba-maza-peen)	Grand mal Psychomotor	Dizziness, blurred vision, drowsiness
Depakene	Valproic acid	Grand mal, petit mal, Psychomotor, Atonic	Nausea, vomiting, and weight gain
Klonopin	Clonazepam (clo-noz-a-pam)	Petit mal	Drowsiness, ataxia, behavior changes
Zarontin	Ethosuximide (eth-o-sucks-a-mide)	Petit mal	Nausea, fatigue, dizziness, and drowsiness

[a] Safety and effectiveness of Tegretol (carbamazepine) for use in children under age 6 years has not been established (Vinning, 1990).

The long-range goal of medication is to eliminate seizures completely without negative side effects. In general, the amount of medication prescribed is based on a rough estimate of the condition's severity and the possibility of complete seizure control. In the drug management of seizures, children generally have a better prognosis than adults. For example, 80% of youngsters with petit mal seizures become seizure-free when put on drug treatment.

In cases for which a specific cause of the convulsive disorder has been identified, appropriate treatment is usually determined easily. In over half of all children with recurring convulsions, however, no cause can be determined. Treatment generally consists of daily doses of anticonvulsive drugs. When the specific convulsive disorder has been identified and the most appropriate drug prescribed, the drug dosage is then increased gradually until control of the seizures is attained. Once the seizures are controlled, that drug dosage is continued. If the seizures recur, the drug dosage is increased further until side effects become evident. If seizures still continue, a second appropriate drug is usually administered, again in gradually increasing dosages until control is gained. Changes of drug dosage are not advised until a given dosage has been tried for at least 7 days.

Seizures usually occur when individuals are not taking medication. The importance of regular, consistent intake of the prescribed drug cannot be overemphasized.

The person with seizure disorder should have a schedule for taking medication, which should be administered in a few daily doses to make the schedule easy to follow.

The physical educator should know when the student is adding, deleting, or changing medication. Parents should be asked to inform the instructor when changes are being made to ensure that physical activities are within the child's safety limits. For example, gymnastic units involving high balance beam activities may not be appropriate without additional spotting.

If a child is having regular seizures (i.e., daily), the physician may be experimenting with the medication. Safety becomes a critical issue and the physical education instructor must be constantly aware of dangers that could arise. This does not mean that the child should be excused from physical education, but rather, that the program must be adapted to compensate for any possible risks.

The adapted physical educator should become familiar with the most common types of medication used to treat seizure disorders.

Phenytoin (Dilantin) is often prescribed for grand mal seizures because it does not sedate or cause sleepiness. Balance and equilibrium may be impaired as a result of overdosage, but the impairment usually disappears within 1 to 2 weeks after dosage reduction. Dilantin may cause blurred vision or double vision, which can be a problem in activities that involve catching balls. A chronic side effect when Dilantin has been administered for a long time is gum hypertrophy, which causes the gums to bleed during tooth brushing. In females, Dilantin may produce excessive hair growth on the extremities and face.

Phenobarbital (Luminal) is prescribed for grand mal seizures, but is not as much used as Dilantin because it causes hyperactivity or irritability in young children and sluggishness in older children. Either side effect is undesirable in school because attention and performance may be impaired. When a child experiences negative side effects from phenobarbital, another drug is prescribed.

Petit mal seizures are usually controlled with the following medications: Ethosuximide (Zarontin) will control simple staring spells or absence seizures. Trimethadione (Tridione) is as effective as Zarontin and has fewer negative side effects.

"Drop" or akinetic seizures are resistant to anticonvulsant drugs, so steroid therapy is often recommended.

The type and amount of medication required are determined by trial and error. The physician may spend a year or more adjusting medications to achieve the proper dosage. The success of the medication plan could likely result in total control of seizures. Vinning (1990) believes, "Probably 70 to 75% of children will ultimately have their seizures completely controlled. Once the seizures have been controlled for 2 or more years, it is reasonable to consider discontinuation of medication" (p. 804). Obviously, the decision to discontinue the use of medicine can be made *only* by the child's physician.

Children may need to bring medications (pills, tablets, liquid) to school. These medications should be kept in a cool place and not be exposed to excessive temperatures. For example, capsules may melt when left in direct sunlight or near excessive heat, and potency may be reduced. All anticonvulsive medications should be kept in one specific school area, such as in a refrigerator in the nurse's office.

The physical education teacher is not expected to administer or alter a student's medication program, but should be familiar with the common side effects of the prescribed drug. Because of the teacher's close contact with the student, she can usually identify whether the individual's performance or behavior has become markedly better or worse. The educator should consult with the nurse and with the parents before and during administration of a medication program.

CONTROVERSIAL ISSUES REGARDING SEIZURE DISORDERS

Physical educators often ask, "What situations or activities precipitate a seizure?" Many of the old, ultraconservative restrictions imposed on children with seizure disorder were based on fears that rarely materialized. The possibility of **head injury** has been the main reason given for excluding students who experienced seizures from physical education activity. The concern was that a blow to the head, either from falling or from being hit, would cause a seizure. The original injurious damage to the brain is nonprogressive, however, and further brain damage is highly unlikely. The chances that a given seizure-prone individual will have a seizure as a result of head injury are the same as for a person who has never had a seizure.

Livingston and Berman (1974) state, "Over the past 36 years, we have followed at least 15,000 young children with epilepsy, many of whom have been under our care during their entire scholastic careers. Hundreds of these patients have played tackle football and many have participated in boxing, lacrosse, wrestling, and other physical activities which render the participant prone to head injuries. We are not cognizant of a single instance of recurrence or aggravation of epileptic seizures related to head injury in any of these athletes" (p. 172).

Hyperventilation is known to produce absence petit mal seizures in some individuals. Forced deep breathing can be used by physicians to induce a petit mal seizure. This is common practice and is used routinely for EEG examination. The question therefore arises whether deep breathing, as experienced in extended periods of running, swimming, fatiguing exercise, and circuit training, brings on petit mal seizures? Henderson (1978) responds, "It is known simple hyperventilation may precipitate a petit mal episode. However, the hyperpnea (abnormal increase in the depth and rate of respiration) of exercise is a precise adjustment to the metabolic needs of the individual related to oxygen requirements and metabolic acidosis.... Evidence is lacking that hyperpnea of exercise precipitates an epileptic attack"... (p. 44). Livingston and Berman (1974) conclude that hyperventilation caused in confined settings (such as a physician's office) is distinctly different from the increased breathing rate induced by physical exercise. They believe that physical activities do not cause an individual to hyperventilate so as to bring on a seizure. In a 3-year-long research project involving seizure-prone individuals and vigorous physical activities, Rose (1973) observed that rapid breathing, when occurring naturally as a result of vigorous exercise, did not increase seizure incidence, and that changes in blood chemistry during exercise appear to have a protective effect that actually reduces the chance of having a seizure. The conclusion is that labored breathing caused by exercise will not bring on seizures.

Emotional or stressful situations are thought to precipitate seizures, but identifying exactly what triggers a seizure is difficult if not impossible. There is no doubt, however, that seizure frequency is linked to the individual's psychological well-being and that seizure cause is related directly to the emotional intensity of a specific situation. Some children can definitely relate seizures to moods, but it is difficult to decide whether a highly stressful state caused the seizure or whether the seizure was caused simply by worrying that an attack might occur.

Hallahan and Kauffman (1991) state the following:

> Research has shown that children with seizure disorders do have emotional and behavioral problems more than most children. One must not, however, conclude that seizure disorders cause emotional and behavioral problems directly. The stress of having to deal with seizures, medications, and stigma, as well as adverse conditions, is more likely to cause these problems. (p. 353)

Among children with seizure disorders, the emotional stress encountered is essentially the same as that observed in individuals who suffer from other chronic disorders such as asthma and heart disease. These psychological barriers consist primarily of anxiety or depressive states or both, feelings of insecurity and inferiority, and antisocial tendencies. If the students can be relieved of strong pent-up emotions and can be offered positive reinforcement through successful participation in physical education activities, then many stressful situations will be ameliorated. Some children are intensely fearful that they will experience a seizure in the presence of their peers. This burden may become so intense that the constant worry charges the brain's electrical impulses to a state of potential explosion. Medication can help to control the child's anxiety, but being active, stimulated, and happy will also help to ward off seizures.

Fatigue is another potential cause of seizures. The physiological effects of fatigue can be analyzed in terms of what happens just prior to the seizure episode. The body is demanding rest and relief from exhausting daily activities. Fatigue is defined as a state of increased discomfort and decreased efficiency, which results from prolonged or excessive exertion. In short, fatigue is the loss of power or capacity to respond to stimulation (Dorland's Illustrated Medical Dictionary, 1988). Few physical education programs reach this combined intensity. If such conditions do occur and if the physical demand is excessive, the child with a seizure disorder should be told to reduce the demand or pace.

Loss of sleep may be a potential cause of seizures. The instructor should look for signs that indicate fatigue. Is the student distinctly more lethargic than the other children? Does he seem overtired and listless? If the student is interested, active, and attentive, all disorder tends to be suppressed.

Many students have seizures only when they sleep. Those who experience seizures while sleeping have fewer problems, physically and socially, and require no restrictions of their daily activities.

About fatigue, Livingston (1963) states, "I have found it very difficult to evaluate the significance of fatigue as a precipitating factor of seizures in epilepsy. However, I believe that the general attitude of treating an individual with epilepsy as if he had tuberculosis or rheumatic fever and consequently encouraging or forcing him to take frequent rest periods *should be discouraged*. I believe that, if possible, the patient should be instructed and encouraged to conduct himself in the same manner as his normal associates" [italics added] (pp. 58–59).

Menstruation has caused seizures in some women. This occurrence is highly individual and is not considered common or even occasional for the majority of females who have had seizures. If menstruation does seem to cause seizures in a given individual, then modified programming during that time is necessary. The woman's medical history will indicate the relationship between menstruation and seizure onset.

An example of a rare seizure is **photosensitive epilepsy**, which is provoked by repetitive flashing lights or lights reflecting off the ripples of water in a swimming pool. Few individuals will have a seizure under these conditions. If, however, a photosensitive individual is present in the class (which would be rare), the child's medical history should list the potential cause, and steps can be taken for program modification.

FIRST AID FOR TONIC-CLONIC GRAND MAL SEIZURES

Teachers are usually enlightened and helpful, and if fully informed about the possibility of a convulsive episode, they review what to do (or what not to do). Cardinal rules are

1. Remain calm. Students assume the same emotional reaction as their teacher. Remember that the seizure is painless for the child.

2. Clear the area so the child is not injured by hard or sharp objects.

3. Do not force anything between the child's teeth.

4. Do not restrain the child. The seizure cannot be stopped once it has begun. Oxygen should not be administered; it may actually prolong the seizure.

5. Cradle the head in your hands to prevent violent banging against the floor. If saliva accumulates, turn the head to the side so it can drain out.

6. Do not call a doctor unless the seizure lasts for more than 5 minutes or is followed immediately by another major seizure without the child regaining consciousness.

7. Stay with the child until all movement has ceased, consciousness has been regained, and confusion has subsided. A small child can be carried to a

rest area; an older youngster may be allowed to lie where he is until able to talk. If tired, the individual should be permitted to rest until normal activities can be resumed.

8. Observe carefully the details of the seizure, which should be reported to the school nurse and to the child's parents.

9. Turn the incident into a learning experience for the entire class. Explain what a seizure is, that it is not contagious, and that it is nothing to cause fear.

GENERAL GUIDELINES FOR TEACHERS

Teachers, like parents, must not be overprotective toward individuals who are seizure-prone. There are few school situations in which the child cannot participate. Safety and common sense should dictate which activities are potentially dangerous.

When a child with seizure disorder is placed in the class, the instructor should plan a short private interview with the student to develop a complete picture of the child. Both the physical education teacher and the school nurse should interview the child. This personal contact demonstrates to the youngster that the teacher is concerned and interested. Too often, educators are embarrassed to discuss disabilities with the individuals involved, perhaps fearing that such discussion might be construed as an intrusion. The following questions can be used as guidelines for the educator's interview with the child:

1. When was the last time that you had a seizure?
2. How often do you have seizures?
3. What causes your seizures?
4. Do you know when you are going to have a seizure?
5. What happens to you when you have a seizure?
6. Do you lose consciousness?
7. How long does your seizure usually last?
8. How do you feel when you wake up after a seizure?
9. Do you take medicine? If so, what kind, and do you bring it to school?
10. Where do you keep your medicine when it's at school?
11. Do the other students know that you have seizures?

Answers to these questions should give the physical educator a thorough understanding of the student's seizure pattern. In most instances the seizure pattern will be consistent, which should alleviate normal apprehension and prepare the instructor to handle calmly a seizure if it occurs.

SOCIAL ACCEPTANCE

The public's attitude toward seizures is a major cause of concern for persons with seizure disorders. Unfortunately, most attitudes include pity and negative feelings as well as a strong belief that seizure-prone individuals should be protected from injuring themselves or others. The uninformed public often entertains inaccurate images of mental deficiencies, physical deformities, and other bizarre abnormalities as typical characteristics of those who have seizures. The informed educator must reinforce the fact that having seizures is *not* contagious and is *not* a progressive condition.

Misconceptions are bred through lack of knowledge about the condition. Physicians who deal with children who are seizure-prone believe that the major problem is *not* keeping the disorder under control medically. Seizure control can usually be accomplished. The real difficulty lies in dealing with the psychological problems surrounding the disorder. For example, parents may be instructed by the doctor to give the child's teacher full details about the seizures, their nature, and frequency. Many parents, however, believe that if the child's classmates know about the condition, they will be suspicious or fearful or will reject the child completely. The physician can help to avoid these problems by explaining the condition to the parents (and the child), thereby reducing the emotional impact of the terms *seizure*, *epilepsy*, and *convulsion*. The adapted physical educator should reassure the parents that their youngster will be helped to achieve normal status in the school environment.

The stigma of seizure disorders may follow the adolescent into adult life if the school does not dispel old fears and myths. Open discussion of seizures with all children helps to establish a positive, straightforward understanding of the condition, thus erasing the mystery and much of the fear. The role of the school, therefore, is to educate, *not* to hide the facts. Ignoring the situation is not acceptable; openly discussing the problem can lead to understanding. Achievement and success in the physical education class can be a strong motivating influence for children who have seizures, especially when the class attitude is one of acceptance and understanding.

PHYSICAL EDUCATION ACTIVITY RECOMMENDATIONS

All children are subject to risks, and in the physical education environment these become more common. Potential dangers must be accepted. Only through the efforts of conscientious teachers who preplan carefully can serious injuries be avoided. As previously discussed, the seizure-prone child must be allowed to participate in physical education; his exclusion from physical education classes or from athletic competition could mean a future as an inactive invalid. Surburg (1990) believes that once an individual's seizures are under reasonable control, that person should lead a normal life and participate in sports and other physical activities.

The key to determining which activities are best for a given child depends entirely on the individual's degree of seizure control. If daily attacks are occurring, the instructor should not use games involving heights, rope climbing, high balance beams, or stair climbing.

Swimming and water skills must be closely supervised. A buddy system should be used, and the "buddy" should understand what her responsibilities are if a seizure occurs. Laidlaw and Richens (1976) state that seizures seldom occur while the person is swimming, even in special schools for children who might be experiencing seizures. If, however, a seizure should occur while the child is in the pool, he should be floated face up with jaw supported. The child who is convulsing need not be pulled onto the pool deck.

Safety should be of major concern when selecting activities for these students. Most youngsters who are seizure-prone in the public schools have their condition under control by regular administration of prescribed medication. They should have few or no restrictions and normal programming is indicated (Brown, 1989).

When the child's seizures are not under control or when the physician is determining correct medication, the adapted physical educator should consider the following: (1) What specific activities are presently scheduled for the student? Will the student be asked to climb ropes or walk on a high balance beam? Will the activity involve lifting weights above the head? Does participation include carrying or lifting other students, as in relays? If so, appropriate spotting techniques, including use of spotting belts, should be used so the individual can participate. (2) Where will the activities take place? Is the playing surface hard, such as a gym or playroom floor, an asphalt court, or a pool deck? What injuries could occur if the student falls? Should the child wear protective headgear? If the area is undesirable and possibly dangerous, the child should be placed in an adapted environment that includes mats or composition flooring. Wrestling rooms and tumbling areas are examples of ideal playing surfaces. These restricted areas are not suitable teaching stations for many physical education activities, however, and the child's program could become restrictive and shortsighted were his physical education limited to this environment for an extended period of time. The instructor's responsibility is to provide a diversified curriculum for a well-rounded motor program.

Most children whose seizures are not under control will probably possess lower motor skill proficiency because they have been excluded from programs and have not developed normal skill levels. Assessment of general motor ability may indicate that they should have a well-rounded developmental concentration involving basic strength, balance, locomotor skills, agility, and eye-hand coordination.

Because a blow to the head will probably not cause a seizure, exclusion from contact sports is uncalled for! General safety precautions used by all students in the physical education and interscholastic programs will suffice for students whose condition is under control.

Livingston and Berman (1974) list the following suggestions for determining which involved students should engage in contact sports: (1) **Frequency of seizures**—People who experience frequent seizures (daily) should not participate.

(2) **Time of seizure occurrence**—People whose seizures occur only in sleep should be evaluated in the same manner as individuals who are not subject to seizures.

If the patient is interested, active, and attentive, all disorder tends to be suppressed. In other words, for the person who is seizure-prone, activity is good therapy. When bored, the child's disorder tends to increase. Fewer seizures are experienced when youngsters are participating in physical activities, including football and baseball. Indeed, abnormalities in the EEGs of seizure-prone patients frequently *increase* during the resting state.

The cardiorespiratory efficiency of children who have seizures should be improved, for one major concern is that overfatigue may cause seizures. Rose (1977) notes that seizures may be related to degree of cardiovascular fitness. A gradual and progressive program to increase fitness and to minimize undue fatigue therefore seems indicated.

SUMMARY

Seizures are chronic disorders of the brain characterized by recurrent attacks involving loss of consciousness or convulsions or both. There are two categories of seizure: (1) symptomatic or acquired, due to specific disease or damage to the brain, and (2) idiopathic, which includes those individuals who have inherited a low threshold for seizures.

Most individuals who are seizure-prone can be aided by medication. Physical activity need not be restricted for the school-age child unless seizures are not under control. For those who have frequent seizures, the adapted physical education teacher should modify the activity or the activity area. Individuals who are seizure-prone should not be excused from physical education activities because of their disorder. Safety is a main precaution in program planning.

The student with seizure disorder may enter the physical education program with below normal levels of physical fitness and motor skills owing to previous excuses from physical education programs. Assessment is necessary to determine appropriate placement.

Continual communication among the physical educator, school nurse, parents, and physician is necessary. When properly understood and medically supervised, the individual can lead a normal life; his condition need not interfere with daily school activities. Too often, people do not understand what happens during a seizure, and stigma and prejudice are directed at the child. This social problem must be dealt with and an understanding attitude developed in classmates. A positive success-oriented physical education experience can contribute greatly to the child's acceptance in the school and community.

REFERENCES

Adams, R. C., & McCubbin, J. A. (1991). *Games, sports, and exercises for the physically disabled* (4th ed.). Philadelphia: Lea & Febiger.

Alvarez, W. C. (1972). *Nerves in collision.* New York: Pyramid House.

Brown, T. R. (1989). Epilepsy in adolescents and adults. In R. E. Rakel (Ed.), *Conn's current therapy 1989* (pp. 781–792). Philadelphia: Saunders.

Coulter, D. L. (1991). Frontal lobe seizures: No evidence of self-injury. *American Journal of Mental Retardation, 96,* 81–85.

Dorland's Illustrated Medical Dictionary (1988). (27th ed.). Philadelphia: W. B. Saunders.

Eichstaedt, C. B., & Lavay, B. (1992). *Physical activity for individuals with mental retardation: Birth through adult.* Champaign, IL: Human Kinetics.

Epilepsy Foundation of America (1990a). *Seizure recognition and first aid.* Landover, MD: The Foundation.

Epilepsy Foundation of America (1990b). *Epilepsy facts and figures.* Landover, MD: The Foundation.

Guyton, A. C. (1971). *Basic human physiology: normal function and mechanisms of disease.* Philadelphia: W. B. Saunders.

–––. (1979.) *Physiology of the human body.* (5th ed.). Philadelphia: W. B. Saunders.

Hallahan, D. P., & Kauffman, J. M. (1991). *Exceptional children* (5th ed.). Englewood Cliffs, NJ: Prentice Hall.

Henderson, J. P. (1978). *Sports and epilepsy,* (R. M. Palulonis, Ed.). Monroe, WI: American Medical Association.

Horvat, M. (1990). *Physical education and sport for exceptional students.* Dubuque, IA: Brown.

Laidlaw, J., and Richens, A. (1976). *A textbook of epilepsy.* Edinburgh, Scotland: Churchill-Livingstone.

Livingston, S. (1963). *Living with epileptic seizures.* Springfield, IL: Charles C. Thomas.

Livingston, S., & Berman, W. (1974). Participation of the epileptic child in contact sports. *Sports Medicine, 2*(5), 170–173.

Mennonite Hospital Tel-Med Program (1992). *Epilepsy* (Audio Tape No. 125). Bloomington, IL: Bro-Menn Health Care.

Porter, R. J. (1990). Epilepsy in adolescents and adults. In R. E. Rakel (Ed.), *Conn's current therapy 1990.* (pp. 790–802). Philadelphia: W. B. Saunders.

Rose, K. (1973). Physical stress and epilepsy: an investigation. *National Spokesman, 6* (6), 6.

–––. (1977). The effect of exercise on EEG and blood chemistry of epileptics. In *The best of challenge* (Vol. 3). Reston, VA: AAHPERD.

Surburg, P. R. (1990). Other health-impaired and nonhandicapped students in adapted physical education. In J. P. Winnick (Ed.), *Adapted physical education and sport* (pp. 269–297). Champaign, IL: Human Kinetics.

Vinning, E. P. G. (1990). Epilepsy in infants and children. In R. E. Rakel (Ed.), *Conn's current therapy 1990* (pp. 802–807). Philadelphia: W. B. Saunders.

Wright, G. N. (1975). Rehabilitation and the problem of epilepsy. In *Epilepsy rehabilitation.* Boston: Little, Brown.

Chapter 16

CEREBRAL PALSY

 School District 42 has just received records for Keith W., who will be moving into the district in the fall. Keith's records show he is 10 years old and eligible for special education services, as he is labeled as having cerebral palsy. Additionally, Keith has experienced tonic-clonic (grand mal) seizures, although these have been controlled and he hasn't had a seizure for 18 months. The records have been turned over to Ron Kruzel, Director of Special Education Programs, who will determine what information is needed to place Keith into the most appropriate learning environments.

Most important are Keith's present levels of performance. Therefore, the teachers who provide direct services (the special education and the adapted physical education teachers) must be given a time line for assessment, program writing, and placement. The school diagnostician might be asked to test the youngster to measure current levels of IQ and social, emotional, and behavioral competency. The physical educator will be asked to give Keith a series of motor and physical fitness tests.

Past medical records will be consulted to determine Keith's state of health. If more than a year has elapsed since his last physical examination, it will be appropriate to ask his parents to have Keith reexamined by a physician before school testing begins. Therapists might be also called upon to evaluate Keith. This is usually not necessary for children with no irregularities, but Keith's combination of spastic cerebral palsy and seizures might give rise to concerns; in particular, if Keith has complications such as abnormal tonic neck reflexes or muscle contractures, it is important to know to what extent they will interfere with normal motor development.

Physical education activities for individuals with cerebral palsy are too often therapy based. Their capacity for developmental exercise and learning physical and motor skills among people with cerebral palsy has been underestimated. The entire physical education experience should be planned to serve the developmental, rehabilitation, recreational, and vocational needs of these youngsters.

Cerebral palsy is also known as Little's Disease, after the London orthopedist William Little (1810–1894). Winthrop M. Phelps, M.D., originally coined the term *cerebral palsy* in the early 1900s. He identified *cerebral* as a causative lesion located in the brain, and indicated *palsy* to be the consequence—loss or impairment of motor functioning.

Approximately 750,000 people in the United States (16 out of every 5000) have some degree of cerebral palsy. One third of these are under 21 years of age. Cerebral palsy is the most frequently occurring physical disability among school-age children. It is estimated that 10,000 babies are born each year with this disorder, and another 2000 acquire it in their preschool years.

A DEFINITION

Cerebral palsy (CP) has been defined as follows: "Cerebral palsy is a clinical picture, usually manifesting itself in childhood, with dysfunction of the brain in which one of the major components is motor disturbance." In addition, cerebral palsy is described as "a group of conditions usually originating in childhood, characterized by paralysis, weakness, lack of coordination, and any other aberration of motor function caused by pathology of motor control centers of the brain. In addition to such motor dysfunction, cerebral palsy may include learning difficulties, psychological problems, sensory defects, convulsions and behavioral disorders of organic origin."

Cerebral palsy is classified by type, topography, and severity.

MENTAL RETARDATION

Because the etiology of cerebral palsy is destruction of brain cells, there is a high incidence of mental retardation. An estimated 60 to 70% of persons diagnosed as having cerebral palsy also possess some degree of mental retardation (Eichstaedt and Lavay, 1992). This, too, will have a negative effect on the child's motor learning ability.

MOTOR DEFICITS

According to Bobath (1966), cerebral palsy is manifested by abnormal tonus (muscle stiffness), abnormal patterns of posture, and abnormal patterns of movement.

Infants who are severely involved are usually diagnosed at birth; more mildly involved children are identified during the early months of life as developmental lags become apparent. Degree of involvement may vary from mild (very little functional incapacity or obvious disability) to severe (little or no functional ability). Brain damage will not worsen, but nothing can be done to restore those brain cells already destroyed. The child will have permanent lesions and will be relegated to a life involving distinct movement problems. Although the disorder is not progressive, physical growth, compounded by paralysis and atrophy, may contribute to development of further deformities.

Bobath and Bobath (1967), experts on the treatment of cerebral palsy, reinforce the importance of suppressing abnormal posture and movement behaviors and enhancing normal patterns. The corrective program requires early intervention, and any delay can cause irreversible structural damage to muscles and joints.

Laskas, Mullen, Nelson, and Willson-Broyles (1985) reinforce the Bobath neurodevelopmental treatment approach when they identify two fundamental premises: (1) motor development follows a sequential order in children both with and without disabilities, and (2) through controlled sensorimotor experiences, normal patterns of motor behavior can be elicited in the child with a damaged central nervous system (CNS).

Individuals with CP must expend extreme energy to make muscles obey their commands. As a result, they may become lethargic and unmotivated when attempting new movement experiences. They require exciting and stimulating motor activities that provide independence through physical education. Early and appropriate psychomotor programs are important, because proper developmental physical education activities can direct the child with cerebral palsy toward a more successful life-style.

SEIZURES

The brain injury that causes cerebral palsy also causes seizures in 35 to 45% of all affected youngsters. Some studies (Healy, 1990) report that 60% of all children with cerebral palsy have seizures. Scarring on the cerebral cortex is the major cause of seizure activity. Two classifications and four types of seizures are commonly found in children who experience seizures. *Generalized*: absence (petit mal), and tonic-clonic (grand mal), atonic (akinetic, drop); *Partial*: complex-partial (psychomotor).

ETIOLOGY

Cerebral palsy is directly related to **brain cell destruction.** The brain controls motor skills by initiating, coordinating, and integrating movement activities of increasing complexity. To do this, the brain must achieve an exacting and delicate balance between many interacting and opposing forces. In cerebral palsy, the damaged brain cannot achieve this balance correctly. Owing to imperfect coordination, the child has an improper balance between voluntary and involuntary controls, stimulating and suppressing influences, and flexion and extension movements.

The cause of cerebral palsy is linked to the time when the brain destruction occurred. These time periods are divided into two major categories with subdivisions: (1) congenital (prenatal and natal, including 2 weeks of neonatal), and (2) acquired (postnatal).

Certain groups of infants, including those with excessive intracranial bleeding, prolonged birth anoxia, very low birth weight, and abnormal neurological symptoms (low APGAR scores) are possible candidates for cerebral palsy (Adams & McCubbin, 1991).

PRENATAL

A major cause of brain damage during the prenatal period is insufficient oxygen reaching the fetus. This occurrence is known as **anoxia** or **hypoxia.** Restriction of oxygen to the mother, as in carbon monoxide poisoning, dense smoke inhalation, or drowning, will affect the fetus directly. The oxygen supply to the fetus is also reduced in cases of maternal anemia, umbilical cord twisting or knotting, or premature separation of the placenta from the uterine wall.

Certain viruses have been identified as the cause of cerebral palsy because they invade the placenta and infect the fetus. An example is the **rubella virus.** The rubella epidemic of 1964–1965 caused death or serious neurological consequences to approximately 50,000 unborn children. Rubella, known as German or three-day measles, has mild symptoms in children beginning with low-grade fever, a rash on the face that spreads over the body, and swelling of the lymph glands. It usually lasts 1 to 3 days with no apparent aftereffects. If, however, a pregnant woman develops rubella within the first 3 months of pregnancy, when the fetal brain is developing, the fetus is threatened. Possible results are miscarriage, premature birth, stillbirth, or birth of a child with a disorder such as cerebral palsy.

Rubeola (regular measles) should not be confused with rubella. Vaccination against rubeola does not provide protection against rubella, and all children should be inoculated against both types of measles. Vaccination reduces the probability of the child's catching the disease at school and exposing the mother.

Cytomegalovirus and **toxoplasmosis** are two major infections that also cause fetal damage when they strike pregnant women. In the United States alone, cytomegalovirus infections damage as many as 2,600 fetuses annually (Alford, 1988). Toxoplasmosis is found in approximately 1 or 2 per thousand live births. Congenital defects resulting from these prenatal diseases include hydrocephalus, microcephaly, and calcifications in the brain. The complications include cerebral palsy, mental retardation, seizures, and diseases of the retina with resultant blindness (Blackman, 1990b).

Another prenatal cause of cerebral palsy is **Rh hemolytic disease** or **erythroblastosis fetalis.** This condition, commonly called the **Rh factor** and usually identified as blood incompatibility between parents, afflicts approximately 2000 babies born in the United States each year. Half of these infants survive but have permanent brain damage. This accounts for about one tenth of all cerebral palsy cases.

The major concern of the United Cerebral Palsy Association is preventing **premature births,** which are associated with brain damage, particularly when the birth weight is 1500 g (3 lb 5 oz) or less.

Sternfeld and Berenberg (1981) believe that the widespread use of newborn intensive care units has saved the life of many prematurely born babies and has helped preserve intact the central nervous system of babies who weigh above 1500 g at birth. New studies conducted during pregnancy and the newborn period are progressing rapidly. For example, ultrasound studies performed during pregnancy now monitor the fetal position. Physicians can tell if the fetus is at risk if, for example, the placenta is in a dangerous position. Caesarian section can then be performed properly without damage to the baby, which might otherwise have occurred. In certain instances, brain surgery can now be done in utero. For example, if the baby is developing hydrocephalus, excess fluid can be drained off before the infant is born.

NATAL (PERINATAL)

This period begins when the mother identifies labor pains, continues through delivery, and terminates when the baby is 2 weeks old. Complications that arise during this time are usually the result of anoxia, prolonged labor, improper use of forceps, small birth canal, breech delivery, or other abnormal birth position. Poor surgical and delivery techniques that contributed to this type of problem in the past have been all but eliminated today.

The United Cerebral Palsy Association warns physicians (particularly obstetricians) that infants born under the following conditions should be closely monitored: (1) abnormal pregnancy (bleeding, infection, toxemia), (2) prematurity (less than 2000 g birth weight or less than 36-week gestation period), (3) difficult labor and abnormal infant pulse and respiration, (4) abnormal respiration and cyanosis occurring after the first 24 hours, (5) seizures, including flexion spasms, developing in the neonatal period, (6) poor feeding and sucking, or more than 15 percent weight loss in the first 10 days of life, (7) excessive sleeping during the neonatal period, and (8) neonatal jaundice for any reason (United Cerebral Palsy Association, n.d., pp. 1–2).

POSTNATAL

The following causative factors may develop after birth: severe blows to the skull, meningitis, encephalitis, ingestion of arsenic or lead, carbon monoxide poisoning, or any other anoxia. Any destroyed brain cells can lead to cerebral palsy.

Blackman (1990a) identifies the most common cause of postnatal brain injury as **child abuse.** In regard to infants and children he states that "physical abuse is the most common type followed by emotional and sexual abuse" (p. 66). Blackman also talks of the "shaken baby syndrome" and believes that over 95 percent of serious head injuries during the first year of life are the result of physical abuse. Violent, whiplash-type shaking followed by dropping or throwing the infant onto a hard surface result in serious bleeding in the brain. The United Cerebral Palsy Association estimates that more than 1,500 cases of cerebral palsy are caused by child abuse each year.

SEVERITY CLASSIFICATION

The severity of neuromotor involvement of individuals with cerebral palsy can be classified according to observable characteristics. *Mild* cases include persons who need no particular care and are probably assigned to traditional physical education classes. They walk adequately and use their arms, although not as skillfully as noninvolved students. They may have difficulty speaking, but they can be understood. *Moderately* involved individuals usually have difficulty with speech and locomotion. Although they usually are able to attend traditional schools, many may need help in everyday living skills. Some will use canes or braces to help ambulation. Others often use wheelchairs as their means of locomotion, and they can maneuver by themselves. *Severley* involved students will always use a wheelchair that is pushed by others or that is motor driven. Most individuals cannot hold or release objects with ease. Speech will be difficult to understand.

TOPOGRAPHIC CLASSIFICATION

Clinical classifications of cerebral palsy are made by reference to involved body parts. *Monoplegia* involves one limb (rare). *Paraplegia* involves the legs only and is usually associated with spasticity. *Hemiplegia* includes the one half of the body involving the arm and leg on the same side and, again, usually includes being spastic. *Triplegia* involves three extremities, usually the legs and one arm. *Quadriplegia* involves all four extremities. Individuals may be spastic, rigid, or athetoid.

PHYSIOLOGICAL CLASSIFICATION

The type of cerebral palsy is determined by observing clinically the child's reflex patterns. Although different forms are associated with damage to a particular area of the brain, this is less important than the clinical observations of physicians, physical educators, and therapists.

SPASTIC

This is the most common type of cerebral palsy, including 50 to 60% of all cases (Healy, 1990). Semmler (1990) states the following:

> The most common type of cerebral palsy seen in birth-to-3-years-old population is spastic CP. Infants with spastic CP are initially hypotonic. At about 8 to 12 months of age spasticity may become apparent, as characterized by increased stretch reflexes, resistance to passive movement with clasp-knife phenomenon, ankle clonus, and increased deep tendon reflexes. (p. 238)

Muscle movements are explosive, jerky, and poorly coordinated. A spastic muscle (hypertonic) is stiff and movements are awkward. **Spasticity** tends to affect flexor, adductor, and internal rotator muscles of the body. The classic picture of an individual with spastic cerebral palsy includes plantar flexion of the feet, which makes the child walk on the toes, flexion of the knees, and flexion of the hips. Flexor muscles in the upper limbs are also spastic and cause finger, wrist, and elbow flexion. The shoulder is usually adducted and internally rotated (Figure 16.1).

Spasticity is characterized by presence of an **increased stretch reflex,** the principal diagnostic sign. The stretch reflex is an increased tendency of the muscle to contract when stretched rapidly; the reflex does not occur when the muscle is stretched slowly. Harris (1978a) states that affected muscles display elevated tone because their stretch receptors have increased sensitivity. When force is applied to stretch the spastic muscle, there is increased resistance to movement, but at a certain point, a rapid decrease in resistance occurs. This is similar to the action of a pocket knife upon opening: there is tension on the blade, but at a certain point, it springs open. Children with

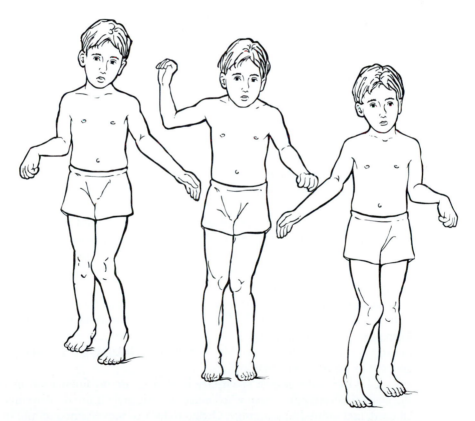

FIGURE 16.1   Typical gait of child with cerebral palsy, spastic diplegia, or paraplegia. Thighs are together (adducted), turned in (internally rotated), and flexed, plus flexion of the knees and tiptoeing (equinus of the feet).

spastic cerebral palsy can hold a limb in either extreme extension or extreme flexion, but they cannot regulate muscle contraction sufficiently to control movements between these extremes.

Another clinical sign is an exaggeration of the deep tendon reflexes (patellar tendon knee jerk) or ankle clonus, which is characterized by a jerking reaction caused by sudden and forceful flexion, or a bending of the foot back toward the leg.

The least restricting form of cerebral palsy is **mild spasticity.** Affected children have no apparent movement difficulties until they begin to ambulate or to try to use extremities in refined tasks. They are usually able to walk, and should be thoroughly tested to determine general motor ability and physical fitness. Many can participate in regular physical education activities.

Children with **moderate spasticity** have differing degrees of muscle tone, ranging from normal to hypertonic. Bigge (1988) points out that children with spastic CP move with less difficulty if activities are done slowly and easily. Furthermore, youngsters have more purposeful movements if they are not overstimulated, overworked, or emotionally stressed. When these children are excited or are trying hard to execute a given task (e.g., hitting a badminton birdie), the high-tone muscles become even more tense. The attempt to move quickly induces an **extensor spasm,** which they cannot control. The muscles that extend or straighten the arms, legs, and body suddenly become extremely tight, throwing the head back, straightening the arms and legs, and stiffening the body. An extensor spasm can literally push the child off a chair (Kieran, Corner, von Hippel, & Jones, 1981).

The child's range of motion is also impaired. The more involved youngsters perform motor skills in a primitive fashion, with little selectivity or refinement. Deformities, such as contractures, can occur. A **contracture** develops when an individual does not, or cannot, voluntarily use certain muscles and joints. The muscles shorten and pull continually until the joint becomes totally closed, often frozen in an immovable position.

The physiological nature of contracture is explained by the fact that muscle tissue will adapt in length to habitually shortened positions over time. Because muscles have the ability to shorten by active contraction, they eventually will adapt to the shortest length if proper stretching exercises do not maintain an adequate range of motion (Cherry, 1980).

Prolonged, gentle manual stretching (elongation) or positional stretching will reduce contractures effectively. Complete range of motion exercises should be performed at the beginning and end of each physical education period. If, after several months of exercise, no measurable change in the joint angle appears, parents should consult an orthopedic surgeon.

Children with **severe spasticity** have little or no fluctuation in muscle tone. Purposeful movement, except when aided, is extremely limited. Movements are small, labored, and limited to midrange. Owing to lack to movement and minimal change of position, these youngsters are prime candidates for contracture deformities. Initiation of voluntary movements is minimal and abnormal reflexes occur frequently.

If the condition has been present for many years, the child with spastic CP is likely to perceive the condition quite differently from the way nondisabled children see themselves. Children with spasticity have no other frame of reference. Consequently, they experience the midrange as a fleeting transitional state; they cannot be expected to exert precise control over movement. The adapted physical educator must provide opportunities for stretching, strengthening, and controlled movement activities for these children.

Spastic hemiplegia is the most common type of cerebral palsy. The main abnormality is in adduction of the hip joint causing flexion on the affected side. The calf muscles are tight and the dorsiflexors are weak, which gives the common appearance of the toe-walker with heel raised. For better control (i.e., dorsiflexion and eversion of the foot), a short leg brace is worn. The upper extremity is also involved; the elbow is flexed, the forearm is internally rotated, and the wrist and fingers are flexed.

The adapted physical education teacher can evaluate the general degree of involvement of a child with spastic hemiplegia by asking this question: "Is the affected hand used for holding, helping, transferring, playing, assisting the dominant hand, or is it completely ignored?"

Teaching Suggestions for a Child with Spastic Cerebral Palsy

1. To relax clenched fists, bend the student's hand down at the wrist.
2. To counteract simultaneous flexion of both legs (when child is creeping), hold back the foot of one leg each time the opposite leg is moved forward.
3. To prevent contractures, avoid activities that stress flexion; encourage the child to change positions frequently.
4. To improve arm extension of the hemiplegic child, hold the affected hand when playing or walking. The thumb will thus be held properly with the arm extended and swung in rhythm.

DYSKINESIA

This type of cerebral palsy includes approximately 20% of all cases of cerebral palsy and is caused by damage to the basal ganglia area, the brain's motor switchboard (Healy, 1990). Dyskinesia consists of three subtypes and was once grouped as a single entity called *athetosis*. **Dyskinesia** is defined as an impairment of the power of voluntary movement, resulting in unwanted, involuntary, fragmentary, or incomplete movements. The first of the subgroups is *athetosis* and includes slow writhing movements, particularly of the wrist and fingers. For instance, the hand may twist repeatedly to one side or the other, then backward, then forward. These children are constantly moving, without selectivity of movement, and they lack control in the midranges. Contractures are not common because muscle tone is in a state of fluctuation. Their gait is often lurching or stumbling. Protective and equilibrium reactions are present, but they are exaggerated and unpredictable.

Speech may be difficult, and the facial expression may be constant grimacing. Communication boards (a board, attached to the wheelchair, with letters, words, and symbols to which the child can point) are commonly used. Newer communication devices are flooding the market today and the computer world has revolutionized communication with more compact units that speak and print.

If the movements are accompanied by more abrupt and jerky movements the person is experiencing *choreoathetosis*. When severe, any activity creates uncontrollable spasms that prevent useful limb function. Individuals will experience involuntary movements that appear to bend the extremity in and then out. These children often seem to make flying motions with the arms and legs when they attempt to move quickly. The third form of dyskinesia is *dystonia* and is characterized by slow, rhythmic movements involving an extremity or the entire body. The unwanted movements in all three subgroups become more prominent when individuals experience high emotional stress or when attempting to "hurry" voluntary movement.

Positioning Suggestions for the Child with Dyskinesia

1. To reduce unsteady and uncoordinated movements, support the child's body to allow concentration on one or two body parts (hand, head, or arm).

2. To reduce unsteady and uncoordinated arm and hand movements, place a hand on the student's shoulder to support or stabilize.

3. To increase movement independence, help the child devise ways to inhibit unnecessary movements (e.g., hold one flailing arm with the other while walking to avoid being thrown off balance by uncoordinated arm movements).

ATAXIA

The individual with **ataxia** exhibits an inability to maintain normal balance compounded by lack of coordination. Depending on degree of involvement, many functions that require postural stability are affected. Activities that require fine hand movements are performed poorly. Walking is characterized by frequent lurches and lunges. These problems are all directly related to damage of the cerebellum, the cause of ataxia.

The cerebellum collects information from moving body parts and determines how momentum affects the movements. Even before each part reaches its destination, the cerebellum sends feedback signals to begin appropriate reversal contractions of opposing muscles to slow and stop movement. This causes the hand, for example, to be brought to rest with ease and accuracy. All movements are essentially pendular; when an arm is moved, momentum begins and must be overcome before arm movement can be stopped. Because of momentum, all pendular movements tend to overshoot. The cerebellum normally prevents this, but in persons with a damaged cerebellum, conscious control does not initiate the proper motor signals to appropriate muscles. The arm thus overshoots and oscillates back and forth several times before it reaches it mark. Guyton (1979) explains this phenomenon: "If a person who has lost his cerebellum tries to run, his feet will overshoot the necessary points on the ground for maintenance of equilibrium and he will fall. Even when walking, his gait will be very severely affected, for placement of the feet can never be precise; he falls first to one side, and then overcorrects to the other side, and must correct again and again, giving him a broken gait" (p. 322).

Ataxia also affects eye-hand coordination, which may be so severely impaired that the child finds it extremely difficult to bounce a ball, strike a badminton birdie, or catch a football. Precise movements are almost impossible owing to excessive overshooting of the arm movement.

MIXED

Due to extensive brain damage, a large percentage (approximately 30%) of children with CP will have a combination of characteristics of two or more classifications. For example, it is common to find an individual who exhibits movements of both spasticity and some form of dyskinesia. Also, it is possible for a person to have ataxic movements along with any of the other types. Generally, one type predominates and makes accurate diagnosis difficult. This problem often results in errors in classification, which could cause uncertainty when writing rehabilitation and activity programs.

INITIAL PHYSICAL EDUCATION PROGRAM CONSIDERATIONS

The aim of physical education for children with cerebral palsy is to improve posture and locomotor function. After a thorough evaluation, level of posture and locomotion development and deficiencies or delays that interfere with further development should be identified.

The Information and Research Utilization Center (1976) identifies the following treatment aims for individuals with cerebral palsy: "(1) improve function by conservative [nonsurgical rehabilitation] as well as active surgical means, (2) prevent deformity, (3) if deformity develops, correct or relieve it, and (4) to achieve the maximum degree of habilation or rehabilitation possible" (p. 146). Habilitation involves the treatment of neuromuscular symptoms, stretching contractures, establishing voluntary control, assessing developmental level and personality factors, and treating other accompanying conditions such as visual, speech, and hearing impairments and seizures.

Too often physical educators have not been involved in planning the motor development program of students with cerebral palsy. Generally, improvement in static control of posture and dynamic control of movement can be obtained by relaxing tight muscles and strengthening weak muscles, thus correcting muscle imbalance. The adapted physical education teacher plays a key role in implementing this type of corrective program.

Perceptual-motor training should also be included. Such training is appropriate for students who are ambulatory or use wheelchairs. Cratty (1989) identifies six major components involved in the learning of perceptual motor skills: (1) impulse control, (2) body image, (3) perceptual-motor competencies, (4) seriation, (5) pattern recognition, and (6) decision making and problem solving. The physical educator plays a major role in the first three. **Impulse control** encompasses relaxation training, controlling movements, and prolonging tasks. **Body image training** includes learning body parts, body planes, and position in space. **Perceptual-motor competencies** include learning balance, agility, locomotor skills, eye-hand coordination skills, and ball throwing, striking, and catching. These perceptual-motor skills often develop very slowly in children with cerebral palsy.

To teach the desired skills, the instructor must start at the child's level of motor development rather than at chronological age development level. The instructor must use teaching skills that enhance the child's learning. For example, physical educators should present tasks in sequential steps that are achievable, using repetition and concrete examples with oral instructions.

Although the ultimate goal is maximum function and independence, short-term goals must coincide with present developmental levels. The child with CP will show only small gains, so the instructor must not set goals too high. Unachievable goals produce only frustration and nonparticipation. Each session must contain activities that allow the child to experience some success.

Development and maturation of the child with cerebral palsy must not be judged in reference to the developmental level of a same-age peer without a disability. The whole child must be considered, and physical components as well as emotional, social, and intellectual aspects of the curriculum must be evaluated. A multidisciplinary approach is important for children with CP because they usually possess additional disabling conditions. The teaching techniques used for dealing with children who are nondisabled or mildly retarded do not always apply. Frequently, the child with cerebral palsy is functioning at a motor developmental level far below the level of walking or running.

Assisting the youngster with cerebral palsy requires a true multidisciplinary approach. The therapist can provide expertise in assessment and rehabilitation of school-age children functioning at the level of able-bodied youngsters who are less than 18 months old. The adapted physical educator must work closely with the therapist during initial assessment and when planning each child's motor program. The related services provided by the therapist are an important part of most cerebral palsy programs and greatly enhance the physical educator's effectiveness.

An individualized program can be developed after a complete assessment of malfunction, which includes manual muscle tests, evaluation of range of motion, status of bones and joints, and evaluation of coordination. The initial assessment and follow-up require careful study by professionally trained individuals.

Owing to the nature of the disability, the child's ability to learn through spontaneous interaction with her physical environment is limited. Objects, symbols, and sensory stimulation must therefore be provided for movement. Specifically, the child must learn basic motor skills, beginning with rolling, crawling, creeping, kneeling, sitting, standing, and walking. The adapted physical educator must teach the child how to move with braces, crutches, or a walker; how to sit while playing on the floor; how to increase limb and body mobility; how to compensate for involuntary muscle action; how to adjust for unresponsive muscles; and how to strengthen other muscles. Developing comprehensive opportunities for the child with cerebral palsy is challenging work for the physical educator.

ASSESSMENT

The initial assessment goal is to determine the level and degree of function already acquired by the nervous system so progress can begin from that point. Because different skills emerge as the child grows, various testing tools are needed for each age group.

Motor skill assessment of the child with cerebral palsy is often the same as assessment used for nondisabled children to age 6 years. The physical educator should be involved in assessment of skills that require muscle tone, strength, and coordination to perform voluntary movement (i.e., rolling over, sitting, walking, running, hopping, and jumping). Defects, as evidenced by failure to perform these tasks at an appropriate age, are specific indicators of the individual's performance level. Performance of these tasks should be acquired progressively during the formative years; inability to perform a task adequately may be normal at age 6 but inappropriate at age 9. Developmental norms for a given task must be understood to assess their significance. An interesting example is cited by Johnston and Magrab (1976):

> A newborn baby responds to stimulus, such as a rattle, by a total body response, that is, flailing of arms and legs and general total body excitement. As the nervous system matures during the next four months, that response is limited and directed to the arms, which reach out in an attempt to grasp the object. This process of inhibition progresses over the years so that by the age of six years the child can do fine finger manipulations with only a minimum amount of overflow movement perceived in the resting hand. This overflow movement is usually entirely lost by age 9 or 10 years. Therefore, at the age of six, there will normally be overflow activity that cannot be inhibited voluntarily, whereas, at the age of nine years, the presence of uninhibited overflow activity is considered abnormal and a sign of possible brain immaturity or dysfunction. (p. 139)

Specific assessment is necessary to determine the degree of maturation and organization of the brain in terms of measurable motor skill performance. A few functional irregularities are not necessarily evidence of significant brain damage. For example, a clumsy child will exhibit distinct motor difficulties, but in most of these children, no brain damage is present.

The purpose of appropriate assessment tools is to determine gross psychomotor abnormalities, which serve (1) to identify existing levels of motor performance, (2) to determine appropriate placement in a least restrictive environment, and (3) to obtain pertinent information for multidisciplinary staffing.

PRIMARY REFLEXES

Basic infantile reflexes are found in newborn children and are necessary for early survival. These reflexes are the source of such necessary functions as breathing, sneezing, coughing, and digesting. Other reflexes play an extremely important role in the development and acquisition of postural skills and voluntary movements. Pediatricians and therapists routinely assess these reflexes to determine the present level of neurological function and the existing level of motor development. Winnick and Short (1985) describe the importance of this information: "If reflexes, when elicited, are uneven in strength, too weak or too strong, or inappropriate at a particular age, neurological dysfunction may be suspected. Various reflexive behaviors are quite predictable and are expected to appear at particular ages and to be inhibited, disappear, or be replaced by higher order reflexes at later ages. Failure of certain reflexes to disappear, be inhibited, or be replaced may inhibit the development of voluntary movement" (p. 50). For example, if children still possess a positive tonic neck reflex at the age when they should be creeping on all fours, the abnormal tonic neck reflex will cause unwanted flexion of the arms or legs and will inhibit creeping.

Zemke (1985) explains that caution must be used when attempting to determine which children still exhibit a primary reflex. She has found that 3- to 5-year-old *nondisabled* children still possess mild levels of asymmetrical tonic neck reflex. This would indicate that the assessment of basic primary reflexes should be done only by highly trained professionals.

Hoskins and Squires (1973) describe 16 developmental reflexes.

1. **Flexor withdrawal**—supine; quick tactile stimulus to the plantar surface of the foot elicits abrupt, uncontrolled flexion of the total lower limb.

2. **Extensor thrust**—supine; child with one leg flexed, opposite leg extended; light pressure applied to ball of flexed foot elicits total, uncontrolled extension of the flexed leg.

3. **Crossed extension**—supine; child with one leg flexed, opposite leg extended; when extended leg is passively flexed, opposite leg extends with adduction, internal rotation of the hip.

4. **Asymmetrical tonic neck reflex**—supine; child actively or passively turns head approximately 90 degrees to one side to elicit extension of limbs on nose side and flexion of limbs on skull side.

5. **Symmetrical tonic neck reflex**—prone; flexion of head (chin to chest) causes flexion of upper extremities, extension of lower extremities. Extension of head causes extension of upper extremities, flexion of lower extremities.

6. **Tonic labyrinthine**—supine; child suspended. The position of face upwards elicits limb extension, or extensor tone in limbs. **Tonic labyrinthine**—prone; child suspended. The position of face downward elicits limb flexion, or predominant flexor tone.

7. **Moro reflex**—supine; several stimuli elicit same response; abrupt loud noise near child's head, sudden movement of supporting surface, or dropping child backwards from semisitting position results in sudden opening (extension and abduction) of upper and lower extremities, with opening of hands, followed by flexion to the midline.

8. **Neck righting**—supine, when head is passively turned and held, thorax should follow. If not, reflex is not present.

9. **Labyrinthine on head**—supine, in suspension, when head is slightly lowered, head and trunk should rise to vertical position.

10. **Plantar grasp**—supine; pressure on sole of foot at base of toes causes flexion of toes.

11. **Positive supporting reaction**—upright; when child is bounced on feet, extension of both lower limbs with plantar flexion of feet occurs.

12. **Placing reaction**—upright; when dorsum of foot brushes table, foot is lifted and placed on table top.

13. **Primitive stepping**—upright; with some weight-bearing on soles of feet, when child leans forward, one foot will step forward, followed by other foot.

14. **Body righting on body**—supine; when child is passively rotated at shoulder or hip, normal, if segmental, rotation of shoulders, trunk, pelvis follows.

15. **Landau**—prone; when child is suspended by chest, head actively or passively dorsiflexes. Extension of trunk and lower extremities is elicited, or ventro-flexion of head elicits flexion of spine and lower extremities.

16. **Upper extremity protective extensor thrust**—upright. When body and head move suddenly toward floor, immediate extension of upper extremities with abduction and extension of fingers to protect head should occur. (pp. 119–120)

The functions to be tested can be separated into three distinct categories: general, prewalking, and walking.

GENERAL ASSESSMENT

Traditional range-of-motion, muscle tone, and muscle strength tests should be included in each student's full evaluation. Body alignment also should be considered, because physical educators are often the first to notice problems such as scoliosis, lordosis, or kyphosis, and leg length differences. Abnormal body alignment should be determined so physical educators can recommend specialized positioning in the wheelchair, assistive standing devices, or adaptations for lying down in proper posture.

Assessment of each child should include the following:

1. Leg length evaluation from the anterior border of the superior iliac crest to the inferior border of the internal malleolus, and from the top of the greater trochanter to the lower border of the lateral malleolus. X-rays (by the physician) that show leg length may be of help.
2. Contractive evaluation, especially of the ankles, knees, and hips.
3. Examination for scoliosis or lordosis.
4. Observation for obvious hearing or vision deficits.
5. Presence of abnormal amount of motor function or activity (hyperactivity and hyperkinesia).
6. Sensory impairment including impaired responses to pain, temperature, and vibration. The inability to recognize objects by touching or feeling them (asterognosis) may be present.

Assessments are the responsibility of the adapted physical educator. Should any of the previous evaluations be difficult or not within the teacher's capability, then direct assistance should be sought from a therapist.

PREWALKING ASSESSMENT

This assessment should be repeated with the student in several positions (supine, prone, sitting on floor, kneeling, and standing). Head control also should be evaluated in all positions, and hip mobility should be evaluated in the sitting position. The student's ability to change position should be noted, and attention should be given to the child's technique for each transition and the degree of difficulty experienced.

The **supine** or **back-lying position** should begin with a warm-up consisting of slow, random movements of the arms and legs. This position minimizes the effect of gravity against which the child with cerebral palsy constantly struggles to maintain postural stability and dynamic balance. Assessment in this position is critical because the fundamental movement problems that interfere with more complex skills can be identified. Particular attention should be paid to the resting position of body parts (when there is no deliberate attempt to move the part), including hips, knees, ankles, elbows, wrists, thumbs, and fingers. The degree of muscle tone needed to maintain these resting positions is determined by moving or attempting to move each joint toward and away from the neutral position. The degree of movement achieved in each direction, the rate at which these movements are made, and the direction against which the greatest resistance is encountered should be noted. The body sides should be compared for imbalance in neuromuscular abnormalities. Note whether the joint positions and distribution of muscle tone are maintained or modified when positions are changed.

Finally, check the child's ability to produce voluntary joint movement. This should be done at points throughout the obtainable range of motion, particularly the extremes. If the child can produce voluntary joint movement, apply slight resistance to determine the strength behind the movement.

Have the student roll over into the **prone** or **front-lying position.** Note arm strength and skills used to roll over. If the child reaches the prone position, note whether there is sufficient neck strength to lift the head off the mat and sufficient control to keep it centered. If unable to lift the head, note whether assistance is required to turn the head to one side so the child can breathe freely.

Have the child assume the **hands and knees position** by using the arms to push up until the shoulders and head are supported by resting on the elbows. If the student is unable to attain this position, place his arms in the proper position and have the child stay in this position. If the student can prop his body weight on the elbows, then have him execute a push-up by extending the elbows. If able to do this, have the student maintain support on the hands and bring the knees up and forward into a kneeling or hands and knees position. If unable to accomplish this, move the student's legs into place. Support the shoulders if necessary, and have the child maintain this position. While the student is in the kneeling position, test for head control by asking him to move his head up and down and from side to side voluntarily.

Have the child reach the **sitting position on the floor** by lowering him into the prone position, then ask the child to roll over into the supine position. (The child's capability determines the amount of assistance required.) From there, place the child in the sitting position by pulling him up by his arms. The child may not tolerate sitting with knees extended because of limited hip flexion. To place the child in a sitting position requires the following technique: While the child is in supine position, bend legs and knees into full flexion position with knees held against chest. When this position has been maintained for 1 min, rock the child forward slowly into an upright position (lift from back of child under shoulders while keeping his knees pressed against the chest). When upright position is reached, the student will be seated with knees flexed, ankles in neutral position, and soles flat on the floor. If the child can tolerate this position, note degree of spine curvature, shoulder protraction, and hip flexion. Assess head control in this position by requesting the child to move his head voluntarily in all directions. Release the child cautiously to determine if he is able to maintain position independently.

If the student is able to tolerate this initial sitting position without marked kyphosis and shoulder protraction, attempt gradually to extend the knees. Determine how far the knees can be extended without losing the sitting position. If the child cannot tolerate the normal sitting position, attempt to teach side-sitting (i.e., resting on one hip and leg with the corresponding arm supporting the upper body). Alternate sides frequently to avoid developing one-sided bias to posture.

The **standing position** is accomplished by lowering the child into supine from sitting and asking the child to roll into prone, and then to rise to the hands and knees position again. If successful, the child should attempt rising to the standing position. The child can grasp a chair to pull up against or to assist with balance. If able to stand by using a chair for assistance, attempt to teach the child to reach the standing position from the hands and knees, without a chair, by raising first one knee and then pushing on the raised knee with one hand and on the floor with the other. If the child is unable to stand alone, then lift and support at shoulders or waist or both to assist with weight-bearing and balance. The flexion-extension positions of the ankle, knee, and hip joints, and any tendency toward increased adductor tone and inward rotation of the femur, should be noted.

Observe whether or not spontaneous arm movements occur to maintain balance. To assess head control while standing, ask the student to move the head voluntarily in all directions (Harris, 1978a).

Figure 16.2 is a motor control assessment chart that uses the basic positions of supine, prone, sitting, kneeling, squatting, and standing.

A complete motor assessment tool, which evaluates motor patterns, was developed by Banham (1978, pp. 112–116) for children with cerebral palsy. Figure 16.3 shows a modified version. Items 1 through 34 can be used for prewalking assessment.

WALKING AND LOCOMOTOR ASSESSMENT

Walking and locomotor assessment should be conducted when the child can stand with reasonable ease. If children are unable to balance but have sufficient lower extremity extensor tone to support body weight, then assist them to walk. During independent or assisted ambulation, observe head control, arm position and movements, trunk stability, pelvic movements, knee and ankle joint positions during swing and stance phases, toe-in or toe-out, tendency to adduct or scissor, and overall quality of gait.

The modified version of Banham's functional motor scale (1978) lists 15 items (see Figure 16.3, items 35–50) that are appropriate for identifying developmental walking levels.

Hoskins and Squires (1973, p. 120) have developed an assessment tool, the *Test for Gross Motor and Reflex Development*, that is validated for use with children with cerebral palsy. The test items shown in Table 16.1 are directly related to the developmental progression for walking.

NAME _____

BIRTH DATE _____ DIAGNOSIS _____

EXAMINER: _____

KEY: 0—Cannot be placed in test posture.
1—Can be placed in test posture but cannot hold.
2—Can hold test posture momentarily after being placed.
3—Can assume an approx. test posture unaided, in any manner.
4—Can assume and sustain test posture in a near normal manner. (Note any abnormal detail)
5—Normal

Test Postures & Movements	NAME:		NAME:		NAME:	
	Date	Remarks	Date	Remarks	Date	Remarks
SUPINE						
1. Hips and knees fully flexed, arms crossed, palms on shoulders						
2. Hips and knees fully flexed a. Extend right leg b. Extend left leg	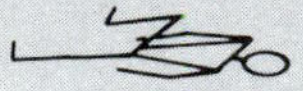 R. L.		R. L.		R. L.	
3. Head raised 						
PRONE						
4. Arms extended beside head Raise head in midposition						

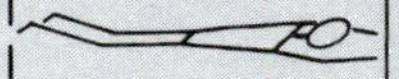

FIGURE 16.2 Cerebral palsy basic motor control assessment chart. (Adapted from materials and test of Karel and Berta Bobath.)

451

5. Arms extended beside body, palms down 						
6. a. Flex right knee, hips extended b. Flex left knee, hips extended	 R. L.		R. L.		R. L.	
7. Trunk supported on forearms, upper trunk extended, face vertical 						
8. Trunk supported on hands with elbows and hips extended 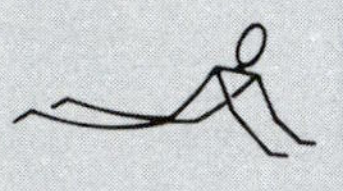						
SITTING ERECT 9. Soles of feet together, hips flexed and externally rotated to at least 45° 						
10. Knees extended and legs abducted, hips 90-100° 						

FIGURE 16.2   (continued)

452

FIGURE 17.5 *continued*

Test Postures & Movements	Date	Remarks	Date	Remarks	Date	Remarks

11. Legs hanging over edge of table
  a. Extend right knee
  b. Extend left knee
	R.
	L.
			R.
			L.
					R.
					L.	

KNEELING
12. Back and neck straight (not hyperextended)
  a. Weight on knees
  b. Weight on hands
	A.
	B.
			A.
			B.
					A.
					B.	

13. Side sitting, upper trunk erect, arms relaxed
  a. On right hip
  b. On left hip
	R.
	L.
			R.
			L.
					R.
					L.	

14. Kneeling upright, hips extended, head in midposition, arms at sides						
15. a. Half kneeling, weight on right knee b. Half kneeling, weight on left knee	R. L.		R. L.		R. L.	
SQUATTING 16. Heels down, toes not clawed, knees pointing in same direction as toes, hips fully flexed, head in line with trunk						

FIGURE 16.2 *(continued)*

453

		R.		R.		R.	

STANDING & COMPONENTS
17. Standing correct alignment

18. Pelvis and trunk aligned over forward leg. Both knees extended
   a. Right leg forward
   b. Left leg forward

19. Bear weight on one leg in midstance
   a. Shift weight over right leg
   b. Shift weight over left leg

20. Heel strike, rear leg extended and externally rotated, heel down. Both knees straight
   a. Right heel strike
   b. Left heel strike

FIGURE 16.2 (continued)

CHILD'S NAME _____ DATE _____

BIRTH DATE _____ AGE _____ IQ _____ FMR SCORE _____

DIAGNOSIS _____ HAD SURGERY: YES _____ NO _____

INVOLVEMENT: GENERALIZED _____ SPECIFIC _____

SEVERE _____ MODERATE _____ MILD _____

RIGHT SIDE _____ LEFT SIDE _____ RECORDER _____

Instructions: Check statements in the appropriate column: True, Completely or Usually; True, Partially or Rarely; Not True or Never, according to observations of the infant made during the preceding week. Allow 2 points for each check mark in the left-hand column (Completely True), 1 point for each check mark in the middle column (Partially True), and no points for check marks in the right-hand column (Not True). Add all the points to give a total score and write the total FMR score in the places indicated on the form.

TRUE USUALLY OR COMPLETELY	TRUE RARELY OR PARTIALLY	NOT TRUE OR NEVER	
			HEAD The child has:
_____	_____	_____	1. Held head steadily when sitting, not letting it flop over uncontrolledly.
_____	_____	_____	2. Lifted head spontaneously, or on request, from lowered position.
_____	_____	_____	3. Raised chin from mat when lying on belly.
_____	_____	_____	4. Raised head from mat when lying on back.
_____	_____	_____	5. Raised head and chest from mat when lying on belly.
_____	_____	_____	6. Turned head to left or right, in search of sound, person or object.
			TRUNK The child has:
_____	_____	_____	7. Sat trunk erect, with or without support.
_____	_____	_____	8. Sat trunk erect, without support, 1 or more minutes.
_____	_____	_____	9. Raised self from lying to sitting position.
_____	_____	_____	10. Rolled unaided from lying on back to side position, spontaneously or when encouraged.
_____	_____	_____	11. Rolled completely over from lying on back to prone position, spontaneously or when encouraged.
_____	_____	_____	12. Pivoted around completely, spontaneously or to attain an object when lying on belly.

FIGURE 16.3   Functional motor scale for children with cerebral palsy. (Adapted from K. M. Banham, Duke University.)

TRUE USUALLY OR COMPLETELY	TRUE RARELY OR PARTIALLY	NOT TRUE OR NEVER	
_____	_____	_____	13. Propelled self forward when lying prone, using arm and body movements.
_____	_____	_____	14. Raised chest from mat supporting body on extended arms, when lying on belly.
			ARMS The child has:
_____	_____	_____	15. Controlled arm movements, directing them toward desired object when reaching.
_____	_____	_____	16. Crawled on hands and knees, trunk away from floor, spontaneously or to reach an object or person.
_____	_____	_____	17. Brought two hands together, spontaneously, manipulating and feeling them.
_____	_____	_____	18. Clapped hands together on request, or in imitation of person clapping
_____	_____	_____	19. Thrown object away with some thrust, not merely releasing hold and letting it drop.
			HANDS The child has:
_____	_____	_____	20. Grasped small objects on contact with hand.
_____	_____	_____	21. Released objects from grasp voluntarily or on request.
_____	_____	_____	22. Held thumb out of palm of either hand.
_____	_____	_____	23. Reached, grasped, and held small object for several seconds.
_____	_____	_____	24. Transferred objects from one hand to the other.
_____	_____	_____	25. Pointed with index finger, or poked it in holes.
_____	_____	_____	26. Picked up tiny objects between first finger and thumb.
			LEGS AND FEET The child has:
_____	_____	_____	27. Flexed legs at knee, while taking hold of toes.
_____	_____	_____	28. Pulled self to standing position, holding furniture or person's hand.

FIGURE 16.3   *(continued)*

TRUE USUALLY OR COMPLETELY	TRUE RARELY OR PARTIALLY	NOT TRUE OR NEVER	
————	————	————	29. Made alternate stepping movements when held with feet touching floor in attempt to move upward.
————	————	————	30. Raised self from sitting to standing, independently, without support of furniture.
————	————	————	31. Sat on floor, knees flexed, legs crossed in tailor fashion.
————	————	————	32. Squatted low, with both knees flexed.
————	————	————	33. Stood erect, hand held.
————	————	————	34. Stood erect, unsupported for half a minute or more.

LOCOMOTION, USING ARMS AND LEGS
The child has:

————	————	————	35. Taken steps sideways, with or without support of hand or furniture.
————	————	————	36. Walked forward, with or without hand support.
————	————	————	37. Walked with both heels touching ground.
————	————	————	38. Walked, legs together, not wide apart to keep balance.
————	————	————	39. Walked across room independently without support of furniture or person's hand.
————	————	————	40. Walked quickly, both heels touching ground, not crossing feet over or scissoring.
————	————	————	41. Walked backwards, independently.
————	————	————	42. Walked up steps with support of wall, rail, or person's hand.
————	————	————	43. Walked up steps independently, or holding rail, wall, or hand.
————	————	————	44. Walked down steps independently without support of wall, rail, or person's hand.

FIGURE 16.3   *(continued)*

TRUE USUALLY OR COMPLETELY	TRUE RARELY OR PARTIALLY	NOT TRUE OR NEVER	
_____	_____	_____	45. Run with hand held.
_____	_____	_____	46. Run about independently without hand support, indoors and outdoors.
_____	_____	_____	47. Moved about independently on wheeled chair or toy, or by propelling self by hands and arms on floor.
_____	_____	_____	48. Raised or pulled self from sitting to standing, unaided.
_____	_____	_____	49. Climbed and seated self on adult chair, unaided.
_____	_____	_____	50. Pedalled tricycle or other pedalled toy without assistance.
_____	_____	_____	TOTAL NUMBER CHECKED
_____	_____	_____	SCORE TOTAL FMR SCORE _____

FIGURE 16.3   (continued)

ACTIVITIES AND REHABILITATION

Developmental and corrective exercises are necessary and should be integral components of all physical education programs for children with cerebral palsy. A study by Bullock and Watter (1980) of 78 children over a 6-month period revealed a decrease of 86% in abnormalities of school-age children and a decrease of 75% in abnormalities of preschool-age children when appropriate developmental and corrective exercises were used. In the control group of children with cerebral palsy who did not do the exercises, a 7% increase in the number of abnormalities was seen in the school-age children and a 14% increase was seen in the preschool-age children. Any delay in programming could leave the child with CP with more severe motor problems than were present when the child entered school.

An important concept to keep in mind when setting goals for the child with spastic cerebral palsy is that proper muscle balance at affected joints must, if possible, be restored. To accomplish this goal, Harris (1978a) advocates relaxing "tight" muscles (i.e., those with hypertonicity) to cause contraction of the weak antagonists. With every movement, therefore, one muscle, or set of muscles, releases tension while the other increases it. If proper muscle balance is present when movement is initiated, changes in tension of both agonistic and antagonistic muscles should improve during motion. The balance of reciprocal muscle action can thus be maintained throughout

TABLE 16.1   A Developmental Progression for Walking

No.	Item
1	Pulls to feet at rail: child can pull to standing position at rail or furniture
2	At rail, lifts foot; child stands holding rail; can lift and replace one foot at a time
3	Cruises: standing at rail or furniture, child moves along sideways holding on
4	Walks, hands held: hold child's hands, and he walks forward
5	Lowers to floor from standing: without "falling," child moves with control to sitting
6	Walks, one hand held: walks with one hand held
7	Walks few steps alone: walks alone without support for two or three steps, then falls or holds on
8	Stands momentarily alone: stands without support briefly, then falls or holds on
9	Walks, starts, stops: initiates walking, steps, and can stop with control
10	Stands independently: stands alone steadily and indefinitely
11	Runs stiffly: runs, but not smoothly and lacks complete control
12	Squats in play: maintaining full flexion of hips and knees, bearing weight on feet, child is able to balance in play
13	Upstairs, one hand held: child can climb stairs if one hand is held
14	Small chair, seats self: child climbs onto a small chair from standing, and sits
15	Downstairs, one hand held: walks downstairs if one hand is held
16	Upstairs, holds rail: child can walk upstairs holding rail with one or two hands
17	Walks and runs: walks and runs well independently, with heel-toe gait
18	Up, down stairs, marks time: brings second foot to lead foot on each step
19	Kicks large ball: kicks a large ball, maintaining balance
20	Jumps with both feet: jumps, keeping two feet together
21	Walks backwards: walks backwards with control at least four steps
22	Walks on tiptoes: walks on tiptoes keeping heels off floor for ten consecutive steps
23	Rides tricycle: rides a tricycle independently
24	One foot, momentarily: can stands on one foot without support for at least ten seconds
25	Jumps high: can jump up off floor with two feet together, at least twelve inches
26	Upstairs, alternate feet: can walk upstairs alternating feet independently
27	Jumps distance: jumps ahead with two feet at least seventeen inches
28	Stands on one foot steadily
29	Downstairs, alternate feet: walks downstairs alternating feet independently
30	Hops on one foot: is able to hop at least five hops

Source: Modified from *Physical Therapy* (Vol. 53:120, 1973) with the permission of the American Physical Therapy Association.

the motion, resulting in better control. Harris has found that when the child with cerebral palsy understands completely how the muscle should work, the child will be able to "feel" variations of tone throughout the midrange. This should teach the child to make distinct movements with controlled acceleration and deceleration.

Relaxation of tight muscles is extremely important. All passive and assistive exercises must use slow and continuous action. Fast movements are contraindicated and usually cause uncontrolled movement.

All affected joints should be moved passively into, or past, the neutral position in the opposite direction from deviation. Place the student in a position so that each joint can be observed, and any pain or discomfort that occurs can be observed or related during the procedure.

During activity, the student should be told what will happen and what is actually happening when joint positions change. Horgan (1980) observes that verbal stimulation and positive involvement in the learning and performance of motor skills is important for children with cerebral palsy: "Motivational reinforcement treatment does in fact aid in the acquisition of motor skills by the spastic child, as shown by the results in this study, that may have important clinical implications. The continued used of motivational or reinforcing stimuli may be profitably adapted to school work, therapy, recreation and activities of daily living. Any method which has the potential for improving the motor function and efficiency of the cerebral palsied child is worthy of consideration" (p. 28).

Applying force smoothly and slowly is absolutely necessary. Prolonged, slow stretching will fatigue the stretch receptors and eventually relax the spastic muscles. The degree of resistance, the time required to bring the joint into the neutral position, and whether any opposing muscle spasms occur are important progress indicators of exercise effectiveness. Harris (1978a) found that when the "slow stretch" process was repeated, the joint was usually more readily brought into the neutral position than on the first day of the program. As the activity program continued over a few months, the abnormal resistance of the originally spastic muscles to stretch was overcome entirely and the joint position was neutralized.

RELAXATION AND STRETCHING EXERCISES

The child should be in a supine position for the following exercises. Because this position is stable, the student can relax, and the teacher can move each joint individually. Children with dyskinesia show less tendency to involuntary movement while resting in this position, and tight muscles of the students with spasticity relax considerably after a few moments of random, passive manipulation of the head and extremities while in the supine position.

Exercises for the foot and ankle. Exercises begin with the ankle brought passively into the neutral position by prolonged, slowly increasing force to the ball of the foot. The calf muscles (gastrocnemius-soleus) will relax during this procedure. Finally, ask the student to bend the ankle backward *voluntarily*.

Knee exercises. Exercises require that the leg be extended passively to the maximum and then slowly extended voluntarily until the hamstrings relax. Gravity can be used by lifting the leg and resting the heel on a low support (rolled-up blanket or mat). The leg's weight will stretch the hamstrings and gradually extend the knee joint, then ask the child to extend the knee voluntarily. Elevate the thigh and hold, then ask the child to extend the knee and align the lower leg with the thigh. As the child's strength increases, the thigh is held at progressively steeper angles.

In most cases, voluntary movements of the ankle and knee joints are possible, even during the first exercise. If voluntary movement occurs, introduce the student immediately to resistance exercises involving movements such as (1) dorsiflexing the ankle while resisting upward movement of the foot and (2) extending the knees in a bilateral extensor thrust with the feet pushing upward against the teacher's midriff.

Exercises for the elbow. Elbow exercises include passively extending the biceps using the prolonged slow-stretch process, and then holding in extended position until relaxation can be felt. The student should flex the elbow first, allowing the forearm to dangle across the chest. The teacher then holds the upper arm and asks the student to extend the elbow and raise the forearm upward. The upper arm should be held in many positions; the force of gravity provides resistance while the procedure is repeated. Finally, to provide resistance, grasp the student's wrist and resist the elbow extension motion.

Exercises for the wrist. Exercises involve slow stretching of the flexors, and while holding the child's forearm, having the child extend the wrist and align the back of the hand with the forearm.

Exercises for the hand and fingers. These exercises require that the child's fingers and hand be closed. In the young child whose upper extremities are involved, normal grasp is not well developed. Palmar grasp (grasping with the hand) is often crude. When the thumb has been held flexed and adducted inside the palm with the fingers flexed over it, the web of the thumb becomes shortened. These fisted fingers can be extended by passively hyperextending the wrist, firmly stroking the back of the hand in a distal-to-proximal direction, and shaking the forearm so the hand is forcibly altered toward wrist extension. Once the fingers are extended, the student should passively "brush" the hands past each other to engage the opposing sets of fingers and pull one open with the other. To aid voluntary finger extension, have the child squeeze the fingers into a fist with maximum voluntary effort while the teacher squeezes down on the child's fisted hand. The "feeling" of extreme opposition to extension provides the child with an awareness against which opening the fingers can be better sensed, or a rebound phenomenon may be involved (Harris, 1978b).

Once the fingers are fully extended, passive manipulation of the child's forearms, as in "drumming" on the chest or abdomen with open hands, keeps them effectively extended. Finally, ask the student to alternately flex and extend the fingers.

When there is voluntary movement in the student's hand, provide games that involve pushing, reaching, grasping, and releasing, followed by activities that require placement and grasp, progressing from crude palmar grasp to pincher grasp. It is best to start with wooden blocks and toys large enough to be picked up easily, but small enough to fit in the student's hand. Progression to smaller objects will occur rather rapidly. Pegboards and cupcake pans are excellent tools for hand and finger development. When the child shows flexion and extension control, use a stopwatch to determine how long it takes the student to complete a task. Objective evaluation for both speed and endurance is then possible.

MUSCLE STRENGTHENING EXERCISES

For proper muscle balance, spastic muscles must be relaxed and their antagonists strengthened. Traditional methods used to stimulate weak muscle action include repetitive tapping, stroking, or brushing the weak muscle. A quick stretch in the direction opposite that of the desired movement, prior to the movement, is particularly effective. The student's voluntary effort is extremely useful. Passive manipulation of the arm or leg in the desired direction may assist the child to understand what is being asked. For true control, the child must understand what movement is being attempted. Clear instructions will establish learned responses. For example, "Press your knees together so you can feel this pillow being squeezed."

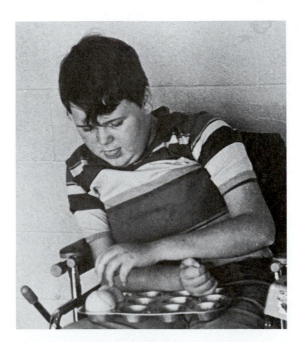

Use of a cupcake pan is helpful when developing hand control. (Photograph courtesy of Photo Associates Limited)

An extensive study by Harris (1978a, 1978b) indicates that development of strength in children with spastic cerebral palsy should be included in all exercise programs: "The subjects responded very enthusiastically to incorporation of newly learned muscle activation and relaxation patterns into activities which they could continue practicing independently in order to sustain proper muscle balance and to strengthen both of the opposing muscles or muscle groups. Exercises such as push-ups, sit-ups, and knee-bends, traditionally used for physical fitness training, were effective in strengthening weak muscles and improving coordination once muscle balance had been approximated through rudimentary single-joint exercises practiced in supine position" (1978a, p. 24).

Development of strength requires exercises and activities involving progressive resistance, which should be matched to the age and status of the child. Motivational and recreational stimuli, from work and conditioning to diversified games and sports, are essential to a stimulating program. Progressions and goals should be written and improvements recorded on colorful graphs and charts. Measurable accomplishments (i.e., how much, how many, how far) are reinforcing, and accurate evaluations fulfill the requirements of a complete individualized educational program.

Muscle strengthening exercises for the head and neck. These exercises should be done in the prone position. The child should be encouraged to roll from the supine to the prone position. Students may "pin" an arm under them when rolling over, but if the shoulder is lifted by the teacher, the child can usually lift the arm high enough to clear it. Prone-lying is one position tolerable to the child with CP if the head can be lifted far enough to avoid covering the nose and mouth. The head may be turned or lifted to one side. If the child is weak, lift the shoulders and place the child in an "elbow-propped" position. The child may require support to perform head and neck exercises. Ask the child to move the head up and down. If neck muscles are too weak to accomplish this, cup the forehead to support the head and ask the child to continue holding it up. The ability to hold the head against gravity, or even to slow the rate at which the head falls, indicates strength development.

Muscle strengthening exercises for the shoulders and upper arms. These should be done with the child in the prone position and supported on the forearms and elbows (i.e., elbow-propped position). When the child can hold this position for a few seconds (increase to 10 sec), place additional weight on the upper back by pressing down on the shoulders. This exercise strengthens the triceps muscles. For additional strength in the triceps and the challenge of a new position, the child should assume the hands and knees creeping position. When able to hold up to 10 sec, increase the child's strength by pressing down on the shoulders.

Muscle strengthening exercises for the abdominals and back. These exercises include isometric contraction of the abdomen, such as "sucking in your stomach" and holding for a 6-sec count. Have the student then assume the supine position and hold the instructor's hands; pull the child to sitting position. By pulling with her own arms, the child uses abdominal muscles. The child should be lowered in the same way, which also uses her abdominal muscles for control. Finally, have the child raise her head and shoulders off the mat and hold this position for a 6-sec maximum count. Repeat.

Straight leg lifts are contraindicated even though they develop strength in the abdominal and hip flexor muscles. The iliopsoas muscle group (major hip flexors) is unusually tight in children with spastic cerebral palsy so additional strengthening is undesirable. Prone leg lifts and prone chest raises are beneficial because they emphasize the action of hyperextension.

Muscle strengthening of the knee joint. Exercises to strengthen the knee joint are necessary for the child to learn to walk. Teaching children to walk by having them walk increases spasticity if they lack sufficient balance and strength to support themselves. Specific quadriceps strengthening exercises in the supine position prepare the child for standing and walking.

Strength in the quadriceps (knee extensors) is gained by extensor thrust exercises against resistance in the supine position. Half knee bends and hopping in place, while supported, should be performed constantly to prepare for independent standing and walking. To develop strength, place the child supine on a scooter board and have him push with the feet. A "stand-box" develops antigravity muscles and balance but does not develop strength when progressive resistance is necessary.

BALANCE IMPROVEMENT

Bobath (1959) believes that upright positioning is a learned response that progresses through specific levels of development: "As the child passes from a stage of primitive reflex activity and learns to right himself and get his balance, he gradually begins to use the automatic patterns for voluntary activity" (p. 13). This concept is extremely important, because many children with CP have neuromuscular conditions that limit head, neck, and body control. These individuals have primitive patterns of abnormal flexion and extension that inhibit normal body posture and foster physical deformities that interfere with further functioning. Abnormal motor patterns interfere with attention to stimuli, perception of stimuli, and voluntary control of responses to stimuli (Hallahan & Kauffman, 1991).

Research in motor control indicates that effective positioning of the body and maintenance of stability are prerequisites to skilled performance. For example, it is difficult, if not impossible, for most performers to execute even the simplest gross or fine motor act effectively (e.g., kicking, throwing, writing, jumping) unless appropriate postural adjustments occur to support such movements (Williams, McClenaghan, & Ward, 1985). These reactions occur automatically in most able-bodied skilled individuals. For such persons, little, if any, conscious attention is given to positioning or balance—allowing the performer to concentrate instead on information related to movement execution. Williams, McClenaghan, and Ward (1985) state that "in certain pathological conditions [e.g., cerebral palsy], stabilizing postural reactions do not occur spontaneously and precision movement of the extremities is, at best, effortful and slow" (p. 171). Williams, Fisher, and Tritschler (1983) believe that for children with motor development delays, postural reactions are often slow and inappropriate, and the execution of skillful movement is difficult and ineffective.

Some children with dyskinesia have difficulty sitting because of involuntary writhing movements and equilibrium reactions that are only partially developed. Stable sitting posture is poor because of the increase in extensor tone (tonic labyrinthine reflex) throughout the body when the head is extended. When the child sits with the head erect, there is a tendency to topple backwards. The most stable sitting position is the reverse tailor position.

Adequate head and trunk control are extremely important when positioning the child. Emphasis should be on symmetry and righting, equilibrium, and protective reactions. The appropriate chair and accessories should place the child in the most normal sitting position possible. This will maintain a posture that inhibits primitive reflexes and allows better control of the head and upper extremities.

When seating a child, the buttocks should be close to the back of the chair to obtain an angle of 90 degrees, thus providing adequate hip flexion. The chair depth should not permit the back of the knees to touch the front of the seat when the child's hips are properly placed. The most ideal position is found by inserting the index and middle fingers between the back of the child's knees and the seat edge; the fit should be comfortable, not too loose or too snug.

The feet should be placed firmly on the floor or on the foot rests of the wheelchair, creating an angle of 90 degrees. Angles greater than 90 degrees (including the knees and hips) generally produce extensor hypertonus due to lack of support at the hips. Tactile and kinesthetic input occur when the feet are in constant contact with a supporting surface. Writing or support boards attached to the chair allow for hand use. The child's forearms should form an approximate 90-degree angle with the upper arm. The desk surface should be $\frac{1}{2}$ to 1 in. (1.25 to 2.5 cm) higher than the child's elbows to provide adequate stability and movement.

All good positioning involves sitting, prone, supine, and standing positions that discourage that child's natural but abnormal reflexes. Most children with spastic tendencies are dominated by flexion movements, so the child should always be placed in positions that discourage flexion activities (i.e., the supine position is suggested, but if the prone position is used, the person should be placed on an incline board so body weight will restrict any flexion activities). Movement skills involving extension, external rotation, and abduction should be integral components of programs for the student with spastic cerebral palsy. For the child with athetosis, whose major actions are usually unwanted trunk extension, positioning should be with flexion, such as placing the student on her side.

Vestibular stimulation is important to improving motor performance of children with cerebral palsy (Ayres, 1975; Ivy & Roblyer, 1980). MacLean, Arendt, and Baumeister (1986) state the following:

> In general, measures of motor functioning and reflexes have shown that rotational vestibular stimulation produces changes beyond those to be expected simply as a function of maturation. . . . In considering the available data, it appears that while the effects of rotational stimulation are fairly modest in terms of magnitude among normal babies these effects could have a profound influence upon the development of developmentally disabled children. (p. 93)

The vestibular mechanism is made up of two kinds of receptors, the **semicircular canals,** which respond to angular acceleration, and **otolith organs,** which respond to linear acceleration. The vestibular mechanism understands where the head is in space; that is, it signals whether the head is upright, upside down, or in some other position. In addition, it is sensitive to sudden changes in direction of body movement. Sage (1984) believes that the vestibular mechanism is also important in the visual component of balance, because it assists in visual fixation during head and body movements.

The biophysics of the vestibular mechanism (semicircular canals) is sensitive only to angular acceleration, that is, a change in angular velocity. These sensitive areas receive stimulation only at the beginning and ending of rotation. The more rapid the change in angular velocity, the greater the angular acceleration stimulus to the semi-circular canals.

The otolithic organs are fluid-filled sacs called the **utricle** and the **saccule.** Each sac has a patch of hairlike nerve endings. The sacs are located between the semicircular canals and feed information into the vestibular nerve, which leads into the auditory nerve. The utricle is approximately horizontal in the upright head and the saccule is approximately vertical. Sage (1984) explains how the otolithic organs function: "Since the hair cells of the utricle are set on a horizontal plane (whereas those of the saccule lie on a vertical plane), the utricle is maximally stimulated when the head is bent either forward or backward.... The saccule appears to be maximally stimulated when the head is bent to the side and when the body is raised or lowered in space" (p. 172).

Chee, Kreutzberg, and Clark (1978) found that semicircular canal stimulation improves gross motor skills in preambulatory children with cerebral palsy, and that stimulation also reduces unwanted reflexes. Striking improvements were seen in equilibrium, gross motor coordination, alertness, and curiosity. In research involving 23 subjects between the ages of 2 and 6 years, including children with athetoid and spastic movements, 16 sessions were given in 4 weeks, using vertical and horizontal circular stimulation. The subjects were rotated at least 60 sec before being stopped to receive the full benefit of the stimulus. These researchers concluded that the treatment enables the vestibuloocular reflex to mature to a level similar to that of normal, ambulatory children of the same age. Not all children, however, are able to tolerate rotary vestibular stimulation. Children with serious cardiovascular disorders and those susceptible to recurrent seizures should not be given this stimulation unless specifically designated by the child's physician.

WALKING PROGRESSIONS

Teaching and assisting with walking are an important part of the physical education program of the child with cerebral palsy. The need for cane, crutches, walker, braces, or other special devices is the physician's decision.

Preliminary strengthening exercises should be included in the program. Preparatory to crutch walking, progressive resistive exercises for the latissimus dorsi, triceps, and biceps are indicated as well as for the quadriceps, hip extensors, and abductors. Rolling, crawling and creeping, sitting, and balance precede ambulation. If the student does not have enough strength in the leg and hip muscles, the child will have negative muscle reactions when the body attempts antigravity actions. Do not encourage the child to try independent walking before initial lower extremity strength is developed.

For students learning correct patterns of gait, parallel bars can be used for balance. Balance is a prerequisite for successful ambulation. The child with CP is often affected by unwanted movements caused by unsteadiness (the muscles react in anticipation of falling). Harris (1978b) describes a technique to aid in standing balance:

> A procedure in which the subjects were continuously thrown off balance, but prevented from falling by a number of surrounding individuals who acted as "catcher" (i.e., who caught them before they tilted very far and returned them to the upright position) had a remarkably relaxing influence on the children. During this procedure, they began to develop compensatory movements of arms and trunk necessary for independent balance. It would appear that the children tense their muscles so much in fear of falling, while attempting to stand entirely on their own, that normal compensatory movements are impossible and they are certain to fall. (In a sense, they cannot stand because they are afraid to fall.) If they are secure in the knowledge that they will not be allowed to fall past a certain point, however, they can develop independent balancing skills. (p. 26)

Once the student has developed sitting control, standing balance, alternating leg movements, forward progression in the parallel bars, and free standing, she is ready for gait training, either unassisted or with crutches, and with or without orthotic devices (braces).

When children use long leg braces, they can begin ambulation by standing in the parallel bars. The hip locks can be opened to allow flexion and extension of the hip joints. Stand behind the child and grasp the wrists. At the count of *one*, move the child's left arm forward to grasp the bar; at the count of *two*, push the right leg forward with the (instructor's) right knee; at the count of *three*, move the right arm forward; and at the count of *four*, move the left leg.

When able to walk in the parallel bars unassisted, the child should be fitted with crutches and placed against a wall to learn standing balance with crutches. With the crutches held properly under the arms and the hip locks open, the child should be instructed to shift the weight and raise the crutches. This procedure should be followed to move away from the wall. Next, have the child walk unassisted with a four-point crutch gait. When this is accomplished, open one knee lock; later, open the other knee lock so the child can develop a normal reciprocal walking pattern.

For the child who does not need braces, toe dragging is a problem. If no abnormality prevents the child from lifting the toes, place bricks or a ladder on the floor to force the child to lift the foot up and over for forward progression. For toeing in, toeing out, and differences in length of step, ask the child to walk in footprints on the floor (painted rubber or plastic). This game can involve several students and works well with young children.

ORTHOTIC DEVICES OR BRACES

Orthotic devices (braces) prevent contractures, restrict unwanted movement, and give support. A passive corrective brace is often used to prevent spastic muscles from reproducing deformity, particularly at night. Night braces prevent deformity from recurring after stretching or surgery. The most common braces are ankle splints for control of plantar flexion deformity (talipes equinus), knee splints to control knee flexion deformity, and adduction splints to control hip adduction contractures. Night braces are not often prescribed for the upper extremities, but a "cock-up" wrist splint is prescribed occasionally to control wrist flexion and improve hand function.

Supporting braces for lower limbs are used to control deformity and to provide walking stability. The basic principles of brace use are simple: If the ankle and foot alone require support, a below-knee brace is used. If the knee also requires support, a long leg brace is used. If hip control is inadequate, a pelvic band is added to the full-length leg brace.

Bracing for children with dyskinesia is controversial. The primary problem is generalized involuntary movement in the trunk and extremities. Secondary problems are weakness and varying degrees of loss of motor control. Fixed contractures are not usually found. For young children with moderate to severe dyskinesia, bilateral double-bar long leg braces with spinal bracing may be used initially. With increased control and maturity, trunk bracing is often removed. Surgical correction of deformities is frequently considered to minimize bracing.

The use of orthotic devices for children delayed in sitting, standing, and walking is recommended because of the benefits of being in an upright position for sitting and standing. Empirical research (Mobility Operations Research Foundation, 1991) gives evidence that orthotic devices which provide standing mobility can have dramatic success with children and teenagers with severe and profound physical and mental disabilities. These researchers were able to increase leg support strength, hip girdle strength, upper body strength (shoulder, arm, hand), and neck strength when providing progressive and daily amounts of standing in the Rifton Mobile Prone Stander. Positive results were found in 5 months with children whose conditions were once considered stable or declining. Areas tested included sitting, standing, weightbearing, walking, independent movement, self-feeding, self-controlled toileting, and communication. During pretesting, the subjects ($N = 11$; age range = 7–16 yrs) passed an average 47 of the 198 skills and in posttesting they succeeded in 133 of the 198 skills, a gain of 275%.

Weightbearing develops better bone formation and stimulates growth, and the vertical position also provides better circulation and prevents postural atrophy. Braces guide the movement of extremities into normal patterns and align skeletal components, minimizing deformities.

SURGICAL TECHNIQUES

If deformity occurs and rehabilitation does not provide positive results, surgery can improve function. Surgical release of contractures, transplant of muscles and tendons, or release of tight joint capsules offers many advantages to children who have severe cerebral palsy. Nerve blocks and nerve crushing also prove beneficial.

Specifically, surgery is done in the following ways: (1) soft tissue surgery to release contractures by dividing tendons, muscles, or joint capsules, (2) neurectomy, the division of selected peripheral nerves to denervate (to deprive the muscle of its nerve supply) spastic muscles, and (3) bone surgery to correct deformity by adding or removing bony parts.

PROGRAMMING FOR CARDIORESPIRATORY IMPROVEMENT

Students with cerebral palsy are sometimes reluctant to walk because of the self-imposed strain placed on the cardiorespiratory system. As ambulation becomes more strenuous, walking tends to decrease and time spent in the wheelchair increases, which means that the more severely involved become totally dependent on wheelchairs for mobility. Such inactivity can cause reduced aerobic capacity and inferior lung function. A vicious cycle is created in which ambulation level and other physical functions decrease continuously.

Rothman (1978) found that when youngsters with spastic cerebral palsy did breathing exercises, they increased their breathing capacity significantly beyond the capacity of a control group that did not do exercises. After exercising for 5 to 7 min each day for 8 weeks, the experimental group's vital capacity was increased by 0.46 liters. The average increase was 31% over pretest values. Rothman used the Bobath treatment, which inhibits abnormal breathing patterns and teaches the child proper breathing technique. The following eight exercises were used in the study:

1. **Diaphragmatic breathing.**[1] This is considered the most important exercise.
2. **Expiratory exercise using abdominal muscles.** While seated, the child blows a Ping-Pong ball across the table for different distances. This exercise enhances cough production and forces expiration.

---

[1]Refer to Chapter 18 for an explanation of how to do correct diaphragmatic breathing.

3. **Inspiration and expansion of the chest.** In the supine position, the child inhales while elevating arms above the head and exhales while lowering arms.

4. **Stimulation of inspiration.** A belt is placed around the lower ribs and crossed in front of the seated child. The child exhales as the belt is tightened and inhales as the belt is loosened.

5. **Strengthening anterior abdominal musculature, especially rectus abdominus.** The child is supine and exhales while bringing knees to chest; inhales as knees are lowered.

6. **Strengthening anterior abdominal musculature, especially rectus abdominus.** A sit-up exercise with knees flexed and feet flat on floor.

7. **Strengthening lateral abdominal muscles and internal and external obliques.** Same as exercise 6, but the child moves an elbow toward opposite knee.

8. Same as exercise 1, but a 5-lb weight is now applied to abdominal area to provide resistance to diaphragm movement.

The exercise schedule is in Table 16.2. The first exercise was performed each day of the schedule. All other exercises were performed for 2 weeks. The exercise schedule allows for the increase in exercise difficulty. These exercises were performed 5 to 7 min per day.

Wall pulleys can be used to develop cardiorespiratory efficiency in the child with cerebral palsy. The use of pulleys is particularly effective for those who are nonambulatory or have great difficulty walking. Physical educators often ask about methods to stimulate cardiorespiratory efficiency if the child cannot run or walk. Even a bicycle ergometer or a stationary bike may not be within the capabilities of a child with CP. Amundsen, Takahasi, Carter, and Nelson (1980) state that wall pulleys and arm exercises are a highly productive way to increase heart rate and systolic blood pressure. The exercise routine is as follows:

- **Wall-pulley pulling** is done while facing the pulleys. Start with the right elbow in full extension and fists pointing at the pulleys. Based on four

TABLE 16.2   **Breathing Exercise Schedule for Individuals with Cerebral Palsy**

Week	Exercise	Week	Exercise
1	1, 2, 3	5	1, 6, 7
2	1, 2, 3	6	1, 6, 7
3	1, 4, 5	7	1, 8
4	1, 4, 5	8	1, 8

counts to a cycle, on count one, the right arm is pulled to approximately full elbow flexion (hand to chest); on count two, the right arm is returned to the starting position; counts three and four are identical to one and two, but with the left arm. These exercises should not be done if the persons are experiencing severe flexion contractures, as commonly found in individuals with spastic CP. Strengthening of the biceps, biceps brachialis, and the coracobrachialis is contraindicated and should not be attempted when developing cardiorespiratory endurance.

- **Wall-pulley pushing** is performed with the student facing away from the pulleys and using the same count. This second exercise is desirable for individuals with spastic cerebral palsy because they need to develop strength in the extensor arm muscles. Repetitions should be counted and recorded. This serves as a measure of existing strength and helps in setting goals for future workouts.

GAMES AND ACTIVITIES TO IMPROVE EYE-HAND COORDINATION AND OBJECT RELEASE

DROPPING OR RELEASING SKILLS

Milk Bottle Drop   Place the milk bottle at the side of wheelchair. Drop clothespins into the bottle—5 chances, 5 points for each successful try. Materials: 1 milk bottle, 5 clothespins.

Waterfall   Drop coins into a glass placed in a bucket filled with water—3 chances, 5 points for each coin that falls in the glass. Materials: 1 bucket, 1 large drinking glass, 25 coins (or metal slugs, disks, or washers).

PUSHING OR SLIDING SKILLS

Miniature Shuffleboard   Slide small disks onto chalk target—3 chances. Disks that stop within designated circles receive 5 points. Materials: 6 checkers or disks, target outline.

Bombs Away   Set large box or wastebasket on the floor at far edge of a table. Slide disks along the table so they fall off far edge. Count number of disks falling into the box—10 chances, 2 points for every victory. Materials: 20 checkers or disks, 1 large box (or wastebasket), 1 long table.

BALL ROLLING SKILLS

Cupcake Bounce   Bounce Ping-Pong balls into cupcake tin or egg carton from a distance of 6 ft — 3 chances, 5 points per successful bounce. Materials: Cupcake pan or egg carton, 6 Ping-Pong balls.

Volleyball Bounce   Bounce volleyball into wastebasket from a distance of 6 ft — 3 chances, 5 points per successful bounce (any type of ball can be used). Materials: 1 wastebasket, 2 volleyballs.

Goal Bounce   Bounce large ball into basket or box positioned 8 ft away — 3 chances, 5 points per ball in the basket. Materials: 1 wastebasket or box, 1 large ball.

UNDERHAND THROWING SKILLS

Coffee Can Toss   Set up 5 coffee cans in irregular order. Throw beanbags or small balls into the cans — 5 chances, 5 points for each bag in a can. Materials: 5 coffee cans, 10 beanbags.

Chair Toss   Toss rings at legs of upturned chair — 5 tosses, 5 points per ringer. Materials: 1 chair, 10 rope, plastic, or wire rings.

Horse Shoe Pitch   Throw 3 rubber or cardboard horseshoes at stake 6 ft from toss line — 5 points per ringer, and 1 point for closest. Materials: 6 cardboard or rubber horseshoes, 1 stake.

TOSSING OR FLIPPING SKILLS

Toss the Discus   Sail paper plate for distance. Measure distance thrown. Materials: Several paper plates.

Paper Plate Flip   Sail paper plates into bushel basket from 15 ft (move closer if necessary) — 5 chances, 5 points for each basket. Materials: Several paper plates, 1 bushel basket.

Ring the Bottle   Toss rubber jar rings at bottles set in triangular shape — 5 chances, 5 points per successful try. Materials: 6 large pop bottles, 12 jar rings.

Card Flip   Toss playing cards into wastebasket set at an angle facing the child. Count number of cards that fall into the basket. Materials: 1 deck of playing cards, 1 wastebasket.

Bottle Cap Pitch   Fill washtub with water, and float a small pie plate. From 5 ft away, pitch the bottle caps (one at a time) onto the plate—5 chances, 5 points per successful try. Materials: Bottle caps, washtub, small pie plate.

LIFETIME SPORT SKILLS AND ATHLETIC COMPETITION

When planning game and sport activities, the following general considerations described by Huberman (1976) are helpful. Children who have spastic cerebral palsy relax with repetitive movements, but persons with dyskinesic cerebral palsy perform better if they relax *before* movement. These children show more accuracy in fine movements, even though their performance is labored and less skillful in larger motor activities. Those with dyskinesic cerebral palsy display the reverse. For example, the child with spastic CP will throw more accurately, but the child with dyskinesia can throw farther and her walking or running is faster and freer than the labored gait of the person who is spastic. Children with ataxia pose a special problem and should, initially, move fewer parts of the body at one time (i.e., keep the rest of the body still when moving the limbs).

In 1978, the first national cerebral palsy competitive sports games were held in Detroit, Michigan. These games provided fun and competition for individuals who ordinarily do not have that opportunity. No entry was withheld because of lack of experience, fear of failure, or fear of embarrassment. Anyone 15 years of age or older and diagnosed as having cerebral palsy could compete.

The National Games of the Cerebral Palsy/*Les Autres* (a French term meaning "The Others") are held annually. Athletes include not only persons with CP (who comprised 90% of the athletes) but also *Les Autres*, a group of individuals with disabilities who are not able to participate in one of the other national organizations governing sports for athletes who are disabled. Eligible physical conditions included (but were not limited to) multiple sclerosis, muscular dystrophy, osteogenesis imperfecta, Friedreich's ataxia, arthrogryposis, skeletal dysplasia, and various forms of cerebral palsy.

The athletes compete in 16 sports, including archery, cycling, golf, horseback riding, table tennis, track and field, soccer, wheelchair soccer, bowling, boccia, basketball, power lifting, swimming, target shooting, cross-country, and slalom.

The United States Cerebral Palsy Athletic Association (USCPAA) has approximately 2000 members. Many individuals with CP are capable of serious athletic competition. Too often, they are expected to possess extremely low levels of motor performance, and traditional physical education activities are considered, mistakenly, to be beyond their reach. Although many cannot compete on an equal basis with nondisabled peers, they can perform identical activities, and with modifications can be integrated into the regular program.

More specific information regarding athletic and sport competition can be found in Chapter 21, Opportunities in Sport.

SUMMARY

Healy (1990) summarizes the problems surrounding this disorder as follows: "Cerebral palsy is the result of a permanent brain injury and is therefore lifelong. While the brain damage itself is nonprogressive, the resultant muscle control problems are not. However, their progress can be halted—or at least postponed—with proper therapy, including frequent elongation (stretching) of stiff muscles and proper positioning. In some cases, surgery is necessary to release tight muscles and tendons, particularly of the ankles and hips, or to treat dislocations of the hips. Other orthopedic disorders, such as scoliosis and contractures of the joints, may become more problematic as the child gets older" (p. 62).

The characteristics of cerebral palsy can range from mild to severe, depending on the child's age and the location and extent of the brain damage. This condition involves general body weakness, paralysis, and an inability to control muscle reflexes. A youngster with mild involvement will appear awkward and clumsy but is able to move easily and freely in a physical education class. Lack of coordination extends to poor eye-hand coordination. A severely involved youngster is unable to sit unaided, speaks unintelligibly, and requires almost total physical care. Most children with CP fall somewhere between these two extremes.

Cerebral palsy is a nonprogressive condition that cannot be cured. The condition is often further categorized as spastic, dyskinesic, or ataxic. The child who has spasticity may be very rigid; the legs scissor and the increased activity of deep tendon reflexes often causes muscle contractures. The child with dyskinesia makes involuntary movements. This child may know where to place balls in a cupcake pan, but arm movements are so uncontrolled and explosive that he frequently misses the pan entirely. The child who has ataxia lacks balance and depth perception. She is unable to stand easily, and when she attempts to take a step forward, as when hitting a ball, she almost falls. Furthermore, her stroke timing is poor.

Children with cerebral palsy also have a high incidence of additional disabilities. Mental retardation is found in at least 60% of all cases. Sensory disabilities are common and include hearing, seeing, and perceptual motor impairment. Speech and communication disorders are encountered often.

The initial assessment of motor abilities and capabilities of these children is an integral part of their physical education programming. Basic motor skills and early childhood activities are commonly included in the program. Many youngsters, because they must expend great energy to make their muscles obey their commands, become lethargic and unmotivated when asked to explore the world of movement through physical education. The adapted physical educator must make sure that the child's program does *not* become a mere extension of the therapy program. The child's physical education should include games, skills, and activities that provide enjoyment, challenge, and stimulation. Finally, evaluation of the child's progress is essential for future planning.

REFERENCES

Adams, R. C., & McCubbin, J. A. (1991). *Games, sports, and exercises for the physically disabled* (4th ed.). Philadelphia: Lea & Febiger.

Alford, C. A. (1988). Chronic perinatal infections and mental retardation. In J. F. Kavanagh (Ed.), *Understanding mental retardation* (pp. 137–148). Baltimore, MD: Brooks.

Amundsen, L. R., Takahasi, M., Carter, C. L., & Nelson, D. H. (1980). Response during wall-pulley versus bicycle ergometer work. *Physical Therapy, 60*(2), 173–178.

Ayres, J. (1975). *Sensory Integration and learning disorders*. Los Angeles: Western Psychological Services.

Banham, K. M. (1978). Measuring functional motor rehabilitation of cerebral palsied infants and young children. *Rehabilitation Literature, 39*(4), 111–116.

Bigge, J. L. (1988). *Curriculum based instruction for special education students*. Mountain View, CA: Mayfield.

Blackman, J. A. (1990a). Child abuse and neglect. In J. A. Blackman (Ed.), *Medical aspects of developmental disabilities in children birth to three* (2nd ed.; pp. 67–70). Rockville, MD: Aspen.

Blackman, J. A. (1990b). Congenital infections. In J. A. Blackman (Ed.), *Medical aspects of developmental disabilities in children birth to three* (2nd ed.; pp. 89–95. Rockville, MD: Aspen.

Bobath, K. (1959). The neuropathology of cerebral palsy and its importance in treatment and diagnosis. *Cerebral Palsy Bulletin, 8*, 13–33.

Bobath, K. (1966). *The motor deficit in patients with cerebral palsy*. London: Clinics in Developmental Medicine.

Bobath, K., & Bobath, B. (1967). The neuro-developmental treatment of cerebral palsy. *Physical Therapy, 47*, 1039–1041.

Bullock, M. L., & Watter, P. (1980). A study of effectiveness of physiotherapy in the management of young children with minimal cerebral dysfunction. *Physical Therapy, 60*(1), 105.

Chee, F. K. W., Kreutzberg, J. R., & Clark, D. L. (1978). Semicircular canal stimulation in cerebral palsied children. *Physical Therapy, 59*(9), 1071–1075.

Cherry, D. B. (1980, July). Review of physical therapy alternatives for reducing muscle contracture. *Physical Therapy, 60*(7), 877–881.

Cratty, B. J. (1989). *Adapted physical education in the mainstream* (2nd ed.). Denver: Love.

Eichstaedt, C. B., & Lavay, B. W. (1992). *Physical activity for individuals with mental retardation. Infancy through adulthood*. Champaign, IL: Human Kinetics.

Guyton, A. C. (1979). *Physiology of the human body* (5th ed.). Philadelphia: W. B. Saunders.

Harris, F. A. (1978a). Muscle stretch receptor hypersensitization in spasticity. *American Journal of Physical Medicine, 57*(1), 16–28.

Harris, F. A. (1978b). Correction of muscle balance in spasticity. *American Journal of Physical Medicine, 57*(3), 123–138.

Healy, A. (1990). Cerebral palsy. In J. A. Blackman (Ed.), *Medical aspects of developmental disabilities in children birth to three* (2nd ed.; pp. 59–66). Rockville, MD: Aspen.

Horgan, J. S. (1980). Reaction time and movement time of children with cerebral palsy. *American Journal of Physical Medicine, 59*(1), 22–29.

Hoskins, T. A., & Squires, J. E. (1973). Developmental assessment: A test for gross motor and reflex development. *Physical Therapy, 53*(2), 117–125.

Huberman, G. (1976). Organized sports activities with cerebral palsied adolescents. *Rehabilitation Literature, 37*(4), 103.

Ivy, A., & Roblyer, D. D. (1980). Vestibular stimulator for handicapped clients. *Physical Therapy, 60*(3), 309–310.

Johnston, R. B., & Magrab, P. R. (1976). *Developmental disorders assessment, treatment, education.* Baltimore, MD: University Park Press.

Kieran, S. S., Connor, F. P., von Hippel, C. S., & Jones, S. H. (1981). *Mainstreaming preschoolers: Children with orthopedic handicaps.* Belmont, MA: CRC Education and Human Development.

Laskas, C. A., Mullen, S. L., Nelson, D. L., & Willson-Broyles, M. (1985, January). Enhancement of two motor functions of the lower extremity in a child with spastic quadriplegia. *Physical Therapy, 65*(1), 11–16.

MacLean, W. E. Jr., Arendt, R. E., & Baumeister, A. A. (1986). Early motor development and stereotyped behavior: The effects of semi-circular canal stimulation. In M. G. Wade (Ed.), *Motor skill acquisition of the mentally handicapped: Issues in research and training* (pp. 73–100). Amsterdam, The Netherlands: Elsevier Science.

Mobility Operations Research Foundation. (1991). *Rifton-For people with disabilities.* Rifton, NY. The Foundation.

Rothman, J. G. (1978). Effects of respiratory exercises on the vital capacity and forced expiratory volume in children with cerebral palsy. *Physical Therapy, 58*(4), 421–425.

Sage, G. H. (1984). *Motor learning and control—A neurological approach.* Dubuque, IA: Wm. C. Brown.

Semmler, C. J. (1990). Developmental disabilities. In C. J. Semmler & J. G. Hunter (Eds.), *Early occupational therapy intervention. Neonates to three years* (pp. 232–261). Gaithersburg, MD: Aspen.

Sternfeld, L., & Berenberg, W. (1981, June 2). *Twenty-five years of cerebral palsy research.* Report at the Board of Directors' Meeting of the United Cerebral Palsy Research and Educational Foundation.

United Cerebral Palsy Association. (n.d.). *Doctor, only through early diagnosis can you control cerebral palsy.* New York: The Association.

Williams, H. G., Fisher, J. M., & Tritschler, K. A. (1983). A descriptive analysis of static postural control in 4, 6, and 8 year old normal and motorically awkward children. *American Journal of Physical Medicine, 62,* 12–26.

Williams, H. G., McClenaghan, B., & Ward, D. S. (1985). Duration of muscle activity during standing in normally and slowly developing children. *American Journal of Physical Medicine, 64*(4), 171–189.

Winnick, J. P., & Short, F. X. (1985). *Physical fitness testing of the disabled—Project UNIQUE.* Champaign, IL: Human Kinetics.

Zemke, R. (1985, March). Application of an ATNR rating scale to normal preschool children. *The American Journal of Occupational Therapy, 39*(3), 178–180.

Chapter 17

CONGENITAL DISABILITIES

Bryan had faced and overcome enormous challenges ever since he was a youngster going into kindergarten. He was born with a congenital birth condition known as spina bifida myelomeningocele which left him paralyzed from the waist down. He has always used a wheelchair to ambulate; in fact, now that he is age 13, his folks have just purchased a new chair that is designed for sport. He is excited because his new light chair gives him freedom that he never had before. In the past, the bulky old wheelchair slowed him down when getting around school and hindered him in his gym class. Mr. Harrier, the physical education teacher, has already listed several new activities in which Bryan can be truly competitive with the other students in class. The teacher is not afraid to let Bryan compete because he knows the implications and contraindications of Bryan's condition. With this knowledge, Mr. Harrier feels secure in developing specific physical fitness and motor skill activities for Bryan.

Congenital refers to any condition that occurs during fetal development. The person with a congenital disability is born with a birth or genetic defect that manifests itself in disability.

Congenital conditions are not necessarily progressive (e.g., spina bifida). Some congenital conditions are progressive but do not necessarily limit life-span (e.g., facioscapulohumeral muscular dystrophy). Some are not only progressive but also terminal; that is, the individual is expected to die in a relatively short period of time. Duchenne muscular dystrophy is one example of a congenital condition that is progressive, in fact relentlessly so, and terminal, and no intervention known at the time of this writing will slow the disease's progress.

Congenital conditions generally remain with the person throughout life, although medical, therapeutic, and educational procedures often lessen the impact that a given congenital condition would otherwise have on the individual's life. On the other hand, certain congenital disabilities are quite remediable. For example, a person with a congenital heart defect may have that condition surgically repaired and henceforth pursue life essentially as though the defect never existed.

Depending on the nature of the child's congenital disability, the adapted physical educator may observe significant interruption in many facets of the child's development. The educator needs to keep in mind, however, that the child, despite his or her congenital disability, is climbing the same developmental ladder as are his or her peers who do not have disabilities. The congenital condition simply makes the climb more difficult, and may often limit the child's progress.

With congenital disabilities, especially when they are significant, there may be a tendency on the part of some people not to be able to see the child through the disability. When this occurs, emphasis in relating to the child is often on disability rather than ability. When this occurs, the child's social and educational progress and horizons often become limited. As always, the child should come before the disability. Ability, not disability, needs to be emphasized. Even when a congenital disability is severe and permanent, perhaps even terminal, appropriate medical attention, therapy, and adapted physical education may readily facilitate the child's physical, motor, and psychosocial development.

Certain congenital conditions have been addressed elsewhere in the text. Some conditions, although congenital, also have acquired counterparts (e.g., amputations). The decision to afford any given condition having a congenital counterpart separate chapter status (e.g., hearing disabilities; visual disabilities) was based on the condition's prevalence among school-age populations and/or the quantity and depth of information deemed necessary to meaningfully address the topic.

MUSCULAR DYSTROPHY

Muscular dystrophy is a degeneration of muscle tissue. As muscle cells degenerate, fat and fibrous tissue emerge. Although the condition appears to be inherited, the cause is not known. In some cases, muscular dystrophy (MD) develops with no previous family history. Such cases are considered to be the result of genetic mutation. Approximately 200,000 persons in the United States have muscular dystrophy (Hopkins, 1985).

Muscular dystrophy is a general term that refers to numerous diseases that cause muscle cell deterioration, and in most cases (depending on the specific disease), result in premature death. Death occurs not because of muscle cell deterioration but from complications, usually involving heart or respiratory failure or both.

Four forms of muscular dystrophy affect school-age children: Duchenne, Becker, limb-girdle, and facioscapulohumeral. The last two will be described only briefly because prevalence does not justify in-depth consideration, but Duchenne and Becker will be discussed thoroughly.

DUCHENNE MUSCULAR DYSTROPHY

Duchenne MD, also called *childhood MD* or *pseudohypertrophic MD*, is an extremely progressive condition and is perhaps the most catastrophic of all childhood diseases. The condition occurs only in males and incidence is 1:3,500 (Urion, 1989). Detailed examination of medical records has not confirmed any report of Duchenne MD in girls (Siegel, 1982). A strong connection exists between the etiology of Duchenne and the inherited recessive X-linked type, which is passed from the mother to her male offspring. The female, who is the carrier, has a 50 percent chance of having a son with Duchenne MD. She also possesses the potential to pass the "carrier" condition on to 50 percent of her female children (Hopkins, 1985).

When physicians attempt to diagnose a child with muscular dystrophy they use a combination of tests, including manual muscle testing, biopsy, electromyogram (EMG), and blood cell analysis. If the blood test reveals an excessively high level of *creatine phosphokinase* (CPK), the cell walls of the muscle tissue are assumed to be breaking down. This leads to the conclusion that the child has Duchenne MD (De Lisa and Tipton, 1979).

Gardner-Medwin (1979) provides insight into this condition. He explains, "Life with the boy with Duchenne MD, for both the affected child and his parents, is punctuated by a series of crises. After the diagnosis itself, the next major crisis to be faced is the moment when he loses the ability to walk, usually between the age of 8 and 11 years. It is found that parents seem to fear this moment more than any other except death itself. Perhaps it is partly because the wheelchair has become the universal symbol of disability, but certainly the loss of their own boy's ability to walk confirms in a graphic and inescapable way the prognosis they have been given and had been hoping against hope might be wrong" (p. 659).

Although symptoms are usually present during the first year of life, they may go unnoticed. Clinical signs develop between the ages of 2 and 6. Early signs include a waddling gate and toe walking (Urion, 1989). The boy may have trouble climbing stairs and difficulty rising from a sitting or lying down position. The clumsiness becomes more prevalent, and there is a tendency to fall more often. The distinctive characteristic of this type of MD is the seeming enlargement (pseudohypertrophy) of calf muscles (Figure 17.1). This is caused by destruction of muscle cells, which are replaced by adipose (fat) and connective tissue. Muscle normally makes up approximately 40 percent of our total body weight. Approximately 33 percent of muscle mass has to be lost for function of the large postural muscles to be impaired. For those with Duchenne MD, the progression of muscle cell loss, resulting in weakness, is rapid with no remission. The proximal muscles, particularly in the pelvic region, begin to lose strength first. These are followed closely by involvement of muscles in the chest, abdomen, and shoulders.

Mild mental disability is associated with muscular dystrophy of the Duchenne type. However, the exact link between Duchenne and mental dysfunction is not understood. According to Avery and First (1989), mental deficiency is present in 25

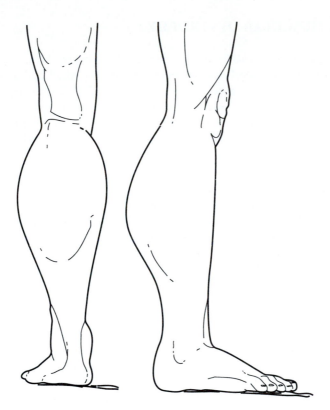

FIGURE 17.1   **Calf manifesting pseudohypertrophy in Duchenne muscular dystrophy.**

percent of boys with Duchenne. The average IQ of boys with Duchenne is reported to be 80 (Avery & First, 1989; Behrman & Vaughan, 1987).

Complications of Duchenne-type MD reflect the severity and extent of muscle weakness. The cause of death in most cases involves the cardiorespiratory system. The child may be unable to cough strongly and may have difficulty clearing secretions. These problems become particularly severe when the boy is immobile in a wheelchair and scoliosis develops. The inability to control the muscles used in breathing results in major complications, including congestive heart failure and stasis pneumonia, which are the most common causes of death (Hopkins, 1985).

At this time no cure exists for Duchenne MD, and no treatment has yet been found to correct the underlying pathology or to stop the progression of the disease (Spiro, 1987). One of the complications occurring as a direct result of muscle weakness is muscle contracture. This is particularly problematic after the youngster becomes a wheelchair user. Owing to a lack of leg use, the foot begins to turn inward and point down (complex equinocavovarus). The ankle joint becomes frozen in place, and the foot becomes totally dysfunctional. After this occurs, putting shoes on the boy is almost impossible. Some controversy exists regarding the use of orthotic devices (braces) by children who are beginning to have difficulty walking. Although each case should be considered individually, some experts reason that if the child will eventually become a wheelchair user, why extend the inevitable? Gardner-Medwin (1979) believes "that the provision of a well-chosen wheelchair, electrically powered if necessary, gives the boy much more practical independent mobility than does 'bracing for ambulation,' that the surgery and the exercises which must be continued use up precious time and energy that might have been devoted by the family to other activities, and that to concentrate attention on walking instead of on activities at which the boy could continue to succeed is psychologically wrong. . . . The boys themselves seem to take to wheelchairs with relief, and indeed with enthusiasm" (p. 661). The Muscular Dystrophy Association stresses that if a youngster is put into a manually operated wheelchair, it is critical that the boy propel himself. This helps to maintain existing muscle strength and thus slows muscle atrophy and its attendant complications.

Other specialists (Whaley & Wong, 1987; Behrman & Vaughan, 1987) take the position that the child should, within reason, ambulate as long as possible. The purpose of prolonging ambulation is to slow the muscle atrophy process so that the child retains as much muscle function as possible for as long as possible. Whaley and Wong recommend that, while disability is yet moderate, the child should ambulate at least three hours per day. They also recommend that the child exercise when bed rest is prolonged, after surgery, or when recovering from an injury. The above recommendation is offered not only to maintain as much muscle function as possible, but also to help overcome tendencies toward obesity that often result from overfeeding and low energy output.

During early stages, affected children may be treated more harshly by peers than are other children with chronic disabilities because the boy exhibits no visible manifestations of the disease. Peers mistake early stages of the illness for ineptness and weakness. The educator must recognize this and enlighten peers to encourage empathy for the child's dilemma.

The earliest signs of Duchenne MD include clumsiness of gait and a tendency to fall. The child may seem to be running "funny." Tiptoeing usually appears early and is caused, in part, by already weakened dorsiflexors. Other early signs of muscle weakness include swaying of the back and protruding abdomen. Gower's sign (named for W. R. Gower, who gave the first comprehensive account in English of the disease in 1879), also an indication of muscular weakness, appears when the child "walks up" the thighs using the hands for support in rising from a sitting position (Figure 17.2) (Behrman & Vaughan, 1987).

As the disease progresses many children become obese, presumably because of overeating and low energy output. Advancing obesity, coupled with decreasing muscle strength, motivates the child negatively, and activity is further diminished. Parent cooperation to reduce food intake is imperative, and activity levels require maintenance to retard fat accumulation.

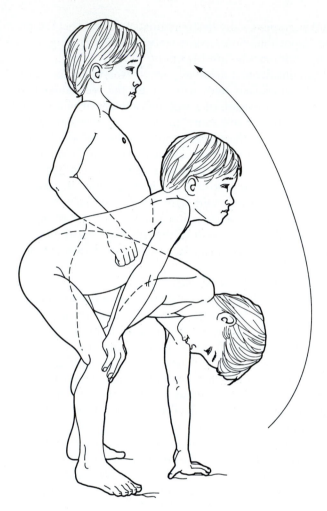

FIGURE 17.2   **Gower's sign.**

BECKER MUSCULAR DYSTROPHY

Becker MD is similar to Duchenne MD in that all persons with the disease are male and the condition is X-linked recessive in its genetic trait (e.g., the mother passes it on to her son). It is less severe than Duchenne and progresses more slowly, although following a similar course. Muscle weakness, however, is less pronounced and much more benign in its outcome. This type is differentiated from Duchenne by later onset (10 to 15 years of age), prolonged ambulatory capability, less severe muscle contracture of the foot and ankle, and nonprogressive scoliosis. Persons with Becker MD often live through the fourth decade of life.

LIMB-GIRDLE MUSCULAR DYSTROPHY

Limb-girdle MD can occur in either sex. It is a slowly progressive muscular dystrophy, usually beginning in childhood, marked by weakness and wasting in the shoulder or pelvic girdle. One girdle usually becomes symptomatic, with the other subsequently becoming involved. Disability typically becomes severe within 20 years. Skeletal deformities and muscle contractures occur late in the course of the disease. The person becomes disabled by middle life, and usually dies earlier than normal.

FACIOSCAPULOHUMERAL MUSCULAR DYSTROPHY

Facioscapulohumeral MD can occur in either sex. Symptoms may appear either in childhood or adult life. Progress of the disease is insidious, interspersed with prolonged periods of apparent arrest. Muscles of the face and upper extremities are primarily involved. The person often becomes aware of the progressive nature of the disease when unable to fully close the eyes, whistle, or drink through a straw. Weakened facial muscles cause a pouting appearance, and speech may become slurred. Persons with this muscular dystrophy typically have a normal life-span.

ACTIVITY CONSIDERATIONS

Persons with *limb-girdle* or *facioscapulohumeral MD* usually survive into adulthood. Quiet forms of recreation, including billiards, table tennis, fishing, and darts, provide activity for those with limited ambulation capability or those who are in a wheelchair.

During school years, activities that develop manipulative skills can prepare the person for clerical or bench-type work. During the advanced stages of limb-girdle or facioscapulohumeral MD, work may require close supervision or a sheltered workshop environment.

Kaneda (1980) believes that owing to the benign course and later onset of *Becker MD* (as compared with Duchenne) a greater potential exists for habilitation and resultant productivity. He states that "contractures and scoliosis are more amenable to conservative treatment...programs should include muscle strengthening and range of motion exercises with special attention to the ankle joint, to retain maximum function for as long as possible" (p. 1485).

For individuals with *Duchenne MD*, the critical point to remember is that the *dystrophy* (i.e., destruction of muscle cells by the disease) cannot be controlled, slowed, or cured (Spiro, 1987). The adapted physical educator must provide activities that will slow muscle *atrophy*, because when dystrophy and atrophy are combined the individual's condition deteriorates at a much faster rate. Strength and range of motion therefore must be maintained, and muscle contractures must, if possible, be reduced. According to Avery and First (1989), "The general aspects of management of children with muscular dystrophy include weight control to prevent the added burden of obesity and physical therapy to prevent contracture and profound weakening" (p. 739).

That range of motion exercise is necessary to prevent disabling muscle contractures is an accepted fact. The value of strengthening exercises, however, has been questioned. Some physicians express concern that short-term strength gains made by exercising dystrophic muscle may be followed by greater weakness in the long run. In other words, the natural muscle cell destruction that takes place during heavy exercise could have a negative effect on boys with Duchenne because they cannot replace destroyed muscle cells as do nondisabled children. This theory is strongly contested by de Lateur and Giaconi (1979), who found that subjects with Duchenne showed no evidence of overwork weakness. Their research used a 30-month follow-up study and concluded that, in addition to range of motion exercises, a program for patients with Duchenne MD may safely contain submaximal strengthening exercises that stay within the comfortable tolerance of the patient.

An analysis of the existing gait pattern is appropriate and should be done for all ambulatory students. Observe the stance and gait semiannually until the boy approaches the point of being unable to walk. The essential limiting factor is muscle weakness, but muscle contracture, itself largely secondary to weakness and abnormal posture, may also play a part. Extensive weakness develops first in the quadriceps muscles and in the extensors of the hips. A little unguarded flexion of the knees or hips while the boy is standing or walking results in "jackknifing" and a sudden fall. Consequently, these joints must remain fully extended whenever they are bearing weight, and at all times the body's center of gravity must be carried directly above them both. This explains the typical posture, the wide-based gait on the toes with the shoulders and head thrust back, inducing the characteristic lumbar lordosis. The boy will often stand squarely on one leg, the other "half-astride," balancing on the plantar-flexed forefoot. This posture usually results in mild but critical contractures of the hip flexors on the side of the "balancing" leg, especially of the iliotibial band (tensor fascia lata). Less often, these contractures develop on both sides, which results in the restriction of full hip extension (as well as adduction) and is the final limiting factor in preventing the boy from walking. At the same time, equinus contractures of the foot develop as a result of the constant equinus posture (standing on the toes), which is necessary for balance. Failure to understand the secondary nature of these contractures has led in some cases to inappropriate surgery in the form of cutting and lengthening of the Achilles tendon (tenotomy), after which the boy is usually unable to walk at all. Although most boys with Duchenne MD develop severe hip and ankle contractures, their ability to walk may be prolonged by continued elongation (stretching) exercises of the hips. A few boys, however, will lose their walking ability without any contractures simply because of extreme muscle weakness. Treatment, therefore, should begin at approximately 5 or 6 years of age. Have the student lie prone on a mat and actively stretch the hip flexor. Ankle contractures are more difficult to prevent. The instructor should stretch the plantar flexors, internal rotators, and adductors. In addition, strengthening exercises should be continued for dorsiflexion, external rotation, and abduction.

The time when the boy is finally *unable to walk* usually occurs between a few months and two years after the child becomes unable to climb stairs. His walking will become increasingly slower and more precarious; he often prefers to walk touching walls and holding on to furniture. He appears to be increasingly anxious about falling. At this point serious consideration should be given to use of a wheelchair.

Breathing exercises are extremely important and should be included, particularly for those in wheelchairs. Breathing is always improved when appropriate posture is maintained. The youngster may have difficulty sitting in the chair because of increased scoliosis or lordosis (a direct cause of weakened abdominal muscles). Diaphragmatic breathing exercises should be taught.

Siegel (1982) stresses the importance of assessing the existing physical fitness condition of the boys. He believes that measuring the strength and functional ability of the child with MD at regular intervals is important. In this way, subtle changes can be noted regarding progressive weakness, and the child's physical education program can be modified appropriately.

Table games and activities that encourage reaching and manipulating small objects should be selected. For young children, an elevated sandbox under which the wheelchair fits will encourage the child's upper extremity use and assist in maintaining manipulative skills. For older students, billiards, modified table tennis, fishing, and darts should be encouraged.

Obesity is a natural result of the combination of reduced exercise and the inability to maintain a desirable balance between exercise and caloric intake. Obesity is also often a result of psychic overeating (a response to anxiety) and parental pampering. The youngster with minimal energy demands should have his caloric intake reduced. When reducing calories, it is essential to ensure that the child's diet still has proper nutritional balance.

Finally, because of the progressively debilitating nature of the disease, emphasis should be placed on enjoying the present. Adapted physical education is a rich source of enjoyment and draws attention away from a treatment-oriented existence.

SPINA BIFIDA

Spina bifida is a congenital anomaly in which the bony casement of the spinal cord fails to close (see Figure 17.3). Spina bifida has replaced poliomyelitis as the major cause of paraplegia in young children (Dumars, 1985). The condition is known to begin developing between the 19th day and 31st day of gestation. The cause of spina bifida remains elusive. For reasons not understood, spina bifida incidence seems to be on the decline (Wolraich, 1987). Myelomeningocele, the most significant form of spina bifida, manifests itself in an average of 1 per 1,000 births in the United States. According to Travis (1976), incidence is three times as common among low socioeconomic whites as it is among high socioeconomic whites. Occurrence in blacks is only half of the combined white incidence. For reasons also not understood, the highest incidence of spina bifida (5 per 1,000) births occurs in England and Wales (Wolraich, 1987).

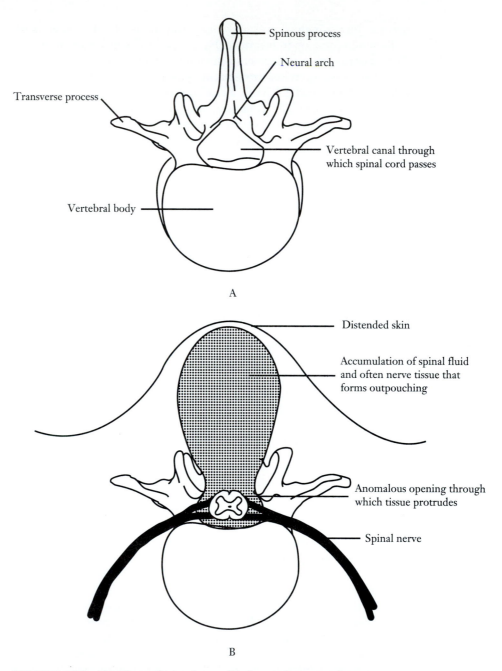

FIGURE 17.3   **(A) Normal vertebrae. (B) Anomalous vertebrae.**

Three categories of spina bifida occur, with specific designations dependent on the tissue that protrudes through the abnormal vertebral opening.

Spina bifida occulta is estimated to occur in 15 percent of the population (Urion, 1989). It is the least serious and is different from the other bifidas in that meninges do not protrude through the defective bony casement. Many people with occulta are asymptomatic, and their condition goes unnoticed until accidently discovered by X ray; spina bifida occulta that is asymptomatic is not considered a significant finding. Sometimes the occulta site may be marked by a dimple and/or tuft of hair. When disability does occur with occulta, neuromuscular disturbances usually manifest themselves in gait abnormalities, foot weaknesses, and bowel and bladder dysfunction. Disability associated with occulta results from abnormal adhesion of the spinal cord to the vertebral malformation (Whaley & Wong, 1987).

Spina bifida meningocele is a hernial protrusion of the meninges through a defect in the vertebral column. The meningocele contains no spinal nerve tissue, and paralysis usually does not occur. Surgical repair generally involves removal of the hernial protrusion. Following successful surgery, the meningocele seldom poses any significant long-term problem (Wolraich, 1987).

Spina bifida myelomeningocele is a hernial protrusion of both spinal cord and meninges through a defect in the vertebral column (see Figure 17.4). In the child with myelomeningocele, the membranes push out at some point along the back. As the spinal cord develops further, it does not follow a straight line but instead pushes out into a membranous sac (-cele), where it does not form in the normal way. Some or all of the nerves coming out of the vertebrae below the sac are not attached properly

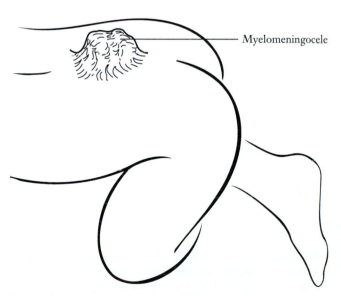

Myelomeningocele

FIGURE 17.4 **Outpouching anomalous vertebrae site.**

to the spinal cord and are thus unable to supply the brain with proper messages (Wolraich, 1990).

In myelomeningocele the spinal cord is subjected to permanently damaging trauma, resulting in partial or total absence of muscle function below the vertebral defect. The higher the site on the column, the more extensive the loss of function. Figure 17.5 reveals muscle function as affected by lesion site. Any complete lesion at T12 or higher results in the person's having no leg movement. Movement affected by any given lesion site as portrayed in the figure is based on the presumption that the lesion at that given site is complete. Incomplete lesions result in exceptions to rules cited in Figure 17.5.

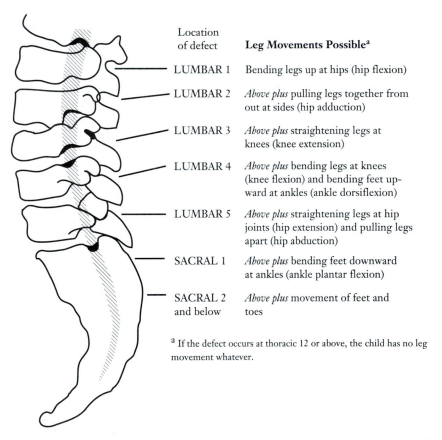

Location of defect	**Leg Movements Possible[a]**
LUMBAR 1	Bending legs up at hips (hip flexion)
LUMBAR 2	*Above plus* pulling legs together from out at sides (hip adduction)
LUMBAR 3	*Above plus* straightening legs at knees (knee extension)
LUMBAR 4	*Above plus* bending legs at knees (knee flexion) and bending feet upward at ankles (ankle dorsiflexion)
LUMBAR 5	*Above plus* straightening legs at hip joints (hip extension) and pulling legs apart (hip abduction)
SACRAL 1	*Above plus* bending feet downward at ankles (ankle plantar flexion)
SACRAL 2 and below	*Above plus* movement of feet and toes

[a] If the defect occurs at thoracic 12 or above, the child has no leg movement whatever.

FIGURE 17.5 **Relationship between level of defect and leg movement in children with spina bifida. Incomplete lesions account for variations among children with myelomeningocele.** (Reprinted with permission of Aspen Systems Corporation, copyright 1990, from M. L. Wolraich. Myelomeningocele. In J. A. Blackman, *Medical Aspects of Development Disabilities in Children Birth to Three*, p. 189.)

Unbalanced muscle pulls may occur whether the lesion is complete or incomplete. Either kind of imbalance in the lower extremities may result in hip dislocation, skeletal deformity, club or rocker bottom feet, and abnormal spinal curves including scoliosis (S curve), lordosis (swayback), or kyphosis (humpback).

COMPLICATIONS THAT ACCOMPANY SPINA BIFIDA

Hydrocephalus (*hydro*, water; *cephalus*, brain) occurs in 80 percent of all myelomeningocele cases (Howell, 1978). Normally, the cerebrospinal fluid travels inside and around the brain and spinal cord and is eventually absorbed into the bloodstream. In spina bifida some interference usually occurs in the circulation and absorption of this fluid. Hydrocephalus is characterized by abnormal accumulation of cerebrospinal fluid within the skull. As a result, pressure on the brain reaches intolerable levels. Enlargement of the head occurs, accompanied by brain atrophy, mental deterioration, and spastic paralysis of the lower limbs.

Surgically implanted shunts or drainage systems in the cranial cavity can release spinal fluid pressure. The preferred procedure, particularly in young children who are still growing, is the ventriculoperitoneal shunt (Williamson, 1987). This procedure allows for implantation of excess drainage tubing between the peritoneal cavity and the brain, thereby allowing the child to avoid unnecessary surgeries while she is growing. Ventriculoatrial shunts through which excess fluid drains into the right atrium are usually reserved for older children who have completed most of their growth or for those who have some abdominal pathology (Whaley & Wong, 1987). Examples of each shunt procedure appear in Figure 17.6. Although an implant does not reverse damage, it can significantly reduce further brain damage.

Children with spina bifida complicated by hydrocephalus likely will have had a shunt implanted to relieve cerebrospinal fluid pressure on the brain. Occasionally, the child will experience shunt malfunction, which is serious and requires prompt medical attention. Shunt malfunction warning signs include the following (Williamson, 1987):

1. Increase in head size
2. Behavioral changes such as extreme irritability or fussiness
3. Increase in sleepiness
4. Seizures
5. Diminished reaction to the environment, or lethargy
6. Forceful vomiting
7. Swelling or redness in skin area around shunt
8. Headaches
9. "Setting sun" eyes (iris only partially visible because of downward gaze)

Deep pressure on the shunt that could alter fluid flow is contraindicated. Also contraindicated are activities in which the person is in the upside down position for

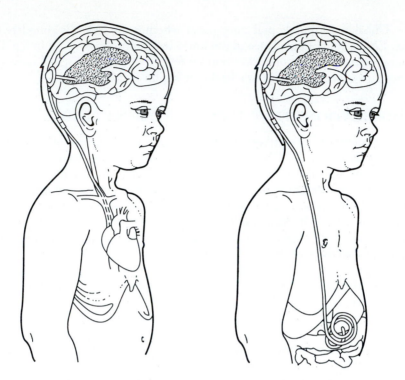

FIGURE 17.6   **Ventriculoatrial shunt (left) and ventriculoperitoneal shunt (right).**

extended periods. This person may disrupt fluid flow and shunt valvular function
(Williamson, 1987).

Another major problem involves uneven muscle pull, which results in paralysis
and deformity of the lower extremities. Fractures are common because affected bones
become weak and brittle and paralysis inhibits the child's ability to react protectively
and prevent injurious falls.

Problems of overweight and obesity often accompany spina bifida. A major
problem associated with excessive weight gain is that it often discourages the person
from being active even more than before and thus marks the beginning of a vicious
cycle.

To some degree, excessive fat weight gain can be a function of paralysis or
paresis that discourages pursuit of an active life-style. Often, however, inactivity that
fosters excessive weight gain is more a function of socialization than disability. People
with disabilities, particularly those with some paralysis or paresis, are often led to
believe that the desire to be active is somehow unreasonable or inappropriate.

The person with spina bifida who does not have typical use of the large lower extremities may need to reduce his caloric intake to maintain or achieve desired weight.
This is particularly true among persons who are relatively inactive. When reducing

calories, for whatever reason, it is important that nutrition remain adequate. This is essential for everyone and particularly for any child who is still growing. Finally, encouraging the person to adopt an active life-style may help the person maintain or achieve desired weight in at least three ways: (1) People who are inactive often consume excessive amounts of food (sometimes calorie-intense junk food) purely out of boredom, whereas active people, at least when exercising, usually are not eating; (2) Exercise will burn calories that would otherwise likely be stored as fat; and (3) Self-esteem that comes from feeling and looking better through exercise may encourage the person to want to continue doing good things (including exercise) for herself.

Bowel and bladder dysfunction (incontinence) occurs in spina bifida as a result of spinal cord trauma. In myelomeningocele in which cord trauma results in paralysis, 90 percent experience bladder and bowel incontinence. This incontinence is not particularly problematic for the child, at least during infancy, but it can become a problem during school years and in adult life.

Most children with myelomeningocele do not feel the urge to urinate, and have no control over the urinary sphincter muscle. This is potentially dangerous because urine cannot be passed. If not cared for, the condition can cause permanent kidney damage or even kidney failure. For the person who has survived major complications associated with spina bifida, including hydrocephalus, prognosis depends largely on avoiding or managing the severity of renal disease (Whaley & Wong, 1987).

In most cases the preferred treatment for urinary incontinence is intermittent catheterization. Catheterized urine drains into a collection bag, which may be affixed to the person's leg or into some other appropriate receptacle. In many instances, children can self-catheterize. In school settings it is important to know who catheterizes if the child does not self-catheterize, and when during the day catheterizing occurs. Although catheterizing is certainly important, care should be taken that, to the extent possible, it does not unnecessarily disrupt the child's school day.

Varying degrees of bowel control can be achieved by children with myelomeningocele. Frequent problems include constipation and fecal impaction. Often, these can be managed by adopting regular toilet habits and regulating diet. A diet high in fiber tends to help alleviate constipation, and sometimes suppositories will be used to soften the stool.

A child with fecal and/or urinary incontinence may be diapered. According to Best (1975), "the teacher of the child with spina bifida will need to be conscious of the physical needs of the child as they relate to bowel and bladder control. If the child is wearing an external collection bag, or if the child attends school wearing diapers, the teacher needs to be alert to the requirements of personal hygiene for the child, not only for cleanliness and infection control, but because of the social implications for the child if he/she is shunned by classmates as a result of odor or altered personal appearance" (p. 55).

The ultimate life expectancy of people with spina bifida is not certain. Recent successful medical treatment is making adult survival increasingly common. In a follow-up of children with myelomeningocele, 80 percent were walking and 20 percent used wheelchairs. Hydrocephalus was arrested in 38 percent of the cases. An IQ of 80 or above was found in 89 percent of the cases. Seventy-nine percent had graduated from high school, and 27 percent pursued postsecondary education (Bleck & Nagel, 1982).

ACTIVITY CONSIDERATIONS

When spina bifida results in nerve damage and limited, unbalanced muscle function, braces equalling the child's body weight historically have had to be worn. This situation has improved significantly in recent years, however, with the advent of relatively lightweight braces fashioned from plastic. The awkwardness of braces regardless of type tends to discourage the child's involvement in movement-centered efforts. The child's motivation to participate in physical activities may match her perceived limited capacity. Perceived limitations may not be accurate, however, but may be simply reflections of the limited expectations that others hold. Past excuses from physical exertion, including physical education, only reinforce inactivity and withdrawal.

Most persons with spina bifida can enjoy pursuits that need not be sedentary. Activities for children who use wheelchairs include darts, fishing, catch, bowling, and archery. Wheelchair basketball provides an excellent activity option when such an opportunity is available. Progressive resistance upper extremity exercises (weight training) are also indicated. When crutch-assisted or other alternative ambulation is possible, the child may participate in modified ambulatory activities. Activities for the child using a wheelchair are also appropriate for the child using crutches or braces who may also participate in modified ball games, low-organized games, and relays. Activity modification varies from child to child. An activity can be modified to suit the child's physical limitations and, when present, the child's mental disability.

When crutch-assisted ambulation is projected to be the ambulation mode over a protracted period of time, Lofstrand crutches are generally preferred over conventional crutches. With Lofstrand crutches, a cuff encircles the upper arm for crutch stability, and no part of the crutch touches the axilla. Conventional crutches encourage the user to "lean" on the crutch where it meets the axilla, and such relentless leaning has the potential to damage nerves innervating the arm that cross the axilla from the torso. The Lofstrand crutch eliminates this problem. When children do walk with the aid of crutches or other assistive devices, it is important to be sure that the device fits the child. Attention to this concern is particularly important when the child is growing rapidly.

Many people with spina bifida will walk as the preferred mode of ambulation part or all of the time. Findley (1983) has stated that walking as a young child is a better predictor of whether the person will walk as an adolescent than is lesion site. Findley observed that children who did not walk outside independently by age 6 typically did not walk even minimally as adolescents. The major implication for practice would seem to be that walking behavior in adolescence and beyond, provided that it is an appropriate expectation, can be facilitated by providing the person opportunities and encouragement to walk when he is young.

In almost all spina bifida cases, swimming is an excellent activity for strengthening muscles and maintaining desirable range of motion. Swimming is particularly valuable because it is enjoyable and permits the exercise of extremities that cannot function under the stress of gravity or weightbearing.

Problems with muscle weakness of the lower extremities must be anticipated from the beginning to avoid development of joint deformities caused by muscle contractures. This can be helped by proper positioning and by range-of-motion exercises. Regular treatments, at least three times per week, will assist in allowing the child to grow stronger and will increase chances for some form of ambulation. Some youngsters will be able to walk without assistance, whereas others will require braces and assistive devices such as canes or crutches. Walking and weightbearing exercises are important to prevent osteoporosis, which could lead to easy bone fracturing.

Upper extremity activities and exercise that conditions arms and shoulder girdle are excellent for children with spina bifida who walk with crutches or who transfer themselves to and from the wheelchair. The adapted physical educator should know the child's capabilities and should understand biomechanical principles so she can educate the child in appropriate techniques for maneuvering in and out of a wheelchair.

Children with spina bifida with unbalanced muscle function will develop debilitating muscle contractures that result in skeletal deformities. Bracing, which minimizes the progress of contractures, and stretching exercises may be prescribed by the child's physician.

Because the child with spina bifida experiences no feeling in affected extremities, the educator must watch for skin irritations and sores resulting from braces or shoes. In some instances, skin irritations and pressure sores have become more problematic with the advent of plastic braces that fit more closely than the older conventional metal kind. Skin breakdowns should be reported to the school nurse, parent, or the child's physician.

Wheelchair use may be necessary in some cases, but many opt for the wheelchair regardless of ability to walk. Some persons perceive themselves as less deviant sitting in the wheelchair than dragging paralyzed extremities along behind crutches. Others recognize that wheelchair ambulation is more efficient. Regardless of the person's ability to walk, standing is physiologically more desirable than sitting. Standing, even for those who cannot walk, improves urinary system function, reduces susceptibility to fractures, improves circulation, and is psychologically beneficial.

In many instances, wheelchair ambulation is desirable regardless of the person's ability to walk with or without assistive devices. Depending on the degree of disability and the demands of the activity in question, walking sometimes may simply be more trouble than it is worth. Although exercise and physical exertion are important for many reasons, most of which are obvious, walking for the sake of walking, particularly when it is unduly fatiguing, frustrating, and inefficient, is quite difficult to justify. Furthermore, the person with spina bifida who walks often manifests a gait that extraordinarily stresses joints. The excessive stress across time (e.g., years) may lead to early onset of osteoarthritis in affected joints. Given this possibility, there may be merit in at least some effort to spare affected joints unnecessary, relentless trauma.

CONGENITAL HIP DISLOCATION

Congenital hip dislocation is a malformation of the hip joint, which results in femoral head displacement from the hip socket (acetabulum) (Figure 17.7). This lesion results from abnormal development of one or all components of the hip joint, including the acetabulum, femoral head, and surrounding capsule and soft tissues (Behrman & Vaughan, 1987). Displacement occurs in three stages:

1. **Unstable stage.** An abnormally shallow acetabulum makes the hip susceptible to dislocation. The affected limb appears shorter than the nonaffected limb. Gluteal and thigh folds may increase in number and prominence on the affected side.
2. **Subluxation stage.** The femur, although still in contact with the acetabulum, rides upward and outward from its acetabular seat.
3. **Dislocation stage.** The femur becomes completely displaced outside the acetabulum.

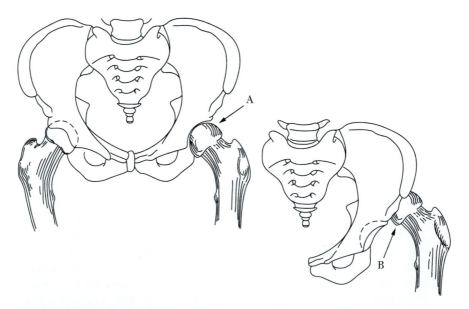

FIGURE 17.7   **(A) Hip susceptible to dislocation (note shallow socket). (B) Hip in dislocation stage.**

Incidence is high among those of Latin descent but is rare among blacks. Incidence is 10 times more common among children who had breech delivery. Incidence is relatively low in cultures that carry infants with legs straddled on the parent's hip, and relatively high in cultures that swaddle the infant's legs together in adduction and extension (Blackman, 1990). The condition usually occurs unilaterally and is more common among girls than boys (7:1) (Whaley & Wong, 1987).

Early identification and management of congenital hip dislocation are important. With early identification and management, the condition is usually reversible. Treatment initiated before 2 months of age yields the highest success rate (Whaley & Wong, 1987). If allowed to progress unchecked, severe arthritis can result, requiring complicated medical corrective procedures. When congenital hip dislocation is left untreated, severe osteoarthritis typically occurs by middle age (Millis, 1987).

The child with congenital hip dislocation walks with a limp (unilateral) or a ducklike waddle (bilateral). In either case, pain may not be evident. Unfortunately, the young child's condition may go unnoticed until limping or waddling becomes apparent when walking commences.

The Trendelenburg test is a diagnostic aid to identify congenital hip dislocation. The child stands on one foot and flexes the nonweightbearing extremity at both hip and knee. When the Trendelenburg test is positive, the nonweightbearing hip tends to sag because weakened thigh abductors on the affected side are unable to support the pelvis in a normal parallel-to-the-ground attitude (Lasko and Knopf, 1984) (Figure 17.8).

ACTVITY CONSIDERATIONS

Efforts to reduce congenital hip dislocation include harnessing, casting, traction, and splinting. Treatment varies with age of the child.

Delayed treatment retards normal hip development, and prolonged dislocation precipitates abnormal development of affected bone and soft tissue. The child whose condition is not treated early will probably need surgical reduction, requiring removal and reconstruction of malformed bone tissue. According to Whaley & Wong (1987), "Successful reduction and reconstruction become increasingly difficult by age 4 and are usually impossible or inadvisable by age 6" (p. 453).

During the course of treatment, the school-age child will have protracted periods of lower extremity immobility. At this time upper extremity exercises should be used to improve energy levels for maintenance of overall physical condition. Actually, any activity that does not traumatize the affected hip should be considered for inclusion in the child's physical education program.

If the child must remain immobile for an extended period, nonlocomotor activities should be brought to the child. When treatment limits interaction with peers, play and learning experiences should be arranged to improve social and emotional growth.

Once mobility is again permitted, swimming is an appropriate activity because it facilitates range of motion development and provides resistance for hip joint

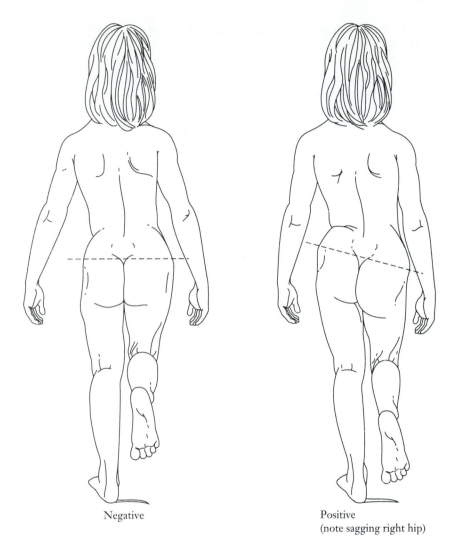

Negative

Positive
(note sagging right hip)

***FIGURE 17.8*   Trendelenburg test.**

muscles when weightbearing is not appropriate. When activity is indicated, the child's physician will prescribe strength and flexibility exercises.

If the child has been immobilized during early childhood when locomotor skills develop and normal posture occurs, opportunities to learn basic locomotor skills and postures should be provided.

The child who has been immobilized for a long period will need to learn social skills if activity and play experiences are to be positive. The adapted physical educator must be empathetic and accentuate the positive, yet limit reinforcement when behavior is inappropriate. The child's classmates must also be helped to understand the child's condition. In this way the physical educator can assist the child in creating positive peer relationships.

TALIPES (CLUBFOOT)

Talipes (clubfoot) is a deformity of the foot characterized by foot malalignment in relation to the leg. The condition may be acquired or congenital, with congenital being the more prevalent. Talipes can occur in conjunction with spina bifida, hydrocephalus, or congenital hip dislocation. Depending on the configuration, the deformity occurs in 1 to 4.4 per 1,000 births. The condition is twice as common in boys as in girls. According to these statistics, talipes is among the most frequently occurring chronic musculoskeletal disfigurements.

Talipes has four cardinal positions: **talipes varus** (foot angled inward or inversion), **talipes valgus** (foot angled outward or eversion), **talipes equinus** (foot angled directly downward or plantar flexion), and **talipes calcaneus** (foot angled directly upward or dorsiflexion) (Figure 17.9).

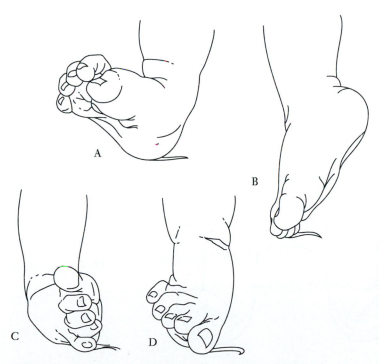

FIGURE 17.9   **Four cardinal talipes positions. (A) Foot angled inward or varus (inversion). (B) Foot angled outward or valgus (eversion). (C) Foot angled downward or equinus (plantar flexion). (D) Foot angled upward or calcaneus (dorsiflexion).**

Combinations of these deformities are often present, with **talipes equinovarus** (foot turned inward and downward) the most prevalent form combination (Millis, 1989).

The clubfoot may be a rigid or flexible deformity, depending on when the clubbing started to occur during pregnancy. The earlier the occurrence began, the more rigid the deformity. Early occurrences tend to result in bone deformities (i.e., in rigidity), whereas later occurrences tend to involve soft tissue and minimum bone abnormality (i.e., flexibility). Regardless of time of occurrence during pregnancy, if left untreated the condition worsens and becomes more rigid.

As with many congenital deformities, early intervention helps ensure a positive prognosis. Early treatment of talipes typically means within hours after birth. Too often, however, prompt treatment that provides greater potential for correction is not followed up with therapy and exercise. Visits to the doctor may become less frequent, and only when serious deformity has reappeared is the child reassessed. It is critical to recognize that talipes tends to recur, and orthopedic management is usually necessary throughout childhood (Behrman & Vaughan, 1987). The adapted physical educator must therefore become alert to cessation or reversal of rehabilitation progress. Interruption in progress requires alerting the child's physician immediately.

ACTIVITY CONSIDERATIONS

Conservative clubfoot deformity correction includes casting or bracing to achieve a more functional anatomical position (Figure 17.10). If the foot does not respond

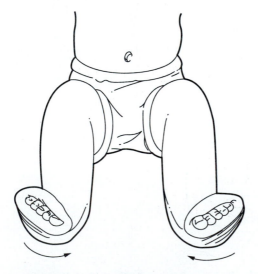

FIGURE 17.10 **Talipes casted into progressively more normal anatomical positions.**

completely, and often it does not, surgical correction may be needed (Behrman & Vaughan, 1987). More rigid deformities (owing to early onset during pregnancy or late postnatal intervention) generally respond only partially to manual pressure. In such cases, surgery is the preferred procedure.

Congenital clubfoot, corrected initially by manual pressure or surgical correction followed by manual pressure, requires constant supervision during the growth years. Progressive exercises to improve muscular condition in the affected foot and in ankle muscles are a valuable adjunct to corrective treatment, but exercise alone does not constitute adequate remedial attention.

No single activity prescription suits all children with clubfoot. Activities must be determined for each child. Severe involvement limits vigorous, weightbearing activity, which may not even be possible for some children. Following casting and bracing, hightop corrective footwear may render vigorous, weightbearing activities awkward. Some children with clubfoot do participate in weightbearing activities, including organized youth sports programs. In any case, the adapted physical educator should encourage vigorous activity involvement when appropriate.

Modification or limitation of lower extremity activity need not limit activity to the upper extremities. When lower extremity activities are limited, however, an activity regimen for the upper extremities can help to maintain a desirable level of fitness and energy.

For a child or adolescent, an abnormality in locomotor patterns results in an emotional disability as significant as the physical disability. The child's clubfoot does not alter his psychosocial and emotional needs. In addition to physical rehabilitation, helping the child establish a positive level of self-esteem is a significant responsibility of the adapted physical educator.

SKELETAL DYSPLASIA

The term *skeletal dysplasia* has replaced *dwarfism*. **Dysplasia** means disorder of growth. Skeletal refers to the skeletal system, where the dysplasia or growth disorder is occurring.

Many etiological factors cause growth inhibition. The most common form is inherited achondroplasia, which is characterized by shortened limbs and height seldom exceeding 1.4 meters (54″)(Avery & First, 1989). The condition occurs in 1 out of 1,000 births. With achondroplasia, the bridge of the nose is flattened and depressed and the forehead may appear to bulge. Hands and feet tend to be foreshortened, but fingers are of normal length.

Skeletal deformities occurring with achondroplasia may require orthopedic management. Abnormal stress on weightbearing joints resulting from unmanaged skeletal deformity may predispose persons with achondroplasia to early onset of osteoarthritis.

Atypical spinal curves are also quite common. These curves may be managed conservatively but at times require surgical intervention. If the person has had a history of atypical spinal curvature requiring management, activities might need to be selected which, while providing adequate exercise, do not unnecessarily traumatize the spine.

Achondroplasia is not associated with deficiencies in intelligence. Apart from mechanical difficulties that shortened stature creates, regular physical and motor activities and typical life pursuits usually characterize the person's interests and achievement motivations.

ACTIVITY CONSIDERATIONS

Foreshortened limbs tend to reduce the individual's motor skill performance to less than typical levels. Typical performance limitations occur in body projection skills because shortened lower extremities reduce force application against a surface (i.e., explosive strength). Likewise, disproportionately short upper extremities reduce potential for distance throwing. Activities that use implements (e.g., golf, tennis, softball, or badminton) create performance problems because the implements are of disproportionately large size. To some degree, this limitation can be overcome by "choking up" on the shaft or cutting down the shaft size.

Using sport implements that require simultaneous arm action (e.g., golf club, softball bat) creates a complication. Disproportionately short arms and a characteristically broad trunk and shoulders necessarily place the implement inordinately close to the body. This trunk and arm compaction significantly inhibits freedom of movement during the swing, thus limiting potential for normal striking achievement.

None of these limitations should be construed as contraindications, but achievement expectations of both child and teacher should be realistically modified. When expectations are modified in accordance with potential, the child can participate safely and successfully in the regular physical education program.

CONGENITAL HEART DISEASE

Congenital heart disease is more common in children than acquired heart disease. Some form of congenital heart defect occurs in approximately 8 of every 1,000 live births (Vargo, 1985). Table 17.1 lists frequency and type of congenital cardiac anomalies.

The fetal heart begins to take recognizable shape during the first trimester of fetal life. This is also when abnormalities develop. The major cardiovascular structure is formed by the 7th week, so severe abnormalities of the heart and major blood vessels usually occur before the 8th week. Rubella, if contracted by the mother during the first 2 months of pregnancy, can cause fetal heart defects. (See Figure 17.11 for a diagram of the fetal heart.)

TABLE 17.1   **Congenital Cardiac Anomalies Seen at Johns Hopkins Hospital Cardiac Clinic, 1963–1972**[a]

Anomaly	Percentage (%) of All Congenital Heart Disease
Ventricular septal defect	26
Pulmonic stenosis	14
Tetralogy of Fallot	11
Atrial septal defect	9
Patent ductus arteriosus	8
Aortic stenosis	6
Coarctation of the aorta	5
Endocardial cushion defect	5
Transposition of the great vessels	3
Total	87

Source: From Freedom, R. M., Pieroni, D. R., and Ho, C. S. Congenital Heart Disease. In *Current Diagnosis 4*, edited by H. F. Conn and R. B. Conn, Jr. Philadelphia: W. B. Saunders, 1974, p. 323.

[a] Total number of patients studied (0 to 16 years) was 2956.

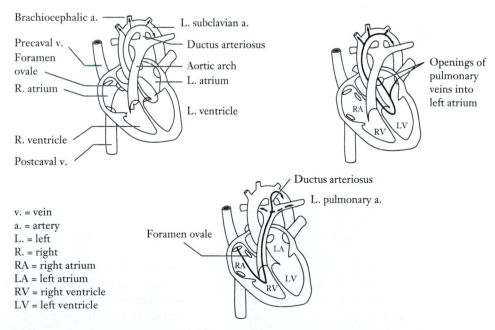

FIGURE 17.11   **Chambers, openings, and circulation in the fetal heart.**

Although specific causes of congenital malformations are largely undocumented, maternal illnesses such as rubella, mumps, or influenza during the first 3 months of pregnancy are known to cause defects. X rays and some drugs have similar detrimental effects. Heart defects, however, are common to all races in all parts of the world. Most inborn heart defects are probably not inherited, but a mother with a congenital heart defect has a 2 percent chance of passing the malformation on to her child.

At least 90 percent of children with congenital heart defects can be categorized in one of four groups. In order of frequency, the groups consist of (1) septal defects, (2) constriction of the aorta, (3) patent ductus arteriosus, and (4) the tetralogy of Fallot (*fal-low*). All are correctable by surgery.

The problem underlying septal defects occurs during formation of the septum, the dividing wall of either the atria or ventricles. An abnormal and ongoing septal opening (**patent foramen ovale**) between the two upper chambers (atria) of the heart is the most common and least important of congenital defects. This condition is an abnormal opening that remains after birth. In fetal development, the normal foramen ovale allows blood to move from the right to the left atrium, bypassing the nonfunctioning lungs. After birth this opening slowly closes, so by the end of the 1st year the opening is sealed. When the opening does not close within the normal time, this slight defect makes it impossible for the child to develop normal cardiorespiratory efficiency. A physician can determine accurately if the defect is present.

Any larger hole in the atrial wall is considered serious and must be corrected surgically for the child to live a normal, active life. Open heart surgery corrects this type of problem.

The most severe congenital heart defect is **tetralogy of Fallot** which produces cyanosis (blueness of the skin caused by lack of oxygen in the blood). The condition is caused by a narrowing (stenosis) of the pulmonary valve leading from the right ventricle to the pulmonary artery. Stenosis of the pulmonary valve restricts the flow of unoxygenated blood to the lungs. As a result, almost 75 percent of the blood returning to the heart may pass directly from the right ventricle into the aorta without becoming oxygenated. Three other changes occur as a result of this condition. First, the septum is shifted to the right, further narrowing the pulmonary opening. Second, an opening develops in the ventricle wall, which allows blood to pass. Third, the right ventricle wall is enlarged owing to the increased pumping action required to force blood through the narrowed pulmonary valve. These four complications gave the condition its name—tetralogy (*tetra*, four).

Surgery is necessary to correct the tetralogy of Fallot defect. Boyd (1971) notes that the child's improvement following surgery is dramatic. Cyanosis and shortness of breath are often eased immediately.

Epstein, Beiser, and Goldstein (1973) stated that in 10 subjects who had complete surgical correction of tetralogy of Fallot, resting cardiorespiratory signs were normal except for small residual ventricular outflow. During upright exercise of sufficient intensity to lower pulmonary arterial oxygen, eight patients showed increased cardiac output, but less than that attained by normal subjects. Residual cardiac dysfunction thus tends to remain despite corrective surgery. In 1976 James, Daplan, and Schwartz studied 43 asymptomatic patients, 1 to 14 years of age, following surgical correction of tetralogy of Fallot. Maximum heart rate and physical working capacity were lower in these patients when they were compared with age-matched controls. Impaired cardiac performance was evident in the individuals who had had surgery. Interestingly, the patients who had surgery while they were young developed more efficient working capacities than the youngsters who had surgery during adolescence.

According to Avery and First (1989), "Everything being equal, all patients with tetralogy of Fallot should electively undergo surgery before 2 years of age" (p. 343). They also stress the importance of early surgical management of tetralogy of Fallot for motor and social development reasons:

> The average toddler is becoming increasingly active at that age and we ... ought to strive to give the child adequate tools for locomotion. Another psychologic issue is the increasing trend to socialize, to play with other children. It's hard to be "one of the kids" if you have to squat every few minutes.

Patent ductus arteriosus is a congenital heart defect that affects approximately 1 in every 5,500 babies. The fetal blood vessel that joins the pulmonary artery and the aorta normally closes immediately in newborn infants—specifically, when the baby takes his first breath. In some babies the vessel may take almost 1 month to close completely. If it fails to close, the condition is known as patent ductus arteriosus. During the first few months the child does not require increased oxygen, but when active walking, running, and jumping begin, the youngster cannot sustain effort because of low cardiac and respiratory reserve. The heart muscle therefore enlarges and the left ventricle hypertrophies because of the excessive work load to pump a greater than normal blood output. Without corrective surgery, people with this condition die between the ages of 20 and 40 owing to pulmonary congestion and increased work load imposed on the heart. Unrepaired patent ductus arteriosus, however, is virtually unknown today in the United States and developed countries. Historically, surgical treatment has involved tying off (ligating) the ductus arteriosus so that the blood flows through normal pathways. Recently, experimental catheterization procedures have been developed that enable placement of umbrellalike devices directly into the anomalous opening. Should this experimental procedure prove effective, surgical repair may no longer be necessary, costs could be reduced, and the person would not be left with a significant permanent scar (Avery & First, 1989).

The abnormal myocardial growth associated with heart defects is distinctly different from the desired hypertrophy of the heart muscle that results from progressive exercise. A healthy heart does and should increase in size when positive aerobic programs are employed.

Many children experience a **heart murmur**. Two out of every three healthy babies have an innocent heart murmur that results from slow development of the circulatory system. This is of no consequence, and most children outgrow these functional murmurs in adolescence (American Heart Association, 1974).

The physician detects a heart murmur with a stethoscope. Murmurs are generally low in intensity and quite difficult to identify. They indicate an imperfection in the heart valves and may sound like indistinct gurglings or hissings as valves close improperly. The blood is being squeezed backward (regurgitated), and not enough blood is being moved forward into the system.

The physician determines which heart murmurs are "normal" and which are associated with heart disease. A serious murmur is often associated with cardiac malformations such as ventricular septal defect, atrial septal defect, and patent ductus arteriosus. Murmurs commonly result when valves are damaged and do not close completely. Rheumatic heart disease is a known cause of acquired heart murmurs.

Children with murmurs generally have lower fitness levels, particularly in activities involving endurance.

Murmurs are also heard in normal hearts. During intense exercise, the blood may flow through the valves and chambers of the heart so rapidly that a turbulence is produced. This turbulence can be heard when the blood in the chamber collides with the incoming stream; it is a phenomenon of no consequence.

When a student has been identified as having a congenital heart defect, the adapted physical educator should refer to the child's medical history to determine if and when surgery was performed on the youngster. If the child underwent surgery several years ago, then the individual may now be able to take part in normal physical activities. The teacher should request a physician's recommendation for activity level for any child who is presently under a physician's care for cardiac conditions.

PHYSICAL ACTIVITY FOR CHILDREN WITH CONGENITAL HEART DEFECTS

Some children with mild heart conditions can participate in organized sports (Gersony, 1975). Students with decreased exercise tolerance tend to limit their activities. Labored breathing (dyspnea), headache, and fatigue in cyanotic youngsters are indications that the activity is too strenuous. Activity intensity should be lowered and smaller gradients established for children exhibiting these symptoms.

For the adolescent with congenital heart disease, Mahoney (1984) states, "The physician should discourage a sedentary lifestyle and encourage physical activity in programs such as physical education but stress with school personnel that the child should be allowed to rest when fatigued" (p. 172). If the student has a dilated heart or significant left or right heart obstructive lesion, the individual should not participate in competitive sports. Participation in such organized sports as baseball, golf, and bowling is acceptable.

The physical educator should look for general warning signs when teaching students with cardiac abnormalities. Common complaints are fatigue, shortness of breath, chest pains, cyanosis (blueness of lips and fingernail beds), and fainting. Poor growth and small chest development also indicate that the child is having difficulty stimulating the cardiovascular system sufficiently.

FUNCTIONAL CLASSIFICATION OF INDIVIDUALS WITH HEART DISEASE

Table 17.2 lists functional classifications of heart disease developed by the American Heart Association. Physicians use these classifications when writing exercise prescriptions, but note that patient classification according to functional capacity gives only part of the information needed to plan individualized activities. An activity recommendation or prescription should be based on information from many sources. The functional classification is simply an estimate of what the person's heart will allow. Classification should not be influenced by the presence of structural lesions or by an opinion as to treatment or prognosis.

THERAPEUTIC CLASSIFICATION OF INDIVIDUALS WITH HEART DISEASE

Table 17.3 lists therapeutic classifications of people with heart disease. These classifications are a guide to permissible activity for each functional class. The therapeutic recommendations should be translated into daily physical activity such as running a number of yards, climbing a number of stairs, lifting a number of pounds, or standing for a limited time. Play programs for each child should be individualized by specifying type and duration of outdoor and indoor activity.

TABLE 17.2 **Functional Capacities of Individuals with Heart Disease**

Class	Description
I	People with cardiac disease who do not have resulting limitation of physical activity. Ordinary physical activity does not cause undue fatigue, palpitation, dyspnea, or anginal pain.
II	People with cardiac disease resulting in slight limitation of physical activity who are comfortable at rest. Ordinary physical activity results in fatigue, palpitation, dyspnea, or anginal pain.
III	People with cardiac disease resulting in marked limitation of physical activity who are comfortable at rest. Less than ordinary activity causes fatigue, palpitation, dyspnea, or anginal pain.
IV	People with cardiac disease resulting in inability to pursue any physical activity without discomfort. Symptoms of cardiac insufficiency or of anginal syndrome may be present even at rest. If any physical activity is undertaken, discomfort is increased.

Source: Adapted from Love and Walthall, 1977, p. 96.

TABLE 17.3   **Therapeutic Classification of Individuals with Heart Disease**

Class	Description
A	People whose physical activity need not be restricted.
B	People whose ordinary physical activity need not be restricted, but who should be advised against severe or competitive physical efforts.
C	People whose ordinary physical activity should be moderately restricted, and whose more strenuous efforts should be discontinued.
D	People whose ordinary physical activity should be markedly restricted.
E	People should be at complete rest, confined to bed or chair.

Differences between functional and therapeutic classifications should be determined. The student's functional capacity does not always determine the amount of physical activity that should be permitted. At the onset of rheumatic carditis, for example, the child may not experience discomfort while playing baseball, but rest is imperative and only sitting activities are allowed. This child would be designated as Class I (functional) and Class E (therapeutic). A discrepancy often exists between the amount of activity that a student can undertake and the activity that should be attempted so the disease is not aggravated. Physical activity is recommended on the bases of amount of effort possible without discomfort and the nature and severity of the cardiac disease.

SUMMARY OF ACTIVITY PLANNING FOR STUDENTS WITH CARDIOVASCULAR CONDITIONS

1. Type of exercise
   a. Should affect overall physical fitness.
   b. Must be aerobic—affect cardiorespiratory system.
   c. Should be gradually progressive.

2. Sample programs
   a. Cooper's aerobics are applicable if discussed with the physician.
   b. Begin mild strength-building exercises, which may include lightweight lifting; progress to rhythmic endurance exercises such as walking, jogging, running, or swimming.
   c. Minimum of three sessions per week; progressive calisthenics, walk-jog activity, noncompetitive group activity.

3. Keys to remember
    a. Each person is different—there are no norms.
    b. Consult a physician before finalizing exercise program.
    c. No exercise alone.
    d. Stop at any sign of fatigue.
    e. Progress slowly and safely.

4. Conditions that contraindicate exercise
    a. Poor exercise environment (e.g., extreme heat, extreme humidity).
    b. For any heart disease patient, stop exercise at first sign of symptoms such as shortness of breath or dizziness.

ROLE OF EXERCISE IN REHABILITATION OF CARDIOVASCULAR DEFECTS

Exercise should not begin until a written prescription is received from a physician. Communication with the physician is necessary before planning physical fitness activities for the student with heart conditions. Abnormalities should be noted, such as condition of heart, septal defects, or cardiac surgery results. All reasons for restricting the person's physical activities should be understood as well as the intensity at which programming should begin.

Physical fitness programs should begin at a low level of physical activity and should continue in a progressive fashion on a daily basis. The individualized program should continue through the logical sequence of passive, assistive, active, and resistive exercises in the supine, sitting, and standing positions. Table 17.4 reviews specific exercise techniques.

TABLE 17.4   **Types of Therapeutic Exercise**

Exercise Type	Description
Passive Exercise	Body part or limb is moved through a range of motion by another person.
Assistive Exercise	Body part or limb is moved through the beginning range of motion by the individual, then the teacher or therapist completes the final phase of exercise.
Active Exercise	Body part or limb is moved by the individual without assistance.
Resistive Exercise	Body part or limb is moved through the range of motion while additional weight or resistance is applied.

Students should be taught to measure their heart rate. This procedure acts as a built-in safety device should the student push herself beyond a safe limit. In addition, attaining an understanding of how the heart responds to and recovers from exercise is a positive learning experience.

BEGINNING PROGRAM OF PROGRESSIVE CALISTHENICS

Begin a cardiorespiratory program with mild bending, stretching, and reaching activities. Weiss and Karpovich (1947) list 42 calisthenics that are graded and designated by energy expenditures (p. 447). These exercises (Figure 17.12) develop cardiovascular endurance and prevent physical deconditioning. The exercises should be done by number and at the designated count per minute to promote the indicated energy cost. Use a metronome for appropriate cadence of the exercise and select only prescribed exercises for a student's program. Exercises that require less energy expenditure should be used for warm-up. Those that require greater energy expenditure should not be used until prescribed by the physician.

PRECAUTIONS

Once the student achieves a minimal level of cardiorespiratory efficiency (as determined by the child's physician), an assessment test should be administered to determine exact degree of fitness.

Be sure the student takes a rest period before participation in the exercise program. Activity must be stopped at onset of fatigue, chest pain, or dyspnea.

Crowe, Auxter, and Pyfer (1981) recommend the following procedures when developing programs for students with cardiac disorders:

1. Reduce exercise cadence.
2. When using progressive exercises, start in a lying down position, then progress to a sitting position and finally a standing position.
3. Keep number of repetitions low.
4. Check for cardiac stress; check heart rate and watch for shortness of breath.
5. Be sure amount of exercise is congruent with student's reaction.
6. Use aerobic exercise within the child's established physical bounds to provide maximum improvement.

*CPM = counts per minute, using a metronome.

Note: The first figure in each exercise shows the starting position for that exercise. All exercises are performed in four counts, except exercise 8, which is performed in eight counts. For example, in exercise 1, the count is: 1, trunk bent right; 2, return; 3, trunk bent left; 4, return.

Exercise 5. Two figures represent each count: 1, elbows back and return; 2, elbows back and return; 3, elbows back and return; 4, elbows back and return.

Exercise 8. The alternate figures in this exercise show the side view.

FIGURE 17.12 Progressive exercise program for rehabilitation of the person with cardiac conditions. (Reprinted with permission from Weiss and Karpovich, 1947, p. 447.)

Ex. No.	CPM*		Energy cost
11)	112		2.6
12)	66		2.8
13)	112		2.9
14)	66		2.9
15)	66		3.0
16)	80		3.1
17)	40		3.2
18)	80		3.3
19)	66		3.3
20)	66		3.4
21)	66		3.6

*CPM = counts per minute, using a metronome.
Exercise 13. Second to fifth figures show first two counts of this exercise: 1, trunk bent right, return half way; 2, trunk bent right, return half way; 3, trunk bent right; 4, return.
Exercise 18. Second and third figures show the side view.
Exercise 19. The right knee is raised in the second figure, and the left knee is raised in the fourth figure.

FIGURE 17.12 (continued)

510

Ex. No.	CPM*						Energy cost
22)	66						3.8
23)	66						3.9
24)	40						4.0
25)	80						4.1
26)	66						4.1
27)	80						4.3
28)	66						4.4
29)	80						4.4
30)	80						4.6
31)	80						4.6
32)	80						4.7
33)	66						4.7

*CPM = counts per minute, using a metronome.
Exercise 30. The second figure shows the side view.

FIGURE 17.12 *(continued)*

511

Ex. No.	CPM*						Energy cost
34)	80						5.0
35)	66						5.1
36)	66						5.1
37)	66						5.7
38)	80						6.4
39)	66						6.5
40)	66						6.8
41)	80						7.8
42)	66						9.3

*CPM = counts per minute, using a metronome.
Exercise 38. Fingers touch toes of the opposite foot. The second and fourth figures show the side view.
Exercise 41. Two figures represent each count; 1, right knee raised and returned, arms circled outward; 2, left knee raised and returned, arms circled outward; 3, repeat count 1; 4, repeat count 2.

FIGURE 17.12 *(continued)*

A TEST AND EXERCISE PROGRAM FOR STUDENTS WITH CARDIOVASCULAR ABNORMALITIES

OBJECTIVES

The test should be usable in the following ways:

1. As conditioning agent and evaluation method
2. As a means to compare pulse rate when student is semiactive with resting pulse
3. To increase cardiovascular efficiency
4. As a home exercise program
5. As an exercise substitute for strenuous activity in physical education class
6. To monitor student's convalescence by measuring overall cardiac efficiency
7. To provide greater student self-confidence

THE TEST

Have the child perform the following:

1. **Chest pass.** Using both hands, pass and catch a large, lightweight ball 15 times to partner. Stand 10 ft from partner.
2. **Knee bends.** From standing position with arms extended straight out, bend knees to half squat position, hold 5 sec, and return to upright position. Repeat ten times.
3. **Inhale-exhale exercise.** Deep breathing exercise:
   a. Stand on toes and inhale through nose to count of 5.
   b. Exhale through pursed lips to count of 10; return to normal standing position, feet spread apart. Repeat 10 times.
4. **Bounce pass.** With both hands, bounce large, lightweight ball to a partner 15 times.
5. **Squat thrusts.** From a standing position:
   a. Take deep knee bend; place hands on floor in front of feet in squat-rest position.
   b. Jump and extend legs backward so body is in front-leaning rest position, with body weight resting on hands and toes.
   c. Return to squat position.
   d. Stand erect; repeat 5 times.
6. **Running in place.** Spot running: Raise and lower feet enough to clear floor. Count right foot contacts only to count of 50.

EQUIPMENT

1. Ruler
2. Lightweight ball (rubber playground ball or basketball)
3. Stopwatch
4. Graph paper

EXERCISE PROCEDURE

Pulse rate is calculated from 1 min stopwatch reading.

1. Have student rest in chair for 5 min.
2. Take student's resting pulse rate.
3. Have student perform six listed semiactive exercises without rest period.
4. When exercises are completed, have student return to sitting position and take student's pulse immediately.
5. Allow a 1-min rest.

SICKLE-CELL ANEMIA

Sickle-cell anemia, a condition in which the red blood cells appear twisted and sickle-shaped, occurs almost exclusively among blacks (8 to 10 percent of the black population in the United States is affected). Inheritance of the defective gene from both parents causes extensive cell sickling with death occurring in 50 percent of the affected population before age 20. This condition is known as true sickle-cell anemia. A milder condition, **sickle-cell trait**, occurs when the defective sickle-cell gene is inherited from one parent only and seldom causes serious or life-threatening complications (Whaley & Wong, 1987).

No effective treatment has been found for individuals with sickle-cell anemia. The severe reduction of hemoglobin causes weakness and an inability to sustain effort, as in chronic anemia. Overexertion or oxygen shortage causes the red blood cells to become sickle-shaped. The cells bunch up in tiny capillaries, impede blood flow, clot, and in the most serious cases, cause death. Because the red blood cells are unusually shaped, delicate, and fragile, they tend to break down and are easily destroyed, thus causing serious anemia.

The general health of an individual with sickle-cell anemia can vary greatly. At times, she may appear to be healthy; at other times symptoms of severe anemia are present. When the disease is most active, the child will seem to be undergoing an acute crisis and the anemia is intensified. At such times, the child experiences sharp abdominal pain (Whaley & Wong, 1987). No medical treatment is available for these painful episodes. The individual's body cannot concentrate urine, so the person requires greater than normal amounts of fluid because dehydration occurs. The child should be allowed to drink a lot of water, particularly when involved in continuous activity. The teacher should remind the student to drink water both during and after the physical education class.

From age 10 to 20 years, the child may experience chronic ulcerations (open sores) on the legs. These usually respond well to antibiotics. The physical educator should stress and encourage thorough showering after activities. If the student has medication and sterile dressings on the ulcerations, fresh medication and coverings should be applied following a shower.

The activity program should be planned with the same constraints as the program for children who have anemic tendencies. If the child with sickle-cell anemia has difficulty keeping up with the peer group, individualized developmental programming with slower progressions is recommended. The National Association for Sickle Cell Disease offers a Sickle Cell Home Study Kit for Families. For further information, contact the Association at 4221 Wilshire Blvd., Los Angeles, CA 90010.

COOLEY'S ANEMIA

Cooley's (Mediterranean) anemia is a hereditary condition in which red blood cells are small, have fragile membranes, and are ruptured easily. This condition is commonly called thalassemia. A mild form develops when the defective gene is inherited from one parent only, and it is of no major consequence to the physical education teacher. When two defective genes are inherited, however, the condition becomes serious and is termed *thalassemia major*. When this condition occurs, severe anemia, skeletal abnormalities, and Down syndrome facial features are present.

The gene responsible for defective hemoglobin formation occurs among eastern Mediterranean peoples and is known as Mediterranean anemia. This condition is found in people of Greek, Italian, and Armenian heritage.

Physical education for these children should consist of slow progressive developmental activities. Routines that induce fatigue or require intense cardiorespiratory exertion are not appropriate. Lifetime skills and games are recommended.

HEMOPHILIA

Hemophilia is a hereditary condition, contracted by males only, in which the blood clots bleeding very slowly or not at all. A cut or bruise can cause excessive bleeding, but the person with hemophilia will not bleed to death from a cut finger. A bump or blow, however, can produce painful internal bleeding into muscles and joints.

The term **hemophilia** is used to identify several different blood coagulation deficiencies that cause indistinguishable bleeding tendencies. Each classification lacks a specific plasma protein. The specific proteins, or factors, that are lacking have been identified and the most common are as follows: lack of factor VIII:C (classic A hemophilia), which includes about 80 percent of all cases, and lack of factor IX (Christmas disease, or B hemophilia), which includes approximately 15 percent of all cases (Hussey & Olive, 1985). Both A and B types are inherited by the son from the mother. Hemophilia is therefore described as a sex-linked recessive trait. The female carries the abnormal trait and has a 50 percent chance of passing the abnormality to a male child. The female carrier also has a 50 percent chance of transmitting the abnormality to a female child, who will not contract the condition but will herself become a carrier. An affected male transmits the condition to all of his female offspring, who become carriers. A male with hemophilia will not, however, transmit the abnormality to his sons. Males must inherit the condition from the mother or, in rare cases, develop hemophilia as a new disease.

Approximately 1 in every 4000 U.S. males will be born with this disease. Of all genetic diseases, hemophilia has the greatest mutation rate; approximately one third of all cases occur in families with no prior hemophilia history (National Hemophilia Foundation, n.d).

Another blood-coagulating abnormality, von Willebrand's disease, affects both males and females. The condition is even more common than hemophilia A if people with milder forms of the disease are included. Factor VIII:VWF is lacking (Goodnight, 1984).

Students who have hemophilia should be classified as having a physical disability. They therefore become eligible for adapted physical education programming.

Until recently, people with hemophilia, given adequate treatment including factor infusion, lived normal or near-normal life spans. From approximately 1981 through 1987, however, persons with hemophilia were subjected unwittingly to HIV infection: People with hemophilia regularly receive transfusions from multiple donors, and prior to the late 1980s donated blood had yet to be screened effectively on a widespread basis for HIV. As of 1987, more than 60 percent of people with hemophilia over the age of 10 tested seropositive for HIV. Currently, factor concentrate is being heat treated, and the likelihood of a person who receives a transfusion being infected with HIV is expected to decrease (Avery & First, 1989).

BLEEDING EPISODES

Any cut, abrasion, or bruise, excessive or stressful movement, or continual use of a joint can cause bleeding in the boy who has hemophilia. The most disabling complications result from bleeding into a joint (hemarthrosis) or muscles (hematoma) (Hussey & Olive, 1985). Approximately 80 percent of all individuals who have hemophilia have had joint hemorrhages. Once bleeding occurs in a joint, it tends to recur. Knees, ankles, and elbows are the most commonly involved joints, although bleeding can also occur in wrists, shoulders, and hips.

MEDICAL TREATMENT OF BLEEDING EPISODES

Treatment involves the replacement of the missing clotting factors by intravenous injection of factor VIII (type A) and factor IX (type B). These factors are contained in plasma, or dehydrated concentrate. In general, moderate and severe hemophilia are treated with concentrate. These injections may be given in a hospital setting or by a parent or the person himself. Individuals generally are taught to administer the "factors" to themselves at home at the earliest sign of bleeding (Goodnight, 1984).

When the concentrate is administered early following the onset of bleeding, the incapacitation period is shortened considerably. The physician may place the affected part in a plaster cast or bulky wrap to restrict movement for a time. Isometric contraction ("muscle setting") without joint movement is appropriate. The physician may recommend crutches if the child's hip, knee, or ankle is involved. Physician contact is strongly suggested prior to the rehabilitation period.

When the youngster begins a strength development program or a cardiorespiratory routine, plasma concentrate should be injected before exercise, which requires that the parent or physician be consulted. New developmental activities could cause joint bleeding, and injections are helpful when bleeding is anticipated. As new muscle strength is developed, it will provide support for joints, and bleeding episodes will become less frequent and less severe. The need for concentrate will be reduced gradually.

Prolonged running and excessive stopping and starting, as in soccer or field hockey, may be too demanding. Slow progressive walking and jogging are recommended. Progressive aerobic programs, as suggested by Cooper, are highly desirable for the individual with hemophilia.

GENERAL FIRST AID FOR STUDENTS WITH HEMOPHILIA

Students who have hemophilia usually know when internal bleeding is occurring, even before swelling or other external signs are evident. The child's statement indicating that bleeding is happening is probably reliable and should be taken seriously.

Because most bleeding involves joints or soft tissue, cold compresses or ice packs should be applied and the body part elevated. This facilitates vasoconstriction and should be continued for 8 to 12 hours following injury. *Aspirin and aspirin-containing compounds should not be given to children with hemophilia* because these medications increase frequency and severity of bleeding in people with coagulation disorders.

Following an acute bleeding episode, the hemorrhage site may be quite painful and temporarily incapacitated. Quick or strenuous movements should *not* be done. *Mild* stretching and *mild* range-of-motion activities are acceptable.

SPECIFIC COMPLICATIONS OF HEMOPHILIA

Hemarthrosis occurs when bleeding into a joint is characterized by a swollen, painful, and slightly warm joint. When lower extremities are involved, weightbearing should not be allowed for 3 to 5 days. Gradual resumption of weightbearing may begin over the next 5 days (Davis, 1975). Swimming and upper body activities that allow the student to sit or lie down are acceptable.

Joint damage occurs from repeated bleeding into the same joint with resultant damage to cartilage and bony structure. Arthritic problems may develop, including limited range of motion, joint stiffness when one position is maintained for a prolonged time, and varying degrees of pain and discomfort. Rehabilitative surgery (e.g., joint replacement, joint bracing, or wedging out of nonosseous contractures) is performed on individuals with severe joint destruction and deformity.

Behrman and Vaughan (1987) state that in addition to joint damage, the muscles weaken. As muscles weaken, joint support diminishes, which makes the joint more susceptible to additional trauma from normal activities with resultant bleeding and greater chronic disability. A vicious cycle is thus established.

Hematoma (muscle and soft tissue bleeding) causes problems because of localized symptoms for which a single dose of concentrate is generally adequate. Bumping the affected area should be avoided. If this happens, ice, compression, and elevation should be administered quickly. Swimming is a fine activity to perform during rehabilitation. If adequate modifications can be made to reduce the chance of reinjury, students should not be excused from physical education.

One complication that sometimes occurs involves the child's biting his tongue. A hematoma generally develops. The student should be forewarned to tell the teacher and the school nurse if this happens.

Hematuria, blood in the urine, occurs often in individuals with hemophilia. It is not life threatening and generally responds to factor replacement injections. Restrictions in the physical education program are not indicated.

PHYSICAL EDUCATION ACTIVITIES FOR THE CHILD WITH HEMOPHILIA

Because educators and parents tend to be overcautious with a child who has hemophilia, many children with this disorder are excluded from regular physical education programs and playground activities. The concern of parents and educators is valid but is not necessarily best for the child. The adapted physical educator is responsible for understanding the adults' concerns and for providing information about activities that will be used in the child's program. The teenage youngster can help by actively avoiding situations that are likely to result in bleeding episodes. In most cases, the individual with hemophilia should be restricted from contact sports. This frequently creates problems in managing the young child who may resent the fact that he is forced to behave differently from his peers.

The educator should encourage and provide activities that are less likely to cause bodily injury (e.g., tennis, golf, badminton, swimming, archery, and jogging). Boone (1974) points out that a number of children with hemophilia play Little League baseball and participate in intramural basketball, soccer, and other sports.

Davis (1975) suggests that avoidance of normal activities because of the possibility of *some risk* is inadvisable: "There is no altogether satisfactory solution to the problem of allowing the patient to experience a 'normal' childhood and at the same time to avoid potentially injurious activity. Encouragement of the hemophiliac to obtain as high a level of formal education as his abilities permit is beneficial" (p. 251).

Because of the multiple problems associated with hemophilia, ideal medical treatment occurs when a team of medical and nonmedical professionals is developed (Carrai & Handford, 1983). The adapted physical educator should be a contributing team member who participates in the development and implementation of the individualized activity and rehabilitation program.

Each male with hemophilia differs in physical ability, severity of joint involvement, and frequency and kind of bleeding episodes. All variables must be considered when the student's individualized physical education program is being planned. For example, a boy who experiences repeated bleeding in the elbow joints should not be placed in an upper body weight-training program because this activity would keep his affected joints chronically irritated. He can, however, participate in isometric exercises that develop similar strength but do not cause unnecessary flexion or extension of the elbow joints. The prescribed program should be flexible enough to accommodate the bleeding variability. The boy should not play tennis or run while recovering from a bleeding episode of the knee. Modified activities such as swimming or isometric weight training while sitting are advisable in that instance. When knee bleeding has stopped and swelling is reduced, he can resume usual activities.

SUMMARY

There are many congenital disorders. In this chapter, we have focused on those that tend to occur among school-age people and those that occur with relative frequency.

Duchenne muscular dystrophy (pseudohypertrophic MD) is a progressive, terminal disease. The condition must not be further complicated by excessive inactivity, which results in yet more physical atrophy. Strength maintenance and range-of-motion development should be major program components.

Spina bifida is a congenital condition that affects the spinal cord directly. The most common and most limiting type is myelomeningocele, which often necessitates constant use of a wheelchair. In addition, paralysis of the lower limbs is present, and bladder and bowel control are often difficult to achieve. Activities involving upper arm manipulation and strength are suggested.

Congenital hip dislocation involves displacement of the femur head out of the hip socket. Activities should be planned that allow the student to exercise in a sitting position. Upper body strength development is suggested.

Talipes (clubfoot) is often encountered in conjunction with spina bifida or congenital hip dislocation. Mild cases involve casting, whereas severe cases require surgery. Following a period of immobilization, activities should involve a progressive exercise program. Walking, jogging, and running are difficult, and the instructor will note marked differences between students. The physician's written prescriptions should guide the rehabilitation activities.

Skeletal dysplasia is a congenital defect caused by inhibition of the growth process. Shorter than average limbs and height are the major characteristics. General activities may have to be adapted, including equipment modifications.

With proper medical treatment and appropriate physical activity, most young people with heart damage or abnormality can live long and productive lives. Restriction of physical activity may be necessary for some but not for others. Many students with heart disease are fully capable of participating unrestricted in the activities of daily life, and some may engage in strenuous activity. In other cases, heart disease may require curtailment of intense physical demands. The physician is the key to program constraints.

Modified activities should be stimulating and interesting, without undue stress.

The more common heart and blood conditions among school-age youth include congenital heart defects, certain congenital anemias, and hemophilia. All have a direct bearing on school attendance and participation in adapted or regular physical education classes.

Rehabilitation and physical education programming for all children with cardiovascular abnormalities are fundamentally similar. Although individual conditions may differ, the heart expresses distress or impairment in a limited number of ways. Many students with mild heart disease do not require program restrictions. Those who do require activity restrictions should experience activity in quantities that stimulate but do not distress the cardiovascular system. The educator should work with the physician to plan a program of permitted and restricted activities, which can be varied depending on the functional and therapeutic classification of each individual. Once a heart condition is identified, the adapted physical educator should provide interesting activities to meet the child's psychomotor needs.

Exercise training for cardiac rehabilitation has been conducted successfully through a number of aerobic exercise programs with duration varying from 3 months to 2 years. Most specialists in exercise rehabilitation agree that an exercise prescription of 50 percent of the maximum VO_2 may be necessary to provide beneficial physiological changes (Woods, 1982–1983). Some individuals may be unable to reach this level of cardiac output because they experience warning signs such as dyspnea, feelings of anxiety, or extreme discomfort before the level is attained. In these cases, training sessions must be adjusted to lower activity levels with anticipation of gradual activity increase in the future.

For children with heart disease, planned programs must begin early in life with special attention devoted to growth and development. The early years are the time when lifelong behavior patterns are established. During this period, birth through adolescence, the caliber of the individual's total life is determined (Amsterdam, Wilmore, & DeMaria, 1977).

REFERENCES

American Heart Association. (1974). *You and your heart.* New York: The Association.

Amsterdam, E. A., Wilmore, J. H., & DeMaria, A. N. (1977). *Exercise in cardiovascular health and disease.* New York: Yorke Medical Books.

Avery, M. L., & First, L. R. (1989). *Pediatric medicine.* Baltimore: Williams & Wilkins.

Behrman, R. E., & Vaughan, V. C. (1987). *Nelson book of pediatrics* (13th ed.). Philadelphia: Saunders.

Best, G. A. (1978). *Individuals with physical disabilities.* St. Louis: C. V. Mosby.

Blackman, J. A. (Ed.). (1990). *Medical aspects of developmental disabilities in children birth to three* (2nd ed.). Rockville, MD: Aspen Systems Corporation.

Bleck, E. E., & Nagel, D. A. (1982). *Physically handicapped children: an atlas for teachers* (3rd ed.). New York: Grune & Stratton.

Boone, D. C. (1974). Physical activity for a child with hemophilia. *Physical Therapy, 54,* 7–12.

Boyd, W. (1971). *An introduction to the study of disease* (6th ed.). Philadelphia: Lea & Febiger.

Carrai, E. B., & Handford, H. A. (1983). Problems of hemophilia and the role of the rehabilitation counselor. *Rehabilitation Counseling Bulletin, 26,* 155–162.

Crowe, W. C., Auxter, D., & Pyfer, J. (1981). *Principles and methods of adapted physical education and recreation* (4th ed.). St. Louis: C. V. Mosby.

Davis, W. E. (1975). Hemophilia and allied conditions. In H. F. Conn (Ed.), *Current therapy 1975* (pp. 752–758). Philadelphia: W. B. Saunders.

de Lateur, B. J., & Giaconi, R. M. (1979). Effect on maximal strength of submaximal exercise in Duchenne muscular dystrophy. *American Journal of Physical Medicine, 58*(1), 26–36.

De Lisa, J. A., & Tipton, M. M. (1979). Exercise effect on creative phosphokinase elevation in motor neuron disease. *Archives of Physical Medicine Rehabilitation, 60*(9), 397–400.

Dumars, K. W. (1985). Approach to genetic disease. In R. B. Conn (Ed.), *Current Diagnosis 7.* Philadelphia: W. B. Saunders, 1985.

Epstein, S. E., Beiser, G. D., & Goldstein, R. E. (1973). Hemodynamic abnormalities in response to mild and intense upright exercise following operative correction of an atrial septal defect or tetralogy of Fallot. *Circulation, 47,* 1065–1075.

Findley, W. J. (1987). Ambulation and the adolescent with myelomeningocele. (Doctoral dissertation, University of Minnesota). *Dissertation Abstracts International* (1983). *44* (9–13), 1704.

Gardner-Medwin, D. (1979). Controversies about Duchenne muscular dystrophy. Bracing for ambulation. *Developmental Medicine and Child Neurology, 21*(5), 659–662.

Gersony, W. M. (1975). Congenital malformations of the heart. In H. F. Conn (Ed.), *Current Therapy 1975.* Philadelphia: W. B. Saunders.

Goodnight, S. H., Jr. (1984). Hemophilia and related conditions. In R. E. Rakel (Ed.), *Conn's current therapy 1984* (pp. 1236–1242). Philadelphia: W. B. Saunders.

Hopkins, L. C. (1985). Muscular dystrophies. In R. B. Conn (Ed.), *Current Diagnosis 7.* Philadelphia: W. B. Saunders.

Howell, L. (1978). Spina bifida. In R. M Goldenson (Ed.), *Disability and Rehabilitation Handbook.* New York: McGraw-Hill.

Hussey, C. V., & Olive, J. A. (1985). Hemophilia and other inherited coagulation disorders. In R. B. Conn (Ed.), *Current Diagnosis 7* (pp. 456–461). Philadelphia: W. B. Saunders.

James, F. W., Daplan, S., & Schwartz, D. C. (1976). Response to exercise in patients after total surgical correction of tetralogy of Fallot. *Circulation, 54,* 671–679.

Kaneda, R. R. (1980). Becker's muscular dystrophy: orthopedic implications. *Journal of the American Orthopedic Association, 79,* 332–335.

Lasko, P. M., & Knopf, K. G. (1984). *Adapted and corrective exercise for the disabled adult.* Dubuque, Iowa: Eddie Bowers Publishing.

Love, H. D., & Walthall, J. E. (1977). *A handbook of medical, educational, and psychological information for teachers of physically handicapped children.* Springfield, IL: Charles C. Thomas.

Mahoney, L. T. (1984). Congenital heart disease. In R. E. Rakel (Ed.), *Conn's Current Therapy 1984.* Philadelphia: W. B. Saunders.

Millis, M. (1989). In M. L. Avery & L. R. First (Eds.), *Pediatric medicine* (pp. 148–161). Baltimore: Williams & Wilkins.

Muscular Dystrophy Association. (1980). *Muscular dystrophy.* New York: The Association.

National Hemophilia Foundation. (n.d.). *What you should know about hemophilia.* New York: The Foundation.

Pearson, H. A. (1975). Sickle cell anemia. In H. F. Conn (Ed.), *Current therapy 1975* (pp. 820–824). Philadelphia: W. B. Saunders.

Siegel, I. M. (1982). *101 questions and answers about muscular dystrophy.* New York: Muscular Dystrophy Association.

Spiro, A. J. (1987). In H. M. Wallace et al. (Eds.), *Handicapped children and youth* (pp. 240–253). New York: Human Sciences Press.

Travis, B. (1976). *Chronic illness in children.* Stanford, CA: Stanford University Press.

Urion, D. K. (1989). In M. E. Avery & L. R. First (Eds.), *Pediatric medicine* (pp. 211–218). Baltimore: Williams & Wilkins.

Vargo, T. A. (1985). Congenital heart disease. In R. B. Conn (Ed.), *Current Diagnosis* 7. Philadelphia: W. B. Saunders.

Weiss, R. A., & Karpovich, P. N. (1947). Energy cost of exercise for convalescents. *Archives of Physical Medicine, 28,* 447.

Whaley, L. F., & Wong, D. L. (1987). *Nursing care of infants and children.* St. Louis: Mosby.

Williamson, G. G. (1987). *Children with spina bifida.* Baltimore: Brook.

Wolraich, M. L. (1987). In H. J. Wallace et al. (Ed.), *Handicapped children and youth* (pp. 254–260). New York: Human Sciences Press.

Wolraich, M. L. (1990). Myelomeningocele. In J. A. Blackman (Ed.), *Medical aspects of developmental disabilities in children birth to three* (2nd ed.). Rockville, MD: Aspen Systems Corporation.

Woods, D. Y. (1982–1983). Exercise rehabilitation in COPD. *Cardio-Gram, 10* (1), 6.

Chapter 18

ACQUIRED CONDITIONS

"Ow, ow, ow, ow," Janet Kruzel complained softly as she was lowered from her wheelchair to an exercise mat on the floor. However painful, the words were welcome. Until 3 months ago, Janet, age 6, was receiving no therapy and was not allowed to take part in any physical activity.

"Lift your arm and we'll count to 10," Mr. Dave Jones told Janet as he cradled her arm in his hands. Janet counted slowly, the pitch of her voice rising in concentrated effort when she got to 6, then relaxing some as she reached 10. "Good job...now try it again," Jones said smiling as he watched her progress through the exercises for the day.

Janet was in pain much of time because of having juvenile rheumatoid arthritis. Her condition had been getting progressively worse, and her parents feared that she would lose the use of her hands and arms because of the intense pain. Medications were helpful, but there were those periods of constant discomfort. Her pediatrician and her physical therapist suggested that it would be best if she had daily exercise to maintain and increase range of motion in her arms and hands, particularly during those times when she wasn't experiencing the extreme pain of the "hot joints."

The opportunity to provide Janet with daily physical education became available because she was entitled to individualized programming. Dave Jones, the adapted physical education teacher, became involved when his principal asked him to develop an appropriate physical education program for Janet. At the I.E.P. meeting, valuable activity suggestions were contributed by Jeff Johnson, the physical therapist. The transdisciplinary team of specialists determined Janet's physical and motor needs and helped Mr. Jones plan her upcoming physical education program.

What is juvenile rheumatoid arthritis? What activities should be provided? What activities are contraindicated? What medical and therapeutic terminology is needed by the physical educator to effectively communicate with other professionals? What other conditions are considered "acquired" conditions, and what basic knowledge is necessary for physical education teachers when developing and implementing physical activity programs?

Acquired conditions are those that occur during or following birth. Recall that *congenital conditions* (Chapter 17) are those occurring during the prenatal (before birth) or gestation (during pregnancy) period. Chapter 17 addressed congenital conditions that occur relatively often among school-age children. As with Chapter 17, the phrase "occurring relatively often" should be construed to mean those conditions about which virtually every *adapted* physical educator should have significant theoretical and practical working knowledge. Among those whose career paths are leading to regular, mainstream physical education teaching, there must be at least entry-level knowledge of acquired disabilities addressed herein, because children with such conditions often will be placed in regular, mainstream physical education. When rare or obscure conditions are encountered, the physical educator, adapted or mainstream, should consult with appropriate therapists or attending physicians.

Children with acquired disabilities today are typically being served in mainstream settings by mainstream physical educators. More than a decade ago, Stein (1979, p. 6) stated that 90 to 95 percent of all children with disabilities could be successfully integrated into regular, mainstream physical education classes. This statement, indeed, has proved prophetic, for such is the case in many places today. Ideally, the mainstream physical educator will have at his or her disposal an adapted physical education specialist for consultation when such need arises. Although this text cannot fully replace the consultation insights and experiences of a veteran adapted physical educator (i.e., one who knows the specific child and circumstances), it should be retained and referenced as an adjunct resource by the mainstream physical educator, who surely will encounter and serve children with acquired disabilities.

Acquired disabilities can range from *mild* to *profound*; such a disability spectrum, for example, is evident among children with juvenile rheumatoid arthritis. Acquired disabilities may be *acute* or *chronic*: *acute* refers to conditions that typically last from days to weeks; perhaps a few months (e.g. a fractured fibula). *Chronic* refers to conditions that typically last many months and, quite possibly, years. Acquired disabilities can be *temporary* or *permanent*. For example, disability resulting from Osgood-Schlatter's typically is temporary, whereas disability resulting from amputation is permanent. Some acquired disabilities are *progressive*, meaning that the condition can become more serious with the passing of time, and some are *terminal*, meaning that the final episode resulting from the condition is death. Acquired Immune Deficiency Syndrome (AIDS) is one such condition in which, at the time of this writing, progression is the rule and death appears inevitable. On the other hand, some acquired conditions may or may not be terminal. One such example is childhood leukemia, in which, at the time of this writing, the 10-year survival rate is approximately 50 percent.

Depending on the nature and extent of the child's acquired condition, the physical educator may observe varying degrees of interruption in the child's developmental progress. The educator needs to keep in mind, however, that the affected child, despite the acquired condition, is climbing the same developmental ladder as her nondisabled peers. Successive rungs of the ladder are likened to sequential stages of development. In the affected child's case, the disabling condition simply makes the climb more difficult and may limit how far up the developmental ladder the child actually climbs. The physical educator who views the child from this developmental perspective is not likely to let the child's specific disabling condition (i.e., label) inordinately influence curriculum, programming, and placement decisions. The guiding principal should be to *treat the child, not the label.* Always focus on and emphasize ability, *not* disability. Even though the child's disability may be significant, emphasis on what the child *can* do virtually always helps ensure accentuation of the positive. Even when the child's condition might be permanent and progressive and perhaps even terminal, appropriate medical attention, therapy, and adapted physical education can facilitate (or at least help sustain) the child's physical, motor, and psychosocial development.

JUVENILE RHEUMATOID ARTHRITIS

Juvenile rheumatoid arthritis (JRA) appears in very young children and affects girls more often than boys. The disease usually appears during middle elementary years, but confirmed diagnoses have been made in 6-week-old infants. JRA is the umbrella term describing a heterogeneous group of chronic rheumatic disorders with onset during childhood. JRA, regardless of the specific type, is typically characterized by inflammation of the synovial lining in joints. As a result of the disease, cartilage and bone tissue may deteriorate. The extent of joint deterioration or permanence of joint dysfunction varies from child to child.

Approximately 250,000 children in the United States are affected by JRA, making it a major disabler among young children (Spencer, 1985). Unlike adults with arthritis, 20 percent of whom experience remission, 60 to 70 percent of children with JRA experience almost complete recovery within 10 years of the disease's onset (Bleck & Nagel, 1982). Approximately one third recover completely, one third experience mild to moderate residual joint dysfunction, and one third experience severe joint dysfunction. Duration of the disease in its active stages is not predictable. Some cases last only months, whereas others persist for years.

In 1977 the American Rheumatism Association established specific criteria for diagnosis of JRA. According to these criteria, the condition appears with symptoms before age 16, and symptoms (i.e., persistent disease activity) last at least 6 weeks. Disease activity appears as observable swelling or effusion (fluid in the joint capsule) of one or more joints and is accompanied by at least two of the following signs at the affected joint site: (1) limited range of motion, (2) heat, (3) pain, or (4) tenderness. Inflammation causing the above symptoms can result in joint deformity and dysfunction. Inflammation from arthritis usually is chronic and persistent.

Frequent remission in JRA indicates that the condition comes and goes. Nearly all children with JRA experience periods when symptoms reduce in severity or disappear. Although X rays and blood tests may still reveal signs of the disease, the child may report feeling quite well. Episodes of disease activity and remission show no consistent pattern. When the child is symptom free or even relatively symptom free, he should be encouraged to take part in most, if not all, *developmentally appropriate* physical education activities. Emphasis is on developmentally appropriate because many children with serious and prolonged involvement with JRA will be smaller and less physically mature than their typically developing CA (chronological age) peers.

Splinting is occasionally the procedure of choice when the purpose is to rest tender joints or prevent or minimize contractures. Typically, removable casts may be used at night or for periods during the day. For example, a wrist splint worn during the day may permit active finger use while protecting the painful or deformed wrist joint from undue trauma.

Consequences associated with having JRA are truly multidimensional. Joint pain and stiffness may become an ongoing distraction for the child, which mitigates against the child's getting and staying on task. To varying degrees, medication schedules can be disruptive. In some cases, the child may self-medicate. In others, this procedure may be the responsibility of school personnel. The child's perception of herself will be influenced, at least in part, by her self-perception of the disease. Further, JRA as perceived by the child and peers will affect both peer and family relationships. The directions these relationships take will depend significantly on attitudes of parents and siblings at home and peers and teachers at school. Suffice it to say that the child with JRA can be disabled as much and more by the attitudes of others as she can be by the disease itself.

A study by Taylor (1987) revealed several important differences of opinion regarding consequences of having JRA among children with the disease, their parents, and their teachers. The researchers found that both parents and teachers tended to focus on physical symptoms associated with JRA. Children with JRA, on the other hand, reported that their major concerns occurred in the areas of peer relationships and self-esteem. This finding suggests that, from the child's perspective, the disease is secondary in importance to being accepted by others. In fact, children in the study were especially reluctant to allow teachers to inform classmates about the disease. According to Taylor (1987), "clearly, children with JRA, like 'healthy' children, do not want to appear 'different' in the eyes of their peers" (p. 189). The impact of this finding on physical educators would seem to be twofold. First, the teacher must try to foster an environment wherein the child with JRA is perceived by all as a person *first* who *happens* to have JRA. Second, the teacher, through physical education, must focus on ability rather than disability so that the child, in a positive environment, develops skills and peer relationships that emphasize similarities rather than differences.

Juvenile rheumatoid arthritis occurs in three forms: systemic, polyarticular, and pauciarticular (Pachman, 1984).

SYSTEMIC ARTHRITIS

Systemic arthritis, often called *Still's disease*, occurs in approximately 20 percent of all cases. Symptoms are systemic (bodywide), hence the disease's name, and include pink rash, swollen lymph nodes, anemia, lethargy, and high spiking fever. These symptoms can occur daily. Arthritis and concomitant joint discomfort often are only minor manifestations of the illness and may not appear until months after other symptoms have come and gone. Given that joint discomfort is not an initial manifestation of systemic arthritis, the disease is often difficult to diagnose. Episodes of this disease may persist for months, disappear, and reappear months or years later. Although complete recovery is not ensured, the prognosis tends to be good.

POLYARTICULAR ARTHRITIS

Polyarticular arthritis (arthritis in five or more joints) affects 40 percent of children with JRA. Severity of pain in affected joints is the child's major symptom. Children with polyarticular arthritis live in pain. Most often, affected joints include knees, ankles, wrists, neck, fingers (Figure 18.1), elbows, and shoulders. When polyarticular arthritis occurs in the jaw, bone growth may be retarded, resulting in a receding chin.

Given that pain is omnipresent in a child with polyarticular arthritis and that movement provokes pain, there is often a tendency for the child to avoid physical activity. The child's defense mechanism, in the face of pain, is often to sit motionless with joints flexed. Persistent flexion in affected joints, if not therapeutically managed, results in chronically disabling skeletal deformities and muscle contractures (Figure 18.2). The extended nature of the disease typically results in the child being small for age and sexually immature.

PAUCIARTHRITIS

Pauciarticular arthritis (four or fewer involved joints) affects approximately 40 percent of all children with JRA. Manifestations of this form of JRA are typically limited to pain and inflammation in affected joints. These children, when compared to those with polyarticular arthritis, appear quite well. Joint damage to affected joints tends not to be permanent even when the disease's duration is lengthy.

The most serious concern with this form of JRA is not joint disease, but inflammation of the iris and muscles controlling the eye. This condition may develop unnoticed, because its onset and progression typically are insidious. Initial symptoms in such instances, because they may be mild, are dismissed as inconsequential. This condition, if left untreated, leads to blindness. Children with red eyes, who rub their eyes often, and/or complain about bright lights should be referred immediately to an ophthalmologist (a medical doctor specializing in diseases of the eye). Early intervention eliminates, or at least minimizes, vision loss. Delayed intervention risks permanent visual impairment or blindness.

Activity Considerations

The child with JRA usually takes medication for joint pain and inflammation. Aspirin is often used because of its effectiveness with relatively few side effects. Side effects

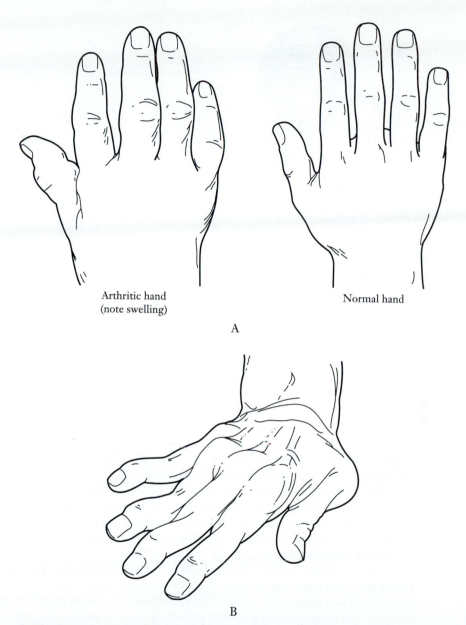

Arthritic hand
(note swelling)   Normal hand

A

B

FIGURE 18.1   **(A) Arthritic hand compared with normal hand. (B) "Swan neck" deformity caused by arthritis.**

FIGURE 18.2   **Child with polyarticular arthritis often prefers
to sit motionless in flexion.**

do, however, occur. The child with JRA who takes aspirin in larger than typical
dosages may experience stomachaches, behavior changes, ringing in the ears, increased bruising following mild trauma, and a feeling of "stuffed-up" ears. It should
be noted that aspirin taken by children has been linked with Reye's (pronounced
"rise") syndrome. However, some physicians still prescribe aspirin, apparently believing that the association between Reye's and aspirin is tenuous at best, and that
the medication's benefits outweigh its risks. Reye's syndrome is an acute, and often
fatal, disease involving brain inflammation and liver enlargement. The physical education teacher should be alert for Reye's syndrome symptoms including persistent
vomiting and unusual irritability in the student (Pachman, 1984).

Sometimes hearing loss, which can occur when aspirin is taken in large dosages,
contributes to maladaptive behavior. Such behavior occurs typically because the child
simply loses track of what he should be concentrating on. If hearing loss is suspected,
the child should be tested to ensure that such loss is *not* due to another cause. Because
acoustics are often poor in physical education environments, the physical educator
should take special care to ensure that the child can hear. Hearing loss associated with
aspirin consumption is temporary and disappears upon cessation of aspirin therapy.

When aspirin fails to provide relief, cortisone may be prescribed. Cortisone,
although it is considered among the most effective arthritis drug therapies, is not
without significant side effects. Growth retardation is among the major side effects
resulting from cortisone ingestion.

Physical movement in appropriate quantities is a staple treatment among children with JRA. Although affected joints do require rest, exercise to help prevent or control deformities and contractures is essential. In preparation for exercise, affected joints may be subjected to warm bathing or paraffin applications. These procedures help reduce discomfort associated with motion, thereby encouraging student compliance with the exercise regimen or activity program.

Mild exercise (i.e., warm-up) should precede more vigorous exercise. Muscle strengthening and flexibility exercises will help control pain and prevent joint deformity. Pain perception, of course, is in part subjective and varies among individuals. A good rule of thumb that can be applied once the teacher comes to know the individual child is to exercise only to, but never past, the threshold of discomfort. Isometric exercises are particularly valuable adjuncts to strength development or maintenance programs because they require muscle contraction while causing little or no movement at the joint. Isometric contractions may be held for 6 seconds at maximum effort. Anderson (1982) recommends that children with JRA engage in isometric exercise twice daily.

Range-of-motion exercises may be active, assistive, or passive, depending on the individual child's need. Stretching should be steady and deliberate, not bouncy (i.e., ballistic). Depending upon the individual child's exercise tolerance, a given stretch may persist for at least 6 seconds. Limb movement activities to maintain or rehabilitate motion can often be done by the child. Care must be taken in such instances to ensure that the child does indeed carry out prescribed exercises. Children often do not see the long-range value of prescribed activities and may be reluctant to inflict discomfort on themselves. Any program that minimizes the effects of JRA will result in some discomfort to the child. The teacher must be patient in working with the child, lest the activity program turn into a battle!

During acute stages of JRA, activities that jar or otherwise traumatize affected joints (e.g., jumping, wrestling, catching heavy objects) are contraindicated. Ideal activities are those that encourage exercise through reasonable ranges of motion and do not traumatize joints. Swimming, tricycling, and bicycling (provided the child does not fall) are good examples.

Children with JRA will often experience mood shifts from day to day. This occurs in part because sometimes the symptoms of the disease are more acute than other times. After a good night's sleep or during the course of days when symptoms are moderate, the child's disposition often shifts toward the positive. Bouts of discomfort from joint pain, on the other hand, may result in the child's becoming fatigued or irritable.

Feelings of fatigue often accompany moderate and severe cases of JRA. A response common among care givers in such situations is to recommend reductions in activity, including rest. According to Ike, Lampman, and Castor (1989), fatigue results only in part from the disease itself. Unnecessary restriction of the child's activity plays a significant role in deconditioning, which in turn exacerbates the child's feelings of tiredness. Joint pain lasting longer than one hour after exercise is an indication that the activity has been too strenuous. In such instances, Ike et al. state that, "alternative or reduced activity such as performing range-of-motion exercises is preferable to complete rest" (p. 136).

PREGNANCY

Not too many years ago, school-age students who became pregnant either did not attend school during pregnancy or were placed (some would say isolated) in special programs provided by the school. Today, it is clearly the rule rather than the exception that school-age students who are pregnant attend school and participate in the regular curriculum with their classmates. Of course, part of that regular curriculum typically includes physical education. Depending upon the course and stage of pregnancy, the student may be placed in regular or adapted physical education. Depending upon the state in which the student resides, pregnancy may or may not be a condition where the option exists, if needed, for special education services. Both mainstream and adapted physical educators in *public schools* should know state education agency policy regarding placement options/obligations (Note the emphasis on *public schools*; private schools in some states are not bound by state education agency mandates).

The school-age student who is pregnant often knows little about the effects and value of physical activity during pregnancy. The March of Dimes (1985) states that "teenagers, especially, may not know or care about improving their health habits. Teenagers under 17 are among the mothers most at risk of having low birth weight babies" (p. 3). This is significant because low birth weight, associated with prematurity, is the number one cause of death during the child's first year of life. Given the importance of appropriate physical activity during this time, physical education can help provide a wellness assist that ensures healthy development for both mother and fetus.

Fitness is always important, and it is particularly important during pregnancy. Yet this is a time when the student may become self-conscious about her body and its changing appearance. This self-consciousness may cause the student emotional discomfort in a physical education setting. Solberg (1988) offers physical educators the following advice to help maintain or improve the student's fitness during pregnancy while avoiding the potential risks of inappropriate exercise:

1. Evaluate your attitude toward the student and her dilemma. Try not to be judgmental.... The challenge now is to achieve a healthy outcome for mother and child.

2. Encourage the student to seek prenatal medical care as early as possible and to have the physician recommend any restrictions that should be placed on physical activity.

3. Help the student understand that, although she may feel self-conscious and awkward about exercising while pregnant, the benefits of maintaining her fitness are substantial. (p. 110)

Activity Considerations

Provided the student is in good health, few activities are contraindicated during pregnancy. However, specific activity restrictions and recommendations should come from the student's physician.

Typically, there should be concern for fitness maintenance or development that serves the student well, not only through pregnancy, but through delivery and after childbirth. The student who has been physically active and fit prior to pregnancy typically can and should remain physically active during pregnancy. A low-fitness student should become more active to facilitate becoming fit, though the student may need to overcome preconceived attitudes toward fitness. For this student, plenty of encouragement and activity level progress characterized by moderation ought to be guiding principles. Any fitness activity well tolerated by the student (regardless of fitness level) and not contraindicated by the attending physician is acceptable.

According to the March of Dimes (1982), ideal weight gain during pregnancy is approximately 25 pounds. However, a small, underweight student may gain less and possibly even lose weight during pregnancy. The student who experiences either of these conditions, especially the latter, should be in close consultation with her physician. Weight loss during pregnancy contraindicates vigorous physical activity. Vigorous activity during pregnancy in the face of weight loss risks premature labor or delivery of a baby that is small for gestation age.

Solberg (1988) recommends non-weightbearing aerobic exercises including swimming and cycling. Exercise should be preceded by a thorough warm-up; this minimizes risk resulting in part from softened ligaments, extra weight, and reduced agility. Recommended exercise frequency is three times per week, 20–30 minutes per session. Strength development should focus on lower back and abdominal musculature.

There is little in the literature to conclude that moderate activity levels during pregnancy are contraindicated. One recurring concern is that exercise might trigger excessive uterine activity that, in turn, might trigger early labor. Veille (1986) concluded from his exercise studies of pregnant women that "none of these women had any increase in uterine activity" (p. 3) and that "exercise itself did not trigger permanent labor in these healthy women." One should, however be cautious with strenuous activity (particularly in hot, humid weather) that heavily concentrates blood in the expectant mother's working muscles. The mother's finite blood supply, concentrated in working muscles *and* near the skin surface (for cooling), may temporarily, but significantly, deprive the fetus of needed oxygen and nutrients.

Finally, there must be concern for the student's fitness *following* delivery. Through physical activity and exercise, the student's body can gradually regain or, if need be, improve upon its prepregnancy figure and condition. This will be particularly important where the decision is made to keep the child, because fitness, both psychological and physical, will play an important role in the student's ability to take care of both herself and the child.

ACQUIRED IMMUNE DEFICIENCY SYNDROME

Acquired Immune Deficiency Syndrome (AIDS) is a condition in which the person's ability to ward off infection is compromised by a virus. The virus has been called Human T-Lympotropic Virus Type III (HTLV 3), Lymphadenopathy Associated Virus (LAV), and Human Immunodeficiency Virus (HIV). Sometimes it is simply called the AIDS virus. The virus is known to be contracted by the intermingling of body fluids, including semen or blood. Ironically, this potentially deadly virus survives only briefly outside the body. Ideal (for the virus) modes of HIV transmission include having unprotected sexual intercourse with multiple partners, sharing contaminated needles among intravenous drug users, or receiving a transfusion of contaminated blood. The latter mode has become increasingly rare with widespread testing throughout the blood supply distribution system.

Today, AIDS is, as it has been, primarily a disease among adults in *high risk* groups, but the fastest growing group of AIDS patients consists of children. Between 1987 and 1988, 416 children under 13 were reported as having AIDS (Quarters report, 1988). The major significance of this statistic is not simply that year's number of reported cases, but that this number represented an 85 percent increase in reported cases over the previous 12-month reporting period. According to the American Medical Association (1988), 75 percent of children with AIDS contract the disease perinatally.

Researchers continue to investigate modes of transmission; however, much remains to be learned. Meanwhile, rumor and myth often prevail, resulting in phobia-driven discrimination against the person known to be infected. Balancing the infected individual's need for anonymity with caregivers' or other principal parties' "right to know" is posing and, in the foreseeable future, will continue to pose difficult philosophical, legal, and ethical questions.

Understanding modes of transmission is critical to separating myth from fact about HIV transmission among persons who work or have social contact with persons who have the HIV virus. Repeated analyses of sources of infection among persons with the HIV virus reveal no cases of transmission attributable to casual or household-type contact, including kissing, changing diapers, wiping noses, sharing toothbrushes, and biting (Dreyfuss, 1987). At least one case, however, receiving widespread media attention, has been reported where transmission resulted from hand-to-mouth contact in a professional setting between a dentist with AIDS and the patient. Even though becoming infected with the HIV virus appears virtually nonexistent beyond aforementioned ideal modes for transmission, steps need be taken to ensure a safe environment. Regarding preventing the disease's transmission, Dreyfuss states that, "(the) goal is to prevent one person's body fluid from invading another's blood stream through mucous membranes or broken skin"(p. 23). Dreyfuss suggests the following:

1. Person with open wounds or dermatitis should always wear gloves when handling another person's body fluids, including urine, vomitus, and excessive blood spills such as nose bleeds or serious lacerations.

2. In the event cloth or tissues become soiled with any of the above, they should be sealed in a plastic bag before disposal.

3. Waste receptacles, particularly in infirmaries and bathrooms, should be lined with plastic and changed as needed, but at least daily.

4. Contaminated surfaces, after they have been initially cleaned, should be disinfected with 70 percent isopropanol alcohol or a freshly mixed 1:10 chlorine solution.

5. Soiled mops should be soaked in a chlorine solution.

6. Any soiled clothing or material that is to be kept should be handled carefully, including laundering in *hot* water that kills the HIV virus. (p. 26)

Disease resulting from HIV infection ranges from no symptoms to AIDS, which is terminal. Typically, death results from infections that are manageable for a normal, healthy immune system. AIDS-related complex is the name given for conditions that occur between showing symptoms and dying of AIDS. Typical symptoms of AIDS-related complex include swollen lymph glands, weight loss, night sweats, and recurrent infections. Death usually results from pneumonia or cancer.

 Activity Considerations

Placement in physical education should be determined according to circumstances unique to the child. Provided the child's social behavior is acceptable, placement can be determined according to the child's motor development and fitness levels. Placing the child in any environment that might unnecessarily provoke the spilling of body fluids is contraindicated. The child should not be placed in a setting where he or a peer might *intentionally* cause bodily harm to another person.

In physical education, mainstream or adapted, it should go without saying that there is no AIDS-specific curriculum. This statement, however, often needs to be articulated and reinforced in view of the fear, myth, and hysteria that often surround AIDS. Such emotions, unchecked, lead to nonessential isolation and dehumanization.

Physical education placement for the student with AIDS should be made, at least in part, on the following considerations:

1. Risk to the student: his/her physical condition, immune status, stamina, and need for special care.

2. Possible risk to (and from) others: open lesions, infections, and inimical behavior including the likes of fighting, scratching, biting.

3. Environmental needs: consideration of the student's age, maturity level and neurological status including control of body functions.

4. Parents' *and* student's wishes regarding placement. (Dreyfuss, 1987, p. 24)

Finally, the prognosis for children with AIDS is poor. Buckingham (1989) recommends interventions that prioritize enhancing life quality over those that prolong a life with little quality. Physical education can well be one of those interventions. Physical education's major role in pediatric AIDS may be one of enhancing the child's psychosocial sense of well-being and worth. Activity may offer the child an important respite from a life that is, otherwise, disease- and treatment-centered. Concerning psychosocial well-being possibly afforded through activity, Buckingham states that "AIDS patients have little time left to enjoy life. Let's not waste this time of theirs by forgetting that they are still living" (1989, p. 117).

ASTHMA

Approximately 9 million Americans have some form of asthma. Although asthma can begin at any stage of life, onset typically occurs before age 15 (Young, Schulman, & Schulman, 1985). This condition, in its various forms, appears more often in boys than in girls. McNichol (1987) asserts that asthma, to various degrees, affects nearly 20 percent of the child population. Most children with asthma are of elementary school age, and the disease appears to subside in many children upon their reaching puberty. Feldman and McFadden (1977) identify asthma as the most common chronic disease of childhood. Hill, Britton, and Tattersfield (1987) indicate asthma to be one of the leading causes of school absenteeism.

People with asthma experience breathing difficulty because air flow through bronchial tubes becomes obstructed. Air flow obstruction results from one or more of the following: (1) swelling of mucous membrane linings, (2) contraction of muscles surrounding bronchial tubes, and (3) plugging of the tubes by mucous.

There are three asthma classifications, each having distinct features:

1. *Extrinsic* asthma usually develops in childhood, although it can occur in adulthood. It is commonly associated with allergies to external materials such as pollens, house dust, mold spores (found in damp areas), and animal hair. Persons with this form of asthma usually have positive skin when tested for allergies (Bierman, Pierson, & Shapiro, 1975).

2. *Intrinsic* asthma, less prevalent than the extrinsic type, is nevertheless commonly encountered in physical education settings. This type includes exercise-induced asthma and psychosomatic asthma.

3. *Mixed* asthma occurs in the person with both intrinsic and extrinsic asthma.

Asthma attacks are often related to environmental conditions. Dust, smoke, smog, and a variety of pollens are among airborne particles that can precipitate an attack. Attacks also can be exacerbated to some degree by the emotional state of the person at the time of the attack. Severity varies according to the presence of factors, both in combination and intensity, to which the individual's respiratory system is sensitive.

Onset of an asthma attack often begins with a cough. Coughing results from mucous formation in respiratory passages and is the body's response to that mucous irritation. Coughing, however, tends to be nonproductive. Treatment, typically prescribed by a physician at some previous time, needs to be administered at this time to curtail the attack or prevent its progressing to a more serious stage. Should an attack progress to the degree that breathing is impaired and *dyspnea* (breathing difficulty) occurs, the child may find that sitting facilitates breathing while medication is administered to reverse the attack. Medications take varying times to act depending on type; the teacher and, where appropriate, the child should be aware of this time lag. This awareness, combined with knowledge of circumstances that provoke an individual child's asthma attack, can facilitate a decision to use medication prophylactically. Typically, the child will be taking medication for asthma on an ongoing basis; however, contingency plans are wise given the likelihood of an otherwise unanticipated attack. Part of such a contingency plan should include (1) knowing the child's medication type and schedule, (2) knowing when the child has last taken the medication, and (3) knowing where that medication is located.

Coughing is the most common complaint among children with asthma (Rimmer, 1989). However, *most* coughing in children is *not* asthma-related. The variety of communicable upper respiratory infections to which virtually all children are exposed accounts for *most* children's coughs. Should any cough in a school-age child last longer than two weeks, particularly when the cough seems exercise-related, asthma should be considered.

Three groups of drugs are currently used to manage asthma. *Theophylline* appears to be most effective; however, it is not without side effects that may contraindicate its use. Theophylline comes in preparations that range from short- to long-acting. Because children are fast metabolizers, the preparation of choice among children is often theophylline of the slow-release type. Theophylline, administered in this form, tends to build up in the child's system, thereby preventing or minimizing the severity of an asthma attack. Side effects associated with this medication include stomach distress, nausea, and vomiting. These side effects may, in turn, precipitate loss of appetite. The primary intervention to reduce the intensities of these specific side effects is to take food at the time the medication is taken. This intervention reduces theophylline's potential for stomach lining irritation. Other side effects include central nervous system overstimulation, including nervousness, hyperirritability, and hyperactivity. Should these symptoms occur when the child is just beginning theophylline therapy, there is cause to consider increasing the dosage to goal level over a *protracted* period of time. This practice helps give the child's body needed time to adjust.

Cromolyn is often prescribed in cases where the child does not tolerate theophylline. Cromolyn's major advantage is that it produces few side effects. Canny and Levinson (1986) estimate that 65 percent of children with asthma respond well to cromolyn. Given this success rate and paucity of side effects, cromolyn has become the drug of choice among many physicians treating children for chronic asthma. Cromolyn usually is inhaled in dry power form and takes approximately 30 minutes to take effect. Cromolyn is helpful in *preventing* exercise-induced asthma attacks *before* they occur. It is not effective in reversing an attack once the attack has begun (Breslin, McFadden, & Ingram, 1980).

Beta adrenergic (beta-2) drugs can be useful both in preventing *and* reversing exercise-induced asthma attacks (Hunt, 1987). Beta andrenergic drugs are available both as oral and inhalant preparations; inhalants, however, appear most effective. The drug, used prior to exercise, helps prevent an attack by bronchodialation resulting from relaxing bronchial muscles. The drug taken during an attack helps reverse that attack by reducing bronchial spasms. Depending on the specific preparation prescribed by the child's physician, the effects of the drug typically last from 3 to 6 hours.

When beta andrenergic drugs are prescribed in aerosol form, there is heightened potential for overuse (i.e., user overreliance or abuse). Because aerosol preparations are fast acting, and because they are so easy to use, there is often a tendency to use the inhaler upon the slightest feeling of discomfort. For this specific reason, many physicians recommend that beta andrenergic drugs in aerosol form not be left in the hands of *unsupervised* children and adolescents.

Should the child's asthma symptoms worsen, dosages of any prescribed medication must *not* be increased prior to consultation with the child's physician. To do otherwise would be potentially injurious to the child's health and promote undesirable attitudes about the indiscriminate use of drugs.

Activity Considerations

Regardless of the type or intensity of activity in which the child is about to engage, the teacher must be reasonably confident that the child is, indeed, taking medications as prescribed. Prevention is *always* better than cure. Children with asthma, specifically, should precede any vigorous activity with a light exercise. This procedure provides the respiratory system graded opportunity to become accustomed to the activity's peak stress level. Exposure to vigorous activity *preceded by warm-up* will help avoid unnecessary asthma attacks and may reduce intensity of those that may occur.

Even if the child is on medication, the child should not be without a bronchodilator when exercising. Should tightness in the chest occur during exercise, the child initially should try to work through the episode. Should asthma symptoms not subside spontaneously, the student may then resort to the bronchodilator. With the parent's permission, the teacher may wish to keep an extra bronchodilator in the event the student does not remember to bring one to class.

If there are times when asthma symptoms seem particularly recurrent, the student may be directed to activities of an *anaerobic* nature. Activities characterized by brief exertion beyond the anaerobic threshold, followed by brief periods of reduced activity or rest, will be less likely to provoke an asthma attack than aerobic activity where exertion occurs over relatively longer time periods. Tennis, badminton, and racquetball are examples of activities which, when played aggressively, cause the student to exercise beyond the anaerobic threshold, but then offer periods of rest where heart and respiration rates can return to near normal.

Aerobic activity is indicated virtually whenever such activity does not materially provoke frequency, duration, or intensity of attacks. Aerobic activity is not to be avoided simply because it can be associated with the onset of coughing or wheezing. In the individual child's case, the question of what serves the greater good must be addressed. Given the vast majority of children with asthma, the greater good, now and for a lifetime, is served when the child, through aerobic activity, learns the values of becoming and staying fit. Guidelines for Prescribing Exercise for Asthmatics (1981) recommend aerobic activity for children with asthma as follows:

1. *Preaerobic exercise warm-up:* Activity should include mild cardiorespiratory activity including walking and easy jogging. At some time during warm-up, the student should engage in muscle strengthening exercises including push-ups, sit-ups, and squat thrusts. Flexibility exercises may include alternate toe touching, side bending, and back arching. Warm-up should last a minimum of 5 minutes. Purposes of warm-up are twofold: they include facilitating bronchodilation to ensure adequate ventilation and raising body temperature to a level that facilitates muscle and vital organ effectiveness during exercise.

2. *Duration:* Aerobic activity sessions should last 30 to 40 minutes provided the individual is reasonably fit. Given an unfit individual, initial exercise bouts of 15 minutes or less may be indicated. Remember, the challenge must be real *but reasonable*, because the ultimate goal is to turn the child on to exercise.

3. *Frequency:* 30- to 40-minute sessions should occur four to five times per week.

4. *Intensity:* Exercise should start at a low level of intensity and increase gradually in intensity as fitness improves. If interval training is used, the work level should be at an intensity that produces a pulse of 70 percent of the maximum heart rate (maximum heart rate may be estimated by the following formula: [220 - chronological age] $\times$ 70 percent). Intensity during the exercise interval may be increased slowly from 70 percent to a maximum of 90 percent. At this point, there should be an interval of less intense activity that reduces the heart rate to 50 to 60 percent of maximum. When using continuous (rather than interval) training techniques, a reasonably fit student should be able to progress gradually to an intensity approximating 85 percent of maximum heart rate.

5. *Mode:* Whenever possible, activities and games of the student's choice should be prescribed. For example, one-wall handball or four-square are game possibilities. Ideally, the child with asthma should be involved in swim training as well. Regardless of activity selection, the program must

focus on increasing the student's aerobic power. A stationary bicycle or hand ergometer could also be utilized.

6. *Progressive Exercise:* Programs should begin with walking. If the student is experiencing exercise-induced asthma regularly, she should start with low-level interval training, using work intervals of 10 to 30 seconds. These intervals should be followed by 30- to 90-second rest intervals. Gradually, the student may progress to higher-intensity interval training. With suitable medication, either continuous or interval training is generally well tolerated.

7. *Preexercise medication:* Preexercise medication is essential for most persons with asthma. Beta-2 or theophylline typically are the preferred agents. They are usually taken at least one hour prior to exercise.

8. *Medication to reverse exercise-induced asthma:* If an attack occurs during exercise, the reaction may be reversed by an aerosol agent. Examples are the beta-2 medications including the common ones, albuterol and metaproterenol.

9. *Warm-down after exercise:* The student should warm down after each exercise session. Vigorous work should not stop abruptly. Low-intensity activity (e.g., walking) should be continued for approximately 5 minutes or until the heart rate returns to within 20 beats per minute of the resting level.

DIABETES MELLITUS

For more than 4000 years, facts have been recorded concerning diabetes mellitus [mell'-a-tus]. It is one of the most common diseases today, affecting approximately 4 million people in the United States, of which 10 percent are children (Malone, 1984). Prevalence of diabetes in children in the United States is 1.6 per thousand (Travis, 1987). The physical educator can, therefore, expect to be in contact with children in school settings who have diabetes.

Diabetes is a major health concern. It is the direct cause of more than 38,000 deaths per year and a contributing factor in another 260,000 deaths annually. Diabetes mellitus ranks third after heart disease and cancer as a leading cause of death in the United States. A child born today has a 1 in 5 chance of developing diabetes. Furthermore, diabetes is increasing at a rate of 6 percent per year. Given that rate of increase, the number of individuals with diabetes will double every 15 years.

DIABETES MELLITUS DEFINED

Diabetes mellitus is *not* a diagnostic term. Rather, it is a term that describes a *symptom-complex*. A symptom is defined as any manifestation of an atypical body function. In effect, diabetes mellitus is the umbrella term for a number of conditions whose symptoms are similar (Travis, 1987). Generally, diabetes mellitus refers to conditions that interfere with the pancreas beta cells' ability to produce and/or the body's ability to use *insulin*. A number of different conditions can produce the diabetes mellitus symptom-complex. Diabetes occurs when the body is unable to properly utilize carbohydrates. This results in an elevated blood sugar level; a condition termed *hyperglycemia*. *Hypoglycemia*, the opposite of hyperglycemia, is a condition wherein sugar concentration in the blood is too low. Depending upon how well the individual's diabetes is managed, both conditions can be experienced by a person with diabetes. Warning signs and treatments for both conditions *are* recognizable, and *must* be recognized by the physical educator in the event either condition occurs. Proper action is essential for the student's well-being.

The body's regulation of blood sugar levels is also affected by the hormone *glucagon* (gloo'-kah-gon). Pancreas alpha cells produce and secrete this hormone. Whereas insulin lowers blood glucose levels, glucagon raises it. Typically, the body activates glucagon during heavy exercise and starvation because, in both conditions, a decrease in blood glucose occurs. In persons with type I (insulin-dependent) diabetes, alpha cells, like their insulin-producing beta cell counterparts, may not be functioning properly. In a study of 14 subjects with and 7 without diabetes, glucagon levels were measured both before and after exercise. Subjects with diabetes were found to possess significantly lower levels of glucagon than did persons without diabetes. Findings suggest that, among persons with type I diabetes, both alpha and beta cells may not be functioning properly (Duncan & Oppenheimer, 1974).

The term *diabetes mellitus* literally means *sweet urine* and refers to an overabundance of sugar in the urine of one whose diabetes is uncontrolled. When an adult develops diabetes, it historically has been designated type II, or mature-onset diabetes (MOD). When diabetes occurs in youngsters (up to 20 years), it historically has been termed juvenile onset diabetes (JOD). In recent years there has been a lessening of reliance on the terms MOD and JOD, because, to some extent, their relationship to age of onset can be misleading. Although infrequent, type I can occur in adulthood and type II can occur in childhood. Brouhard (1987) refers to type I as *insulin-dependent diabetes mellitus* (IDDM) and type II as *noninsulin-dependent diabetes mellitus* (NIDDM). Preference for these designations over MOD and JOD stem from the fact that people with type I *always* require insulin replacement, whereas people with type II do not necessarily require insulin replacement. Among persons with type II, the condition can often be managed through diet, weight loss, exercise, and oral medication. Table 18.1 shows differential characteristics associated with type I (IDDM) and type II (NIDDM) diabetes.

SUSPECTED CAUSES OF DIABETES

Many investigators have demonstrated that persons who have diabetes come from families with a history of diabetes. Simply looking at family history, however, falls short of truly facilitating determination of whether diabetes is a function of genetics,

TABLE 18.1   **Diabetes Characteristics**

	IDDM (Type I)	NIDDM (Type II)
Age at onset	< 40 yrs (80% > 20 yrs)	> 40 yrs
Sex predilection	None	Female
Nutritional status	Normal/Thin	> 60% Obese
Clinical onset	Rapid (> 80%)	Insidious
Degree hyperglycemia	Marked	Mild to moderate
Ketonemia-ketonuria	Present	Absent
Insulin replacement	Absolutely necessary	Often optional
Stability of disease	Labile	Stable
Response to oral drugs	Uncommon	Common

Source: Travis, Brouhard, & Schreiner, 1987, p. 18.

environment, or some combination of both. Studies of twins suggest, but do not conclusively demonstrate, that genetics may be a factor. According to Travis et al. (1987), monozygotic (identical) twins show higher incidence of each twin having diabetes than do dizygotic (fraternal) twins. Because monozygotic twins are more closely genetically matched than are their dizygotic counterparts, the interpretation is that genetics does, in some way, play a role. Travis et al. also state that, "although these studies suggest that genetic factors are involved in the diabetic state, exact mechanisms of genetic transmissions are unknown" (1987, p. 9).

Another factor that may influence the onset of diabetes is an autoimmune disorder. In certain autoimmune disorders, the body fails to recognize its own tissue and manufactures antibodies to destroy tissue that the body perceives as being foreign. One theory suggests that when cells perceived by the body to be foreign are *pancreatic beta cells* (where insulin is manufactured), antibodies destroy these cells. Such destruction is believed to destroy the beta cells' ability to manufacture insulin, and diabetes is the result. The autoimmune theory's validity is reinforced by the observation that antibodies capable of attacking pancreatic beta cells are present in a sampling of 67 percent of people newly diagnosed with insulin-dependent diabetes.

A number of studies have proposed a relationship between viral illness and the onset of diabetes. The viral theory has been linked by some to the autoimmune disorder theory. The belief is that a viral infection is the perpetrator that triggers an autoimmune disorder that, in turn, brings about the onset of diabetes.

Further support for the viral theory comes from studies indicating that, in the Northern Hemisphere, the onset of type I diabetes occurs most frequently in fall and winter. Highest frequency for the onset of type I diabetes in the Southern Hemisphere occurs May through August. Note that these respective periods of onset, by hemisphere, are almost precisely 6 months apart. In the respective hemispheres, the months cited above are those when viral respiratory disease are most prevalent in the population (Travis et al., 1987).

COMMON CHARACTERISTICS OF TYPE I DIABETES

Type I will remain the primary focus of our diabetes discussion and recommendations, because type I appears most often in school-age people. Also, of the two general types of diabetes, type I typically is more difficult to monitor and control.

Children with type I generally are insulin-dependent from the time of diagnosis. In the absence of insulin, sugar accumulates in the blood in excessive amounts. In effect, the body becomes unable to utilize glycogen (resulting from carbohydrate intake) for fuel. In this situation, the body resorts to fat for fuel. A problem arises here, because, for proper fat combustion, a certain proportion of carbohydrate must be burned simultaneously. Incomplete fat combustion, resulting from carbohydrate unavailability during combustion, produces toxic acid waste products. These wastes, known as ketones, result in a condition known as *ketosis* or *acidosis*. In uncontrolled diabetes, ketone concentration becomes very high, and a strong acid effect known as *ketoacidosis* occurs. This creates an emergency situation, requiring insulin administration. Failure to administer insulin may result in diabetic coma or death. Table 18.2 presents symptoms of hyperglycemia, resulting from absence of insulin, and hypoglycemia, resulting from the presence of insulin in excess.

EMERGENCY TREATMENT OF HYPOGLYCEMIA

Immediate intake of carbohydrates is needed to counteract a hypoglycemic reaction. The person will improve quickly after eating or drinking any form of sugar. The Juvenile Diabetes Foundation suggests the following treatment for an individual experiencing hypoglycemia (i.e., insulin reaction):

TABLE 18.2   Comparison of Hypoglycemic and Hyperglycemic Reactions

Warning Signs	Hypoglycemic Reaction (Insulin Reaction)	Hyperglycemic Reaction (Diabetic Coma)
Onset	Sudden	Gradual
Skin	Pale, moist	Flushed, dry
Behavior	Excited, nervous, confused	Drowsy
Breath	Normal	Fruity odor (acetone)
Breathing	Normal to rapid, shallow	Deep, labored
Vomiting	Absent	Present
Tongue	Moist, numb, tingling	Dry
Hunger	Present	Absent
Thirst	Absent	Present
Pain	Headache	Abdominal
Sugar in urine	Absent or slight	Large amounts

1. Give some form of sugar immediately. This will rapidly increase blood sugar level. Use any of the following: sugar cubes, skim milk or fruit juice (approximately $\frac{1}{2}$ cup), soda pop (approximately $\frac{1}{2}$ cup, but not diet pop), or candy (equivalent to 6–8 sugar-sweetened Life Savers). The person may need coaxing to eat.

2. Improvement should be evident within 10 minutes. At that point, give additional food and have the person resume normal activities.

3. If the student fails to improve, call parents, physician, and emergency medical assistance.

EMERGENCY TREATMENT OF HYPERGLYCEMIA

Hyperglycemia, also called diabetic coma or diabetic acidosis, is relatively rare. It can occur, however, if the person with diabetes seriously departs from prescribed diet and/or fails to take insulin.

In contrast to fast-developing hypoglycemia, hyperglycemia progresses slowly over many hours or several days. Common symptoms are fatigue, sluggishness, or general lethargy (Seltzer, 1977). Need to urinate will increase; therefore, the instructor should take note of the person's increasing requests to use the restroom. One telling sign of hyperglycemia is the fruity odor of the person's breath.

A student who persists with these symptoms or lapses into a coma must receive immediate medical assistance. If the child is comatose, *only* a trained nurse or physician is qualified to administer insulin.

MONITORING AND CONTROLLING BLOOD SUGAR LEVELS

The person whose diabetes is well controlled will exhibit the following characteristics:

1. Feeling of physical well-being
2. Normal weight, maintained by a well-balanced diet and exercise
3. Negative urine tests
4. Negative blood sugar tests

Ideally, children with diabetes should be taught by their physicians to understand diabetes. This instruction should be reinforced by parents and teachers. The child should understand the role of diet, exercise, and insulin in self-management of diabetes. The child, as soon as possible, should be taught skills required for urine and blood sugar self-testing and insulin injection.

INSULIN AND EXERCISE

People with diabetes who exercise regularly, when compared to nonexercising peers, maintain lower blood sugar levels and increase the effectiveness of available insulin

(Ubel, 1985). Insulin injection sites should vary according to the specific activity in which the person will be participating. This recommendation is based on differences in insulin absorption rates of working and nonworking muscles.

Hard-working muscles need more fuel (glucose). However, insulin injected directly over hard-working muscles is absorbed more rapidly than that injected over resting muscle. A resulting precipitous drop in blood sugar level may produce a tendency towards hypoglycemia. Persons with diabetes should check with their physicians regarding preferred injection sites according to specific activities in which they plan to engage. The physician may recommend, for example, that a person planning to play tennis, basketball, or volleyball (i.e., sports in which both leg and arm muscles are heavily involved) inject insulin directly above muscles of the abdomen.

When activity is expected to be less than normal, insulin should be increased. For greater than normal activity, prior ingestion of carbohydrates is advised. If exercise is long and strenuous, hourly snacks may need to be taken to ensure adequate blood sugar level maintenance. Also, due to increased carbohydrate metabolism during prolonged and/or strenuous activity, the person may need to adjust the insulin dosage downward. As always, when adjusting medication dosages, prior consultation with a physician is advised.

Activity Considerations

Regular physical activity is essential in the physiological and psychological management of diabetes. This is particularly true of young people with type I diabetes. According to Wentworth and Hoover (1981), "Most physicians encourage active participation in exercise, physical education, and extracurricular school sports. Uncomplicated diabetes should never be a reason to exclude a child from activity" (p. 43GE).

Coping with the psychological aspects of diabetes is especially important for children so affected, because exclusion from activity prompts feelings of isolation. Diabetes need not be a barrier to a full and happy life-style. Misunderstandings, however, on the part of the child, peers, and adults often lead to the child with diabetes believing that he can never be like other children. Attitudes become more disabling than clinical manifestations of the disease. The child with diabetes and the child's associates should learn early on that the *only* difference between persons with and without diabetes is pancreas cells that do not produce insulin. Above all, the child should be perceived as a child first; one who happens to have diabetes; not a diabetic child (Figure 18.3). Travis et al. (1987) states that "when professionals use the adjective 'diabetic' to describe such persons, it is small wonder that many children see themselves as a composite of what they feel is the disease itself" (p. 123).

Weight control often is associated with diabetes. Children with type I diabetes are generally underweight and smaller than their peers. Overweight is more often associated with type II. Arkey (1978) emphasizes that youngsters with type I must consume adequate calories to ensure normal growth and maturation. Physical education for children with type I should include strength-development activities that

THE CHILD WITH DIABETES MELLITUS   THE DIABETIC CHILD

FIGURE 18.3   **Consequences of Ways in Which Child Is Perceived.** (Source: Travis, Brouhard, & Schreiner, 1987, p. 39)

facilitate weight gain through enhanced musculature. Need for strength development among boys with type I is reported by Cunningham and Etkind (1975). Their data indicate that boys with type I score significantly lower on measures of strength than do their nondiabetic peers. In interpreting these data, one should, however, recall that children with type I often are small for chronological age, and that a small child's strength may be typical for one of that child's stature.

   Cardiovascular fitness also must be emphasized. Some children with diabetes possess very low levels of cardiovascular fitness and may need to begin an aerobic program by walking. The National Heart, Lung, and Blood Institute has developed a 12-week progressive walking program (Table 18.3). This program is appropriate for people whose cardiovascular fitness is, as yet, underdeveloped. The walking schedule should be undertaken at least three times per week, and each session should be preceded by a stretching warm-up. Should the individual find any one day's walking activity particularly tiring, then that day's exercise regimen should be repeated during the subsequent exercise session. Following the repeated session, the individual, during the next exercise session, should be capable of progressing to the next level (Krosnick, 1984).

TABLE 18.3   Twelve-week Progressive Walking Program

Week	Warm-up (Slow Walking) (min)	Exercise (Brisk Walking) (min)	Cool Down (Slow Walking) (min)	Total Time (min)
1	5	5	5	15
2	5	7	5	17
3	5	9	5	19
4	5	11	5	21
5	5	13	5	23
6	5	15	5	25
7	5	18	5	28
8	5	20	5	30
9	5	23	5	33
10	5	26	5	36
11	5	28	5	38
12	5	30	5	40

Source: Modified from Krosnick, Spring 1984, p. 5.

Risk of infection is heightened among people with diabetes. When blood sugar is high, white blood cells' effectiveness in fighting infection becomes compromised. Infection may be particularly problematic in lower extremities (i.e., where blood is circulating farthest from the heart). Foot cleanliness is a must, and the teacher should be on the lookout for any kind of skin lesion.

Few, if any, activity modifications need be made for the child whose diabetes is controlled. Modifications likely would need to be considered while the specific plan to control the individual's diabetes is being developed and/or when, for whatever reason, the child's fitness or skill levels are dramatically below average.

The physical educator should be aware that the child with diabetes may need more fluids than other youngsters. This is because blood sugar levels, when higher than normal, draw needed water from body tissues. Amounts of water lost depend on activity level, fitness level, and climatic conditions. A good rule of thumb is for the teacher to ensure water intake every 15 minutes during strenuous activity.

Should the child become sick or vomit during activity, an imbalance involving insulin and blood sugar may have occurred. In such instances, the child should be excused from further activity. In addition, the school nurse and the other teachers should be notified to watch for continuing symptoms during the remainder of the school day.

LIMB DEFICIENCY

Limb deficiency has far-reaching consequences physically, motorically, and psychosocially. Depending on the site or sites of limb deficiency, physical and motor impairment may range from relatively mild to relatively severe. In addition, psychosocial implications influence the child's feelings toward self and his feelings toward others, and others are influenced in their feelings toward the child. Developing a positive psychosocial attitude in the child and in how others react to the child will create a positive environment in which the child can grow and develop. Because children (and adults) tend to be very conscious of even slight differences that set them apart from others, the obvious limb deficiency presents a significant psychosocial dilemma.

Classmates of a child with a prosthesis may reject that child unless the teacher provides a positive setting and acceptance. Kieran, Conner, Von Hippel, and Jones (1981) make the following suggestions: "Children are often more straight forward in their questions and explanations than adults are. If a child is somewhat accepting of the handicap, he or she may act as a 'teacher,' explaining what happened and how the prosthetic device (if any) works. Touching the disfigured area often helps to satisfy young children's curiosity. Once the curiosity has been satisfied, the children will probably play together like all other children" (p. 56).

Limb absence may be either *acquired* or *congenital*. Acquired amputation refers to limb loss by accident (traumatic amputation) or surgery (surgical amputation). Surgical amputation most often occurs owing to a malignant bone tumor. The child with an acquired amputation was born with an intact body, but has experienced a problem subsequent to birth necessitating amputation.

Congenital amputation refers to missing limbs or portions of limbs at birth. Characteristics of the various congenital limb amputations are **amelia** (absence of limb or limbs), **hemimelia** (congenital absence of all or part of distal half of limb), and **phocomelia** (congenital absence of proximal portion of limb, the hands or feet being attached to the trunk by a small bone).

Congenital amputation may be transverse, taking the limb in full cross-section, or paraxial (Greek for "along the axis"), taking only a side or center portion of the limb (Figure 18.4).

Males incur more amputations from all causes at the rate of 2:1 from disease, 10:1 from trauma, and 1.2:1 from congenital causes and tumor (Dunham, 1981). The three major causes of amputation that most directly affect school-age individuals are cancer, trauma, and congenital deformity. Trauma involves crushing injuries or lacerations that are so extensive that reconstruction is not possible. The destroyed tissue and attendant loss of blood may threaten the person's life. Amputation resulting from **congenital deformity** is performed when the limb is not capable of functioning and there is extensive loss of nerve supply or muscle power. Individuals with congenital underdevelopment or malformation of the limbs have been helped by amputation of the nonfunctional limb and fitting of a prostheses.

Activity Considerations

When amputation is elective and planned in advance, physical conditioning activities should be provided in preparation for surgery and convalescence. Following convalescence and return to the physical education setting, the child will need psychosocial

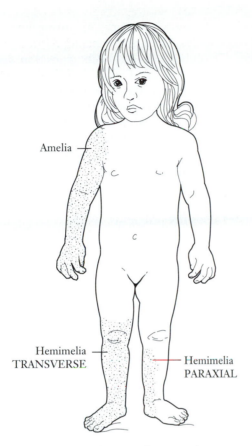

Amelia

Hemimelia
TRANSVERSE

Hemimelia
PARAXIAL

FIGURE 18.4   **Types of amputations.**

support as well as physical and motor rehabilitation. The educator should discuss the child's amputation with classmates to satisfy their curiosity and alleviate apprehension about the amputee. This effort will help to resolve social problems for the amputee and his peers.

Recommended activities for the amputee involve moving the joints above the amputation site as pain permits. Stretching activities prescribed by the physician following surgery and return to school usually are done by, or in cooperation with, a physical, occupational, or kinesiotherapist. Moving the affected limb through reasonable ranges of motion and strengthening appropriate muscles will prevent debilitating contractures that can occur following amputation.

The following list of progressions is designed for a below-the-knee (BK) amputee. A mat program is a combination of exercises that involve different functional skills such as rolling, crawling, and kneeling. Such skills are commonly taught in a sequence that follows their normal development in childhood. Each section of this mat program for a unilateral amputee stresses skill development. The exercises build on one another to increase strength and coordination. The activities are (1) rolling,

(2) assuming a long sitting position, (3) seated push-ups, (4) moving forward, backward, side to side in a long sitting position, (5) assuming a kneeling posture on all fours, (6) crawling and resisted crawling, (7) assuming a high kneeling position, and (8) balance activities in a high kneeling position (O'Sullivan, Cullen, & Schmitz, 1981).

Maintaining proper range of motion in the limb is vital to achieving correct body mechanics, and the strengthening of appropriate muscle groups allows for eventual motor control and management of the artificial limb or **prosthesis** (Figure 18.5). The sound limb and all unaffected body parts should be exercised as well to maintain a desirable physical condition. Lower extremity amputees need activities to strengthen upper extremities for crutch or cane walking.

Children with congenital amputations may have had few opportunities for pre-prosthetic care or motor skills enlightenment. It is important to note that comprehensive early attention facilitates a positive prognosis. As the child continues to grow and develop, regular evaluation serves as the basis for prosthesis fitting, refitting, and activity prescription. The adapted physical educator, by virtue of professional preparation and practical or clinical experience, can provide valuable input by evaluating the child's progress as related to potential and prognosis.

When attempting to understand prosthetic devices, the adapted physical educator should determine if modifications are possible that will allow the youngster to take active part in a specific skill or game. In many cases, the person who makes the prosthesis, called the prosthetist (pros′ thet ist), will offer suggestions for adapting the artificial equipment. For example, the split hook is an extremely functional hand substitute that can be modified to add a device on which a baseball glove is securely attached and easily opened and closed by the player.

A new type of artificial equipment that is becoming popular is the myoelectric prosthesis. This equipment involves movement of the artificial limb through an elec-

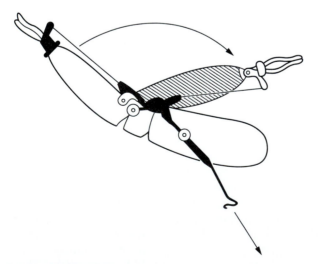

FIGURE 18.5   **Above-the-elbow (AE) prosthesis.**

tric signal initiated by the person. At present, such prostheses are generally reserved for light work, with the conventional prosthesis used as a back-up for heavy-duty tasks. Shaperman (1985) has found, however, that myoelectric hands have greater grip strength than those operated by body power. In reference to the traditional prosthetic devices operated by body power, Adams et al. (1982) state the following: "The stump is used as a source of energy for control of the prosthesis .... Force and motion can be obtained by means of a cable that is connected between the prosthetic device and a harness across the chest or shoulder" (p. 51).

PROBLEMS OF BALANCE

Balance appears to pose one of the most pervasive problems confronting people with amputations, particularly newly acquired amputations who are in the early stages of rehabilitation. Initially, the child is not accustomed to the limb's absence and its effect on the body's center of gravity. Learning to manage the prosthesis can be disconcerting also because of its awkwardness in not moving counteractively to the other member. Normal arm counteraction for balance in walking or running is complicated by limb absence and prosthetic replacement.

For people with lower extremity amputations, balance is a problem particularly when amputation is above the knee (AK). Below-the-knee (BK) amputees often walk quite normally with little or no indication that the limb is missing. Generally, the

Below-the-elbow (BE) prosthesis.

level of lower extremity amputation and whether the amputation is AK or BK will determine the child's balance capabilities and skill development. These factors should serve as a guide in selecting appropriate activities.

Swimming.   Swimming is an enjoyable and valuable activity for children with amputations. It serves to condition and to ensure that affected body segments can move through the desired range of motion. Depending on need, swim fins may be strapped to the limb or to a special prosthesis to enhance performance and enjoyment.

Problem of Increased Perspiration.   Amputees encounter increased perspiration during activity because the amputee's cooling surface is reduced owing to missing a limb or limbs. Encourage the person to wear lightweight clothing to reduce fatigue and to absorb perspiration. On days that are warm or humid or both, this problem needs to be monitored closely.

Low Energy Output and Obesity.   Because of low motivation and low self-concept, many children with amputations adopt a sedentary behavior pattern. Although amputation may limit movement and decrease efficiency to some degree, low energy output nevertheless tends to be a characteristic behavior even among unilateral below-elbow amputees. This suggests that in some cases the sedentary behavior pattern may be a function of attitude rather than of disability.

Some people, particularly those with BK amputations, become obese with age as a result of inactivity. This tendency should be countered with an activity program that is both satisfying and within the individual's potential.

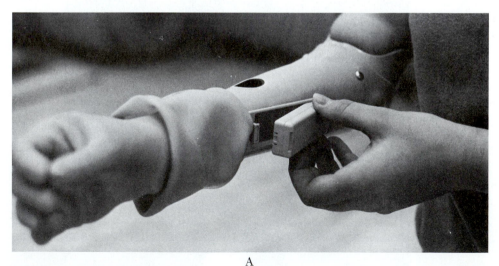

A

(A) Battery activates servo.

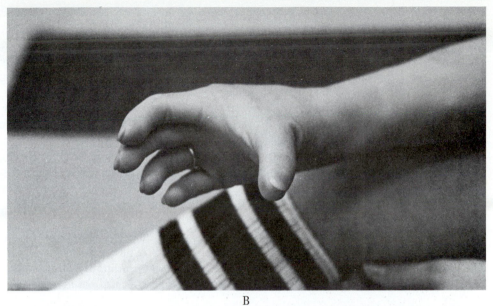

B

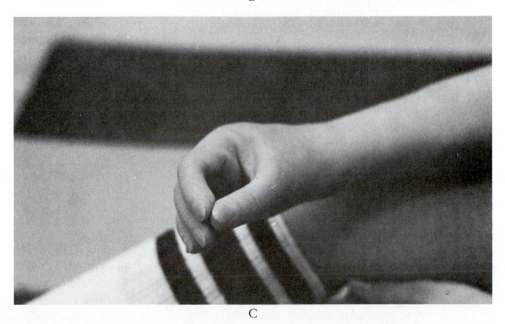

C

(B) Tensing the stump causes prosthetic hand to open. (C) Relaxing the stump causes hand to close.

Lasko and Knopf (1984) stress the importance of developing appropriate levels of cardiorespiratory efficiency: "The aerobic capacity of the amputee should be maintained as much as possible. Swimming is an excellent choice for even the bilateral amputee. Swim fins may be attached to the stumps by special prostheses. Arm crank ergometry may be another choice for those with limited weight bearing capabilities" (p. 198).

Increasing energy output is important, because good muscular condition is required to manage the prosthesis. Limited muscular strength and endurance render the prosthesis unmanageable and encourage sedentary behavior.

Among amputees with low energy whose sedentary behavior appears more a function of attitude than disability, a negative self-concept is probably the culprit. Children who have been treated as invalids will reflect the limited expectations of those adults around them. Telling children through words and deeds that they are invalids becomes a self-fulfilling prophecy.

Many amputees with low energy can achieve physical and motor proficiencies well beyond their present performance levels. The adapted physical educator should be patient but persistent, empathetic but gently prodding to help these children find enjoyment, success, and improved self-image through movement.

Playground Activities and Sports.   Surprisingly, children with amputations often enjoy participating in climbing and hanging activities. For those with upper extremity amputations, this presents a unique challenge because the pull against the prosthesis, which occurs in hanging activities, is identical to the force exerted to remove the appliance. Resourceful children do discover ways of stabilizing the prosthesis so it will not come loose. Individuals with below-the-elbow amputations become proficient climbers by using a forceful tensing of the stump in the prosthesis socket to hold it in place.

Children with amputations can participate in many sports, depending on each specific case. Skiing is one activity that appears to be gaining favor among those with unilateral lower extremity amputations. Persons with unilateral upper extremity amputations can participate in baseball or softball when they learn to catch and throw with the same hand. This is done by catching the ball, tossing it into the air, quickly tucking the glove under the affected arm, catching the ball with the unaffected hand, and throwing it. Those with upper extremity amputations with controls that open and close the hook learn to time opening the hook by tossing beanbags for distance or accuracy or both (Bleck and Nagel 1982, p.20). A person with lower extremity amputations can enjoy archery and weight training.

While engaging in sports, some individuals will discard their prosthesis because it gets in the way. If removal of the prosthesis has the physician's approval, there should be no other cause for concern. Under such circumstances, the person is often the best judge of how she performs most efficiently.

When introducing a variety of activities, do not overprogram the individual so that he never becomes proficient at any one activity. Enjoyment of an activity is determined by the child's skill in that activity. Realistic activity selection should reflect some variety but also some focus so the child can develop skill.

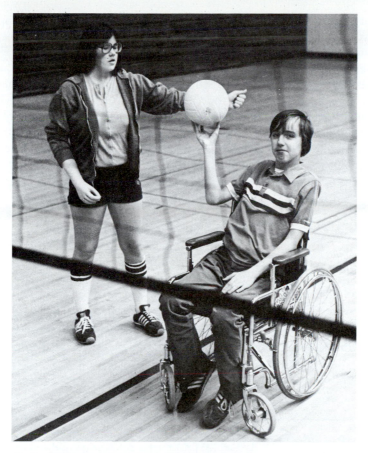

**Girl with below-the-elbow amputation uses nonimpaired arm
to serve while boy with muscular dystrophy "sets up" ball.**

SPINAL CORD INJURY

Spinal cord injury is not a musculoskeletal condition; it is a neuromuscular condition. The disability is not caused by a dysfunction of either muscle or bone, but by trauma to the spinal cord nerves that innervate skeletal muscles. The condition is being seen increasingly in schools and is characterized by chronic, permanent orthopedic disability.

In the United States, the leading cause of death between ages 1 and 25 is accidents. Many persons who undergo accidents sustain permanent injuries, particularly to the spinal cord. When permanent spinal cord injury occurs, disability results below the injury site in the form of muscle paralysis (Figure 18.6). This happens because the nerves responsible for innervating those muscles do not function owing to spinal cord trauma.

Generally, the higher the site where trauma on the spinal cord occurred, the more pervasive the loss of muscle function. Permanent injury to the neck area (cervical vertebrae) will involve all four limbs (quadriplegia). Permanent injury to the spinal cord below the neck will involve the lower extremities (paraplegia). When the lesion is complete, loss of function below the injury site will be total. In some instances, the lesion may be partial only, resulting in *some* residual muscle function below the injury site. For example, some people with quadriplegia (i.e., people with cervical lesion) are able to walk.

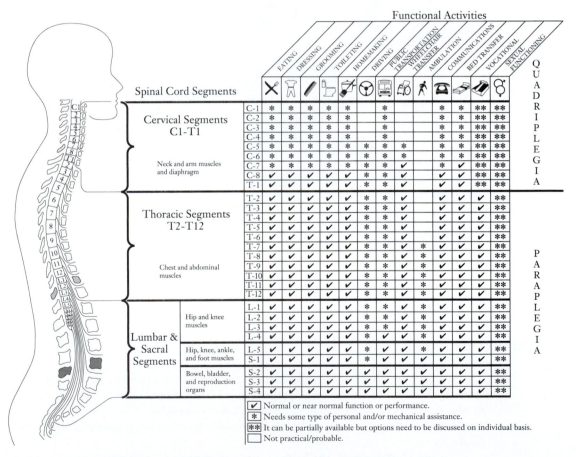

FIGURE 18.6   Functional activity for spinal cord injuries. (Used with permission of the Harmarville Rehabilitation Center, Pittsburgh, PA 15238)

Prior to spinal cord injury, opportunities for educational, psychosocial, and physical and motor development were probably normal. This should be considered a plus in helping the person who faces post-accident rehabilitation and adjustment, for the skills of noninvolved extremities will remain intact (Tindall, 1985). When involvement is partial, rehabilitation may restore function according to potential with modifications occuring in sport skills, equipment, and rules to restore and continue participation.

Although spinal cord injury is significant, persons with this injury generally do not encounter multiple disabilities or the degree of complications experienced by those with other orthopedic impairments (i.e., muscular dystrophy is progressive; cerebral palsy may affect intelligence, vision, and speech; arthritis is painful; leg paralysis may accompany spina bifida). Fewer complicating conditions mean that spinal cord injury often is more manageable and responsive to rehabilitation than other orthopedic conditions.

Historically, persons with spinal cord injury have been relatively active in developing and maintaining physical and motor proficiencies and sport skills. Such activity levels began shortly after World War II when soldiers returned paralyzed from war injuries. These active life-styles over the years have provided positive role models for others who have sustained spinal cord injury.

Beyond physical education, opportunities to participate in sports are expanding. National wheelchair athletic associations are active in many sports. Several states have formed adapted athletic associations so athletes with orthopedic impairments can engage in interscholastic athletic competition (see Chapter 21, Opportunity in Sport).

Activity Considerations

Activities that use primarily noninvolved or partially involved extremities are appropriate. Although the available options are more varied for persons with spinal cord injury located lower on the spinal cord, many options do exist for persons with higher site lesions. Persons with higher site lesions are now engaging in activities and sports previously considered inappropriate or not possible. White water kayaking, racquetball, tennis, and skiing are among these expanding opportunities. Further information regarding sport opportunities and activities can be found in the publication *Sports n' Spokes*. Another organization that supports activity opportunities is Courage Center, 3915 Golden Valley Road, Golden Valley, MN 55422.

Finally, yet another excellent source of programming for individuals with disabilities is found in the journal *Palaestra: The Forum of Sport and Physical Education for the Disabled.* This periodical is edited by Dr. David Beaver and can be obtained by writing to P.O. Box 508, Macomb, IL 61455.

The person with spinal cord injury often can participate in the physical education mainstream, sometimes with and sometimes without modification. Bowling, table tennis, archery, weight lifting, and swimming may be performed with little modification. Many racket and ball games require only modest modifications for participation. For example, in softball, the participant may play a position that requires minimal amounts of rapid mobility (e.g., pitcher). On offense play, the person may bat as others do, and "run" a distance that challenges the batter and the fielders. In court and racket games, the ball might be permitted to bounce more than once and still be considered playable. Such rule modifications should be applied only as needed to equalize the challenge for all players.

Should the disability limit the student's grasping functions, several modifications are appropriate. A rack ("the third hand") can be mounted on a wheelchair so a bowling ball is "held" until needed. Pushing devices can be purchased or made to give added control and strength to enable the nonimpaired hand and arm to impart more velocity. Tape or Velcro on paddles, mallets, or rackets provides grip assistance.

In track and field activities, only jumping events will be inappropriate. Participation in putting and throwing events is both possible and desirable, though the weight and dimensions of the projectile may require modification. When appropriate, a softball or baseball might replace the shot put. Participation in running events often requires little or no modification, except for the wheelchair. In some instances, an efficient wheeler may move even faster than a conventional runner. Distances should be modified to equalize opportunities and challenges. When wheelchair and other participants engage in highly mobile activities, the chair must not impose unnecessary risk or produce interference for other athletes.

Sometimes positive results can be achieved when nondisabled students use wheelchairs or crutches to participate in races with the student with spinal injuries. The activity should, however, remain appropriate for all participants so the educational integrity is not compromised.

The participant with spinal cord injuries needs to learn to move in and out of the wheelchair independently. Based on the student's capabilities, the physical educator should teach him efficient ways to exit and enter the chair and how to right himself after a fall during active play. To develop exit and entry skills, the student must develop arm and shoulder muscle strength. Isometric grip activities, flexed arm hang, pull-ups, and dips are appropriate exercises.

The National Wheelchair Athletic Association, to equalize competition for persons with spinal neuromuscular conditions, has developed a participant classification system. The system is revised periodically to make it more sensitive to different degrees of residual muscle function. The system classifies participants by lesion site (This classification is discussed in Appendix C and Chapter 21).

REFERENCES

Anderson, R. (1982). Exercise in management of arthritis and rheumatoid diseases. *Cardio-Gram, 9*, 3.

Arkey, R. A. (1978). Current principles of dietary therapy of diabetes milletus. *Medical Clinics of North America, 64*, 655–662.

Bierman, C. W., Pierson, W. E., & Shapiro, G. G. (1975). Asthma in childhood. (Ed.), H. F. Conn in *Current Therapy 1975* (pp. 695–699). Philadelphia: W. B. Saunders.

Bleck, E. E., & Nagel, D. A. (1982). *Physically handicapped children: an atlas for teachers* (3rd ed). New York: Grune and Stratton.

Breslin, F. J., McFadden, E. R., & Ingram, R. H. (1980). The effects of cromolyn sodium on the airway response to hypernia and cold air in asthma. *American Review of Respiratory Diseases, 122,* 11–16.

Buckingham, R. W. (1989). *Care of the dying child.* New York: Continuum.

Canny, J. G., & Levinson, H. (1986). Management of asthma—A Canadian perspective. *Chest, 190,* 465–525.

Cunningham, I. N., & Etkind, E. L. (1975). Let the diabetic play. *JOPER, 46,* 40–42.

Dreyfuss, K. R. (1987). What about AIDS? *Camping Magazine, 59,* 23–26.

Duncan, T. G., & Oppenheimer, H. E. (1974). New discoveries in disabilities reported. *ADA Forecast, 27,* 15–18.

Dunham, C. S. (1981). Amputations. In R.M. Goldenson (Ed.), *Disability and rehabilitaion handbook* (pp. 36–45). New York: McGraw-Hill.

Feldman, N. T., & McFadden, E. R., Jr. (1977). Asthma therapy old and new. *Medical Clinics of North America, 61,* 1239–1250.

Guidelines for prescribing exercises for asthmatics (1981). *The Physician and Sports Medicine, 9,* 51.

Hill, R. A., Britton, J. R., & Tattersfield, L. E. (1987). Management of asthma in schools. *Archives of Diseases in Childhood, 62,* 414–415.

Hunt, C. H. (1987) Exercise induced asthma. *Delaware Medical Journal, 59,* 609-610.

Ike, R. W., Lampman, R. M., & Castor, C. W. (1989). Arthritis and aerobic exercise: A review. *The Physician and Sports medicine, 17,* 128–138.

Kieran, S.H. (1981). *Mainstreaming preschoolers: Children with orthopedic handicaps.* Belmont, MA: CRC Education & Development.

Kieran S.S., Conner, F.P., Von Hippel, C.S., & Jones, S.H. (1981). *Mainstreaming preschoolers: Children with orthopedic handicaps.* Belmont, MA: CRC Education & Human Development.

Knox, K. R. (1975). Management of the diabetic child. In H. E. Conn (Ed.), *Current Therapy 1975,* (pp. xx-yy). Philadelphia: W. B. Saunders.

Krosnick, A. (1984, Spring). Walk your way to health. *Diabetes 1984,* p. 5.

Lasko, P.M., & Knopf, K.G.(1984). *Adapted & corrective exercise for the disabled adult* (Ed.). Dubuque, IA: Eddie Bowers.

Malone, J. I. (1984). Diabetes mellitus in childhood and adolescence. In R.E. Rakel (Ed.), *Conn's Current Therapy 1984,* (pp. 456-459). Philadelphia: W. B. Saunders.

March of Dimes. (1983). *Be good to your baby before it is born.* White Plains, NY: Author.

March of Dimes. (1985). *Low Birthweight.* White Plains, NY: Author.

McNichol, K. (1987). Asthma in the younger child. *Australian Family Physician, 16,* 559–562.

O'Sullivan, S.B., Cullen, K.E., & Schmitz, T.J. (1981). Physical Rehabilitation: Evaluation and treatment procedures. Philadelphia: F. A. Davis.

Pachman, L. M. (1984). Juvenile (rheumatoic) arthritis. In R. B. Conn (Ed.), *Conn's Current Therapy,* (pp. 235-239). Philadelphia: W. B. Saunders.

Quarterly report to the Domestic Policy Council in the prevalence and rate of the spread of HIV and AIDS in the United States. (1988). *Journal of the American Medical Association, 259,* 2657–2661.

Rimmer, J. H. (1989). A vigorous physical education program for children with exercise induced asthma. *Journal of Physical Education, Recreation, and Dance, 60,* 91–95.

Seltzer, H. S. (1977). Urinary glucose tests—A consumer's guide. *Diabetes Forecast, 30,* 25–27.

Shaperman, C. (1985). Myoelectric stimulation of prosthetic limbs. In R.B. Conn (Ed.), *Current diagnosis* 7 (pp. 840–846). Philadelphia: W.B. Saunders.

Solberg, E. (1988). Can I be excused from gym? I'm pregnant. *Physical Educator, 45,* 109–111.

Spencer, C. H. (1985). Juvenile rheumatoid arthritis. In R. B. Conn (Ed.), *Current Diagnosis* 7, (pp. 345–349). Philadelphia: W. B. Saunders.

Stein, J. U. (1979, June). The mission and the mandate: Physical education, the not so sleeping giant. *Education Unlimited.*, p. 27–29.

Taylor, J. (1987). School problems and teacher responsibilities in juvenile rheumatoic arthritis. *Journal of School Health, 57,* 186–190.

Tindall, S.C. (1985). Trauma of the central nervous system. In R.B. Conn (Ed.), *Current diagnosis* 7 (pp 421–429). Philadelphia: W.B. Saunders.

Travis, L. B., Brouhard, B. H., & Schreiner, B. (Eds.), (1987). *Diabetes Mellitus in children and adolescence.* Philadelphia: W. B. Saunders.

Ubel, E. A. (1985, April 21). Cure for diabetes? *Health on Parade*, p. 12.

Veille, C.B. (1986). *Research shows that pregnant women can safely continue to exercise.* Bethesda, MD: The National Institutes of Health.

Young, S. A., Schulman, S. A., & Schulman, M. D. (1985). *The asthma handbook: A complete guide for patients and their families.* New York: Bantam Books.

Wentworth, S. M., & Hoover, J. (1981). The student with diabetes. *Today's Education, 156,* 42–44GE.

Chapter 19

SEVERE, PROFOUND, AUTISTIC, AND MULTIDISABLING CONDITIONS

Jeff is 8 years old and goes to Edgewood Elementary School and is in the regular first-grade class. Jeff does not speak and does not walk. His school experience includes close contact with several support team members, including his regular first-grade teacher, a special education classroom teacher, a teacher-aide, the adapted physical education teacher, the school nurse, and several nondisabled classmates who help him get around the school in his wheelchair.

Jeff's basic needs include feeding and toileting. In spite of his profound and multidisabling condition, this youngster has learned to make his wants and needs known through a communication board; he is able to maneuver through the school halls in his electric wheelchair; and he is learning to feed himself independently. Jeff lives at home with his family, including his younger twin sisters, who are 3 years old. He enjoys participation in all family activities, including going to Wrigley Field to see the Chicago Cubs baseball team (he particularly enjoys Ryne Sandberg, of whom he has a personally autographed photo). He likes eating in fast-food restaurants, going to shopping malls, fishing in the small pond in the local park, playing modified soccer with his classmates, and at home running his electric train set by using multiple switches, levers, and large buttons (all of which were modified by his dad).

Jeff has had extensive physical therapy since he was a newborn infant. The physical therapist is an active member of his multidisciplinary planning, teaching, and rehabilitation team. Since his birth, Jeff's parents have been directly involved in the writing and implementation of his Individualized Family Service Plan. Jeff goes daily to both traditional physical education class with his first-grade classmates and also to a 30-minute adapted P.E. class with six other youngsters who have disabilities. His physical education (motor) annual goals are being addressed in both P.E. classes, but more specifically in the adapted P.E. class. He likes his school and his friends and truly seems to be a happy and growing youngster.

The above scenario is upbeat and provides us with a picture of educational opportunities available today for individuals with multiple disabilities. In fact, this story about Jeff is true. He lives in Northbrook, Illinois, and was the youngster to whom the second edition of this book was dedicated. The 1987 dedication read as follows:

> Special recognition is given to one youngster as he embarks on his road in life. His birth announcement reads: "Jeffrey Daniel Jones was born at 5:41 P.M. on November 26, 1984. Shortly after his birth he developed complications which left him a very sick baby. The serious nature of the problems indicate that Jeff will require special care for his entire life. We are nervous and excited about the prospect of providing the love and care necessary for his life to be as full as it possibly can be." (Eichstaedt & Kalakian, 1987 xii)

There is no question that the laws of the country have provided youngsters with severe, profound, and multidisabling conditions with a much brighter future than even a few years ago. Nietupski and Robinson (1990) take a closer look at the past.

> For those who have not had the opportunity to know individuals with severe or profound [disabilities], the mere thought of this type of [disabling] condition conjures up thoughts of state hospital wards or county homes filled with low-functioning people who sit motionless, if nonambulatory, or wander aimlessly, if ambulatory, around white-walled day rooms with little to do. Though these nightmarish settings may still exist in some parts of the world...persons with severe or profound [disabilities] can be viable members of today's society. The pictures mentioned above come in the majority of situations only from bad dreams or from memories of bygone days, when our technology and educational prowess were more primitive. (p. 227)

Youngsters with severe, profound, autistic, and multiple disabling conditions may be impaired in nearly every facet of life. Many of these individuals have marked intellectual, learning, and behavior disorders, and others have physical or sensory impairments. Semmler (1990) states the following:

> Young children who are severely delayed are likely to have physical, neurological, or sensory anomalies in addition to delays. They may show poor health, feeding problems, and poor growth. Initially, many will be extremely hypotonic, and they may appear to be deaf or blind, even if there are no apparent abnormalities of the eyes or ears. (p. 236)

Most individuals with severe or profound disabilities have conditions that transcend the single-disability categories. The needs of these children cannot be met by one profession. The very nature of these disabilities extends equally into the fields of special education, physical education, therapy, medicine, psychology, and social services. Because these individuals present such a mixture of characteristics and need many professional perspectives, it is not surprising that numerous definitions and intervention strategies are used to describe and treat them. The role of physical education must not be underestimated because of the necessity of providing daily motor activities in addition to those of physical, occupational, or kinesiotherapy.

DEFINITION

Hardman, Drew, Egan, and Wolf (1990) use a cross-categorical definition of severe and profound/multiple disorders:

> Individuals with severe and profound/multiple disorders exhibit physical, sensory, intellectual, and/or social-interpersonal performance deficits that range beyond three standard deviations below the average on normative and criterion-referenced assessments. These deficits are not limited to any given setting but are evident in all environmental settings and often involve deficits in several areas of performance. Cause(s) is more likely to be identifiable at this level of functioning, but exact cause(s) may be unknown in a large number of cases. Individuals with functional disorders at this level require both substantially altered patterns of service and treatment and modified environmental accommodations. (p. 229)

PREVALENCE

A difficulty arises when attempting to identify the number of children classified as severe/profound or multidisabled who are provided educational services. Many students are included with those labeled as mentally retarded or physically disabled. The U.S. Department of Education (1991), in its report of 1989–1990, lists students between 6 and 21 with *multiple disabilities* as 87,956, representing 2.1% of all students with disabilities.

ETIOLOGY OF SEVERE/PROFOUND OR MULTIDISABLING CONDITIONS

There is little doubt that destruction to the central nervous system (brain, brain stem, cerebellum, and spinal cord) results in a myriad of disabling conditions. The degree of impairment is proportional to the level of damage; that is, the more cells that are destroyed, the lower the functioning of the individual, and the greater the likelihood of two or more disabling conditions (i.e., mental retardation, cerebral palsy, and convulsive seizures). All prenatal, perinatal, and postnatal causes of brain damage can be included in the list of etiologies. Additionally, children with Down syndrome, although not possessing brain damage, will often experience several disabling conditions (i.e., mental retardation, congenital heart defects, visual and hearing impairments).

With reference to individuals with mental retardation, the classification of *severe* indicates, in part, that the person has an IQ somewhere between 20 and 35, whereas the profound label refers to an existing IQ range between 1 and 20. Both labels indicate that these persons will usually function at chronological ages (CA) below 4 years of age. The implication is that these individuals will possess very low levels of intelligence and will be very slow in learning both cognitive and motor skills. Any additional physical disability will further delay learning and attainment of developmental and motor milestones. It is estimated that, within the classification of mental retardation, the subgroups of severe and profound include approximately 8% of all children with mental retardation (Patton, Payne, & Beirne-Smith, 1990).

It should be noted that children may have multiple disabilities and not be mentally retarded, as is often found with children having dyskinesic (athetoid) cerebral palsy. These youngsters could have significant motor dysfunction, they may be nonambulatory, or they may have little or no speech, and yet they may have average or above-average intellectual ability. Thus, motor programs for them would not be complicated by a lack of understanding but instead by an inability to control voluntary movement.

Prematurity is often associated with multidisabling conditions. Goldson (1992) estimates that between 200,000 and 250,000 infants (2% to 9% of those born each year in the United States) will be born prenatally (less than 37 weeks gestation and/or less than $5\frac{1}{2}$ pounds) and will require neonatal intensive care. The premature infant, at best, is physically immature and demonstrates less organized adaptation to the environment and has more immature motor patterns. Goldson (1992) states the following: "The premature infant is forced to live in an environment for which he or she is not ready and is an organism whose biologic systems are being asked to differentiate and integrate stimuli for which he or she is unprepared" (p. 34). These "premies" are often found to have had complications such as anoxia (lack of oxygen), intracranial hemorrhage, persistent fetal circulation, and pulmonary problems. All of these abnormalities are potential causes of brain damage.

A comparatively new cause of extensive prenatal brain damage is that of cocaine use by pregnant females. This problem results in what is termed as a *"crack baby."* Newald (1986) found common clinical signs, including hyperirritability, poor feeding patterns, high respiratory and heart rates, increased tremors and startles, and irregular sleeping patterns. The negative effects on infants with this condition were observed by Schneider, Griffith, and Chasnoff (1989). They found both at birth and after 4 months of age that cocaine-affected infants exhibited frequent tremors (especially in the upper extremities) and increased extensor muscle tone (especially in the lower extremities). Primitive reflexes normally integrated by 4 months were often still present. These researchers concluded, using previously established risk categories, that approximately 40% of the cocaine-exposed infants studied were designated "high risk" for motor developmental dysfunction, as opposed to 2% of a control group. To highlight the findings of this study, it can be stated that cocaine-exposed infants were approximately 40 times more likely to be identified as "high risk" children for motor developmental dysfunction than nonexposed infants.

EDUCATIONAL PROGRAMS

With the implementation of P.L. 99-457 (1986) and its successor P.L. 101-476 (I.D.E.A., 1990), intellectual and motor development programs for infants, toddlers, and young children "at risk" are not only legally required but are considered essential for the free and appropriate education of these little ones. Today, children and teenagers with multidisabling conditions are being provided with educational services that directly relate to life skills. For the teenagers, programs are geared to help in the transition from public school to adulthood. Wolery and Haring (1990) have found that although no hard-and-fast rules exist about what constitutes adequate curriculum domains, the following areas are common:

- *Domestic skills*—self-care skills (toileting, eating, dressing), home management skills (food preparation, laundry, house cleaning), and related skills needed for independent community living
- *Communication skills*—actions related to receiving and sending messages between individuals
- *Community living skills*—skills related to mobility and accessibility within the community and use of community facilities
- *Recreation and leisure skills*—skills related to occupying time in socially acceptable and enjoyable ways
- *Vocational skills*—abilities related to securing and maintaining employment that is not demeaning, but monetarily significant (p. 257)

An ongoing debate exists today as to where individuals with disabilities between birth and 21 are best educated. Some professionals believe that every child, regardless of the severity of the disability, must be educated with his peers in a "mainstreamed" environment. Examples include (a) Regular Education Initiative (REI), (b) Parents for Inclusive Communities ("Inclusions"-PIC), and (c) Choices. The first (REI) is designed for students with mild disabilities, whereas the last two are targeted toward those with severe and profound disabilities (Eichstaedt & Lavay, 1992).

Although the trend is strongly leaning toward total integration, many teachers and therapists believe that individuals with the most serious involvement are being given inferior and less effective programs because of an "all or none" philosophy (Eichstaedt, 1992). Infants and toddlers, who have been identified as "at risk," are in most cases sent to special programs and have little opportunity to be integrated with nondisabled peers simply because no programs exist (under the auspicious and financial support of the local public school system). Thus, as can be hoped for, substantial growth and development will result from the special education early childhood programs, which could allow for appropriate integration by the time the children are old enough to enter regular preschool and kindergarten classes.

THE ROLE OF PHYSICAL EDUCATION

For individuals with severe/profound (S/P) or multidisabling conditions, educational goals should center on the attainment of significant levels of physical strength, cardiorespiratory endurance, balance, and mobility, and eye/hand coordination. Dunn, Morehouse, and Fredericks (1986) state the following: "Programs must be developed and instruction individualized to help the severely handicapped overcome, to the greatest extent possible, their functional deficits. The expression *severely retarded* communicates clearly that these individuals need and will benefit from physical education programs which are well designed and systematically implemented" (p. 4).

Both fine and gross motor skills will need to be taught because they are involved in the accomplishment of all activities within every projected life skill, and especially in physical education and leisure skill development. Moon and Bunker (1987) state the following: "Motor development is highly sequential and interdependent and is influenced by an individual's physical fitness, body awareness, posture, and functioning level of the central nervous system. Nevertheless, there is ample evidence that even a profoundly retarded person can be taught not only fundamental gross and fine motor activities, but also complicated fitness and sports skills" (p. 232).

ASSESSMENT OF MOTOR DEVELOPMENT

For infants with S/P disabilities, traditional methods of intelligence testing are virtually useless. If tested, they tend to be given IQ scores at the extreme lower end of the continuum. Heward and Orlansky (1992) state the following: "Knowing that a particular student has an IQ of 25 is of little value in designing an appropriate educational program. Educators of students with severe handicaps tend to focus on the specific skills that a child needs to learn, rather than on her intellectual level" (p. 371).

Although intelligence testing is questioned, at least regarding its use, the determination of existing levels of motor performance appear to have merit. Meaningful motor assessment can provide information for the development of appropriate motor programs for individuals with severe or profound disabilities, a point not argued by most experts. In reference to the testing of these children, Snell (1991) states the following: "I think of assessment or testing as being an evil necessity; necessary for educators.... When assessment is used properly, its findings provide valuable guides for instructors, parents, and others who work with persons with disabilities. However, assessment findings are only valuable if they are accurate, if they are meaningful to the individual's current and future life, and if they are actually used" (p. xi).

Due to the severity and impairment of physical and mental performance, standardized, norm-referenced test batteries are difficult to administer and interpret. Browder (1991) states the following: "When the disability is such that an individual's curriculum needs to focus on the practical everyday skills in life, assessment procedures typically shift away from norm-referenced tests to informal tests involving observation and interview" (p. 27). At best, test batteries such as the *Peabody*, the *Brigance*, and the *Denver* are only effective in the hands of trained specialists such as physical/occupational therapists, school psychologists, or diagnosticians. Many adapted physical education specialists will possess the necessary expertise to assess early motor development levels, but most traditional physical education teachers will need to rely on the information provided by these professionals.

Existing levels of performance of individuals with S/P disabilities are generally within the range of infant through early childhood (birth through 5 years), thus knowledge of developmental milestones of infants, toddlers, and preschool children is necessary. For example, development progresses from head to foot, from proximal to distal (e.g., hip to foot), and from midline outward (e.g., shoulder to hand). Individuals must experience movement on their own (or with the assistance of a parent or teacher), as this practice provides information to the brain and establishes motor learning. This informal or formal practice often involves hours and hours of trial and error by the individuals. Without this practice, they cannot attain minimal levels of strength, coordination, and balance and thus will not progress upward to the next developmental milestone. Although some individuals with profound disabilities may be older, they still are seriously lacking in motor performance and in some cases are functioning as infants and toddlers. The most pressing problem for the teacher becomes one of providing *appropriate* motor programs commensurate to the existing level of each individual. Again, it should be emphasized that activities must be age appropriate. For a review of developmental motor milestones of infants and young children, refer to Chapter 4.

NEGATIVE RESULTS OF HYPOACTIVITY

Individuals with S/P conditions move very little on their own (hypoactivity) but would seem to be content to lay in their beds or just be pushed around in their wheelchairs. These individuals become real challenges for the physical education teacher. There is an obvious need to provide ongoing movement activities, ones that provide for basic motor skill and strength development. The teacher should be reminded of the progressive techniques used in rehabilitation.

- *Passive*. The teacher moves the student's arms, legs, and head through the full range of motion. The student is unable to provide any assistance.
- *Assistive*. The teacher allows the student to begin an action and the teacher completes the movement because the student cannot finish it (e.g., reaching upward to touch a ball).
- *Resistive*. The student moves a body part through the full range of movement as the teacher applies resistance such as putting a small weight around the student's wrist or ankle.

The above techniques are used to increase blood circulation, to stimulate muscle and joint proprioception, and to increase range of motion.

It is imperative that range-of-motion activities be continued to reduce the chance of muscle and joint contractures developing (in some cases, these contractures are already present). Conditions such as spastic cerebral palsy or cerebral vascular accident (e.g., a "stroke" resulting in hemiplegia) will produce these contractures. One should be reminded that muscle and joint contractures develop when individuals do not, or cannot, voluntarily move a limb. Over a period of months and years of little or no use, the muscle fibers of the affected limbs shorten and reduce usefulness to virtually nothing. The physiological nature of a muscle and joint contracture is explained by the fact that muscle tissue will adapt in length to habitually shortened positions over time. Muscle tissue has the ability to shorten by active contraction, thus muscles eventually will adapt to the shortest length if proper stretching exercises do not maintain adequate range of motion (Adams & McCubbin, 1991). Daily stretching (elongation) exercises are usually done at least two times a day (BID). (Refer to relaxation and stretching exercises found in Chapter 16, Cerebral Palsy.) In some cases surgery is the only option to reduce these unwanted contractures.

For infants with severe or profound brain damage, Hunter (1990) suggests that passive range-of-motion exercises should be initiated as soon after birth as tolerated, including shoulder external rotation and abduction, forearm supination, wrist extension, finger extension, and thumb abduction: "All range of motion exercises should be done gently to prevent soft tissue damage; these movements should not cause the infant to cry" (p. 89). Blackman (1990) describes infants with multiple muscle and joint contractures:

> Babies are sometimes born with various joints compressed and positioned at abnormal angles (arthrogryposis). The congenital deformity is caused by neuromuscular problems in the fetus, too little amniotic fluid, or structural abnormalities of the uterus—all of which inhibit the fetus from moving in the uterus....Mild cases are treated by passive exercises; more severe cases may require gradual correction of deformities by splints, casts, or surgery. (p. 217)

GROSS MOVEMENT

Severe brain damage can leave individuals with abnormal body tone such as hypertonia or hypotonia. *Hypertonia* (stiffness) results from damage to the brain that causes excessive muscle tone. This characteristic is seen in a child with spastic quadriplegic cerebral palsy who walks on her toes with a scissors gait, including unwanted and jerky movements of the arms. The problem is generally noted with equal degree of stiffness (high tone) through the trunk, neck, and all limbs (Bigge, 1988). Activities and exercises should be used that reduce the tightness. The problem areas include abnormally strong muscle flexors, internal rotators, and adductors. Thus, the instructor should stress the actions of extension, external rotation, and abduction.

Hypotonia is characterized by an unwanted degree of "looseness or floppiness." Infants born with this condition are referred to as "floppy babies"; it is commonly found in children with Down syndrome. Hypotonia is a condition that slows all movement, including running, jumping, and quick actions. Muscle-strengthening activities must be used, thereby stabilizing joints and allowing the muscles to move more effectively (Eichstaedt & Lavay, 1992).

Gross movement activities are to begin as soon as possible, and appropriate activities should be taught to the parents by the physical education teacher or the therapist. Parents must learn how to administer the motor program, thus helping to ensure that the child will receive the extra sessions that are desperately needed. Also, including the parents in the planning and implementation of a program (Individualized Family Service Plan-IFSP) is required by the mandates of P.L. 101–476 (I.D.E.A.).

Specific activities include allowing the child to move about freely and giving assistance only when necessary. In the early months, rolling, scooting, and crawling allow the child to use the entire musculoskeletal system. For example, place the youngster on his back and guide him into rolling over from back to front, and also front to back. Individuals with severe or profound disabilities will need sensory stimulation, including input from seeing, hearing, touching, and being touched. Instructors must never forget that without intervention (i.e., manipulation, stimulation, and verbal encouragement) these individuals would likely do nothing but "vegetate" and become lost in their world of inactivity. Their only response to the outside world would be based around a need to satisfy hunger, a comfortable room temperature, pleasant sounds, and dry diapers. In some cases of profound retardation, individuals may not progress past the stages of infantile or primary reflexes without stimulation from other people. The desire or need is simply not present.

BEHAVIOR MODIFICATION

Behavior modification is often necessary to control and eliminate unwanted behaviors that interfere with learning. Also, negative or maladaptive behaviors can become so prevalent that integration with other people becomes impossible. For example, whenever Lanny experiences stress (e.g., something he does not want to do), he reaches into his pants and looks for satisfaction through masturbation. This action is so socially inappropriate and undesirable that teachers would not even consider taking the individual into places with other people. Thus, integration and mainstreaming are not possible until this behavior is eliminated and replaced by socially acceptable actions.

Several socially unacceptable behaviors include vomiting at will, rumination (vomiting and swallowing vomitus), pica (eating inedible objects such as cigarette butts), and coprophagia (eating feces). Why individuals do these bizarre actions is almost beyond comprehension, yet care givers are constantly battling weird behaviors and *must* address the problem. The maladaptive behavior is fulfilling a need that is not being met within the limited world of these individuals. A person seeking out and eating cigarette butts might indicate that he was hungry, but this is not the case, because the person will do this after having eaten a full meal. An inner drive, for no identifiable or obvious reason, is satisfying a basic need of the individual.

Browder (1991) provides a list of questions pertaining to problem behaviors:

- Is the behavior life-threatening or does it cause irreversible physical harm to the individual?
- Does the behavior interfere with learning?
- Is the behavior likely to become serious if not modified?
- Is the behavior dangerous to others?
- Is the behavior of concern to care givers?
- Is the behavior not improving or getting worse?
- Has the behavior been a problem for some time?
- Does the behavior interfere with community acceptance?
- Would other behavior improve if this behavior improved?

The key to reducing and replacing unwanted behaviors begins by determining, for each individual, his *desirable* basic "wants," possibly including foods (cookies/apples), objects (a velvet cloth/battery vibrator), sounds (cassette player/radio), personal contact with others (touching/stroking), movement (rocking/swinging), or voices (soft pleasant comments). Rooms or places, such as a dim-lighted bedroom or the warm water of a swimming pool, spa, or shower may give some individuals extreme satisfaction. Instructors must also be aware that any of the above may also cause extreme discomfort and could bring about negative responses. The physical education teacher should consult with each individual's special education teacher to determine which activities or objects are positive reinforcers and which are not. Hopefully, this information will have been shared at the multidisciplinary meeting when the IEP or the IFSP was being developed.

With the above reinforcers ("wants") well defined, the instructor should use them to reward individuals when appropriate behavior is given. In turn, the reinforcer is taken away when unwanted actions occur. Constant monitoring of an individual's actions is necessary. That is, the teacher must keep accurate records of appropriate and inappropriate behaviors. This information will provide a clear picture of the progress being made (or not made) and will thus provide reasons for continuing, modifying, or discontinuing the present program.

STEREOTYPIC BEHAVIOR

Behavior that is undesirable, but not injurious, may include repetitious and stereotyped actions such as

- *Mouthing* (putting hands and fingers in the mouth)
- *Body rocking*
- *Head movements* (moving head back and forth)
- *Wall or floor patting*
- *Finger "flipping"*
- *Object manipulations*

It is hypothesized that individuals perform these behaviors to provide some degree of proprioceptive or vestibular stimulation. The secret to eliminating annoying behaviors is to find positive actions that enable the individuals to gain similar but positive satisfaction.

SELF-INJURIOUS BEHAVIOR

It is estimated that between 5% and 15% of individuals with severe or profound disabilities exhibit self-injurious behavior (SIB) (Favell, McGimsey, & Snell, 1982). Examples of SIB include hand biting, head banging, scratching, eye poking, and hair pulling of both one's own self and of others (e.g., teachers). This problem is evident and must be terminated. Obviously, the most immediate concern is for the safety of the student. She cannot continue to hurt herself because the incidents could cause permanent damage and in some extreme cases result in death. The next priority would be to eliminate injury to others. A specific list of methods used for reducing self-injurious behavior is provided in Chapter 11.

AUTISM

Individuals with autism generally exhibit functioning levels of individuals with severe/ profound and multidisabling conditions. Autism is a developmental disorder that begins in childhood and often continues into adulthood. The condition profoundly affects social and emotional behavior, language, cognition, activities, and interests. Various labels used to describe this condition include *infantile autism, childhood autism,* or *Kanner's syndrome* (Baroff, 1991). Youngsters who have autism face a complicated and difficult road when attempting to attain functional levels of physical, educational, social, emotional, recreational, and vocational activity. There is disagreement as to how these individuals should be classified. For example, in some schools, these students may be put into classes with children labeled as learning disabled/behavior disordered, or possibly with students with severe or profound mental retardation. The difference is that each of the above groups will be taught by different classroom teachers whose expertise may or may not include children with autism. For physical education teachers, who teach in noncategorical settings, the label means little except to imply that these children will bring with them extremely low levels of motor performance and unusual behavior characteristics. For identification purposes, the U.S.

Department of Education (1991) requests students with autism be listed as "Other Health Impaired," whereas the state of Illinois has a separate classification titled as "Autistic." At one time these youngsters were included under the classification of seriously emotionally disturbed.

The etiology of autism is unknown (idiopathic) but indications are that there is brain "dysfunction." Autism occurs in approximately one child in 2,000 (Schor, 1990). For children to be diagnosed as having autism, the American Psychiatric Association's Revised Third Edition of the *Diagnostic and Statistical Manual of Mental Disorders* (DSM-III-R) (1987) lists the following criteria:

- Onset usually by the age of 3
- A pervasive lack of responsiveness to others
- Abnormalities of communication, both verbal and nonverbal forms
- A very narrow range of interests and activities that tend to be pursued in a rigid and compulsive fashion

In current psychiatric terminology, autism is classified as a *pervasive developmental disorder* rather than as a psychosis or a mental illness.

Characteristics of Students with Autism.   Individuals with autism display various degrees of nonconformity. Some are extremely withdrawn and show little or no interest in other children or adults. Normal activities of age peers usually do not excite them. They are often described as being "in a shell" or "living in a world all their own." The child with autism seems to look through, or past, people, and it is difficult to "catch their eye."

Some youngsters never speak; others can talk or repeat words and phrases. The repetitious statements often make no sense, as do their responses to questions from other students, teachers, or parents.

Some of these youngsters are hyperactive, always on the run and into everything; others sit long periods without moving. Still others may go back and forth between the extremes. Some move with ease and are sure-footed, running and climbing as well as anyone in class; others persist in strange self-stimulating movements such as rocking back and forth, flipping their fingers, clapping their hands, or taking unusual poses. Some will hurt themselves (self-injurious behavior), for instance, by banging their heads, biting their hands, or poking their eyes. Hallahan and Kauffman (1991) describe the actions of self-stimulation often found:

> Behavior that is stereotyped, repetitive, and useful only for obtaining sensory stimulation is common. . . . Such self-stimulation can take a nearly infinite variety of forms (swishing saliva, twirling an object, patting one's cheeks, flapping one's hands, staring at lights). These children often exhibit such behavior so constantly that it is extremely difficult to engage them in any other activity. (p. 195)

MEDICAL TREATMENT OF AUTISM

Volkman (1989) believes that medications are extremely helpful in reducing unwanted behaviors of children with autism:

> No medications have yet been developed that "cure" autism. Rather, medications are sometimes used to treat specific symptoms when they interfere with education or pose a potential danger to the child. For example, medication may be prescribed to treat a self-abusive behavior like head banging or to treat behavior like continual hand flapping which can interfere with education....Because each medication has a range of side effects, it is important to balance the potential benefit of the medication against its risks....Probably the most common side effect is sedation or sleepiness. A child may become overly sedated and be unable to benefit from her educational program. (pp. 56–57)

Implications for Physical Education for Children with Autism.   Because children with autism cannot relate to external phenomena, they must be taught in small groups. During early stages or when symptoms are severe or both, individual instruction will be required.

Virtually all children with autism experience significant difficulty in understanding spoken language. In providing verbal directions to children with autism, always speak to the child in simple terms.

The child with autism functions best in individual activities. Dual or group activities, including team participation, often exceed the child's ability to understand the dynamics of participation. When the child does participate as a group member, activities should not require extensive interpersonal cooperation. For example, participation in basketball might be inappropriate, but participation with a group in swimming, jumping on the trampoline, or tumbling might be suitable. These youngsters are receptive to being led through an activity such as jogging. The instructor or another student can hold the child's hand or arm and start jogging. The teacher should record the beginning and ending time and the distance covered. Positive verbal reinforcement should be given continually during the run. The child usually will terminate the experience when fatigued. By accurately recording progress and by making sure that the child jogs at least every other day, the instructor can assume that cardiovascular efficiency will improve.

Montileone (1983) was successful in gaining the attention of a child with autism when he would "mirror the youngster's movements." The child tended to become very interested in what was happening and seemed to want to continue this experience.

When the child with autism does exhibit superior abilities in a specific area of motor performance, the teacher should capitalize on such abilities. Allowing the child an opportunity to excel will provide a sense of accomplishment and recognition by others.

Activities for children with autism must be monitored closely owing to an apparent inability of these youngsters to relate to pain. Care must be taken to ensure that the child does not aggravate an injury, new or old, simply because the child does not relate to pain.

SUMMARY

Motor programming for individuals with severe, profound, autistic, and multidisabling conditions begins by understanding the functioning level of the students, including both mental and physical limitations. Most students with S/P labels will possess excessive brain damage; intellectual functioning is likely to represent the lowest levels and thus is likely to leave students with minimal ability to understand verbal instructions. Most will have the intellectual capabilities of infants, toddlers, or preschoolers. Although not all students will experience extreme mental impairments (e.g., a dyskinestic (athetoid) cerebral palsy, nonspeaking, and nonambulatory), their physical disabilities will provide extreme challenges to the physical education teacher. These students will have only mild or no mental retardation and will understand verbal instructions and be able to assist the teacher in many ways, although their bodies will be unable to perform voluntary movement with ease and control.

For individuals with autism, the following characteristics exemplify common behaviors:

- Impaired or complete lack of social and emotional relationships
- Repetitive non-goal directed body motions or behaviors (i.e., constant rocking, hand waving in front of face, head banging)
- Resistance to change and extreme distress when minor changes in environment or routine are undertaken
- Peculiar perceptual and motor experiences such as "looking through" people, not seeing certain objects, not hearing some sounds and overreacting to others, hyperactivity or passivity, apparent insensitivity to pain
- Severe speech and language difficulties
- Mental and motor retardation in some areas, often accompanied by superior skill in other areas

The prognosis for children with autism is not encouraging. Presently, approximately one half of all individuals with autism require special residential settings. Despite the statistics, these people should have full opportunity for successful physical education participation and recognition, because success in the motor domain could likely contribute to integration and normalization.

Physical education programs should be developed with each student's basic motor needs in mind, that is, activities which emphasize sensory stimulation, range of motion, neck, hand and arm strength, sitting and standing balance, and eye/hand coordination. All activities, including games, should concentrate on these immediate needs. Individualized annual motor goals and short-term objectives become the basis for each child's program. The physical education teacher must always remember to include games and activities that are age appropriate. Finally, each individual must experience new challenges, fun, and enjoyment when taking part in physical education.

REFERENCES

Adams, R. C., & McCubbin, J. A. (1991). *Games, sports, and exercises for the physically disabled* (4th ed.). Philadelphia: Lea & Febiger.

American Psychiatric Association. (1987). *Diagnostic and statistical manual of mental disorders* (3rd ed; revised). Washington, DC: The Association.

Baroff, G. S. (1991). *Developmental disabilities: Psychosocial aspects.* Austin, TX: Pro-Ed.

Bigge, J. L. (1988). *Curriculum based instruction for special education students.* Mountain View, CA: Mayfield.

Blackman, J. A. (1990). *Medical aspects of developmental disabilities in children birth to three* (2nd ed.). Rockville, MD: Aspen.

Browder, D. M. (1991). *Assessment of individuals with severe disabilities* (2nd ed.). Baltimore, MD: Brookes.

Dunn, J. M., Morehouse, J. W., Jr., & Fredericks, H. D. B. (1986). *Physical education for the severely handicapped.* Austin, TX: Pro-Ed.

Eichstaedt, C. B. (1992, March). *Legal implications of teaching and coaching individuals with disabilities.* Paper presented at the 1st annual conference on Adapted Physical Activity, Western Illinois University, Macomb, IL.

Eichstaedt, C. B., & Kalakian, L. H. (1987). *Developmental/adapted physical education: Making ability count* (2nd ed.). New York: Macmillan.

Eichstaedt, C. B., & Lavay, B. W. (1992). *Physical activity for individuals with mental retardation: Infancy through adulthood.* Champaign, IL: Human Kinetics.

Favell, J. E., McGimsey, J. F., & Snell, R. M. (1982). Treatment of self-injury by providing alternate sensory activities. *Analysis and Intervention in Developmental Disabilities, 3,* 83–104.

Goldson, E. (1992). The neonatal intensive care unit: Premature infants and parents. *Infants and Young Children, 4,* 31–42.

Hallahan, D. P., & Kauffman, J. M. (1991). *Exceptional children* (5th ed.). Englewood Cliffs, NJ: Prentice-Hall.

Hardman, M. L., Drew, C. J., Egan, M. W., & Wolf, B. (1990). *Human exceptionality: Society, school, and family* (3rd ed.). Boston: Allyn & Bacon.

Heward, W. L., & Orlansky, M. D. (1992). *Exceptional children* (4th ed.). New York: Merrill/Macmillan.

Hunter, J. G. (1990). Orthopedic conditions. In C. J. Semmler & J. G. Hunter (Eds.), *Early occupational therapy intervention: Neonates to three years* (pp. 72–121). Gaithersburg, MD: Aspen.

Montileone, T. (1983, July). *Movement exploration activities.* Paper presented at the annual convention of the American Corrective Therapy Association, Houston, TX.

Moon, M. S., & Bunker, L. (1987). Recreation and motor skills programming. In M. E. Snell (Ed.), *Systematic instruction of persons with severe handicaps* (3rd ed.; pp. 214–244). New York: Merrill/Macmillan.

Newald. J. (1986). Cocaine infants: A new arrival at hospital's step? *Hospitals, 60,* 96.

Nietupski, J. A., & Robinson, G. A. (1990). Severe and profound mental retardation. In J. R. Patton, J. S. Payne, & M. Beirne-Smith (Eds.), *Mental retardation* (3rd ed., pp. 227–259). New York: Merrill/Macmillan.

Patton, J. R., Payne, J. S., & Beirne-Smith, M. B. (1990). *Mental retardation* (3rd ed.). New York: Merrill/Macmillan.

Schneider, J. W., Griffith, D. R., & Chasnoff, I. J. (1989). Infants exposed to cocaine in utero: Implications for developmental assessment and intervention. *Infants and Young Children, 2,* 25–36.

Semmler, C. J. (1990). Developmental disabilities. In C. J. Semmler & J. G. Hunter (Eds.), *Early occupational therapy intervention: Neonates to three years* (pp. 232–261). Gaithersburg, MD: Aspen.

Snell, M. E. (1991). Foreword. In D. M. Browder, *Assessment of individuals with severe disabilities* (2nd ed.; pp. xi–xiii). Baltimore, MD: Brookes.

Schor, D. P. (1990). Autism. In J. A. Blackman (Ed.), *Medical aspects of developmental disabilities in children birth to three* (2nd ed.; pp. 7–10). Rockville, MD: Aspen.

U.S. Department of Education. (1991). *Thirteenth annual report to congress on the implementation of the Individuals With Disabilities Education Act.* Washington, DC: Office of Special Education Programs, U.S. Office of Special Education and Rehabilitative Services.

Volkman, F. R. (1989). Medical problems, treatments, and professionals. In M. D. Powers (Ed.), *Children with autism: A parents' guide* (pp. 55–77). Kensington, MD: Woodbine House.

Wolery, M., & Haring, T. G. (1990). Moderate, severe, and profound handicaps. In N. G. Haring & L. McCormick (Eds.), *Exceptional children and youth* (5th ed.; pp. 239–280). New York: Merrill/Macmillan.

Part 4

SPORTS

Chapter 20

SWIMMING FOR THE
STUDENT WITH DISABILITIES:
ADAPTED AQUATICS

I guess I will never forget the time, some years ago, when a little guy with cerebral palsy looked up at me with big blue eyes from where he was resting, propped up in the corner of the pool, and said, "You know something, Louise! This is the only place in the world where I can walk!" ... It just tore me up! But it was true; for him, with his disability, walking was impossible on land, but the water provided the support, lessened the need for weight bearing and balance, and made it possible for him to have independent mobility. It was the freedom from disability, a time to achieve. Looking from his perspective, there was no question about why he should be in the water.

(Priest, 1982, p. 2)

The most desirable physical education programming includes instruction in swimming. In fact, Public Law 101-476 specifically identifies water skill development as a part of all physical education curricula. Swimming, therefore, should be used to develop the physical and motor needs of students with disabilities.

GOALS AND BENEFITS OF A SWIMMING PROGRAM
FOR STUDENTS WITH DISABILITIES

The primary goal is to teach students with disabilities to swim or to swim better. In addition, students should learn water safety and that the swimming experience is fun.

Physiological, psychological, and social benefits can be gained from swimming, which provides these benefits for all individuals, both disabled and nondisabled. Swimming activities give youngsters opportunities and experiences not possible in any other environment. Buoyancy and ease of movement in water occur because of (1) reduced gravity, (2) less weight on joints, (3) less strength needed for movement, and (4) easy attainment of the independent standing position. These contribute to greater participation in basic skills. The physical benefits of swimming include better coordination, more endurance, improved range of motion, strengthened muscles, and effortless muscle performance.

Swimming can be used to develop social acceptance of the child with disabilities and is an important way to improve the child's self-image. These youngsters often possess distorted or negative feelings about themselves. One's self-image, the subjective picture of one's physical appearance, is influenced both by self-observation and by noting the reactions of others. To the teenager with disabilities particularly, overt impairments may be discouraging because they not only limit the motor skill repertoire but may also promote a devalued sense of self. Depressed physical and psychological development may follow. For example, Pagenoff (1984) found that a 14-year-old student with spastic cerebral palsy was exceptionally different from her peers in her approach to many activities. Fearing failure, the youngster refused to perform many activities both in treatment and extracurricularly. Her development of self-esteem and performance skills was therefore limited. The girl in Pagenoff's study was quoted as saying: "I'm deformed, no one wants me around. I can't do what my friends can." A 2-day-a-week program was planned for the girl for an 8-week-period. To ensure optimal participation and performance, it became necessary to restrict the immediate area surrounding the pool during treatment sessions because the student refused to perform swimming activities when her mother or any outside observers were present. After completing the program, in addition to positive physiological and motor skill improvement, Pagenoff found that "the most significant changes were noted in self-image. The patient became an active participant in planning the pool sessions. . . . Although body image continued as a concern, the patient began participating in the presence of pool observers and other guests" (p. 472). Steinbrunner (1982) agrees with Pagenoff about the benefits of a swimming program: "There are secondary characteristics which often flow out of good [swimming] programs. One of them is the building of confidence in an individual. . . . I think this is more important in working with special populations than the actual program itself" (p. 28).

Mayse (1991) endorses the use of swimming as an excellent medium for improving movement skills and developing physical fitness for individuals with disabilities. She describes different terms commonly used for water exercise, including aquadynamics, water aerobics, aquacise, hydroaerobics, and aquafitness. These terms refer to programs promoting physical fitness activities in swimming pool settings:

> While some individuals can determine for themselves desirable levels of fitness and then work hard to attain such goals, others, due to the nature of their disabilities, need assistance to structure and carry out fitness activities. Administrators, parents, teachers, and community leaders should become more active in implementing water exercise programs for persons with disabilities. (p. 54)

SAFETY CONSIDERATIONS

It is widely recognized that drowning is the second leading cause of accidental death among children under 5 years of age (Langendorfer, 1990).

Some students with disabilities pose unique problems and challenges directly related to their disabling condition. These problems affect the student's personal safety and the ability to learn water safety skills. The normal pool hazards are increased because the youngster with a disability often has vision difficulties, balance problems, impaired sense of direction, space, or distance, and may lack muscular control. Any one of these disabilities creates a potentially dangerous situation that should not be overlooked. For example, a child with cerebral palsy may have extreme difficulty walking on a wet, slippery deck.

The American National Red Cross (1977a) lists these suggestions for poolside safety:

1. Individuals with balance difficulties should always be assisted in walking on wet decks and ramps.

2. Wheelchairs should be used whenever possible. Carrying children, even small children, is unsafe on wet, slippery decks.

3. Wheelchairs should be locked in place at poolside before the student is taken out of the chair or returned to it.

ROLE OF THE LIFEGUARD

The adapted aquatics program requires constant student supervision. Lifeguards should be trained to be aware of specific complications that may arise as a result of disabling conditions. They should be told which children experience seizures and should understand the procedure to be followed if a child has a seizure in the locker room or shower area, on the pool deck, or in the water (American National Red Cross, 1974). Procedures to follow when a seizure occurs are discussed later in this chapter.

The lifeguard's first responsibility is to ensure each student's safety. The person who is lifeguarding an adapted physical education class must *not* have any other teaching or leadership assignments.

To ensure complete communication between swimming teacher and lifeguard, all water policies should be written and understood by all regular and substitute guards. When dealing with students with disabilities, nothing should be left to chance. Most problems can be avoided if everyone understands clearly what must be done. This includes procedures for acquiring medical help: who should phone a physician, what physician should be called, what instructions should be given to locate the pool area.

When a student is using a personal flotation device (PFD), the lifeguard must be reminded that this apparatus does not make the child water safe. Gross (1987) believes that a buoyancy aid does not take the place of a lifeguard, but rather, the PFD increases need for supervision, because both the swimmer and the device need constant observation.

FACILITIES FOR THE SWIMMER WITH DISABILITIES

Most pools are not suitable for both individuals who are disabled and nondisabled. Indeed, most pool facilities require adaptations to provide an acceptable program. The American National Red Cross (1977a) identifies some of the necessary adaptations as follows: "Generally, specific adaptations are to overcome problems such as architectural barriers, water depth, temperature adjustment, and the ever-present problem of getting some less mobile individuals into the water. It is far better to adapt existing facilities than it is to forego programs for the lack of special facilities"(p. 110).

LOCKER ROOMS, DRESSING AREAS, AND SHOWERS

Specific federal guidelines pertaining to standards for locker rooms, showers, and swimming pools are described in detail in the 1990 Americans with Disabilities Act (ADA). These regulations include all components of Section 504 of the Vocational Rehabilitation Act of 1973.

Students with disabilities often need assistance and special accommodations to prepare for a swimming class. Youngsters with physical impairments must remove braces, which often requires assistance. The student should be encouraged to assist in this process with minimum help from the instructor. A classroom teacher or the therapist should show the swimming instructor how to remove prosthetic devices.

Students who are blind may have difficulty with combination locks found on most dressing room lockers. Key locks are more appropriate, and lockers or baskets should be easily located. Special locks are not necessary for all students and should be provided only when a student is spending an inordinate amount of time trying to get into the locker. Opening a lock may be a valuable learning experience but should not shorten swimming time excessively.

When undressing and dressing, students should become as independent as their disability allows. The American National Red Cross (1977a) offers the following advice on dealing with youngsters who are retarded: "Aides [and teachers] in the dressing room can provide a real service to retarded children and their families by encouraging the child and teaching competence in self-help. The aids should reward, in some way, any act that approximates desired behavior. For example, half a knot tied in a shoelace is better than none. Verbal approval is in itself a reward" (p. 98).

The locker room should be on the same level as the shower room and pool, with no curbs or stairs. Aisles should permit easy movement of wheelchairs. All benches should be securely fastened to the floor in locker room and shower areas. All lockers should be large enough to accommodate braces. Durfee (1977) also suggests that a 3 × 5 ft table be available in the locker room to assist students who cannot bend over easily to pick up an article from the floor.

Wheelchairs should be available in locker and pool areas. These chairs should not become dirty from daily school activities. They should be the "stripped-down" collapsible kind that can be pushed directly down the pool ramp into the water.

Astroturf or other thick nonskid material should be used on floors and pool decks. Smooth paint and nonskid patches or paint do *not* provide a safe enough walking surface. The shower room should contain safety railings.

POOL DECK

The deck should be wide enough to permit passage of two wheelchairs. The surface must consist of a nonskid material that meets safety standards; that is, a child using crutches or canes will not slip and fall.

The water level should be not more than 12 in. below the pool deck, or more desirably, at the same level as the deck to permit easier entry and exit from the water. This is particularly important for students using pool ladders.

Regardless of water level, all pool edges should have a slightly raised lip to minimize danger of wheelchairs slipping into the water.

POOL EQUIPMENT

Getting the students in and out of the water easily and safely is important. Ideally, the pool should have wide, broad steps with hand rails for entering, exiting, resting, and learning. A wheelchair ramp from deck to pool floor should be provided. The ramp should be flush with the pool wall, but out of the way of those swimmers who are not using wheelchairs. Hand rails should be installed on the ramp sides to enable students on foot or in wheelchairs to pull themselves up the ramp or to control their descent.

Hydraulic or hand-cranked lifts are extremely helpful for lowering or raising students in and out of the water. Manual lifting of students is considered a technical violation of the Americans with Disabilities Act (1990), which prohibits lifting or carrying individuals to circumvent requirements to make facilities barrier-free and accessible to all. The intent of this law is not to restrict students with disabilities from the water, but to demand that school boards and public pool managers be aware of and provide appropriate and accessible facilities.

Should a child with a disability be unable to enter the water by hydraulic lift (because of inability to sit in *any* chairlike device), then it is appropriate to lower the child by lifting and handing the child to another individual who is already in the water. To do this, a stable body position must be maintained by the person who is lifting, and proper balance support is required for the person being lifted. Using proper hand positions and firm grips to support the child is also important.

Resting platforms, such as small benches, should be located in the shallow end of the pool. These facilitate teaching and help students (e.g., double amputees) to grasp the sides of the pool.

WATER TEMPERATURE

A comfortable pool setting, not loud or noisy, can help relieve any anxiety the child might have. Air temperature and water temperature are also critical. Water temperature will have a decided impact on how the child accepts the situation and should be carefully controlled. The more severe the child's impairment is, the warmer the water should be.

Authorities disagree about the ideal water temperature. The American National Red Cross (1977a) recommends that the temperature for swimmers with disabilities be between 78 and 84 °F (26 and 29°C). Their publications also state that a higher water temperature may be desirable for some individuals, especially for students with severe cerebral palsy or people with specific orthopedic problems. Durfee (1977) states that the ideal temperature is between 88 and 90 °F (31 and 32°C) in summer and 91 and 93°F (33 and 34°C) in winter. Harris (1978) suggests that the water temperature should be between 96 and 100°F (36 and 38°C) for individuals with hypertonic, spastic cerebral palsy. Greenshaw and Sadler (1988) found that youngsters with disabilities between the ages of birth and 6 years responded best when water temperatures were between 90 and 95°F.

If the water temperature can be regulated to accommodate the activity levels of different groups of students, it should be adjusted to maximum comfort level for each group in turn. Youngsters who cannot move about quickly will need higher water temperatures, shorter periods in the water, or activities that increase participation.

THERAPEUTIC BENEFITS

Lian and Goyette (1988) describe the therapeutic benefits of swimming:

> Water feels good and is good for the body and health. Water provides plenty of sensory stimulation, such as different water temperatures, water movement, the feeling of being free, and the sounds and visions in and around the swimming pool. Just being in the water is relaxing and exhilarating at the same time. People with spastic conditions become more relaxed with less muscle tone when they are in warm water, while limp persons become more alert with higher muscle tone when they feel the movement of the water....Movement in the water seems effortless, muscles relax and mental tension fades away. (p. 12)

Lasko and Knopf (1984) endorse rehabilitation exercises in the water. They use the term **hydrogymnastics** to refer to a medically prescribed therapeutic exercise program performed in the water. In hydrogymnastics, the water is used as a therapeutic modality to habilitate individuals with disabilities: "Many people prefer Hydrogymnastics because it occurs in warm water (92–93°F). It is believed that warm water decreases pain and induces relaxation. With this decreased pain, many clients can see noticeable improvements in their range of motion" (p. 176).

GENERAL TEACHING TECHNIQUES

The instructor should be aware of each child's disability and the important characteristics that each child exhibits, because many students must rely on the instructor for physical support. The educator, therefore, must be continually aware of the child's comfort and safety needs.

For individuals with disabilities who need a one-on-one teaching situation, the best results are attained by having an assistant or aide work with each child. Durfee (1977) suggests that the supervising teacher provide specific learning instructions and serve as demonstrator and roving assistant. This allows the teacher to assist many swimmers and aides with suggestions and comments.

BASIC TEACHING FACTORS

The American National Red Cross (1977b) identifies three factors that are basic to teaching swimming to persons who are disabled. The individual with a disability must be able to (1) make the physical and mental adjustment to the water in relationship to the skill being learned, (2) find and maintain good body position for each skill, and (3) practice each skill with adequate teacher correction.

The *first basic factor* recognizes that each child must become totally adjusted to the water. Grosse and McGill (1979) explain that many individuals with disabilities have had little or no exposure to swimming pool settings: "Nervousness, excitement, fear, or just concentration can increase muscle tensions, limit further voluntary movements and increase involuntary actions. Therefore, the primary goal in water adjustment is to make the individual comfortable in water" (p. 3). It is thus important that the child's first experience in the swimming pool be both nonthreatening and enjoyable. Durfee (1977) stresses that it is important "to teach self-confidence before skills, for once the child is comfortable, mentally and physically, learning is absorbed and retained at a quicker and deeper learning level" (p. 2).

Fear of water is a natural response of many youngsters, both disabled and nondisabled. Each child comes to the experience with preconceived ideas. Students with disabilities may not understand the dangers or the potential joys of swimming. If the youngster is openly afraid of the water, the instructor is responsible for helping the child feel relaxed so the student can gain confidence and eventually enjoy playing in the water. Some students may be afraid of getting in the pool or of having water splashed in their faces. Newman (1976) suggests the following technique when dealing with an extremely frightened child: "Do not be distressed, even if it takes many sessions in the water, talk to him, reassure him, just walk into the pool carrying him while allowing him to cry it out.... If a child feels that you like him, he soon loses his reluctance to respond to you. *Never try to reason a child out of his fears*" (p. 5).

GAMES AND ACTIVITIES TO OVERCOME FEAR OF THE WATER

Lawrence and Hackett (1975) discuss using games and activities to move a child into a water learning environment:

> Feelings of self-confidence acquired by participation in activities and games are so important to handicapped children that the leader should modify activities in any way that will allow for maximum participation. This may mean abolishing some very traditional rules or ignoring standard team "positions," in order to incorporate all eager participants. The leader will soon discover that most of the well-known games can be modified or even eliminated, while the essence of the games is preserved. The joy on the players' happy faces is far more rewarding and important than strict adherence to rules. (p. 87)

The following games and techniques were developed by Durfee (1977) to overcome students' innate fear of water.

1. Use toys (e.g., boats) to help the children get their minds off initial fears.
2. Gently pull the swimmer into the water from a sitting position on the pool side by saying, "Humpty Dumpty sat on the wall...Humpty Dumpty had a great FALL!" Many rhymes can be used in this fashion.
3. To reduce fear and have fun while getting wet, sing and play "London Bridge" and "This Is the Way We Wash Our Hair."
4. Push floatable objects, such as oranges, apples, grapefruits, Ping-Pong balls, and plastic milk bottles, in relays and races.
5. Spit water over heads to learn not to swallow and to have fun squirting and blowing water with the mouth.
6. Other suggested activities include the following:
   a. Throw a sponge at a plastic milk bottle.
   b. Throw small balls into a floating bucket.
   c. Play target toss, increasing the difficulty by slowly moving the target away.
   d. Carry a Ping-Pong ball in a spoon.

 e. Push a balloon with only the chest, only one hand, only the head.

 f. Carry a piece of paper or a cloth flag without it getting wet.

 g. Carry or balance an object on the head.

PREBEGINNER TECHNIQUES

Langendorfer (1990) identifies a newer trend developing in the area of teaching pre-beginner swimming techniques: "One of the more profound, yet subtle, changes in infant/preschool aquatic programs is the gradual shift away from teacher-centered methods of instruction toward more child-centered, developmental programs...it is inadequate to teach young children as if they were miniature adults, that teaching traditional strokes was less important than permitting young children to learn through play" (p. 37).

 For some youngsters with disabilities, entry into a large pool may be inappropriate until they develop a basic enjoyment of the water. This is often true of children who are severely involved. Lawrence and Hackett (1975) recommend several alternative methods for introducing prebeginners to the water. They state that a child's first exposure to water can occur in almost any setting and under varied conditions. Children experience water fun by splashing and playing in a wading pool or in a large tub or bucket. Their suggested interactions to facilitate water orientation include the use of tub toys, animals, boats, and soap containers:

1. Which is your favorite toy? Why do you like it best?

2. What does your favorite toy do? Show me.

3. Can you show me the smallest toy you have in the tub?

4. Does it float or sink? Let me see.

5. How many of the toys in your tub float? Count them for me.

6. Can you tell me how many of them do not float?

7. What colors are your boats?

8. Make a bridge with your body and see if your boat can float under it. (p. 24)

 The American National Red Cross (1977a) has some excellent exercise suggestions for prebeginners using sponges:

1. Let it fill with water, squeeze it out, and wipe your face.

2. Let it fill, don't squeeze it out, and wipe your face.

3. Let it fill, place it on top of your head, don't squeeze it.

4. Let it fill, place it on the teacher's head, and squeeze it.

5. Let it fill, place it on your own head, and squeeze it.

6. Play a sponge-toss circle game with the other class members. (pp. 158–159)

Once the prebeginner feels secure in basic water orientation, established levels of advancement should be followed. Figure 20.1 shows skill breakdown progression charts.

The *second basic swimming factor* identified by the Red Cross involves learning how to maintain an efficient body position in the water. The instructor must teach those skills that enable students to learn breath control, prone float, back float, turning over, and changing direction (American National Red Cross, 1977a).

Some youngsters with disabilities have difficulty maintaining a standing or floating position because their disability causes irregular and unwanted movements. Children with cerebral palsy require special attention, and many individuals with disabilities may need some form of **personal flotation device (PFD).**

PFDs such as rubber tubes, inflatable vests, swimsuits with built-in air pockets, water skiing life jackets, or regular life preservers can be used for effective teaching and learning. These devices enable the student to assume and maintain correct body position. Each child's abilities and disabilities must be analyzed when selecting the appropriate PFD and determining how it will aid the student. Instructors should ask themselves the following questions:

1. Can the child stand alone in the water (e.g., muscular dystrophy, spina bifida)?

2. Does the child have extreme balance problems (e.g., ataxic cerebral palsy)?

3. Does the child have uncontrollable flexion movements (e.g., spastic cerebral palsy)?

4. When in supine position, will the child's head submerge due to involuntary hyperextension (e.g., athetoid cerebral palsy)?

5. Does the child have sufficient neck strength to hold up the head (e.g., muscular dystrophy)?

When using any PFD, several important factors need to be considered. The device must fit correctly and be secured properly every time it is used. This is particularly true for young children, children with mental retardation, or those youngsters with physical disabilities that may impair their ability to fasten the device correctly. Also, the instructor will need to check all aids on a regular basis during the class. Gross (1987) suggests the following: "Movement of the swimmer as well as movement of the water tend to alter the fit of most buoyancy aids. Remember, individuals who are severely disabled are probably not going to be able to indicate something is wrong, nor are they going to be able to help themselves if they become trapped inside of or slip completely out of their flotation devices" (p. 56).

Newman (1976) questions the use of PFDs:

Personally, I do not use swim aids, with the exception of swim tubes. . . . I do use kick boards and swim tubes (rubber inner tubes) since they are not fastened on the child's

SUGGESTED SKILL BREAKDOWN BELOW BEGINNER LEVEL

LEVEL I

THE STUDENT WILL:

___ 1. Enter pool via ladder with assistance.
___ 2. Leave pool via ladder with assistance.
___ 3. Sit on deck and enter pool with assistance.
___ 4. Climb on deck from pool with assistance.
___ 5. Bob up and down in water to chin level with support of two arms of instructor.
___ 6. Bob up and down in water to chin level with support of one arm of instructor.
___ 7. Bob up and down in water to nose level with support of one arm of instructor.
___ 8. Bob up and down in water to forehead level with support of two arms of instructor.
___ 9. Bob to top of head with support of one arm of instructor.
___10. Put mouth on surface of water and blow bubbles.
___11. Walk width of pool with support of instructor.
___12. Walk width of pool unassisted.
___13. Run width of pool with support of instructor.
___14. Run in water width of pool without support.
___15. Pick up ring off bottom with foot.
___16. Move arms in crawl movement with aid of instructor on deck of pool.
___17. Do crawl arm movement while standing in water facing side of pool.
___18. Use crawl arm movement while walking across pool in water.
___19. Play catch with plastic balls with instructor in water.
___20. Kick legs while instructor tows student.
___21. Kick legs using kickboard with assistance.

Date completed _____

Student's name _____

Instructor's name _____

LEVEL II

THE STUDENT WILL:

___ 1. Climb down ladder unassisted.
___ 2. Climb up ladder unassisted.
___ 3. Enter pool from deck unassisted.
___ 4. Leave pool from water unassisted.
___ 5. Bob up and down in water without support of instructor, using bobbing progression in Level I.
___ 6. Bob down deep and touch ankles and jump up high in air and maintain balance, using both arms to balance body.
___ 7. Touch bottom of pool.
___ 8. Open eyes underwater and count instructor's submerged fingers.
___ 9. Sit on bottom of pool.
___10. Put face on surface of water and blow bubbles out of *mouth.*
___11. Put face on surface, blow mouth bubbles, roll head to side (one ear underwater), take breath of air, repeat five times.
___12. Hang onto side of pool in prone position and kick legs ten times, using a straight-arm support.
___13. Pick up ring off bottom with hand.
___14. Hold onto side of pool in supine (back) position and kick legs.
___15. Assume prone (front) floating position with two-arm support of instructor. Regain footing.
___16. Jump into pool from crouched position.
___17. Jump into pool from standing position.
___18. Assume back floating position with two-arm support of instructor. Regain footing.
___19. Use kickboard unassisted.

Date completed _____

Student's name _____

Instructor's name _____

FIGURE 20.1   Skill breakdown progression charts. (Excerpt from *Methods in Adapted Aquatics,* copyright ©1977 by The American National Red Cross, reprinted with permission.)

body and are more easily discarded; they are only used for part of a swim lesson. Swim tubes have two uses: (1) For children who will never swim independently, but who can learn to become water safe and actually swim strokes in a tube, to provide him pleasure and a sense of independence; they can also join in swim games and often come up with unique methods of attaining goals; and (2) as a play activity toy during play period, as they are not attached to the body, there is not a feeling of dependence, as new skills are achieved children tend to rely on the tubes less often. (p. 163)

Bradley, Fuller, Pozos, and Willmers (1987) warn that PFDs may not give adequate support if used as a life jacket for some individuals with disabilities. From their study, they conclude that the PFDs on the market today are not safe for individuals with physical disabilities. They stress that those available for use do not provide correct positioning in the water and are difficult to put on.

The *third basic swimming factor* cited by the Red Cross involves teaching techniques to develop specific skills. Swimming programs almost always group students by ability classifications such as beginner, advanced beginner, intermediate, and advanced. Both students who are disabled and nondisabled should be placed in the group that is most compatible with their swimming ability level. This concept reinforces the philosophy of individualized instruction because the child's ability determines placement in the least restrictive environment. Many students with disabilities are able to take advantage of mainstream swimming opportunities.

Helpful teaching points include the following:

1. Most students with impairments do not want to be babied or pitied.

2. Ask students about their disabilities, their capabilities, their range of movement, their fears, and their interests.

3. Do not do for students what they can do for themselves.

4. Keep verbal directions short and simple. Remember that constant repetition can be boring. Make practice sessions short and change activities often. Let students use a variety of movement skills, and most important, vary actual skill practice with games and stunts.

5. Teach new skills early in the lesson before fatigue sets in.

6. When teaching young students and students who are mentally retarded, remember that demonstration by other children rather than adults is more effective. Many children love competition and will attempt a skill that another child is demonstrating.

7. Look for signals that indicate learning has stopped.

8. Read the medical clearance sheet for each student to ensure that the physician's suggestions are being followed.

9. Reinforce the student continually with constructive feedback and performance corrections.

These teaching methods emphasize success. It is important that students experience success quickly at whatever level of skill they possess. In planning an individual program, consider carefully the skills to be taught. Activities must be planned so the student is reasonably challenged without creating undue pressure to complete the task. Although success is critical, skills to be learned must not be so simple that the student loses interest.

Specific skill progression should be noted and recorded. Figure 20.2 is a typical evaluation sheet. The skills to be learned will vary from student to student. The instructor should record comments for each student.

Meyer (1991) has developed specific behavior tasks when teaching children with disabilities to enter the water, walk the width of the pool, and exit the pool. (See Table 20.1.)

EVALUATION SHEET

Name			Diagnosis	

Movements indicated			Movements contraindicated	

Skills	Number of Times	Distance	Amount of Time	Manner
Entering pool				
Walking across pool				
Putting face in water				
Blowing bubbles				
Bobbing				
Face float, assisted				
Back float, assisted				
Kicking with board				
Beginner arm motion				
Face float alone				
Back float alone				
Use of life jacket				
Beginner crawl				
Safety skills				
Instructor's comments:			Date:	

FIGURE 20.2   **Evaluation form for specific skill progression.** (Excerpt from *Adapted Aquatics*, copyright ©1977, The American National Red Cross, reprinted with permission.)

TABLE 20.1   Task Analysis for Entering the Pool, Walking in Water, and Exiting the Pool

I. Given a pool, the learner will climb down and up ladder to enter and exit at a point where water is waist deep:

   1. Locates ladder
   2. Turns back to water
   3. Grabs railing
   4. Lowers one leg onto rung
   5. Lowers opposite leg onto rung
   6. Holds rail until firmly on pool bottom
   7. Stands in water
   8. Completes task

II. Given a pool, the learner will slide into the water at a point where water is waist deep:

   1. Locates shallow end of pool
   2. Climbs out of chair, crutches, etc.[a]
   3. Sits on edge of pool
   4. Twists body around to stomach
   5. Bends at waist
   6. Grips edge
   7. Lowers body down slowly
   8. Stands on pool bottom[a]
   9. Holds onto edge
  10. Completes task

III. Given a sensory cue, the learner will walk through chest-deep water the entire width of the pool:

   1. Stands along edge
   2. Steps forward with left foot
   3. Reaches forward with right arm
   4. Steps forward with right foot
   5. Reaches forward with left arm
   6. Looks straight ahead
   7. Completes task

Source: Adapted from Meyer, 1991.

[a] If appropriate.

Putting the face under water usually proves to be difficult for most beginning swimmers. This apprehension should be expected. The two most important concepts to be taught are that: (1) water will not hurt the eyes, and (2) a mouthful of water can be spit out.

The old and simple technique of wiping water out of the eyes is very successful with beginners. The youngsters should be told to wipe the fingers downward over the eyes to remove water. Some experts suggest that this method teaches students bad habits because one cannot wipe the eyes while swimming. A more effective method involves blinking several times.

Newman (1976) suggests that breath control exercises be incorporated in the first swimming lesson. She cautions that "this does not mean that a child will blow bubbles or that he will at that time even put his face in the water. There may be many small steps to climb and problems to solve before he actually learns this skill. Some small children with handicapping conditions cannot even blow a small puff so that the act of blowing must be taught. Small easy-to-blow whistles, noisemakers, candles, and party pop-outs usually motivate a child to attempt to blow. The instructor should not be discouraged if this first step in swim training takes a month or more to accomplish. When blowing practice is consistent, most children learn" (p. 6).

Another teaching suggestion involves the students practicing breath control out of the water. The instructor times the youngsters and encourages them to increase the length of time they can hold their breath (e.g., 5, 10, 15, 20, and 25 sec).

Games that allow the student to become accustomed to putting the head totally under the water are as follows:

1. Have student submerge face only (up to, but not including, the ears) in the water, and identify whether the instructor's submerged fist is open or closed. When the student is able to see clearly underwater, use number of fingers for a more difficult challenge.

2. Tap two metal objects together underwater to encourage the student to listen and think (count) underwater. Breath holding is also practiced in this activity.

3. Have student try to sit on the bottom.

4. Have student attempt a jellyfish float, and also a dead man's float.

5. Have student retrieve objects from the bottom of the pool. This develops associative skills such as breath control, eye opening, eye-hand coordination, movement, and self-confidence.

6. Place a weight in the student's hands (a lifesaving brick is ideal), and have the student go underwater. Later, put the brick underwater and ask the youngster to pick it up.

Children often have difficulty putting their heads underwater. Table 20.2 lists the teaching progressions to use for youngsters with disabilities.

Swimming instructors are often reluctant to use artificial pieces of equipment because these implements do not allow for natural development of skills. For individuals with disabilities, Green and Miles (1987) strongly encourage the use of masks, fins, and snorkels for the teaching of basic swimming skills:

Use of mask, fins, and snorkel together with some adaptations of traditional skill progressions and teaching style, enabled disabled students to master the front crawl. Equipment was initially used to compensate for disabilities. Removing individual

TABLE 20.2   **Task Analysis for Putting the Head Underwater**

I. Given a sensory cue, the learner will bend forward and submerge the entire head under water for 10 sec:

    1. Takes deep breath
    2. Bends forward
    3. Places entire head in water _____ sec
    4. Places entire head in water _____ sec
    5. Lifts head out of water
    6. Completes task

II. Given a sensory cue, the learner will exhale into the water each time the face is submerged:

    1. Inhales above water
    2. Lowers head to water
    3. Exhales above water
    4. Exhales with lips touching water
    5. Exhales with mouth in water
    6. Exhales with face in water
    7. Completes task

Source: Adapted from Meyer, 1991.

pieces of equipment during stages of learning enabled students to concentrate on the subtask at hand with a reduced amount of interference from their individual disabilities. (p. 15)

PATTERNED ARM AND LEG MOVEMENTS

This technique is designed to teach basic swimming movements to students with disabilities who usually do not have the physical or mental capability to understand or accomplish coordinated skills. Difficulty arises when the student is asked to move two or more body parts at the same time. Newman (1976) believes that when a child with a disability uses the large muscles and is told which body parts are being used, the youngster realizes for the first time that he has a right and a left arm, and a right and a left leg. He also learns the meaning of directions such as in-out, up-down, back-front, and bend-straight.

Incorporated in this teaching method is the hands-on approach—the instructor moves the student's arms and legs through the basic positions. To assist learning, the instructor should sit on a step in shallow water and hold the student in a back float position, making sure the child's ears are submerged. Newman (1976) explains: "All movements should be slow and rhythmic. Do each pattern at least five times. Counting out loud is one way to keep your movements steady. The child should be patterned passively until his own muscles take over. Patterning is especially beneficial for children with coordination problems" (p. 10).

Basic arm and leg strokes should be repeated until the child can successfully complete the skill alone. When a physical disability restricts the child from accomplishing a correct movement, the instructor should note this irregularity and realize that the child will be attempting certain strokes with a modified movement similar to the original pattern.

Swimming can be taught using a multisensory approach. For example, the instructor can simultaneously use two or more senses, thereby increasing the chance that learning will occur. The following techniques, can be used when teaching swimming to students with disabilities:

1. **Assistive:** Guidance of body parts through movements provides kinesthetic (proprioceptive) feedback from the muscles to the brain, allowing the child to feel and sense her body parts as they move. An example of this teaching approach would be the teacher's turning of the child's head as rhythmic breathing is practiced.

2. **Tactile:** Touching of body parts enables the child to sense the part to be moved, such as the arm to be used in stroking or the leg to be kicked. Tactile reinforcement facilitates visual or verbal stimuli or both.

3. **Visual Stimulus:** The eyes are stimulated through demonstrations and simple visual aids, enabling the child to reproduce the movement by imitation. Good demonstrations and simple visual aids are effective instructional methods.

4. **Verbal Stimulus:** The ears are stimulated through the spoken word. Simple and accurate word descriptions of the activity to be performed should be used. Oral instruction should reflect the child's level of understanding.

5. **Abstract Stimulus:** Use of stimuli, such as signals, signs, numbers, and colors, requires the student to receive, interpret, and transfer those stimuli into actions.

ASSISTIVE EQUIPMENT

A strap with one end tied to a plastic gallon jug and a slipknot on the other end is helpful for strengthening lower extremities. The strap length depends on depth of water. While standing against a support (e.g., wall or railing) in waist-deep water, the swimmer inserts one foot in the slipknot. The swimmer then pulls the jug underwater. The stress exerted against the limb can be regulated by filling or emptying the jug. Thick plastic jugs work best.

Passive range of motion can be achieved in many ways. One way is to place a swim fin on the affected hand, foot, or both, then to move the body so water resistance will push-pull the flipper and limb.

Swim fins or flippers can be used for swimmers with lower extremity anomalies or spasticity to develop a stronger dolphin kick and flutter kick. The fins allow the swimmer above-average speed with minimum effort while strengthening the lower limbs. Diving masks help swimmers to see underwater, a new experience for many. A snorkel may aid swimmers who cannot get their faces above water to breathe properly while swimming (Durfee, 1977, p. 4).

TECHNIQUES FOR THE STUDENT WITH MENTAL RETARDATION

Students with mental retardation can usually learn most basic swimming skills if they can *remember* which skill is being taught or reviewed. Words and phrases must be reinforced continually because the child often forgets what was taught only the day before. The instructor's vocabulary should be carefully adjusted to the student's intellectual level. For example, the student with mild mental retardation will understand and remember better than if moderately mentally retarded. The child's intellectual level, *not* chronological age, should dictate the terminology used. Most teenage students with moderate mental retardation function at an IQ level equivalent to that of a 6- or 7-year-old nondisabled child. Behavioral and learning characteristics of the two groups are the same and include short attention span, an inability to follow detailed explanations, and a tendency to be egocentric.

Adjustments also must be made in selection of teaching techniques. It is important to establish safety rules, repeat them often, and never change them. A structured environment in which students know what to do and what not to do provides a feeling of security. Establish a pattern for poolside procedures such as walk in, sit on deck, and wait for command to enter water.

Some students may exhibit a real fear of the pool environment; others will show none at all. Both groups need careful, clear directions and sound instruction. If a youngster becomes belligerent or uncooperative, the child may not understand what is being taught. The instructor should explain the skill or situation in a positive way that is easily understood.

The student with severe mental retardation has intellectual characteristics similar to those of a nondisabled child under 4 years of age. Students with severe or profound mental retardation often possess other disabling conditions, such as epilepsy or cerebral palsy, and therefore need special considerations when being taught to swim. These youngsters progress more slowly, display longer stages with no apparent development, and are less consistent in using and building on information that appeared to be learned. In teaching these youngsters, it is suggested that instructors should (1) use wider limits of time and patience, (2) break learning experiences into small units, and (3) provide a stimulating, multisensory, enthusiastic atmosphere.

Skills must be segmented and the teaching approach modified. It is necessary to task-analyze basic skills into the simplest components and develop entirely new progressions to be successful. Motivation should include basic behavior modification techniques, including visual, verbal, tactual, and taste reinforcers.

Most students who are severely or profoundly disabled seem to lack a sense of fear and thus require close supervision. The instructor should make very few assumptions about what the students understand because these youngsters lack the ability to remember specific dangers of a swimming pool environment. They commonly jump into deep water and make no effort to move or swim. They may remain underwater and make no effort to come up for air. Close, individualized supervision is imperative (1:1 ratio) for these students.

Water adjustment activities such as those described for prebeginners earlier in this chapter are necessary.

TECHNIQUES FOR THE STUDENT WITH CEREBRAL PALSY

When teaching the child with cerebral palsy, repetition must be stressed. Newman (1976) suggests that new skills be introduced early in the lesson because children with cerebral palsy tire quickly and chill easily. This is particularly true initially until the youngster develops greater strength and endurance.

Contractures, immobilized joints, and limited range of motion require modifications of normal swimming movements. Proper execution of the stroke is not important. The goal should be for the student to learn the skill in the best way possible and then to strive for greater efficiency of movement. PFDs may be effective for some students, but overdependence on them should be avoided. Many individuals cannot walk without braces or crutches or use wheelchairs. Learning to stand and walk in water is possible and can be taught in chest-deep water. Students should be instructed in how to use their hands to make finning, sculling, or winging motions. These same movements are also used to teach supine floating skills.

Students with severe impairments tend to draw the knees to the stomach, making it difficult to float in either the front or back position. PFDs are recommended for these individuals.

Each student must be assessed to determine ability to control the head in the prone or supine position without involuntary movements. A child who exhibits strong hip flexion or head and neck hyperextension movements must be watched carefully. A common reflex found in individuals with cerebral palsy is described in the American National Red Cross literature (1977a) as follows: "A prone body position results in an upward thrusting of the head and neck. The supine position results in a hyperextension of the head and neck back into the water" (p. 50). Youngsters with this particular problem require close hands-on supervision by the instructor or aide to prevent submersion when attempting a particular skill. The fear that results from accidental submersion will inhibit the child's desire to continue.

Once the child has made some physical and mental adjustments and has learned to put her head underwater, swimming instruction can begin. The easiest stroke for most students with cerebral palsy is the back float position. This requires movement by finning, sculling, or winging the arms, or by modifications of these. The legs are moved by flutter kicking.

Recovery from the back float position is easier for the person with cerebral palsy than recovery from the prone position. Instruction to recover from the back float position should therefore be taught first.

TECHNIQUES FOR THE STUDENT WITH SPINA BIFIDA OR TRAUMATIC PARALYSIS

Students with spina bifida or traumatic paralysis often exhibit lack of bladder or bowel control (incontinence) and paralysis of the legs.

At one time, these individuals were not allowed to participate in swimming activities. These students, however, gain valuable benefits from aquatic activities. For some, swimming may be the only form of recreation within their capabilities. All phases of swimming are appropriate for these students. From a sanitary point of view (i.e., contamination of pool water), new techniques that control seepage more effectively can correct this concern.

Because of inability to control excretory functions, many people who have disabilities do not wish to participate in swimming programs. Embarrassment and fear of an accident in the pool area have kept many individuals from this activity. The instructor must make a conscious effort to convince students to participate. As a result of spinal cord impairment or damage, proper innervation to the lower body does not occur. These students usually cannot sense when the bladder or bowel needs emptying. They also cannot voluntarily relax the external sphincter muscles that control urination and defecation. In addition, muscle strength, which assists in voiding waste materials, may be lacking. Most children with spinal cord injuries who cannot control bladder function have, however, usually been taught bowel training and use of a urine collection bag early in life.

URINARY INCONTINENCE

When students are unable to control urination, they often use urine collection bags. For females, a tube (catheter) is inserted directly into the urethra to allow drainage through a flexible tube into a bag. Males commonly use a condom catheter, which connects the condom with a urine collection bag. The bag can be detached from the catheter and clamped off while swimming. All students should empty the bag prior to pool entry to prevent pool contamination.

FECAL INCONTINENCE

Diapers or plastic rubber pants under a child's swimsuit are usually sufficient if bowel incontinence is a problem. Both should fit snugly to ensure sanitation and a neat appearance.

Individuals who are unable to control bowel function often require surgery. An artificial opening, or *stoma*, is made in the abdominal wall to excrete body waste. There are three types of operation, or *ostomy:* an ileostomy, a colostomy, and a ureterostomy. With proper management, the ostomy is only a minor inconvenience to the individual (Adams & McCubbin, 1991).

Ostomy appliances consist of a plastic disk to which a pouch is attached. These devices are simple, comfortable, nonirritating, inexpensive, inconspicuous, odor free, and leakproof. Attachment to the body is accomplished with contact adhesive cement, double-faced adhesive disks, or karaya gum rings. A belt or waterproof tape is often used to reinforce adhesion. Odor is controlled by special deodorants (Smigielski-Curry, 1990).

Questions about bladder or bowel program, collection bags, or catheters should be addressed directly to the student. If the student is too young to understand the procedures or is unable to communicate effectively, the child's parents or a physician should be consulted.

SPECIFIC SWIMMING SUGGESTIONS

It is important that each student's balance point be found. Because of each student's distinct disabling condition, locating the child's balance point aids in developing the proper floating position for that individual. Newman (1976) stresses that learning the floating position is necessary because it teaches the child the concept of buoyancy necessary to swimming on the back and to safe skill practice. "The ability to float on the back when tired or frightened is of utmost importance. Until the balance point is determined it will be impossible to perform a back stroke, if at all. No two students are alike. One may be paralyzed from the waist down; another may have some use of the legs; one may have legs of different lengths; often the older child has a fused back; plus other differences" (pp. 39–40).

CONCERNS RELATED TO STUDENTS
WHO EXPERIENCE SEIZURES

The swimming pool can be particularly hazardous for individuals who have seizures or a convulsive disorder. Before these students are taught to swim, the following questions must be answered: What type of seizure disorder does the child have? Are the seizures completely controlled by medication? If not, are seizures frequent or do they occur rarely? The child's parents, physician, and medical records should supply answers to these questions.

Generally speaking, the student with infrequent seizures should be allowed to swim if the instructor is aware of the condition and knows simple first aid techniques to employ in the event of a seizure (see Chapter 15 on seizures and convulsive disorders).

The necessary precautions include alerting the lifeguard about specific children who could experience seizures. A buddy system should be used, and the buddy should know what to expect, what to do, and who to call if a seizure occurs.

Because swimming is considered a strenuous activity, it has been suspect of bringing on seizures. This outdated concept is not valid. In fact, physical activity and high levels of physical fitness tend to ward off seizures.

GENERALIZED TONIC-CLONIC SEIZURE (GRAND MAL)

During a tonic-clonic seizure, the student will hold his breath momentarily and so will not inhale water. The instructor (or buddy) should roll the child onto his back and tilt the head backward while supporting the back with the forearms. The child should not be removed from the water unless this can be accomplished easily. In fact, the water may provide a soothing atmosphere in which the child's thrashing movements present no danger.

Do *not* use a portable oxygen unit to administer oxygen during a grand mal seizure, unless the student has stopped breathing.

SWIMMING PROGRESSIONS

Table 20.3 outlines a progressive system of swimming instruction.

ENDURANCE SWIMMING

Swimming has traditionally been a popular sport for the development of cardiorespiratory efficiency; individuals with disabilities can experience similar rewards. As with other types of aerobic conditioning, much depends on the intensity of effort, the duration of each session, and the length of the entire program (Shephard, 1990). Frieden (1989) found she could increase the endurance levels of her 15 students (ages 14 to 18) who were labeled as moderately, severely, and profoundly mentally retarded. The swimmers were required to perform an adapted front crawl, completing a distance of one mile, over a 4-month period. Once a week, each swimmer swam as many laps as possible in a 25-minute session. Each lap consisted of 25 yards.

> During the first few sessions, participants showed slow lap rates, shortness of breath, poor body position, and low stamina. Many were required to start a lap over because they had touched the side of the pool or put their feet down on the bottom and stood up.... During the beginning...the average total laps per session were quite low (from 4 to 8). By the end of the program, averages were much higher (from 6 to 16). Thirteen of the 15 participants achieved the objective of one mile total distance. Two students completed three quarters of a mile. (pp. 54, 60)

TABLE 20.3 Swimming Instruction: A Progressive System

First Level: Making Mental and Physical Adjustments to Water	Second Level: Maintaining Constant Motivation to Learn and Survive (Drownproofing)	Third Level: Propulsion	Fourth Level: Coordinated Stroking	Fifth Level: Challenging Advanced Skills	Sixth Level: Achievements
1. Talk to swimmer. Let swimmer trust you. Self-confidence is delicate to teach.	1. Assistants and aides provide good one-to-one motivation and decrease need for flotation devices.	1. Prone glide (pushing off bottom or edge with legs or arms to go from point A to point B).	1. Dog paddle (with face submerged).	1. Object recovery (toys, weights, etc.) from varying depths.	1. Earn swimming certificates and cards for achievements. Award Red Cross skill cards to those who qualify (local organizations or camps may issue their own cards).
2. Use safest, easiest method for each person to enter and exit from water.	2. Prone float and recovery.	2. Sculling, finning, and winging: a. Walking b. Face down c. On back	2. Elementary backstroke (works well with hemiplegia).	2. Swimming between instructor's legs (one or many instructors).	2. Present water shows to demonstrate accomplishments before an audience of family and friends (themes are effective if incorporated into show).
3. Face in water: a. Inhale air through mouth. b. Exhale through nose (bubbles release air and keep water out, thus avoiding sinus irritation). c. Hold breath. d. Open eyes underwater (pick up pennies, count instructor's fingers).	3. Gradual depth progression—from steps, to shallow, to deep.	3. Flutter kick.	3. Crawl (with rhythmic breathing).	3. Underwater distance swimming.	3. Include: a. Individual demonstrations b. Relay races c. Underwater races
	4. Survival float (jellyfish or dead man's float): a. Rhythmic breathing b. Rhythmic bobbing	4. Breaststroke kick— frog kick, modified whip kick.	4. Breaststroke (with rhythmic breathing).	4. Jumping, diving, or falling from side into water.	
	5. Back float (provides best position to survive).	5. Dolphin kick.	5. Sidestroke (with rhythmic breathing).	5. Use of mask, fins, and snorkel.	
		6. Modified kicks.	6. Modified or combined strokes.	6. Disrobing and inflating clothes to survive.	

Source: Adapted from Durfee, 1977, pp. 4–7.

601

Competitive swimming for individuals with disabilities is usually accomplished against other athletes with similar disabilities. Excellent swimming competition, such as in the Special Olympics for persons with mental retardation, or the Paralympics for those with differing degrees of paralysis, are held at local, regional, national, and international levels. A more complete picture of athletic competition is found in Chapter 21, Opportunities in Sport.

SUMMARY

Major goals of a swimming program for students with disabilities include enjoying water activities, learning how to swim, and improving swimming performance.

A good swimming program should provide periods of training and periods of relaxation for improving and maintaining balance, gait, muscular strength and endurance, power, agility, coordination, and flexibility. Socialization and emotional well-being also should improve.

An individualized swimming program needs to follow a written plan like any other activity area. Assessment is the critical first step in planning the program. Each student's physical, intellectual, emotional, and social development determines the specific activities, skills, and strokes to be taught.

Some students will progress as rapidly as their nondisabled peers and should be allowed to develop at a rate appropriate for them. Youngsters with severe disabilities progress at slower rates, and small accomplishments are satisfying and rewarding.

Instructors must remember that children who are nondisabled control their arms and legs willfully, but youngsters with physical disabilities, especially those with cerebral palsy and brain damage, find this difficult. Many children with disabilities receive great pleasure and a sense of achievement simply from splashing or moving their arms and legs in the water. Small enjoyable progressions often lead to positive experiences that reinforce future learning. Newman (1976) states: "Everything is relative. That which is good for one is bad for another....Just learning to propel and move around the pool in a swim tube is a thrill beyond words for many of these children. Avoid the trap of judging things in terms of your [the teacher's] interests, abilities, and experiences rather than those of the children with whom you work" (p. 169).

Progressions can begin by introducing students to the water through activities involving water-filled buckets, sponges, sprinkling cans, and shallow wading pools. The most important objective is to help the child develop a positive attitude toward water learning. Simple games provide an ideal learning experience. With slight modifications, most land games can be played in the water. These activities, along with water games and stunts, provide stimulating, challenging, and enjoyable opportunities for students.

Critical points for the beginning swimmer include balance, buoyancy, and propulsion.

When writing the individualized swimming program, progressions for children without disabilities can be used as a guide and modified appropriately. Because children with disabilities have specific impairments, each program should be designed to complement the individual's unique abilities. Effective instruction requires initiative, imagination, and patience when teaching swimming to students with disabilities. Instruction must be slow, deliberate, progressive, and specific.

Langendorfer (1989) lists three recent developments and practices in adapted aquatics for young children with disabilities. These include (1) new measurement and assessment approaches, (2) development and use of IEPs, and (3) inclusion of developmental task analysis procedures in curricular and teaching design of adapted preschool aquatics.

The importance of an individualized swimming program is emphasized in the following statement by a student who is severely disabled (Kuechler, 1978):

> I used to stand and sit in the wheelchair using the rail in the pool. To learn to swim, I used a life preserver. Then I used an air collar around my neck. Now I swim without the collar, with my hands in the air. I can swim on my back without anything to keep me floating. I kick my legs and use my back to swim. I hold onto the rails and push back and forth with body and hands to turn circles, and to swim in a straight line. I swing my left hand over my head to swim. At first I was afraid of the water when I was standing up and sitting down in the wheelchair. I was not afraid when I started using the life preserver. Then I used the collar which I liked so I wouldn't get water in my ears. I was afraid to swim without the collar at first, but not now. Now that I know how to swim, I enjoy the water. (p. 8)

REFERENCES

Adams, R. C., & McCubbin, J. A. (1991). *Games, sports, and exercises for the physically disabled* (4th ed.). Philadelphia: Lea & Febiger.

American National Red Cross. (1974). *Swimming for the handicapped—A manual for the aide.* Washington, DC: American National Red Cross.

American National Red Cross. (1977a). *Adapted aquatics.* Garden City, NY: Doubleday & Company.

American National Red Cross, (1977b). *Methods in adapted aquatics—A manual for the instructor.* Washington, DC: American National Red Cross.

Bradley, N. J., Fuller, J. L., Pozos, R. S., & Willmers, L. E., (1987, May/June). PFD's personal flotation devices. A lifejacket is a lifejacket...not necessarily so, especially if you're disabled. *Sports 'N Spokes*, 23–25.

Durfee, E. (1977). Teaching persons who are handicapped to swim. *Occasional Papers of the National Easter Seal Society for Crippled Children and Adults, 25*, 1–10.

Frieden, D. (1989). Weaver mile lap fitness swim. *Palaestra, 5*(2), 52–54, 60–62.

Green, J. S., & Miles, B. H. (1987). Use of mask, fins, snorkel, and SCUBA equipment in aquatics for the disabled. *Palaestra, 3*(4), 12–17.

Greenshaw, A., & Sadler, B. (1988). Whale...wet happenings and learning experiences. *Palaestra, 5*(1), 10–11, 13–15, 31.

Gross, S. (1987). Use and misuse of flotation devices in adapted aquatics. *Palaestra, 4*(1), 31–33, 56–57.

Grosse, S. J., & McGill, C. D. (1979). Independent swimming for children with severe physical impairments. *Practical Pointers, 3*(2), 1–15.

Harris, F. A. (1978). Correction of muscle balance in spasticity. *American Journal of Physical Medicine, 57*(3), 123–138.

Kuechler, T. (1978). I swim in a straight line. *Bethesda Messenger, 69*(3), 8.

Langendorfer, S. J. (1989). Aquatics for young children with handicapping conditions. *Palaestra, 5*(3), 17–19, 37–40.

Langendorfer, S. J. (1990). Contemporary trends in infant/preschool aquatics—Into the 1990s and beyond. *Journal of Physical Education, Recreation, & Dance, 61*(5), 36–39.

Lasko, P. M., & Knopf, K. G. (1984). *Adapted and corrective exercise for the disabled adult.* Dubuque, IA: Eddie Bowers Publishing.

Lawrence, C. C., & Hackett, L. C. (1975). *Water learning: A new adventure.* Palo Alto, CA: Peek Publications.

Lian, M. G., & Goyette, A. L. (1988). Adapted aquatics for people with severe multiple disabilities. *American Rehabilitation, 14*(3), 12–13, 31–32.

Mayse, J. S. (1991). Aquacise and aquafitness for adapted aquatics. *Palaestra, 7*(2), 54–56.

Meyer, J. R. (1991, October). *Using behavioral objectives when teaching swimming to children with disabilities.* Paper presented at the annual meeting of the Illinois Association for Health, Physical Education, Recreation, and Dance, Arlington Heights, IL.

Newman, J. (1976). *Swimming for children with physical and sensory impairments.* Springfield, IL: Charles C. Thomas.

Pagenoff, S. A. (1984, July). The use of aquatics with cerebral palsied adolescents. *The American Journal of Occupational Therapy, 38*(7), 469–473.

Priest, L. (1982). *Adapted aquatics teaching methods.* Indianapolis: Council for National Cooperation in Aquatics.

Shephard, R. J. (1990). *Fitness in special populations.* Champaign, IL: Human Kinetics.

Smigielski-Curry, P. A. (1990). Bowel and bladder management. In J. A. Blackman (Ed.), *Medical aspects of developmental disabilities in children birth to three* (2nd ed.). Rockville, MD: Aspen.

Steinbrunner, D. (1982). The process of leadership development. *Adapted Aquatics—Leadership Development.* Indianapolis: Council for National Cooperation in Aquatics.

Chapter 21

OPPORTUNITY IN SPORT

"But, Mom, why can't I go out for the team? I can run farther than the other guys on the freshman cross-country team. You know how Dad and I have been working out all summer. Even yesterday, we ran eight miles and I wasn't even tired. I know I'm blind, but that doesn't keep me from being good enough to run for the team." Mrs. March didn't have a good reason for telling her son that he shouldn't go out for the team, but the ever-nagging questions always came to her, questions typical of a parent who has raised a child with a disability: What if Bobby gets hurt? What if the coach doesn't watch him carefully? What if the other boys make fun of him? Who will be there if he needs something? His dad and I have always been available to encourage and give him the extra help he needed. Mrs. March continued to silently wonder: Would it be possible? Are there other athletes who have disabilities and still are able to participate? How do they get along? I remember hearing about another boy in a town near here who was blind and he wrestled on his high school team. Okay, maybe Bobby is ready. I'm going to call the high school today and talk to the cross-country coach.

Mrs. March was about to make one of the biggest choices of her young son's life—athletic competition—toward developing a full quality of life for an individual with a disability.

A major goal of physical education is to prepare the individual to become physically active and remain so throughout life. For many, this means having the opportunity to participate in a variety of sports experiences. Participation may be informal and among friends or organized, formal, and competitive.

Historically, the opportunity to participate in sport programs has been an option mainly for people without disabilities. People with disabilities often did not have the physical education background that develops sport skills and enables a person to follow an active life-style.

With sport opportunities for people with disabilities emerging and prospering, physical educators must exert leadership to help the trend gather momentum. Timely leadership from concerned professionals is important to ensure that the trend will maintain a proper course.

SPORTS PARTICIPATION AND MAINSTREAMING

Sports opportunities for people with disabilities should not automatically conjure up images of people in special programs. Public Law 101-476 calls for a physical education program conducted in the least restrictive environment. Physical education is defined in the law as participation in individual and group games and sports, including intramurals and lifetime sports. A reasonable interpretation of the law requires the school to implement mainstreaming in sports, including athletic programs, and in physical education programs.

A major concern in mainstreaming in sport and athletic programs is whether all participants, both with and without disabilities, can experience reasonably safe, successful participation. At first mention the phrase *safe and successful participation for all* prompts concern primarily for the athlete with a disability. Mention of similar concerns for athletes without disabilities results at first in wrinkled brows. Consider, however, the athlete without disability who comes in physical contact with a participant wearing an artificial limb. Impact of an artificial limb, depending on configuration and materials, can inflict serious injury to bone and soft tissue. This does not suggest that participants in athletic contests may not sustain injury, but rather that no one should sustain injury resulting from exposure to undue risk.

AMERICANS WITH DISABILITIES ACT OF 1990 (ADA) AND ACCESS TO OPPORTUNITIES IN SPORTS AND ATHLETICS

ADA states that no person shall be denied access to a given program purely because that person has a disability. If the disability does not influence participation materially, the person is entitled to participate in a regular program. When disabilities do materially influence participation and when athletic participation is an opportunity afforded people without disabilities, the providing agency must offer substantially equal participation opportunities for those who have disabilities. The relevant passage from ADA is as follows:

> A recipient may offer to students with disabilities...athletic activities that are separate and different from those offered to nondisabled students only if...no qualified student with a disability is denied the opportunity to compete for teams or to participate in courses that are not separate or different.

EXAMPLES OF ACCESS DENIAL

Alberts (1984) reports that the American Medical Association (AMA) has established medical eligibility guidelines for student athletes. Disabilities listed for disqualification from athletic competition included uncontrolled diabetes, jaundice, active tuberculosis, enlarged liver, absence of a paired organ, and sensory impairments. Based on these AMA recommendations, many athletes with disabilities historically have been denied the right to participate in school athletic programs. According to the American Academy of Pediatrics' (AAP) policy statement regarding recommendations for participation in competitive sports, "The list has become increasingly obsolete due to changes in both safety equipment and in society's attitudes toward the rights of athletes to compete despite a medical condition that may increase the risk of straining and injury or aggravating a preexisting medical condition" (AAP, 1988, p. 165).

The AAP takes the position that determination of whether sports participation will be beneficial to the individual must be determined on an individual basis. The AAP asserts that this decision is best made by the parent and athlete in consultation with the physician. The AAP has evaluated sports according to degree of strenuousness and likelihood that there will be contact, and this evaluation is intended to help the physician, parent, and athlete arrive at an informed decision regarding desirability of competition in a given sport for a given athlete. The AAP asserts, as one might expect, that the physician's judgment should remain the final arbiter in determining appropriateness of participation.

Denial solely on the basis of having a disability is in strict violation of ADA. Each case must be judged on its unique characteristics. For example, in the federal district court decision of *Grube v. Bethlehem Area School District 550* (1982), the court ruled that a male high school senior who had only one kidney should be able to play on the interscholastic football team. The court decided that the plaintiff had provided enough medical and statistical evidence to indicate that participation would not be harmful to himself or others.

In yet another case (*Hollonbeck v. Board of Education of Rochelle Township*), Scott Hollonbeck asserted that his school district had denied him opportunity to participate in competitive sports solely because of his disability ("Disabled Athlete...", 1988). Scott, who was paralyzed when struck by a van in 1984, began participating in competitive wheelchair athletics as part of his rehabilitation following his injury. Subsequently, he began training regularly with his high school's track team. Eventually, Scott began racing as an "exhibition runner" during his high school's track meets. Scott, however, was not granted full status as a competitor by his high school, and Scott and his father charged the high school with discrimination. Scott's position was that the high school should be compelled to allow him full competitor status alongside able-bodied teammates or provide him opportunity to compete against other athletes who use wheelchairs. The court ruled that a multidisciplinary board composed of school officials that denied Scott the opportunity to compete was not qualified to assess Scott's fitness for competition. The court ruled that the Board of Education had denied Scott his civil rights, and that he was entitled to opportunity to compete as a full and equal member of the able-bodied team or be provided meaningful opportunity to compete against athletes who use wheelchairs.

Historically, persons with mental disabilities have often been denied access to sport and athletic programs simply because of their disability. In certain states, high school leagues or athletic associations have relied on academic eligibility requirements to exclude students with such disabilities from regular program participation. These exclusions are objectionable on philosophical grounds; they are now considered invalid on legal grounds as well. If, for example, a student with a mental disability posts the fastest 100-yard dash time for the school and if that person's disability does not otherwise negatively affect the quality of anyone's participation in the track program, then the person with mental disability is entitled to full participation in the regular track program.

WHEN SPECIAL SPORT PROGRAM PARTICIPATION IS INDICATED

Students with disabilities who, for legitimate reasons, cannot participate in regular sport programs but who can benefit from modified participation are entitled to such opportunities. In addition, ADA ensures that special programs must be of the same educational quality as regular programs. To match the quality of regular programming, special programs require acceptable budgets; equitable access to facilities, equipment, and supplies; and quality coaches whose professional preparation and remuneration are comparable to those of coaches for the regular programs. For many reasons (e.g., conflicting educational philosophies, inflation, categorical discriminations), opportunities for students with special needs to participate in special athletic programs will not always evolve voluntarily. As cited above, considerable debate and, in some cases, litigation have resulted when student athletes with disabilities have sought athletic experiences.

CONCERN FOR PARTICIPANT DIGNITY IN MODIFIED SPORT

The avowed purpose of virtually every sports program for people with disabilities is to provide participants meaningful opportunities to participate and compete. Modified sports programs are intended for persons who, because of disability, would probably be unable to participate meaningfully in programs intended primarily for people without disabilities.

The question of dignity arises when one considers the impact of modified sport on self-esteem of the participant. Of course, the intent is that such impact should always be positive, but is this always the case? William Rush is an adult (age 26) who has athetoid cerebral palsy. He cannot talk, walk, or use his hands. His level of involvement is severe. His insights are instructive to anyone who might organize and promote athletic experiences for persons who have disabilities (1983).

Rush recounts being signed up for a United Cerebral Palsy sports competition. He arrived to find that he had been signed up to compete in, among other events, swimming, motorized wheelchair race, and bean bag toss. He stated the following:

> I vigorously protested the bean bag toss because people have been trying to get me to throw a bean bag ever since age five. After years of prodding, I still couldn't throw a bean bag. My family and I had accepted it, so why couldn't the "professionals" accept it? (p. 96)

His point seems well taken on two grounds. First, he recounts a history of bean bag throwing, not much of which seems to have been particularly rewarding. He seems to be asking, when is enough, enough? Second, bean bag tossing in the minds of some, perhaps including Rush, is child's activity. Because adults typically do not throw bean bags for self-expression, those who do who happen to have disabilities may be reinforcing negative stereotypes of people who have disabilities.

While on the way to the competition, a friend and coparticipant in the meet remarked to Rush, "They have a knack for talking us into doing things that we don't really want to do, if you know what I mean" (p. 99). Rush recalls coming in last in a three-person race and being congratulated for coming in third. He states, "I knew that coming in third in a three-man race was coming in last. I resented the artificiality of the congratulations" (p. 98). He recalls feeling little pride in coming in first in a 25-meter swimming competition with a winning time of eight minutes. Further, he recalls a spectator near him relating to his aide "How could I cope with a child that different?" (p. 99) Finally, he recalls overhearing a meet volunteer referring to the volunteer experience as baby-sitting.

The above is not intended to diminish the validity of sport opportunities for people who have disabilities. It is intended simply to reveal some of the potential pitfalls associated with modified sports competition that might at least be avoided and perhaps even eliminated.

RISK SPORTS

With some notable exceptions, people with disabilities have tended not to participate in activity and sport experiences that one might characterize as risky. Risk, of course, is relative. For example, while both bicycling and skydiving might be characterized, in part, as risky, most people likely would be less reluctant to ride a bicycle than jump out of an airplane.

A number of activities that seem risky often are, in fact, less risky than they might appear. If the person perceives the activity as risky, that activity, in that person's mind, is indeed risky. Two dilemmas arise with perceived risk: (1) The person may unduly perceive risk in activities that are actually quite safe, or (2) the person may approach potentially risky activities with reckless abandon. In either case, the teacher or leader needs be available to ensure the person's safe, successful participation.

Participation in risk sports can be beneficial particularly to people who characteristically are not risk takers. Where risk is largely perceived, but the activity is really quite safe, the successful participant may grow in confidence and self-esteem. A number of organizations, though technically they do not promote activities traditionally called sport, provide participants opportunities to take measured risks. Such programs are termed *adventure-based* and often are offered in wilderness settings. Outward Bound and Wilderness Inquiry are but two examples of such programs.

Lathen, Stoll, and Hyder (1988) surveyed persons with physical disabilities to determine interest in risk sports participation. From a list of 19 possible risk activity experiences, the top five included rafting, bicycling, backpacking, winter camping, and canoeing. Desire to participate in specific risk activities appeared dependent on a combination of the following variables: (1) the individual's past experience with risk sports participation, (2) whether the individual's immediate family participated in risk sports, and (3) whether the individual was acquainted with other individuals with disabilities who participated in risk sports.

Risk sports participation seems positively associated with previous risk sport participation experience, and these experiences appear associated with whether family and friends (i.e., peers) likewise participate. The implication for practitioners is that participation in risk sports would be a viable option for persons with disabilities if opportunities could become available.

SELECTED EXAMPLES OF SPORT AND ATHLETIC OPPORTUNITIES

In recent years, those athletes whose disabilities do not affect their involvement in regular programs are already participating. Some persons with limited lower extremity function participate in gymnastics and skiing. Attesting to successful participation in the regular program are the place kicker in football who has an upper extremity amputation, the woman archer who, shooting from a wheelchair, qualified for and competed in the U.S. Olympic trials, and the wrestler who is blind. In the case of these individuals, ability rather than the disability was the criterion. It would be difficult to quantify the numbers of persons with asthma or diabetes whose disabilities, when managed, allow safe, successful participation in regular programs.

For some individuals, placement in regular sport programs is not appropriate. When modified programming is needed, programs must exist or be created to meet those needs.

Perhaps the program most visible to the general public is the **Special Olympics.** This program, supported by the Joseph P. Kennedy Jr. Foundation, exists so that people with mental disabilities can have opportunity to gain positive experiences through athletics. Although the Kennedy Foundation provides the Special Olympics impetus, participating individuals and their groups, schools, and agencies whose efforts and support make the Special Olympics work must be recognized as well. The Special Olympics program encourages athletes, when appropriate, to "graduate" to participation in regular programs.

A skier with an amputation has modified poles that function as outriggers. (Photograph courtesy of Courage Center, Golden Valley, MN)

Special Olympics competition opportunities also are available for athletes who, in addition to having a mental disability, also use a wheelchair (Eichstaedt & Lavay, 1992). When athletes with physical disabilities participate in Special Olympics events, they often participate in the same events and heats as athletes who do not use wheelchairs. In effect, athletes who are stand-up runners and athletes who are wheelchair runners often compete against each other in the same race. Special Olympics is not as concerned with the athlete's mode of ambulation as it is with each athlete having a reasonable opportunity to achieve success. If a wheelchair runner and a stand-up runner compete side by side, either athlete should have reasonable opportunity to come in first (Burkett, 1988).

The point needs to be clearly made, however, that many athletes who use wheelchairs do not compete in, nor are they eligible for, Special Olympics competition. The only time an athlete who uses a wheelchair in competition is eligible for Special Olympics competition is when the athlete also has a mental disability. Among the general public, there often is the misconception that all sports for persons with disabilities are termed (or offered through) Special Olympics. This simply is not true, and it is in part the responsibility of mainstream physical educators, adapted physical educators, and allied professionals to work vigorously to dispel this common misconception.

For many years, students with mental disabilities have had the opportunity to participate in Special Olympics programs, but people with other types of disabili-

A skier with a lower extremity amputation wearing prosthesis (left extremity) and skiing on two skis. (Photograph courtesy of Courage Center, Golden Valley, MN)

ties have not had similar opportunities. In response to these persons' needs, several modified sport programs and modified sport associations have emerged.

People who have cerebral palsy, who have had a stroke, or who have brain damage with motor dysfunction (either congenital or acquired at any age) are eligible for competition sanctioned by the United States Cerebral Palsy Athletic Association (USCPAA, 1989). Athletes with disabilities other than cerebral palsy may participate in USCPAA competitions provided the athlete also has a confirmed diagnosis of cerebral palsy. USCPAA has an 8-class classification system that groups athletes for competition according to functional ability. The goal of the classification system is to provide that people with reasonably like degrees of motor involvement compete against each other. Athletes are classified for competition according to answers to a series of questions relating to daily living skills and tests of motor involvement. But a few examples of sports offered by the USCPAA are archery, bicycling (and tricycling), boccie, horseback riding, power lifting, swimming, track and field/cross-country running, and wheelchair team handball. For further information about USCPAA, contact the organization's national office at 34518 Warren Road, Suite 264, Westland, MI 48185.

The United States Amputee Athletic Association (USAAA), founded in 1981, offers athletic competition for people whose amputations are congenital or acquired. Athletes are classified for competition according to a 9-level classification system based on amputation site (Poretta, 1990). Examples of USAAA sports include track and field, weight lifting, archery, cycling, basketball, volleyball, and swimming. Athletes in USAAA competition participate with or without prostheses depending on amputation sites. Athletes with double above the knee (A/K) amputations or combined upper and lower extremity amputations compete without prostheses. Various national wheelchair sports associations permit athletes with amputations to compete in their sanctioned events. For example, the National Wheelchair Athletic Association (NWAA) permits athletes with amputations to compete in swimming. Similar accommodations have been made by the National Wheelchair Basketball Association and the National Wheelchair Tennis Association.

The United States Les Autres Sports Association (USLASA) offers competitive sports for persons with disabilities who are not being accommodated at all or accommodated fully by other sports organizations. *Les Autres* in French means "the others." *Les Autres* conditions include muscular dystrophy, multiple sclerosis, osteogenesis imperfecta, and Guillain-Barre syndrome. Like other sports organizations, USLASA has its own classification system. USLASA athletes participate in wheelchairs and standing up. Athletes who use electric wheelchairs compete against other athletes who use electric wheelchairs. USLASA offers competitions in weight lifting, track and field, swimming, volleyball, and basketball.

In Minnesota, there is the **Minnesota Association for Adapted Athletics.** This association was organized to provide modified competitive athletic experiences for students with physical disabilities. Participants, who are in the 7th through 12th grades, may be ambulatory or in wheelchairs. Disabilities range from muscular dystrophy, cerebral palsy, and congenital abnormalities to spina bifida and quadriplegia. Participation is coeducational and may merit a school athletic letter. Opportunities are offered in adapted floor hockey, soccer, whiffleball, and other seasonal sports. Among MAAA's major goals is that the organization eventually become absorbed by the state agency that administers public and private school interscholastic athletic competition. Thus far, this goal has not been achieved. At this time the only athletes with disabilities who participate in sports sanctioned by the Minnesota State High School League are those who can safely and successfully participate in regular programs. Athletes with disabilities whose disabilities preclude meaningful participation on regular athletic teams, at this time, are not being embraced by the state high school league. Similar sanctions prevail throughout the nation and would seem to raise significant legal issues concerning equal protection under the law and

An athlete using a wheelchair to participate in Minnesota Association for Adapted Athletics floor hockey contest. (Photograph courtesy of Courage Center, Golden Valley, MN)

discrimination solely on the basis of disability. MAAA has more than a 10-year history of providing modified sports programs and communicating with the state high school league. For more information about this organization and competitive activities offered, contact the Minnesota Association for Adapted Athletics, % Courage Center, 3915 Golden Valley Road, Golden Valley, MN 55422.

Many adapted sport and athletic opportunities are sponsored by organizations outside the school setting. The **United States Association for Blind Athletes** (USABA) sponsors competitions at the local and national level. At present, no age limits are specified for participation in any USABA-sponsored sport. USABA sports include goalball, swimming, wrestling, gymnastics for women, Judo, power lifting, tandem cycling, and track and field. Winter sports include skiing (nordic and alpine) and speed skating. Recently, USABA has introduced new demonstration sports including basketball, archery, and race walking. To be eligible for USABA competition, an individual must have no more than 20/200 visual acuity in the better eye after

Goalball, one of the sports sanctioned by the U.S. Association for Blind Athletes.
(Photograph courtesy of Courage Center, Golden Valley, MN)

correction, or a visual field arc in the better eye, after correction, of no more than 20 degrees, or both. Participants are classified for competition by degree of visual impairment.

Another sport organization for persons who are visually impaired or blind is the **National Beep Baseball Association** (NBBA). Beep baseball uses an official 16-in. softball that contains a high-pitched audible beeping device. After batting a fair ball pitched by a sighted player, the participant runs to a cone-shaped base that buzzes when the umpire determines that the ball is fair. The batter must arrive at the base before a defensive player fields the batted ball. If the batter prevails, a run is scored for his team. If the ball is cleanly fielded before the batter touches base, the batter is out. Approximately 25 teams are active in national level NBBA competition in the United States and Canada. Outside NBBA auspices, approximately 100 teams play recreationally and competitively in the United States, Canada, and other countries.

The **National Wheelchair Basketball Association** (NWBA) has promoted and sponsored wheelchair basketball since shortly after World War II. Impetus for formation of the organization came after World War II when veterans, who returned from the war with spinal cord injuries, acted on their desires to play the game they enjoyed before the war. Consequently, the NWBA was formed in the late 1940s. It

National championship women's wheelchair basketball sanctioned by the National Wheelchair Basketball Association. (Photograph courtesy of Courage Center, Golden Valley, MN)

is the oldest wheelchair sports organization in the United States. Today, wheelchair basketball truly is an international sport; international wheelchair basketball tournaments typically include teams from the United States, Israel, Argentina, Great Britain, Germany, Canada, Holland, Sweden, and France. In 1976, The NWBA legislated to admit women to the heretofore all-male organization. Both men's and women's teams compete regularly at the local through international levels.

The NWBA has a three-class classification system based upon degree of disability. The classification process assigns each player a number, 1–3. One represents a relatively greater degree of disability. Three represents a relatively lesser degree of disability. To ensure that participants with relatively greater disability have opportunity to play, NWBA allows no more than 12 points on the floor during play.

Some 10 years after inception of the NWBA, the **National Wheelchair Athletic Association** (NWAA) was formed. The NWAA also has a long and extensive history of promoting competition among athletes who use wheelchairs. Events sanctioned by the NWAA are staged regionally throughout the country. Regional events provide immediate participation opportunities and, in addition, opportunity to qualify for national competition in track and field, swimming, table tennis, weight lifting, and archery. Each June national competitions are held in which participants vie for national honors and for berths on the U.S. Wheelchair Athletic Team, which competes in the International Stoke-Mandeville Games. These games are staged annually in England except during Olympic years, when the games are traditionally held in the host country of the Olympics. These games are called the Paralympics. The NWAA classification system, as with other sports organizations' classification systems, is administered to all participants to ensure that athletes with comparable disabilities (not necessarily comparable athletic talent) compete against each other.

Many participants in NWAA-sanctioned events do not use wheelchairs for daily ambulation. These are persons who cannot participate in a meaningful manner in regular sports events because of a permanent physical disability of the lower extremities. The NWAA has implemented a classification system based on spinal cord injury site that enables participants to compete on an equitable basis against athletes with a similar degree of disability. The classification system has undergone modifications periodically that have resulted in an increase in the number of competitive classes. Assignment to a competitive class requires a specially certified judgment by a physical therapist or physician. For more information about the NWAA, contact the organization at 3595 E. Fountain Blvd., Suite L-1, Colorado Springs, CO 80910.

There are also national wheelchair associations for bowling, tennis, and softball. For more information about sport and athletic opportunities for disabled wheelchair athletes, contact the national office of the Paralyzed Veterans of America, 4330 East West Highway, Suite 300, Washington, DC 20014.

Space does not permit mention of all the associations, activities, and sport opportunities available to athletes with disabilities. In this chapter, we have merely touched on available opportunities.

A FINAL WORD ABOUT COMPETITION

The thought of athletic competition for people with disabilities, particularly those whose disabilities are substantial, causes mixed emotions. We perceive competition as being neither good nor bad. As with any competitive experience, the quality of the experience is no better than the participant's readiness for it and the quality of the leadership that provides the experience with direction.

Any individual's athletic endeavor must be judged by the quality of the effort. A second, third, or last place finisher who put forth great effort has achieved more than a first place winner who did not try his or her hardest. Winning is certainly one of many desirable outcomes of any competitive activity, but it is not the only outcome. The label "winner" should not necessarily be reserved only for those who take first place. Any effort to organize competitive experiences, particularly within the educational setting, should ensure that all second-place winners are not perceived as losers.

When the need to win is viewed in proper perspective, many desirable outcomes are achievable. Competition often means travel, staying overnight, self-reliance, self-discipline, expanded social contacts, and an opportunity to demonstrate ability and excellence to people who are important in the participant's life.

Finally, each athletic opportunity needs to be evaluated on its own merits. The following questions will assist in evaluating such programs:

1. Will the program result in the most good for the greatest number?
2. Does the emphasis on athletics and competition detract from the fulfillment of other, equally important needs?
3. How is winning placed as a priority in evaluating program and individual success?
4. Is there a classification system to equalize opportunities for success? Is the system sensitive to each participant's circumstances?
5. With reference to long-range outcomes, are the skills that receive primary emphasis ones that will have lifelong value?
6. Does the desire to excel in the activities of an athletic organization influence unnecessarily the emphasis of the recipient's physical education program?
7. Are opportunities for people with disabilities to participate in sport programs substantially equal to those available to persons without disabilities?

SUMMARY

Opportunity in sport is not a new phenomenon for people with disabilities. Among the early opportunities were those developed in response to the activity interests of veterans who became paralyzed in World War II. Only recently, however, have such opportunities become available to people with disabilities under direct school sponsorship. Such opportunities are likely to increase in response to growing public awareness and assertiveness of people with disabilities. Consensus is growing that the school or agency that provides sport programs for the able-bodied but not for students with disabilities is in direct violation of ADA (federal civil rights legislation protecting people with disabilities from arbitrary discrimination).

Participation guidelines can help the educator to determine when a student with a disability might safely and successfully participate in the regular sport program. Guidelines should also be developed that suggest ways of modifying selected activities so the athlete's participation neither jeopardizes her/his own nor anyone else's safety nor compromises the activity's integrity for participants.

Many specific organizations and athletic associations sponsor and promote sport opportunities for people with disabilities. For individuals with spinal cord injury or cerebral palsy, classification systems foster equitable competition among athletes with similar degrees of disability.

A relatively recent trend is the emergence of state high school adapted athletic associations. This trend is emerging in response to growing need for formal adapted sports participation opportunities under school sponsorship. At present, these associations are often administered apart from the state high school associations or leagues that sponsor athletic activities for nondisabled students. In all probability, many state-adapted athletic associations eventually will become integral to the state associations that govern athletics for the able-bodied. This absorption process will occur largely owing to recognition that state high school athletic associations, which provide for the able-bodied student, should not deny students who have disabilities an opportunity to benefit educationally from athletic experiences.

REFERENCES

Alberts, C. L. (1984). Section 504 of the rehabilitation act and the right to participate in school athletic programs. *Educational Considerations, 11*(1), 23–26.

American Academy of Pediatrics. (1988). Recommendations for participation in competitive sports. *Physician and Sports Medicine, 16,* 165–167.

Anderson, N. E. (1986). An athlete's reflection. *Palaestra, 2*(2), 25–26.

Burkett, L. N. (1988). The physically disabled athlete in Special Olympics. *Palaestra,* ISSOG, 23–24.

——Disabled athlete barred from competing wins victory in New York federal court. (1988, August 25). *Occupational Therapy Week,* pp. 5–6.

Eichstaedt, C. B., and Lavay, B. H. (1992). *Movement activities for individuals with mental retardation.* Champaign, IL: Human Kinetics.

Grube v. Bethlehem Area School District 550. Federal Supplement 418 (D. Penn. 1982).

Lathan, C. W., Stoll, S. K., and Hyder, M. (1988). Do physically disabled persons desire participation on risk sports? *Palaestra, 4,* 19–23.

Poretta. D. L. (1990). In J. P. Winnick (Ed.), *Adapted physical education and sport,* Champaign, IL: Human Kinetics.

Rush, W. L. (1983, Spring). Dignity challenged by sports meets. *Accent on Living,* pp. 96–100.

USCPAA. (1989). *Classification and sports rules manual.* Westland, MI: USCPAA.

GLOSSARY

Absence seizure Also called petit ("petty") mal. It is characterized by a blank stare, beginning and ending abruptly, lasting only a few seconds. These seizures occur most commonly between the ages of 4 and 12. Approximately one third to one half of these children will also have tonic-clonic grand mal seizures.

Acuity Sharpness or clarity as related to seeing, hearing, or touching.

Acute Disease or condition having a quick onset and a short duration.

Adapted physical education Modification of traditional physical education activities to allow students with disabling conditions or low levels of physical or motor ability to participate safely, successfully, and with satisfaction.

Adaptive behavior The degree to which individuals meet standards of personal independence and social responsibility expected of their chronological age and cultural group.

Adventitious (acquired) deafness Severe reduction in hearing as a result of illness or trauma after one is born with normal hearing.

Age appropriate The development of learning activities that corresponds with the individual's chronological age.

Allergen A substance that causes an allergic reaction (same as *antigen*).

Allergic rhinitis Inflammation of the membrane of the nose caused by allergens and resulting in the common condition of hay fever.

Allergy Hypersensitivity to substances that are inhaled, ingested, injected, or absorbed.

Amblyopia A reduction in vision that is not correctable by glasses or contact lenses and that is not caused by obvious structural or pathological eye defects.

Amelia Absence of a limb or limbs at birth.

Amniocentesis Process of removing amniotic fluid from the pregnant woman for the purpose of genetic analysis. The technique is used to detect birth defects.

Anemia Condition in which the red blood cells do not have enough hemoglobin, thus creating a loss of energy and decreased ability to sustain effort.

Annual goals General statements of student outcomes projected over the school year.

Anorexia nervosa An obsession with thinness, obtained from starving to become extremely thin. The individual, usually female, eats very little and continues to lose weight in spite of being dangerously underweight.

Anoxia Insufficient amount of oxygen often resulting in brain damage.

Antigen A substance that produces an allergic or asthmatic reaction (same as *allergen*).

Aphasia Difficulty in using or comprehending spoken language.

Apraxia Difficulty or inability to perform skills that require purposeful motor or movement tasks.

Arthritis Inflammation of and pain in the joints.

Arthrogryposis A congenital condition characterized by rigid and curved joints; joints fixed in flexed position.

Asthma A condition caused by violent contraction of the bronchial tubes because of allergies, exercise, or other irritations and resulting in wheezing, coughing, and breathing difficulties.

Astigmatism   A curvature defect of the eye that impedes the focusing of rays from a luminous point at a single point on the retina but instead spreads the rays out as a line.

Asymmetrical tonic neck reflex (ATNR)   An infant reflex, which occurs when the head is turned, and causes extension of the arm on the face side and flexion of the arm on the skull side (called "fencer thrust").

Ataxia   Clinical term for the type of cerebral palsy characterized by defective muscular coordination, often involving balance difficulties that result from damage to the cerebellum, pons, or medulla.

Athetosis (dyskinesia)   Clinical term for the type of cerebral palsy characterized by slow, wormlike movements, and involving a continual change of position of the fingers, toes, hands, arms, and head.

Atlantoaxial instability (AAI)   Orthopedic condition found in approximately 12% to 22% of individuals with Down syndrome. It is characterized by a misalignment of the 1st and 2nd cervical vertebrae, which could cause permanent damage to the spinal cord during hyperflexion or hyperextension of the head and neck.

Atonia   Lack of muscle control often found in individuals with cerebral palsy and Down syndrome ("floppy baby" syndrome).

Attention deficit hyperactivity disorder   Commonly associated with the old term *hyperactivity*. The American Psychiatric Association does not refer to children as "hyperactive" without also attaching the label "attention deficit." Also, children are found to possess major problems involving inattention, hyperactivity, and impulsivity.

Audiologist   A specialist who measures hearing ability.

Aura   A warning sensation (e.g., vertigo, noises, flashes of light, burning, or numbing) that precedes a convulsive seizure.

Autism   A disorder usually diagnosed between 2 and 4 years of age and generally characterized by extreme withdrawal, language impairment, refusal to speak, obsessive demand to keep the environment stable, and monotonous repetition of motor actions.

Behavioral objectives   Statements of conditions, actions, and criteria that have not been mastered by the student. These objectives are directly related to long-term or annual goals.

Behavior modification   A systematic approach using methods designed to alter observable behaviors, including increasing, decreasing, extending, restricting, and maintaining behaviors.

Bilateral   Pertaining to or affecting both sides of the body.

Binocular   Using both eyes to see an object, thus fusing two images into one.

Blind   Cannot see a bright light from 3 ft away.

Blindness   Legal definition: acuity of 20/200 or less in the better eye with corrective lens, or restriction of the width of the visual field to an angle no greater than 20 degrees.

Body image   Ideas and feelings that individuals have about their bodies and the relationship of their body parts.

Body righting   Primitive infant reflex that enables segmental rotation of the trunk and hips when the head is turned.

Borderline mentally retarded   Those individuals who possess an IQ of 70 to 85. They are not considered legally handicapped.

Bronchospasm   Spasmodic contraction of smooth muscle surrounding the bronchial tubes caused by allergic reaction; directly related to an asthmatic attack.

Bulimia An obsession with thinness, obtained from vomiting and using laxatives to remove food from the body before it is digested. Often called binge-and-purge behavior.

Cataract A condition in which the normally clear eye becomes cloudy or opaque.

Catheter A tube inserted in the bladder through the urethra to allow urine to drain from the body.

Central deafness An abnormality of the central nervous system that prevents one from hearing, although the hearing apparatus is functionally normal.

Cephalocaudal development Gross motor development beginning with the head and progressing down the axial skeleton to the feet.

Cerebral palsy A condition characterized by lack of control of voluntary body movement and caused by damage to the brain. The condition is nonprogressive and occurs in infancy and childhood.

Chromosomes Small rod-shaped or v-shaped bodies that appear in the nucleus of a cell during cell division and contain the genes, or hereditary factors, of the cell. Humans normally have 46 chromosomes comprised of 22 pairs of autosomes and 2 sex chromosomes. A common chromosome abnormality is Down syndrome.

Chronic A condition having gradual onset and long duration.

Cochlea A spiral tube, resembling a snail shell, located in the inner ear. It transmits sounds to the cochlear nerve.

Colostomy A surgical opening in the intestine that allows fecal matter to pass into an external collection bag.

Conductive hearing loss Loss of function of the organs of the ear to transmit sound to the inner ear. Most conditions are greatly improved by use of a hearing aid.

Congenital Present at birth.

Contracture Abnormal shortening of a muscle owing to extreme lack of use or paralysis; commonly results from spastic cerebral palsy, cerebral vascular accident (stroke), or spinal cord injury (paraplegia).

Contraindication Any undesirable or improper treatment (e.g., strengthening exercises for flexor muscles of involved limbs of a child with spastic cerebral palsy is contraindicated).

Coxa plana A degeneration of the head of the femur (commonly called Legg-Calve-Perthes disease).

Criterion-referenced test Measures a student's performance compared with a preestablished, behaviorally stated criterion. These tests are particularly useful in evaluating special populations to which available norms are not applicable.

Cultural-familial retardation A general classification of mental retardation with no biological brain damage, presumably associated with family history of borderline retardation or mild retardation and a home environment that is either depriving or inconsistent with the general culture. It is believed to be the major cause of most individuals with mild mental retardation.

Cystic fibrosis An inherited condition that is generally fatal in childhood; characterized by overproduction of mucus, which causes progressive lung damage, and by impaired absorption of fat and protein. Youngsters become less able to exercise and have frequent respiratory symptoms such as coughing and wheezing.

Cytomegalovirus An infection transmitted to the fetus while the mother is pregnant, causing a devastating generalized infection, often including encephalitis. Subsequent damage to the developing brain often causes severe mental retardation.

Deaf   No measurable hearing (90 dB loss).

Developmental approach   Matching instruction to ability, as measured by developmental milestones.

Developmental age   An individual's approximate age in terms of cognitive and/or motor development and maturation, regardless of chronological age.

Developmental milestones   Progressive activities that a child is expected to perform such as sitting, crawling, creeping, standing, walking, running, jumping, skipping, throwing, and catching.

Developmental period   The time when structural growth begins and ends, from conception to approximately 18 to 20 years.

Diabetes mellitus   A disorder of the pancreas characterized by inadequate production of insulin, which leads to high levels of sugar in the blood. Two basic types of diabetes mellitus are identified: juvenile onset (type I) and mature onset (type II).

Diplopia   Double vision, or the seeing of two images, when the eyes are focused on one object.

Directionality   Feeling or perception of direction in space.

Direct service   Instructional opportunities provided for students with disabling conditions by certified teachers. Physical education is a direct service. Recreation and physical or occupational therapy are not direct services.

Discrimination   The intellectual ability to determine variations in sensory stimuli.

Disinhibition   A problem of staying on task, with random shifts in paying attention and daydreaming.

Distractibility   Objects of situations that cause a student to lose concentration. Some common distractions are extraneous noises, bright colors, toys or equipment other than those the student is working with, other students or instructors, and especially, unfamiliar adults.

Dorsiflexion   Bending the foot upward.

Down syndrome   A condition resulting from a chromosomal abnormality. Characteristics commonly include mental retardation (IQ between 40 and 55); abnormal shortness of hands, feet, trunk, arms, and legs; hyperflexibility; and frequently, congenital heart defects, hearing impairments, and visual disabilities.

Duchenne muscular dystrophy   A condition that destroys voluntary muscle fiber, which is replaced by fat and connective tissue. Inherited by males, the condition usually causes death before age 25. Also called pseudohypertrophic muscular dystrophy.

Ductus arteriosus   A fetal artery between the aorta and the pulmonary artery. When failing to close, it results in an abnormal mixing of oxygenated and unoxygenated blood in the newborn. (A congential heart defect: patent ductus arterious)

Dwarfism   A hereditary, congenital disturbance of growth and maturation, which causes inadequate bone formation and results in abnormally shortened limbs, normal trunk, small face, and lordosis. (Now called skeletal dysplasia)

Dyskinesia   *See* Athetosis.

Dyslexia   Neurological dysfunction usually causing a serious reading problem.

Dysrhythmia   A lack of ability to achieve and maintain rhythmic performance.

Educable mentally retarded (EMR)   *See* Mildly mentally retarded.

Effusion   Filling of a body part with fluids.

Electrocardiograph   An instrument used to record heart rates; also called ECG and EKG.

Encephalitis   An acute viral infection causing high body temperatures and severe inflammation of the brain. A common cause of mental retardation, cerebral palsy, and convulsive disorders.

Epilepsy   An involuntary increase in electrical impulses in the brain, which results in seizures; caused by damage to the brain or by inherited factors. Epilepsy is now more appropriately called *seizure disorder* or *convulsive disorder*.

Equilibrium reactions   The innate ability to maintain an upright position when the center of gravity is moved suddenly out of its base of support.

Etiology   The study or understanding of the cause of a disease or condition.

Extinction   A behavior management technique involving removal of reinforcers that previously followed the behavior. The technique may also involve removal of the individual from the activity or area.

Extrinsic   Coming from the outside.

Factors   Chemical agents that cause blood to coagulate. Factor VIII or IX is usually missing in a male who has hemophilia.

Fading   The process of gradually removing assistance when helping a student perform a task or learn a skill.

Feedback   Verbal, gesture, and/or physical consequences given immediately after the individual responds to a cue.

Fetal alcohol syndrome   Defects to the developing fetus due to excessive alcohol consumption during pregnancy causing mental retardation, facial anomalies, or heart defects in the child.

Flaccid paralysis   Condition characterized by extreme weakness or absence of muscle tone.

Fragile X syndrome (Bell-Martin syndrome)   A chromosome abnormality that accounts for up to 10% of all cases of mental retardation.

Galactosemia   An abnormal elevation of the concentration of the carbohydrate galactose in the blood. The condition leads to death in infancy or mental retardation.

Generalized tonic-clonic seizures   *See* Grand mal.

Genu recurvatum   Hyperextension of the knee, causing improper posture.

Genu valgum   Knock-knee.

Genu varum   Bowleg.

Glaucoma   An increase of fluid pressure inside the eyeball, causing decreased vision and potential blindness.

Goal   An annual or long-term observable behavior (e.g., to improve explosive leg power to the 30th percentile).

Goal ball   A highly competitive game played by individuals who are blind using a sound-emitting, air-filled ball.

Grand mal   A form of convulsive (tonic-clonic) seizure that includes a tonic phase (stiffening), a clonic phase (violent, whole body contractions), and a recovery phase (postictal). The individual remembers or feels nothing during the seizure.

Heart murmur   Sound made by backward flow of blood through defective heart valves.

Hemiplegia   Paralysis of one side of the body as occurs in a cerebral vascular accident (stroke), or affecting one side of the body as in cerebral palsy.

Hemophilia   Inherited condition affecting males only and characterized by the absence of blood coagulation factor VIII or IX, thus causing the blood not to coagulate.

Hydrocephalus   A condition that develops when spinal fluid accumulates in cerebral ventricles. If not immediately and continuously drained (i.e., shunted), fluid accumulation can produce enlargement of the infant's skull and possible brain damage.

Hyperactivity   A condition in children in which they always seem to be in motion. Sitting or standing still for any length of time is difficult or impossible. Such children routinely interfere with other children. Hyperactivity is a type of attention deficit disorder.

Hyperglycemia   Abnormally high level of blood sugar, commonly associated with diabetes mellitus and indicating a need for insulin.

Hyperopia   Farsightedness, usually correctable with glasses or contact lenses.

Hyperreactivity   Allergic response to an external or internal allergen.

Hypertrophy   Increased size or enlargement of a body part or organ.

Hyperventilation   Abnormally prolonged, rapid, and deep breathing, frequently used as a test procedure in the medical diagnosis of absence petit mal seizures.

Hypotonia   Reduced muscle tone often found in individuals with Down syndrome. Infants born with this condition are commonly termed "floppy babies."

Hypoxia   Insufficient amount of oxygen, also called anoxia.

Idiopathic   Denoting a disease or condition of unknown cause.

Individualized educational program (IEP)   A program specially designed to meet the educational needs (including physical and motor needs) of a specific child.

Individualized family service plan (IFSP)   A written plan of instruction based on a multidisciplinary assessment of each infant's and toddler's needs; includes an evaluation of family needs. This plan is mandatory for infants and toddlers as described in P.L. 101-476, Individuals with Disabilities Education Act of 1990.

Innate response system   Natural, primitive reflexes that the human infant possesses at or shortly after birth.

Insulin   Hormone produced in the beta cells of the islets of Langerhans in the pancreas. Insulin allows glucose to pass through cell membranes. Without insulin, the cells do not receive appropriate amounts of glucose and cease to function.

Intrinsic   Coming from inside the body.

Isometric exercise   Muscle contraction without movement of body parts, often used in rehabilitation when movement is not indicated but muscle strength is desired. Also called muscle setting.

Isotonic exercise   Muscle contraction with body part movement through a range of motion.

Kinesiotherapist (RKT)   In cooperation with a physician, a kinesiotherapist applies principles, tools, techniques, and psychology of medically oriented rehabilitation to assist individuals with various physical and mental conditions to accomplish prescribed treatment objectives.

Kinesthesis   Awareness of body position in space as indicated by proprioceptors found in muscles, joints, and tendons.

Kyphosis   Increased thoracic curve (also called humpback).

Laterality   An internal awareness of both sides of the body.

Least restrictive environment   The best possible learning environment for an individual with disabling conditions, preferably an environment shared with people who are nondisabled.

Legg-Calve-Perthes disease   *See* Coxa plana.

Lordosis   An increase in the forward curvature of the lumbar region of the spine (also called swayback), and often causing lower back pain.

Mainstreaming   Placement of students with disabling conditions in traditional classes with students who are nondisabled.

Manual communication   A technique, including fingerspelling and sign language, used by individuals who are hearing impaired.

Meningitis (bacterial)   A highly contagious disease affecting the covering of the brain and spinal cord (meninges), and often leading to permanent damage.

Meningocele   A protrusion of the covering of the spinal cord (i.e., meninges) through an abnormal opening in the vertebra. The spinal cord does not protrude outward, and physical impairment is slight.

Mental age   Level of mental development measured by standardized IQ tests.

Mental retardation   Significantly below average general intellectual functioning (less than 70 IQ) existing concurrently with deficits in adaptive behavior, all manifested during the developmental period.

Mildly mentally retarded (EMR)   Individuals with IQ between 50 and 70 who also exhibit maladaptive behavior. Includes approximately 60 percent of all individuals with mental retardation.

Mobility training   Specialized approach to teaching travel techniques to individuals who are blind. Use of the long cane is often emphasized.

Modeling   Demonstration of a task, skill, or desirable behavior for the benefit of another student.

Moderately mentally retarded (TMR)   IQ between 35 and 50. Approximately 29 percent of all individuals with mental retardation are in this category. About 40 percent of individuals with Down syndrome are in this classification. Also called trainable mentally retarded (TMR).

Mononucleosis   An acute infectious disease caused in 90% of cases by the Epstein-Barr virus, and characterized by fever, malaise, sore throat, and liver dysfunction. Enlargement of the spleen can occur.

Monoplegia   Neurological involvement of one limb, common in cerebral palsy.

Moro reflex   Protective opening and closing of an infant's arms and legs when a loud noise is heard. Also called "startle reflex."

Mosaicism   A rare type of Down syndrome (1% to 2%) in which an abnormal separation of chromosome 21 occurs after conception. All future divisions of the affected cells result in cells with an extra chromosome. The extent to which the individual has the features of Down syndrome depends on the percentage of body cells with the extra 21st chromosome.

Muscle setting   Tensing of a muscle without movement of body parts. Often used when a limb is isolated in a plaster cast.

Muscle testing   A subjective technique used by physical therapists to evaluate muscle strength and performance.

Muscular dystrophy   An inherited disease characterized by loss of muscle fiber. The most common and destructive type is Duchenne, or pseudohypertrophic muscular dystrophy. (*See also* Duchenne muscular dystrophy.)

Myelomeningocele   The most serious type of spina bifida in which the spinal cord protrudes into a sac on the surface of the back, thus causing paralysis or lower extremity impairment. Bowel and bladder control are affected.

Myopia   Nearsightedness.

Neonatal   Time period between birth and 1 month.

Neurosis   A psychological disorder that can include anxiety, obsessions, phobias, or hysteria.

Normalization   Providing opportunities for individuals with disabling conditions to be involved directly with nondisabled peers; can include activities of everyday life that are consistent with the norms and patterns of mainstream society.

Norm-referenced test   The measurement of an individual's performance in relation to the performance of a representative peer group composed of individuals with specifically defined characteristics such as age, gender, and/or specific disability.

Nystagmus   Uncontrollable rhythmic jerking of the eyeballs when turned sharply sideways.

Obesity   An increase in body weight beyond the limitation of skeletal and physical requirement; a result of an excessive accumulation of adipose tissue (fat) in the body.

Orthopedics   Branch of surgery including the practice of straightening deformed or injured body parts by use of orthotic or exoskeletal devices (braces).

Otitis media   Chronic inflammation of the middle ear, which can lead to balance or coordination problems.

Parachute reflex   A small child's automatic protective extension of the arms when he falls suddenly forward or to the side. This reflex is often delayed in children with cerebral palsy.

Paraplegia   Paralysis or involvement of the legs and lower trunk caused by brain damage or spinal cord injury, commonly in the lumbar region.

Perception   A process involving the reception of sensory input and converting the information in the brain to data for use or memory storage.

Perseveration   An undesirable behavior characterized by persistent repetition of a meaningless, irrelevant, or inappropriate word, phrase, or movement.

Petit (pet tee) mal   A mild form of seizure characterized by sudden, brief blackouts of consciousness (hardly more than a few seconds long) followed by immediate recovery. Also called absence seizures, this type of seizure occurs mostly in childhood and adolescence.

Phenylketonuria (PKU)   A genetic condition characterized by an inability to metabolize phenylalanine, an amino acid that is essential for optimal growth in infants. If untreated, it results in severe brain damage and mental retardation.

Phobia   Any persistent abnormal dread or fear.

Polyarticular rheumatoid arthritis   An arthritic development affecting all or most of the body joints.

Positive reinforcer   A reward given when appropriate behavior is observed.

Positive supporting reaction   Neonatal reflex that causes the legs to extend and the feet to point downward when the young child is bounced on the feet.

Premature   Infants delivered before 37 weeks, and/or weighing 2,500 grams ($5\frac{1}{2}$ pounds) or less.

Profoundly mentally retarded   IQ between 1 and 20. Includes approximately 4% of all individuals with mental retardation. Of that 4%, most have other serious disabling conditions, including seizures.

Prognosis   Prediction of the probable outcome of a disease or condition.

Prompt   A cue or stimulus, usually in the form of physical guidance, that occasions a response of a proper behavior.

Prosthesis   An artificial appliance or limb.

Protective extensor thrust   *See* Parachute reflex.

Pseudohypertrophy   An increase in size of a body part without true muscle hypertrophy. Commonly observed in the calf muscles of a boy with Duchenne muscular dystrophy.

Psychogenic deafness   No sound is heard, although the hearing organs are normal; often the result of an emotional response.

Psychomotor seizures   A seizure classification characterized by inappropriate actions, irrelevant speech, and random ambulation.

Public Law 89-313 Amended Title I of Elementary and Secondary Education Act (1965)   Federal law providing grants for state-supported schools for students with disabilities.

Public Law 90-538 Handicapped Children's Early Education Assistance Act (1968)   Federal law establishing experimental preschool programs as demonstration projects of children with disabilities.

Public Law 93-112 Amendments to Vocational Rehabilitation Act (1973)   Federal law emphasizing provisions for most severely disabled individuals, including *Section 504*—the Bill of Rights for individuals with disabilities. This law ensured accessibility to public buildings and programs.

Public Law 94-142 Education of the Handicapped Act (EHA) (1975)   Federal law that increased federal commitment to providing free and appropriate education for all students with disabilities (ages 3–21) in least restrictive environments. The law mandated that all needed supplementary aids and services be provided, the rights of children with disabilities and their parents be protected, and states and localities provide effective education for children with disabilities. Included were protections of due process procedures for parents and children, the individualized educational program (IEP) and evaluation, hearing rights, and appeal. Mandatory physical education is found in this law.

Public Law 98-199 Amendments to Education of the Handicapped Act (1983)   Federal law extending discretionary grants, established new programs for transition of teenagers into adult life, and providing financial incentives to expand services for infants and toddlers from birth to 3 years of age.

Public Law 99-457 Amendments to Education of the Handicapped Act (1986)   Federal law requiring that children with disabilities, ages 3 to 5, be served, even in states that do not provide public education for children that young. *Part H* of the law authorized funds to states to develop statewide interagency programs of early intervention services for infants and toddlers with disabilities and their families.

Public Law 101-476 Individuals With Disabilities Education Act (IDEA) (1990)   Federal law that changed the name of P.L. 94-142 and replaced the word *handicapped* with *disabled*. The *Infants and Toddlers with Disabilities Program*, the *Preschool Program* that originated as part of P.L. 99-457, and all other parts of the original P.L. 94-142 are now incorporated into P.L. 101-476.

Quadriplegia   Paralysis or involvement of both arms and legs.

Reinforcement   Following a desired behavior, the instructor responds positively so the behavior is likely to recur.

Related services   Special services that are needed to fulfill the educational, physical, emotional, or social needs of students with disabilities. Physical and occupational therapy are examples of related services.

Retardation   *See* Mental retardation.

Rheumatoid arthritis   A condition characterized by inflammation of the joints, usually accompanied by deformity of the hands and fingers.

Rhinitis   The common cold, including inflammation of the nasal passages and mucous membranes.

Righting reflexes   Automatic or involuntary reactions of an infant or small child to regain original position when suddenly moved or pushed.

Rigidity   Classification of cerebral palsy involving extreme difficulty when attempting limb movement.

Rubella (German measles)   In children, a mild viral infection lasting 3 to 4 days. In pregnant women during the first trimester, the infection is serious and produces fetal abnormalities including defects of the heart, eyes, brain, bone, and ears.

Schizophrenia   Abnormal personality accompanied by less than adequate contact with reality.

Scoliosis   Lateral deviation of the spine in the shape of an "S," reverse "S," "C," or reverse "C." Deviation can be caused either by functional or structural problems. Functional deviations can be corrected by physician prescribed programs implemented by a physical educator.

Section 504   *See* Public Law 93-112 Vocational Rehabilitation Act of 1973.

Sensory input   All information received by the body through the senses, that is, seeing, hearing, kinesthesis, and vestibular and tactual input.

Sensory-motor response   A combination of sensory input, brain integration and interpretation, and motor output. Feedback completes the total perceptual-motor act.

Severely mentally retarded   IQ between 20 and 35. Includes approximately 7% of all individuals with mental retardation. These individuals are considered dependent; they function at a mental age of 3 to 5 years.

Shaping   Reinforcement of small progressive steps that lead to a desired learner behavior.

Short-term instructional objectives   Statements of observable criteria used to meet annual or long-term goals, always incorporated in an individualized educational program (IEP).

Sickle-cell anemia   A severe inherited form of anemia, occurring mainly among the black race and characterized by fragile, sickle-shaped red blood cells. Sickle cell "trait," a much milder condition, occurs when only one parent passes on the sickle-cell gene to the child.

Somatotype   A particular type of body composition (i.e., ectomorph, mesomorph, or endomorph).

Spastic   Cerebral palsy classification characterized by hard, jerky, uncontrolled movements. An increased stretch reflex is present and muscle contractures are common. The greatest percentage of individuals with CP fall into this classification.

Spatial relations   Identification of objects in space as they relate to the body.

Special Olympics International (SOI)   The largest and most visible sport organization in the world for people with mental retardation.

Spina bifida   A congenital opening in the vertebral column, often with the protrusion of the meninges. If the meninges do not protrude, the type is called occulta.

Status epilepticus   Seizures that last for more than 30 minutes, or when one seizure immediately follows another. Most commonly associated with tonic-clonic (grand mal) seizures.

Stereotyped behavior   Complex, repetitive movements that appear to be nonfunctional, especially hand movements, rocking, object twirling, or head banging; "blindisms." It is common among individuals with severe or profound mental retardation or nonverbal infantile autism.

Strabismus   A condition characterized by the eyes not being directed simultaneously to the same object as a result of an imbalance of the muscles of the eyeball. Crossed or deviated eyes are examples.

Stretch reflex   Muscle contraction as a reflex to sudden muscle movement. Increased stretch reflexes are commonly found in individuals with spastic cerebral palsy, thus making controlled movement extremely difficult.

Symmetrical tonic neck reflex (STNR)   An infant reflex in which the arms flex when the head is hyperflexed; also, when the head is hyperextended, the legs will flex. The locomotor process of creeping becomes extremely difficult when this reflex persists beyond the normal time frame of infancy. Children with cerebral palsy often have this difficulty.

Tactile   Pertaining to touch.

Talipes equinus   Walking on the toes or front portion of the foot.

Talipes valgus   Walking on the inside of the foot.

Talipes varus   Walking on the outside of the foot.

Tetralogy of Fallot (fal-oh)   Congenital heart defect involving four different defects.

Time out   A behavior modification technique of excluding or removing a child from an activity, or denying the opportunity to participate for a specific period of time.

Tinnitus   A ringing or roaring sound in the ears.

Total communication   A communication technique used by the hearing impaired that includes signing, fingerspelling, speech reading, and speaking.

Toxoplasmosis   A congenital infection transmitted from mother to fetus often resulting in cerebral calcification, mental retardation, seizures, hydrocephalus, or microcephaly.

Trainable mentally retarded (TMR)   *See* Moderately mentally retarded.

Translocation   A rare type of Down syndrome where there is an added leg of chromosome material to the 14th, 15th, or 22nd pair, often resulting in mental retardation.

Trisomy 21   The most common type (approximately 95%) of Down syndrome in which the 21st pair of chromosomes has three legs instead of the normal two, resulting in mental retardation and other distinct characteristics. (*See also* Down syndrome.)

Tympanic membrane tubes   Tubes that are inserted into the ear drums (tympanostomy) to drain excessive fluid in the middle ear that is a result of chronic otitis media.

von Willebrandt's disease   A congenital bleeding disease inherited as an autosomal dominant trait, characterized by a prolonged bleeding time, and resulting from a deficiency of coagulation Factor VIII.

INDEX

633